D1798058

INCOME DISTRIBUTION AND HEALTH IN A NORTH INDIAN VILLAGE

Income Distribution and Health in a North Indian Village

MIKE SHEPPERDSON

Avebury

Aldershot · Brookfield USA · Hong Kong · Singapore · Sydney

Published by
Avebury
Ashgate Publishing Limited
Gower House
Croft Road
Aldershot
Hants GU11 3HR
England

Ashgate Publishing Company
Old Post Road
Brookfield
Vermont 05036
USA

British Library Cataloguing in Publication Data

Shepperdson, Mike
Income Distribution and Health in a
North Indian Village
I. Title
339.20954

ISBN 1 85628 036 5

Library of Congress Catalog Card Number: 94-74548

Printed and bound by Athenæum Press Ltd.,
Gateshead, Tyne & Wear.

Contents

TABLES

MAPS AND FIGURES

PER CAPITA INCOME, ECONOMIC GROWTH, AVERAGE LIFE EXPECTANCY AT BIRTH AND CRUDE DEATH RATE, 177 NATIONS 1988

LIFE EXP. AT BIRTH	NATION	CRUDE DEATH RATE	% DECREASE CDR 1965-88	GNPPC US$	% gpa GNPPC 1965-88
78	Japan	7	0	21,021	4.3
	Iceland			20,190	3.3
77	Hong Kong	5	17	9,220	6.3
	Canada	7	12	16,960	2.7
	Netherlands	8	0	14,520	1.9
	Italy	9	10	13,330	3.0
	Switzerland	9	10	27,500	1.5
	Spain	9	+12	7,740	2.3
	Greece	10	+25	4,800	2.9
	Norway	11	+10	19,990	3.5
	Sweden	12	+20	19,300	1.8
76	Australia	7	22	12,340	1.7
	*CUBA	7	12		
	Israel	7	+17	8,650	2.7
	France	9	18	16,090	2.5
	USA	9	0	19,840	1.6
	Channel Is.			6.000+	NA
	Cyprus			6,260	NA
75	*Costa Rica	4	50	1,690	1.4
	N. Zealand	8	11	10,000	0.8
	Finland	10	0	18,590	3.2
	Austria	11	15	15,470	2.9
	Belgium	11	8	14,490	2.5
	UK	11	8	12,810	1.8
	W. Germany	11	8	18,480	2.5
	Denmark	12	+20	18,450	1.8
	Puerto Rico			2.200-5,999	NA
	Barbados			6,010	2.3
	Martinique			2,200-5,999	NA
	Luxembourg			22,400	4.1
	Brunei			6,000+	NA
74	Singapore	5	17	9,070	7.2
	Ireland	9	25	7,750	2.0
	Portugal	9	10	3,650	3.1
	*Dominica			1,680	0.6
	Guadeloupe			2,200-5,999	NA
73	Kuwait	3	57	13,400	-4.3
	Taiwan	5		3,500+	c7.0
	**Jamaica	6	33	1,070	-1.5
	E. Germany	13	7		
	Fr. Guinea			2,200-5,999	NA
	Antigua+B			3,690	0.6
	Malta			5,190	7.4
	Guam			6,000+	NA
72	*Panama	5	44	2,120	2.2
	ALBANIA	6	50		
	*Chile	6	45	1,510	0.1
	YUGOSLAVIA	9	0	2,520	3.4
	Uruguay	10	0	2,470	1.3
	*POLAND	10	+43	1,860	NA
	BULGARIA	12	+50		
	Fr. Polynesia			6,000+	NA

LIFE EXP. AT BIRTH	NATION	CRUDE DEATH RATE	% DECREASE CDR 1965-88	GNPPC US$	% gpa GNPPC 1965-88
71	U.Arab Emirates	4	71	15,770	NA
	**Sri Lanka	6	25	420	3.0
	Trinidad	6	25	3,350	0.9
	Argentina	9	0	2,520	0.0
	CZECHOSLOVAKIA	12	+20		
	*Fiji			1,520	1.9
	*St. Lucia			1,540	2.7
	Macao			2,200-5,999	NA
	Reunion			2,200-5,999	NA
70	*Malaysia	5	58	1,940	4.0
	N. KOREA	5	58		
	Venezuela	5	38	3,250	-0.9
	S. Korea	6	45	3,600	6.8
	**CHINA	7	30	330	5.4
	ROMANIA	11	+22	(2,560)	NA
	USSR	11	+57		
	HUNGARY	13	+18	2,460	5.1
	**St. Vincent + G			1,200	2.0
	Seychelles			3,800	3.2
	Qatar			9,930	NA
	Virgin Is.			6,000+	1.9
69	*Mexico	6	45	1,760	2.3
	Grenada			1,720	NA
	St. Kitts + Nevis			2,360	3.6
68	**Colombia	6	45	1,180	2.4
	Bahrain			6,340	NA
	Bahamas			10,700	1.0
	N. Caledonia			6,000+	NA
67	**Paraguay	6	25	1,180	3.1
	**Botswana	7	63	1,010	8.6
	*Mauritius	7	12	1,800	2.9
	*Belize			1,500	2.4
	Suriname			2,460	1.1
66	*Jordan	6	71	1,500	NA
	**Tunisia	7	56	1,230	3.4
	**Dominican R.	7	46	720	2.7
	**Ecuador	7	46	1,120	3.1
	VIETNAM	7		100-545	NA
	**W. Samoa			640	NA
	**Tonga			830	NA
	Neths. Antilles			6,000+	NA
65	*Syria	7	56	1,680	2.9
	**Thailand	7	30	1,000	4.0
	Brazil	8	27	2,160	3.6
	**Sao Tomé + P			490	-0.1
	**Cape Verde			680	NA
64	**WORLD AVERAGE**	10	29	3,470	1.5

LIFE EXP. AT BIRTH	NATION	CRUDE DEATH RATE	% DECREASE CDR 1965-88	GNPPC US$	% gpa GNPPC 1965-88
64	Oman	7	71	5,000	6.4
	NICARAGUA	7	56	(830)	-2.5
	**Philippines	7	42	630	1.6
	Saudi Arabia	8	60	6,200	3.8
	Algeria	8	56	2,360	2.7
	**Honduras	8	53	860	0.6
	**Turkey	8	47	1,280	2.6
?	Lebanon	8	33?	546-2,199	NA
	**Solomon Is.			630	NA
	**Vanuatu			840	NA
63	Iran	8	56	2,200-5,999	NA
	Iraq	8	56	(3020)	NA
	**Zimbabwe	8	53	650	1.0
	**El Salvador	8	28	940	-0.5
	**Egypt	9	53	660	3.6
	**Guyana			420	-4.4
62	**Guatemala	8	53	900	1.0
	MONGOLIA	9	44		
	Peru	9	44	1,300	0.1
61	**Indonesia	9	55	440	4.3
	**Morocco	9	50	830	2.3
	Libya	9	47	5,420	-2.7
	S. Africa	10	38	2,290	0.8
60	MYANMAR	10	44	(200)	NA
	**Maldives			410	2.3
59	**Kenya	11	45	370	1.9
58	**India	11	45	340	1.8
57	Namibia	12	45		
56	**Cameroon	13	35	1,010	3.7
	Lesotho	13	28	420	5.2
	Comoros Is.			440	0.6
	Swaziland			810	2.2
55	**Pakistan	13	38	350	2.5
	**Haiti	13	35	380	0.4
	Kiribati			650	NA
54	Papua NG	12	40	810	0.5
	Ghana	13	28	400	-1.6
53	Tanzania	13	41	160	-0.5
	Zambia	13	35	290	-2.1
	Côte d'Ivoire	14	36	770	0.9
	Togo	14	36	370	0.0
	Bolivia	14	33	570	-0.6
	CONGO PR	15	17	910	3.5
	Gabon	16	27	2,970	0.9
52	Zaire	14	33	170	-2.1

LIFE EXP. AT BIRTH	NATION	CRUDE DEATH RATE	% DECREASE CDR 1965-88	GNPPC US$	% gpa GNPPC 1965-88
51	Benin	15	38	390	0.1
	Nepal	15	38	180	NA
	Nigeria	15	35	290	0.9
	S. YEMEN	15	35	430	NA
	Bangladesh	15	29	170	0.4
50	Cent. Afr. R	15	38	380	-0.5
	Sudan	16	33	480	0.0
	Madagascar	16	27	190	-1.8
	Liberia	16	20	(450)	NA
49	Burundi	16	33	240	3.0
	LAO PDR	17	26	180	NA
	Rwanda	18	+6	320	1.5
48	Senegal	16	30	650	-0.8
	MOZAMBIQUE	17	37	100	NA
	Bhutan	17	26	180	NA
	Uganda	17	10	280	-3.1
47	Burkina Faso	18	31	210	1.2
	Mali	19	30	230	1.6
	Somalia	19	27	170	0.5
	N. Yemen	20	26	640	NA
	Malawi	20	23	170	1.1
	ETHIOPIA	20	0	120	-0.1
	Djibouti			546-2,199	NA
46	Chad	19	32	160	-2.0
	Mauritania	19	27	480	-0.4
	Equatorial Guinea			410	NA
45	ANGOLA	20	31	(470)	NA
	Niger	20	31	300	-2.3
44	Gambia			200	1.1
43	Guinea	22	24	430	NA
42	S. Leone	23	26	(300)	NA
40	Guinea-Bissau			190	-1.9
NK	KAMPUCHEA	20	or less	100-545	NA
	AFGHANISTAN	29	or less	100-545	NA
	<u>$PCI</u>				
76	6,000-27,500 H	9	10	17,080	2.3
68	2,200-5,999 UM	8	33	3,240	2.3
65	546-2,199 LM	8	38	1,380	2.6
60	100-545 L	10	38	320	3.1
	<u>REGIONS</u>				
67	LATIN AMERICA	7	42	1,840	1.9
66	EAST ASIA	7	36	540	5.2
64	EUR,M.E.+N.AFR	10	33	2,000	2.4
57	SOUTH ASIA	12	40	320	1.8
51	SUBSAHARAN AFR	16	27	330	0.2
64	WORLD	10	29	3,470	1.5

* Asterisks indicate nations with disproportionately high LE in relation to low PCI; GNPPC = Gross National Product Per Capita; gpa = growth per annum. Current or past socialist nations IN CAPITALS. Sources: WB 1990; UNDP 1990.

1 Health theories and inequalities

Given that world income and health seem to be improving (and mortality has certainly been falling), what has been happening to inequalities in income and health? If a majority of the world's population has indeed increased their income and general living standards (and if even income distribution may have improved in some quarters), has there been a commensurate improvement in health, judged in terms of the four major criteria of mortality, morbidity, health care and use of health care in relation to need? If health has improved (commensurately with income or even only marginally), have the improvements been equally distributed between nations, regions, classes, castes, genders and other categories or has there been a widening or narrowing of pre-existing inequalities? Which health criteria (mortality, morbidity, health care or use-need) were most unequal in the past and which have undergone most change in inequality? Kuznets and other economists have addressed analogous questions on economic growth and its effect on income distribution and some have concluded that nations move from relative income equality in their initial underdeveloped state to less equality in an intermediate, medium income and development phase, progressing to greater equality in the third phase. Townsend (1988) has found some evidence of increasing inequality of health between social classes in Britain as both income and health have improved generally. Townsend is a sociologist who seems genuinely surprised to find health inequalities increasing in modern Britain, with its welfare State and expensive National Health Service. The evidence from Britain could suggest that India, especially rural India, might have less health inequality now but that it can look forward to increasing health inequalities in the future.

This book is primarily a study of the political economy and health anthropology of a medium-sized village within a three-hour bus ride of Lucknow, the capital city of the state of Uttar Pradesh (or 'Northern State'). The intention is quite deliberate to avoid reporting on a rural microcosm in total isolation from its regional, national and international context, but the inclusion of chapters on the political economy of India and of UP has lengthened the story and perhaps the resulting web is not entirely seamless. The choice of an Indian village for study may be justified both in demographic and theoretical terms. At least 622 million people (one in nine of us) live in Indian villages. Such villages, especially in UP, are arguably near the beginning of their 'medical transition' and as such should provide information on the nature of health and health inequality in the early or middle stages of the process towards a high standard of health. The residents of Basauli are mostly poor and middle peasants in a nation whose average per capita income is moderately low ($340 in 1988), whose annual economic growth (1.8% betweeen 1965 and 1988) has been only slightly above the world average but whose crude death rate is only slightly greater than the world average. India has reduced its CDR from 16 in 1965 to 11 in 1988. This represents a reduction of 45% in 23 years (roughly two percentage points per year) and was considerably faster than the world average (29%) and slightly faster than the poor nation average (38%).

Definitions and Indicators of Health

Definitions of health range from very broad philosophical ones to narrow physiological approaches. Health may be equated with 'physical, mental and social wellbeing'; with capacity to perform anything from a basic minimum of functions necessary for survival to an enormously wide range of highly complex functions; or with high performance on measuring such things as height, weight, blood pressure, pulse rate, blood sugar and serum cholesterol levels, lung function and eyesight.

Health indicators include various measures of mortality; morbidity; health care; the relationship between use of health care and morbidity (or need for health care); and, finally, the quality and effectiveness of health care. Mortality indicators include the crude death rate; stillbirth, perinatal, neonatal, postneonatal, infant and maternal mortality rates; and standardised mortality ratios (SMRs) which allow for comparisons between different social classes, regions or other categories, holding other variables (such as age, sex and occupation) constant. An SMR is also the ratio of the observed mortality rate in a subpopulation to the mortality rate expected from the total population, multiplied by 100. The average SMR for the whole population is 100.

Morbidity indicators include incapacity for (or absence from) work; restricted activity in a two-week or other reference period; acute or short-term sickness; restricted activity in terms of either longstanding or longstay (chronic) sickness; and limiting, longstanding illness.

Indicators of use of health care include the number of GP and outpatient consultations; and standardised patient consultation ratios (SPCRs). Even more important are indicators which show whether those who have most need of health care actually receive it. For example, a use-need ratio can be calculated by dividing the number of GP or other consultations by the number of restricted activity days, each in a two-week or other reference period. Other such indices include the Hospital Outpatients Department (OPD) Index and the GP Index. Both of these measure consultations, relative to prevalence of chronic handicapping illness in a population.

HEALTH THEORIES

Variations in health can be explained in terms of different kinds of factor, from the most basic and 'natural' (such as genetic) through to the most 'artificial' and complex (such as politics and health care systems). These types of factor include: biological, genetic or physical; demographic; natural or physical environment; sociocultural patterns; the 'political economy'; and the nature of health care, in all its many guises. Basch (1990) reviews many of these factors.

Biological and Physical Factors

Biological factors include chromosomal abnormalities such as the extra chromosome inherited by children with Down's syndrome. Perinatal and neonatal deaths are more related to biological factors and, arguably, postneonatal and subsequent deaths are more related to socio-economic factors, especially the more the infant survives beyond the first 28 days. Usually neonatal deaths increase relative to postneonatal deaths as countries become more developed. Other important physical factors are low birthweight, lack of breastfeeding and early weaning. The rapid progress in the relatively new science of genetics offers serious hopes of conquest of the many diseases which arise from genetic abnormalities.

Demographic Factors

Demographic factors include maternal age, with higher risk of infant death when mothers are teenagers or aged 40 plus; early marriage of the mother; high parity, with high risk for the seventh or higher order baby born; non-use of contraception and consequent lack of spacing between births (especially if there is less than two years between them); dissonance between current and desired number (and also age-sex composition) of children; and early death of the mother. In countries where infant deaths form a large proportion of total deaths, then demographic factors may be particularly important. The same is true of countries with a high ratio of old persons.

Environmental Factors

Environmental factors include the climate, seasonality, vegetation, housing, water supply, sanitation, radiation and pollution.

Chambers (1981) emphasises the seasonality of climate, production, income, nutrition, health and accessibility of health services. Poorer persons, especially poorer villagers (since the effect of seasonality, especially on incomes, seems obviously greater in the rural sector), may be subject to greater seasonal fluctuations in income and in health and there may be a specially high seasonal income elasticity of demand for health services among the poor. In other words, the poor spend more on their health at certain times of year either because they are more ill at these periods or because a seasonal rise in income enables them (at last) to spend something on a health problem which has been troubling them for some time and which arose initially in an earlier season of low income. This expenditure may absorb a high proportion of the rise in income.

Hopper (1957) found that agricultural labourers in Senapur, a village in eastern UP, had least work in May and in the latter part of July. He also noted that

> illness showed a marked seasonal cycle, with the village most healthy in February and early March. The beginning of the hot weather toward the end of April brought fever and eye trouble that claimed a toll of 3% of the available working time. The monsoon saw an increase in malaria and other moisture-responsive diseases and resulted in a mid-July illness rate of 10% of available time. The 1954 monsoon delivered less than the usual precipitation and this may have been the reason why the village was spared any severe outbreaks of malaria, typhoid or cholera, usually expected in late August and September. Nevertheless illness declined from July's high to a fairly constant 5 or 6% until the cooler weather in mid October, when it dropped to 3%. Cold weather in December saw an increase again to 5 or 6% for the period studied. The incidence of sickness at this time was especially high among the lower economic groups of the village who reported most of the illness recorded. This declined steadily during January to around 1% in mid February (1957:290-1).

Sociocultural Factors

Sociocultural factors include education, religion, caste, family and peer group (see Helman 1990, especially chapter 12). Sociocultural explanations may also emphasise the personal ideas and behaviour of the individual, including intelligence, education, skills, 'lifestyle', thoughtfulness and responsibility. Ill-health may be seen as deriving from 'excessive consumption of harmful commodities, refined foods, tobacco and alcohol, or by lack of exercise, or by their under-utilization of preventive health care, vaccination, ante-natal surveillance or contraception' (Townsend 1988:110). However, a crucial sociocultural variable such as education is highly dependent on class and the inter-relationship between 'materialist' and sociocultural factors is quite complex and their relative effects not easily separable.

In India an important sociocultural variable obviously has to be caste. Djurfeldt (1976) reports heavier drinking by scheduled caste males in a Tamil village and most got drunk once a week. In autumn and winter they drank varnish or 'French polish'. Drinking reached its peak after the harvest when labourers' incomes were highest. Higher castes drank less frequently and women and children almost never. In other areas such as Rajasthan, most drinking (and opium consumption) appears to be done by high castes, especially Rajputs.

Hasan (1979) has also studied health in a village of Uttar Pradesh - a village 16 kilometres south of Lucknow, and he lays major stress on sociocultural (and environmental) factors. He relates cholera, typhoid, dysentery and diarrhea to indiscriminate defecation and points to Muslim-Hindu differences over defecation outside the home. Skin ailments, notably ringworm and prickly heat, relate to bathing habits and only Bhagats bathed daily. Cosmology and theory of disease varies with religion. Barbers' instruments were not sterilised between shaves and Muslims shared the huqqah and sometimes eating vessels, as an expression of brotherhood. Vitamin B deficiency followed the replacement of parboiling or hand-pounding by mechanical milling of rice. Iron deficiency followed substitution of factory sugar for traditional gur and this led to anemia in those infected with ankylostomiasis. Beliefs about 'hot' and 'cold' foods lead to inappropriate diets at particular seasons, times of day or of the body's cycle and certain food combinations were avoided or enjoined. 'Cold' foods include cow's milk, sugarcane juice, leafy vegetables (sags), carrots, water chestnuts (singhare) and curd (dahi). 'Hot' foods include buffalo milk, pulses (such as arhar dal), raw sugar and gur, meat and eggs. Certain items, especially meat and alcohol, were prohibited for certain castes. Caste status also affected choice of occupation, physical tasks related to occupations, sexual practices, performance of prayers, disciplines and rituals. Caste mobility often led to changes in behaviour. Disease was regarded as mainly a random event though a breach of a taboo might cause leprosy, dropsy or VD. Sorcery might bring diarrhea to children, spirit intrusion might cause tetanus whilst the evil eye and the wrath of gods or goddesses might cause diseases like smallpox in the past and chicken pox in the present. Ghost intrusion caused psychosomatic illness, arising from, say, a fright whilst walking home in the dark and leading to sweating, fever, mental upset and loss of weight.

Smucker notes a significant tendency for low caste Hindus and also Muslims to live closer to 'dispensaries' and concludes that 'this is possibly a reflection of the concentration of Muslims in larger villages which are also likely sites for dispensaries' (1980:327). Helman (1990) analyses sociocultural factors and health, and even incorporates some analysis of political economy in this second edition.

Political and Economic Factors

Political and economic factors include international and national systems of production, distribution (especially distribution of wealth, income and commodities) and consumption. The systemic factors relate to the nature of the international political economy, the nation-state and the type of economic system (eg. whether communist, socialist, mixed economy or capitalist). Systemic factors include 'the healthiness of the State' and consciousness on health issues, as well as the health education, awareness and knowledge of State functionaries, including politicians, civil servants, judges, academics, journalists and other media persons. Production includes the nature of agricultural production and of the cropping pattern (eg. whether crops provide 'healthy' foods, 'unhealthy' foods, non-food or drugs); relative quantities and prices of commodities, including international and rural-urban terms of trade; prices of food, soap, pharmaceuticals, mosquito nets and other health-related commodities; the nature of production of pharmaceuticals, medical equipment and technology (eg. whether national or multinational; monopolist or competitive; and whether allopathic or based on other medical systems). Industrial production may involve new and dangerous processes, changed conditions and amenities at work, including less security and stability of employment, migration and longer distance to travel, less association with co-workers and lowered levels of job satisfaction and of general self-fulfilment.

Apart from agricultural and industrial production, 'tertiary output' in the service sector encompasses the production of health care, including the degree of State involvement in this and also the social recruitment, training, deployment, remuneration and class structure of various health and health-related professions and occupations.

The distribution of wealth, income and commodities obviously relates to the distribution of health. Key commodities include food, water, sanitation, housing, clothing, transport, health care, medicines, drugs and other leisure items. Other commodities may be more collective, including buildings and town and rural planning, with implications for community participation. Sen's theory of endowments and entitlements (from ownership, production, labour, exchange, transfer payments and inheritance) was originally devised to explain vulnerability to famine but it can also be related to more general health conditions than the singular, extreme but still recurrent cases of famine-induced mortality.

Equally, the theory of income and health developed by Cornia and Jolly (1987) in particular relation to the health effects of structural adjustment and stabilisation programmes has a much wider relevance. The relationship between poverty lines, minimum nutritional levels and basic health requires further exploration. A rise in income may involve high income elasticity of demand for harmful as well as healthy consumption. Increased income may also facilitate increased expenditure on medical care but ignorance may lead to poor choice from a bewildering range of medical treatment, and also serious delays in seeking effective treatment. Payment of labourers 'in kind' may be beneficial when food prices are high, but partial payment in cooked meals for the employee may disadvantage non-employed members of the household who miss out on these food payments.

The 1993 World Development Report is devoted to health and priority is given to governments fostering 'an economic environment that enables households to improve their own health. Growth policies (including, where necessary, economic adjustment policies) that ensure economic gains for the poor are essential' (World Bank 1993:iii). But the emphasis is on growth, not redistribution.

Materialist explanations are not politically homogeneous and range from Marxist, 'Marxian' and Marxist-feminist to Fabian or democratic socialist. One variant has examined the nature of capitalism and particularly the effect of economic fluctuations ('the business cycle') on health. Brenner and Eyer have come to virtually opposite conclusions. Brenner (1973, 1976 and 1977) finds that US recessions have, after a time lag of two to five years, produced increases in foetal, infant, maternal and national mortality rates. Brenner and others regard unemployment as a source of low income and 'stress' which in turn affect mortality. Navarro and others also point to the reduction in State expenditure, especially on health care and other welfare services, during recessions. Eyer (1975, 1977 and 1984), on the other hand, argues that the boom phase in the capitalist business cycle induces overcompetition, overwork (including excessive overtime), 'stress' and increased consumption, especially of painkiller and stimulant drugs. All this serves to raise mortality, without any significant time lag.

Djurfeldt (1976) provides a strong theoretical statement in favour of a political economy approach to explaining ill health in a Tamil village. Unfortunately, the study was conducted in an untypical year of exceptional drought and also the authors failed to collect data on the relationship between class and disease. On the other hand, Simmons (1978 and 1982) found that tetanus (the cause of 66% of neonatal deaths in rural Kanpur and Etawah between 1965 and 1969) was highest among the largest landowners, particularly those who owned several animals. Concentrations of tetanus bacillus increase with animal contact, with manuring of soil, and with use of dung for plastering walls, for cooking and for dressing the umbilical stump of newborn babies. Simmons claims that the explanatory model for other killer diseases of neonates is more biological and that mortality from these diseases was declining.

Eyer (1984) has suggested that richer peasants in China may be among the healthiest classes or categories in the world, partly because they enjoy reasonable nutrition and other benefits of rural living and farming without the disadvantages of stress and other negative factors associated with capitalism and more commercial agriculture and without the even greater health risks of the fully modernised, urbanised and industrialised society, particularly of the more capitalist MDCs (see also Chen Junshi 1990).

International and national changes in political economy, health policy and medical care mean differential benefits for particular classes and categories (such as 'Green Revolution' farmers, labourers - especially agricultural labourers, rural landlords, industrial workers, informal sector workers, professionals, managers, government employees and members of the armed forces). Some categories may be mostly upward mobile, such as many middle peasants, car workers (and, more generally, skilled manual workers), workers in financial, banking and related services, (and, more generally, white collar workers). Others may be downward mobile such as many agricultural labourers, some rural landlords, traditional craftsmen, university and other teachers, hunter-gatherers (and, more generally, tribal peoples).

Gender may engender even greater health inequalities than income and social class (see PC 1988; WB 1990; and UNDP 1990). Jeffery (1979 and 1989) and Sharma (1980) document the problems of women in northern India. Jeffery (1989), writing on childbearing in two Bijnor villages in western UP, records severe and fairly general difficulties for women. Others, such as Simmons (1982) and Smucker (1980) allege that neglect leads to higher female mortality among infants and hint fairly heavily about female infanticide. Hopper (1957) noted non-celebration of female births, less mourning of female infant deaths, slower resort to medical care for girls but similar survival rates up to the age of ten. By 1988 life expectancy at birth in India was the same (58 years) for both sexes. (Only China, Bhutan and Nepal now have lower life expectancy for females.)

Jeffery (1989) focuses particularly on the problems of the bahu (wife or daughter-in-law), especially in the transitional phase when she moves from the loving, natal environment of her parental home and village to the unfamiliar, more segregating, demanding, laborious and not necessarily always very friendly household of her husband's parents in a strange and often quite distant village. This focus on the strains endured by newly wedded young women (usually mere teenagers) is a reminder of the more general question of the points in the individual life or family cycle when stresses and strains on particular family members, whether female or male, may increase sufficiently to affect their health.

Health Care Factors

Health care factors include whether medical services are public or private; mainstream or so-called 'alternative' systems; professional, 'traditional' and informal or 'self-care'; and whether they are effective or not.

Relative Influence of Different Types of Factor

The relative influence of different types of factor is obviously a complex question and accordingly difficult to assess. The task is not made any easier by imprecise boundaries between some types of factor. For example, education may be seen as both a sociocultural and political economy factor. The sheer multiplicity of factors affecting health does not help either. However, it seems likely that biological factors become increasingly important as countries develop and neonatal deaths exceed postneonatal deaths among infants and senile dementia and other diseases of senility increase among the old. Sociocultural factors may become at first less important and technological, quick-fix health care factors more important as poor countries become richer and income inequalities make political and economic factors more important in influencing health. Then, as nations become rich enough for most of their populations to afford (at least in theory) to maintain good health, sociocultural factors may again assume greater importance. However, ill health which derives from increased consumption of harmful foods and drinks, tobacco, alcohol and harder drugs may be attributed equally to sociocultural ('lifestyle') changes and to the political economy which legitimises and facilitates mass production and distribution of such commodities to satisfy the changes in people's tastes which occur when people's incomes begin to exceed the basic minimum level necessary to maintain good health, ie. when people begin 'to have more money than health sense'.

INTERNATIONAL VARIATION IN HEALTH

The table shows 1988 data on life expectancies at birth and crude death rates in 121 member countries of the World Bank, 10 non-member countries, Puerto Rico, and also 45 out of 55 smaller countries with populations of less than a million. Inclusion of small countries increases the 'sample' size, but at some cost in terms of quality of data. Countries have been ranked by life expectancy because this should be a more accurate indicator of relative health than crude death rate since LE is based on age structure and age-related mortality. The main disadvantage is that life expectancy is a non-empirical datum, expressing a likely outcome if certain assumptions hold true. On the other hand, while the crude death rate does express empirical realities, its main weakness is that, without standardisation, it does not allow for the large international differences in age structure, especially the much larger ratio of old persons in MDCs. It is to be hoped that the WHO and other agencies can soon start publishing international data on standardised death rates. Average life expectancy ranged from 78 years in Japan and Iceland down to only 40 years in Guinea-Bissau. Crude death rate reaches a minimum of 3 in Kuwait and its maximum in Guinea, Sierra Leone and probably also Kampuchea and Afghanistan (all over 22). Changes in crude death rate during the period from 1965 to 1988 ranged from a huge reduction of 71% in the United Arab Emirates and Jordan to a formidable increase of 57% in the USSR. Average per capita income varied from $100 in Mozambique to $27,500 in Switzerland. Average annual economic growth in the period from 1965 to 1988 exceeded 6% in six countries (Hong Kong, Singapore, Malta, South Korea, Botswana and Oman) and was seriously negative in Kuwait, Jamaica, Nicaragua, Guyana, Libya, Ghana, Zambia, Zaire, Madagascar, Uganda, Chad, Niger and Guinea-Bissau. Overall, life expectancy rises from an average of 60 in poorest nations to 76 in richest nations, whereas CDR varies only slightly with PCI. Regionally, OECD countries have the highest life expectancy (76), followed by Latin America (67), East Asia (66), South Asia (57) and Africa (around 50 or less?).

PER CAPITA INCOME, ECONOMIC GROWTH, AVERAGE LIFE EXPECTANCY AT BIRTH AND CRUDE DEATH RATE, 177 NATIONS 1988

LIFE EXP.AT BIRTH	NATION	CRUDE DEATH RATE	% DECREASE CDR 1965-88	GNPPC US$	% gpa GNPPC 1965-88
78	Japan	7	0	21,021	4.3
	Iceland			20,190	3.3
77	Hong Kong	5	17	9,220	6.3
	Canada	7	12	16,960	2.7
	Netherlands	8	0	14,520	1.9
	Italy	9	10	13,330	3.0
	Switzerland	9	10	27,500	1.5
	Spain	9	+12	7,740	2.3
	Greece	10	+25	4,800	2.9
	Norway	11	+10	19,990	3.5
	Sweden	12	+20	19,300	1.8
76	Australia	7	22	12,340	1.7
	*CUBA	7	12		
	Israel	7	+17	8,650	2.7
	France	9	18	16,090	2.5
	USA	9	0	19,840	1.6
	Channel Is.			6.000+	NA
	Cyprus			6,260	NA
75	*Costa Rica	4	50	1,690	1.4
	N. Zealand	8	11	10,000	0.8
	Finland	10	0	18,590	3.2
	Austria	11	15	15,470	2.9
	Belgium	11	8	14,490	2.5
	UK	11	8	12,810	1.8
	W. Germany	11	8	18,480	2.5
	Denmark	12	+20	18,450	1.8
	Puerto Rico			2.200-5,999	NA
	Barbados			6,010	2.3
	Martinique			2,200-5,999	NA
	Luxembourg			22,400	4.1
	Brunei			6,000+	NA
74	Singapore	5	17	9,070	7.2
	Ireland	9	25	7,750	2.0
	Portugal	9	10	3,650	3.1
	*Dominica			1,680	0.6
	Guadeloupe			2,200-5,999	NA
73	Kuwait	3	57	13,400	-4.3
	Taiwan	5		3,500+	c7.0
	**Jamaica	6	33	1,070	-1.5
	E. Germany	13	7		
	Fr. Guinea			2,200-5,999	NA
	Antigua+B			3,690	0.6
	Malta			5,190	7.4
	Guam			6,000+	NA
72	*Panama	5	44	2,120	2.2
	ALBANIA	6	50		
	*Chile	6	45	1,510	0.1
	YUGOSLAVIA	9	0	2,520	3.4
	Uruguay	10	0	2,470	1.3
	*POLAND	10	+43	1,860	NA
	BULGARIA	12	+50		
	Fr. Polynesia			6,000+	NA
71	U.Arab Emirates	4	71	15,770	NA
	**Sri Lanka	6	25	420	3.0
	Trinidad	6	25	3,350	0.9
	Argentina	9	0	2,520	0.0
	CZECHOSLOVAKIA	12	+20		
	*Fiji			1,520	1.9
	*St. Lucia			1,540	2.7
	Macao			2,200-5,999	NA
	Reunion			2,200-5,999	NA
70	*Malaysia	5	58	1,940	4.0
	N. KOREA	5	58		
	Venezuela	5	38	3,250	-0.9
	S. Korea	6	45	3,600	6.8
	**CHINA	7	30	330	5.4
	ROMANIA	11	+22	(2,560)	NA
	USSR	11	+57		
	HUNGARY	13	+18	2,460	5.1
	**St. Vincent + G			1,200	2.0
	Seychelles			3,800	3.2
	Qatar			9,930	NA
	Virgin Is.			6,000+	1.9
69	*Mexico	6	45	1,760	2.3
	Grenada			1,720	NA
	St. Kitts + Nevis			2,360	3.6
68	**Colombia	6	45	1,180	2.4
	Bahrain			6,340	NA
	Bahamas			10,700	1.0
	N. Caledonia			6,000+	NA
67	**Paraguay	6	25	1,180	3.1
	**Botswana	7	63	1,010	8.6
	*Mauritius	7	12	1,800	2.9
	*Belize			1,500	2.4
	Suriname			2,460	1.1
66	*Jordan	6	71	1,500	NA
	**Tunisia	7	56	1,230	3.4
	**Dominican R.	7	46	720	2.7
	**Ecuador	7	46	1,120	3.1
	VIETNAM	7		100-545	NA
	**W. Samoa			640	NA
	**Tonga			830	NA
	Neths. Antilles			6,000+	NA
65	*Syria	7	56	1,680	2.9
	**Thailand	7	30	1,000	4.0
	Brazil	8	27	2,160	3.6
	**Sao Tomé + P			490	-0.1
	**Cape Verde			680	NA
64	WORLD AVERAGE	10	29	3,470	1.5
64	Oman	7	71	5,000	6.4
	NICARAGUA	7	56	(830)	-2.5
	**Philippines	7	42	630	1.6
	Saudi Arabia	8	60	6,200	3.8
	Algeria	8	56	2,360	2.7
	**Honduras	8	53	860	0.6
	**Turkey	8	47	1,280	2.6
?	Lebanon	8	33?	546-2,199	NA
	**Solomon Is.			630	NA
	**Vanuatu			840	NA
63	Iran	8	56	2,200-5,999	NA
	Iraq	8	56	(3020)	NA
	**Zimbabwe	8	53	650	1.0
	**El Salvador	8	28	940	-0.5
	**Egypt	9	53	660	3.6
	**Guyana			420	-4.4
62	**Guatemala	8	53	900	1.0
	MONGOLIA	9	44		
	Peru	9	44	1,300	0.1
61	**Indonesia	9	55	440	4.3
	**Morocco	9	50	830	2.3
	Libya	9	47	5,420	-2.7
	S. Africa	10	38	2,290	0.8
60	MYANMAR	10	44	(200)	NA
	**Maldives			410	2.3
59	**Kenya	11	45	370	1.9
58	**India	11	45	340	1.8
57	Namibia	12	45		
56	**Cameroon	13	35	1,010	3.7
	Lesotho	13	28	420	5.2
	Comoros Is.			440	0.6
	Swaziland			810	2.2
55	**Pakistan	13	38	350	2.5
	**Haiti	13	35	380	0.4
	Kiribati			650	NA
54	Papua NG	12	40	810	0.5
	Ghana	13	28	400	-1.6
53	Tanzania	13	41	160	-0.5
	Zambia	13	35	290	-2.1
	Côte d'Ivoire	14	36	770	0.9
	Togo	14	36	370	0.0
	Bolivia	14	33	570	-0.6
	CONGO PR	15	17	910	3.5
	Gabon	16	27	2,970	0.9
52	Zaire	14	33	170	-2.1
51	Benin	15	38	390	0.1
	Nepal	15	38	180	NA
	Nigeria	15	35	290	0.9
	S. YEMEN	15	35	430	NA
	Bangladesh	15	29	170	0.4
50	Cent.Afr. R	15	38	380	-0.5
	Sudan	16	33	480	0.0
	Madagascar	16	27	190	-1.8
	Liberia	16	20	(450)	NA
49	Burundi	16	33	240	3.0
	LAO PDR	17	26	180	NA
	Rwanda	18	+6	320	1.5
48	Senegal	16	30	650	-0.8
	MOZAMBIQUE	17	37	100	NA
	Bhutan	17	26	180	NA
	Uganda	17	10	280	-3.1
47	Burkina Faso	18	31	210	1.2
	Mali	19	30	230	1.6
	Somalia	19	27	170	0.5
	N. Yemen	20	26	640	NA
	Malawi	20	23	170	1.1
	ETHIOPIA	20	0	120	-0.1
	Djibouti			546-2,199	NA
46	Chad	19	32	160	-2.0
	Mauritania	19	27	480	-0.4
	Equatorial Guinea			410	NA
45	ANGOLA	20	31	(470)	NA
	Niger	20	31	300	-2.3
44	Gambia			200	1.1
43	Guinea	22	24	430	NA
42	S. Leone	23	26	(300)	NA
40	Guinea-Bissau			190	-1.9
NK	KAMPUCHEA	20 or less		100-545	NA
	AFGHANISTAN	29 or less		100-545	NA
	$PCI				
76	6,000-27,500 H	9	10	17,080	2.3
68	2,200-5,999 UM	8	33	3,240	2.3
65	546-2,199 LM	8	38	1,380	2.6
60	100-545 L	10	38	320	3.1
	REGIONS				
67	LATIN AMERICA	7	42	1,840	1.9
66	EAST ASIA	7	36	540	5.2
64	EUR,M.E.+N.AFR	10	33	2,000	2.4
57	SOUTH ASIA	12	40	320	1.8
51	SUBSAHARAN AFR	16	27	330	0.2
64	WORLD	10	29	3,470	1.5

* Asterisks indicate nations with disproportionately high LE in relation to low PCI; GNPPC = Gross National Product Per Capita; gpa = growth per annum. Current or past socialist nations IN CAPITALS.
Sources: WB 1990; UNDP 1990.

The table shows the incidence of varying levels of life expectancy for 167 countries and crude death rate for 130 countries. As many as 43 countries have moved out of the high death rate category since 1965 and 29 have joined the category of lowest CDR (3 to 7 per 1000). All nations with a CDR of 10 or less have an average life expectancy of at least 60 and nearly all countries with a high CDR have an average life expectancy of less than 50. The bimodal distribution for LE in countries with a medium CDR is mainly because some rich countries have high LEs but medium death rates, arising from a high ratio of old people. As might be expected, the rate of decrease in CDR between 1965 and 1988 correlates more with current CDR itself than with LE. Indeed, the CDR fell more rapidly in medium and low LE countries than in countries with high or very low LE. The concentration of rapid decrease of CDR in countries which have now attained a life expectancy of 60 to 69 is particularly noticeable, especially when 40% rather than 30% is used as the threshold of rapid decrease.

The following data on PCI show that no rich countries had a LE of less than 60 and in only 8 out of 50 poor countries did the LE reach 60. Two poor nations (Sri Lanka and China) had both achieved a LE of 70 or more by 1988, showing that a low PCI need not be an insuperable obstacle to improving health. The highest performer of all is Costa Rica, achieving a LE of 75 with a PCI of $1690. However, the figures show that PCI correlates much more closely with life expectancy than with CDR. Eighty-two percent of richer countries (those with a PCI of $2200 or more) enjoyed very high life expectancies whereas only 36% of (a smaller sample of) richer countries had very low death rates. Richer countries predominated most in the low CDR category (8 to 10 per 1000) and only eight rich countries had very low CDRs of 7 or less.

For the remaining variables, data were available on fewer countries and the number of countries reporting is given in the final column. Economic growth correlates highly with both LE and (negatively) with CDR. The pattern is similar for both except that far more countries with a medium CDR managed to equal or exceed the world average for economic growth than was the case for countries with medium life expectancy. Analysis of the relationship between income distribution, poverty and health is more problematic, both because of the even smaller sample size, variation in timing, and also because the data need to be treated with considerable caution (see WB 1990:258). Briefly, there seems to be very little correlation between income distribution and life expectancy and, for two out of the three indicators, higher crude death rates are associated with higher incidence of greater equality of income. However, there is no data on income distribution for the high mortality countries. In the case of the third indicator, the Gini coefficient, there appears to be no relationship with either life expectancy or death rates, but the sample size was only 28 and included only one country with a low life expectancy and none with a high death rate. On the other hand, relatively low urban and especially relatively low rural poverty correlate strongly with higher life expectancy and, to a slightly lesser extent (especially in the case of urban poverty), with lower CDR (Cf. World Bank 1993:40 which refers to a study of 22 LDCs which found that variation in poverty, defined as under $1 a

PER CAPITA INCOME, ECONOMIC GROWTH, INCOME DISTRIBUTION, POVERTY AND HEALTH, 176 NATIONS 1988

	Number or Percentage of Nations									
	LIFE EXPECTANCY AT BIRTH					CRUDE DEATH RATE				
	HIGH 70-78	MEDIUM 60-69	LOW 50-59	VERY LOW 40-49	TOTAL	V.LOW 3-7	LOW 8-10	MEDIUM 11-15	HIGH 16-23+	TOTAL
No.of countries, Popn 1M+ 1965						7	31	24	68	130
No.of countries, Popn 1M+ 1988	49	33	26	21	129	36	34	35	25	130
Change in No. of countries 1965-88						+29	+3	+11	-43	0
CDR 1988 VERY LOW, 3-7	21	15			36					
LOW, 8-10	15	18			34*					
MEDIUM, 11-15	13		22		35					
HIGH, 16-23+			4	21	25					
% countries with CDR decrease of: 30+% 1965-88	24%	88%	73%	38%	52%	67%	52%	57%	36%	54%
40+% 1965-88	18%	79%	19%	0%	31%					
$ GNP PER CAPITA 1988										
RICH $6,000-27,500	34	5			39	8	10	7	0	25
UPPER MIDDLE $2,200-5,999	19	8	1		28	4	10	2	1	17
LOWER MIDDLE $546-2,199	10	30	7	3	50	18	11	5	2	36
POOR $100-545	2	6	20	22	50	3	2	16	22	43
TOTAL No. OF COUNTRIES	65	49	28	25	167	33	33	30	25	121
% countries $2,200+	82%	27%	4%	0%	40%	36%	61%	30%	4%	35%
ECONOMIC GROWTH, 1965-88										
No.of countries reporting GNP PC % gpa	50	34	24	16	124	30	27	15	102	
% countries GNP PC 1.5+% gpa 1965-88	78%	65%	29%	19%	57%	77%	60%	52%	20%	57%
					Percentage of countries					
INCOME DISTRIBUTION, 1979-87 PERIOD										No.of countries
Poorest 20% Hhs got 6+% Income	50%	33%	80%	NA	49%	14%	60%	75%	NA	41
Richest 20% got less than 8 x Poorest	58%	13%	57%	NA	45%	20%	48%	79%	NA	55
Gini Coefficient 0.45 or less	56%	54%	60%	0%	54%	57%	50%	60%	0%	28
POVERTY INCIDENCE										
Urban Poverty 30% or less	100%	60%	36%	50%	55%	67%	70%	38%	44%	47
Rural Poverty 50% or less	83%	71%	37%	22%	51%	75%	71%	31%	33%	51

*Includes Lebanon, LE not known, probably about 64.
Sources: WB 1990; UNDP 1990.

day at 1985 purchasing power parity prices, and in per capita public spending on health was important in explaining variation in life expectancy). The World Bank continues that, 'because fewer people live in poverty as average incomes rise, there is generally a strong link between incomes and health status. Across countries, more than 75 percent of the difference in health is associated with income differences. Indeed, this relation is not merely associative but causal and structural: income growth leads directly to better health. In a sample of 58 developing countries, a 10 percent increase in income per capita, all else being equal, reduced infant and child mortality rates by between 2.0 and 3.5 percent and increased life expectancy by a month ..... [Within countries] a 10 percent advantage in income reduces infant mortality by between 1 and 2 percent in Nigeria, Sri Lanka, Thailand and several Latin America countries and by as much as 4 to 8 percent in Côte d'Ivoire and Ghana' (1993:41).

The data shown on page 12 suggest that LE and CDR correlate with each other quite highly and, unsurprisingly, that CDR correlates with the rate of decrease in CDR. Life expectancy correlates highly with per capita income, quite highly with recent economic growth and with low rural poverty, less so with low urban poverty and not at all with more equal income distribution. However, the World Bank claims that change in income distribution within countries can help increase life expectancy: 'in industrial countries life expectancy depends much more on income distribution than on income per capita, and it has been rising faster in countries with improving income distribution. Japan and the United Kingdom had similar income distributions and life expectancies in 1970, but they have diverged since then. Japan now has the highest life expectancy in the world and a highly egalitarian income distribution. In the UK, where income disparity has widened since the mid-1980s, life expectancy is now more than three years shorter than in Japan' (1993:40). On the other hand, Japan's PCI has also increased, to be 63 per cent higher than that of the UK. In addition, such a comparison of only two countries is obviously very selective. Crude death rate correlates highly and negatively with recent economic growth (though less so than does life expectancy), fairly highly with rural poverty and less so and negatively with per capita income and positively with urban poverty. Insofar as there is any relationship between more equal income distribution and CDR, it seems to be negative, with more medium mortality countries having less inequality. However, there were no data on income distribution for the 25 high mortality countries, apart from a high Gini coefficient of 0.59 for Sierra Leone. The inclusion of data on these countries would probably show that there is no significant trend relationship between income distribution and CDR.

More sophisticated analysis of international variation needs to compare health status and trends in countries with differences in political economy, rate and recency of industrialisation, level of debt and wider economic crisis, structural adjustment and/or stabilisation programme, upward or downward mobility and level of 'human (social?) development', human rights record and political stability. Overall, rich countries have the highest life expectancies and lower middle income countries the lowest crude death rates. Ten countries reduced their CDR by 50% or more in the period between 1965 and 1988.

HEALTH INEQUALITIES

The following section analyses international health inequalities, especially between poorest and richest nations, and also intra-national health inequalities between social or occupational classes in Britain (or, more accurately, mostly in England and Wales). The main sources for this are the annual reports of international agencies, notably the World Bank and the UNDP, and the seminal work of Peter Townsend (1988).

Measurement of Inequality

The most accurate representation of inequality would be an index which expresses inequality across the whole range of the population. The Gini coefficient is such an index (eg. for income distribution) and, though it also has its limitations, a comparable index for health distribution would be useful (indeed, see Le Grand 1989). Here a much cruder index will be used, expressing the performance of the lowest category as a percentage of that of the highest. For example, if the lowest category has an Infant Mortality Rate of 72, and the highest reports an IMR of only 9, then the index of inequality is 72 divided by 9, multiplied by 100 (ie. 800). In cases where the inequality involves the poorest category having a lower figure (as in the case of life expectancy) and the ratio emerges as less than 100, then the gradient of inequality is derived by dividing it into 100. For example, in 1988 male life expectancy in poor nations was 82% of that in rich countries. If 82 is divided into 100, the gradient of inequality emerges as 122 and these 'inverted gradients' are shown in brackets in the tables. Gradients or indices of inequality range from complete equality (100) to extremely high inequality: the highest recorded here is 5500, ie. the rich country PCI averaged 55 times the PCI of poor countries. As a rough guide to degrees of inequality, the following scale attempts to describe them, albeit purely arbitrarily:

Gradient of Inequality
(Relative Disadvantage of Poor as % of Rich)

Under 100	100	101 -150	151 -250	251 -400	401 -800	801 -5500+
Negative Gradient	Equality	Low	Medium	High	Very High	Extremely High

This is not meant to be a sophisticated approach and statisticians will point out quite correctly that the gradient will depend on factors such as the range of values, the number in the sample, the number of categories and the choice of thresholds between categories.

Per Capita Income or Development Level of Nations and Health

The first table shows data on income, mortality and health care for the 121 large World Bank countries, divided into four income categories, and the second table shows inequalities for the 130 UNDP countries (mostly the same as the 121), divided into three categories based on so-called 'human development'. The final columns show the ratio of performance of the poor or low development countries in relation to rich or high development countries.

The third table summarises the indicators of inequality or 'gradients'. The income inequality had the highest gradient and was higher between countries categorised in terms of income than development. The income gradient had steepened for development categories between 1976 and 1987 but use of parity purchasing power reduced the gradient from 3,083 (ie. nearly 31 times more income) to 1,223. Only one mortality indicator had a comparably high gradient and that was maternal mortality (approximately 5,127 between poor and rich nations). The next highest gradient was for child mortality and this had actually increased between high and low development categories since 1960. The gradient for mortality of female children was somewhat higher than for males. The gradient for the IMR of rich and poor nations in 1965 was higher than for the

INTERNATIONAL GRADIENTS IN HEALTH AND HEALTH CARE, BY INCOME CATEGORIES, 121 NATIONS

		RICH	UPPER MIDDLE	LOWER MIDDLE	POOR	TOTAL	POOR AS % OF RICH
$ MINIMUM GNP PC		6,000	2,200	546	100	100	
$ MAXIMUM GNP PC		27,500	5,999	2,199	545	27,500	
No. OF COUNTRIES		25	17	36	43	121	
AV. $ GNP PER CAPITA 1988		17,080	3,240	1,380	320	3,470	2 (5,338)*
CDR 1965		10	12	13	16	14	160
CDR 1988		9	8	8	10	10	111
% OF POPN.AGED 0-14, 1988		20.5	33.4	38.0	35.7	33.4	174
IMR 1965		25	82	107	124	97	496
IMR 1988		9	42	57	72	57	800
RISK OF DYING BY	M	12	55	75	97	77	808
AGE 5 (CMR) 1988	F	10	46	64	89	69	890
MATERNAL DEATHS PER 100,000 LIVE BIRTHS 1980 UNWEIGHTED AVERAGES		11	107	246	564	278	5,127
RANGE OF MATERNAL MORTALITY		2-52	12-550	12-1000	44-2000	2-2000	
MALE LIFE EXPECTANCY AT BIRTH	1965	67	59	54	48	54	72(140)
	1988	73	65	62	60	63	82(122)
FEMALE LIFE EXPECTANCY AT BIRTH	1965	74	62	57	50	57	68(148)
	1988	79	70	67	60	65	76(132)
POPN.PER PHYSICIAN	1965	940	2,380	4,910	9,760	6,630	1,038
	1984	470	1,220	3,030	5,580	4,070	1,187
POPN. PER NURSING PERSON	1965	470	2,190	2,190	6,010	4,000	851
	1984	140	680	1,090	2,200	1,600	1,571
DAILY CALORIE SUPPLY	1965	3,083	2,629	2,458	1,993	2,321	65(155)
	1986	3,376	3,117	2,846	2,384	2,653	71(142)

* Figures in brackets in the final column show 'inverted' gradients of inequality ie. where the figure for the poor is less than that for the rich.
Source: World Development Report 1990.

INTERNATIONAL GRADIENTS IN HEALTH, BY LEVEL OF HUMAN DEVELOPMENT, 130 NATIONS 1960-88

		HIGH	MEDIUM	LOW	INDUSTRIAL	DEVELOPING		LOW AS % OF HIGH
		HUMAN DEVELOPMENT			COUNTRIES		WORLD	
$ GNP PER CAPITA	1976	4,350	540	180	4,850	450	1,800	4(2,417)
	1987	9,250	690	300	10,760	650	3,100	3(3,083)
$ PARITY PURCHASING POWER (REAL GDP PC)	1987	11,860	2,370	970	14,260	1,970	4,110	8(1,223)
% MOTHERS BREAST-FEEDING AT ONE YEAR	1980-7	NA	60	72	NA	64	NA	
MATERNAL MORTALITY	1980-7	37	130	460	24	290	250	1,243
UNDER 5 MORTALITY	1960	67	209	285	46	243	218	425
	1988	27	72	170	18	121	108	630
IMR	1988	20	51	107	15	79	71	535
% LOW BIRTHWEIGHT	1982-8	8	9	25	6	17	15	312
% 12-23 MONTHS WASTED	1980-8	NA	10	16	NA	13	NA	
% 24-59 MONTHS STUNTED		NA	43	44	NA	42	NA	
% 0-5 YRS UNDERWEIGHT		NA	32	42	NA	38	NA	
LIFE EXPECTANCY AT BIRTH	1960	68	48	42	69	46	53	62(162)
	1975	71	61	49	71	57	61	69(145)
	1987	73	67	55	74	62	65	75(133)
HEALTH EXPENDITURE AS % GNP	1960	2.2	0.8	0.6	2.2	0.9	2.0	27(367)
	1986	4.6	1.5	0.8	4.7	1.4	4.2	17(575)
$ PARITY PURCHASING POWER, PRIVATE EXPENDITURE ON HEALTH PER CAPITA 1985		82.5	11.8	4.2	90.9	7.1	33.0	5(1,964)
% POPN. WITH ACCESS TO HEALTH SERVICES	1985-7	NA	75	47	NA	61	NA	
% POPN.1977-87 BELOW:								
URBAN POVERTY LINE		NA	16	40	NA	27	NA	
RURAL POVERTY LINE		NA	18	55	NA	35	NA	
% BIRTHS ATTENDED BY HEALTH PERSONNEL 1983-8		94	61	30	99	42	51	32(313)
% 1-YEAR OLDS IMMUNISED	1987	76	81	55	75	68	69	72(138)
POPN. PER DOCTOR	1984	600	2,300	8,800				1,467
POPN. PER NURSE	1984	300	1,500	2,600				867
NURSES PER DOCTOR	1984	3.6	1.9	4.3				119

'Inverted' gradients of inequality are given in brackets in the final column.
Source: UNDP Human Development Report 1990.

INTERNATIONAL GRADIENTS IN INCOME, HEALTH AND HEALTH CARE, BY PER CAPITA INCOME AND LEVEL OF DEVELOPMENT

INDICATOR		YEAR	POOR AS % RICH COUNTRIES	LOW AS % HIGH DEVELOPMENT COUNTRIES
$ GNP PER CAPITA OR LEVEL OF DEVELOPMENT		1976		2,417
		1987		3,083
		1988	5,338	
$ PARITY PURCHASING POWER OR REAL GDP P.C.		1987		1,223
MATERNAL MORTALITY RATE		1980	5,127	1,243
CHILD MORTALITY RATE	TOTAL	1960		425
	MALE	1988	808 M)	
			)	630 TOTAL
	FEMALE	1988	890 F)	
INFANT MORTALITY RATE		1965	496	
		1988	800	535
% LOW BIRTHWEIGHT		1982-8		312
LIFE EXPECTANCY AT BIRTH	MALE + FEMALE	1960		162
	MALE	1965	140	
	FEMALE	1965	148	
	MALE + FEMALE	1975		145
	MALE + FEMALE	1987		133
	MALE	1988	122	
	FEMALE	1988	132	
CRUDE DEATH RATE		1965	160	
		1988	111	
PARITY PURCHASING POWER, PRIVATE EXPENDITURE ON HEALTH PER CAPITA		1985		1,964
POPN. PER NURSE		1965	851	
		1984	1,571	867
POPN. PER DOCTOR		1965	1,038	
		1984	1,187	1,467
GOVT. HEALTH EXPENDITURE AS % GNP		1960		367
		1986		575
% BIRTHS ATTENDED BY PROFESSIONAL		1983-8		313
DAILY CALORIE SUPPLY PER CAPITA		1965	155	
		1986	142	
% OF ONE-YEAR OLDS IMMUNISED		1987		138

Sources: WB 1990; UNDP 1990.

CMR of development categories in 1960, and the increased gradient between rich and poor nations for the IMR (800) had increased beyond the development categories CMR gradient of 630 and had come very near the income categories CMR gradient (of about 849) by 1988. The gradient for low birthweight (312) was much lower than for the IMR (535). The CDR had the lowest gradient (down from 160 in 1965 to 111 by 1988) and was somewhat lower than the gradient for life expectancy at birth which had fallen from 144 to 127. As in the case of the CMRs, the female gradient for life expectancy was at least 8 percentage points higher. The remaining figures show an extremely high gradient for private expenditure on health (1,964) and for supply of both nurses (1,571) and doctors (1,187). The gradient for nurses had almost doubled by 1984.

Inequality in relative government expenditure on health (expressed as a percentage of GNP) was much lower but the gradient also had increased from 367 in 1960 to 575 by 1986. In 1990 rich and developing countries spent $1500 and $41 respectively on health per person, a very steep gradient of 3,659%. The gradient for professional attendance at births was high (313) but it was low (138) for immunisation of one-year olds, an area of rapid recent improvement in LDCs. Finally, daily calorie supply had a gradient slightly in excess of that for life expectancy (142 compared with 127) but the calorie gradient had fallen from 155 in 1965 to 142 in 1986.

Social Class and Health in Britain

Health inequalities within a nation have begun to be studied particularly intensively in Britain where data, though by no means unproblematic, are more available than elsewhere. Britain had the seventeenth highest per capita income in the world by 1988 and, though its relative income and power has been declining, it still has been maintaining economic growth slightly above the world average. Its health standards have been improving considerably, including since the government pioneered a National Health Service in 1948, but the decrease in CDR since 1965 has been extremely modest (8%, compared with a world average of 29%).

The gradient for the difference between the median final income of the richest and poorest deciles in Britain was 151 (the average for 1961 to 1975). The three tables show national class gradients for mortality between about 1930 and 1984 and for morbidity, health care and use-need, mainly in the 1970s. The class gradient indicates the ratio of the unskilled manual or social class V to the professional or social class I. As may be expected, the figures in the first table show smaller gradients between social classes within nations than between categories of nations, whether based on per capita income or level of development. For example, the international and national gradients for IMR in the 1965-72 period were 496 and 258 respectively. By the 1980s the respective gradients were 800 and about 239. Inequalities of mortality within Britain were greatest for deaths from respiratory diseases, lung cancer and motor accidents, infant mortality, CDR for those aged 15 to 64, SMR for children aged 1 to 14, postneonatal deaths and stillbirths. Gradients were smallest for deaths due to ischaemic heart disease and cerebrovascular disease, for perinatal deaths and for SMRs of adults (with a decline in gradient as adult age rises). The trend over time poses various problems of data availability and comparability (arising partly from re-classification of occupations), but most indicators of mortality show some degree of increase in inter-class inequality. The exceptions are IMR (marginally down by 1984); postneonatal mortality (down from a gradient of 202 in 1975 to

178 in 1984 but subject to considerable fluctuation from one year to the next); and age-standardised death rate for those aged 15 to 64 (which fell between 1961 and 1971 but was still very much higher than in 1951). The figures for morbidity reveal a similar range of gradients, from 568 down to 116. Inequality was higher for absence from work and associated chronic sickness (all over 200), whereas no inter-class differences for acute or short-term sickness exceeded 200. The gradients for use of GP and hospital services were mostly lower than for morbidity, indicating a shortfall between compensatory use of health care and the almost invariably higher need for health care by the unskilled. For example, unskilled manual males had nearly three times as much chronic sickness as professionals, with the gradient standing at 292. Lower class men did use hospital inpatient and GP services more than professionals but the gradients (178 and 238 for hospitals and 132 and 146 for GPs) hardly compensate for three times the amount of chronic sickness. The standardised patient consultation ratios for specific diseases are interesting in themselves, in that they reveal wide variations in class gradient. The mortality ratios shown in brackets demonstrate that, for some diseases, the mortality gradient far exceeds the morbidity gradient (as in the case of bronchitis, respiratory TB and pneumonia) and yet for some diseases (such as ulcers, coronary disease and cancers) the reverse was true. Finally, the use-need ratio and related indices confirm the already observed dissonance between relative need and relative use of health services by the unskilled manual category. The inequality was least for acute illness (especially female) and was much higher for chronic illness, whether measured in relation to use of either hospital outpatient or GP services. In both cases female inequality was nearly 50 percent higher than male inequality and peaked at 323 in the case of consultation by women at hospital outpatients (Cf. 286 for GP consultation). Overall, inequality of chronic morbidity ranged from 200 to 348 whereas the acute morbidity gradient was appreciably lower (116 to 200). Because the use of hospital inpatient care and GP consultations was much less unequal than was warranted by the very unequal levels of chronic morbidity between classes, one finds that the use-morbidity indices are particularly unequal in relation to chronic handicapping illness. If the figures for Scotland are typical of Britain as a whole, then female use of inpatient care by the unskilled class was insufficiently unequal (166) to compensate for the very high class difference in chronic sickness (348). The gradient of outpatient consultation to chronic handicap remains high, at 323. Note, however, that here this comparison of morbidity, health care and use-morbidity is based on different years and regions. Male social class V use of hospital beds was significantly higher but not sufficiently so to reduce the inequality of the OPD index below 217. Both acute sickness and GP consultation were more equal between classes and so it is to be expected that the GP use-need indices would also be fairly equal and particularly so for women.

Townsend (1988) identifies four theories which help to explain inter-class inequality in health. Two of these theories are, firstly, the materialist or structuralist approach (which Townsend favours) and, secondly, the (less radical) sociocultural perspective. These have already been outlined briefly, earlier in this chapter. The remaining two so-called 'theories' perhaps resemble methodological footnotes as much as 'grand theory'. The first, the 'artefact explanation' focuses on the artificiality and complexity of the key variables (class and health) and the unlikelihood of any causal significance in their interrelationship. Britain's economic growth has led to a decline in the proportion of unskilled and semi-skilled workers and a commensurate increase in the proportion of professional and other higher class workers. (One might also mention the reduction in class V workers as numbers of unemployed increase.) It is argued that depletion of social class V (and class IV) leaves a hard core or 'sink' of the least able and least healthy in the lower social classes, as the more able succeed in becoming upward mobile. Presumably, the more successful the strategy for economic growth, the more concentrated and the more relatively unhealthy becomes the minority of unskilled left at the bottom of the occupational hierarchy.

The remaining theory, natural and social selection, seems integrally related to this view of health inequality as a purely 'statistical artefact'. This 'Darwinian' approach is also concerned with upward and downward social mobility and attributes this primarily to health. In other words, it is not class which determines health but rather health which determines class and especially the social class people move into during adulthood. (Common sense suggests that there is a two-directional reciprocal relationship between class and health.) However, one further possibility is that the richest and poorest have the worst health and middle income persons the best (see Lerner 1969). Townsend and others seem both surprised and cautious over the apparent increase in inequality of mortality over time, given the undisputed general fall in mortality and, in some respects, in morbidity. However, it seems just as plausible to posit that, in an age of falling mortality, the richer, more educated and more privileged members of the upper classes will improve their health at a much faster rate than the lower social classes, especially if successive governments fail to focus on the health problems of the lowest classes and also if government policy on health tends to dwell exclusively or disproportionately upon the National Health Service, the size of the budget allocated to it and on similar shibboleths. The more that academic and public debate can be displaced onto no doubt entirely desirable discussion of sectoral issues such as NHS management (especially the degree of marketisation and commercialisation which is necessary to optimise resource use), the more the dominant classes, the government and other interested parties can distract people from focusing on much wider and more fundamental multisectoral issues, including wealth and power distribution, and their effect on both health-related behaviour and ultimately on health itself.

INTERNATIONAL AND NATIONAL GRADIENTS IN HEALTH, WB/UNDP COUNTRIES + UK 1930-88

INDICATOR	1950-59	1960-69	1970-79	1980-86	1987 or 1988
INTERNATIONAL					
INCOME					
GNP PC					5,338
GNP PC			2,417*		3,083*
REAL GDP PC (PARITY PURCHASING POWER)					1,223
MORTALITY					
MATERNAL MORTALITY RATE				5,127;1,243*	
CMR		425			849 630*
IMR		496			800 535*
LE FEMALE		148			132
LE MALE		140			122
LE TOTAL		144 162*	145*		127 133*
CDR		160			111
HEALTH CARE					
POPULATION PER NURSE		851		1,571 867*	
POPULATION PER DOCTOR		1,038		1,187 1,467*	
DAILY CALORIES SUPPLY PER CAPITA		155		142	
BRITAIN					
INCOME					
FINAL PERSONAL INCOME PER HH (TOP 10% AS % OF POOREST 10%)	1,394; 1,013; 948; 772				
MORTALITY					
IMR (250 IN 1930-32)	221		258	c239	
CDR, AGED 15-64			244		
STANDARDISED MORTALITY RATIO, AGED 1-14			219M 175F		
SMR, MALES AGED 15-64 (123 in 1930-32)	137	188	178	c243	Ages 20-64
adjusted		169	161		
SMR, FEMALES AGED 15-64		176	165	c196	
AGE STANDARDISED DR, 15-64	133	163	156		
MORBIDITY					
AV.WORKDAYS LOST PER PERSON P.A. THROUGH ILLNESS OR INJURY			520		
CHRONIC SICKNESS INDICATORS			200 TO 348		
ACUTE SICKNESS INDICATORS			116 TO 200		
HOSPITAL CARE INDICATORS			166 TO 238		
GP CARE INDICATORS			118 TO 146		
USE-NEED HOSPITAL OUTPATIENT USE: CHRONIC ILLNESS			217 to 323		
GP CONSULTATION: CHRONIC HANDICAPPING ILLNESS			200 TO 286		
GP CONSULTATION: DAYS RESTRICTED ACTIVITY, 2 WEEKS			120 TO 135		

* Countries with low 'human' development as a % of performance of countries with high 'human' development. M = Male; F = Female. Sources: WB 1990; UNDP 1990; Townsend 1988.

NATIONAL GRADIENTS IN MORTALITY, UK OR ENGLAND AND WALES 1930-84

	UNSKILLED(S.C.V) AS % OF PROFESSIONAL (S.C.I.)					
INDICATOR	1949-53 M = MALE	1959-63 M	F	1970-72 M	F	1979-83 or 1984 T
SMR, 15-64, DEATH, BRONCHITIS	503			522		
SMR, 15-64, DEATH, PNEUMONIA	283			476		
SMR, 15-64 DEATH, LUNG CANCER				297		
IMR (250 in 1930-2)	221			250 258 M + F	270	c239 (1984)
CDR, 15-64, 1971				248	241	
SMR, DEATH, RESPIRATORY TB	247					
SMR, DEATH, INFLUENZA	240					
SMR, 15-64, DEATH, MOTOR VEHICLE ACCIDENTS				226		
SMR, 1-14				219	175	
POSTNEONATAL DEATH * GRADIENT INCREASING 1949-72				202 M + F (1975)		186(AV 1975-84) 178 (1984)
SMR, 25-34 *	145M	177		196		
STILLBIRTH				194 M + F		c210(1984)
SMR, 35-44 *	146M	171		180		
SMR, 45-54 *	126M	155		161		
SMR, 15-64 (MALE 123 in 1930-32)	137M	188	176	178	165	c243 c196
adjusted		169		161		(Ages 20-64)
SMR, 15-64 DEATH, CEREBROVASCULAR				170		150 (AV 1975-84)
PERINATAL DEATH *				c150 M + F		
AGE-STANDARDISED DEATH RATE, 15-64	133M (1951)	163 (1961)		156(1971)		
SMR, 15-64 *	112M	135		141		
SMR, 15-64 DEATH, ISCHAEMIC HEART DISEASE				126		

* Social Classes IV and V as % of I and II
SMR Standardised Mortality Ratio
Source: Townsend 1988.

GRADIENTS IN MORBIDITY, HEALTH CARE AND USE-NEED, UK 1955-6 AND 1970s

INDICATOR	YEAR	UNSKILLED MANUAL AS % OF PROFESSIONAL		
MORBIDITY		T	M	F
WORKDAYS LOST PER PERSON PER YEAR THROUGH ILLNESS OR INJURY.	1972	568		
	1971	472		
ABSENCE FROM WORK (Persons per 1000 Popn. due to illness or injury in 2 week ref.period)	1972	471		
Rounded to nearest 10 persons	1977	c300		
CHRONIC SICKNESS RATE (Persons per 1000 Popn. reporting limiting longstanding illness, all ages).	1976		292	348
LIMITING LONGSTANDING ILLNESS (Persons per 1000)	1971-6		299	317
ABSENCE FROM WORK (Persons per 1000).	1971	238		
LONGSTANDING ILLNESS (Persons per 1000).	1972-6		204	260
LIMITING LONGSTANDING ILLNESS.	1984		200+	200+
ACUTE SICKNESS RATE (Av. Days Restricted Activity per person per year, all ages)	1976		200	131
ACUTE SICKNESS DAYS PER PERSON.	1972-6		196	133
ACUTE SICKNESS RATE (Persons per 1000 Popn. in a 2 week reference period).	1971-6		129	116
HEALTH CARE				
HOSPITAL STANDARDISED BED-DAY RATIO, SCOTLAND	1971		238	166
HOSPITAL STANDARDISED DISCHARGE RATIO, SCOTLAND	1971		178	168
NO.OF CONSULTATIONS OF GPs PER 1000 POPN.	1971-6		146	118 (1972-6)
PERSONS CONSULTING A GP PER 1000 POPN.	1971-6		132	120
HEALTH CARE, SPECIFIC DISEASES (MORTALITY GRADIENTS 1949-53 IN PARENTHESES)				
STANDARDISED PATIENT CONSULTATION RATIOS (SPCRs) AGED 15-64				
BRONCHITIS (503 FOR MORTALITY)	1955-6		298	
GASTRIC + DUODENAL ULCER(197)	1955-6		242	
PNEUMONIA (283)	1955-6		189	
MALIGNANT NEOPLASMS (120)	1955-6		148	
INFLUENZA (240)	1955-6		129	
CORONARY DISEASE/ANGINA (60)	1955-6		104	
RESPIRATORY TB (247)	1955-6		89	
DIABETES MELLITUS (78)	1955-6		83	
HYPERTENSION (82)	1955-6		74	
USE-MORBIDITY				
HOSPITAL OPD INDEX (Ratio of Hospital Outpatient Consultation Rate to Prevalence of Chronic Handicapping Illness among Adults).	1970-2		46 (217)	31 (323)
GP INDEX (Ratio of GP Consultation Rate to Prevalence of Chronic Handicapping Illness among Adults).	1970-2		50 (200)	35 (286)
USE-NEED RATIO (GP Consultations divided by Days Restricted Activity in a 2-week reference period).	1974-6		74 (135)	83 (120)

Sources: OPCS 1978; Townsend 1988; Blane 1986.

CONCLUSION

In general, health is influenced by biological, demographic, environmental, sociocultural, political economy and health care types of factor. In India, particular variables within this typology of factors which influence health include genetic defects arising from parental malnutrition, high parity, poor housing, water supply and sanitation, caste, religion and communal conflict, illiteracy, low education (especially inadequate health education), the 'unhealthy State', rural class structure and poverty, seasonality of income and of disease, male dominance and relatively expensive and inadequate health care.

International variation in life expectancy and in crude death rate was analysed in some detail. Average life expectancy was found to be related to per capita income, economic growth and poverty incidence, especially rural poverty. Life expectancy apears not to be related to income distribution and particularly not to the Gini coefficient which measures inequality across the whole range of persons or households. Crude death rates also correlate with per capita income but less significantly and less consistently than does life expectancy. The relationship between economic growth and CDR resembles that for life expectancy, except for countries with medium mortality. Poverty, especially rural poverty, correlates with mortality but less so than it does with life expectancy. Low mortality actually correlates with more unequal income distribution, when expressed in terms of either the absolute or the relative income share of the poorest quintile.

Inequalities of income, mortality, morbidity, health care and use of health care relative to morbidity or need were compared for rich and poor nations and also for professional and unskilled manual classes within Britain. Comparative figures for some of the more important indicators were:

INDICATOR	GRADIENT OF INEQUALITY	
	INTERNATIONAL	UK
Real PCI	1,223	772
MMR	1,243 to 5,127	NA
CMR	849	(197) Ages 1-14
IMR	800	c239
LE	127	NA
CDR	111	(244)Ages 15-64
Male SMR, ages 20-64	NA	c243

Comparison of such international and intra-national inequality confirms what might be expected, namely that international inequalities tend to be greater, particularly for real income and maternal, child and infant mortality. However, crude death rates have been equalising and are now almost equal between rich and poor nations, mainly because of differences in age structure. Life expectancies are less equal than crude death rates but are also becoming more equal and are already fairly equal.

The level of inequality also varies according to which type of indicator is used, as the following table shows. None of the health inequalities were as large as the income differences, except for the very wide international range in maternal mortality. Given the larger international inequalities anyway, it is hardly surprising that differences in degree of inequality between indicators is greater for nations than for classes. Unfortunately, international data on morbidity have not been analysed but are becoming increasingly available (see WHO 1989).

INDICATOR		GRADIENT OF INEQUALITY	
		INTERNATIONAL	UK
INCOME	Real PCI or Parity Purchasing Power	1,223	772
MORTALITY	General Mortality	111 to 133	156 to 244
	Infant & Child Mortality	535 to 849	175 to 200
MORBIDITY	Absence from WORK through illness or injury	NA	520
	Chronic sickness	NA	200 to 348
	Acute sickness	NA	116 to 200
HEALTH CARE	Health care	851 to 1,571	NA
	Hospital care	NA	166 to 238
	GP care	NA	118 to 146
USE-NEED	GP & Hospital Consultation relative to Chronic Handicap	NA	200 to 323
	GP Consultation relative to Acute sickness	NA	120 to 135

International inequality of health care parallels income inequality and always exceeds mortality inequality. The British data show very high inequality for income and sickness absence and high inequality of chronic morbidity and of consultation relative to chronic handicapping illness. General and infant mortality share similar medium ranges of inequality. So do British health care indicators and most indices of acute sickness (especially in terms of persons rather than days of sickness). Class equality is greatest for number of sick persons and for GP consultations relative to days of restricted activity. Inequality rises for use of hospital outpatient care and, to a lesser extent, of GPs, relative to chronic illness. In other words, inequality seems to be worse for more serious events such as premature death (in LDCs) and chronic illness (and proportionate care) in Britain.

The next table shows relative inequalities for male and female indicators.

CLASS GRADIENT OF INEQUALITY

INDICATOR	MALE	FEMALE	FEMALE INEQUALITY AS % OF MALE
Scot. Hospital Outpatient: Chronic	217	323	149
UK GP index (Chronic)	200	286	143
UK Longstanding illness	204	260	127
UK Chronic sickness	292	348	119
Intl. Life expectancy	122	132	108
UK IMR, 1970-2	250	270	108
UK CDR, 15-64	248	241	97

Female inter-class inequality exceeded male inter-class inequality most in the case of consultations relative to chronic handicapping illness and also in the case of the numbers of chronically sick persons. International inequality of life expectancy and UK inequality of IMR were also higher for females but only marginally. For other UK indicators, especially on acute sickness, hospitalisation, use-need of GPs and SMRs at all ages, female inequalities were lower than male. In short, women in social class V are at their greatest disadvantage (compared with the relative disadvantage of social class V men) in chronic sickness and use of health care relative to that chronic illness. Women in the poorest nations suffer analogously in relation to life expectancy but to a smaller extent.

Health gradients differ for the various age categories. Internationally, inequality is currently similar for both infant and child (or under five) mortality - both very high, around 800. In the UK the infant mortality gradient is much less (about 239?) but seems to attract much more academic and political attention from Townsend and others than the international gradient, which is about three times the British national gradient. Gradients for SMRs of adult males were lower than for children in 1970-2 and declined consistently with age in 1970-2 and, with one exception, in 1949-53:

CLASS GRADIENT OF INEQUALITY OF MALE SMR

IMR Age category	0-1	1-14	25-34	SMR 35-44	45-54	55-64	TOTAL
SMR of S.C. IV & V as % S.C. I & II 1970-2	250*	219	196	180	161	141	178
1949-53	221*	NA	145	146	126	112	137
% Points increase 1949-53 to 1970-2	29	NA	51	34	35	29	41

Source: Townsend 1988:60   * Female and Male

These inequalities appear to have increased in the 20-year period and the increase was particularly marked for the 25 to 34 age category.

British gradients also differed according to the disease, and were highest for respiratory diseases, lung cancer and ulcers. The range of inequality was much wider for mortality (up to 522) than for morbidity (up to 298) and there was not always any correlation between mortality and morbidity gradients for the same disease.

Finally, the table shows changes in the inequality gradients over time. Comparison is made less satisfactory by the lack of congruence in the time periods for different indicators and, though the rate of change has been reduced (rather ambitiously) to a single annual rate in the final column, comparability is obviously impaired. However, the figures show that inequality has been increasing faster at the international level than within Britain and that the rate of unequalisation was speedier for at least two health indicators (above all for nurse provision but also for IMR) than even for money income per capita. (Income unequalisation between rich and poor nations has almost certainly been faster than the 2.5% per year between the high and low 'human development' countries shown here.)

INDICATOR	TIME PERIOD	GRADIENT OF INEQUALITY: EARLIER	GRADIENT OF INEQUALITY: LATER	% CHANGE	% POINTS CHANGE PER YEAR
*					
Intl.Popn.per nurse	1965-84	851	1,571	85	4.4
Intl. IMR	1965-88	496	800	61	2.7
Intl. GNP Per Capita (Human development)	1976-87	2,417	3,083	28	2.5
UK SMR, Males aged 15 (or 20) to 64	1931-84	123	c243	98	1.8
Intl. CMR (Human development categories)	1960-88	425	630	48	1.7
Intl. Popn per doctor	1965-84	1,038	1,187	14	0.8
UK SMR, Females aged 15 (or 20) to 64	1961-84	176	c196	11	0.5
UK IMR	1931-84	250	c239	-4	-0.1
Intl. Life expectancy	1965-88	144	127	-12	-0.5
Intl. CDR	1965-88	160	111	-31	-1.3
UK Personal final income per hh.	1961-75	1,394	772	-45	-3.2

In the UK, male adult SMRs appear to have been growing less equal between 1930-2 and 1984, at the fastest rate of any indicator and over three times faster than comparable female unequalisation. International inequalities in doctor provision have been growing five times slower than inequality of nurse provision. Changes in (medium) IMR inequality in the UK appear quite negligible, over a 53-year period. Inequalities in international life expectancy and especially CDR have fallen significantly since 1965 and UK income inequalities (at the extreme deciles) had fallen sharply (down 3.2% per year), at least until 1975.

JAMMU
&
KASHMIR
CHINA
PAKISTAN
HIMACHAL
PRADESH
TIBET
PUNJAB
HARYANA
DELHI
NEPAL
SIKKIM
ARUNACHAL
PRADESH
BHUTAN
UTTAR
PRADESH
RAJASTHAN
ASSAM
NAGAL
MEGHALAYA
MANIPUR
BIHAR
BANGLA
DESH
MIZORAM
WEST
BENGAL
GUJARAT
MADHYA PRADESH
CALCUTTA
TRIPURA
BURM
ORISSA
MAHARASHTRA
BOMBAY
ANDHRA
PRADESH
BAY OF
BENGAL
GOA
KARNATAKA
MADRAS
ANDAMAN AND NICOBAR ISLANDS
(INDIA)
LAKSHADWEEP
(INDIA)
KERALA
TAMIL NADU
0
200
400
600
800 km
SRI
LANKA

2 Power, income distribution and health in India

Recent analysis of the political economy of India relates this mainly to economic (especially industrial) growth, rural development and poverty (especially rural). Mitra (1977), Toye (1981) and Bardhan (1984) present respectively CPI(M) Marxist, neo-Keynesian dirigeiste and econometric Marxian emphases on industrial growth, especially through public investment. Frankel (1978) highlights the gradualness and incompleteness of the socialist transition and Jha (1980) gives a partly neo-Gandhian explanation for low growth. Lipton (1977) and Brass (1990) approach rural poverty from a neo-populist perspective, using neoclassical economics and political modernisation theory respectively. All these writers have informed the debate but none are entirely persuasive on class dominance and all except Brass mainly ignore the non-class factors in State dominance (such as family, faction, caste, religion, gender and region). Emphasis on another non-class factor, the rural-urban dichotomy, varies. The dominant class is seen as either (1) a single class eg. the 'feudal' class (by the CPI) or, more often, the capitalist bourgeoisie (by the CPI-M and the majority of Indian communists?); or the 'urban class', as in Lipton (1977); or the 'intermediate class', as in Jha (1980); or (2) two classes, eg. the urban and rural bourgeoisies, as in Mitra (1977), or the metropolitan and national bourgeoisies, as in dependency theories; or (3) a coalition or alliance of three classes, eg. the dominant proprietary classes consisting of industrial capitalists, professionals, including white collar workers, and rich farmers, as in Bardhan (1984); the metropolitan and national bourgeoisies, plus the 'feudal' class, as perhaps in Alavi (1975, and 1983, relating to Pakistan); and various less specific 'multi-class' coalitions (which often refer more to political support for the ruling party than to the dominant class per se). In practice only Alavi of those mentioned is

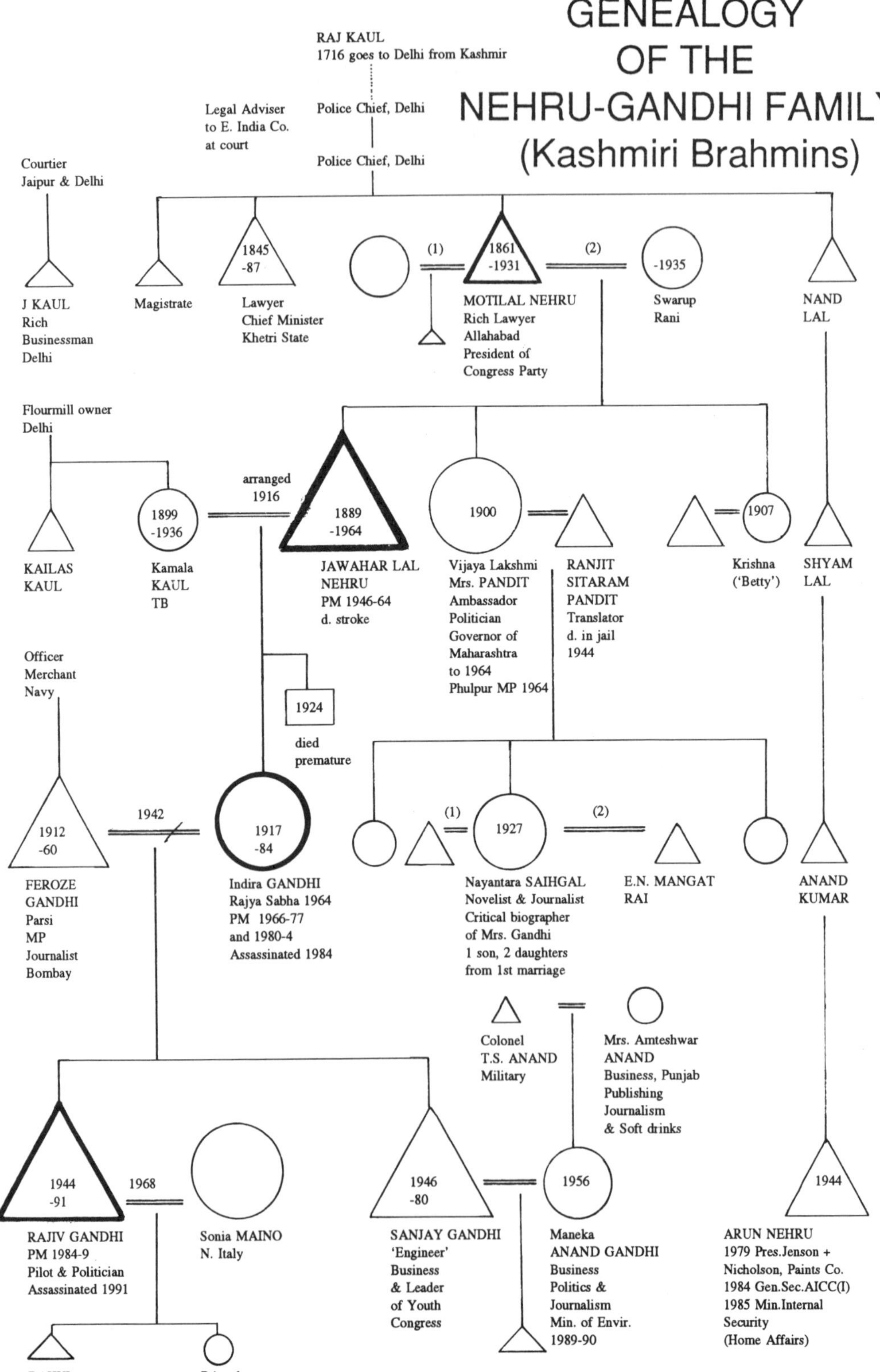

GENEALOGY OF THE NEHRU-GANDHI FAMILY (Kashmiri Brahmins)
RAJ KAUL
1716 goes to Delhi from Kashmir
Police Chief, Delhi
Legal Adviser to E. India Co. at court
Police Chief, Delhi
Courtier Jaipur & Delhi
J KAUL Rich Businessman Delhi
Magistrate
1845 -87
Lawyer Chief Minister Khetri State
(1)
1861 -1931
(2)
-1935
MOTILAL NEHRU Rich Lawyer Allahabad President of Congress Party
Swarup Rani
NAND LAL
Flourmill owner Delhi
arranged 1916
1899 -1936
1889 -1964
1900
1907
KAILAS KAUL
Kamala KAUL TB
JAWAHAR LAL NEHRU PM 1946-64 d. stroke
Vijaya Lakshmi Mrs. PANDIT Ambassador Politician Governor of Maharashtra to 1964 Phulpur MP 1964
RANJIT SITARAM PANDIT Translator d. in jail 1944
Krishna ('Betty')
SHYAM LAL
1924
died premature
Officer Merchant Navy
1942
1912 -60
1917 -84
(1)
1927
(2)
FEROZE GANDHI Parsi MP Journalist Bombay
Indira GANDHI Rajya Sabha 1964 PM 1966-77 and 1980-4 Assassinated 1984
Nayantara SAIHGAL Novelist & Journalist Critical biographer of Mrs. Gandhi 1 son, 2 daughters from 1st marriage
E.N. MANGAT RAI
ANAND KUMAR
Colonel T.S. ANAND Military
Mrs. Amteshwar ANAND Business, Punjab Publishing Journalism & Soft drinks
1944 -91
1968
1946 -80
1956
1944
RAJIV GANDHI PM 1984-9 Pilot & Politician Assassinated 1991
Sonia MAINO N. Italy
SANJAY GANDHI 'Engineer' Business & Leader of Youth Congress
Maneka ANAND GANDHI Business Politics & Journalism Min. of Envir. 1989-90
ARUN NEHRU 1979 Pres.Jenson + Nicholson, Paints Co. 1984 Gen.Sec.AICC(I) 1985 Min.Internal Security (Home Affairs)
RAHUL
Priyanka

a sociologist and Lipton's 'urban class' includes several urban classes and arguably the rural landlords. Jha's 'intermediate class' is perhaps even more disparate and includes smaller, family, private and less regulated companies, shopkeepers, traders, lenders, the self-employed, some government workers and professionals as well as rich (and perhaps some middle?) farmers who market a surplus.

Class analysis can neglect the importance of personality, family and faction. The genealogy shows the extremely dominant Nehru family, which includes three Prime Ministers who, by 1994, had ruled ruled India for over 38 out of 47 years of independence, two central Ministers and at least two MPs (see Ali 1985 and Brass 1990). Other families operate (less successfully) as provincial dynasties and factions are important at provincial, district and village levels.

Caste

Caste is also very important in both Indian politics and in the composition of the dominant class coalition (ie. the classes which supply both the personnel to the State institutions and also the non-functionaries in civil society who still influence the actions of State functionaries). Castes may be categorised according to varna, landownership, political dominance, occupation and entitlement to positive discrimination. Thus the 3,000 or so jatis may be categorised as twice-born (Brahmins or Kshatriyas), Vaisyas and Sudras; upper ('élite'), middle (sometimes called intermediate) and lower; or Forward, Backward and Scheduled. Relying on the now ancient census figures of 1931, India divides approximately into nearly 18 percent upper or forward castes; nearly 44 percent Hindu middle or backward castes (including 19 percent intermediate and 4 percent depressed); over 16 percent non-Hindus (mostly middle status, including nearly 8 percent now defined as 'backward'), 15 percent scheduled castes and 7.5 percent scheduled tribes (see Table). In oversimplified terms, this is an 18 percent-59 percent-23 percent split between upper, middle and lower status categories. Numerically important forward categories include Brahmins (5.5%) and Rajputs/Thakurs (3.9%); Marathas, dominant in Maharashtra (2.2%); Vaisya castes, including Banias (1.9%); the highly educated Kayasthas (1.1%); and Jats (1%) - who are Sudras and may even claim backward status. Other forward castes include Bhumihars in UP and Bihar, and Nayars in Kerala.

Some middle castes belong to the dominant rich and/or middle peasant landowning category, such as the Reddis and Kammas in Andhra, the Patidars and Kunbis in Gujarat and the Jats of Punjab, Haryana and western UP. 'Non-Brahmin' castes such as the Nadars and Mudaliars supplanted Brahmins in Tamil Nadu well before 1947.

The backward castes (or 'class') include most of the Sudra varna, the most numerous middle ranges of the Hindu hierarchy, plus over half the non-Hindus. The Constitution provided for possible positive discrimination towards them and policies such as reservation of scholarships and jobs for them on similar lines to those already established (and largely accepted) for the scheduled have provoked bitter and violent controversy in some states and increasingly, especially in 1990, nationally. The Mandal Commission divided the 3,248 backward castes into two categories, the 'intermediate' and the 'depressed'. The backwards in fact covers at least 52 percent of the population - much more, if one includes those upper middle castes and categories still seeking registration as backward. The intermediate castes include Sudra dominant and major landowning castes such as the Lingayats and Vokkaligas in Karnataka. Both of these castes have been listed as backward at various times. Non-dominant, landowning backward castes include Ahirs/Yadavs, Kurmis and Gujars in UP and Bihar, Bishnois in Haryana, and Kshatriyas (including Kolis) in Gujarat. Some forward castes (such as the Jats) align themselves with the backward castes in the increasingly acute conflict over political dominance, land, education and white-collar jobs. In some states, notably Karnataka, both Congress (changing its caste strategy) and Janata or other opposition parties have each owed their majority to support from the backward castes.

APPROXIMATE % DISTRIBUTION OF CASTE CATEGORIES IN POPULATION, BASED ON THE 1931 CENSUS

MODERN CATEGORY	BRAHMIN KSHATRIYA + VAISYA	SUDRA	SCHEDULED		HINDU TOTAL (EXCL.STs)	NON HINDU	TOTAL
			CASTES	TRIBES			
FORWARD CASTES (Aghla)							
Brahmin	5.5	Kayastha 1.1					
Bhumihar							
Rajput/Thakur	3.9	Jat 1.0					
Maratha (Maharashtra)	2.2	Other 2.0 or less					
Vaisya incl. Bania	1.9						
TOTAL FORWARD	13.5 +	4.1 or less			(17.6)		17.6
NON-HINDU NON-BACKWARD (BUT MIDDLE STATUS)						7.7	7.7
BACKWARD CASTES (Pichchla)							
INTERMEDIATE BACKWARD							
Landowning or cultivating castes		6.4					
Market gardening castes		2.1					
Pastoral, excl. Shepherds		2.5					
Military, excl. Rajputs		1.8					
Weavers		1.4					
Oil Mongers		1.4					
Potters		1.1					
TOTAL INTERMEDIATE BACKWARD		19.6			(19.6)	6.8	26.4
DEPRESSED BACKWARD					Scavengers Muslim: Ex-criminal + nomadic tribes; Shepherds		
TOTAL DEPRESSED BACKWARD		24.1			(24.1)	(1.6)	25.7
TOTAL BACKWARD CASTES		(43.7)			(43.7)	(8.4)	(52.1)
SCHEDULED			15.1	7.5	(15.2)	(0.7+)	22.6
TOTAL	13.5	47.8	15.1	7.5	(76.5)	(16.1)	100.0

Note: In 1981 the proportions were: Muslims 11.4%; Christians 2.4%; Sikhs 2.0%; scheduled 15.7%; and scheduled tribes 7.8%

Source: GOI, Mandal Report 1981:235.

Various Commissions on the Backward Classes have reported, including Mandal in 1980 and Venkataswamy in 1986 at the national level and Bakshi (1976) and Rane (1983) in Gujarat. These commissions have deliberated on such crucial questions as the criteria for eligibility, identification of backward castes and occupations, and the percentage of jobs and other goodies to be reserved for them.

The 'scheduled' castes (15.7%) refers to the avarna or ex-untouchables (or Harijans) who were originally listed on a 1935 schedule of categories entitled to positive discrimination which was established in principle by the 1950 Constitution. This includes reservation of about 15 percent of seats in legislatures, scholarships, jobs and promotions. These benefits have served to coopt an elite within the scheduled castes and usually to secure scheduled support for Congress. They have also antagonised many backward castes who regard themselves as equally underprivileged and deserving of aid as the average scheduled and much more so than rich scheduled. (This raises the important question of congruence and articulation between caste and class.)

The 'scheduled' tribes (7.8%) are the most disadvantaged and exploited category but positive discrimination towards them has been taken up even less than by the scheduled castes and aid has more often been misappropriated or diverted than in the case of the scheduled castes. This applies particularly to tribals in areas like north-central India (especially Madhya Pradesh, with 12 million tribals) where they form a minority of the population. In the north-east tribals have benefited from being a majority and from geopolitical and military considerations affecting central policy and State allocation of resources to border areas.

Over 16 percent are non-Hindus, of which most (11.4%) were Muslims in 1981. Muslims are divided by caste (including some having backward status), by sect (Sunni and Shia), by religious philosophy and law (Deoband and Aligarh), and class, orthodoxy or progressiveness and region. Many Muslims are lower class workers, including handloom weavers, artisans and craftsmen as well as agricultural and other labourers. Support for Congress has been substantial but has become increasingly volatile, due to factors such as communal tension, riots, higher Muslim casualties in such riots and increasingly partisan and violent action by Hindu-dominated police and paramilitary forces. Christians (2.4%), with their foreign connections, mostly try to maintain a low political profile, except in Kerala and the northeast. Sikhs (2%) dominate the richest state (Punjab) and the virtual civil war there brought Sikh fundamentalism, communalism, terrorism and a high casualty rate close to the national capital. The Green Revolution and consequent structural (especially class) changes and shifts in income and welfare have been postulated as contributing to the communal and secessionist conflict in Punjab but class is only one element in a complex conflict which has been intensified by Congress intervention in, and manipulation of, Akali Dal factions.

SOCIAL COMPOSITION AND STRUCTURE, INDIA 1947

% OF LABOUR FORCE	CATEGORY	% OF NATIONAL INCOME
(18)	NON-VILLAGE ECONOMY	(44)
0.06	British officials and military British capitalists, plantation owners traders, bankers and managers	5
0.94	Native princes Big zamindars and jagirdars	3
	Indian capitalists, merchants and managers	
	The new Indian professional class	3
17	Petty traders, small entrepreneurs, traditional professions, clerical and manual workers in government, soldiers, railway workers (1M), industrial workers (3M), urban artisans, servants, sweepers and scavengers	30
(75)	VILLAGE ECONOMY	(54)
9	Village rentiers, rural money-lenders, small zamindars, tenants-in-chief	20
20	Working proprietors, protected tenants	18
29	Tenants-at-will, sharecroppers, village artisans and servants	12
17	Landless labourers, scavengers	4
7	TRIBAL ECONOMY	2
100	TOTAL ECONOMY	100

Source: Maddison 1971:69

Class

The 1981 census showed that, out of 245 million who were economically active (excluding Assam), 153 million worked in agriculture, hunting, forestry and fishing. A further 25.1 million worked in manufacturing, 18.6 million in community, social and personal services, 12.2 million in trade, restaurants and hotels, 6.1 million in transport, storage and communications, 3.6 million in construction, 1.7 million in finance, insurance, real estate and business services, 1.3 million in mining and quarrying, and nearly one million in electricity, gas and water. A further 22 million were in other activities or were marginal or unemployed.

Analysis of class in India can be even more variable and confusing than caste analysis. Here classes will be categorised as upper, middle or lower. The urban upper classes include the metropolitan or foreign bourgeoisie (including the World Bank, foreign governments and businesses, especially multinational companies); non-resident Indians (NRIs); the large, national (ie. resident Indian) bourgeoisie; the medium mainly regional bourgeoisie; and senior bureaucrats and professionals. The rural upper class includes former maharajas, rajas, talukdars, zamindars and other 'feudal' former tax-gatherers and landlords; other landlords; large or rich or capitalist (ie. hiring non-family labour) farmers (or peasants); and traders and moneylenders. Large, rich farmer status implies ownership or cultivation of at least 10 acres of average quality land (or perhaps Rs 40,000 of land and other assets?)

The middle classes comprise the 'petite bourgeoisie', the salaried, including middle and junior bureaucrats; the self-employed, including small shopkeepers, traders and owners of small, private industrial firms and other private businesses; and middle peasants, owning 5 to 10 acres of average quality land. (The average areas of owned and cultivated land per household were about 4.2 and 5.4 acres respectively in 1971.)

The lower classes include the industrial working class; artisans; urban labourers and unemployed manual workers; poor farmers, including small peasants (owning 2.5 to 5 acres), marginal farmers (1.25 to 2.5 acres) and submarginal farmers (less than 1.25 acres); tenant farmers, including sharecroppers (who usually retain less of the total crop than contract tenants paying a fixed amount, though this obviously depends on the percentage share and the fixed amount agreed); agricultural and non-agricultural labourers, including the totally landless and also bonded labourers who are 'enslaved' to an employer (eg. landlord, farmer or brickworks owner) who has advanced them money at high interest rates.

Urban Classes

Expositions on the nature of the dominant class or coalition by Bardhan (1984) and others give insufficient attention to changes in power over time. For example, foreign influence on the Indian State was high in the 1950s (partly because of aid and the colonial transition), decreased in the late 1960s and has increased after the 1973 recession, the IMF loan in 1980 and recent liberalisation. Only about 500 of the 2,500 public limited companies account for most of the trading on India's various stock exchanges, and 100 of these are subsidiaries of multinational corporations. The largest primarily foreign-owned company in 1982 was the Indian Tobacco Company, with sales of nearly Rs 6 billion. In terms of sales ITC ranked thirteenth among public and private sector companies. Other major MNCs include Hindustan Lever, Dunlop, Ashok Leyland and ICI, but MNCs are relatively less powerful in India than many LDCs. The already considerable political influence of major monopolists and business 'dynasties' such as the Tatas, Birlas, Mafatlals, Thapars, Singhanias, Shri Rams, Bangurs, Kirloskars, Modis, Sarabhais, Nandas, Mahindras, Bajajs, Ambanis, Iyengers and Shaw Wallace has almost certainly increased during the liberalised 1980s. Industrial capitalists have benefited, over a longer period, from import substitution policies, manipulation of industrial licensing (perversely), weak control or relaxation of control of monopoly and low food prices (and thus cheap wage goods). Their benefits have increased further since the liberalisation process accelerated after Rajiv's accession in 1984.

Over 230 million Indians now live in urban areas and perhaps more than 80 million of these belong to an educated, urban middle class. This includes 16 million government employees; four million at the centre, six million in the states and the rest in quasi-government and local government. At the pinnacle are up to 10,000 IAS and nearly 3,000 IPS officers, whose power increased during the emergency but has declined vis-a-vis the politicians since then. The police (over one million), the paramilitary (over a quarter of a million) and the armed forces (1.3 million) employ well over 2.5 million persons. The military are used at least 40 times per year to quell civil disturbances but have not otherwise so far intervened overtly in day-to-day politics. Brahmins, Kayasthas and other upper castes with high access to education are disproportionately represented in the professional class.

Professional bureaucrats have benefited from their regulation of foreign exchange, control of monopoly, licensing of industrial capacity, supervision of credit allocation and investment decisions and rationing of inputs. Bureaucratic power and the prices chargeable for bribery and corruption have both increased. Bureaucrats, including some upper class ones, can siphon off some of the resources of development and anti-poverty programmes which were ostensibly aimed at the lower class. In addition, government employees have insisted on 'dearness allowances' to keep their salaries in line with inflation. In 1977 central government employees received wages nearly five times the average per capita income but maximum pre-tax pay fell from 117 to 70 times average PCI in the 1960s. Some also benefit from subsidised food prices and other policies alleged to reflect 'urban bias'. The professionals, many of them hailing from Brahmin and other upper caste anti-business backgrounds, come into fairly frequent conflict with industrialists and traders who are seeking permits, licences, information and other publicly allocated resources. The professionals also have a vested, employment interest in further expansion of the public sector and their socialist rhetoric barely conceals their own vested class interests. The professionals can, by accident or design, divide or fragment the business class according to how (whimsically or otherwise) it distributes its favours. On the other hand, the analogous power of the professional bureaucrats over the rich farmers, even from the state capitals, is attenuated by geographical distance, poor communications and the sheer scale of numbers and variety of local circumstances controlled by the rich farmers on the spot. Professionals may influence administered prices, procurement, restrictions on grain movements and trade between states as well as distribution of scarce inputs but they have lost various battles for land reform - except in states like Karnataka where upper caste professionals with very little land allied with smaller farmers from backward castes to neutralise richer, dominant middle caste farmers (particularly from the Lingayat and Vokkaliga communities?).

The middle classes are referred to as the 'intermediate class' by Jha (1980). This seems an extremely numerous, disparate and amorphous range of occupations and social categories. Jha argues, not entirely convincingly, that members of the 'intermediate class', especially small, private firms, have benefited from being outside the formal, regulated economy and from being too small for regular government inspection and control. Many have benefited from speculation and hoarding, other illegal and quasi-legal operations, including tax evasion and avoidance, activities in the parallel economy (such as laundering 'black' money into party political funds or into extravagant, non-developmental projects such as new five-star hotels and urban real estate), smuggling and organised and other crime.

The lower classes include 23 million industrial workers, of whom 8 million work in the low-paid, small-scale sectors. The urban lower classes have benefited from the subsidised prices of foodgrains, sugar and other basic items sold in ration (or 'fair price') shops.

Rural Classes

Whatever the political links between urban and rural sections of the upper, middle and lower classes, the complexity of rural class structure requires separate analysis. Just as there is often considerable vagueness about caste status (especially in the large, middle ranges), so terms like large, rich, middle and small/poor peasants/farmers are bandied about without sufficient definition. As with caste, several overlapping hierarchical frameworks exist. The lower table on page 51 shows the percentage distribution of landownership in various years, using data from the National Sample Surveys. The trend between 1953-4 and 1971-2 was for over half the landless to have become marginal or submarginal owners and for about a fifth of large owners to have become small or medium or even marginal owners. By 1975 the rural agricultural population was divided into nearly 8 percent very large owners (20 or more acres); nearly 11 percent large owners (10 to 20 acres); over 16 percent medium owners (5 to 10 acres); 18.5 percent small owners (2.5 to 5 acres); nearly 16 percent marginal owners (1.25 to 2.5 acres); nearly 19 percent submarginal or below subsistence farmers (less than 1.25 acres); and over 12 percent owning no land at all. In 1975 the proportion below the poverty line decreased with holding size but only fell below 50 percent after 5 acres and only below 30 percent after 20 acres. This suggests that owners with similar sizes of holding may vary widely in income and perhaps even class. The figures indicate that 35 percent of the rural agricultural population owns at least 5 acres per household. Brass (1990) estimates that in most states 20 percent of the rural population controls an economic holding of between 5 and 25 acres. These mainly upper and intermediate castes form a dominant rural class which controls local institutions, including panchayats, cooperatives and to a large extent the lower ranks of the police and lower revenue officials.

The highest rural class, the so-called 'feudal' class of rajas, talukdars and zamindars has certainly lost considerable wealth and power, through abolition of zamindari, intermediate tenures, tax farming, princely purses and other Nehruvian, 'anti-feudal' measures. On the other hand, many ex-princes and ex-zamindars are still prominent in Indian politics and former Prime Minister V.P. Singh is himself the adopted son of an ex-zamindar. It is highly debatable whether Bardhan is justified in referring to a 'phantom' feudal class, especially in the Hindi belt. Brass claims that

> the cumulative result of the legislation to abolish intermediaries and to limit the size of landholding has been to curtail significantly the political and economic control over the land of the former big zamindars and talukdars, to perpetuate the local political and economic influence of the major élite proprietary castes such as the Brahmins, Rajputs, Jats and Bhumihars in north India, and to enhance the major cultivating castes of middle status, particularly the Ahirs (Yadavs) and Kurmis in north India, the Jats of western UP, Haryana and Punjab, the Marathas in Maharashtra and the Kammas and Reddis in Andhra (1990:282-3)..... Such power and wealth as exists in the Indian countryside belongs to the land controlling castes. In some districts and localities in the country, particularly in north India, ex-landlords with extensive and illegal holdings remain powerful and have even extended their sway politically over large segments of a district or even over an entire district. Where they are descendants of former princes or local rajas and especially where they maintain some of the traditions of local kingship by acting as the benefactors and protectors of the local populations, they draw up traditional loyalties which cross both class and caste boundaries to a considerable extent (1990:330).

Some Zamindars have established trust funds to build large schools as a means of evading land reforms and of winning local support.

Rich peasants or farmers are generally seen as having improved their position, partly at the expense of the 'feudal' class, partly through the Green Revolution and partly through exploitation of the rural poor. Adult suffrage in 1947 enhanced the power of controllers of rural 'vote banks' and Congress became dominated by a less narrowly urban range of professional and other categories. Zamindari abolition in the 1950s increased their land and relative power and no doubt some of the smaller zamindars fell down into the rich farmer category. Through control of state governments they successfully blocked other land reforms (especially the reduction of land ceilings) in most states and had a strong influence on agricultural policies. They monopolised access to subsidised inputs, such as irrigation, electricity, tractors, diesel fuel, fertilisers, rural credit and seeds (especially the new HYVs and particularly wheat, not least in the richest state, Punjab). They enjoyed rising output prices for foodgrain, consequent improvements in the terms of trade between agricultural and nonagricultural commodities and negligible taxation on rising wealth, incomes and profits. They were the initial, if not necessarily the exclusive, beneficiaries of the Green Revolution, which certainly involved economies from high risk-taking, whatever the truth about 'economies of scale'. More subtly, perhaps, as new technologies and policies are introduced, the differential benefits to various rural classes have shifted over time. Bardhan claims that rich farmers can exercise hegemony over the small and medium family farmers (2.5 to 10 acres?) because the latter also benefit from subsidised input and inflated output prices - though, arguably, later on?

The rich farmers are clearly the most numerous of Bardhan's three dominant classes and, perhaps partly because of their size and heterogeneity, there seems to be most disagreement about their position and power. Bardhan notes that 'the industrial capitalist class, the rich farmers and the professions all belong roughly to the top two [income] deciles of the population' (1984:54) though this rather suggests that they form rather less than 20 percent of the total population, i.e. less than about 170 million in 1990. The rural population in 1990 was about 622 millions and, if the proportion of cultivators of 10 acres or more is still 13.1 percent (as it was in the 1976-7 agricultural census), then about 81.5 million belong to the rich farmer class. Add on, say, 10 million or more professionals (both civilian and military), including white-collar workers and up to a million industrial capitalists and the dominant coalition could include nearly 100 million persons!

Inevitably, such a large class of up to 85 million rich farmers is divided internally. There are differences of caste, religion, region, language, culture, faction, political party, crops, economic interest and ideology. They can unite on common interests of higher prices and no reform of the agrarian structure but they are deeply disunited on other matters, especially access to public resources, including inputs and reserved seats in colleges and jobs in government. Overall, Brass (1990) claims that the weakening from centrifugal, disuniting forces helps explain the net aggregate disadvantages accruing to the rural population of all classes.

However, Bardhan, in analysing the various divergences of interest between his three dominant, proprietary classes, regards the conflict 'between the urban industrial and professional classes on the one hand and the rural hegemonic class of rich farmers on the other' (1984:54) as the sharpest and most overt. This conflict focuses particularly on unfavourable terms of trade between agriculture and industry and on urban parasitism (especially of bureaucrats, intellectuals - particularly leftist ones, and the inefficient public industries they tend to support and man). Meanwhile the urban classes deplore the negligible taxation of the rural rich.

Frankel argues that the Green Revolution has strengthened the dominance of the rich farmer castes and that commercialisation has led to class polarisation and class conflict, especially between rich peasants ('the kulaks') and their farm labourers. Brass (1990) raises the question of the extent to which the rich farmers are capitalist and employing labour. In fact the rich farmers include ex-zamindars, capitalist employers and family peasant farmers. Leftist critics of the rich farmers claim that the rural capitalist exploiters of labour provide a political lead not only to the rich peasants but also to the middle peasants (with 2.5 to 10 acres). Brass dissents from this and concludes that Nehruvian, industrialising and centralising policies of Congress have produced a neglect of agriculture which hardly suggests political strength of rich and/or middle peasants. However, he also argues, not entirely consistently, that, though the Congress bias towards industry has weakened the 'former landlord class', Congress patronage and protection has been extended to 'the new class of independent rural landowning proprietors' (1990:271).

Middle peasants presumably refers to small owners (2.5 to 5 acres) and medium owners (5 to 10 acres). There is much propaganda and theorising about the 'rise' of the middle peasants who are also mainly of middle caste (including backward) status. Brass instances middle peasant farmer movements in Maharashtra (such as that of Sharad Joshi) and in UP (such as the Jat, Tikait) as evidence that the middle (and richer) peasantry are not part of a dominant, exploiting class. Nevertheless, Congress still tries to coopt dissidents from the rich and middle peasantry into the ruling coalition through appeals to caste. Chapter 3 describes this process in UP, increasingly a cockpit of middle peasant, middle caste politics.

The rural lower classes include mini-owners (ie. marginal and submarginal owners), tenants and landless labourers. Male agricultural workers as a proportion of the rural workforce increased from somewhere between 13 and 16 percent in 1961 to over 21 percent in 1971. They too are often also divided by caste and the various other factors discussed already. They have benefited from extremely modest land redistribution, and Bardhan estimates that only 0.6 percent of total cultivated area has been involved); 'trickle down' from the Green Revolution; a plethora of rural development, employment and anti-poverty programmes, including 'loan melas' and other hyperpopulist gestures which can only benefit a minority. Desai, Gough, Byres and others have emphasised peasant protests but Brass (1990) can identify only seven major peasant uprisings since 1947. All of these have involved tribals, have been localised to parts of districts within a single linguistic region and have been led by Communist party cadres. He claims that they all preceded the Green Revolution which he dates, rather arbitrarily, as having started in 1967-8. The implication is that these uprisings came before any class polarisation arising from depeasantisation and/or proletarianisation which might be attributable to technological and other changes introduced during the Green Revolution. Brass concedes that there has been serious rural violence in Punjab, in much of Bihar (especially in tribal areas and also particularly in Bhojpur district) and in Thanjavur district in Tamil Nadu.

Conflict and terrorism in rural Punjab is now so serious that many farmers are migrating to the relative security of the urban areas and the main question is the extent to which this very bloody conflict (which is also post-Green Revolution) is related to agrarian change and class conflict. Brass claims that class conflict has mainly occurred in backward, not Green Revolution, areas and has involved disputes 'over wages, not over land' (1990:308). He concludes that 'no stable power base can be built upon the poor and the landless' (1990:310) but this seems to ignore the example of West Bengal (where a CPI(M)-led Left Front had by 1994 ruled for 17 continuous years) and the (less stable) example of Kerala.

% DISTRIBUTION OF POPULATION BY CASTE, CLASS AND LANDOWNERSHIP, INDIA

CLASS	UPPER CASTE		MIDDLE CASTE Upper	 Lower	SCHEDULED CASTE + TRIBE	TOTAL OWNED
UPPER CLASS 10+ acres owned per Hh	Metropolitan bourgeoisie; Nehru (BR) family	Non Hindu non- Back- ward	Intermediate Backward	Depressed Backward		Very large 20.1+acres 7.9%
	Brahmin, Kshatriya & Vaisya business. BR, KAYASTHA professional bureaucrats Bhadralok (W.Bengal)		Sudra business		Scheduled business	Large 10.1 to 20 acres 10.7%
	BR,K + V Feudal incl. BHUMIHAR BR,K + V Rich farmers		Sudra Feudal Sudra Rich Farmers incl. JAT and JAT Sikh		Sched. Rich Farmers	MAX OVERALL 20%
MIDDLE CLASS 2.5 to 10 acres owned	5 to 10 acres MEDIUM FARMERS	7.7% or less	JAT farmers BISHNOI LINGAYAT PATIDAR/KUNBI REDDI/KAMMA NADAR/MUDALIAR Sudra Middle Peasants	 AHIR/YADAV KURMI GUJAR		Medium 5 to 10 acres 16.3%
	2.5 to 5 acres SMALL FARMERS		JAT Sikh farmers + Punjabi farmers (Av. 3.8 acres)			Small 2.5 to 5 acres 18.5% TOTAL 34.8
LOWER CLASS 0 TO 2.5 acres owned			Sudra Poor Peasants			Marginal + sub marginal 0 to 2.5 acres 46.6%
Marginal 1.25 to 2.5						marginal 1.25 to 2.5 acres 15.7%
Submarginal 0.1 to 1.25						submarginal 0.1 to 1.25 acres 18.6%
Landless	BR landless labourers	7.7%	MUSLIM SIKH	11.4% 2.0%	CHAMAR landless labourers Bonded labs. Tribals	No land 12.3% TOTAL 46.6
TOTAL	17.6% incl. 5.5% BR 3.9% RAJPUT & 1.4% MARATHA; BHUMIHAR		Non Hindu non Backward Non Hindu Intermediate B. Non Hindu Depressed	7.7 6.8 1.6	15.1 SC 7.5 ST	100%
			NON HINDU Hindu Intermediate Hindu Depressed	16.1 19.6 24.1	22.6 SC/ST	
			TOTAL BACKWARD	52.1		
	17.6 UPPER		NON-HINDU AND HINDU INTER + DEPRESSED	59.8	22.6 SC/ST	100

Ultimately, it is necessary to try to assess which of the nine broad categories (encompassed in the matrix of 3 class categories x 3 caste categories shown in the table) have improved or worsened their economic and political position. This is, of course, extremely difficult to assess in such broad terms. The conventional wisdom seems to be that: (1) change between classes has been small and gradual; (2) there has been differential change within classes, including within the upper class and also within the dominant upper class, upper caste category; (3) the middle class, middle caste category has become the most assertive, whether this refers to the middle and small peasant farmers (which includes many Punjabi and Jat Sikh farmers) and/or the backward castes; (4) the increasingly assertive middle ranks have not achieved power at the centre nor in many states and, even in states where they have achieved power, that power has not been longlived; (5) the lower class has not benefited very much and certainly not as much as the scale of programmes and political rhetoric might suggest; and (6) there has been differential change within the lower class and especially within the lower class, lower caste category.

This is all rather vague but some particular examples may help to reduce the level of generalisation, even if some of the comments may be debatable and certainly not conclusive. Overall, the four most likely alternative trends are: (1) the upper class has retained or even increased its dominance; (2) the middle class has improved its position either at the expense of the upper class; (3) or mainly at the expense of the lower class; (4) the lower class has significantly improved its position.

Arguably, the upper class, upper caste dominant coalition has undergone some internal changes. Independence increased the power of the Indian national business class vis-a-vis the metropolitan bourgeoisie, though the latter has made some degree of a comeback, as MNCs have increased their penetration in the 1980s. Until 1991 the Nehru family and the central politicians had increased their power in relation to the professional bureaucrats and the more rural-based state politicians. The rich farmers have taken some of the land and power of the 'feudal' class. In terms of caste, upper castes other than the larger and traditionally dominant ones (such as Brahmins, Bhumihars and Rajputs) have increased their political activity and power. The upper class has widened its caste base even further than this already wide range of upper castes and now includes more coopted persons from the middle and scheduled castes. The upper class includes most of the richest 20 percent.

The middle class is numerically and politically much more dominated by rural classes and especially by the small and medium peasants. Middle class, middle caste peasants already dominate rural politics in some states like Karnataka, Andhra and Tamil Nadu and the larger middle castes in particular have been increasing their power at provincial level in these states and also in Punjab, Gujarat and intermittently in UP and Bihar. There is much manipulation, manoeuvring and coopting of middle class leaders by the dominant class and it is too early to write of a major, permanent advance by the middle class, backward castes and their middle peasant majority. Perhaps about 35 percent of the population belong to this category.

Finally and briefly, the scheduled castes have benefited more than the scheduled tribes. However, many of the policies and programmes are aimed at individual beneficiaries (through reservation of scholarships, seats, jobs and promotions; through redistribution of small plots; through Antayodhaya, IRDP and the many other programmes which provide grants and loans) and so the benefit is inevitably selective (probably to the richer, more assertive and more progressive elements?) and the effect may often be to coopt the scheduled leaders and cream off the more dynamic members who rise into the middle class. Galanter (1984) implies that many of the scheduled legislators who win reserved seats tend to over-compensate, over-conform and to be too overawed by their upper class (usually Congress) patrons. The lower class probably includes at least 47 percent of the population and may exceed 50 percent. Given that in some years the proportion of the population below the poverty line has exceeded 50 percent and given that structural class position must also bear some relation to income, this seems a reasonable assumption. Clearly, class and caste categories need to be related to income distribution. Class and income do not always correlate and, for example, some lower class tenants may cultivate more land and receive more income than some middle class small owner-farmers. However, it will be worth examining the changes in income distribution between the top two, the middle four and the bottom four deciles to gain some kind of rough indication of change in income between classes.

Political Parties

The classes, castes and other categories discussed so far are the key contributors to the rise, fluctuation or fall of the many political parties in India. The political arena consists of a national level in a highly centralised, federal State which is constantly on its guard against assertions of power from the 26 states and, to a much lesser extent, the 6 union territories. The arena also includes 412 districts, over 5,000 blocks and nearly 560,000 villages. Elections to the national Lok Sabha are held in at least 545 parliamentary constituencies (which mainly correspond to districts) and nearly 480,000 polling stations. Elections to the 27 Vidhan Sabhas or legislatures are held in 3,997 constituencies in 25 states plus Delhi and Pondicherry. The population in 1994 was over 900 million and 256 million out of a total electorate of 400 million voted in 1984. Constitutionally, the states control policy on agriculture, education, law and justice, health, welfare and local government.

The consciousness, organisation, articulation, mobilisation and strength of classes varies considerably. The upper classes have benefited from continuity of the Nehru dynasty and of the Congress party, from the relative congruence of class and caste, from the improvement in transport and communications technology (especially recently of telephone and electronic communication) and from a common language (English, 'the associate additional official language'), plus widespread knowledge of the official language, Hindi, in the north. Lower

% SHARE OF VOTES BY MAIN PARTIES, GENERAL ELECTIONS TO LOK SABHA, INDIA 1952-84

PARTY AND DATE FORMED	1952	1957	1962	1967	1971	1977	1980	1984
CONSERVATIVE								
Bharatiya Jana Sangh (BJS)1951	3.1	5.9	6.4	9.4	7.4	-		
Bharatiya Janata Party (BJP)1980							-	7.8
Swatantra 1959			7.9	8.7	3.1			
REFORMIST								
Indian National Congress (INC)1885	45.0	47.8	44.7	40.7	43.7			
INC (Indira) or Congress(I) 1977						34.5	42.7	48.1
INC (Organisation) or Congress (O)					10.4	1.7	5.3	1.6
INC (Urs) or Congress (U)								
INC (Jagjivan Ram) or Congress (J)								
INC (Socialist) or Congress (S)								
Janata Party 1977						41.3G	19.0	6.9
Bharatiya Lok Dal(BLD)1974								
Janata Party(Secular or JNPS)							9.4	6.0
Lok Dal 1969 + 1979								
Dalit Mazdoor Kisan Party (DMKP)								
SOCIALIST								
Praja Socialist Party(PSP)1951	5.8	10.4	6.8	3.1	1.0			
Kisan Mazdoor Praja Party(KMPP)1981								
Socialist 1948?	10.6		2.7					
Samyukta Socialist Party (SSP)1964				4.9	2.4			
COMMUNIST								
Communist Party of India(CPI) 1928	3.3	8.9	9.9	5.2	4.7	3.8	3.6	2.8
CPI (Marxist) or CPI(M) 1964				4.4	5.1	4.3	6.1	5.9
OTHER PARTIES, esp.local & regional	16.4	7.6	10.4	10.1	13.8	9.8	8.5	14.1
INDEPENDENTS	15.9	19.4	11.1	13.7	8.4	5.5	6.4	8.1
Voters as % Total Electorate	45.7	47.7	55.4	61.3	55.3	60.5	57.0	64.1

% OF TOTAL LOK SABHA	1952	1957	1962	1967	1971	1977	1980	1984
BJS/BJP + Swatantra	0.6	0.8	6.5	15.2	5.7			0.4
Congress + Congress(I)	74.4	75.1	73.1	54.4	68.0	28.4	66.7	76.6
Janata + JNP(S),LD + DMKP						54.4	13.6	2.4
Socialist, PSP, KMPP + SSP	4.3	3.8	3.6	6.9	1.0			
CPI + CPI(M)	3.3	5.5	5.9	8.1	9.3	5.4	8.9	5.2
Other parties, including Congress(O,U,J + S)	9.6	6.3	6.9	8.6	13.3	10.1	9.1	14.6
Independents	7.8	8.5	4.0	6.7	2.7	1.7	1.7	0.9
TOTAL NO. OF SEATS	489	494	494	520	518	542	529	542

G = Governing party when not Congress; % vote of largest opposition party underlined.
Sources: Khan 1989:62-3; Brass 1990:69

classes have been divided by the same range of factors as the upper class and even more so by region, culture and language. For example, it is fortunate for Congress and unfortunate for the Communists that Andhra, Kerala and West Bengal are so geographically distant from each other and that their populations speak three entirely different languages. There are about 3,000 'mother tongues' in India, including at least 14 official state languages and a further 19 languages each spoken by over a million persons.

Whatever the problems of class articulation, the turnout in Indian elections has risen from 46 percent in 1952 to 64 percent in 1984 and candidates now come from a wider range of upper castes and also increasingly from the larger backward castes, particularly the middle status, agricultural backward castes and the lower status artisan, service and smallholder backward castes (Brass 1990:91).

Regional parties (especially in Tamil Nadu) and the CPI(M), in Kerala and West Bengal, have mobilised the backward castes in some states but in most states 'the leading land-controlling castes of élite or middle status' (1990:91) remain dominant. In 'UP and Bihar, the old élite castes of Brahmans, Rajputs and Bhumihars have remained dominant in the Congress, which itself has remained the dominant party, while the middle and lower backward castes have been mobilised by the opposition, first by the socialists in the 1950s and 1960s, then by the Lok Dal in the 1960s and 1970s' (1990:91).

The table shows the details of the five main types of political party and their performance in the ten general elections between 1952 and 1991. Usually at least six national and as many regional and local parties have gained 2 percent or more of the total votes and at least some seats. Currently, the range of types of party includes one or two conservative parties (including one communally inclined Hinduist party). Conservative parties have attracted between 3 percent and 18 percent of the vote in the various elections. There are three or four reformist or social democratic parties, of which Congress (I) is itself of course the most supremely successful example. Reformist parties have secured between 41 percent and 78 percent of the vote and the Congress share has ranged from 34 percent to 48 percent of this mainstream, centripetal vote. Until 1971 there were also at least two major socialist parties but the rise of the reformist, populist and middle caste, middle peasant parties (of which the Lok Dal is the exquisite example) put paid to the socialist parties and their previous supporters are now mostly dispersed among the reformist parties. Support for the socialist parties sank to 3 percent by 1971 but it had been 16 percent in their heyday. The two communist parties have never pulled in more than 10 percent of the vote. They began with only 3 percent in 1952 but averaged over 8 percent between 1952 and 1984. The regional parties have attracted a vote that has fluctuated from 8 percent to 16 percent of the total. Centralisation and central government intervention in (and often contemptuous treatment of) state governments (not least of Congress Chief Ministers and administrations) have contributed to the rise of new regional parties and their total vote reaching 14 percent in 1984. Finally, there has been no such fluctuation of revival in the Independent vote, which has declined from a peak of 19 percent in 1957 to a mere 8 percent in 1984.

The most important conservative party has been the Bharatiya Jana Sangh and its successor, the Bharatiya Janata Party. Their support has come from merchants, traders, urban shopkeepers, other businessmen, professionals, junior civil servants (including policemen), students and other urban categories, as well as former maharajas, rajas and zamindars, plus big landlords and rich and middle peasants. The BJP is particularly strong in the north and especially in the six states of the Hindi belt, plus Delhi. Caste leadership comes from the upper castes, especially Brahmins and caste support from the middle status, cultivating castes. Religious support is almost exclusively Hindu and even a sizeable number of Hindus regard the BJP as a communal party.

VOTING IN GENERAL ELECTION, INDIA 22-26 NOVEMBER 1989

	M.VOTES	SEATS
Congress (I)	115	193
Janata Dal	50	141
Bharatiya Janata Party	33	88
CPI (M)	19	32
Telugu Desam	10	2
CPI	7.5	12
Bahujan Samaj Party	5.7	3
AIADMK	4.5	11
Akali Dal (Mann)	2.3	6
Revolutionary Socialist Party	1.8	4
Forward Bloc	1.2	3
Jammu and Kashmir National Conference (Farooq)	NA	3
Jharkhand Mukti Morcha	NA	3
Indian Muslim League	NA	2
Nominated (Anglo-Indians) by the President	-	2
Unattached, Independent and others	NA	22
Vacant (14 in Assam + 4 deaths)		18
TOTAL	NA	545

Sources: Europa 1990; Keesing's Archive 1989

VOTING IN GENERAL ELECTION, INDIA MAY-JUNE 1991

Congress (I)	226
Bharatiya Janata Party	119
Janata Dal	55
CPI (M)	35
Telugu Desam	14
CPI	13
AIADMK	11
Jharkhand Mukti Morcha	6
Samajwadi Janata Party	5
Shiv Sena	4
Revolutionary Socialist Party	4
Forward Bloc	3
Indian Union Muslim League	2
Asom Gana Parishad	2
Other Parties	8
Countermanded due to death of candidate or violence	12
Results withheld or elections not held (Punjab and Jammu & Kashmir)	24
Nominated by the President	2
TOTAL	545

Source: Keesing's Record of World Events 1991:38287

Its connections with the militant Rashtriya Swayamsevak Sangh attracts even more serious accusations of fascism. In 1989 the BJP took Hindu votes from Congress (I) and had enough seats for the Janata Dal-led National Front coalition to need to seek its support. In November 1990 disagreements over reservation policy, the Ayodhya temple and other issues led to withdrawal of support and the collapse of the Janata Dal government. Though the BJP has not explicitly opposed the Mandal Report and reservation for the backward castes, the policy is seen as deeply divisive, particularly among Hindus, and also threatening to the interests of the upper castes, who will lose jobs to the backward castes.

The other major conservative party was Swatantra which arose to fight the perceived rise of State socialism and public sector expansion in industry during the second plan. The party was promoted by urban big business (which was then still heavily dominated by Bombay and western India). Its class support came from former rajas and zamindars and from landlords, whilst caste support was mainly upper caste and especially landed Rajputs in the north.

Before 1947 the Congress party was dominated by urban professionals, particularly upper caste lawyers like Nehru, Gandhi and Patel. The professionals were supported by the smaller landlords, owner-farmers and the upper tenantry who together controlled Congress organisation at the district level. Congress leaders came from the Brahmin caste in nearly all areas, from the Kayasthas in the north, from Banias in many regions and from other high castes elsewhere. Since 1947 leaders have come from mainly upper or middle status land-controlling, dominant rural castes, especially in the north, where Brahmins, Rajputs/Thakurs and Bhumihars are frequently dominant. Elsewhere Marathas have monopolised rural power and served to make Maharashtra the only state with unbroken Congress rule. In Karnataka Lingayats and Vokkaligas are the two dominant, middle castes which have mostly supported Congress until fairly recently. Now in a few states, especially Karnataka and also Gujarat, where there have been greater realignments and shifts in caste voting, Congress has acquired some lower caste leaders. Congress is supported by the commercial and industrial class in north Indian cities and by former landlords, richer farmers and the poorest. The stereotype of the normal electoral coalition for Congress is the upper castes (especially Brahmins and increasingly Rajputs, in the north), plus lower caste (especially scheduled) dependants and other minorities, especially the Muslims (and particularly the more liberal, secular and even Marxist adherents). More progressive Congress leaders (like Urs in Karnataka) widened the caste appeal to less dominant, more backward castes than the also backward but still very much dominant Lingayat and Vokkaliga castes. (Urs deprived Lingayats of backward status in 1979 and both castes were given a special, less serious category of backwardness in 1986.)

The High Caste-Low Caste-Muslim formula of Congress has been changing since the 1970s and the battle is on for the support of the numerically large and economically rising category of middle peasants and/or middle/backward castes. For example, Gujarat in 1976 saw a 'KHAM' strategy to gain the support of 'Kshatriyas' (a wide range of middle castes claiming Kshatriya status), 'Harijans',

Adivasis (tribals) and Muslims. Ministries were awarded to members of the backward castes, especially lower middle 'Kshatriyas' such as the Kolis. Gujarat was previously dominated by the élite and upper middle agricultural castes (especially the Patidars and Kunbis) and they have been largely supplanted by lower backward 'Kshatriyas'. The latter now dominate the state government, with the support of other backward castes and the scheduled castes and tribes.

The Congress party has won eight out of ten general elections up to and including 1991. The party averaged 43.4 percent of the votes cast in the first eight elections. Given the incomplete development toward individual choice in elections and also given the size of the electorate, parties have to appeal to large blocs of voters such as those in caste and religious categories. The following hypothetical figures illustrate the percentages of the total population from various social blocs which might be necessary to give Congress 43 percent of the vote:

	High Caste	Back-ward	Scheduled		Muslim	Total
			Caste	Tribe		
1. hypothetical % of total electorate voting Congress	8.0	13.0	10.0	4.0	8.0	43
2. approx. % of total population	15.3	52.4	15.7	7.5	11.4	100
1 as a % of 2	52	25	64	53	70	43

These are imaginary figures and obviously the real figures will vary with the size of the vote and with related fluctuations in support by particular blocs. For example, it is estimated that only about 50 percent of Muslims (not 70%) voted for Congress in 1984, after communal riots and a strongly pro-Hindu (anti-Sikh and anti-Pakistan) electoral campaign. The next election is due in 1996.

There have been various groups which have splintered off from Congress to form rival parties. Two of these were named after their founders, respectively Devaraj Urs and the scheduled caste leader, Jagjivan Ram. Urs appealed particularly to the backwards and Ram to the scheduled. Apart from this, it is likely that the splinter parties from Congress appeal to a similar cross-section of Indian society as does Congress but that they play on factional and other divisions within the upper echelons of the dominant élite.

The other reformist parties (the BKD, BLD, Lok Dal, Janata and now the Janata Dal) have appealed primarily to the rural voters and especially to the (rising?) middle and also to the rich peasants and/or the middle and lower backward castes. Their support has been mainly in the north (especially in the Hindi belt) and the appeal of a Jat leader like Charan Singh to Jats, Yadavs, Kurmis and Bishnois has epitomised in a quite archetypal way how a new, populist political party could mobilise a fairly narrowly defined but numerous category. The Lok

Dal succession of parties originally began in the late 1960s to challenge the Congress, Nehruvian, urban and industrialising hegemony. The Lok Dal emerged as the main opposition party in the late 1960s and early 1970s but it did more damage to the Jan Sangh and even more particularly to the socialist parties of the north, who declined after 1967 and virtually disappeared after 1971. The outcome in most of the Hindi belt has been Congress one-party dominance for most of the time, with some opposition but of a highly fragmented and mostly ineffective kind. In 1990 the Janata Dal ruled in UP and Bihar and both Chief Ministers were Yadavs, conforming to the aggressive stereotype which many people have of Yadavs.

The socialist parties, including the Samyukta Socialist Party, have drawn their support from the middle and lower backward castes, especially in Bihar and UP. One socialist Chief Minister of Bihar, Karpuri Thakur, came from the Nai (barber) caste, which is lower backward.

The communist parties have been led by urban professionals and intellectuals who have, since the end of the Telengana revolt in 1950, adopted a parliamentary and reformist, multi-class strategy. Particular appeal has been made to industrial workers, the urban working class (especially in the major and more industrialised cities), the landless rural poor (notably by the CPI(M) in Kerala) and tribals. Some landed and dominant peasant castes (such as the Reddis or Kammas in Andhra) have found it convenient to support the communists against a rival dominant caste. CPI strength has been in Kerala, West Bengal and Bihar whilst the CPI(M) currently leads a coalition in West Bengal and also did so earlier in Kerala and Tripura. It has mobilised the lower backward and even the scheduled castes in Kerala and West Bengal. Brass sometimes prefers to stress political historical factors rather than contemporary socio-economic processes in explaining present day political actions. This somewhat evolutionary, anti-functionalist approach underlies his explanation of the current distribution of Communist party strength as being in areas where Congress dominance of the nationalist movement was weakest. (This begs the question <u>why</u> Congress was historically weak in such areas .....)

Communist governments in West Bengal and especially in Kerala have been much more successful in achieving agrarian reform, including reduction of ceilings on landownership, tenancy (especially for jotedars in West Bengal) and improved pay and conditions for agricultural labourers. Policies have increased employment and incomes of the poor in these two low income states.

Regional parties (and also, incidentally, 'national' parties with a mainly regional or subnational base), appear to have particularly benefited from 'the rise of the middles'. Backward caste support to the DMK and AIADMK in Tamil Nadu is the major example of such support leading to the displacement of Congress. Other long established regional parties include the Akali Dal (supported by Jat Sikhs) in Punjab and the National Conference (dominated by Muslims) in Jammu and Kashmir. Newer regional parties include the Telugu Desam in Andhra (led by a Kamma) and the Asom Gana Parishad, supported by Assamese Hindus who have violently opposed infiltration by Bengali and Bangladeshi Muslims.

The vote for Independent candidates has more than halved and the number and percentage of successful candidates has radically shrunk to only five MPs (1%). The demise of the Independent MP suggests the triumph of modern, 'machine' party politics but it may also signify a progressive move away from dependence on 'feudal' and rich and powerful (though often also very able) local magnates.

Government in the 26 States

A federal system, even one with strong central powers as in India, should facilitate some regional variation and possibly mitigation of monolithic national patterns of class and caste dominance and no doubt it does to some extent. However, the weaker and more insecure the feelings of central government (especially under Mrs Gandhi), the more it has interfered in, manipulated and even suborned state governments. Chief Ministers have been appointed by the Prime Minister and the High Command without local votes or even much consultation in some cases. They have spent inordinate amounts of time in Delhi lobbying and waiting to see central ministers and have been summarily dismissed or undermined by various Machiavellian ploys. Instruments of interference have included state governors who have become embroiled in the party and factional politics of the states they are supposed to oversee. President's Rule has been imposed nearly 40 times and sometimes has remained in force for several years (as in Punjab). The national Emergency affected all states between June 1975 and March 1977, though the south suffered less. Congress has also manoeuvred to gain some modest influence by electoral pacts such as those with the DMK parties in Tamil Nadu. The power of the state legislatures has declined and many Chief Ministers minimise the length of assembly sessions and rule through ordinances as much as they can. Brass claims that "state legislatures have been generally fragmented, unstable and so opportunistically motivated that few governments can stay in power if a state legislature is allowed to remain in session for more than a few weeks" (1990:312). When confidence does fade, then many still avoid putting this to a parliamentary vote in the house and prefer to 'parade' government supporters (sometimes kept confined in a safe place to prevent their seduction and defection) before the governor. Defections by dissident and non-Ministerial and non-preferred members of the ruling party have been common but Rajiv Gandhi's anti-defection amendment to the Constitution in 1984 has made this more difficult for members of the larger parties. (Defection of less than a third of a party's members requires them to seek re-election.)

The majority of states do not have fully competitive party systems. Maharashtra and Gujarat in the 1980s were dominated by a single party, Congress. In the six Hindi states plus Orissa Congress also dominated but this preeminence was not based on a homogeneous social structure and a reasonably united dominant caste (such as the Marathas in Maharashtra) but rather depended upon a fragmented and disunited variety of opposition parties who partly reflected the social heterogeneity and division in those states. In four of them, including UP and

CHANGES IN WEALTH + INCOME DISTRIBUTION + POVERTY, INDIA 1960-90

INDICATOR	1960 -65	1965 -70	1970 -75	1975 -80	1980 -85	1985 -90	OTHER
AV.ACRES OWNED PER HH	5.0 (1961)		4.2 (1971-2)				6.2 (1953-4)
GINI COEFFICIENTS	1961-2		1971-2				1953-4
LANDOWNERSHIP	.68		.68				.68
FARM SIZE	.58		.59 to .64				.69
URBAN CONSUMPTION EXPEND.	.35	.33	(.32)	.34(77-8)			.38 (1951-5)
RURAL CONSUMPTION EXPEND.	.30	.29	(.29)	.34(77-8)			.34 (1951-5)

<u>INCOME DISTRIBUTION</u>

Source:	Todaro 79	WB 1979	WB 1990		
% SHARE OF QUINTILES	1965	1975-6	1983	1989-90	% CHANGE 1965-90
RICHEST 20% HHS (Q1)	48.9	49.4	41.4	41.3	16
QUINTILE 2	19.6	20.5	22.0	21.3	+9
QUINTILE 3	14.3	13.9	16.3	16.2	+13
QUINTILE 4	10.5	9.2	12.3	12.5	+19
POOREST 20% HHS (Q5)	6.7	7.0	8.1	8.8	+31
Ratio of Richest 20% Hhs to poorest 40% Hhs	2.8	3.0	2.0	1.9	

<u>% POVERTY</u> 1960-61 PRICES

	1960 -65	1965 -70	1970 -75	1975 -80	1980 -85	1985 -90	OTHER
RURAL (<Rs 180 P.A.)	42	53	(44)	39 (77-8)			
URBAN (<Rs 240 P.A.)	42	46	(42)	41 (77-8)			
TOTAL							
MALE AGRIC.LABS. AS % RURAL MALE LABOUR FORCE	15.8 (1961)		25 to 30 (1971)		24.0 (1981)		14.3 (1951)
FARM SERVANTS PER 100 HOLDINGS			36 (1971-2)				14 (1953-4)

Sources: Sundrum 1987; WB 1979 and 1990:236; Todaro 1979; Chenery 1975.

PERCENTAGE DISTRIBUTION OF WEALTH, LAND AND ASSETS, RURAL INDIA 1961-82

PERCENTILE	ASSETS IN RURAL AREAS			% OF OWNERSHIP HOLDINGS		
	1961	1971	1981-2	1953-4	1961-2	1971-2
96-100				37.3	36.1	35.4
91-5				15.1	15.6	15.6
91-100	51.4	51.0	49.5	(52.4)	(51.7)	(51.0)
76-90				23.6	24.6	25.2
71-90	27.6	30.9				
51-75				17.6	17.8	17.8
31-70	18.5	16.1				
26-50				5.4	5.5	5.4
0-25				1.1	0.5	0.6
21-30) 11-20)	2.4	1.9				
0-10	0.1	0.1	0.4			

Source: Sundrum 1987:177 and 183, based on GOI, 6th Plan 1980:8, RBI and NSS, Rounds 8,17 and 26.

Bihar, the largest opposition party mustered less than 25 percent of the votes. In the remaining nine major states, power has swung between two parties or coalitions of parties over a longish period. Opposition to Congress has been successful when the lower class has supported the CPI(M), as in Kerala and West Bengal. The dominant, landed castes (Lingayats and Vokkaligas) and the backward castes have supported Congress (I) and then Janata in Karnataka, forcing Congress (I) to seek the support of the backwards. Brass notes that 'during the succession struggles after 1965 between Mrs Gandhi and her rivals, the central Congress leadership in several states moved to displace upper caste leaders from state Congress organisations and replace them with backward caste persons to mobilise the votes of the latter castes to defeat its rivals in the state Congress and in the opposition' (1990). However, he concludes that, even in states with backward and low caste governments, the dominant, landed castes (usually two or more per district) retain power at district, block, cooperative and village level. One exception is West Bengal where CPI(M) penetration of village panchayats has led to the replacement of the dominant, landed classes by smaller landholders, teachers and social workers. Central government intervention in state government has served to discredit and weaken both and it has certainly not prevented agrarian reform becoming a 'cruel farce', delivering pitiful remnants of 'barren, unproductive or alkaline soil' (1990:253) to those too poor to develop them.

To summarise, both central and state government has been dominated by reformist parties and particularly (especially at the centre) by the Congress (I) which has, arguably, been moving to the right. There have been brief, unstable interregna by a populist, pro-rural party (Janata 1977-80) or a similar coalition (the Janata Dal and the National Front 1989-91). There have been intermittent Left Front, communist led coalitions in Kerala and also a more enduring CPI(M)-led Left Front government in West Bengal which returned in 1977 and still continues in 1993. The implications of mainly reformist government for wealth and income distribution, poverty and health will now be briefly explored.

Rural Wealth Distribution

The table shows that there had been very little change in distribution of rural assets (debt and investment) or of land at least up to 1971-2.

The Gini coefficient for landownership remained at the very high level of 0.68 between 1953-4 and 1971-2. Bandyopadhyay (1986) reports that 7.3 million acres have been declared surplus under the ceiling laws. Nearly 5.0 million acres (79%) have been possessed by the government and 4.4 million have actually been distributed to nearly 3.4 million persons - an average of 1.3 acres per recipient. Of the area distributed, nearly 44 percent has been allotted to scheduled castes and tribes, who comprise nearly 55 percent of all beneficiaries. Of the area not distributed, 6 million acres are involved in litigation and nearly 0.9 million acres are reported to be unfit (or unavailable) for cultivation. Referring to operational (rather than ownership) holdings, he calculates that the number of marginal (under 2.5 acre) farmers increased from 36.2 million in 1970-1 to 50.5 million in 1980-1. If the 3.2 million beneficiaries of land reform are excluded, then this represents an increase of 11.1 million marginal farmers or a rate of marginalisation of 4 percent per year (twice the rate of rural population growth). The land declared surplus constitutes less than 2 percent of total cultivated area, whereas estimates of potential surplus have been as high as 8 per cent. Bandyopadhyay explains the shortfall by: (a) provision for holding up to twice the ceiling limit by families with over five members; (b) provision to give a separate ceiling limit for major (ie. adult) sons of the family; (c) provision for treating every shareholder of a joint family, under applicable personal law, as a separate unit for ceiling limits; (d) exemption of tea, coffee, rubber, cardamom and cocoa plantations and of lands held by religious and charitable institutions beyond normal ceiling limits; (e) Benami (in someone else's name) transfers to defeat the ceiling law; (f) misuse of exemptions and miscalculation of lands; and (g) non-application of appropriate ceilings of lands newly irrigated by public investment (1986: A51). In May 1985 a conference of state ministers suggested that ceilings be lowered to 12.4 acres per family for irrigated land with two crops, 18.5 acres for irrigated land with one crop and 29.6 acres for dry and other land.

National Income Distribution

The national distribution of income appears to have changed very little between 1965 and 1975-6 but World Bank data indicate an improvement by 1983. The share of the richest decile fell by 24 percent between 1965 and 1983, including 20 percent after 1975-6. However, the next richest decile actually increased their share by 7 percent overall. The percentage change in the share of the various percentiles between 1965 and 1983 was:

	Richest 10%	Next Richest 10%	Richest 20% 1	Quintiles 2	3	4	Poorest 20% 5
% change in income share 1965-83	-24	+7	-15	+12	+14	+17	+21

Sources: Todaro 1979; WB 1979 and 1990.

This shows that, apart from the richest 10 per cent, all other percentiles improved their share and that the degree of improvement increased, the poorer the percentile. The performance of quintiles 2 and 3 (the non-dominant, 'middle classes'?) is particularly noteworthy, since their increases in shares (12% and 14% respectively) was on top of an already sizeable share. The higher increases in the bottom two quintiles are less impressive when seen in relation to the low initial share and bearing in mind that nearly all of the bottom 40 percent were still below the poverty line in 1984-5. Even so, there appears to have been a net transfer of over 8 percent of total household income between 1975-6 and 1983. Data for 1989-90 show nearly 9 percent increase in the share of the poorest quintile but also a slight increase in the share of the richest decile. India differed little from China and in fact the poorest quintile in India fared better.

Income distribution in India is not as equal as in Eastern Europe nor as unequal as in some Latin American countries but is of medium inequality, similar to the rest of South Asia.

% SHARE OF TOTAL HOUSEHOLD INCOME, SELECTED COUNTRIES 1980s

COUNTRY AND YEAR	RICHEST 10%	R20% RICHEST 20% 1	QUINTILE 2	3	4	P20 POOREST 20% 5	R20% ÷ P20%	R20% ÷ P40%
HUNGARY (1983)	18.7	32.4	22.8	18.7	15.3	10.9	3.0	1.2
BANGLADESH (81-2)	24.9	39.0	21.8	16.8	13.1	9.3	4.2	1.7
JAPAN (1979)	22.4	37.5	23.1	17.5	13.2	8.7	4.3	1.7
INDONESIA (1987)	26.5	41.3	21.5	16.0	12.4	8.8	4.7	1.9
INDIA (1965)		48.9	19.6	14.3	10.5	6.7	7.4	2.8
INDIA (1983)	26.7	41.4	22.0	16.3	12.3	8.1	5.1	2.0
INDIA (1989-90)	27.1	41.3	21.3	16.2	12.5	8.8	4.7	1.9
PAKISTAN (84-5)	31.3	45.6	20.6	15.0	11.2	7.8	5.8	2.4
CHINA (1990)	24.6	41.8	24.4	16.4	11.0	6.4	6.5	2.4
UK (1979)	23.3	39.5	25.0	18.2	11.5	5.8	6.8	2.3
SRI LANKA (85-6)	43.0	56.1	18.4	12.1	8.5	4.8	11.7	4.2
PERU (1985)	35.8	51.9	21.5	13.7	8.5	4.4	11.8	4.0
BRAZIL (1983)	46.2	62.6	18.6	10.7	5.7	2.4	26.1	7.7

Sources: WB 1990:236-7; WB 1993:296

Rural Income

Rural income is more often represented by consumption expenditure, which is both more easily monitored through the regular and large-scale surveys of the National Sample Survey, and is less susceptible to fluctuation than income. Real rural consumption expenditure per capita, using 1970-1 prices, increased by 40 percent between 1950-1 and 1977-8. This represents an average annual simple increase of 1.5 percent (Cf. 3.2 percent for value of agricultural production).

Sundrum summarises National Sample Survey annual data on average consumption expenditure per capita for three income categories between 1950-1 and 1977-8. The quinquennial averages show that there was steady but really quite marginal redistribution up to 1973-4 but reversion to the 1960-5 position in 1977-8.

PERCENT OF TOTAL RURAL CONSUMPTION EXPENDITURE, INDIA 1950-78

Fractile	1950-5	1955-60	1960-5	1965-70	1973-4	1977-8	% points change 1950-74	% change 1950-74
Richest 20%	41.8	41.5	39.6	38.8	36.9	40.1	-4.9	-11.7
Middle 40%	38.6	38.2	38.5	39.1	40.3	38.3	+1.7	+4.4
Poorest 40%	19.5	20.2	21.8	22.1	22.8	21.6	+2.1	+10.8
Index of Average Consumption Expenditure (1950-1=100)	103	111	121	125	132	140	+29	+28
Richest 20% as % of Poorest 40%	214	205	182	176	162	186		

Source: Sundrum 1987: 143, based on NSS Reports.

The largest increase in the average share of the poorest occurred between 1955-60 and 1960-5 which was also the quinquennium when average consump-tion expenditure shot up the most. There was very little improvement for the poorest in the late 1960s when average consumption expenditure increased very little. Caution needs to be exercised over any trends in the 1970s, since Sundrum only provides data for two isolated years, 1973-4 and 1977-8 (years of high and very high agricultural production respectively). The consumption data suggest some slight improvement for the middle and especially the bottom 40 per cent, even after the partial regression in 1977-8, but any significant long-term shift in rural income distribution looks rather improbable, up to 1977-8. The figures also provide some support for Kakwani's claim that inequality of consumption per capita has tended to increase in periods of high economic growth. Sundrum shows that the Gini coefficient for rural consumption expenditure has been much lower and thus more equal than that for landownership (0.68). The Gini coefficients for food (and especially foodgrain) consumption have been lower still and only consumption of non-foodgrain foods has been more unequal than general consumption. The average Gini coefficient for rural consumption expenditure in 1951-5 was 0.34 (11 percent lower than the urban GC) and this fell by 15 percent to 0.29 by 1970-4.

The largest decrease in rural inequality appears to have occurred in the early 1960s:

Period		1951-5	1955-60	1960-5	1965-70	1970-4	1977-8
Gini Coefficient	Rural	.34	.33	.30	.29	.29	.34
	Urban	.38	.37	.35	.33	.32	.34

Sources: Sundrum 1987:140; Kohli 1987:84.

Kakwani (1990) claims that intra-state rural inequality fell rapidly between 1977-8 and 1983 but inter-state rural inequality increased from at least 1972-3 until 1983. Theil's index of inequality of consumption actually shows a very marginal decrease in intra-state inequality and a significant increase in inter-state inequality.

Rural Poverty

Measurement of poverty incidence is influenced by the price index or deflator used; regional variations in prices; the definition, criteria and threshold of poverty and of the 'poverty line'; concentration on the poor or the 'ultra-poor'; focus on income or on (the more stable) consumption expenditure; and the weighting of consumption of household members in relation to that of adult male equivalents. This partly explains the variation in estimates of poverty incidence, including some of the differences in estimates for the same year which are mentioned below. These discrepancies are less serious as long as the trends in incidence are tolerably in parallel. There is wide agreement with Ahluwalia (1978) that poverty, especially rural poverty, is closely related to fluctuations in agricultural production. It is thus not easy to detect long-term trends amid the annual ups and downs, which can be quite sharp, as in 1965-6 and 1971-2. Insofar as a trend in poverty incidence is discernible, it seems to be mostly downward, from around 50 percent in the late 1960s to an average of 42 percent in the early 1960s and 53 percent in the late 1960s. The peak incidence of rural poverty was the famine year in 1966-7 when it reached 57 per cent. The Green Revolution was under way by 1967-8 and poverty fell from 56.5 percent in that year to 51.0 percent in 1968-9. The rate then fell slowly until 1971-2 when it dropped seven percentage points to 41 per cent. Since then it has not exceeded 50 percent and has more often been nearer 40 per cent, as in the most recent year, 1984-5, for which data are easily available. Urban poverty until recently has been comparable with rural rates but has never exceeded 50 percent and particularly avoided the sharp increases during harvest failure and famine. However, data for 1977-8 and 1983-5 indicate that urban poverty may have fallen from 41 percent to 28 per cent, whereas the rural rate still seemed stuck around the 40 percent mark.

Ultimately, health and health indicators must be affected by numbers rather than percentages of poor. The number of rural poor = total population x percent rural population x percent poor. Thus in 1984-5 the rural poor = 762 million x 0.73 x 0.40 = 222 million. This was 44 million more rural poor than in 1956-7, even though the incidence of poverty had dropped by 14 percentage points.

Kakwani (1990) shows poverty incidence for four years between 1972-3 and 1983. Though isolated years obviously cannot be taken as reliable evidence of a steady trend, the figures do show a significant decline in poverty (from 60% to 48%) after no change in the first consecutive year. A comparable decline is also observed for the ultra-poor (those receiving Rs 480 or less annual consumption per person as against Rs 600 or less for the 'normal' poor). The ratio of ultra-poor declined from 42 per cent to 30 percent but the numbers of poor and ultra-poor were still 255 and 160 million respectively in 1983. The poverty gap ratio which, crucially, measures the distance below the poverty line, also fell for both the poor and the ultra-poor.

INEQUALITY AND POVERTY, RURAL INDIA 1972-83

	1972-3	1973-4	1977-8	1983
Rs ANNUAL REAL CONSUMER EXPENDITURE PER CAPITA 1973-4 PRICES	636	622	680	740
INDEX OF REAL CONSUMER EXPENDITURE PER CAPITA	100	98	107	116
THEIL'S INEQUALITY				
Within state inequality	14.2	12.3	15.1	13.8
% contribution of within state inequality to total inequality	(92)	(93)	(91)	(88)
Between state inequality	1.3	0.9	1.5	1.8
% contribution of between state inequality to total	(8)	(7)	(9)	(12)
POOR				
Head-count ratio (%)	60.5	60.5	56.3	48.4
Million Poor	264	269	269	255
Poverty Gap Ratio	19.5	18.8	17.5	13.8
Watts Measure	27.0	26.7	23.2	18.9
ULTRA POOR				
Head-count ratio (%)	42.1	41.3	37.9	30.3
Million Ultra-poor	184	183	181	160
Poverty Gap ratio	11.3	10.9	9.9	7.3
Watts Measure	14.9	14.4	12.5	9.4

Source: Kakwani 1990 (31 March):A3.

Kakwani concludes that

> in general, the reduction in poverty is more for the ultra poor than for the poor, and the magnitudes of reduction in poverty are higher for the period 1977-8 to 1983 than for the former period 1973-4 to 1977-8. This is an interesting result because 1973-4 to 1977-8 was a period of higher growth (2.7%) with increasing inequality, whereas the 1977-83 period was characterised by a somewhat lower per capita growth of consumption (1.7%) but accompanied by a substantial decrease in inequality. The decrease in inequality was the major factor which led to a substantial reduction in poverty in the second period (1990:A5).

The period from 1977-8 to 1983 'witnessed a spate of anti-poverty interventions'.

Inequality of consumption per capita actually increased in 11 out of the 15 major states between 1973-4 and 1977-8 but decreased in 12 of these states between 1977-8 and 1983. If 1983 refers to 1983-4, this was a year of high and much increased foodgrain production, widely acknowledged to be a key correlate of poverty reduction. Poverty incidence fell in 13 states between 1973-4 and 1977-8 and in every major state except Bihar between 1977-8 and 1983. Six states saw poverty reduced by 30 percent or more between 1972-4 and 1983: Andhra 45 percent decrease, Gujarat 44 percent, Punjab 40 percent, Kerala 36 per cent, Haryana 32 percent and Maharashtra 30 percent. Total poverty declined at an annual rate of 1.8 percent between 1973-4 and 1977-8 and this decline would have been 4.2 percent but for the increase in inequality which added to poverty incidence by 2.4 percent per year. From 1977-8 to 1983 inequality decreased and contributed 0.5 percent towards a total annual reduction in poverty incidence of 2.7 percent. The IRDP and other strategies against poverty accounted for this 0.5 percent and the remaining 2.2 percent decrease is attributed to economic growth. Kakwani claims that, despite slower growth in the latter period, the change was from increasing to falling inequality from 1977-8 and 'the poverty ratio fell largely due to a decline in inequality in most states' (1990: A11).

Major programmes to alleviate poverty accounted for 9 percent of plan outlay but only 1 percent of GDP in 1987-8:

	Rs BILLION
1. Credit-based self-employment: IRDP	19.0
2. Wage employment:	
a) National Rural Employment Programme (NREP),	7.8
b) Rural Landless Employment Guarantee Programme (RLEGP),	6.5
c) Maharashtra Employment Guarantee Scheme (MEGS),	2.6
3. Area development:	
a) Watershed Development,	2.4
b) Drought Prone Area Programme (DPAP),	0.9
c) Desert Development.	0.5
TOTAL MAJOR PROGRAMMES AGAINST POVERTY	39.8

The largest investment was in the Integrated Rural Development Programme which provided an average of Rs 4,471 to 4.2 million beneficiaries. During the period from 1980 to 1985 Rs 50 billion were distributed to 17 million families and by about 1988 IRDP had reached 25 percent of all rural households. The NREP and RLEGP have absorbed only 9 percent of total unemployment among the rural poor, but have provided 40 percent of incremental rural employment. Kakwani lists other criticisms, including that works are not sufficiently useful, concentrating on 'unproductive' infrastructure such as roads and schools rather than on soil conservation or watershed development; that the public works were badly timed and located; that the assets created were both of poor quality and non-beneficial to the poor labourers who had created them; and that wages were lower than budgeted, owing to 'leakages' and corruption. Maharashtra's Employment Guarantee Scheme has been much more successful, both in employing women and in reducing gender differences in wage rates. However, recent moves to pay statutorily fixed minimum wages may have adverse effects, especially in reducing the self-targeting character of the scheme. If the MEGS increases its previously quite low wage rates, then it will no longer be so certain to attract only the very poorest rural workers and could begin to spread its benefits to less needy, lower middle peasants.

In general, poverty alleviation programmes seem to have been, paradoxically and perversely, less effective in poorer states. In fact India's poor were quite concentrated in regional terms in 1983. Only three states (UP, Bihar and WB) accounted for nearly 47 percent and six states (add MP, Maharashtra and TN) spoke for nearly 71 percent of India's total poor. Six (partly different) states - Bihar, MP, TN, WB, Assam and Kerala, had experienced low growth of foodgrain production up to about 1985 and these states encompassed 51 percent of India's poor. UP's foodgrain growth has been rapid, if a little erratic, but the eastern region provides a major concentration of poor. The fairly recent introduction of HYVs of rice has begun to benefit eastern UP.

Overall, Kakwani concludes that the poverty-reducing effects of rapid economic gowth can be (partly?) nullified by a sharp rise in consumption inequality, such as appears to have happened between 1973 and 1977. From the mid-1970s policies incorporated more anti-poverty or poverty alleviation interventions. Consequently,

> during the period 1977 to 1983, average consumption grew slowly, but consumption inequality fell in many states, and the reduction in the incidence of poverty was greater in magnitude than in the earlier period of high growth [from 1973 to 1977] ..... the beneficial impact of a reduction in inequality is more pronounced for the ultra poor than for the poor and by the same token a worsening of inequality hurts the ultra poor proportionately more than the poor (1990: A15-16).

It is highly probable that the anti-poverty strategies from about 1975 contributed to the decline in inequality which occurred in many states between 1977 and 1983. The poverty ratio has been responsive to reduction in income inequality (through anti-poverty programmes) as well as to economic growth and this is especially true for richer states and for the ultra poor in all states.

The Green Revolution and Health

Much of the discussion of the Green Revolution has focussed on its effect on class formation, class structure, employment, income and also on the environment. In fact the GR has probably had more effect on health than on any other aspect of life in India, both directly through increased food production and also through increased farm and other incomes. The main benefit has perhaps been in enabling India to support a much larger population (mostly at pre-existing or even slightly lower levels of food intake) rather than to make very dramatic improvements in nutrition (except in the north-western heartland of the GR). Even in Punjab and Haryana 'cultural lag' and other factors have conspired to make health improvements disproportionately slow in comparison with rapid agricultural growth and the rise in income to levels twice that of all-India. In fact Punjab and Haryana only rank fifth and seventh in general health status, though they rank second and fifth in terms of life expectancy. Haryana has a bad record for mortality under the age of four and still had a high CBR (36) in 1985.

The 12 percent increase in life expectancy between the 1960s and 1986 was only just above average (10%) in Punjab and actually appears to have been zero in Haryana. Reported cases of malaria were highest in these two irrigation-infested states, followed by somewhat lower rates in Gujarat, Karnataka and Himachal Pradesh. Shiva (1991) analyses the relationship between changes in the political economy and the environment of Punjab.

Tobacco Production

India is the third largest grower and producer of unmanufactured tobacco and the fifth largest exporter. In 1985-6 production reached 0.44 million tonnes, including 0.1 million tonnes of Virginia tobacco. Tobacco exports in 1986-7 earned India about Rs 1.7 billion. Cultivation provided employment and income for at least 69,000 growers on nearly 102,000 hectares (see Nath 1985).

Food Availability

Food availability is measured mainly in terms of grams of cereals and pulses per person per day. Using quinquennial averages, there was a 1 percent fall in total cereal and pulse availability between 1961-5 and 1981-5. Cereal availability increased by 4 percent but pulses declined by a serious 34 per cent. Cereal and pulse availability fell by 4 percent and 20 percent respectively in the late 1960s and, whilst the Green Revolution moreorless restored cereal availability to 1961 levels, pulse production has continued to decline, albeit at a slower rate. The long-term stagnation in cereal availability is compounded by very sharp fluctuations, such as the 14 percent fall in 1966, the 10 percent drop in 1973 and the 12 percent nosedive in 1979-80 (which helped to destroy the electoral chances of Janata in 1980).

GRAMS PER CAPITA NET AVAILABILITY OF CEREALS AND PULSES, INDIA 1956-85

PERIOD	GRAMS PER PERSON AVAILABLE PER DAY			
	CEREALS	PULSES	TOTAL	INDEX
1956	300	70	431	100
1961-65	400	61	461	107
1966-70	385	49	434	101
1971-75	399	44	443	103
1976-80	399	43	442	103
1981-85 (P)	418	39	457	106
1976-80 as % 1961-65	111%	56%	106%	

Source: Brass 1990: 291.

INDICES OF FOOD AVAILABILITY, INCOME, RURAL POVERTY AND CDR, INDIA 1950-89

YEAR	PER CAPITA NET AVAILABLE GRAMS AND INDEX (1956=100) CEREALS | PER DAY	PULSES	RS NET NATIONAL PRODUCT PER CAPITA AT 1970-1 PRICES + INDEX (1950-1 = 100)	RS RURAL CONSUMPTION EXPENDITURE PER CAPITA AT 1970-1 PRICES + INDEX (1950-1 = 100)	INDEX AGRIC. NDP PER CAPITA AT 1970-1 PRICES (1970-1 = 100)	RURAL POOR AS % RURAL POPN.+ INDEX OF FALL IN % POOR (1956-7 = 100)	INDEX OF FALL IN CDR (1956 = 100)
1950-1			Rs 467	Rs 381			
1952				103			
53				104			
54				110			
55				111			
56	360g grams	48g	109	108			22.8 per 1000
57				110	98	54%	
58				108	91	107	
59				116	100	114	
60				115	96	119	95
61	110	98	120(1960-1)	120	101	128	94
62	110	88		119	98	127	
63	106	85					
64	111	73		118	94	118	
65	116	76		128	100	113	112
66	100*	69	120	122	84*	100	117
67	100*	56		121	81*	94*	
68	112	80		128	92	95*	
69	110	67		128	90*	106	123
70	112	74		128	94	109	131
71	116	73	136	132	100	111	135
72	116	67			97	124	126
73	106	58			88*	120	132
74	114	58	133	132	93	115	136
75	101	56					130
76	104	72					134
77	107	62					136
78	117	65	149	140	99	128 or 106E	138
79	120	64	154P				144
80	105	44	143P		Bad		146
81	115P	53P	150P				145
82	115P	56P	154P				148
83	110P	56P	155P				148
84	121P	59P	163P		Good	126E	145
85	118P	55p	166QE			126	148
86							151
87							153
88							153
89						(148P)	

P = Provisional; QE = Quick Estimates; E = Estimate; * Years of low performance.
Source: Brass 1990:291 Data in base years for indices are underlined.

DEMOGRAPHIC INDICATORS, INDIA AND CDR/IMR, CHINA 1871-1990

YEAR	LE T	LE M (IN FIRST YEAR OF DECADE)	LE F	CBR SRS	CDR SRS	NATURAL INCREASE	MILLION POPN	IMR SRS	CMR 1-4 YEARS	CDR CHINA (IMR)
				PER 1000 POPN						
1871-81	25				(40)			(278)		
1881-91	24.6	23.7	25.6	48.8	39.6	9.2		(287)		
1891-1901	25.0	24.6	25.5	(46)				(292)		
1901-11	23.8	23.6	24.0	49.2	42.6	6.6	238	(295)		
1911-15	20	22.6	23.3		30.2	-0.3	252	204		
1916-20	NA				38.2			219		
1921-25	25*	19.4	20.9		26.3		251	173		
1926-30	27				24.6			178		
1931-35	32	26.9	26.6		23.6	10.4	279	174		
1936-40	NA				22.3			161		
1941-45	33	32.1	31.4		22.5	13.3	319	161		
1946-50					18.7			134		
1949					24					
1950							358			
1951	?	32.4?	31.7?	39.5?	27.4	12.5	361			
1952							366			
1953							373			
1954							380			22
1955							387	c146?	(1951-61)	
1956				41.7	22.8	18.9	394			
1957							402			
1958							411			
1959							420			
1960	43	43	42	43.7	24.0	19.7	429	165	26	21
1961		41.9	40.6	45.0	24.1	20.9	439			(IMR 165)
1962							450			
1963							463E			
1964							469?			
1965	45	46	44	45.0	20.0	25.0**	475	150		
1966				41.1	18.9	22.2	487			
1967				(41.8)			499			
1968				(41.4)	(c15?)		511	137?		
1969				37.6	17.6		527	140?		
1970	48			36.8	15.7	21.1	539	129	21	16
1971		46.4	44.7	36.9	14.9	22.0	548	129		
1972				36.6	16.9	19.7	564DY	139		
1973				34.6	15.5	19.1	576DY	134		
1974				34.5	14.5	20.0	588DY	126		
1975	50			35.2	15.9	19.3	601DY	140		12
1976	49.4?	50.1E	48.8E	34.4	15.0	19.4	613DY	129		
1977	51			33.0	14.7	18.3	626DY	130		
1978	52.3E	52.5E	52.1E	33.2	14.1?	19.1	639DY	127		
1979	52			33.1	12.8	20.3	660DYNS	120		
1980	52.1	52.6	51.6	33.3	12.4	20.9	675DY	114		
1981	52			33.2	12.5	20.7	685/690DY	121	17	
1982	55	55	54	33.8	11.9	21.9	705DY			7
1983	55	56	54	33.7	11.9	21.6	720DY	105		6.8
							743DYSON	DYSON 125-135		(IMR 49)
1984		56.1	57.0	33.9	12.6	21.3	736DY	104		6.7
1985	56.6	56.7	56.6	32.9	11.8	21.1	762/751DY	97		6.7?
1986				32.6	11.1	21.5	766DY	96		6.7
										(IMR 32)
1987				32.0	10.8	32.3	781DY	95	10	6.7
										(IMR 32)
1988	58	58	58	32.0	10.8 or less	21.2?	816/797DY WB	97		6.6
1989				29.1T	10.4T		830E			
1990					10.4T		852E			7.6T
1991	60	60	60		10		870E	90		
1996	64T	64T	64T	21T	9.0T	12.0T		60T		
2000	63.3T	64.7T		23.1T	8.2T or 9.0T	12.0T	1007P	60T		
2025							1350P			
2100							1600P(Stationary Popn will be 1862 M)			
% CHANGE 1901-88	+144			-35	-75			-52 to -67		

DEMOGRAPHIC INDICATORS, INDIA AND CDR/IMR, CHINA 1871-1990 (continued)

YEAR	LE T	LE M (IN FIRST YEAR OF DECADE)	LE F	CBR SRS	CDR SRS	NATURAL INCREASE	IMR SRS	CDR CHINA
				PER 1000 POPN				
1901-11							200 to 300	
1911-20							292 to 212	
1921-30	26.7	26.9	26.6				176	
1931-40							178	
1941-50		37.7	36.7	39.9	27.4	12.5	148	
1951-60	41.2	41.9	40.6	45	22.8		139	
1961-70	46.3	47.1	45.6	41.2	19.0	22.2(or more)	(151DYSON) 129SRS	
1971-80	c50	c50.1	48.8	34.4	14.7	22.0(or less)	129	
1981-85	55.4	55.6	55.2	33.5	12.1	(21.2)	118	6.8
1986-90	58.0	58.0	58.0	32.0	10.8		c100E	(6.6)

T Target SRS Sample Registration Scheme DY UN Demographic Yearbook
DYNS Demographic Yearbook, New Series * 1921 ** Peak of Natural Increase
Sources: Visaria 1983:501; ICSSR 1981:229 + 231; Cassen 1978:145; Dyson 1984; Jeffery 1985; UN 1974:518-19 and 1980:464-5; UNICEF 1981; ESCAP 1985; GOI, Ministry of Welfare 1981; WB 1983, 1984, 1990 + 1993.

HEALTH IN INDIA

Mortality

The main sources of demographic data on India are the decennial population census (with the latest in 1991); the civil registration system, relatively undeveloped in most states; the Sample Registration System (SRS) which uses a fixed sample over time and is the most reliable source; and demographic surveys by the National Sample Survey (NSS) which changes its sample areas from one round to another.

The table shows changes in life expectancy, vital rates, population size, and infant and child mortality rates, plus some intermittent data on the CDR and IMR in China. The figures show that, for most demographic indicators, India's situation in 1988 has improved by two to three times that prevailing in 1901-11:

	TOTAL LE_0	MALE LE_0	FEMALE LE_0	CBR	CDR	NI	MILLION POPN.	IMR
1901-11	23.8	23.6	24.0	49.2	42.6	6.6	238	295
1988	58.0	58.0	58.0	32.0	10.8	21.2	816	97
1988 as % 1901-11	244	246	242	65	25	321	343	33
% Improvement	144	146	142	(54)	(294)	(221)		(204)
% Improvement p.a.	1.8	1.8	1.7	-0.4	-0.9	3.9	3.0	-0.8

The CDR has fallen more than the IMR and both have improved less than average life expectancy at birth (as one would expect).

Life Expectancy

Average life expectancy at birth increased between 1871 and 1988 by at least 136 percent or an annual average increase of 1.2 percent. The annual increase to 1951 (ie. mainly during the later colonial period) was only about 0.35 percent, compared with an average of about 2.2 percent per year between 1951 and 1988.

TOTAL, MALE AND FEMALE LIFE EXPECTANCY AT BIRTH, INDIA 1871-1996

YEAR(S)	LIFE EXPECTANCY AT BIRTH			FEMALE AS % OF MALE LE	% DECENNIAL CHANGE IN TOTAL LE	% ANNUAL CHANGE IN TOTAL LE	COMMENT & AVERAGE LE IN LDCs
	T	M	F				
1871-80	25						
1881	(24.6)	23.7	25.6	108	-1.6	-0.2	
1881-90	(25.0)	24.6	25.5				
1891	(25.0)	24.6	25.5	104	+1.6	+0.2	
1891-1900	23.8	23.6	24.0				
1901-10	23.0	22.6	23.3	103			
1901	23.8	23.6	24.0	102	-4.8	-0.5	
1911	(23.0)	22.6	23.3	103	-3.4	-0.3	
1911-15	20						
1911-20	(20.2)	19.4	20.9	108	-12.2		FLU EPIDEMIC 1918-19
1921	25	19.4	20.9		+8.7	+0.9	
1921-25	(20.0)	19.4	20.9	108			
1921-30	26.7?	26.9	26.6	99**			
1926-30	27						
1931	(26.8)	26.9	26.6	99	+7.2	+0.7	
1931-35	32						
1931-40	31.8	32.1	31.4	98			
1941	(33)	32.1	31.4	98	+23.1**	+2.3	1930s
					INCREASE		
1941-50	(32.0)	32.4	31.7	98			
1951	(32.0?)	32.4	31.7	98	-3.0	-0.3	
1951-60	(41.2)	41.9	40.6	97			
1960	43	43	42				
1961	(41.2)	41.9	40.6	97	+28.8***	+2.9	1950s PEAK
1961-65	(46.4)	47.1	45.6	97			LDC AV c51
1965	45	46	44	96			
1970	48	50	49				
1971	(45.6)	46.4*	44.7*	96*	+10.7	+1.1	LDC AV c55
1975	50				(+11.8)	(+2.0)	
1976	(49.4E)	50.1E	48.8E	97	(+8.3E)	(+1.7E)	LDC AV 57.5
1970-75	49.8	50.5	49.0	97			
1977	51						
1978	52.3E	52.5E	52.1E	99			
1976-80	52.3	52.5	52.1	99			
1980	52.1	52.6	51.6	98			LDC AV c59.5
1981	52				+14.0**	+1.4	1970s
1982	55	55	54				
1983	55	56	54				LDC AV 62
1985	56.6	56.7	56.6	100**			
1988	58	58	58	100	(+11.5)	(+1.6)	WORLD AV 64
1991	60	60	60		(+15.4)	(+1.5)	
1981-86	55.9	55.6	56.2				
1996	64T	64T	64T	1981-96:	(+23.1T)	(+1.5T)	
% INCREASE							
1881-1988	136%	145%	127%			+1.2	

* 1971 data based on 10% rural + 20% urban sample. T = Target
** or *** Turning points or rapid increase.
Sources: Chatterjee 1988; GOI, Office of Registrar-General; Agarwal 1989; Ruzicka 1984; Mitra 1978; WB 1993:300.

Until 1921 the LE appears to have fluctuated between 20 and 25 and only rose significantly in the 1930s, reaching 33 by 1941. The annual rate of increase may have been as high as 2.3 percent from 1931 to 1941. After a decade of no significant change in the 1940s there followed the fastest ever improvement in India's LE. Life expectancy increased from about 32 in 1951 to about 41 in 1961, an annual increase of 2.9 percent (far higher than economic growth per capita). In the 1960s the rate of increase slowed to 1.1 percent per year and this may be connected with the peaking of population growth in this decade (2.5% in 1965). The annual rise in LE accelerated again to 1.4 percent in the 1970s, as population growth began to decline from its peak and the Green Revolution improved general nutrition in the 1970s.

The annual increase in LE perhaps even rose to 1.6 percent between 1981 and 1988. The current LE in 1990 is estimated to be 60 and the target of 64 for 1996 implies a continuation at a similar rate of about 1.3 percent per year. Even then, India's average LE will still be at least 14 years shorter than that of Japan.

Chatterjee pinpoints some fundamental disagreement among demographers over trends in LE during the 1950s and 1960s:

YEARS	ANNUAL INCREASE IN LIFE EXPECTANCY				% DECREASE IN CDR
Source:	Registrar-General; and WHO 1982		Visaria 1969; Adlakha & Kirk 1974		Ambannavar 1975
	Male	Female	Male	Female	% Total
1951-60	0.94	0.89	0.45	0.42	12% (1951-61)
1961-70	0.45	0.41	0.87	0.75	21% (1961-71)
1971-80	0.31	0.31			

Sources: Chatterjee 1988:32-3; Ruzicka 1984.

In general, the influence of health expenditure and health care on salubrity has to be questioned but it is still worth comparing levels of investment in health and changes in LE during nine periods of planning:

PLAN	1	2	3	Annual Plans	4	5	Annual Plan	6	7
YEARS	1951-6	56-61	61-66	66-69	69-74	74-79	79-80	80-85	85-90
Health as % Total Plan	5.0 (3.3)	4.6 (3.0)	2.6	2.1	2.1	1.9	1.82	1.86	1.88
Approx % Increase in LE per year	2.9 Investment in Health Care	2.9	1.1	1.1	(c1.7E) GREEN REVOLUTION	1.4	1.4	1.6 Higher Economic Growth	(c0.8)

Note: In 1984-5 all levels of government spent Rs 20.8 billion (3.9% of total government expenditure) on health. This paid for over 1 million hospital beds, nearly 300,000 physicians, 5,372 Primary Health Centres and nearly 38,000 Health Subcentres. The military budget for 1989-90 was Rs 130 billion.

It is very noticeable that the fastest increase in LE coincided with the initial high levels of investment in health of the first two plans. The other periods of acceleration seem to coincide with the Green Revolution from about 1967-8 and with the more rapid annual growth in GDP in the 1980s (5.2 percent from 1980 to 1988, compared with only 3.6 between 1965 and 1980).

Female life expectancy appears to have exceeded male (by roughly from 2 to 8 percent) until the 1920s. From the 1920s until about 1985 female LE was 1 to 3 percent below that of males, which may reflect a larger male share both in the benefit of economic growth and in the general increase in LE that occurred after 1931. Globally, it is unusual for females to have a lower LE than males and it is interesting (and also anomalous?) that the maximum female inferiority of LE occurred in 1961, after a decade of the most rapid increase in general LE that India has probably ever experienced. By about 1985 LE seemed to have equalised between the sexes but the causes are unclear.

SEX RATIO, INDIA 1901-81

Year	1901	1911	1921	1931	1941	1951	1961	1971	1981
Females per 1000 Males	972	964	955	950	945	946	941	930	933
Decennial Change		-8	-9	-5	-5	+1	-5	-9	+3

Source: Mitra 1978:493.

Crude Death Rate

CDR usually fluctuates much more than CBR which shows a more regular trend. Both Ruzicka and Dyson (1984) were worried that mortality decline began to slow down during the later 1960s and during the 1970s (and especially between 1972 and 1978?). However, the subsequent data (at least the official data) seem to suggest that these fears may have been groundless and in fact the official data (which may not be reliable) indicate that the CDR fell more rapidly in the 1970s than during any decade since the post-influenza years 1921 to 1930. Indeed the rate of decrease appears to have been accelerating since 1946-50, with the possible exception of the 1950s: the CDR fell by 17 per cent, 23 percent and about 22 percent in the sixties, seventies and eighties respectively.

CHANGES IN CRUDE DEATH RATE, INDIA 1871-1988

PERIOD	AVERAGE CDR	% CHANGE FROM PREVIOUS PERIOD	COMMENT
1871-81	(40)	Not worth calculating:	
1881-91	39.6	Apparently nil between	
1891-1901	(46)	1871-81 and 1911-20?	
1901-11	42.6		
1911-15	30.2		
1916-20	38.2	+26	Influenza Pandemic
1921-25	26.3	-31**	After the Flu
1926-30	24.6	-6	
1931-35	23.6	-4	
1936-40	22.3	-6	
1941-45	22.5	+1	War; Bengal Famine
1946-50	18.7	-17*	
1951-55			
1956-60	(23.4)		
1961-65	(22.0)		
1966-70	(17.4)		Rural 17.7 1968-70
1971-75	15.5	-11	Rural 17.1 (-3+%)
1976-80	13.8	-11	Rural 15.0 (-12%)
1981-85	12.1	-12	Rural 13.3 (-11%)
1986-90	(10.8E)	-11 1986-88	
1921-30	(25.4)	-33**	
1931-40	(23.0)	-9	
1941-50	(20.6)	-10	
1951-60	22.8	+11?	
1961-70	19.0	-17	(-12% in Ambannavar 1975)
1971-80	14.7	-23*	(-21% in Ambannavar 1975)
1981-88	(11.4E)	(-22E)	
1990 Target	10.4 T	(-17T)	
2000 Target	9.0 T	(-13T)	

Sources: As for the earlier table, plus Ambannavar 1975; see also Chatterjee 1988:32-3.

_Despite the impressive long-term downward trend, there continues to be some annual fluctuation, including a 6 percent increase as recently as 1984 (causes unknown). However, there have only been three years since 1970 (1972, 1975 and 1984) when the figures indicate a rise in CDR.

The data on vital statistics for males and females given in Mitra (1978:493) show that the male CBR was higher between 1891 and 1921, equal between 1921 and 1941 and then lower than the female CBR from 1941 to 1971. The trend was much less regular for CDR, with male mortality exceeding female in 1901-11, 1921-4, and 1951-61 and equalling female in 1941-51. The net result of these differential rates has been a steady decline in the sex ratio so that females per 1000 males have fallen steadily from 972 in 1901 to 930 in 1971. Apart from a very minimal upturn in 1951 (possibly attributable to normal margins of error in measurement), 1981 was the first recorded increase in the sex ratio this century and even this (3) was only half the average decrease (6) in previous decades.

Rural CDR

The rural CDR since 1971 has been roughly 10 percent higher than the national rate. The rate of decrease appears to have parallelled the national decline during the 1970s. In 1978 the rural CDR was 15.3, ie. 63 percent more than the urban CDR of 9.4. This was still the lowest rural-urban differential in CDR during the 1970s.

Infant Mortality

The infant mortality rate from 1871 to 1911 averaged about 288 per thousand. Since then the rate has more than halved, from over 200 to less than 100, between 1911 and 1990:

Quinquennium beginning	1911	1916	1921	1926	1931	1936	1941	1946
Av. IMR	204	219	174	178	174	161	161	134
IMR Change/1000		+15	-45	+4	-4	-13	0	-27+E

Quinquennium beginning	1951	1956	1961	1966	1971	1976	1981	1986
Av. IMR	146	(156)	129	(138)	134	124	107	100E or less
IMR Change/1000	+12					-10	-17	-7+E

The IMR declined from an average of 146 in the 1951-61 decade to 129 in the 1961-71 decade but the downward trend then appeared to be faltering during the 1970s. Yet the largest decrease since 1946-51 occurred in the late 1970s. This either means that the official figures are over optimistic or that Dyson and Ruzicka, writing in 1982, were too pessimistic about the late 1970s.

The IMR is almost certainly measured even less accurately than the CDR and in any case it probably has tended in the past to fluctuate much more than the CDR. However, since 1970 the official IMR has risen more than marginally in only two years (1972 and 1975). Despite the fears of Dyson and Ruzicka, it does appear that the average IMR fell from 124 between 1976-80 to 107 between 1981-5. This fall coincided with anti-poverty programmes, the Expanded Programme of Immunisation, introduction of Community Health Workers and other improvements in Primary Health Care.

Like LE, which began with female superiority until 1925, IMR was also lower for females until about 1972 and is now about equal.

Urban-rural inequality of IMR is much greater than any gender difference. The national gradient of inequality of IMR between the rural and urban sectors was 185 percent in 1978 and the gradient was actually 232 percent in a high IMR state like Rajasthan.

The data show a 10 percent increase in the late 1970s neonatal mortality over the rate in the early 1970s. Whereas in the 1970-4 period neonatal deaths comprised 54 percent of total infant deaths, this rose to an average of 60 percent in the next four years (Cf. 80 percent in Sweden). A high NMR ratio is one indicator of a more 'developed' pattern of IMR. However, in India neonatal deaths are mainly due to congenital problems, birth injuries and tetanus, whilst postneonatal mortality follows infectious diseases and/or malnutrition. Thus success in tackling the problem of tetanus can lead to an <u>increase</u> in the ratio of postneonatal deaths. (Some would perhaps argue that it merely postpones a neonatal death to the postneonatal stage?).

GENDER AND INFANT MORTALITY, INDIA 1881-1983

Year(s)	1881-91	1891-91	1901-11	1911-15	1931-35	1941-50	1959	1969	1970	1971	1972
National Female IMR as % of Male	86	88	91	98	93	92	90	NA	96	100*	112*
Rural Female IMR as % of Male								112*	97	101*	114*

Year(s)	1973	1974	1975	1976	1977	1978	1979	1980	1981	1982	1983
National Female IMR as % of Male	102	93+	100	108	107	107	101	102	101	98	100
Rural Female IMR as % of Male	102	99	99	110	107	108	102	102	100	100	101

Rural Infant Mortality

Since 1970 the rural IMR has usually been about 10 points higher than the national IMR. As with the national rate, the rural rate rose sharply only in two years (1972 and 1975). However, the female rate diverged widely from the male only in 1969 (112%) and 1972 (114%) and the only other large divergence occurred in 1976 (110%), a year when IMR fell to 1973-4 levels. By 1981 the gender difference had disappeared.

Child Mortality

Life table probabilities show a 50 percent decline in mortality of those aged between 1 and 5 in the period from 1941-50 to 1961-70. Ruzicka (1984) surmises that there was little decline in rural child mortality during the 1970s. The risk of dying under the age of 5 had declined from 199 per thousand between 1975 and 1980 to 119 per 1000 by 1988.

Crude Birth Rate

The crude birth rate has fallen from nearly 50 in 1901 to about 44 in 1960 and 32 by 1988. The family planning programme began in 1954 but there appears to have been no reduction in the CBR until the late 1960s and early 1970s when there were decreases of 12 percent and 10 percent respectively. This rapid decline (of nearly one point per 1000 each year) decelerated to a decrease of 6 percent in the late 1970s and to no decrease at all in the post-emergency period from 1977 to 1985. From 1986 to 1988 India experienced a modest fall of 4 percent in CBR.

CHANGES IN CRUDE BIRTH RATE, INDIA 1881-1988

PERIOD	CBR	% Change from previous period
1881-91	49.0/48.8	
1891-1901	46.0	-6
1901-11	48.0/49.2	+4+
1911-21	49.0	+2
1921-30	46.0	-6
1931-40	45.0	-2
1941-50	NA/44.0	-2
1951-60	(41.6?)/41.7	-5 (or less?)
1961-70	(41.2)/40.0	-1? Rural 38.9 1968-70
1971-80	34.5	-16?
1981-90	(33.0)	-4 1981-88
1981-90	(33.0)	-4 1981-88
1941	45.0	
1951	43.0	
1960	43.7	
1961	45.0	+3
1965	45.0	0
1966-70	39.7	-12 Rural 38.9 1968-70
1971-75	35.6	-10 Rural 37.2 (-4%)
1976-80	33.4	-6 Rural 34.7 (-7%)
1981-85	33.5	0 Rural 35.0 (+1%)
1986-88	(32.2)	(-4)

Sources: As for the earlier table showing annual data, plus Mitra 1989:492.

In 1986, after 32 years of family planning, still only 37 percent of 133 million eligible couples used contraception (compared with 74% in China). Population growth has averaged more than 2.2 percent per year since 1965 and is currently much higher than China's 1.3 percent even though India has fewer married women of reproductive age. India is expected to have a marginally larger population than China by the time it reaches a stationary state (of 1,862 million).

Rural CBR

The rural CBR fell from 39.0 in 1968 to 34.3 in 1985 and only in 1975 was there a recent significant year-on-year increase in CBR. The official data show a particularly high decrease in 1973 and 1974 (35.9) from 38.4 in 1972. A fall of 2.5 points in one year seems suspiciously high but it did coincide with low agricultural production in 1972-3. The CBR fell to 34.3 by 1977, moved marginally upwards to 35.5 by 1982 (as the post-Emergency backlash against family planning took effect) and then had edged downwards to 34.3 by 1985. Overall the rural CBR only fell by 4.7 points in the 17 years between 1968 and 1985, a piffling annual reduction of 0.28 points per 1000.

Maternal Mortality

The rural MMR averaged 394 per 100,000 births in the 1970-3 period. The national rate was estimated to be still 500 in 1980 (Cf. 44 in China).

Class, Income and Health

The most frequently used evidence on the relationship between class, income and health is the Registrar-General's report on rural infant mortality in 1978 (see Ruzicka 1984 and the table on page 72). This is not entirely satisfactory and there are no direct data on income and class, only on utilities possessed and on type of occupation. The evidence shows that Muslims and Tribals (surprisingly) both had a considerably lower rural IMR but scheduled castes had the highest IMR. Literacy of the mother was associated with a much lower IMR and mother's possession of 6 to 10 years education actually reduced the IMR to 64. Most rural households used a lamp or lantern and had a medium level of IMR (119). Households that used oil lamps (and were thus presumably poorer) had an average IMR of 163 and households with electricity experienced a much lower IMR of 87. Oddly, source of water appears to make less difference than source of lighting (a better proxy for income?). Age of the mother at marriage was strongly related to IMR. Finally, the occupation of the household head seems to be very weakly associated with IMR, but with the trend in the expected direction. However, the occupational categories need disaggregation and are not all that helpful for the sociologist.

Jain reproduces data on income variations of average and low birthweight in New Delhi 1969-70 and Calcutta 1976-7. The income gradients of incidence of low birthweight were very similar: 152 percent in Delhi and 157 percent in Calcutta. The income gradient of low birthweight (2500 grams or less) was 105 percent in Delhi. (The gradient here expresses poorest as a percentage of richest, who were fewer.) However, nearly 17 percent of the richest category in Delhi and over 7 percent of the richest in Calcutta had babies with low birthweight (see

Ghosh 1977 and Daṣ 1981, data reproduced in Jain 1988:106).

CLASS, INCOME AND RURAL INFANT MORTALITY IN INDIA, 1978

	CLASS OR INCOME				
	V.HIGH	HIGH	MEDIUM	LOW	TOTAL
	RURAL INFANT MORTALITY				
Muslim					108
Hindu					136
Total					c137
Scheduled Tribe					113
Scheduled Caste					159
Years Education of Mother		6-10	0-5		
		64	105		
Literacy of Mother			LITER-RATE	ILLI-TERATE	
			90	132	
Source of Hh Lighting		ELEC-TRIC	LAMP OR LANTERN	OIL LAMP	
% of total		18%	56%	23%	100%
		87	119	163	c137
Source of Drinking Water	TAP	HAND PUMP	WELL	POND/TANK/ RIVER	
	103	105	137	105	c137
Age of Women at Marriage		21+	18-20	<18	
		90	132	156	
Occupation	NON WORKER	WORKER	WORKERS: FARMER FISHERMAN HUNTER LOGGER & RELATED WORK	WORKERS: PRODUCTION AND RELATED UNLESS TRANSPORT, EQUIPMENT OPERATION & LABOUR	
	134	142	143	150	c137

Sources: Ruzicka in Dyson 1984:26; GOI, MOW 1986:23

HEALTH VARIATION BETWEEN STATES IN INDIA

India has a federal structure and the constitution makes the states primarily responsible for health. In 1994 there are 26 states (now including Delhi) and 6 union territories but the seven most populous states accounted for 66 percent of the total population in 1981. India is such a diverse and continental federation of highly heterogeneous constituent states that it provides a further 'laboratory', additional to international comparison, for examining variations in health standards and for seeking possible explanations, including the relevance of income distribution and poverty incidence.

The table shows an attempt to rank health status in the 17 major states, using LE, CDR, IMR, CMR and (more controversially) CBR.

HEALTH INDICATORS AND APPROXIMATE HEALTH RANKING OF INDIAN STATES, 1974-86

APPROX. HEALTH RANK / STATE (RANK ORDER IN PARENTHESES)	LE_0 1986	CDR 1985	IMR 1985 (*1983)	CMR (0-4 YEARS) 1974-6 RURAL	CMR (0-4 YEARS) 1974-6 URBAN	CBR 1985 (*1979-81)	TOTAL RANK POINTS (T)	AVERAGE RANK T ÷ 6
VERY HEALTHY								
1. KERALA	65.5(1)	6.5(1)	31(1)	20(1)	15(1)	23.3(1)	6	1.0
HEALTHY								
2. (KASHMIR)			71*(4)	34(3)	15(2)	31.3*	9	(3.0)
3. KARNATAKA	56.3(3)	8.8(3)	69(2)	33(2)	16(3)	29.6(6)	19	3.2
4. MAHARASHTRA	56.3(4)	8.4(2)	68(3)	36(4)	26(5)	29.0(4)	22	3.7
5. PUNJAB	60.5(2)	8.9(4)	71(5)	37(5)	26(6)	28.5(3)	25	4.2
6. TAMIL NADU	53.4(6)	9.5(6)	81(8)	48(6)	27(7)	24.7(2)	35	5.8
7. HARYANA	54.8(5)	9.1(5)	85(10)	48(7)	22(4)	35.7(10)	41	6.8
MEDIUM HEALTH								
8. W. BENGAL	52.0(9)	9.6(7)	74(6)			29.4(5)	27	6.8
9. (HIMACHAL PRADESH)			80*(7)			31.6*	7	(7.0)
10. ANDHRA PRADESH	53.1(7)	10.3(8)	83(9)	54(9)	36(12)	29.9(7)	52	8.7
11. (ASSAM)			94*(11)	49(8)	33(10)	32.7*	29	(9.7)
12. GUJARAT	52.4(8)	10.8(9)	98(12)	58(11)	37(13)	33.0(9)	62	10.3
UNHEALTHY								
13. ORISSA	49.1(11)	14.0(11)	132(16)	56(10)	30(9)	30.7(8)	65	10.8
14. RAJASTHAN	51.9(10)	13.2(10)	108(14)	64(13)	28(8)	39.7(14)	69	11.5
15. MADHYA PRADESH	49.0(12)	14.2(12)	122(15)	63(12)	34(11)	39.4(13)	75	12.5
16. BIHAR	46.0(14)	15.0(13)	106(13)			37.8(12)	52	13.0
17. UTTAR PRADESH	46.2(13)	15.8(14)	142(17)	86(14)	48(14)	37.6(11)	83	13.8
INEQUALITY GRADIENT: UNHEALTHY STATES AS % OF KERALA	(135)	222	394	336	233	159		
INDIA	c57.0	11.8	c97			32.9		

Sources: Kakwani 1990:A13 for LE; GOI, MOH 1988:152-3 for CDR and CBR: GOI, MOW 1986 1986:22 for IMR; Bardhan 1984:88 for CMR.

There is quite high (but by no means complete) correlation between these various indicators and so ranking the states does not seem too difficult. For example, Kerala ranks first on all health counts and is really in a league of its own. Membership of division two, states with high health status, also seems clearcut, though the inclusion of Kashmir on the basis of less data may be questionable. (Kashmir's health appears similar to that of its richer neighbour, Punjab.) The exclusion of West Bengal from the high category is justified on the grounds of its having a significantly lower LE and of taking LE to be the most important indicator of health. On the other hand, Rajasthan has been included in the low category in spite of its relatively higher LE.

There are a few major inconsistencies between indicators for individual states. Tamil Nadu ranks sixth overall but had the second lowest CBR (24.7) in 1985. This was nearer to that of Kerala than any of the others in the high health status category. Haryana ranks seventh overall but had a high IMR and a very high CBR in 1985. Conversely, West Bengal had a lower CBR than would be expected from its overall medium ranking. Andhra had a relatively high LE and relatively low CBR. Gujarat also ranked quite high on LE but low on infant and child mortality. Orissa ranked well on CBR and urban child mortality but second worst on IMR. Rajasthan's record is perhaps even more uneven and it is interesting that Rajasthan has increased its LE more than any other major state since the 1960s, by 19 per cent. UP occupies the bottom position for all the health indicators used here, except CBR (which is still high in absolute terms). UP's marginal superiority over Bihar in LE is so slight as to be within the bounds of error in measurement.

Chatterjee (1988:60-1) provides a ranking of 17 states, based on rural needs for health improvement. Using an index constructed from the CDR, rural IMR and size of the rural population, she identifies four categories:

1) Lowest priority: Himachal Pradesh, Kerala and Kashmir.
2) Low priority: Assam, Maharashtra, Karnataka, Punjab and Haryana.
3) Second highest priority: West Bengal, Andhra Pradesh, Tamil Nadu, Gujarat and Orissa.
4) Highest priority: UP, Bihar, Madhya Pradesh and Rajasthan.

Returning to inequality gradients, the penultimate row of the table on page 73 shows the performance of the five unhealthiest states, relative to Kerala. The figures show that regional inequality in India is highest for IMR (394%), then rural CMR (336%) and CDR (222%). Child mortality in the urban sector is less unequal (233%) than in the rural sector and CBR (159%) has a lower range than CDR. The interstate gradient for life expectancy at birth in 1985 was 135 percent. This compares with the gradient of 127 percent between rich and poor countries and 133 percent between high and low 'human development' countries in 1988 (see Chapter 1). These figures are remarkably similar but the gradient between the highest international performer (Japan, with an LE of 78) and the lowest category (eg. Ethiopia, with an LE of around 47) is nearer 165 percent, confirming the expected higher gradient between individual nations than between regions within a nation. However, regional health gradients may be higher in countries with significantly lower national averages for life expectancy than that possessed by India.

The table on pages 77-78 shows the actual social composition and development performance of India, of the healthiest state (Kerala) and of the unhealthiest (UP). The last four columns present indices of average development for the four categories of state, ranked according to health in the earlier table. The averages used are unweighted. For example, the second row shows that the one very healthy state had a population size 6 percent below the average whereas the five unhealthy states had an average population size which was more than twice that of the mean for the major Indian states. Indeed, health status seems to be negatively related to population size and it is significant that the unhealthy category includes the two most populous states. There is less variation in the ratio of members of scheduled castes and tribes and hardly any variation at all in the ratio of scheduled castes (except in the case of Kerala). However, there is a clear trend of better health in states with fewer members of scheduled castes and tribes. The same hardly applies to scheduled castes alone. The positive association with the Muslim share of the population seems both surprising and beyond simple explanation. The proportion of agricultural labourers in the male labour force is also positively related to health but this seems perverse and the relationship certainly needs to be explored. Kerala emerges as highly untypical on this indicator (as indeed on so many others). Superficially, one might surmise that the high concentration of labourers (and, incidentally, of unemployment) in Kerala has contributed to the political pressure leftwards. The ratio of immigrants reveals no smooth trend and the connection with health is likely to be at least two separate processes: richer states attract more migrants and also it is sometimes claimed that migration induces stress and consequent ill health. (Areas with more than 10 percent of their population immigrant include Delhi, Assam and several other northeastern states, Haryana, Punjab and W. Bengal: these areas, plus also Maharashtra, have been foci of considerable conflict and violence between locals and immigrants.) The average sex ratio does not vary between categories of state, except that Kerala has a ratio of females which is 11 percent above the national average. The contrast between Kerala and UP is particularly marked.

Health seems clearly related to per capita income, except that Kerala itself has a PCI 25 percent below the national average (but still higher than that of the unhealthy states). Health seems much more related to economic growth since 1970-1 than to the actual PCI in 1983-4. The relationship with distribution of land appears perverse, with higher inequality in the healthiest state. This is difficult to explain and one can only point out that the range in Gini coefficients is relatively small (though the absolute levels are all fairly high, by international standards) and the inequality in Kerala may have been reduced to some extent since 1971-2, when these data were produced.

The size of the ceiling for landownership which has been specified in the land reform legislation of different states also does not seem to bear much relation to health. This is not very surprising since ceiling sizes are related to non-equity factors such as quality and availability of land as well as to population density and land-population ratios. The structure of farm sizes is also not clearly related to health, though Kerala has a minuscule proportion of farms over 25 acres and a somewhat higher proportion of small and marginal farms (below 5 acres), compared to the rest of India. Average farm size also seems unrelated to health, though again Kerala is untypical in having farms about a quarter the size of the national average. The two indices of inequality of consumption actually show higher disparity in the healthier states though the trend is not a smooth one. This perverse relationship arises partly because consumption inequality is accentuated in the richer states but this does not account for the relatively unequal consumption in Kerala and as late as 1983. As in the case of the international comparison, it does seem that income (or consumption) distribution has very little effect, at least in isolation, on average health standards. There is a stronger (but still fairly weak) association between poverty incidence and health. However, the second set of figures, for 1983-4, and the 1983 data for the ultra-poor (80 percent or less consumption of that of the poor) show hardly any variation, except in the case of the five unhealthiest states. Just as health is more closely related to growth in PCI than it is to a recent level of PCI itself, so health correlates more with the decrease in poverty incidence between 1972 and 1983 than it does with the actual incidence of poverty in 1983. The range of the fall in poverty between healthier and sicker states is very wide but the trend is not a smooth one. The range is comparable for literacy (and even much wider for female literacy) and there is a very smooth trend of positive association.

LEVELS AND INDICES OF ASPECTS OF DEVELOPMENT RELATED TO HEALTH, INDIAN STATES

HEALTH STATUS	LEVEL OF DEVELOPMENT (RAW DATA)			INDICES, USING UNWEIGHTED AVERAGES ALL-INDIA = 100				
				VERY HEALTHY	HEALTHY	MEDIUM HEALTHY	UNHEALTHY	
STATES	INDIA	KERALA	UP	KERALA	KASHMIR KARNATAKA MAHAR. PUNJAB TAMIL N. HARYANA	WB HIMACHAL ANDHRA ASSAM GUJARAT	ORISSA RAJ. MP BIHAR UP	INEQUALITY GRADIENT: UNHEALTHY AS % OF KERALA
No. of States	25	1	1	(1)	(6)	(5)	(5)	
MILLION POPULATION PER STATE 1981	27	26	111	94	113	123	217	231
SOCIAL COMPOSITION 1981								
% Scheduled Caste & Tribe	23.5	11.0	21.4	47	78	94	126	268
% Scheduled Caste only	15.8	10.0	21.2	63	100	108	103	163
% Muslim	11.4	21.2	15.9	186	159	137	76	41
Ag. Labourers as % Male Labour 1971	30	46	22	153	107	100	87	57
% Immigrants from outside the state	4.8	1.4	1.8	29	137	130	64	221
Females per 1000 males	933	1032	885	111	99	100	100	90 (111)
INCOME								
Net Domestic Product PC 1983-4	2344	1760	1567	75	111	94	66	88 (114)
% gpa NDP PC 1970-1 to 1983-4	1.6	2.0	0.7	125	119	50	44	35 (286)
WEALTH DISTRIBUTION								
Gini Index, Landownership 1971-2	.68	.74	.64	109	99	100	91	83
Max. Ceiling, Irrig. Acres 1986	(24)	15	18	64	102	83	95	148
% Operational Holdings:								
25+ acres 1980-1	2.4	0.1	0.4	4	158	79	162	4050
0.1-5 acres 1980-1	74	96	87	129	84	99	93	72
Av. acres, operational holding 1971-2	5.4	1.3	3.8	24	133	96	100	417
Gini Index, Consumption 1983	(.29)	.33	.29	115	103	91	101	87
Theil's Measure of Inequality of Consumption Expend. PC 1983	(.14)	.19	.14	137	104	81	103	75
POVERTY*								
% below PL (<Rs 600 pa) 1983	38	40	49	83	77	88	108	130
% below PL 1983-4	37	27	45	73	70	73	119	163
% Ultra Poor (<Rs 480 pa) 1983	30	22	31	73	73	77	110	151
% decrease in ratio below PL 1972-83	20	36	17	180	135	155	75	42 (240)
SOCIAL DEVELOPMENT								
% Male Literacy 1981	47	74	39	157	136	104	85	(185)
% Female Literacy 1981	25	65	14	260	124	112 or less	60	(435)
HEALTH CARE								
Rs. Public Expend. PC on Health, 1986-87	(30)	29	19	99	116	108	80	124
1982-83	33	37	17	112	142	130	85	76 (132)
1976-77	(19)	25	10	131	113	106	77	59 (169)
% gpa PC Expend. on Health, 1976-87	(4.5)	1.7	6.7	38	102+	102+	109	35 (286)

LEVELS AND INDICES OF ASPECTS OF DEVELOPMENT RELATED TO HEALTH, INDIAN STATES (contd.)

STATES	INDIA	KERALA	UP	KERALA	KASHMIR KARNATAKA MAHAR. PUNJAB TAMIL N. HARYANA	WB HIMACHAL ANDHRA ASSAM GUJARAT	ORISSA RAJ. MP BIHAR UP	INEQUALITY GRADIENT: UNHEALTHY AS % OF KERALA
HEALTH								
Life Expectancy at birth 1986	57.0	65.5	46.2	115	99	92	85	(135)
Male Life Expectancy 1961-70	(49.3)	59.3	44.0	120	106	95	94	(128)
CDR 1985	11.8	6.5	15.8	55	76	84	122	222
Total IMR 1985	97	31	142	32	76	86	126	394
Rural IMR 1983	114	35	166	31	77	82	114	368
Urban IMR 1983	66	26	100	39	86	88	120	308
Female Rural IMR 1961-70	(139)	62	259	45	82	97	131	291
Rural Child (0-4) MR 1974-6	(c49)**	20	86	41	82	110	137	334
Urban Child (0-4) MR 1974-6	(c27)**	15	48	53	80	128	128	242
Neonatal MR as % IMR 1976-8	61	62	56	98	100	103	92	(107)
CBR 1985	32.9	23.3	37.6	71	90	94	112	158
Child-Woman Ratio per 1000 women 1981	546	409	629	75	96	93	110	147

Averages in parentheses for India and all averages for categories of states are UNWEIGHTED.
* Data for 1983 from Kakwani (1990); for 1983-4 from GOI MOH 1988. ** Median.

Sources: GOI, MOW 1986:4-8,22,30,112-13; Brass 1990:189, 223 + 258; Chambers 1988:44; Bandyopadhyay 1986:A54-5; GOI, MOH 1988:151-3; Kakwani 1990 (31 March):A5-6, A13; Dyson 1984:5, 22-3; Sundrum 1987:195; Agarwal 1989 (28 Oct.):WS 47; Visaria 1985:1353-4; Bardhan 1984:88.

Expenditure per capita on health care in 1976-7 shows a closer relationship to health standards in the mid 1980s than does analogous expenditure in 1982-3. By then Kerala was no longer the biggest spender on health services. There was little variation in growth of expenditure between 1976-7 and 1986-7, except that it was much lower in Kerala. By 1986-7 Kerala ranked only ninth in health expenditure per capita, compared with first in 1976-7.

Kakwani (1990) concludes that there appears to be no systematic relationship between health expenditure per capita by 14 state governments and such health indicators as LE and IMR. However, the three lowest spenders on health (UP, MP and Bihar) also have poor health. Analysing health expenditure per capita by state governments in 1976-7 and life expectancy in 1986, he finds that 'the elasticity of LE to expenditure was [only] in the range 0.13 to 0.37. Infant mortality, however, is weakly related to expenditure and not at all to its growth rate' (1990:A15). This tends to confirm that the allocation of expenditure between health programmes (eg. to immunisation and to nutrition) is more important than aggregate expenditure. The World Bank shows that in 1990 the public sector share of total health expenditure in India was as low as 22%, compared with 60 percent both in the world as a whole and also even in established market economies. The next lowest, in the rest of Asia, was 39 percent (WB 1993:52).

Finally, various individual health indicators are presented, mainly to check that they correspond reasonably well with the aggregated assessment of health. In all cases except two indicators (both minor ones), there is a smooth trend and in some cases the range between the healthiest state and the five unhealthy states is very wide indeed. It is noticeable that, for virtually every indicator, the 'medium' health category performs below the all-India average. The widest range of values and the largest inequality appears in the IMR figures, especially the IMR for 1985 when mortality was nearly four times higher in the unhealthy states than in Kerala. In descending order, the other inequality gradients were high (251 to 400) for all IMR indicators and also for rural CMR; medium (151 to 250) for urban CMR and total CDR and CBR; and low (101 to 150) for the child-woman ratio, life expectancy and the neonatal mortality ratio. All these inequality gradients are, however, accentuated by comparing the five worst performers with a single state which has exceptionally high standards of health. If the three states with the highest IMR are compared with the three states with the lowest IMR, the inequality gradient is lower. The gradient has changed over time: it was high (287%) in the 1960s, fell to an average of 223% in the 1970s and rose again to an average of 241% in the 1980-5 period. There has been considerable fluctuation in this inequality gradient, ranging from 204% in 1976 to 254% as late as 1982. The inter-state inequality does not appear to be related to national fluctuation in IMR.

Comparing Kerala and UP, the inequality gradients for urban and rural CDRs in 1979-81 were 160% and 250% respectively.

Changes in Life Expectancy at Birth between Major States

In 1951-60 four states had a life expectancy at birth which was very low (40 to 49) and six states had extremely low LEs (below 40). By 1986 Kerala had attained an upper medium LE of nearly 66 and Punjab a medium level of over 60. The majority of eight states (and also probably Assam) had a low LE (50 to 59) and four states (Orissa, MP, UP and Bihar) still retained a very low LE of between 46 and 49 years, ie. comparable to LE in the least developed (mainly African) nations. By 1986 average life expectancy in Kerala was 42 percent higher than in Bihar and UP.

Though Kerala has had the highest LE since at least the 1960s, the most rapid increase in its LE may have occurred as early as the 1950s, the period when India as a whole appears to have made the most accelerated improvement in its life expectancy. In the period between 1961-70 and 1986, LE in both Kerala and India has been prolonged by 10 percent but the highest increases have occurred in states which had a very low and still have a low LE (especially Rajasthan, Gujarat and Karnataka) and two states (Orissa and UP) which have moved upwards by 16 percent from the extremely low to the very low category. Haryana presents an interesting case of zero improvement (Cf. Punjab with 12 percent increase) and Bihar appears to have figures which are bizarre, if not downright incredible. (Cf. Kakwani 1990 who gives data suggesting nearly 9 percent improvement in LE in Bihar between 1976 and 1986.)

LIFE EXPECTANCY AT BIRTH, INDIAN STATES 1951-86

STATE + LEVEL OF LIFE EXPECTANCY 1986	1951-60		1961-70		1976	1981-6 PROJECTED		1986	1961-70 TO 1986
	M	F	M	F	T	M	F	T	% INCREASE
HIGH									
KERALA	39.1	40.7	59.3	59.3	61.7	69.9	65.2	65.5	10
MEDIUM									
PUNJAB	43.3	41.1	55.5	53.0	58.4	64.3	64.3	60.5	12
LOW									
KARNATAKA	41.1	41.6	48.8	48.7	54.5	61.1	60.2	56.3	15
MAHARASHTRA			50.2	50.6	53.5	60.7	59.8	56.3	12
HARYANA			57.0	52.7	52.9	59.6	61.4	54.8	0
TAMIL NADU	39.1	40.7	49.9	47.9	50.3	57.8	58.2	53.4	9
ANDHRA			47.2	48.0	47.9	60.0	56.1	53.1	12
GUJARAT	41.0	40.1	44.4	44.4	50.2	58.3	55.3	52.4	18
W.BENGAL			49.0	50.9	49.6	56.3	57.0	52.0	4
RAJASTHAN	42.1	40.5	44.0	43.2	49.3	55.4	54.8	51.9	19
VERY LOW									
ORISSA	37.1	35.3	42.6	42.2	44.0	51.9	54.1	49.1	16
MADHYA			47.0	46.8	46.9	51.5	53.2	49.0	4
UP	37.1	34.8	44.0	35.8	42.8	46.9	51.1	46.2	16
BIHAR	36.3	36.8	53.5	47.8	42.3	52.3	55.2	46.0	-9(?)
OTHER									
ASSAM	37.0	38.4	47.3	48.9					
GRADIENT OF INEQUALITY (Kerala as % of Very Low)	106	114	127	137	140	138	122	138	
INDIA			(52)	(52)	(c50?)	(56)	(54)	(c57)	10
Sources:	Sinha and Lahiri 1976		Dyson 1979 + 1984		Kakwani 1990	GOI, MOH 1988		Kakwani 1990	

Comparison of health in the various states of India inevitably raises questions of political economy and its influence on health, since the states vary considerably in their social composition, class structure, configuration of political parties, orientation and durability of the dominant party or coalition, economic strategy and policies, including those related to health. There is a need to arrange the states into types, according to their political economy. It is relatively easy to identify the more 'radical' states, such as Kerala, West Bengal and Tripura, and the more conservative ones, such as UP, MP and perhaps Rajasthan. Kohli (1987) compares the political differences between leftist W. Bengal, reformist Karnataka and conservative UP and assesses their effect on incidence of poverty. Nossiter (1986) has compared the communist and Left Front governments in India. There is a need for a full inter-state comparison of health and social development. Whilst socialist orientation has coincided with very impressive attention to and improvement in the health of Keralans, this has not been the case in West Bengal. West Bengal has only improved its LE by 4 percent since the 1960s and has slipped from fifth to ninth in the league table of life expectancy yet on the other hand it still ranks sixth lowest for IMR, seventh lowest for CDR and fifth lowest for CBR. West Bengal continues to have one of the highest (possibly the second highest?) incidences of poverty and probably the third largest number of both poor and ultra-poor. It had the third worst record for reducing poverty incidence between 1972 and 1983, but half of this period antedates the accession to power of the Left Front in 1977. West Bengal reported medium inequality in consumption and was similar to the all-India average in 1983. (Kerala in fact had the second highest inequality in consumption.) West Bengal ranked tenth in terms of health expenditure per person in 1986-7, compared with fourth in 1976-7. Growth in health expenditure per person has actually been the second slowest between 1976-7 and 1986-7. (Expenditure per capita on health in Tripura was higher than in any major state except Rajasthan in 1982-3 but all ten of the northern and northeastern minor states recorded higher amounts and geopolitical, military, new statehood and 'catching up' factors complicate any assessment of what is happening in the smaller and frontier states. The CDR in Tripura had fallen below 9 by 1983.)

However jerky, uncertain and sometimes rhetorical the transition to socialism may have been in Kerala, there is no disputing its success in improving health and thus being in a much better position to reduce fertility. Chatterjee (1988) articulates some current concern about possible health deterioration in Kerala. Success on the health front to date has not been solely due to political and economic factors such as serious implementation of (still fairly modest) land reforms; politicisation of the working (and indeed the labouring) class and higher (indeed, inflationary) wages; and the improvement in the education, employment, income, health care, family planning protection and overall status of women, including female labourers. Kerala also benefits from its environment which facilitates good drainage and sanitation; its sociocultural characteristics, including strong Christian and (relatively modern) Muslim influences; a more active economic role for women, as in most of South India (see Dyson 1983); a settlement pattern with relatively weak boundaries between the rural and urban sectors and with many large villages which facilitate the provision of an infrastructure of PHCs and SHCs; and modernised, relatively effective health services, including more use of paramedicals and community participation.

Though India still has, by international standards, a medium life expectancy, it has moreorless halved its crude death rate between 1965 and 1990. Critics may still argue that (1) the official data on mortality are overoptimistic in their inaccuracy and, when information is incomplete, it tends to omit the worst states or the poorest and least healthy categories; (2) national averages conceal differential rates of improvement in the various states (as has already been clearly demonstrated) and classes (for which evidence has yet to be adduced); and (3) reductions in mortality can be achieved through relatively expensive (and sometimes very inappropriate) high technology, curative approaches but these do not guarantee and may even help to minimise comparable reductions in morbidity. Indeed, reduced mortality among the rich (and even also among the poor) can actually coincide with the same or even increased levels of morbidity, especially among the poor and those with least access to modern or over-modernised health care. In September 1994, an outbreak of mainly pneumonic plague spread from the slums of Surat in Gujarat to Delhi and elsewhere and was disrupting education, leisure, tourism and the economy. It was also threatening to have international repercussions, including effects on richer people in MDCs.

KUMAON
UPPER DOAB
UTTAR
Delhi
ROHILKHAND
OUDH
LOWER DOAB
Lucknow
GORAKHPUR
PRADESH
BUNDELKHAND
VARANASI
BI

HIMACHAL PRADESH
UTTAR KASHI
TEHRI GARHWAL
CHAMOLI
DEHRA DUN
HARYANA
TIBET
PITHORAGARH
SAHARANPUR HARDWAR
GARHWAL
ALMORA
MUZAFFAR NAGAR
BIJNOR
NAINITAL
NEPAL
MEERUT
GHAZIABAD
MORADABAD
RAMPUR
DELHI
PILIBHIT
BAREILLY
BULAND SHAHR
SHAHJAHANPUR
KHERI
BUDAUN
ALIGARH
MATHURA
ETAH
BAHRAICH
SITAPUR
FARRUKHABAD
FIROZ ABAD
MAINPURI
HARDOI
SIDDHARTH NAGAR
MAHARAJ GANJ
RAJASTHAN
AGRA
UTTAR
GONDA
LUCKNOW
BARABANKI
BASTI
GORAKHPUR
UNNAO
DEORIA
ETAWAH
KANPUR DEHAT
KANPUR NAGAR
PRADESH
FAIZABAD
SULTANPUR
RAEBARELLI
MAU
AZAMGARH
JALAUN
FATEHPUR
PRATAPGARH
BALLI
JAUNPUR
GHAZIPUR
JHANSI
HAMIRPUR
BANDA
ALLAHABAD
VARANASI
BIHA
MIRZAPUR
LALITPUR
MADHYA PRADESH
SONBHADRA

3 Politics and health in Uttar Pradesh

This chapter will describe the social and economic composition of Uttar Pradesh; the political parties which represent caste, class and other interests in the state; the brief political history of the at least 27 administrations which have ruled UP in the past 47 years; some of the policies which have influenced the distribution of resources; and some aspects of health policy and of the health status of people in UP. The sections on politics obviously owe much to the various works of Paul Brass who has been studying UP for the past 30 years.

Uttar Pradesh, with a population of about 135 million in 1990, is the most populous of the 26 Indian states. It exceeds the scale of most sovereign nations and there is occasional, though not yet very serious, discussion of bifurcation. With no less complex problems than large LDCs like Indonesia and Pakistan, UP has to deal with them within the constraints of a federal structure and a political system in which interference from the centre, both by government and by parties, has increased in frequency and in arbitrariness. Despite its strategic importance in India's culture, history and politics, and despite having provided India with eight of its ten Prime Ministers, UP's State Domestic Product per capita declined from 93 percent of the all-Indian average in 1950-1 to 74 percent in 1975-6 and to 69 percent by 1984-5 (Saha 1983: 46-8; EIU 1989: 20). Political deterioration has also been severe and perhaps second only to that of neighbouring Bihar (on which, see Kohli 1991). Health standards have improved since nearly four million died in the United Provinces during the epidemic of 1917-8, but UP remains one of the largest concentrations of unhealthy people on this earth. Despite this, health hardly seems to be a prominent issue in the politics of UP.

THE SOCIAL AND ECONOMIC COMPOSITION

Between 1775 and 1856, when the British annexed the kingdom of Avadh ('Oudh'), the East India Company took control of virtually all of what is now Uttar Pradesh. In 1902 the NW Provinces were integrated with Avadh to form the United Provinces of Agra and Oudh which were renamed Uttar Pradesh (Northern Province) in 1950. The state covers an area of about 500 by 200 miles and may be divided into at least six regions (see map), of which the most populated and politically most important are the Western, Central and Eastern Plains. The conventional wisdom emphasises the economic superiority of west over east in UP, but this oversimplification should not mask both the serious underdevelopment (especially social) of central UP and also the considerable intra-regional differences in income and development. Nevertheless, the 20 western districts are more irrigated and have larger farms which are more capitalised (and capitalist?), more mechanised and more productive. Kohli suggests that economic divisions (such as a commercialised class of peasants) are more important in the west and caste and other primary groups are more politically significant in the east (1987: 190). Eastern UP has more tenancy, fragmentation of holdings and bonded labour. There is also more industry in the west (which adjoins and runs into the Delhi region), though there are some sugar mills and other, newer, factories in the east. Annual growth in crop output averaged 1.75 percent between 1950-3 and 1974-7 and only in the period from 1962-5 to 1968-71 did the growth rate (2.8%) rise above that of population. Many of UP's factories are ageing sugar and textile mills, with among the lowest labour productivity in India (GOUP, 1983-4 Plan, 1982: 5).

In 1962 there were only 268,000 workers in larger industry, but Papola (1985) claims that from about 1978 both investment and diversification began to increase. By 1984 there were at least 389 large and over 5,400 small factories and also nearly 96,000 small-scale industry (SSI) units. Industrial employees totalled 1.26 million, including 15, 17 and 67 percent in the large, small and SSI sectors respectively. The new, larger factories are mainly in engineering and agro-based production. The central government had invested about Rs 30 billion in at least 15 projects, including production of fertilisers, electronics, heavy machinery, chemicals and precision instruments. A sizeable ratio of the industrial investment has been concentrated in Rae Bareli and Sultanpur districts, where Mrs Gandhi and her sons had their constituencies. One of four gas fertiliser plants has been built in Amethi, Rajiv Gandhi's constituency, and this cost over Rs 10 billion. Brass (1984) recounts how the most powerful Raja in Gonda district, a Congress (I) MP, successfully pressurised Mrs Gandhi to 'award' a French telecommunications factory not just to his constituency, but to a site within two kilometres of his palace.

Brahmins and Thakurs accounted for 9.2 percent and 7.6 percent of the population in the 1931 census and they probably still own about 40 percent of the land. Many of the Rajas, Talukdars and large Zamindars were Brahmin or Thakur, though a few came from medium castes such as Bania or from even lower medium castes such as Kurmi. Eleven of the 16 individuals who have filled the post of Chief Minister, on 15 occasions out of 24, have been Brahmin (10) or Thakur (4). Brahmin Chief Ministers have tended to select Brahmin councils of ministers and Brahmins have also tended to dominate Congress (I) committees at the district and block level. Brass (1981) suggests that Brahmin loyalty to Congress (I) may override caste loyalty. Thakurs can be either complementary, 'secular' complements to the 'priestly' Brahmins or else their rivals in political games which sometimes demand rather crude alternation (or expectation thereof) between a Brahmin and a Thakur figurehead. (This has also been true in institutions like the civil service, police and universities, and had tended to become the pattern for selection of Chief Minister in the 1980s.) In 1984 there were 29 Brahmins and 8 Thakurs holding the position of chairmen of the Congress (I) district committees out of a total of 59 (now 63) districts. Other high castes accounted for a further 3.6 percent of the population in 1931 and nearly a fifth of the population belonged to a high or 'élite' caste.

Other important castes include the Bhumihars who own land in the east and claim rough equality with Brahmins; Banias who dominate much of trade, business and industry; Kayasthas who are highly educated and thus prominent in government and education; and Tyagis. Jats, Bhumihars and Tyagis comprised 2.1 percent of the population in 1931. Altogether, 46 percent came from the middle castes which include: Yadavs or Ahirs (herdsmen) who comprised 7.8 percent of the population in 1931; Kurmis who comprised 3.5 percent; Jats, who are less numerous but own considerable land in the west, especially in the 8 Upper Doab districts; and Gujars and Koris. Many members of the medium castes are also medium to large peasants, owning 5 to 20 acres of land (especially in the west) and some, particularly Jats and Yadavs, have expressed their increasing wealth and power by supporting opposition parties such as the Lok Dal. In 1984, 26 chairmen of the Lok Dal district committees were Yadav. Other middle castes have been more divided politically, with some supporting the quasi-communal Bharatiya Janata Party. There was resentment that the UP government was ignoring the recommendation of the Mandal Commission to provide 27 percent of government posts for the 'backward' castes and that among the numerous victims of 'fake encounters' with the police were members of the 'backward' castes. Congress policies have benefited the 'backward' castes but the latter have not continued to support Congress, especially after 1967, partly because Congress had not given them enough. This is mainly because Congress has had to try to appeal to the widest possible range of castes and not just to the highest and lowest castes, as it sometimes seems.

In 1971 Muslims constituted 15.5 percent of the total population and were a higher proportion in urban areas and western districts, reaching nearly 50 percent of the population in some large cities in Rohilkhand. Muslims have tended to vote as a bloc for Congress (I) but the issues of sterilisation and slum clearance alienated many Muslims during the Emergency. In the 1980 election for the legislative assembly, Muslim candidates won 18 seats, including six for Lok Dal. Since 1980 there have been serious communal riots in western cities such as

Aligarh, Moradabad and especially Meerut. These led to strong Muslim accusations of partiality and harassment against the Hindu-dominated Provincial Armed Constabulary, the paramilitary mobile police force in UP. Muslims have not voted for the Jan Sangh or the BJP because of their strong associations with Hindu communalism. Muslim leaders in eastern UP have traditionally opposed Congress (I), and in 1980 some voted for the Lok Dal. However, in 1984 Muslims were not keen to support the Lok Dal, because of its championing of the backward castes, who are seen as rivals of Muslims in competition for government patronage and assistance.

About 23 percent of the population belong to scheduled castes and there is also a tiny proportion of members of scheduled tribes, mainly in Kumaon and in Mirzapur district. The scheduled castes are more organised in terms of state-wide caste associations and have thus traditionally been a safe 'vote bank' for Congress (I). Up to 1967 at least, the scheduled caste associations served as agencies for distribution of Congress patronage, in return for votes. Scheduled caste MLAs in the reserved seats were non-militant and had no power in the Congress organisation. In the 1980 parliamentary election nine of the 18 seats reserved for scheduled caste candidates were won by the Lok Dal and there was some support for Janata. However, in the state elections Congress (I) won 71 of the 92 reserved seats in June 1980. The Janata government of UP suspended the practice of reservation in promotions (as distinct from appointments) in government service. As Galanter (1984) makes clear, reserved promotions arouse more antagonism from other castes than do reserved appointments. Congress (I) has since then introduced 18 percent reservation in both recruitment and promotion and claimed to have increased this to 22 percent in 1982. Over half of all the scheduled belong to one caste, the Chamars or Jatavs, as the more politicised and more modern members, especially in the west, prefer to be called. In 1931 Chamars constituted 12.7 percent of the total population. The Chamars are the best educated and more politically conscious of the scheduled but are mainly agricultural labourers, marginal farmers in rural areas and leather workers, factory workers, cycle-rickshaw drivers and labourers in urban areas. They have mainly voted for either the Republican party or for Congress (I). The relatively few members of scheduled tribes in UP have no political significance.

The class situation is complex and complicated further by the caste and other factors. Brass describes how the British established two entirely different systems of land revenue administration in Oudh and in the NW Provinces. In Oudh rights of revenue collection and ownership over the land were granted primarily to a small body of Talukdars, most of whom controlled areas comprising a large number of villages. Their control was both economic and political since the Talukdars of Oudh retained some of the attributes of petty local chiefs. In the rest of the province, the land was settled with individual Zamindars or with joint Zamindari bodies where the latter existed. Some of the individual Zamindars farmed the revenue of hundreds of villages, as did many of the Talukdars. The big Zamindars also tended to wield both economic and political power. In the joint Zamindar areas, economic and political control tended to be exercised over small areas, comprising a mahal or estate of one or a few villages. The joint proprietors generally belonged to a single caste lineage which maintained economic and political dominance over other caste groups in the villages under their control.

Altogether, there were more than two million Zamindars in UP, most of them collecting only a few rupees in revenue from tenants to whom their smallholdings were rented. In 1947 there were 390 very large Zamindars who received over Rs 10,000 in annual land revenue. These included most of the 256 Talukdars who lived in and virtually ruled what used to be Avadh. There were also a further 5,503 large Zamindars who received land revenue of between Rs 1,000 and Rs 10,000. A further 24,000 or so received Rs 250 to Rs 1,000 and two million petty Zamindars received less than Rs 250 in land revenue. The petty Zamindars overlapped with the 12.8 million peasant households which existed in 1952. In 1947 the Zamindari Abolition Committee had found that 2 percent of landholdings exceeded 16 acres, 17 percent contained 5 to 16 acres and the vast majority (81%) consisted of less than 5 acres. In 1977-8 there were 9.42 million self-employed agricultural households and 1.93 million self-employed non-agricultural households. There were also 2.91 million households defined by the NSS as agricultural labourers and a further 0.77 million households of non-agricultural labourers. According to NSS definitions, 19.6 percent of households were mainly employed as labourers of one kind or another. The landless constitute about 20 percent of the population but the proportion is higher in the west. The class composition of UP is unclear and confused by multiple occupational and class membership within households (and even by individuals?), and by ambiguities and changes in official definitions of occupational and employment status.

OCCUPATIONAL AND CLASS COMPOSITION OF RURAL HHs IN UP, 1947-52 AND 1977-8

	1947-52			M = Million			1977-8
390	Very large ex-Zamindars (incl. 256 ex-Talukdars)						
5,503	Large ex-Zamindars						
24,259	Medium ex-Zamindars (NB. total 112,000 villages)						
30,152	TOTAL ZAMINDARS						
2.0 M	Petty ex-Zamindars			Acres landholding 1947			
	Large owners	0.26	M	16.1+	1.03	M	Other rural employment
	Medium to large owners	2.18	M	5.1 to 16	1.93	M	Self-employed non-agricultural
	Small owners	10.37	M	5 and under	9.42	M	Self-employed agricultural
TOTAL PEASANTS		12.80	M		12.38	M	
3.4 M	Rural labourers (1931)				0.77	M	Non-agricultural labourers
					2.91	M	Agricultural labourers
					3.68	M	TOTAL LABOURERS
GRAND TOTAL (16.51)					16.06		TOTAL HOUSEHOLDS

In addition, in 1977-8 there were 1.2 million urban households self-employed and 1.55 million employed in other urban work, presumably mostly paid in wages and salaries.

One relatively recent study of agrarian class in UP is that of Shrimali (1981) who seems biased by his CPI perspective and his use of quota sampling of villages. Brass, particularly in his writings of the 1960s, when he was strongly influenced by the modernisation theories of Weiner and others, has tended to play down class differences and to give major emphasis (some would say over-emphasis) to factions, which are seen as bridging people of different classes. Hardiman (1982) has been particularly critical of the concept of the 'Great Indian Faction', suggesting that factions are really a form of inter-class collaboration. Pandey (1978) has characterised Congress political activity among the peasants in the 1930s as an example of 'imperfect mobilisation' and has claimed that sometimes it was the peasants leading the Congress rather than the reverse.

Since the Kisan Sabha (Peasant Assembly) was first formed in UP in the 1930s, there has been some mobilisation of peasants and peaks of activity seem to have included 1938, the later 1940s, 1958, the mid-1960s, and the 'land-grab' movement of the 1970s, especially 1971. Lower class unity has been diminished by the splitting away of the Kisan Congress in the 1940s, by the formation of the Khet Mazdoor Sabha (Agricultural Labourers Assembly) in 1959 and by the splitting of the Communist party into CPI and CPI(M) - with associated splitting of the Kisan Sabha into analogous wings, in 1964. There has also been a trend for each of the many other political parties, including even the conservative ones, to form their own (often temporary) peasant organisation, especially just before elections. The lower agrarian classes thus remain divided by class itself, by caste, by political party affiliation and by strategy. Vertical divisions of class include family, clan, religion, sect, region, village, ward and even hamlet. Shrimali complains that the Kisan Sabha distanced itself from the middle peasants on the grounds that the capitalist transition in agriculture was complete and therefore the true enemy was no longer just the 'feudal' landlords but now comprised the rich peasants, who were liable to be supported by the middle peasants in any class struggle.

The Congress Socialist Party leaders appear to have been small landlords and upper tenantry, who sought to control the increasing radicalism of the Kisan Sabha in the late 1940s. The latter concentrated on the land issue and conflicts over abolition of land revenue or over input and output supplies and prices were regarded as 'deviationist'. As a result, support for the Kisan Sabha narrowed down to the poor peasants and agricultural labourers, particularly those in the poorer east. The Kisan Sabha became dormant in the more prosperous west and only campaigns such as those for higher sugarcane prices seem to have united rich and poor peasants. Insofar as the poorest and most deprived labourers have been able to migrate to the Green Revolution areas of Punjab, Haryana and western UP, this may have also reduced, or at least temporarily removed, some of the tension between classes in the east. Shrimali concludes that by 1979 the ex-Zamindars had actually benefited most from changes since 1951. The majority, ie. middle and smaller peasants, had benefited much less and the tiny owners and the poorest the least.

Shrimali claims that the ex-Zamindars have become big owner-farmers and have allied with the newly emerging, rich farmers (presumably from the 'rising, middle castes') to seize the benefits of government development programmes. Hasan also claims that, 'with the creation of only one type of tenurial right in 1974, the distinction between Zamindars and new proprietors became increasingly blurred' (1989: 257). The middle and smaller peasants have been less well equipped to seize these benefits and, though they may have gained absolutely, they have lost out in relative terms and they feel suitably cheated. Some have fallen into the category of tiny owners and the poorest, through demographic and other causes, and the numbers of landless have increased, both absolutely and proportionately, and particularly among the lower castes.

Joshi has argued that 'agrarian policy has only contributed towards the restructuring of the landed class, more specifically to the ousting of the paternalistic, semi-feudal landed class by a more production-oriented but aggressively acquisitive landed class' (1974: 328). Brass points to how the middle and rich peasants have benefited most from the Green Revolution, particularly from 1967 onwards, and how the entry of non-Congress parties into government at exactly the same time has obliged greater inter-party competition for the support of this increasingly rich and influential class, who also happen to come mainly from the middle castes, especially from the Sudra castes, which form a sizeable proportion of the so-called 'Backward Classes'. Brass notes the effects of the concentration of the Green Revolution in the west and of inappropriate industrialisation on low castes and landless labourers. Yet in the western constituency of Meerut he finds that conflicts between different leading proprietary castes and also between the scheduled and these leading, proprietary castes and also within the rich farmer category mean that 'these issues and conflicts intersect with each other in such a way as to prevent a polarisation of class conflict' (1981: 27). The dominance of the landed castes continues and 'the scheduled castes should be regarded more as pawns than as a powerful force in their own right. All the landed castes share an interest in thwarting the economic and political demands of the low castes' (1981: 28). Brass suspects that many of the Chamars and other scheduled castes would have preferred to have voted for Congress (I) in the 1980 parliamentary elections, but their Jat and Gujar employers directed their votes to the Lok Dal. In the central and backward district of Gonda the conflict was between Thakur and Brahmin descendants of two of the largest Talukdars in the district. In this election both middle and lower castes were 'pawns'. His visit to five constituencies in 1980 led Brass to conclude that 'the landed castes continue to be politically dominant in the UP countryside and constitute the central core of support for all leading political parties' (1981: 34). Lower caste voters have to seek protection, patronage and other favours: 'In many cases, their votes can be purchased' (1981: 35). Brass concludes that the lower castes are not, and show no signs of becoming, an independent political force, as thcy have become in Kerala. Politics in north

India involves tactics of coalition, division and cooption of particular caste groups and their leaders rather than class-caste polarisation,

> for it is primarily a conflict based on different economic interests. The future political strategy of the Congress, therefore, will probably be to divide the middle castes ..... to attempt to build inter-caste coalitions that cut across either [caste] status or economic differences or both. Class polarisation, therefore, is unlikely to occur as long as the Indian regime is based upon open, competitive elections (1981: 37).

The persuasiveness of this argument is reduced, though not necessarily eradicated, by the fact that somewhat greater class mobilisation in Kerala has occurred within an open, competitive framework.

Though Shrimali and Brass differ fairly sharply in their political background and theory, and though their analysis and explanation of events also differs, their separate views seem to justify the conclusion that rural class conflict in UP has been intermittent, varying from low to moderate intensity and attenuated by the existence of a variety of other conflicts, some of them cross-cutting and some less so. One of the latter is the conflict between dacoits (and other criminals) and the police (and other agents of rural authority and power). In the early 1980s the problem of dacoity and of 'law and order' in general was defined by public and government alike as the foremost policy issue. Another related question was that of crimes ('atrocities') against scheduled persons and Shrimali shows that registered cases of such crime averaged over 6,300 per year between 1975 and 1977, including an average of 189 such murders each year. Some writers have sought to link crime, and especially dacoity, to class conflict, unemployment of educated youths and other politico-economic factors. Dacoity is, legally, a crime committed by a gang of five or more persons and it was considered to be most common in about eleven districts of south-west UP, which are defined officially as 'dacoit-infested'. In 1981-2 the police of UP were engaged in a major campaign to eradicate dacoity and had adopted an aggressive shoot-to-kill policy which was in sharp contrast to the softer, subtler approach of neighbouring Madhya Pradesh, where dacoits were given every encouragement to surrender peacefully to face trial and receive gentler treatment in prison than would normally be the case in UP. In June 1981 the UP government had even been obliged to postpone an important by-election because 40 companies of police were involved in anti-dacoit activities. A government statement on the achievements of its first two years in office claimed that 1,703 dacoits had been 'liquidated' and 14,000 others arrested in 4,880 'encounters' (Pioneer, 14 January 1982). A later administration also issued a statement on the achievement of its first hundred days and again results against dacoits featured prominently: 121 dacoits 'eliminated' and 1,582 arrested from 493 'confrontations' (Pioneer, 13 November 1982). Many critics of the government, not least persona non grata in rural areas, were complaining of 'fake encounters' and of the police and rural political bosses exploiting the dacoit issue to settle personal, political and other scores.

Overall, the failure of the lower classes to organise in UP has been a problem of identification, unification, mobilisation and choice of strategy. Many peasants may be unsure of their own objective class position (which may in any case change with their day-to-day struggle to survive); even those who are sure of their class identity are constrained from uniting with others of the same class, by caste and other horizontal divisions and by a host of vertical divisions, not least of which is the vast geographical distance between east and west; those who do unify can be discouraged or distracted from mobilisation by landlord and police terror or by being absorbed into multiclass coalitions within political parties led by upper and middle class persons; and those who succeed in mobilising may still be divided and diverted by the sheer variety of agrarian and other issues which require delicate decisions over strategy and priorities.

POLITICAL PARTIES

The incomplete articulation of classes in UP may be partly a cause and partly a consequence of the symptomatic profusion and duplication of political parties, most of which tend to appeal to a few 'core castes' but which nearly all also seek to appeal to the widest possible range of classes, especially given that the Congress (I) party has so often been so successful in such a multiclass appeal. Indeed, so successful was this appeal in the period up to 1967 that Brass found factions much more significant than class in dividing the Congress party. He argues that factions link up the particularisms of family, caste, village, school ('classmate') and friendship network (inter alia) with the relatively more universal and 'modern' political party. Instead of seeing factions as cutting across class solidarity, Brass sees factionalism as partly positive in linking the poor with the powerful via patrons, brokers, bosses, criminals, dacoits and/or faction leaders. When a single party becomes as dominant in the political system as the Congress party had done by 1960, then factionalism within the dominant party intensifies and the opposition parties (including socialist ones) even begin to behave rather like factions themselves.

Factions can recruit on a multicaste basis and, given that a majority in the state assembly has required from 34 to 42 percent of the votes and that the most numerous caste, the Chamars, comprised less than 13 percent of the population of the United Provinces in 1931, political parties must appeal to more than three castes or communities, in virtually all areas. Certain castes are identified more with particular political parties but no caste is homogeneous in its party support. Up to 1967 and probably since then no major political party in UP has operated exclusively in the state and all the major parties were 'national' parties or at least north Indian parties. Brass notes the high proportion of votes going to minor parties and independents, many of whom are dissidents who have left the Congress party. This contributes to the instability of the party system, which has been 'characterised by a single-party dominance, opposition fragmentation and continued evidence of an absence of allegiance on the part of many politicians and voters of any party' (1984: 240). Socialist opposition was stronger than communist at least until 1969 but 'there has been a constant movement of political leaders from the Congress to the Praja Socialist Party, from the PSP to the Socialist Party, and very often from one of the socialist parties back to the Congress' (1984: 249).

The interparty conflict could be represented as merely a version of factionalism within the dominant class and/or between the élite castes. At least 40 percent of MLAs represent landed interests. The core of loyal support for any particular party is very small and, conversely, the state has a high and volatile, floating vote which swings more widely between parliamentary elections than the Indian electorate as a whole, though always in the same direction as the national trend. Victory margins in individual constituencies tend to be relatively small and often explicable in mainly local terms. Swings may run in opposite directions in different constituencies and regions of UP. All this suggests that class associations, like caste associations, are weakly developed. The strongest class associations appear to be the textile trade unions and the cane cooperative unions. The political party system fails to reflect the main class struggles partly because these are far from being clearcut anyway; because Congress is adept at disguising its true class interests and at obfuscating any tendencies towards clarification of class issues (eg. the use of smothering, paternalistic euphemisms like the 'weaker sections'); because, until recently, Congress could, if need be, resort to intimidation, repression and manipulation of the state institutions it usually controls; and because opposition parties are even less united in UP than elsewhere.

Brass attempts some periodisation of the recent political history of UP. From 1947 to 1955 there was one-party dominance (by Congress), relative unity within Congress under Pant's eminent leadership and some conservative reforms, including Zamindari Abolition. In 1955 Pant was called to the central cabinet and Congress leadership passed to 'second rank' leaders, party managers from the organisational wing. One-party dominance continued but subject to increasing internal conflict and factionalism. Government became increasingly weak, there was corresponding lack of development and by the election of 1967 there was widespread unrest and no clearcut Congress majority. Brass (and also Frankel 1978) treats the 1967 to 1969 period as a watershed, involving a transition from one-party dominance to two-party competition, particularly between Congress (I) and the various political party incarnations of Charan Singh. This transition happened to more or less coincide with the start of the Green Revolution in UP and Brass links the agricultural growth with the rise of the middle castes and/or peasants and their rise in turn is used to help explain the continued decline of the socialist vote and the rise to dominance of the Lok Dal and its predecessors. The period between 1967 and 1969 was itself an interregnum, consisting of non-Congress coalition and shaky Congress government, in a period of maximum instability. The transition is said to have switched the main focus of political debate from urban-rural priorities to competition for the support of three main strata within rural society - the élite castes, the middle castes/peasants and the rural poor and landless and/or minorities, consisting mainly of scheduled castes and Muslims. Agricultural growth and rising prosperity, especially in western UP, increased the already considerable demographic and political importance of the middle castes/peasants and obliged the major parties to bid for their support with more and more populist concessions. This greater bid for the middle peasant vote reached its climax in 1977 and 1980, when there were big swings in the parliamentary elections, swings far bigger than in other parts of India and perhaps larger than can be explained purely in terms of successive reactions of the electorate to Emergency excesses or to Janata incompetence.

Despite an apparent increase in the class dimension of conflict, especially in competition for the votes of the rural middle class, Brass (1981) emphasises that the élite castes had still retained much of their dominance up to 1980 and the socialist parties continued to be divided, in disarray and decline. Hasan claims that

> appeals to caste and community [especially religious] loyalty have prevented mobilisation based on an alliance by the oppressed, cutting across castes. This was best exemplified by the strategy of the Lok Dal to mobilise middle and backward castes on social and political issues which were the main source of their grievance against Congress rule. On balance, the emergence of middle and backward castes as a dominant force under the aegis of the Lok Dal may have been of negative consequence in UP's quest for social transformation and equality (1989a: 257).

Brass has also chronicled the divisions, mergers and further splits which have beset the socialist parties in UP, especially in 1955, 1962-5 and 1971-4, which have ultimately weakened the left in UP and contributed to the decline in the socialist vote. He emphasises the strongly factional divisiveness within parties which might be expected to be more ideological and less personalised than parties like Congress and shows how the extreme egoism and opportunism have served to compound the effects of ideological differences between the leaders of the socialist parties. In addition, the intellectualism and relative lack of grassroots base, organisation and support have also contributed to the failure of the socialists in UP. He also traces a trend, dating from about 1970, soon after the bifurcation of the Congress party in 1969, whereby Mrs Gandhi increasingly intervened in the politics of UP (and other states) and treated the fortunes of Congress government in UP and at the centre as more and more indissolubly interlinked. This has complicated what was already a highly complex political situation in UP and has added yet another destabilising factor in a situation of already decreasing stability. There has been increasing centralisation, interference by and dependence on central government, exemplified in cynical exchanges of personnel between Union cabinets and UP ministries. The increased interdependence between Delhi and Lucknow has probably served to reinforce the already existing predominance of western UP.

The Congress (I) Party

Congress (I) has ruled UP for at least 38 out of 47 years since 1947. Rural and district leaders of the Congress party come from the dominant castes, especially the Brahmins, Kayasthas and Thakurs. Urban leadership and financial support come from professionals, merchants, businessmen and industrialists, such as the textile and sugar mill owners. Support has usually tended to be higher among urbanites or Muslims or scheduled castes such as the Chamars, Jatavs, Koris and Pasis. Congress support had already declined by 1969 when the division within the party increased Congress dependence on segments of the locally dominant, landowning castes. The increasing threat from Charan Singh and a succession of his parties, representing the middle castes and/or peasantry, reinforced the pre-existing tendency of Congress to recruit its following from the highest and lowest strata and from the minorities. Mrs Gandhi's greatest attempts at centralisation and intervention in state politics were frustrated by a (perhaps associated?) decline in local knowledge and authority. Brass concludes that, in the 1980 parliamentary elections in Deoria and Gonda districts, 'the Congress leadership in Delhi sought allies from the most powerful local families with the greatest economic and/or political resources. The Congress operates more than ever before through existing structures of local power, which its economic policies are supposedly designed to eliminate' (1984: 209). The party uses patronage and local structures but also resorts to populist slogans and policies and exploitation of social dramas, crises and 'atrocities' to gain a following. Brass suggests that 'the system, therefore, shifts back and forth between jobbery and demagoguery and fails to confront effectively major issues concerning the economic future of India and the spread of lawlessness and violence in the countryside' (1984:223).

The Congress appeal is more broad based than those of other parties and is arguably more class-oriented than other non-socialist parties but it is still, like the others, more explicitly directed at particular castes and communities. Insofar as it casts its appeal so widely and is trying to devise policies to please so many and varied categories (some of them quite volatile in their support and increasingly voracious in their demands), Congress is paradoxically the most vulnerable to periodic large losses of support.

The Jan Sangh

The Jan Sangh (People's Assembly) was founded in 1951 and represented conservative, Hindu and commercial interests. Its leaders were merchants, shopkeepers and other businessmen of Brahmin, Rajput, Kayastha and Vaishya castes in the urban areas and big landlords elsewhere, especially in Avadh (ie. central UP) and in pockets of eastern UP. In western UP urban leaders are Vaishyas and Kayasthas who could make little appeal to a rural population typified by Jats and Gujars. However, in eastern UP urban leaders had more rural connections and often even shared the same caste as the rural majorities. Jan Sangh support has come from the urban small business and trading communities; those urban dwellers with a somewhat better education but in the medium of Hindi and tending to be anti-western and also opposed to the westernising élite led by the Nehrus; and the rural and urban propertied classes in general. The party was tightly organised and well disciplined, with support from groups such as especially the notorious Rashtriya Swayamsevak Sangh (RSS). Kohli comments that 'with its base in urban traders and shopkeepers, with its "morning exercises" and hymns glorifying health, India and Hinduism; and with its "brown shirt drills", the disciplined orientation of the Jan Sangh evokes the interwar fascist parties of Europe in more than a superficial way' (1987: 204).

Despite being an 'élite party' with not much hope of a mass base, the Jan Sangh was the only opposition party to have significantly increased its vote by 1967. Support declined slightly in the 1970s but it still rose to power as the second most powerful, but still distinctly junior partner, in the Janata coalition of 1977 to 1979. It lost this second place in the coalition in early 1979. In 1980 the party became the Bharatiya Janata Party and won nine MLA seats. In the late 1980s the BJP has exploited the communal issue (especially the temple-mosque dispute at Ayodhya in UP) and has risen to become the main opposition party in India and the ruling party in some Hindi states. This represents a serious threat to Muslims, to the 'secular State' and not least to Congress credentials as defender of this.

The Swatantra Party

The Swatantra (Freedom) Party was another conservative, landlord party which existed between 1959 and about 1974, with its base in Avadh. Its peak support occurred in 1962 and 1967, with nearly 5 percent of the vote.

Lok Dal (also BKD, BLD and DMKP)

The Bharatiya Kranti Dal (Indian Revolutionary Party) was founded by Charan Singh in April 1967 after his defection from the Congress government and party. The title 'revolutionary' was something of a misnomer and the strongest support came from middle or so-called 'backward' castes, such as Jats in the west and Yadavs and also Kurmis, Koris and Muraos across the state, and also from other middle peasants, holding five or more acres, especially in the western districts and particularly in the Upper Doab. (In fact Jats were not actually listed officially as 'backward' in UP.) Duncan (1988) suggests that the BKD ignored agricultural labourers and marginal farmers, focussing on farmers holding between 2.5 and 27.5 acres. The BKD secured 21 percent of the votes in the state elections of 1969. In 1974 the name was changed to Bharatiya Lok Dal (Indian People's Party) when Raj Narain merged the Samyukta Socialist Party with the BKD in what amounted to a dismantling of the socialist movement in UP. This merger brought in the support of Yadavs from the central and eastern districts and made the former BKD more balanced in its regional bases. Narain had the support of cultivating castes in the east. The BLD lacked much of a formal structure below the district level, even in the western districts, and support for the BKD-BLD-Lok Dal-DMKP series of parties has been mainly focussed on Charan Singh and his personal and populist championing of the kisans. Hasan claims that, 'unlike the Congress which followed a multi-class strategy of mobilisation, the BLD applied the SSP model of mobilisation and concentrated more on specific groups' (1989a: 261). The BLD needed to expand beyond rich surplus farmers and so it pitched its appeal to backward castes, especially lower backwards in the east, with social grievances. Singh (a Jat) even posed as an 'old Yadav' in the east. The Lok Dal appeal to caste has renewed Congress politics of caste but behind this there is actually a class conflict between newly rich middle peasants who are refusing minimum wages to their labourers, demanding begar, evicting them from small plots allotted by the government and committing 'atrocities' against them. The Lok Dal has exploited middle caste/middle peasant grievances against both upper castes and urban trading castes.

In 1977 the Janata Party was formed nationally and in UP this led to the union of the BLD and the Jan Sangh, bringing in the middle and rich peasants of central UP and also some disaffected Muslims and scheduled. In 1979 Charan Singh left the Janata Party and formed the Lok Dal which gained solid adherence from Jats and the more numerous Yadavs in the 1980 parliamentary elections. In 1984, after many false starts in attempts to unify the opposition for the coming elections, the Lok Dal merged with the Democratic Socialist Party (led by an ex-Congress ex-Chief Minister, H.N. Bahaguna). This Dalit Krishak Mazdoor Party (Oppressed Peasant and Worker Party) won only two seats in the parliamentary election but recovered to gain 85 seats in the assembly election of March 1985. In November 1985 Charan Singh suffered a stroke and his long delayed retirement from politics, at the age of 83, became inevitable. He died in 1987 but his son has returned from the USA to take a prominent role in the party.

The Republican Party

The Republican Party is the successor to the Scheduled Castes Federation, associated with Dr Ambedkar. The RP is dominated by the most numerous, scheduled caste, the Chamars or Jatavs, who are mostly landless labourers, and the party appears to be stronger in the west.

Socialist Parties

Various socialist parties have risen and fallen, including the Socialist Party (1948), the Kisan Mazdoor Praja Party (1949), the Praja Socialist Party (1952) and the Samyukta Socialist Party (1964). These have been subject to, or have arisen out of, fairly frequent splits and mergers, which Brass regards as evidence that even the supposedly more ideological and leftist parties are vulnerable to the prevailing factionalism. The Congress Socialist Party was formed in 1934 and included some prominent Congressmen, and was more or less tolerated within the Congress Party. In 1948, as Congress policies were seen as too conservative by some members of the CSP, about a fifth of them left to form the Socialist Party. In 1949 the Jan Congress and the Kisan Mazdoor Praja Party (led by Acharya Kripalani, ex-President of the National Congress Party) were formed, only to be united in June 1951. After gaining a total of nearly 18 percent of the vote in 1952, the SP and KMPP joined to form the Praja Socialist Party. In 1955 Lohia, Limaye and others left the PSP to form a new, 'non-Congressist' SP, because the Awadi declaration had introduced cooperation between Congress and the PSP. In 1957 the two parties won almost 22 percent of the total vote, the PSP securing 14.5 percent and the SP, fighting as 'independents', winning 7.4 percent. In the 1962 election the two parties gained over 20 percent, with the PSP share falling to 11.9 percent (whilst the CPI vote rose from 3.8 percent to 5.4 percent). In December 1962 the PSP and SP suddenly and rather unexpectedly merged in the UP assembly to form the Samyukta (United) Socialist Party. The national leadership of the SP was upset because the PSP was prepared to agree to the SP election manifesto of 1962 but not the party's constitution, basic principles and discipline. The national conference of the SP later accepted the merger but without approving it. By March 1963 there were growing divisions within the SSP over the status of English, over 'backward caste' reservation, over relations with the Jan Sangh and the CPI and over disruptive tactics in the assembly (which most ex-PSP MLAs refrained from joining). This disagreement over parliamentary tactics precipitated the reformation of the SP, leaving most of the ex-PSP members in the SSP.

In June 1963 some ex-PSP considered joining Congress and in September 1963, after Asoka Mehta, the national leader of the PSP, had accepted the post of Deputy Chairman of the Planning Commission, some PSP did join Congress. Mehta was forced to resign from the PSP and he also formally joined Congress in June 1964. At the same time Lohia led a hasty remerger of the SP with the PSP to renew the SSP, but issues of leadership, organisation and policy were not properly agreed. This left the PSP weakened and split three ways: those accepting a union with the SP; those moving towards Congress; and those wishing to preserve the PSP as a democratic socialist party in opposition to Congress. In January 1965 some ex-PSP leaders opposed Lohia's 'non-Congressism' with its consequence of alliance with rightist parties like the Jan Sangh and leftist parties like CPI, and revived the PSP. However, in UP many former members of the PSP remained within Lohia's SSP, which continued to be the main socialist opposition party in the state. These manoeuvres left the PSP severely weakened and in fact it gained only 4.1 percent of the vote in 1967, compared with a more respectable 10.2 percent for the SSP. This was particularly disappointing, given the low (32%) vote for Congress itself, which had been declining since the 48 percent achieved in 1952. There soon followed the non-Congress coalition government and the rise of Charan Singh's middle caste/middle peasant party. In 1969 the PSP (1.7%) and SSP (7.8%) fared even worse than in 1967. In August 1971, having won only three seats in the national elections, the SSP and PSP reunited to form the SP but by December 1972 the SSP was recreated at Patna. The SP remained the stronger of the two, but both were weakened by this further split. In 1974, before the assembly elections, Raj Narain led the SSP into a merger with the (non-socialist) BKD to form the BLD, which won 21 percent of the vote. Later, in June 1980 Bahaguna's Democratic Socialist Party won 11 seats.

This brief and incomplete history of mergers, coalitions and splits within the socialist movement in UP shows how parties with explicitly socialist labels have become smaller and less significant. This complicated chronology of fission and fusion among socialists tends to support the Brass theory of factional politics, but it should be remembered that some of the changes arose out of politics outside UP itself; that it is difficult for parties to appeal to or command a majority of support from such large and heterogeneous populations as those of UP (and indeed beyond); that factionalism can also be based on (or rationalised by?) ideology and policy as well as by the more traditional and personal dynamics which are stressed by Brass. He claims that, at least up to 1967, the socialist (and communist) leaders in UP were western-educated intellectuals and the leftist MLAs were middle peasants or petty Zamindars from the districts which had a density of more than 560 persons per square mile in 1951 and correspondingly small holdings. These districts included Deoria, Gorakhpur, Ballia, Azamgarh, Ghazipur, Jaunpur and Allahabad, where current densities mainly exceed 1,000 per km^2 and average holdings amount to only one or even half an acre per person. The socialist parties try to appeal to the peasant proprietors, including the 'backward classes' (eg. Yadavs and Kurmis), the high caste Bhumihars, and also landless labourers.

In the early 1960s the SP demanded abolition of land revenue for 'uneconomic' holdings; annulment of fictitious partitions of land by large owners, designed to avoid confiscation; price restraint for manufacturers; an end to the official use of English; and reservation of 60 percent of both administrative jobs and seats in the legislature for the 'backward' castes.

The PSP manifesto of 1962 included free bhumidhari rights for sirdars; a landownership ceiling of 20 acres; nationalisation of the sugar and power industries; aid to small and medium industries, including protection from competition by large industries; and protection and encouragement of Urdu.

By the mid-1960s the socialist base in eastern and central UP was declining as they pursued social issues appealing to Kurmis and Yadavs and eventually the socialist strategy merged with that of the Lok Dal.

Communist Parties

There are two communist parties in UP and the rest of India. The Communist Party of India (Marxist) represents a national split from the CPI in 1964 and is ostensibly the more radical, refusing to collaborate with bourgeois parties such as Congress. In UP the CPI commands considerably more support, in a Congress-dominated state, but the combined voting strength of the two communist parties has never risen above the peak of 5.1 percent in the 1962 state elections and 4.5 percent of the vote in the 1967 national election. The increase in votes between 1952 and 1962 mainly reflected an increase in the number of candidates. The CPI had 14 MLAs and the CPI(M) one MLA in the 1967 state assembly. Communist strongholds include the eastern districts of Azamgarh and Ghazipur (8 MLAs in 1962) and the city of Kanpur (especially workers in the textile mills). The more progressive and radical Muslims at Aligarh Muslim University in the west are also sometimes accused of being communists. Brass reports that, at least up to 1967, 'the Communists have been more inclined to support the Congress on many issues than have either the PSP or the Socialists' (1984: 254).

Other Parties

In May 1982 other parties represented in the state assembly included the Janata Party (7 seats); Congress (S) and Congress (J) - with 7 and 3 seats respectively; and the Shoshit Samaj Dal (Exploited Association Party) with one seat. There were also six Independent MLAs. Finally, the non-party Chipko movement in Uttarakhand is perhaps worth mentioning as an example of mildly militant rural protest in UP. In March 1973 many scheduled tribes and others combined in an area of the Himalayan foothills to protest against environmental, social and other costs of indiscriminate and illegal felling of trees by contractors, supposedly on behalf of the Forest Department. Such contractors often have links with senior politicians in still forested states such as UP, MP and Himachal Pradesh.

TWENTY-SEVEN ADMINISTRATIONS IN 47 YEARS

There has been a succession of 24 administrations under Chief Ministers, plus three periods of Presidential Rule between August 1947 and November 1993. The 24 administrations under Chief Ministers have drawn upon 16 individuals as Chief Minister. Until April 1990 the average length of any one government, including Presidential Rule, had been only 1.7 years, whilst Chief Ministers averaged about 1.8 years per administration and individual Chief Ministers with two or more administrations an aggregate average of 2.8 years. Periods of Presidential Rule lasted for about 12, 4 and 11 months respectively. The average duration of administrations in the postcolonial period as a whole has not been so short, mainly because of the long, seven-year administration of Pant. Whereas from August 1947 to March 1967 there were only seven administrations and four individuals filling the position of Chief Minister, from March 1967 to April 1990 there had been 16 administrations (plus two periods of Presidential Rule) and 12 individuals as Chief Minister. The average length of an administration had thus more than halved from 2.9 to 1.4 years (1.3 years, including Presidential Rule). The current trend appears to be towards even shorter administrations than this, with eight administrations in the 1980s. There have been ten Brahmin Chief Ministers (seven individuals), three Bania (all C.B. Gupta), four Thakur (four different individuals), two Kayastha (both Sampurnand), two Jat (both Charan Singh) and three Yadav (M.S. Yadav twice). In other words, 19 Chief Ministers have been from the higher castes, five from the middle castes and none from the lower or scheduled castes.

Pant (August 1947 - December 1954)

Pant was a Brahmin who had been the first Congress Chief Minister of the United Provinces from 1937 to 1939. In 1947 he provided a stable, mature but conservative lead to UP until he was incorporated into the national cabinet after 1954.

The Minister for Revenue in the first post-independence government of UP was Charan Singh, a western Jat who had served as a junior member on the Zamindari Abolition Committee of 1948. Charan Singh became the main force behind the Zamindari Abolition Act of 1951. Apart from seeking to abolish the system of 'feudal' intermediaries in the collection of land revenue and to simplify the tenurial system, Charan Singh aimed to promote peasant proprietors of moderate, but 'economic' size. Brass notes that,

> while his colleagues in the Pant ministry were establishing bases in the party organisation through the use of government patronage, Charan Singh was following a somewhat different course. He did not hold portfolios that controlled important sources of patronage. He did, however, differ from his other colleagues in having a strong policy orientation, with an emphasis on protection of the middle peasantry, with whose interest he became identified increasingly over time (1984:305).

In February 1953 Charan Singh opposed the increase of irrigation charges which had a particularly adverse effect on the western farmers. He wrote the Chief Minister a note on this but the difference of view neither received publicity nor did it divide the government significantly.

Sampurnand (December 1954 - December 1960)

Pant was succeeded by Dr Sampurnand, a Kayastha teacher and Sanskrit scholar from the Kashi Vidyapith at Varanasi. He represented a move from a national, conciliating and moderately secular leader with some 'charisma' to a more provincial, Hindu revivalist, political patron and manager, who failed to remain aloof from intra-party factions. Sampurnand 'led a group that was solidly based upon the rural support of élite castes in the countryside' (Brass 1984:307), and in a note to Pant in 1953 he had pointed out how their policies were alienating the upper class and the Brahmin, Rajput/Thakur, Bhumihar, Kayastha and Vaishya 'communities' which had been the greatest supporters of the Congress in the past. He had opposed giving benefits to the landless and very small landholders on the grounds that such categories would continue to oppose Congress, no matter how many benefits they received.

Sampurnand offered Charan Singh the portfolios of Transport and Cooperation (the latter providing major powers of patronage) but Singh preferred to retain his existing and important position as Minister of Revenue. He wished to promote his vision of a rural democracy of yeoman peasants, to extend Zamindari Abolition to the few remaining areas as yet uncovered by the 1951 Act, and to begin consolidation of holdings - all part of what he termed 'the bourgeois democratic revolution'. Charan Singh's initial disagreement with his Chief Minister arose over not being offered the Agriculture ministry, but it was soon articulated in policy terms. It was in 1956 that Singh defied party orders and presided over a conference of backward castes, the first overt sign of their impending politicisation. Brass, who was friendly with Charan Singh and had access to his private papers, gives a detailed insight into the Charan Singh critique of the Sampurnand administration. Charan Singh 'argued that the state was heading towards bankruptcy ..... that the government was providing favours to big industrialists at the expense of the general public, that the bureaucracy had expanded and bureaucratic corruption had increased, that food production had declined, and that consolidation of landholdings had been stopped' (Brass 1984:308). Singh also recorded his opposition to 'joint' (ie. cooperative) farming. He prepared a statement in connection with his resignation on 21 April 1959, in which he concluded that, 'unfortunately for Uttar Pradesh, the villages are a sealed book to its Chief Minister' (1984:308). He chose not to deliver this statement. Sampurnand had already had nine other ministers resign in November 1958. Charan Singh joined the C.B.Gupta faction after his own resignation and Gupta won the party elections in October 1960. By December 1960 Sampurnand had himself resigned.

Gupta (December 1960 - October 1963)

C.B.Gupta was a bachelor lawyer from Aligarh district who was also a factional leader and a conservative Bania, with strong links with urban, commercial and industrial interests. Brass notes that he 'was known to have had good relations with the prominent industrialists of the state, but he was also known to be quite blunt in his remarks and in his policy towards the millowners when necessary'. In the mid-1950s Gupta's machine included both local leaders personally loyal to him and also minority factions based primarily on regional but also to some extent on caste support - such as K. Tripathi and Charan Singh. In December 1962 the central government related the cane price to the recovery rate of sucrose and this probably would have amounted to a marginal reduction in the price paid to sugarcane farmers, especially in the east, where sucrose content was lower. Gupta successfully opposed the central government on this. Overall, however, Gupta was a faction leader who relied on an 'urban-financed organisational machine' (Brass 1984:308). He consequently soon ran into difficulties with

Charan Singh, his Minister of Agriculture. Brass describes the debate between them:

> The major policy issue that arose during the Gupta government concerned a proposal, introduced in response to demands from the Planning Commission to the state governments to increase revenues from agriculture, to impose a surcharge of 50 percent on the land revenue in UP ..... [There was an increasingly bitter correspondence between the Chief Minister and his Minister of Agriculture between March and September 1962.] In these letters and statements, Charan Singh argued: (1) that the tax [ie. effectively an increase in land revenue of 50 percent] was an unjustifiable burden on the peasantry who, he insisted - against the prevailing notions - were already paying their full share of taxes in relation to urban classes and groups; (2) that, even if it were true, as proponents of the measure argued, that rural per capita income had increased, this did not justify a 50 percent increase in the land revenue; (3) that even if the increase in rural income had been substantial, it was not wise to absorb it through taxation and, thereby, reduce the purchasing power of the peasantry, which would harm the entire economy; (4) that the necessary resources could be acquired by other means than the proposed tax, such as through government economy or through an increased tax on urban incomes; and (5) that an increase in land revenue would be a political liability for the Congress.
>
> In place of the proposed 50 percent surcharge on the land revenue of all landholders, Charan Singh suggested a plan that he had for long wanted to implement, namely a new campaign to persuade sirdars (tenants of the state) to acquire bhumidhari (full proprietary) rights in their lands by paying [in advance] a single payment of ten times their land revenue. As for those sirdars who still refused to acquire bhumidhari rights, Charan Singh proposed that their land revenue be increased by one third. In an exchange of confidential correspondence with C.B.Gupta on this proposal, Gupta responded: (1) that Charan Singh's own proposal contradicted his claim that the peasants had no taxable capacity since he was himself proposing that the poorer peasants pay an increased land revenue; (2) that arguments based on low rural per capita income figures were irrelevant since the new tax was to be levied only on landholders; (3) that rural people were paying far less than their fair share of taxes, compared to urban residents; (4) that the current incidence of land revenue was only 2 percent of state agricultural income and the proposed tax would increase that proportion by only 1 percent[-age point]. Moreover, Gupta argued that Charan Singh's proposals were designed to protect the interests of a privileged rural class, the bhumidhars, and to discriminate against urban classes.

> As the correspondence [proceeded] ..... increasing emphasis was placed on the distinction between rural and urban classes and on their incomes and taxable capacities. Charan Singh continued to argue that urban classes, even if they were paying higher taxes, could afford to do so because their incomes were much higher than rural incomes and that the manufacturing, commercial, transport, and service sectors produced much larger surpluses than the agricultural sectors. Moreover, he pointed out that urban people received many amenities provided by the state that rural people did not, such as electricity, roads, railways, post and telegraph services, and the like ..... his counter-proposal for saving state revenues through economy in government expenditure was directed in part at urban groups for he complained that, since independence, the numbers of government servants had increased by three times and of gazetted officers by four times and he noted that 'our official machinery, at least in the higher reaches, is overwhelmingly drawn from the cities'. Gupta in reply again disagreed that urban persons had a greater ability than rural people to absorb new taxes and pointed out that central government taxes also hit urban dwellers more than rural people. Charan Singh's relentless opposition to the tax measure, however, and his symbolic framing of the issue as one involving a defence of rural life and rural economy persisted to the end, even after a compromise was introduced, reducing the surcharge to 25 percent and exempting dwarf [ie. under one acre] landholders (Brass 1984: 309-10).

The debate represented a clear ideological difference between Gupta, the urban, industrialising, central development planner, prepared to squeeze the peasants in the process, and Charan Singh, the populist, committed to building a prosperous rural democracy, based on bhumidhars or full proprietary peasants as the leading class and on rural, labour-intensive and small-scale industrialisation.

Kripalani (October 1963 - March 1967)

Gupta resigned as part of the Kamraj Plan and, as his successor, he nominated Mrs Kripalani, the Brahmin wife of a prominent Gandhian socialist. She had no roots in UP and Gupta hoped to control her. However, she established her own faction which was independent of either the Gupta faction or the other Brahmin-led faction of Tripathi. Charan Singh resumed his position as Minister of Agriculture until 1965, when his portfolio was reduced to Animal Husbandry, Fisheries, Forests and Local Self-Government. This change exacerbated his earlier dissatisfaction at the lack of ministerial coordination of all aspects of agricultural policy.

The Kripalani government proved very unpopular and it owed its lack of success to factionalism within the ruling party; three failed monsoons; food shortage and minor famine; rising food and other prices and urban, particularly middle class, disaffection; Muslim discontent, particularly over the non-recognition of Urdu as the second official language; peasant antagonism to the 25 percent surcharge on land revenue (introduced in 1963 only but then reimposed to pay for defence costs after the war with Pakistan in 1965); business antagonism, with goldsmiths and jewellers objecting to the Gold Control Order and traders angry over police raids to catch hoarders, profiteers and black marketeers; anger among fundamentalist Hindus over the alleged neglect of the issue of cow slaughter; and general weariness with continuing corruption, which thrived under a relatively weak government.

Higher food prices affected particularly the middle and lower middle class of urban, salaried employees. Many of the half a million state employees were actually on strike during the election period in 1967, as they, along with teachers in private colleges and in state secondary schools, agitated for an increase in their dearness allowances. There was also student unrest, possibly fomented partly by their teachers. Muslim discontent could now be channelled through a new organisation, the Majlis-e-Mushawarat, which was openly hostile to Congress and supported non-Congress candidates of various parties.

Gupta (March - April 1967)

The Gupta and Tripathi factions patched up their differences for the election of March 1967 and Mrs Kripalani went off to be elected as an MP in Delhi. Urban, middle class revolt against rising food prices and other factors combined to reduce Congress seats from 249 to 198. Mrs Gandhi prevailed upon Charan Singh to allow the unanimous election of Gupta, in order to try to form a Congress government. The opposition parties meanwhile united to form the Samyukta Vidhayak Dal (United Legislative Party) with a 33-point common programme, which included abolition of land revenue and an increase in dearness allowances. Gupta was still able to form a government but made the mistake of selecting mainly his own, predominantly Brahmin and Bania, supporters and of not giving Singh the Agriculture portfolio. Charan Singh refused to join and on 31 March 1967 he and 16 others, representing mainly Jats and Ahirs, defected to form the Jan Congress, which later became the Bharatiya Kranti Dal (BKD). By 6 April 1967, Gupta had resigned and Charan Singh headed an SVD coalition. The only significant act of the Gupta government was the abolition of the surcharge on land revenue, and the demise of the Gupta administration marked the end of an unbroken period of nearly 20 years of Congress dominance in UP.

Charan Singh (April 1967 - February 1968): Samyukta Vidhayak Dal

The new coalition government of the Samyukta Vidhayak Dal included Charan Singh's Jan Congress, the Jan Sangh (which had taken votes, especially in urban constituencies, from Congress), the SSP, the CPI, Swatantra, and the Republican Party. It therefore represented a very wide political spectrum. Seven of the 28 ministers and deputy ministers came from the 17 Jan Congress MLAs and a further six were selected from the Jan Sangh. A minister from the CPI even went so far as to state that he did not expect, for many years to come, very big differences between the Jan Sangh and the Communists. This accommodation between left and right was occurring at a time of major unrest in the urban areas. The 33-point programme of the SVD elicited the support of all parties in the coalition, except that the Jan Sangh could only agree to the 'encouragement' of Urdu rather than to its official recognition. Concessions to the various protest movements included release of political prisoners, and judicial enquiries into charges of corruption against Congress ministers and into police firings. Unpopular measures and taxes, such as grain procurement orders and previous increases in taxes and land revenue were withdrawn. Even a communist minister was willing to agree to delay the introduction of state trading in foodgrains, for an 'experimental period' of two years. In a situation of acute food shortage, inflation and manifest and widespread public unrest, there were strong external pressures for parties of different ideology to pull together. The new government soon ran into trouble over several issues, including procurement, land revenue and abuse of their portfolios by the Jan Sangh ministers. The cabinet had decided to procure 0.5 million tons of foodgrain. This was opposed by the organisational, party wing of the Jan Sangh (the largest party in the coalition) and also by an ad hoc inter-party interest group of big farmer MLAs and MLCs:

> The Jan Sangh ministers maintained cabinet responsibility on the issue and succeeded in persuading members of their organisational wing to refrain from making public announcements opposing procurement. However, the objections of the inter-party legislative group, which itself included many Jan Sangh members, were satisfied only by a compromise whose effect was to reduce the amount of foodgrains to be procured from 0.5 million to 0.2 million tons. Again, however, no major defection from the government or from government supporters in the Assembly occurred on this issue (Brass 1984: 112).

The next issue led to temporary resignations but again was resolved:

> The demand for land revenue abolition was a major public commitment of the Samyukta Socialist Party especially and one to which all other parties had committed themselves in the formation of common programmes ..... The Chief Minister, Charan Singh, was a man who had well-formed views on the issues of both land revenue and state financial resources in general. He refused to agree to abolish the land revenue completely until alternative resources could be found. The result was a stalemate and a crisis in the UP government which threatened to bring the government down. An initial decision on the issue was taken by the UP government in July [1967], by which it was agreed that 50 percent of the land revenue would be abolished on holdings up to 6.25 acres, beginning after the current Kharif crop. [In

> 1947 this would have included over 85 percent of all holdings.] Internal divisions in the SSP on the issue developed, however, and the SSP continued to insist on further concessions. The crisis in the government continued for several months, leading ultimately to an SSP-CPI alliance on the issue and their joint resignations from the government. Again, however, on the land revenue issue, as on the procurement issue, a compromise was reached which permitted the return of the two parties to the government at the end of October, 1967 (Brass 1984: 113).

Despite this, the problems of the Charan Singh ministry continued to mount, particularly with increasing opposition from the SSP-CPI on the left and from the Jan Sangh on the right. There was also fluidity of allegiance in an Assembly which included at least 54 independents and/or party defectors.

> A central source of strain arose out of attempts by the Jan Sangh ministers to use their portfolios, particularly those of the Cooperation, Local Self-Government and Education departments, to nominate members of the Jan Sangh party to powerful district cooperative, local government and education institutions. Open dissatisfaction with the actions of the Jan Sangh ministers was expressed on several occasions by members of all parties in the SVD. A second source of strain related to the efforts of a faction in the SSP led by Raj Narain, an MP, to assert a dominant role in state SSP politics and in the SVD government. In those efforts, the SSP adopted agitational tactics to pressure the SVD government while continuing to support the government in the legislature (1984: 122).

The CPI ministers resigned on 20 November 1967,

> ostensibly because of differences with the Chief Minister on issues related to the use of police in political agitations and the release of government employees and others who had been jailed for their activities in various agitations in the past. Although the CPI ministers withdrew from the government, they continued to support the government in the Assembly. The SSP contingent continued in the government until January 6, but increasingly oriented its activities toward public agitations on the land revenue issue, on the release of government employees held in detention, and on the demand for elimination of English from use for government purposes (1984: 122).

Perhaps significantly, the rightist party was the last to desert Charan Singh: the break came when the Chief Minister reshuffled the Jan Sangh portfolios without the consent of the party leaders, taking away from them both Cooperation and Self-Government and replacing them with relatively less powerful and more innocuous portfolios, such as Public Works and Animal Husbandry. The Jan

Sangh accepted the reshuffling without withdrawing from the government, but the party leaders now joined with some of the SSP leaders in calling for the resignation of Charan Singh and his replacement by a new leader (1984:123).

The Swatantra party, the Republicans, the BKD and the Independents continued to support Charan Singh; the Jan Sangh demanded his replacement; and the SSP, PSP and CPI were divided on the issue. By this time Charan Singh was beset with so many problems that on 18 February 1968 he chose to resign without a vote of no-confidence. On 26 February 1968 the Governor of UP declared President's Rule. The SVD and Congress tried to form a majority but 'the Governor ultimately decided that no stable government was possible and dissolved the Assembly on April 16' (1984: 123). Brass concludes that 'the SVD coalition lost its cohesion primarily through intra-party divisions on the leadership question which affected most of the parties in the coalition; and through inter-party conflict for power, outside the cabinet and the Assembly, in the districts where local party activists maintain a continuing struggle for local power' (1984:124). 'The North Indian party systems which have replaced the Congress-dominant systems have proved incapable of providing stable, effective government in the first two years of coalition politics' (1984:132). Brass attributes the instability to a combination of multiplicity of small parties (and independents) which reflect the myriad social divisions, traditional power bases and personal factions in a large and heterogeneous state; inter-party conflict; intra-party conflict, and especially factionalism within all parties and especially within the Congress party; opportunism, 'virtuoso' politicking and political entrepreneurship; policy conflicts and ideological rigidities (though he gives little weight to these factors); personal animosities, sometimes longstanding and even dating from childhood; and conflict over power within the state government and at district, block and lower levels.

Brass emphasises that the period between 1967 and 1969 represented a watershed in UP politics, during which Charan Singh formed his Bharatiya Kranti Dal and the UP Congress party split, just as it had done nationally. Brass presents Charan Singh as a man of integrity, with clear ideas on policy, especially on agrarian issues, who was able to appeal to and articulate a more definable mass base of middle peasants and/or 'backward' castes, especially Jats and Ahirs/Yadavs. Consequently, he was able to win 21 percent of the vote and 98 seats in the mid-term state elections of February 1969. The BKD became by far the largest opposition party and this meant that

> agrarian issues and interests became more central than they had been during the Nehru period and it became necessary for competing political forces to pay closer attention to the distinctive interests of different social classes and castes in the North Indian countryside (Brass 1984:302).

It may not be accidental that these apparent changes in the political system coincided with major technological and economic changes associated with the Green Revolution. Charan Singh's earlier championing of the middle peasants had been through private memoranda, letters, books and anonymous press releases, as 'befitted' a cabinet minister. His new party provided a more public platform for his populist ideology and for a new, more explicit power struggle between agrarian classes. Brass concludes that,

> whereas in the Congress governments, issues could often be framed in terms of the interests of the peasantry in general, against urban, industrial, commercial and bureaucratic interests, some of the issues that arose between 1967 and 1971 in the coalition governments that often included parties of both the right and the left had the potential for dividing the poor peasantry from the middle and rich peasants and the landless from the landowning peasantry (1984: 317).

President's Rule (February 1968 - February 1969)

Gupta (February 1969 - February 1970)

In February 1969 state elections were held and Congress increased its vote marginally from 32 to 34 percent. The BKD secured 21 percent of the vote and became the largest opposition party, with especially strong support in the west. C.B. Gupta was able to form an administration which survived for nearly a year, until the national split in Congress led to the formalisation of the already existing divisions between the Gupta and Tripathi factions within the UP Congress party. Gupta became part of the national Congress (Organisation) and the weaker Tripathi headed the UP branch of Congress (R) which became Congress (I).

Charan Singh (February - October 1970): Coalition of Bharatiya Kranti Dal and Congress (I)

There followed a coalition between the BKD and Congress (I), led by K. Tripathi, in which Charan Singh again became Chief Minister and declared to the press that priority would be given to agricultural production and 'the interests of big traders or businessmen and big industrialists or financiers shall be given a second place'. As promised in the 1969 Manifesto of the BKD, the new government moved to reduce land ceilings from 40 to 30 acres, but with no major redistribution of land to the landless. 'At the same time, however, he dealt very firmly with the "land grab" movement of the CPI and SSP, which sought by forcible action against allegedly illegal holders of large estates to symbolise the plight of the landless and to grab lands for them' (Brass 1984: 319).

> Charan Singh's second government was a coalition government with the Congress (I). It was marked by conflict, tension and persistent

> manoeuvring for advantage by the two parties throughout. During the eight months in which the government was in power, Mrs Gandhi played an active role, directly and indirectly , in decisions concerning the fate of the UP government, which affected critically the fate of her rule and that of the Congress at the Centre, which at that time was functioning with a precarious majority in Parliament. In fact, it was clear throughout that Kamalapati Tripathi, the state Congress leader, could take no initiative without consulting the Centre. The fate of the UP government became, in effect, a contest between the political skills of Mrs Gandhi and Charan Singh that presaged a similar contest in 1979 when Charan Singh became Prime Minister with the support of Congress (I) (Brass 1984: 319).

This period in 1970-71 probably marked another political watershed, which this time changed centre-state relationships just as the earlier one in 1967 is said to have changed urban-rural and intra-rural relationships:

> In 1970 and 1971, state politics in UP became much less autonomous than they had been in the 1950s and 1960s and central and state politics more closely linked than before ..... For the first time in the history of the state, both the formation and termination of a government were considered critical for the future of the Union government, which played a determining role in both outcomes. Since then, the state of UP has not been considered a separate arena in which political forces acted relatively autonomously, but a base of power for the stability of the Union government that must be maintained at all costs. The closer interlinking therefore of political conflicts and policy issues in Lucknow and Delhi is related also to transformations in the dynamics of the federal system itself (Brass 1984: 331).

The coalition in UP fell apart when Mrs Gandhi reacted angrily to the failure of three BKD members of the Rajya Sabha to give crucial lasting support to the 24th Constitutional Amendment Bill, which aimed to abolish the privy purses of the princes and which had been passed in the Lok Sabha on 2 September 1970. Charan Singh had already agreed, 'against his better judgement' to Congress demands to abolish land revenue on marginal and very small holdings. There had also been counter-charges of postponing the nationalisation of sugar factories in UP and of each coalition partner being in the sway of the sugar mill barons, not to mention milking them for campaign funds. Brass describes how Congress tried to portray the BKD as champions of the princes and their purses:

> Charan Singh argued that the Congress stand was only a political stunt, that it represented a 'breach of faith' of the original agreement [with the princes in 1947], whose abrogation might ultimately threaten the right of private ownership of property in the country. In fact, Charan Singh

> argued, the Congress was falsely putting itself forth as hostile to the former rulers when there were several ex-rulers in its ranks. Moreover, its attack on the privy purses diverted attention from its partiality to the 'big capitalists and industrialists', whose income tax arrears alone were equivalent to 180 times the amount of the privy purse [C. Singh 1970: 19] (Brass 1984).

Charan Singh also mentioned his role in the enactment of Zamindari Abolition in UP and his prevention of the sort of loopholes that had permitted ejectment of tenants in other states. Behind the rhetoric, the BKD represented the interests of the 'self-sufficient peasantry' who could afford to pay traditional land revenues and did not need to hold more than 30 acres. The BKD also supported small industry against large units, such as textile mills, which the party considered should be reserved for export production. Congress, on the other hand, ingratiated itself with the smaller and marginal peasants by compelling Charan Singh to accept elimination of land revenue on holdings of 3.12 acres (5 bighas) or less. (In 1947 this would have included about 67 percent of total holdings.) Congress accused Charan Singh of favouritism towards the Jat and other backward castes in administrative postings, whilst the BKD accused Congress of identification with the élite castes.

As the conflict between the upper and middle castes became more explicit, an independent Khet Mazdoor Sabha (Land Labourers Assembly) was established in 1970, designed exclusively for agricultural labourers and calling for land reform. In some eastern districts, scheduled castes added social and caste conflict to the class struggle, by refusing to remove animal carcasses or to attend births. This proved very unsuccessful because it led to a new alignment, involving closer alliance between middle and even poor peasants and the upper castes. There were violent reprisals, as caste and communal divisions merged with those of class. The Republican Party, with its strong base among the scheduled castes, continued to organise such social protests, but the main peasant leaders backed down and recommended concentration on land, wage and class struggles.

T.N. Singh (October 1970 - March 1971): Coalition of BKD and other parties

Mrs Gandhi engineered the downfall of the second Charan Singh administration in October 1970. T.N.Singh then led another shortlived coalition of the BKD, Congress(O), Swatantra, Jan Sangh and the SSP. The SSP had differed with the BKD over land revenue in earlier coalitions and this time they pressurised the government into extending the exemption so that no farmer holding 6.25 acres or less would pay land revenue. The coalition was eventually defeated in the legislature on 30 March 1971.

Congress governments (April 1971 - January 1977)

There then followed three successive Congress (I) governments headed by Brahmins, with the BKD as the main opposition, in UP. Both central and UP governments sought more support from the poorer peasants and the landless than from the middle peasants, who were increasingly identified with the BKD and other opposition parties. Land ceilings were reduced to 18 acres of irrigated land per family and the range of ceilings for non-irrigated or otherwise less productive land was brought down from a range of 42 to 148 acres to between about 18 and 48 acres per family. The 20-point programme, introduced after the declaration of the Emergency in June 1975, included the enforcement of land ceilings and the UP government showed slightly more vigour against former big Zamindars and Talukdars than earlier governments, which had allowed extensive estates to survive. The UP government also took over the wholesale trade in wheat and this antagonised not only the traders but also all peasants with a marketable surplus. Aid to the rural poor, the landless and the small farmer was provided through rural public works and special programmes. Provision of jobs, allotment of house sites and drinking water wells and distribution of land ceiling surplus was made to the scheduled. Brass concludes that, from 1971 onwards, Charan Singh became identified with agricultural priority, high farm prices and benefits to the backward castes, thus favouring the so-called 'kulaks' overall whilst the 'Congress, which depended even more heavily on rich peasant and ex-landlord support, downplayed its reliance on these social forces while employing its policies for the poor, the landless and the scheduled castes' (1984: 326). Singh also opposed abolition of princely purses and nationalisation both of the sugar industry and the wholesale wheat trade in 1971.

Brass claims that 'the Congress has increasingly mobilised the support of the dominant castes of Brahmins, Rajputs and Bhumihars, who continue to be the most powerful landed castes in the north Indian countryside' (1984:329), whilst providing Integrated Rural Development and other aid to the rural poor and landless. Congress distributed surplus land and house sites to the poor from 1971 to 1974 and also passed reformist laws (which were mostly not implemented), giving 2 or 3 biswas (thirtieths of an acre) of gaon sabha or ceiling land. The Congress party has sought to blame 'atrocities' against lower castes on the backward castes and their BKD/Janata/Lok Dal leaders, whereas the actual pattern of intercaste violence is much more complex and 'not necessarily tied to class struggles in the countryside' (1984: 320).

> In the struggle among the landed castes, the Congress and the BKD/Lok Dal have been fairly evenly divided, which means that the low castes hold the balance electorally. In these struggles, the Congress, with its dual base among the élite landed castes and former landlords and the rural poor, has continued to hold the edge against the BKD/Lok Dal, with its base primarily among the middle peasant castes (1984: 330).

While the BLD appealed mainly to landowners, Congress used a broad-based strategy which helped win over even sections of the backward castes, especially their younger leaders who were attracted by power and patronage. Opposition parties can only offer them party positions. Hasan notes that

> in the late 1970s the Congress leadership managed to wean away sections of the Yadavs by appointing them to important positions in the party, to undercut the monopoly of Brahmins. Likewise, in the 1980s the Congress deepened the division in the ranks of backward castes by weaning away Kurmis and Gujars in central UP by gradually increasing the representation of these groups in the party (1989: 263-4).

Two backwards were appointed to the council of ministers in 1985 and Congress offered Yadavs tickets in constituencies where the Lok Dal had not. Backward caste leaders continued to denounce the remaining Brahmin monopoly of power within the Congress party and even threatened to demand a separate state. 'However, the greatest effect of the challenge from the Jat-led backward castes was to unite the upper castes, as apparent in the renewed cooperation between Brahmins and Thakurs since 1980. Before that the Thakurs were not an important component of the Congress coalition ..... In spite of its best efforts Congress failed to win over the backward castes' (Hasan 1989:264) and they voted for the Lok Dal in the 1980 elections, almost irrespective of the caste of the candidates. Lok Dal increased its influence in western UP in the 1980 elections and from 1980 to 1983 about 25% of the MPs, MLAs and block pramukhs were Lok Dal. However, the Congress leadership and the bureaucracy remained firmly high caste.

Tripathi (April 1971 - June 1973)

Kamalapati Tripathi, as weakest of the three faction leaders in the UP Congress party in 1967, was left to form the Congress ministry of 1971.

> He remained in power for more than two years, but he left office in discomfort after a mutiny of the state police forces in 1973 had to be suppressed by the Indian army. He was required to leave office by Mrs Gandhi and was then replaced by one of his erstwhile, but none too faithful, followers, H.N.Bahaguna ..... Under the control of Mrs Gandhi and the amorphous Tripathi group forces, the composition of the leadership became much less diverse than it had ever before been. Although Mrs Gandhi in UP and elsewhere attempted with some success to identify the Congress with the interests of the poor and the low castes, the state and district leadership of the Congress in UP became much more of a Brahmin affair than even before. Tripathi, Bahaguna and Tiwari were all Brahmins. Five of the 15 ministers in Tripathi's government (including Tripathi) were Brahmins. Thirty-eight of the 75 District

Congress Committee (DCC) and City Congress Committee presidents in 1973 were also Brahmins. The most notable under-representation was of the middle proprietary castes. There were no Jat presidents, only two Yadavs, and only two Kurmis (Brass 1984: 304).

Bahaguna (November 1973 - January 1976)

Mrs Gandhi chose H.N. Bahaguna to replace Tripathi. He was an outspoken defender of Muslims. Brass claims that his ineffectiveness as leader and his egocentrism helped move Mrs Gandhi to replace him.

Tiwari (January 1976 - January 1977)

N.D. Tiwari was appointed Chief Minister by Mrs Gandhi about six months after she had declared the Emergency. The initials N.D. were sometimes explained as 'New Delhi' Tiwari because, perhaps even more than the usual Chief Minister, he was so often courting Mrs Gandhi and the High Command in New Delhi. Or as 'Nothing Doing' Tiwari insofar as he was said to be unsympathetic to sofarish (nepotism) and patronage networks. Tiwari is considered to have been very close to Sanjay Gandhi and to have been a particularly ardent implementer of Sanjay's family planning obsessions. Brass describes him as 'a policy-oriented but totally non-political man who lacked any political bases of his own'. He was later Planning Minister and Industries Minister in the central cabinet. In January 1977 Congress lost heavily in the elections, securing only 32 percent of the votes and the lowest ever number of seats.

R.N. Yadav (January 1977 - February 1979): Janata coalition led by the BLD and Jan Sangh

In January 1977 the Janata party was elected in UP and a new Chief Minister, Ram Naresh Yadav, became the third Chief Minister of UP from a backward caste. Janata was an unstable alliance of the Bharatiya Lok Dal (the former BKD) and the Jan Sangh, both of which drew support from middle and rich peasants and the backward castes. However, the Jan Sangh was a much more organised and disciplined party than the Bharatiya Lok Dal. Yadav proved to be a weak Chief Minister. He sacked his Jan Sangh ministers in January 1979 partly because proposals for organisational elections within the UP Janata party threatened to give an advantage to the better organised Jan Sangh. Banarsi Das was chosen as another compromise (and also weak) Chief Minister who was acceptable to both the Bharatiya Lok Dal and its new partner, Congress for Democracy. To a large extent UP politics continued to be dominated by national, especially Janata, politics in nearby Delhi and probably more energy was put into travel between Lucknow and Delhi than into policy formulation. Das introduced hardly any new policies. Janata pleased the rich farmers by supporting high sugarcane prices to offset the losses caused by the poor monsoon of summer

1979; by increasing the procurement price of wheat; and by abolishing the tractor trolley tax. Land reform was virtually dumped. Das was about to end the reservation of promotions for the scheduled when the Janata government fell, but Charan Singh did not oppose reservation of jobs for the scheduled so long as the backward were also included. Congress did not implement the Janata decision. Yadav had been a tahsil court lawyer and he lacked either charisma or an independent political base or an identifiable political stance. His chief merit was a lack of political enemies. His BLD dominated the UP Janata government and represented primarily the rural population, especially the middle and rich peasants, particularly those producing commercially. Kohli points out that the Yadav administration depended mainly on civil servants for its policies and that, as long as resources were allocated to the rural sector, no questions were asked about which rural classes actually benefited. In practice, public investment was used to 'buttress the profitability of commercial farmers, especially those in the western half of the state' (1987:202). Overall, Kohli concludes that the UP Janata regime was 'a fragmented regime of shifting alliances through which the better-off kisans became politically significant' (1987: 211). Janata introduced various agrarian measures in February, including simplification of land tenure to two categories (Bhumidhari and Asami) and also a Debt Relief Act. The Debt Relief Act of 1977 liquidated the debts of landless agricultural labourers, marginal farmers and rural artisans, as well as other poor, receiving an annual income of less than Rs 2,400 per household. Richer households which had paid twice the capital sum borrowed were also discharged from further payment. Small farmers had their debts scaled down and repayment was subject to a moratorium. Shrimali (1981) claims that, like the Regulation of Moneylending Act of 1976, the new law failed to inhibit many moneylenders from pressing for payment. Among various events which damaged the Janata government was the killing of at least 15 agricultural labourers who were employed at the G.B.Pant Agricultural University. The Vice-Chancellor was a Jat and the incident was presented as Jat police firing on lower caste labourers.

Das (March 1979 - February 1980): Janata coalition led by the BLD and the CFD

Banarsi Das, also from the Bharatiya Lok Dal and speaker of the Legislative Assembly, succeeded Yadav as Chief Minister. In January 1980 Mrs Gandhi was able to exploit the 'Narainpur incident' and the alleged atrocities against Muslims and the scheduled castes. By February 1980 the President of India had dismissed the UP government (and those in nine other states) and imposed Presidential Rule until elections could be held in June.

President's Rule (February - June 1980)

V.P. Singh (June 1980 - July 1982)

In June 1980 Congress recovered to secure nearly 37 percent of the vote and

Vishwanath Pratap Singh was selected as Chief Minister. Singh ('Raja Sahib') comes from a Thakur ex-Zamindar family in Allahabad district and is thus an old family friend of the Nehrus. He cultivated a reputation for integrity and for threatening to resign if government aims (especially on law and order) were not achieved. He initiated a vigorous 'shoot to kill' campaign against dacoits which involved many deaths (and also many accusations of 'fake encounters' and exploitation of the campaign to exterminate other enemies of the police and of local landlords). He avoided resignation in December 1981 after some degree of 'success' had been achieved in eliminating various gangs. Soon afterwards his brother, a High Court judge, was shot in the forest by dacoits. In July 1982, after another large scale massacre of lower caste villagers by dacoits, V.P.Singh chose the opportunity to resign from a post in which he at least appeared to have become increasingly unhappy. He was widely hailed as having displayed a conspicuous integrity, especially in not clinging to public office in the manner in which many other Congress Chief Ministers were doing. He subsequently became Central Minister of Commerce under Mrs Gandhi, Minister of Finance and then of Defence under Rajiv Gandhi. He eventually resigned in protest over alleged corruption scandals and emerged as the new Prime Minister in 1989. From at least 1980 the Chief Minister has increasingly used a helicopter to travel around the state: a prestigious but ultimately alienating mode?

Misra (July 1982 - August 1984)

The successor to V.P.Singh was Sripat Misra, the speaker of the Vidhan Sabha. He was chosen by Mrs Gandhi, perhaps partly to alternate Brahmin with Thakur and also to secure a pliable, compromise candidate who was not identified with either the Thakur faction of V.P. Singh or the faction of Lokpati Tripathi, the Health Minister. Misra achieved little and, as by-election results in UP became more and more unfavourable to Congress (I), he was replaced by a (rather reluctant?) Central Minister of Industries, N.D. Tiwari, who had also been Chief Minister in 1976-7.

Tiwari (August 1984 - September 1985)

When Tiwari was drafted into UP to beef up the ailing Congress government in the final months before the national elections due in January 1985, he was accompanied by another central minister, V.P.Singh, who was appointed President of the UP Provincial Congress (I) Committee and was charged with galvanising a very dormant party into readiness for the elections. The seemingly cynical movement of senior Congress personnel in this way suggests a decreasing seriousness given to the post of Chief Minister of even large states like UP. The extreme difficulty of the job dictates that Chief Ministers should rule for at least four or five years to hold out even the remotest hope of modest success. With the assistance of seven general secretaries, Singh began compiling a list of 200 'local issues' which would need to be 'tackled' before the election. The emphasis on approaching the election through local, rather than statewide, issues is worth noting.

Tiwari proclaimed that 'everyone knows that I am a development man. My government will ensure that the minimum needs of the people are met'. He spent five of his first eight days in office waiting for Mrs Gandhi and the High Command to approve his choice of ministers. His deliberations were not eased by having 35 ex-ministers and over 200 MLAs visiting his Delhi bungalow to lobby for a ministry. He eventually chose 48 persons, including 18 ministers, 26 ministers of state and four deputy ministers. These included five new ministers and 13 other new recruits. Among the senior ministers retained were those for Industry and Irrigation, B.B.Singh, and also for Health, L.Tripathi. Singh is a Thakur leader from the east who was considered close to Rajiv Gandhi and Arun Nehru. Tripathi is a Brahmin and the son of Kamalapati Tripathi, the senior Working President of Congress (I) and responsible for supervising the national election campaign of 1984.

Tiwari cultivated a Chief Ministerial style which included long (16-hour) working days at the files and an emphasis on conspicuous decisiveness and implementation. His staff claimed that he had passed 6,000 orders, including 1,200 major decisions, in the first two months. He had also chaired at least a dozen meetings of the council of ministers, toured 20 districts and authorised government programmes worth Rs 3 billion.

Two months before the general election which was now fixed for December 1984, the Finance Minister of UP admitted that 'we do believe in political expediency. Any Finance Minister who completes his five-year term will enforce strict financial discipline in the first two years, maintain status quo for the next two years and resort to relaxation and concessions in the last. We will not hesitate to arrange funds for any development programme' (IT, 31 October 1984). In the previous two months the government had agreed to spend at least Rs 3.44 billion, which included immediate clearance of arrears in paying farmers who had sold sugarcane to the mills (Rs 0.9 billion); repair or installation of electricity generation and distribution (Rs 0.75 billion); equity participation in over a hundred joint (public and private) sector industrial projects (Rs 0.7 billion); new rural link roads, including 700 begun on Gandhi's birth anniversary (Rs 0.7 billion); regularisation of all temporary government employees; revival of zila parishads by nominating office-bearers and providing grants to enable them to begin development work (Rs 0.2 billion); rural bank loans of Rs 6,000 each to 100,000 poor borrowers at 4 percent interest, also on Gandhi's birth anniversary (Rs 0.15 billion); two-phased electricity supply to all electrified villages (Rs 0.15 billion); and repairs to 40 percent of the 17,000 state-owned tubewells (Rs 0.04 billion). The electoral strategy also included daily contact with general managers of electricity plant and with selected district magistrates; use of the seven general secretaries to interview the 350 MLAs and also the MLCs; and use of up to 50,000 party workers to gather information and grievances from the villages. The party workers were paid a token honorarium. The strategy was based on two principles, delegation of spending power to 'opinion leaders' and targeting of decisions to where they will have the most impact on power brokers, communities or income categories. As part of this strategy, the government allotted funds to Block Development Committees which equalled the land revenue paid by landowners within each block. This entailed payment of Rs 0.3 million each to 839 normal size blocks and Rs 0.45 million each to 41 large blocks by 31 December 1984. This was to be spent on water supply, school buildings and maintenance of street lighting. In addition Gaon Sabhas were empowered to spend Rs 0.1 million each on development and construction, without prior official approval, and urban committees somewhat smaller amounts. By this strategy the government had provided increased powers of patronage for at least 5,000 political functionaries, such as village pradhans, block pramukhs, MLAs and MPs.

Other pre-election schemes included an increase in wages paid in kind to 700,000 rural workers (raised from one to two kilograms of foodgrain per day) which cost Rs 0.13 billion; and bonus payments to those 40,000 government employees who were receiving Rs 1,600 or less per month. This bonus was equivalent to 18 days' salary and cost Rs 0.4 billion. The government also agreed to pay four additional instalments of dearness allowance which became due between 1 January and 1 June 1984. The government also provided benefits to cobblers, barbers, tailors, rickshaw-pullers, bullock cart owners and artisans, partly in an effort to win back the dwindling support of the Scheduled and Muslims. The council of ministers also established a corporation to finance industrial entrepreneurs from the minorities (such as the Muslims), through seed capital and equity participation. This new corporation joined the 70 already existing state corporations in UP.

Since the Congress (I) was particularly worried about western UP and the threat of the Lok Dal, the government took over the management of 12 'sick' sugar mills which 'secured' the employment of 5,000 workers and led to the clearing of Rs 0.05 billion of unpaid arrears to sugarcane farmers. The Chief Minister also ordered sugar mills to clear a further Rs 0.91 billion of cane arrears, much more than any previous administration. Private mills refused, until the government offered financial support and 'persuaded' banks to advance them loans. Mills were exempted from having to hand over Rs 0.23 billion which had been collected in purchase tax from growers and the Reserve Bank of India wrote off Rs 0.1 billion of debt and advanced a loan of Rs 0.12 billion.

The opposition parties failed to form a united front but the Lok Dal and the smaller Democratic Socialist Party (led by Bahaguna and Raj Narain) eventually joined to form a new party, called the Dalit Mazdoor Krishak (Oppressed Labourer and Peasant) Party. Whereas the 'index of opposition unity' had risen to 91 in the heyday of 1977, it was only 56 in 1984. The DMKP fielded 67 candidates and the Rashtriya Sanjay Manch (National Sanjay Platform), a new party led by the widow of Sanjay Gandhi, contested 63 seats. Other parties which competed included the Bharatiya Janata Party (54 candidates), Janata (41), CPI (3) and Congress(S), also with three candidates. Altogether there were 1,204 candidates, an average of 14 candidates per seat and thus even higher than the all-India average of 10 candidates per seat. Congress (I) exploited national issues of external and internal security, as well as the sympathy vote for the son of an assassinated Prime Minister. The result was a landslide victory, with Congress winning 83 seats and the DMKP winning the remaining two seats. The Congress (I) share of the vote rose from 36 to 51 percent. The DMKP had clearly failed in its appeal to the backward castes, as had the RSM appeal to the Muslim vote and the Janata and BJP bid for Brahmin, Thakur, urban and middle class support.

For the Vidhan Sabha elections in March 1985, there was a great rush of applicants for party tickets: a staggering 80,000 plus for 425 Congress (I) candidatures and over 5,000 for the DMKP. Altogether, 1,146 candidates were selected by the various opposition parties, including 375 by the BJP and 150 by the RSM. This meant that the opposition was split at least three ways in most constituencies. In addition, the former Chief Minister, Ram Naresh Yadav, left the DMKP and put up his own candidates.

The Congress (I) faced fresh problems of internal division because only 0.5 percent of applicants could be supplied with the party ticket. Among the nearly 80,000 unsuccessful applicants were 153 of the 306 sitting MLAs. Some of those rejected either refused to campaign or else filed rebel candidatures. Congress (I) candidates were originally promised election expenses of Rs 50,000 but this was reduced to Rs 10,000 (and no jeep) when the strategy switched to a much lower-key campaign.

The distribution of Congress (I) tickets involved lobbying by the factions of Chief Minister, N.D.Tiwari, and of Irrigation Minister, B.B. Singh. After the election, the contest for Chief Minister was expected to be between B.B. Singh and Lokpati Tripathi, but Tiwari continued in the office for a further 9 months.

In March 1985 the Congress (I) secured 42 percent of the votes and won only 266 seats, about 30 less than it had controlled when the state assembly was dissolved. Whereas in 1980 the party had increased its share of the vote marginally from 35.9 percent in the national election to 36.9 percent in the state election, this time their vote fell from 51 to 42 percent. If the large Lok Sabha constituencies are broken down into their state assembly segments, then a repeat of the voting in the national elections would have yielded 383 seats for Congress (I). As it was, the badly demoralised Dalit Mazdoor Krishak Party was able to recover considerable ground, winning 85 seats, 16 more than it had won in 1980 as the Janata (S). In eastern UP the Congress (I) did particularly badly whilst the Janata party did well in ten districts dominated by Thakurs.

B.B. Singh (September 1985 - June 1988)

On 23 September 1985 Tiwari resigned after only 416 days in office and was replaced by Bir (or Veer) Bahadur Singh, the Minister of Irrigation and leader of the more powerful (Thakur) faction within the council of ministers. Whereas Tiwari might be characterised as the smooth Delhi operator, Singh has been described as a 'rustic politician from the crime-infested district of Gorakhpur'. As such, he may, however, be better qualified to fight the battles of being Chief

Minister in a state like UP. He certainly began in characteristically aggressive and abrasive style, suspending over 50 officials for dereliction of duty during the first month. He also ordered the gates of the Lucknow secretariat to be closed and locked at 10.15 am every day, so that even some ministers were excluded when they arrived late. Singh put his chief rival, Tripathi, in charge of a council of ministers committee to supervise flood relief, allegedly so as to tie him down with a thankless and impossible task of solving the misery of the floods. Tripathi was instructed to remain in the flood area and was constrained from making his usual frequent visits to Varanasi (the family seat of many prominent Brahmins in UP) and Delhi. All ministers were told to curtail their previously frequent visits to Delhi. Obervers suggested that the initial discipline and drive for increased efficiency would be followed by rewarding loyalists with senior posts. Since Singh initially appointed only 17 ministers, compared with Tiwari's 48 and since a dozen posts of departmental secretary and of managing director of state corporations were due to fall vacant, Singh was in a position to widen his support.

B.B. Singh was the fourth Chief Minister of UP since June 1980. The sequence had been one Thakur, two Brahmins and then another Thakur. It was widely acknowledged that B.B. Singh was a close supporter of Arun Nehru, a Brahmin and third cousin of Rajiv Gandhi, and that Nehru's then great influence with the Prime Minister helped secure Singh's appointment. Nehru was asked about the frequent switching of Chief Ministers for reasons other than loss of confidence of the legislative party. He replied that 'there are party priorities. Sometimes you have to shift people for better jobs. Many Chief Ministers may not like to continue personally. And nobody is imposed from above. The Prime Minister has made it very clear that Chief Ministers have complete independence in the matter of selecting their cabinet but they must perform' (IT, 31 Oct. 1985: 35).

In 1988 following the Congress defeat in the June by-elections in UP, Rajiv Gandhi replaced Chief Minister Bir Bahadur Singh with central finance minister N.D. Tiwari, who came back at short notice from a visit to London.

It may have been coincidental that during rule by a Chief Minister from eastern UP a powerful farmers' movement emerged in western UP, led by a 'charismatic peasant'. In January 1988 Mahindra Singh Tikait and his Bharatiya Kisan Union began agitation for higher crop prices and reduced electricity and irrigation charges. Tactics included 80,000 farmers besieging the Divisional Commissioner's office in Meerut; then 'militant non-cooperation', including non-payment of electricity bills and taxes; and later 100,000 farmers occupying the Delhi Boat Club lawns for a week.

Tiwari (June 1988 - December 1989)

In June 1988 V.P. Singh (Jan Morcha) gained a large majority over the Congress (I) candidate in a Lok Sabha by-election at Allahabad. This was a humiliating defeat in Nehru-Gandhi territory and it is alleged that Rajiv Gandhi directly ordered B.B. Singh to resign. N.D. Tiwari gave up his central ministry at

Finance and Commerce to become Chief Minister for the third time. B.B. Singh was given the central ministry of Communications. Tiwari retained 12 of Singh's 13 ministers and expanded the number to 46 in early July.

M.S. Yadav (December 1989 - June 1991)

In November 1989 elections were held in UP (and four other states) at the same time as the general election. V.P. Singh won nationally and the Janata Dal and other National Front parties formed only the second non-Congress government. In UP's state elections the Janata Dal won 204 seats out of 425, followed by 94 Congress (I) and 57 Bharatiya Janata Party. The relatively new Bahujan Samaj Party won 13 seats, the communist parties 8 and the Lok Dal only 2. On 4 December Mulayem Singh Yadav became UP's fourth Chief Minister from a backward caste. Yadav proved to be a tough, aggressive but not always very tactful defender of secular values and of Muslim rights, as the BJP exploited the Ram Janmabhoomi issue and the Ayodhya crisis deepened. In January 1990 the new central government called for all state governors to resign and this included the Muslim who had been governor of UP since 1985. In October 1990 the Ayodhya mosque site was invaded by Hindu militants and shortly after a 'truce' was agreed between the UP government and the Vishwa Hindu Parishad.

K. Singh (June 1991 - December 1992)

The central government of V.P. Singh was rocked by the worsening dispute over Ayodhya and by controversy over his determination to introduce reservation in 27 percent of public sector jobs for the lower castes. His outspoken deputy, Devi Lal, a Jat who represented the backward castes, campaigned against such reservations and Singh eventually dismissed him in August. In November 1990 V.P. Singh was replaced by Chandra Shekhar, who led another weak government, based on his small faction of Janata Dal dissidents and dependence on the support of Rajiv Gandhi and Congress (I). Shekhar resigned in March 1991, unwilling to pay the political price of Congress support. He continued as caretaker until elections in May 1991, when Rajiv Gandhi was assassinated and P.V. Narasimha Rao was recalled from virtual retirement (and convalescence after open heart surgery) to head a new Congress (I) government. In May and June 1991 state elections were held and the Bharatiya Janata Party won 211 seats, followed by Janata Dal 91 and Congress (I) 46. The Samajwadi Janata Party (dissident faction of the Janata Dal) won 30 seats, the Bahujan Samaj (Majority Society) Party 12 seats and the communist parties 5. The BJP had increased its number of seats from 57 in 1989, an enormous victory for communalism and ostensibly a relegation of class struggle and also, to a large extent, of caste conflict.

The main thrust of policy was for law and order (especially campaigns against 'mafia dons' in western UP) and against corruption, cheating and encroachment. There was little emphasis on development.

President's Rule (December 1992 - November 1993)

On 6 December 1992 the Babri mosque was destroyed by Hindu militants. All over India an estimated 1,200 were killed (two-thirds Muslim) and 5,000 injured in sectarian violence, probably the worst since independence. The UP government had, in an unprecedented fashion, failed to uphold a Supreme Court order to protect the Babri mosque, despite having given a formal assurance that it would do so. The Chief Minister resigned and later the same day the central cabinet met in emergency session and ordered the immediate dismissal of the BJP-controlled government in UP. President's Rule was declared for the third time and the state governor, chief secretary and the civil service once again undertook to administer the state on behalf of the President.

On 10 December the Bajrang Dal, the Rashtriya Swayamsevak Sangh, and the Vishwa Hindu Parishad were banned, along with two Islamic organisations.

In the state elections of November 1993 the BJP (177 seats) was in effect defeated by a lower caste alliance of the Samajwadi (Socialist) Party and the Bahujan Samaj Party (176 seats). Congress (I) and Janata Dal each won 28 seats and their support enabled M.S. Yadav, the SP leader, to become Chief Minister, for the second time.

One immediate interpretation was that Hindu voters, especially from the lower castes, had 'rejected upper caste efforts to unite Hindus under a fundamentalist banner' (Guardian, 29 November 1993) and were prepared to join forces with Muslims against Brahmins and 'upper caste Hinduism' in both the BJP and Congress (I). The leaders of the SP and BSP were, respectively, M.S. Yadav, a secular Yadav (lower middle) and Kanshi Ram, a lower caste, virulent foe of the high castes, campaigning on a caste rather than religious basis. Turnout increased from 49% in 1991 to 57%. The BJP gained 16 extra seats in the west but the SP-BSP made much greater gains in the east (73 extra seats) and in central UP (25) and also itself gained 17 in the west. The frenetic secular-cum-populist, local issues approach of Mulayam Singh Yadav appealed particularly to rural voters, especially as he changed his image from abrasive Hindu-baiter to moderate Sanatani Hindu, devotee of Hanuman and Krishna (IT, 15 December 1991). Villagers objected to political exploitation of Ram, feared economic chaos and communal conflict and were nervous of increased police power as a consequence of all this. The mathematics of 21% Scheduled, Muslims 19% and Yadavs 17% seemed to have added up, in electoral terms. Many 'Other Backward Castes' (OBCs) seem to have shifted from Janata Dal (1991) to BJP (1991) to SP-BSP in 1993. Urban voters divided more on religious lines, seeing the SP as a 'Muslim party' whilst rural voters divided more on caste lines. Urbanites fear Yadav 'gangsterism' in the villages.

M.S. Yadav (from November 1993)

CRIMINALISATION OF POLITICS AND POLITICISATION OF PUBLIC INSTITUTIONS

Some of the more pessimistic observers in UP take the view that UP is 'going the Bihar way' and they point to the deterioration in standards of political behaviour, the apparent increase in criminalisation of politics and the pervasive intrusion of party politics (criminal or non-criminal) into a wide range of institutions which they consider should be free from or 'above' party politics. These include the IAS, the PCS, the IPS, the judiciary, the universities and other educational institutions. It no doubt also includes institutions of health care, but their politicisation appears to receive less coverage in the media and elsewhere.

Political standards are set from the top, by the Governor, the Chief Minister, ministers and by the president of the ruling party. In 1982 the Governor was an 82-year old Thakur who displayed very little independence. Chief Ministers have been becoming more and more dependent on the Prime Minister and their tenures increasingly short. The criticisms of Chief Ministers apply a fortiori to the state ministers. There has been proliferation of ministries and the concentration of powers of patronage in certain ministries (such as Home, Industries, Education and Cooperation); there has been division of ministries in order to reallocate such powers, often at the expense of the functional coordination of policy; and the proliferation of ministries to as many as 46 can mean that more than one minister has political interests in the same district, leading to increased politicisation of the district administration and heightened factionalism. Attempts at administrative decentralisation have led to ministers being made responsible for particular divisions or districts, but this frequently leads to more politicisation, arbitrary interference, administrative confusion and disputes between ministers rather than to development. The post of Health Minister is valued because it gives power over an important profession; it gives control over up to 12 percent of the recurrent budget and patronage over many government employees; and it affords access to medical facilities for the Minister's family and members of his social and political network. Finally, leadership from the head of the ruling party becomes difficult when the Provincial Committee of Congress (I) had gone through 8 presidents between 1980 and August 1984.

MLAs have always been predominantly rural. As the rural areas themselves become more criminal, violent and 'dacoit-infested', so have their political representatives. It was alleged that in 1984 at least 150 of the 425 MLAs, especially from the Congress (I), had criminal records and that many more had contacts with the criminals and dacoits of their areas. For some this represented a voluntary association of mutual benefit but for others it was an involuntary accommodation which seemed necessary for political and perhaps personal survival. Sanjay Gandhi's selection of candidates in 1980 was frequently blamed for the high rate of criminals among Congress (I) MLAs. It may be argued that some MLAs have acquired so-called 'criminal records' through 'courting arrest' and other political activities. This may be true, but the fact that some MLAs were linked in with liquor shop barons and other mafia-like gangs and that several ministers were widely acknowledged to have links with dacoits and that one minister's family was growing illegal opium, all suggest that standards have deteriorated from the time of Nehru and Pant. Among many abuses are the extravagant claims for travel and medical expenses by MLAs. It was alleged that during 1982-3 the 425 MLAs spent Rs 12 million in free rail coupons and consumed free medicines valued at Rs 25 million - an average total cost of over Rs 87,000 per MLA. (The average per capita income in UP in 1984 was less than Rs 2,000.) The Health Minister claimed Rs 244,000 in travel expenses and the Chief Minister took medicines worth Rs 15,000. Favourite medicines of MLAs included antibiotics such as Septron, analgesics such as Tendril, Paracetamol, tonics and vitamin tablets, especially Becosules and other B complex formulations. Many of these medicines are presumably given to their political supporters. These perquisites seem particularly unnecessary since each MLA, from April 1984, has received a constituency allowance of Rs 1,250 per month, a salary of Rs 500 per month and an increased daily allowance of Rs 60. This could provide a minimum of Rs 24,000 and a maximum annual income of nearly Rs 42,000. In addition, they receive heavily subsidised housing with free water, electricity, two telephones, free bus passes, free rail travel within UP and up to 19,000 kilometres per year subsidised travel outside UP. The official work of an MLA can occupy him for as little as 50 days per year. Since 1975 all MLAs have been required to state their assets and liabilities but only 23 did so in 1983 and not all of these did so accurately (IT, 31 May 1984: 46).

Tucker (1970) and Misra (1982) both document the demoralisation and deterioration within the Indian Administrative Service. The politicisation of the police has become even more serious (IT, passim and especially 31 October 1984; 15 July 1984: 23; and 31 July 1985: 15; see also Brass 1984: 196). District politicians need to control the local police, to protect themselves from criminal intimidation and for a host of other purposes. The UP government needs to control the police, especially in marginal constituencies, and it was alleged that 30 senior superintendents and superintendents were transferred a few months before the 1984 election. Political interference in police appointments and transfers appears to have become so disruptive that the Director-General of Police was said to have taken the rather unorthodox step of circulating a semi-official letter in 1985 which directed his subordinates to ignore any transfers not routed through the DGP. At least 27 out of 52 SPs and SSPs had been transferred after less than 18 months in one post.

Baxi (1982) and Galanter (1984) highlight some of the problems facing the judiciary. Capitalism generates litigiousness and litigation and in June 1978 there was a backlog of 133,000 cases pending at the UP High Court in Allahabad. The judiciary face quantitative overloading and qualitative mixing of a great diversity of cases (see Galanter 1984) and corruption and political interference compound the main internal problems of the legal processes. There was increasing political influence on the judiciary under Mrs Gandhi but it has been resisting more successfully than certain other Indian institutions. There is a growing attempt to control the press, by censorship during the Emergency and by distribution of bribes and favours since. The favours include subsidised house plots, travel grants and other perquisites (see IT and Pioneer).

POLICIES ON WEALTH AND INCOME DISTRIBUTION

Since 1947 various policies and laws have been introduced, which have affected the distribution of wealth and income. These have included the famous Zamindari Abolition and Land Reform Act of 1951; ceilings on landholdings; redistribution of communal village lands; consolidation of holdings; changes in land revenue, other taxation and rates for irrigation water; facilities for credit and for debt relief; prices and organisation of government procurement of foodgrain, sugarcane and other crops; and minimum wages for agricultural labourers.

Zamindari Abolition

Congress won a large majority in the 1946 election, with a programme which included abolition of landlordism. A committee was established in August 1946 and it reported in 1948. In July 1949 a bill was introduced, passed in January 1951 but it took until July 1952 to come into operation, after blocking litigation by Zamindars had been defeated in the High Court and Supreme Court. These six years gave the larger and more organised Zamindars ample time to protect their interests.

Shrimali states that in 1947, 'although all agricultural land was owned and held by Zamindars, only some fifth of the land was held by them as sir and khudkasht. Even this was not all under their direct cultivation; a sizeable part of it was let out ..... only 1.5 percent of landlords paid a land revenue above Rs 250 a year and owned 58 percent of land, while 85 percent of them paid land revenue of Rs 25 or less' (1981: 363). The distribution of size categories of Zamindar in 1947 was as follows:

Rs land revenue payable	Number of Zamindars	% of total Zamindars	M Rs land rev. payable	Av. Rs L.R. per Zamindar
10,000 +	390	*	15.6	40,077
5,000 - 9,999	414	*	2.9	7,077
250 +	(30,142)	1.5	(39.4)	1,305
50 - 249	133,221	6.6	13.7	103
25 - 49	142,890	7.1	5.0	35
1 - 24	1,710,530	84.8	10.0	6
1 - 249	(1,986,641)	(98.5)	(28.7)	14
TOTAL	2,016,783	100	68.1	34

Source: Shrimali 1981. There were 256 Talukdars in Oudh, after the talukdari settlement.

Shrimali has summarised this important act and its effects:

> All intermediaries between the State and the cultivator (Proprietor or Tenant) were done away with and the land was vested in the State. All landlords (intermediaries) whose rights, title or interest in any estate are acquired, have been paid compensation at the uniform rate of eight times the value of the net assets; no distinction has been made between the bigger and the smaller intermediary. In addition to the compensation, rehabilitation grant on graded rates, ranging from one to twenty times of the net income has been allowed to intermediaries (landlords), other than Thekadars, paying annual land revenue up to Rs 10,000 [ie. the smaller Zamindars: some of the larger ones had been paying over Rs 10,000. Indeed, 27 such landlords in Rae Bareli district accounted for 62 percent of total land revenue in the district]. The grant is largest for the lowest income and smallest for the larger income-receiving landowners. Thus, landowners paying annual land revenue up to Rs 10,000 received both the compensation and the rehabilitation grant. These landowners, however, were allowed to continue to reclaim their entire sir, khudkasht and groves et cetera, which they could claim and prove to be under self-cultivation; though they were not allowed the right of resumption of land under that pretext.
>
> The Act abolished the multiplicity of [over 41 types of] tenure ..... and introduced only three main types of tenures, viz. Bhumidhar, Sirdar and Asami .....
>
> (i) The Bhumidhar is a peasant proprietor having permanent, heritable and transferable rights in his holding; the right to transfer being subject to the condition that the purchaser or donor may not have more than 12.5 acres of land. He has also the right to use the land for any purpose whatsoever, and is not liable to ejectment. All landholders, who had sir in their cultivatory possession, ie. not sub-let (except in the case of proprietors who suffered from certain disabilities) automatically became bhumidhars of the land in their possession and paid the revenue direct to government. [Former intermediaries or landowners became statutory bhumidhars in respect of sir and khudkasht land automatically and without payment, but others, called voluntary bhumidhars, had to apply and acquire their bhumidhar rights by depositing ten times the land revenue.] The bhumidhar [of either kind] cannot sublet his holding or any of its part except when he is a disabled person (minor, widow, disabled or a defence personnel) ..... [sub-letting can lead to dispossession].
>
> (ii) The Sirdar also has permanent, heritable interest in his holding, but this is not transferable. He can use his land only for agriculture, horticulture and animal husbandry and is liable to be ejected if he violates

this provision. He has, however, the option of acquiring bhumidhari rights in his holding at any time by paying into the treasury a sum equivalent to ten times his annual land revenue at the hereditary rate of rent whereupon his future land revenue would be reduced to half. [Payment in instalments entailed payment of twelve times the land revenue.] ..... With the latest amendment in the Act [1977], sirdars have been granted bhumidhar rights even without having to deposit ten times land revenue.

(iii) The Asami is either a lessee of a disabled bhumidhar or [of] a sirdar or is a tenant of the gaon sabha (village community) ..... He is actually a sub-tenant or shikmi kashtkar. His right in land is neither permanent nor transferable; it is only heritable [ie. he is an occupancy tenant?]. An asami's land would also be deemed to be abandoned if it is allowed to remain unused for two consecutive years [as in the case of sirdar] ..... The asami can become sirdar, if after expiry of the term of the lease, the landowner fails to file a suit and execute a decree for ejecting him from that land. On becoming sirdar, he can acquire bhumidari rights (Shrimali 1981: 165-7).

A fourth interim type of tenure, Adhivasi, existed until the amendment of 1954, when these ex-tenants of sir land were able to become themselves sirdars and pay land revenue, equivalent to the earlier rent.

Since February 1977, there have been only two tenurial categories, bhumidhar and asami, sirdars becoming bhumidhars without having to pay ten times the annual land revenue. (Many had in effect already paid 25 times this, over the years.) Only a third of the original sirdars had opted to convert to bhumidhari.

The weaknesses of Zamindari Abolition included the repossession by Zamindars of land which they had been renting out but now claimed to have been self-cultivating. Shrimali claims that less than 15 percent of the 10.2 million acres recorded as landlords' sir and khudkasht was actually being cultivated by them in 1951. As a result of this repossession, he alleges that 'the Zamindars were finally able to grab 8.14 million acres, ie. 79.5 percent of the total land recorded as sir and khudkasht' (1981: 187). Secondly, the cost of acquiring bhumidhari rights on their sir and khudkasht land was nothing to those who were bhumidhars already on most of their land and yet was 10 and 15 times the annual land revenue for sirdars and adhivasis. Indeed, sirdars wishing to become bhumidhars had to pay 20 times the land revenue between June 1969 and June 1976. By 1973-4, still 53 percent of the taxable land was sirdari, because sirdars regarded the cost of conversion too high in relation to the return in terms of reduced land revenue. Thirdly, the landlords were paid, in the form of bonds, much higher compensation than the committee recommendation. All landlords, of whatever size, were paid a uniform eight times the annual net income from the land rather than the recommended, graduated scale of three times for big landlords and up to 25 times annual net income for small landlords. Fourthly, a graduated 'rehabilitation grant' was paid to medium as well as to small landlords, since the ceiling was fixed at land revenue of Rs 10,000 rather than Rs 5,000. Fifthly, there was discrimination and differentiation in the new land revenue rates. Ex-Zamindars paid a quarter of the local circle rate for self-cultivated lands, adhivasis paid eight times this ex-Zamindar rate, others paid four times this rate and even sirdars who paid the amount necessary to become bhumidhars still paid twice the rate paid by ex-Zamindars. It is claimed that the land revenue paid by the holders of the new, consolidated forms of tenure was equivalent to the amount which they had previously paid as rent to the Zamindar. Sixthly, the prohibition of letting and sub-letting (batai) of most land has been sidestepped by resort to fake 'partnership' (sajhedari) which was permitted by the new act. Seventh, there was no ceiling on landownership and consequently hardly any land was made available for redistribution. Shrimali uses NSS data to show an appreciable increase in tiny (under one acre) and marginal (under 2.5 acre) holdings between 1953-4 and 1971-2. Eighth, the legislation was followed by a tide of 1.5 million cases of land litigation. Finally, there was provision for the Land Management Committees, set up under the 1947 Panchayat Act, to redistribute surplus transferred land to the gaon sabha. These committees usually included no landless labourers and, since they were dominated by upper caste Pradhans, they achieved very little for the landless. Shrimali claims that 'the bulk of the land grab of the gaon samaj land was effected' by the rich and powerful in the 1950s before the secret ballot and slightly wider representation was facilitated, if not actually achieved, in village government. Investigation of land allotted between 1964 and 1967 revealed that 59 percent of cases were irregular and this alone led to the filing of 177,000 lawsuits and cancellations of 174,000 allotments.

Brass concludes that Abolition 'merely confirmed all actual cultivators -whether Zamindars or tenants - in the possession of their lands on a new legal basis. The benefits to the holders of new legal titles were mainly psychological' (1965: 12). Absentee landlords (who lacked sir and khudkasht) and the biggest Zamindars and Talukdars lost some land but Brass concurs with Neale and Reeves and others that abolition 'changed very little either in the agrarian structure or the pattern of political domination in UP' (1965: 12):

> The Act has had very little effect on the condition of the former tenants and the petty zamindars, except that the tenants now pay their land revenue directly to the state and they have greater rights of ownership over the land they cultivate. The large landlords are deprived of their rights to collect revenue, but they retained lands in their private possession and received compensation for the lands taken away from them ..... The continued influence of the former big zamindars and Talukdars in the countryside is an important factor in contemporary party politics in UP (1984: 232).

Ahmed and Saxena claim that Brahmins gained ownership of land that they had previously controlled only as intermediaries and Kohli adds that this further cemented the Brahmin support for Congress (I). The Act 'essentially substituted the state government as zamindar in place of the landlords' (1984:279).

Landownership Ceiling

The Zamindari Abolition Committee found that in 1947 nearly 38 percent of holdings were under one acre and nearly 56 percent under two acres:

ACRES OWNED	0-0.5	0.5-1	1-2	2-3	3-4	4-5	5-10	10-16	16-25	25+	TOTAL
% TOTAL HHS	21.5	16.3	18.0	11.6	8.1	5.7	13.2	3.6	1.6	0.9	100
CUMULATIVE % TOTAL HRS	21.5	37.8	55.8	67.4	75.5	81.2	94.4	98.0	99.6	100.5	100
% TOTAL AREA	2.2	3.8	8.1	8.7	8.7	7.6	26.1	13.2	8.6	12.9	100

Source: Shrimali 1981: 142

Despite the obvious inequality, the 1951 Act imposed no ceiling on existing landownership because it had been argued that there was little surplus available for redistribution and in any case redistribution would arouse major discontent. In addition, Charan Singh, the Minister for Revenue and a major influence on the bill, was keen to eliminate both the Zamindar class and also 'uneconomic' holdings, leaving a peasant class of 'economic holdings' of between about 2.5 and 30 acres. However, the Act restricted landowners from expanding their future holdings beyond 30 acres (amended to 12.5 acres in 1958). The Kisan Sabha in 1958 and the Praja Socialist Party in 1962 called for a ceiling of 20 acres. The first Imposition of Ceiling on Land Holdings Act was passed in 1960 and this restricted ownership of fair quality land to 40 acres per person or a maximum of 64 acres per family, excluding grove land, when family size exceeded 5 persons. NSS data show that in 1961-2 the average holding in UP was 4.7 acres and so the ceiling was more than eight times the (declared) average. The effect of the Act was further weakened by various loopholes, including delayed enforcement; staggered implementation by districts; family subdivisions; benami transfers (ie. covert transfers to an unnamed agent); and some backdated registration of such transfers. Out of over 50 million acres of taxable land, 1.4 million acres was expected to be surplus but only 0.11 million acres was officially claimed to have been redistributed. Brass (1965) estimates that the ceiling could yield a maximum distributable surplus of only 1.3 percent of the total cultivated area and prior conversion of such surplus to groves of fruit trees could easily eliminate even this slender surplus. In theory, the prime beneficiaries were supposed to be agricultural cooperatives, newly formed by agricultural labourers, but the fact that the landless were debarred from membership of such cooperatives made this rather difficult until criticism by the

Sanwal Committee of 1969 led to a change in the law. When Congress (I) returned to power in April 1971, the government was influenced by a report on vast, illegal holdings by former Zamindars and Talukdars. One means of evasion had been to set up bogus educational and other 'trusts' to conceal holdings of 500 acres and possibly more (Brass 1981: 28). Until 1973 a landowner could retain 128 acres plus groves, orchards and various categories of land which was exempt from the ceiling legislation. In about May 1972 the ceiling was reduced to 18 acres of irrigated land and up to 48 acres of less productive land per family. The Bharatiya Kranti Dal did not oppose this amendment, but Charan Singh criticised its 'retrospective effect' and the inadequacy of a land redistribution strategy, compared with rural industrialisation. He supported distribution to the scheduled castes, especially those whose holdings could be raised to the threshold of 'viability' (2.5 acres). Brass notes that Charan Singh, by favouring a minimum holding of 2.5 acres and a maximum holding of 27.5 acres, encouraged 'the locally dominant landed proprietors ..... who, according to the 1971 agricultural census, constitute approximately one third of the landholding classes and control approximately 70 percent of the land' (1984: 315). Singh sought to avoid land-hungry class conflict by siphoning surplus labour into small, rural industries. The new ceiling yielded a further surplus of 0.12 million acres, of which only 0.04 million acres were redistributed, according to Shrimali (1981). He implies that land grabbing, encroachment and trespass on the land of the poor more than cancelled out the effects of even this minimal redistribution and thus concentration of landownership and class differentiation had actually increased.

The report of the Sanwal Committee on Tarai Lands in 1969 found that there were about 5.5 million acres of gaon sabha land, including at least 1.8 million acres which could be redistributed without using land 'reserved for planned use' (Shrimali 1981: 399). Brass claims that ceilings were lowered and implementation of the ceiling laws became more rigorous during the Emergency, especially against former big Zamindars and Talukdars. Priority was given to distribution to landless from the scheduled castes. The government claimed in 1982 that 1.92 million persons had been given 1.74 million acres of gram sabha and ceiling lands (Pioneer, 14 January 1982) but village committees are reputed to have been corrupt in distributing surplus land to their favourites. Kohli concludes that 'it is doubtful if landowners in UP have ever lost lands of significance due to the "land ceilings" legislation. Most likely, the only lands that changed hands following land reforms were those for which governmental compensations were close to the market value' (1987: 214). He estimates that during a high point of land reformism (between 1972 and 1977) only about 116,000 acres (0.7%) of cultivated land was actually redistributed. Conversely, Montgomery (1992) suggests that land reform has encouraged the growth of a middle class of farmers: the largest landowners sell land to pre-empt total loss through confiscation under impending enforcement of ceilings on land holding. If the elected power of Congress (I) proved impotent against the economically dominant classes, then the election of Janata by medium and rich landowning peasants led to the virtual suspension of land reforms as a policy goal.

Lease of Land

The 1951 Act prohibited sub-letting (shikmi), leasing out or giving land on sharecropping (batai), except when the owner was disabled, widowed, a minor or defence personnel. This (rather unrealistic) prohibition has not been observed, partly because of the loophole of 'partnership' (sajhedari) or fixed-cash tenancy, which was legal until 1974. Shrimali's survey of 17 villages in 1976 found that 13 percent of households were at least partly sharecroppers and in eastern UP the ratio was 19 percent. Most had only annual contracts and very little security. In most areas the batai paid to the landlord was half the gross crop (see Bliss 1982 for an economic analysis of tenancy). Kohli points out that 'UP is one of the few states in India where, over time, area under tenancy has actually increased as a proportion of the total cultivated area' (1987: 213). In 1970-1 about 13 percent of cultivated land and about 20 percent of the rural population was involved in tenancy even though all tenancy was technically illegal. The area under illegal batai (sharecropping) as a percentage of area under all tenancy also increased from 54 percent in 1953-4 to 81 percent in 1970-1.

Consolidation

The Consolidation of Holdings Act was passed in 1953 and UP was one of at least three northern states where the process was still proceeding in 1982. (It was almost complete in UP by 1987.) Shrimali alleges that rich peasants have taken better quality land from poor peasants. Several thousand complaints were brought before the legislative assembly.

Land Revenue

Various issues related to land revenue have occupied a major, indeed a quite disproportionate, place in policy and in wider political debate and action. The issues have included the level of land revenue, surcharge and related taxation on land; graduation of rates, especially between size and tenurial categories; and the threshold of exemption.

Brass has provided a particularly full account of the key discussion on land revenue. In 1953 Charan Singh, as Minister of Revenue, wrote a note, expressing reservation over a proposed increase of 50 percent in charges for irrigation water. Instead, he proposed that the land revenue should be increased by a third for sirdars only and that water rates should be increased by a third to all tenures. Brass explains that Singh was peeved because the majority of tenants had refused to pay the Rs 50 or so per acre in order to convert their sirdari into bhumidhari tenure (which would reduce their annual land revenue from about Rs 5.5 to less than Rs 2.5 per acre). Singh's proposal which was biased in favour of the irrigated, western districts and against sirdars (who were probably more recalcitrant about conversion to bhumidhari in the poorer, eastern districts?) was not accepted by the council of ministers.

During the 1950s the government was reluctant to tax the rural sector. However, in 1960, when C.B. Gupta became Chief Minister and needed to meet Third Plan expenditures to follow the Planning Commission's recommendation for state governments to increase taxation of agriculture, the Landholding Tax Bill was introduced, after much deliberation, on 4 September 1962. Originally, this proposed a 2.5 percent tax on the capitalised value of landholdings and this effectively amounted to a 50 percent increase in the land revenue on the 62 percent of all holdings which were over one acre. The proposal provoked a political storm and, after consultation with the Planning Commission, the exemption was extended to landholdings of eight acres or less, ie. 90 percent of all landholdings. Many MLAs found this also unsatisfactory, partly because it might encourage fragmentation of holdings. In late October the Emergency Surcharge on Land Revenue and Rent Bill was presented, with only a 25 percent increase in land revenue and exemption narrowed down again to the holdings of one acre or less, which are most common in the east. This was passed on 10 December 1962. Brass points out that this controversy ranged widely, both in time (over 6 months) and in political space (to the Prime Minister, Union cabinet ministers and the Planning Commission). The total amount of extra taxation at stake could not have been much more than Rs 120 million or about 11 percent of the necessary plan revenue. Nevertheless, the issue aroused strong disagreement within the UP cabinet and a prolonged and increasingly acrimonious debate between the Chief Minister and his Agriculture Minister, Charan Singh. The latter reminded Gupta that the government had promised the bhumidhars in 1951 that their land revenue would not be increased for 40 years. Singh also revived his hobby-horse about increasing the tax on the sirdars to pressurise them into bhumidhari. Like the critics of the bill from the opposition parties (of all ideologies), Singh complained of undertaxation of the urban sector, and the government imposed new urban taxes before the rural land tax proposals came up for discussion. Gupta argued that, since Singh was himself proposing increased taxation for sirdars (who were mostly poor peasants anyway?), he could hardly sustain his claim that there was no taxable capacity in the peasant sector. He also pointed out that existing land revenue absorbed only 2 percent of agricultural income and suggested that Singh was protecting a privileged, bhumidhar 'class'. They disagreed profoundly on the urban-rural issue, with Charan Singh complaining of excessive urban expenditure and expansion in government employment.

The argument was revived in September 1963 when the government attempted to extend the Emergency Surcharge Bill (which had been widely assumed to be a temporary expedient) for a further year. A change-over of Chief Ministers provided a convenient break and the new Chief Minister lost no time in withdrawing the bill. However, the surcharge was re-imposed in 1965, after war with Pakistan, and this added to the growing anti-Congress feeling which was expressed in the 1967 elections. The new, but shortlived, Gupta administration withdrew the surcharge in March 1967.

At this point, the wheel turned full circle and there was a situation in which there was a non-Congress coalition, led by Charan Singh, which now found itself having to refuse to abolish land revenue altogether! From April 1967 the Samyukta Socialist Party led a campaign to persuade the new Samyukta Vidhayak Dal coalition ministry to implement this, as one of the 33 points in the coalition programme. Charan Singh, for all his populism, refused to abolish land revenue completely until alternative sources of revenue could be found and eventually in July the cabinet reduced the land revenue by half for owners of up to 6.25 acres, ie. probably about 85 percent of all holdings. A crisis ensued and it was only after a compromise proposal that the SSP and CPI ministers rejoined the cabinet in October. Brass comments that Charan Singh

> was faced with a demand from the Left parties that would benefit principally the poorest peasants, would affect the middle peasantry only marginally, but would withdraw substantial revenue from the state exchequer ..... [He] who had opposed any increase in land revenue by the C.B. Gupta government, now opposed any reduction in it. While he did not support any increases in land revenue, he saw no reason why the middle peasants should not continue to pay the traditional, and very modest, land revenue charges that also provided the principal basis for maintaining the peasants' records of title to their lands (1984: 318).

In 1970, as leader of an uneasy coalition between the Bharatiya Kranti Dal and Congress (I), Charan Singh, against his better judgement, agreed to abolition of land revenue on holdings of less than 3.125 acres, ie. probably about 67 percent of holdings. In May 1971 the BKD-led government of T.N. Singh raised the exemption to 6.25 acres. Charan Singh later opposed a Congress land development levy which sought to increase land revenue on a graduated, progressive scale related to acreage owned. He opposed it now because it exempted owners of less than 3.5 acres and opposed agricultural taxation partly because of the effect of the reduced ceiling on land holdings. The threshold of exemption was again reduced to 3.125 acres at a still later date and in 1981 the government was considering the abolition of any exemption from land revenue.

Shrimali shows that the income from basic land revenue remained very stable, ranging from Rs 206 million to Rs 213 million, between 1955-6 and 1973-4, in the plains:

LAND TENURE, AREA AND LAND REVENUE, UTTAR PRADESH 1955-6 AND 1973-4

Year	M. acres	Av. Rs land rev. per acre	M. Rs land rev.	M. acres	Av. Rs land rev. per acre	M. Rs land rev.
		BHUMIDHAR			SIRDAR	
1955-6	14.0	2.49	35	30.3	5.63	170
1973-4	19.6	2.63	51	26.6	5.75	153
		ASAMI			TOTAL	
1955-6	0.29	4.06	-	47.2	-	206
1973-4	0.36	3.53	-	49.8	-	206

Source: Shrimali 1981:202. The data only include the plains districts of UP.

These figures show that the ratio of area of bhumidhari only increased from 30 to 41 percent during this 18-year period. In 1977 the tenures of sirdari and bhumidhari merged and this presumably led to a fall in land revenue. Shrimali also shows that land revenue rates were graduated on a regressive scale, not only in relation to tenure, but also in effect according to size in 1970-1:

Acres holding	0-0.5	0.5-1	1-2	2.5	5-6.25	20-30	40-50	50+
Average Rs land revenue per acre, 1970-1	5.72	5.32	5.06	4.85	4.60	3.43	2.4	1.8
Rate as % of 50+	318	296	281	269	256	191	133	100

Source: Shrimali 1981: 204

This regressive graduation was presumably because of the higher proportion of sirdars among smaller and poorer owners. However, the average basic land revenue was taking away less than 1 percent of the value of gross agricultural output in the early 1970s and, since the rates were not tied to inflation, this ratio fell as crop values rose. For this, and other reasons, Brass seems fully justified in concluding that 'the state government has been unable to tax the peasantry' (1984: 327). Attempts have been made to impose development levies and the like but these have also aroused controversy quite disproportionate to their revenue potential. In the late 1970s about 40 percent of state revenue came from sales tax on consumer items and this probably accrued mainly from richer elements of the urban sector, though such a tax is regressive.

Irrigation Water

The supply and price of irrigation water are important issues. The canal water rates were increased by 50 percent in 1953, at the same time as Panchayat and District Boards imposed taxes and sought to realise arrears. Campaigns against both led to the restoration of the old rates for small canals, an increase of only 24 percent for other canals and remission in several districts. Realisation of the tax arrears was also suspended or postponed for five years in most districts. By 1981-2 there were also said to be over 18,000 state tubewells, mostly powered by electricity. Consumers of whatever wealth and capacity were all charged the same minimum rate, in a regressive system. Since 1969 the State Electricity Board has ceased to fit meters to tubewells and charges are based on connected horsepower rather than on units consumed. By 1982 only about 30 percent of tubewells had accurate meters and partly because of this, the recorded average annual running hours per tubewell had declined from 2,300 hours in 1976-7 to 900 hours in 1981-2. This had led to a fall in annual revenue to about Rs 91 million, a decrease of over 30 percent (Northern India Patrika, 20 May 1982).

Earlier, a government statement claimed that they had 'sided with the farmers and, disregarding the pressure put by the industrialists, supplied power to farmers for timely irrigation by imposing cuts on their factories. It resulted in the record production of 24.5 million tonnes of foodgrains last year. The irrigated area also increased by 25 percent this year' (Pioneer, 14 January 1982).

Credit

Credit, especially to the so-called 'weaker sections' expanded considerably during the 1970s and, more recently, through the IRDP. The Agricultural Credit Act of 1973 made it possible for all agriculturalists, including sirdars and asamis (?), to alienate their land or other property to obtain bank credit. In the inceasingly competitive party political battle between 1971 and 1977, Congress (I) introduced subsidised loans and other schemes, through the Marginal and Small Farmer Development Agencies. Janata's Debt Relief Act of 1977 was intended to liquidate the debts of landless agricultural labourers, marginal farmers and rural artisans, as well as those whose annual household income was less than Rs 2,400 (ie. well below the poverty line). Richer households which had paid double the amount of the original loan were also discharged from further requirement to pay. Small farmers had their debts scaled down and made subject to a moratorium on repayment. Shrimali (1981) claims that this act, like the Regulation of Moneylending Act of 1976, had no immediate positive effect and that moneylenders were continuing to press for repayment. A negative effect was the drying up of private credit flows to the poor. Kohli (1987) documents the negligible contribution of the Small Farmer Development Agency to poverty reduction during the Janata period.

Procurement of Crops

The organisation, level and pricing of crop procurement are other issues which have been politically important. The new cabinet of Charan Singh in 1967 decided to fix a procurement target of 0.5 million tons of foodgrain but this aroused the opposition of the larger, richer farmers, especially the wheat producers of the western districts, Charan Singh's main power base. The relatively high target would entail the sale of their wheat at below market prices. The opposition was expressed through the organisational party wing of the Jan Sangh, plus an ad hoc inter-party group of big farmer MLAs and MLCs. Though the Jan Sangh ministers avoided public controversy, the opposition was strong enough to force a compromise, entailing a reduction of the target to 0.2 million tons (Brass 1984: 112). Charan Singh himself had 'favoured a graduated procurement policy that drew most heavily from the biggest farmers' (Brass 1984: 319).

Between 1971 and 1977 Congress took over the wholesale trade in wheat and this upset both the private traders and also the larger farmers. Charan Singh opposed this and also in 1972 urged that the procurement price for wheat should be increased from Rs 73 to Rs 90 per quintal, to cover rising costs. Generally, the government, especially at state level, increases procurement prices somewhat above the level recommended annually by the Agricultural Prices Commission. Between 1979-80 and April 1982 the procurement price for wheat increased from Rs 115 to Rs 142 per quintal. Even then, there were complaints in Parliament that it was much lower than the import price of Rs 187 per quintal and landed cost of over Rs 200 (Pioneer, 29 April 1982). The Indian Express commented that 'the consumer-oriented APC has drained out resources from the farmer sector to the industrial sector. In October 1980 the prices of agricultural products relative to that of manufactured goods was only 78 percent against 87 percent a year earlier. Since March 1979 industrial prices have been rising faster than agricultural prices, forcing more and more farmers to slide below the poverty line' (28 October 1982). In November 1982 the APC raised the recommended price to Rs 155 per quintal. The APC terms of reference were revised in 1981 to include transport costs and changes in terms of trade. In August 1982 the government, in order to maintain its national food subsidy at Rs 7 billion, had to raise the issue price in fair price shops from Rs 145 to Rs 160 per quintal (and from Rs 155 to Rs 185 for roller flour mills).

Sugarcane is a major cash crop in UP but it has a political importance which is disproportionate to its economic, nutritional and health value. Its political significance is obvious, since up to 3 million out of over 9 million farmers grew sugarcane and most of these belonged to 135 or more registered cooperative cane unions. In 1982-3 there were 4.2 million acres under sugarcane. Growers had many complaints, including low prices and delays both in purchase and particularly in payment. Shrimali mentions a major strike, involving 1.4 million growers in 1953, and demands included bonuses for earlier years; higher prices (including for gur); uniform prices, regardless of distance from the mill; payment of the cane cess; crushing of all available cane; and both a guaranteed quota of 500 quintals to all and particular preference to smaller growers. Brass (1965) describes the complex politics of sugar in Deoria district and concludes that cross-cutting conflicts prevented sugarcane growers from becoming effectively organised and so the expression of their demands was accordingly sporadic. In September 1982 the APC recommended continuation of the previous procurement price of Rs 15.5 per quintal, but added a new allowance of two rupees per quintal for transport. However, the UP government again raised this to Rs 20.5 per quintal in the east and to Rs 21.5 in western and central districts. It also introduced a scheme for growers to bond up to 85 percent of the level supplied to the mill in 1981-2. The 91 mills would pay the growers through banks and permanent passbooks had been issued to the growers, presumably to reduce time wasted on renewing them. In September 1982 the sugar industry nationally owed the growers about Rs 700 million, a record debt following a bumper crop. The high price of sugarcane encouraged UP farmers to increase the acreage from 3.8 million to 4.2 million acres in 1982-3, even though there was over-production in 1981-2. Excess acreage of sugarcane reduces foodgrain acreage and, since the mills have only the capacity to crush about a third of the sugarcane, in 1977-8 many farmers (probably mostly the smaller and less influential ones) were forced to sell to gur and khandsari producers who only paid Rs 3 to Rs 6 per quintal compared with a mill price of about Rs 13. (Some of the surplus may also be used as a cheap, partial payment of agricultural labourers.)

It is clear that the UP government has been quite generous to sugarcane (ie. mainly richer) farmers but that generosity has to be constrained by the need to keep the mostly ancient and decrepit sugar mills solvent and to hold down the consumer prices for sugar (especially for the monthly ration supply).

Wages of Labourers

The Minimum Wages Act was passed in 1948 and it began to be applied to agricultural labourers in UP in 1954. Shrimali and also Nayyar (1977) both show that, despite this, real wages for most tasks have stagnated or actually fallen.

Many agricultural labourers, especially in eastern UP, are paid in kind, and some are also provided with a tiny plot of land, to secure the attachment of the labourer to the farmer-employer. Shrimali claims that 'about 30 percent [of agricultural labourers] reported that they are physically assaulted by the employer' (1981: 261), apart from other abuse, threats and harassment. The Indian Express (6 December 1981) mentioned that the UP and three other state governments were interested in initiating a minimum wage of Rs 240 per month for all categories of workers.

In 1976 the central government passed the Bonded Labour Act and eradication of bonded labour was one of Mrs Gandhi's famous '20 points'. Many of those bonded by debt to employers are from the scheduled categories and in 1982 there was still a sizeable, but unknown, number of bonded labourers in UP.

OFFICIAL MINIMUM AND ACTUAL AVERAGE WAGES OF LABOURERS, UTTAR PRADESH 1954-81

YEAR	RANGE	1954	1961	1969-70	1972	1975	Nov. 1981
Official minimum wages Rs per day	Max.	1.0	1.8		3.5 Large farms	6.5 W. region	8.5* (West)
	Min.	1.0	1.5		2.5 Small farms	5.0 Poorer regions	6.5 (East)
Actual aver., at current prices			1.31			2 to 6.5	2 to 6.5
Actual aver., at constant 1960-1 prices			1.31	1.32			

* The big farmers did not provide lodgings and clothes, as in Punjab and Haryana, where minimum wages were Rs 14 and Rs 10 per day, respectively. Many labourers in western UP have migrated from eastern UP.

Sources: Shrimali 1981: 256; Indian Express, 30 November 1981.

Kohli (1987) notes the neglect of wage and employment schemes for the landless during the Janata period. The Food for Work Programme received no state-level funds and central funds were frittered on non-development. In the west Jat landowners increased their power over the scheduled who had begun to benefit from the '20-point' programme.

Capital and Income Distribution

Shrimali (1981) claims that land concentration has increased in UP since 1950. He bases this assertion partly on evidence from the 17 villages which he surveyed but, since these villages appear to have been chosen partly for their Communist party links or for signs of agrarian conflict, and they thus seem to be a biased sample which may yield unrepresentative results.

CONCENTRATION OF LANDOWNERSHIP, UTTAR PRADESH 1950-75

YEAR	1950	1953-4	1961-2	1971-2	1975
Coefficient of concentration of landholding	.63	.64	.72	.68	.68
Population	17 villages	UP	UP	UP	17 villages

Source: Shrimali 1981: 371

However, it is perfectly possible for market forces and private land transfers to have been at least balancing the very slight tendency towards deconcentration, set up by the highly ineffective land reform legislation. There has been no long-term reduction in poverty incidence but some decrease in poverty intensity (the Sen index) in UP between 1957-8 and 1973-4. There was also some decrease in the Gini Ratio of inequality of consumption. Despite agricultural growth, per capita availability of foodgrains had only improved from 510 to 570 grams per day between 1950 and 1979, but 1979 was a bad harvest year. The cereals availability had increased significantly but this was almost cancelled out by the halving of availability of pulses. Sarvekshana (1983) provides details of the NSS survey on expenditure in UP in 1977-8. This showed that 37 percent of rural and 35 percent of all households spent less than Rs 600 per capita. Assuming the poverty line to have been about Rs 656 per capita, then 49 percent of the rural and 47 percent of all households were below this line. Over 1 million households (5.8%) spent an average of less than Rs 360 per person in 1977-8 and all but 60,000 of these households of extreme poverty were rural (Sarvekshana 1983: S102). Kohli estimates that in 1979-80 there were about 40 million persons (about 50%) and 8 million households below the poverty line, including 20 million living in households of marginal farmers and sharecroppers and 20 million members of households of landless labourers. Kohli concludes that

> tenancy is probably higher in the eastern UP, while the proportion of the landless is higher in the western half. Any strategy for alleviating rural poverty in UP would have to keep these regional variations in mind. While the unionisation of the landless for higher wages and small-farmer programme would be most suitable for the western half, tenancy reforms and investment in agrarian infrastructure, such as irrigation, would be needed as a beginning in the eastern parts (1987: 213).

There was a relation between per capita expenditure and nutritional intakes in rural India and rural UP in 1972-3. The figures show that standards were consistently higher in rural UP than in rural India and that in both rural areas nutritional intake rose steadily with per capita expenditure. It appears as if about 50 percent of rural householders in UP had an average intake of 2,429 calories or less (ie. on or below the rural 'poverty' level of nutrition). Intake of fat among the poor was very low but protein intakes were adequate for all but the poorest 6 percent.

ASPECTS OF HEALTH POLICY IN UTTAR PRADESH

The sixth plan outlines the health objectives for UP from 1980 to 1985 (GOUP 1980: 493). More than Rs 3 billion (3.3% of the total plan) was allocated to health, including 54 percent to rural health services. However, the plan aimed to increase the number of hospitals/dispensaries from 4,183 to 5,216 whilst primary health centres would only rise from 907 to 1,007. The largest increase was planned for subcentres: from 7,640 to 14,640. There was also later a grandiose plan for another very expensive postgraduate teaching hospital in Lucknow which was mooted in 1982, as a memorial to Sanjay Gandhi.

In 1981 the size of the sixth plan was reduced from Rs 92 billion to Rs 62 billion and it was reported that the largest cut occurred in the Health Department. The implications were that 764 doctors, previously assigned to government service, would have to go into private practice; that 1,520 nurses, 3,523 midwives and 1,074 sanitary inspectors (out of 1,154 being trained) would not be able to find jobs in government service. There would also be a surplus of 1,401 pharmacists and 719 laboratory assistants. After all the cuts there actually remained only 84 approved posts for sanitary inspectors.

The Ministry of Works and Housing is responsible for drinking water supplies, through the state corporations, Jal Nigam (Water Corporation) and Jal Sansthan (Water Works). A programme to provide piped water began as part of the Minimum Needs Programme in 1971-72. A survey then showed that 32 percent of the 112,561 villages in UP suffered from scarcity of drinking water (not to speak of quality). The World Bank offered a loan of $40 million for a commercially organised and centralised programme and in June 1975 the UP Jal Nigam was established, using the existing Local Self-Government and Engineering Department as the basis. Jal Nigam seems to have given priority to urban projects and by 1980 water supplies 'covered' 89 percent and sewerage schemes 'covered' 46 percent of the urban population. There were still 602 towns in UP without sewerage. Priority in rural areas was being given to plains villages with a source 1.6 kilometres or more distant and to hill villages with a water source 0.8 kilometres or more distant; to plains villages with water tables below 20 metres or hill areas with a water source 100 metres up or down from the village site; and to sources susceptible to cholera, typhoid, guinea-worm and other water-borne diseases, or to sources excessively saline or with a high content of iron or fluoride. In addition, a modest pilot project to instal water (pour-?) flush latrines in Mal block, Lucknow district by the Planning, Research and Action Institute was set up. By 1983 the PRAI was said to have succeeded in building about 800 dry latrines, costing about Rs 300 each. These included a cement squatting plate, an angled drop to a hole about 2 metres deep and one metre in diameter. Most takers were given a 25 percent subsidy and the 'weaker sections' were given 50 percent. The majority of those installing latrines were richer and upper caste villagers. The latrine pit lasted for three years when five persons used it.

During the 1970s there was a gradual increase in the number of acceptors of various types of contraception and, from 1973, of abortion ('medical termination of pregnancy') in UP. There has been relative and increasing importance of the IUD, conventional contraceptives (ie. mainly condoms or nirodhs) and sterilisation. The number of sterilisations is claimed to have risen from 129,000 in 1975-6 to 838,000 in 1976-7, followed by only 13,000 in the next, post-Emergency year. Everyone knows the damage done to the family planning campaign by the Emergency but later there was a steady build-up to at least the 1975-6 acceptance rate by 1981-2.

The backlash against vasectomy which began during the Emergency had still not entirely died down by 1982. Since males were 'no longer coming forward', the emphasis was on female sterilisation, especially by laparectomy. Apart from other regressive implications for male-female relations, laparectomy cost more (Rs 25 compared with Rs 5 for a vasectomy in 1982), used more skilled labour, and more scarce and expensive equipment, involved more medical risk and lacked the option of at least theoretical reversibility. In addition, it may take both the women and the PHC doctor away from their home or work for at least a day.

There was an the increase in immunisation within the Maternal and Child Health Programme from 1970-1 to 1981-2. Out of 32 million activities, 11.2 million involved immunisation of pregnant mothers and children against Tetanus Toxoid; Diphtheria, Pertussis and Tetanus; and Diphtheria and Tetanus. A further 8 million or so activities were concerned with treatment for nutritional anemia and 11 million with prevention of blindness. The remaining 2.6 million were deliveries and prevention of polio, typhoid and TB. There was a dramatic increase in treatment of children aged 1 to 12 for nutritional anemia in 1981-2 and there was also a marked (and unexplained) fall in the number of deliveries by auxiliary-nurse-midwives in that year.

Medical supplies in 1983 were provided by 11 government companies but the

Central Medical Stores sent exactly the same supplies to each of the 57 districts, with their differing needs, leading to wastage of unwanted medicines. There was a strong feeling that the ordering of medicines should be decentralised, especially since district Medical and Health Department plans and budgets have been decentralised since 1961.

An investigation by the Vigilance Department in 1984 revealed that, out of Rs 300 million spent on government purchase of medicine, Rs 50 million went on substandard or non-delivered goods. The Directorate of Health Services would claim despatch of supplies before they had even received them at headquarters. Substandard drugs would be distributed even when suspect samples were due to be sent for laboratory analysis. Between 1974 and 1982 drug importers examined over 12,000 medicine samples and found 150 totally spurious and a further 1,300 substandard. In 1981 the central drug controller directed the state government to punish manufacturers, suppliers and buyers of spurious drugs but no action had been taken two years later.

The Drugs and Cosmetics Act of 1945 requires the state government to order the withdrawal of the entire batch if samples of a medicine are shown to be faulty. This has not always happened. The rules also require that in UP a minimum of 17,000 samples have to be lifted from over 350 drug manufacturers and 4,000 chemists each year but up to 1983 the sampling had never exceeded 14,000. Between 1974 and 1982 over 40 percent of manufacturers and retailers were untouched by sampling. The Comptroller and Auditor General also found that goods had either been supplied to the Health Department which had not been ordered or had been purchased from suppliers other than those on the approved list.

By 1980 the corruption in the Health Department attracted sufficient political attention to oblige government action. Between 1980 and 1982 over a hundred doctors were 'charge-sheeted' for buying spurious drugs, indiscipline and negligence but none were actually dismissed. Six doctors and a drug manufacturer were arrested but subsequently released.

HEALTH IN UTTAR PRADESH

In 1982 figures from the Central Bureau of Health Intelligence showed UP to have both the highest fertility and mortality of any state in India. The crude birth rate (for 1980-1?) was 40.4 per thousand and the death rate was 20.2 per thousand (Pioneer, 8 August 1981). In addition, the IMR was 168 per thousand births, compared with 128 in all-India. Though progress in UP has lagged behind that of certain states in India, the postcolonial situation is still much better than that of 1918, when an estimated 3.9 million people died in the United Provinces during the great influenza epidemic which itself killed off two million. By the early 1970s the CDR had fallen to somewhere between 22 and 24, ie. nearly half the rate in 1920. In 1973 the urban rate had fallen to around 13 and the rural rate to around 20. There then appears to be no trend towards reduction in mortality (urban or rural) until the late 1970s, when total CDR fell to 16 in 1979, but the CBHI figure rose to 20 again for 1980-1 (?).

The infant mortality rate in UP continued to be above 150 during the 1970s and showed no clear signs of long-term decline in rural or urban rates. The urban IMR was lower but always 110 or more. The rural rate was always at least 165, actually reached 213 in 1972 and also, like the urban rate, lacked a clear trend. It was still 172 in 1978. There was some but by no means close correlation between the rural and urban rates with an annual average of 65 excess infant deaths per thousand live births in rural areas over urban. The proportion of neonatal deaths in total IMR was the same (54%) in rural areas as in urban, though rural levels were higher. It is perverse that in the year of highest infant mortality, 1972, the neonatal proportion fell to 47 and 46 percent in rural and urban areas respectively. The relative proportion of neonatal deaths may be expected to increase if UP reduces its overall IMR in the future. This fluctuation in the proportion of neonatal deaths was greater in the rural areas and may provide some further support for theories which stress environmental and economic factors in the causation of mortality in UP, ie. neonatal deaths may occur more often in response to genetic and medical than to political economy and sociocultural factors.

TEN MAIN REPORTED CAUSES OF INFANT DEATH, UTTAR PRADESH 1979

REPORTED CAUSE OF DEATH	RURAL UP			RURAL INDIA	URBAN UP		
	M	F	T	T	M	F	T
1. TETANUS	39.5	28.1	30.6	14.2	26.7	19.2	23.2
2. PNEUMONIA	11.0	12.6	11.8	6.4	13.3	13.6	13.4
3. PREMATURITY	8.5	9.2	8.8	8.9	14.0	9.7	7.7
4. DYSENTERY	5.2	8.8	7.1	5.0	6.6	9.7	7.7
5. INFLUENZA	5.1	6.9	6.0	5.1	4.1	8.4	6.1
6. TYPHOID	6.1	3.2	4.6	2.3	3.5	2.5	3.0
7. DIARRHEA	2.6	2.3	2.4	2.9	1.8	6.8	4.2
8. JAUNDICE	1.5	3.1	2.3		-	-	-
9. BRONCHITIS	1.0	3.5	2.3	1.9	3.5	1.4	2.5
10. DIPHTHERIA	2.3	1.9	2.1		2.6	2.9	2.8
11. MALARIA	-	-	-	3.6	0.7	3.6	1.6
12. OTHER RESPIRATORY	-	-	-	6.0	-	-	-
TOTAL REPORTED	82.0	79.6	78.0	56.3	76.7	77.8	76.5
NOT REPORTED	17.2	20.4	22.0	43.7	23.3	22.2	23.5
TOTAL	100	100	100	100	100	100	100

Source: Registrar-General 1983, reproduced in Jain 1988:100-1

The survey of IMR in 1979 showed that 30 percent of rural infant deaths and 23 percent of urban infant deaths were attributed, by non-medical respondents, to tetanus. Another major cause of death is likely to be unclean water supply:

WATER SUPPLY, LOCATION AND INFANT MORTALITY RATE, UTTAR PRADESH 1979

WATER SUPPLY	TAP OR HAND PUMP		WELL, POND, TANK OR RIVER	
LOCATION	URBAN	RURAL	URBAN	RURAL
IMR	95	140	156	182

Jain (1988) refers to Khan's research, showing that piped water and concrete flooring reduced postneonatal mortality in rural UP. Most of the deaths from tetanus are likely to have been neonatal and many may have arisen from cutting the umbilical cord with a dirty sickle or other unsterilised instrument.

Rural infant mortality in 1968 and 1969 was highest in UP, exceeding the total and female rates in the next highest state, Gujarat, by 22 and 28 percent respectively. In 1981 only about 10% of women were vaccinated against tetanus. Jain (1988:34) claims that in UP immunisations against tetanus rose from 0.4 million in 1977-8 to 1.3 million by 1984-5, leading to a dramatic fall in IMR by 14 points between 1984 and 1985. This was a major contributory factor in the national IMR falling from 104 to 95. Average life expectancy in about 1971 was also lowest in UP (41 years) and for women it was only 38 (22 years shorter than in Kerala). In 1980 over 56 percent of male and 66 percent of female deaths occurred in those aged 0 to 4 (Cf. 46% nationally, for both sexes). Under five mortality has declined generally but the reduction was lower for rural females than rural males, for urban than for rural overall, and for total females than for total males. The under 5 mortality rate for all females improved relatively in 1980. Cassen notes that the three states with highest male-female ratios in the 1971 census - Punjab, Rajasthan and Uttar Pradesh, are also the three with highest excess female mortality, as measured by the ratio of female to male deaths at ages 0 to 9 and 15 to 49; and the one state with more females than males (Kerala) has lower female than male mortality (1978a: 148).

The table shows that adults from UP in 1980 were significantly shorter and lighter than adults in Punjab. UP women aged 40 were particularly light, weighing 15 percent less than their Punjabi peers.

AVERAGE HEIGHTS AND WEIGHTS OF ADULTS, UTTAR PRADESH AND PUNJAB 1980

		UTTAR PRADESH		PUNJAB	
	AGE	M	F	M	F
Av. centimetres height	18-40	163.2	152.8	164.6	155.3
Av. centimetres height	40	160.5	150.7	164.8	154.3
Av. kilograms weight	18-40	49.8	43.9	54.8	48.0
Av. kilograms weight	40	47.6	41.5	53.4	49.1

Source: Bardhan 1984:88

On the other hand, Gopalan (1985) suggests that Kerala's nutrition in 1980 was substandard and even, in some respects, inferior to that of UP. Comparison of incidence of low body weight and height among adults in UP and Kerala shows that Kerala had a higher rate of low weight for four out of five age categories whilst UP had a higher proportion of persons with short stature for three of the five age categories.

AGE AND LOW WEIGHT AND HEIGHT, UTTAR PRADESH AND KERALA 1980

	% under 38 kg		% under 145 cm	
Age Category	UP	KERALA	UP	KERALA
No. in sample			(1577)	(1781)
20-24	17	20	22	20
25-29	20	21	25	20
30-34	24	23	22	22
35-39	25	26	25	24
40-44	26	34	26	30

NB: Weights of 38 kg and heights of 145 cm are said to be the thresholds for risk during pregnancy in poorer countries.

Source: NNMB (1980), reproduced in Gopalan (EPW 1985: 164).

Morbidity

UP is the heartland of the Hindu religion, with many pilgrimage centres. One major health problem is raised by the Kumbh Mela (Fair) which is held every 12 years at Hardwar and also the smaller Ardh Kumbh Mela every six years at Allahabad. Such a gathering can attract over 15 million pilgrims and tourists and cholera vaccination is supposed to be compulsory at entry points. In 1981 there were over 11,500 reported cases of gastroenteritis and at least 1,500 of these proved fatal. There were also over 660 cases of cholera that year. The health staff required for such a mela was nearly 300 but not all the posts were usually filled in time.

Government data on the reported cases, deaths and case fatality rates for selected communicable diseases in 1980-2 indicate the very high fatality rates for tetanus, diphtheria and meningococcal infections. There were over half a million reported cases of dysentery in 1982 and no doubt many more unreported. In an investigation in the mid-1980s, the Vigilance Department found that, out of 0.9 million drinking wells, over 0.2 million had not been disinfected twice a month as required, even though funds were disbursed for that purpose. Significantly, the highest number of deaths occurred in these non-disinfected areas.

In Shahjahanpur district over 600 people died of malaria during 1983 (allegedly in only a two week period), compared with only 173 deaths in the rest of India. This provoked a furore in the state Assembly and the Minister of Health ordered suspensions, dismissals and disciplinary action against 100 senior doctors, particularly in the Malaria Department. They were charged with negligence and financial irregularities in the purchase of medicines.

There had been acknowledgement of the existence of a malaria epidemic in Bihar, but the UP Minister of Health chose to deny the existence of one in his state. UP had spent over Rs 400 million on the National Malaria Eradication Programme but still the prevalence was said to have risen by 70 percent in 1983.

A report by the Comptroller Auditor General of India blamed the UP health officials for this resurgence and indicated corruption and failure to spray priority areas of mosquito breeding, where the Annual Parasite Index (API) exceeded two persons per 1,000. Deaths proved to be highest in these neglected areas. In fact the Malaria Department, between 1979 and 1983, had actually concentrated on districts with APIs of less than two, whilst malaria-prone districts were not fully covered by the prescribed three sprayings per year. Some insecticides were sub-standard and an enquiry by the Public Accounts Committee seemed to suggest that the NMEP officials had failed to send suspected samples to Delhi for a second analysis. The enquiries of the Comptroller Auditor General of India and of the Public Accounts Committee showed that, despite a 20 percent rise in NMEP expenditure, the target of three sprayings per year had not been achieved. Again, out of a target of 4 million blood samples in eight malaria-prone districts, only 1.8 million were taken and, for over 70 percent of these, they were examined in a period varying between a week and two months. In 1980-1 over 10 million cases of suspected malaria were treated without any examination of their blood samples. Even though separate malaria dispensaries were opened in all 57 districts, none managed to collect even 50 percent of their target of blood samples. The bulk of the 170,000 positive cases reported between 1980 and 1982 occurred in the richer and only partially sprayed districts of western UP. This regional discrepancy may have been partly due to differences in irrigated area.

The malaria epidemic first struck Shahjahanpur district in August 1983 and in April 1984 rural dispensaries were still receiving over 100 patients each per day. Doctors were found to be absent from duty during the crisis. In Nigohi block doctors were unwilling to go to affected villages because these were knee-deep in flood water. Medicines were out of stock and it was six weeks later, in October, before medical aid, albeit inadequate, was provided. On 30 September 1984 the Chief Medical Officer accompanied the District Magistrate on a tour of the district and an attempt was made to blame the deaths on encephalitis and Japanese encephalitis (which had killed several hundred people in Gorakhpur and Deoria districts in 1978). State officials continued to deny that the deaths were caused by malaria. Over 12,000 positive cases were found in Shahjanpur district and most had not been properly treated. None of the 12 Primary Health Centres had enough anti-malaria medicines. Over 40 percent of village houses had not been sprayed once, never mind the twice prescribed. Despite ample supplies of insecticide, the heavily waterlogged areas had not been sprayed. Nor had any of the wells been disinfected weekly. On 20 December 1983 the UP Health Minister sacked four PHC doctors and suspended the Chief Malaria Officer of the district. Government doctors threatened strikes and dharnas (sit-down demonstrations) and in March 1984 more than six doctors' unions threatened to paralyse the medical services of the state (IT 1984).

Conclusion

This analysis of politics and health in Uttar Pradesh suggests the prime importance of political economy to health in UP: (1) the lower castes and classes are only weakly organised and their interests are inadequately articulated both within and beyond the political party system; (2) policies have been designed to preserve a relatively undisturbed, increasingly precarious and currently interrupted dominance of the Congress (I) and the upper class and caste interests which it mainly represents; (3) parties opposed to Congress (I) have sometimes outbid the latter in their populism and their devotion to the rural sector but such redistribution as has gone to the rural population has been rather indiscriminate in class terms, wasteful and relatively ineffective; (4) redistribution of capital and income has been insufficient to make any very significant contribution to improving either nutrition or health; (5) the subject of health has been low on the political agenda, despite the widespread prevalence of ill-health, probably even among richer inhabitants of UP; (6) mortality has halved since 1920 but it continues to be relatively high, especially in the rural areas, among infants and females of most ages, and particularly when compared with India as a whole; and (7) there are very significant contrasts between the political economy and health status, inter alia, of UP and more progressive states like Kerala.

Partly in consequence, Uttar Pradesh continues to have by far the largest population with such a very low life expectancy on this planet.

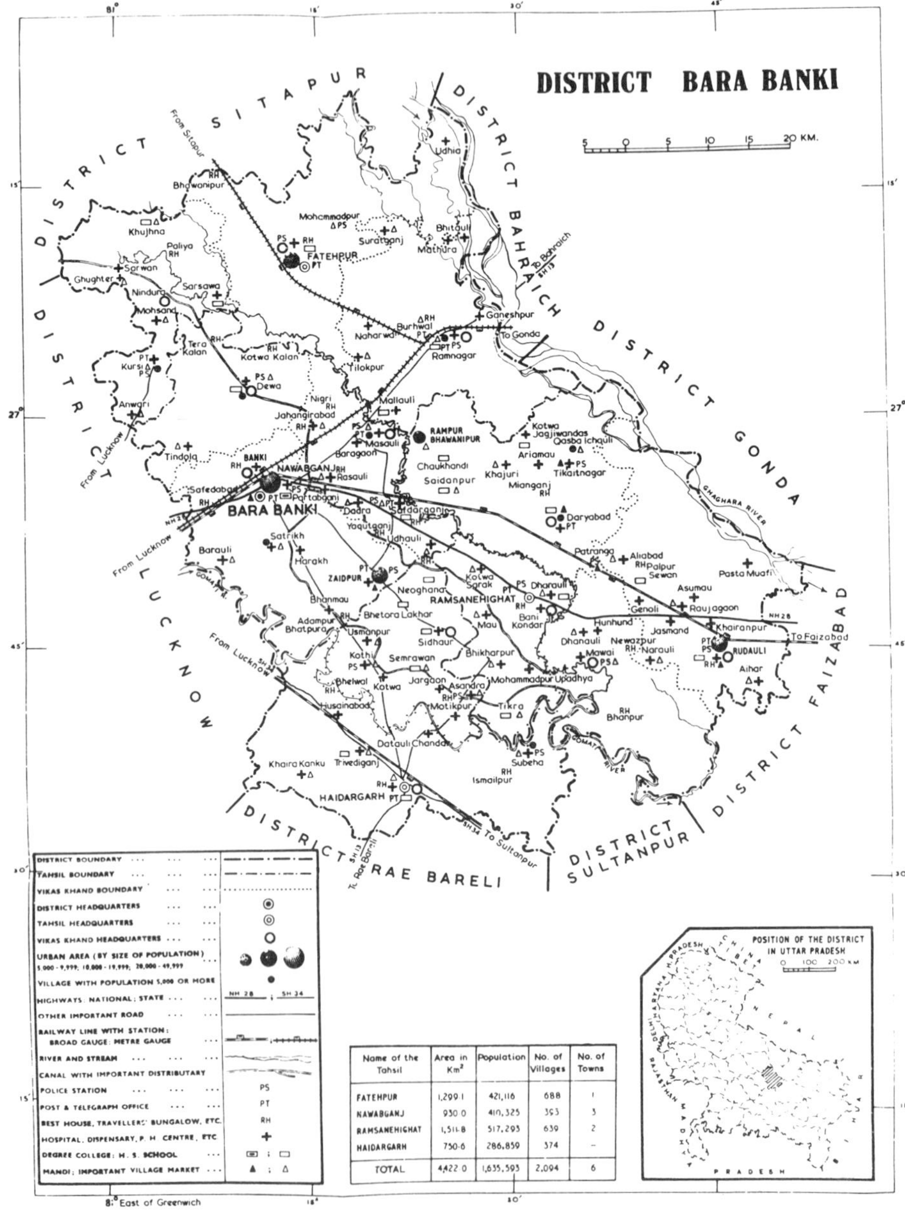

Name of the Tahsil	Area in Km^2	Population	No. of Villages	No. of Towns
FATEHPUR	1,299.1	421,116	688	1
NAWABGANJ	930.0	410,325	393	3
RAMSANEHIGHAT	1,511.8	517,293	639	2
HAIDARGARH	750.6	286,859	374	–
TOTAL	4,422.0	1,635,593	2,094	6

4 A village in Central Uttar Pradesh

It was decided to select Barabanki district for the fieldwork partly because this was adjacent to Lucknow, where the researcher's family stayed for the initial months, and partly because the Institute of Public Administration had close ties with this district. The District Magistrate kindly took the researcher with him on one of his tours of inspection and a village in Suratganj block, in the north-east of the district, was selected. There were several reasons for selecting this village. Firstly, an 'interior' location was desired, where villagers normally had no immediate access to district level medical services. Secondly, the village needed to be within easy cycling distance of a Primary Health Centre so that it could be visited from the village. Thirdly, the village should possess caste and class heterogeneity but not exceed a population of 2,000 persons. Fourthly, it should have an intelligent and sympathetic Pradhan (Chairman) who could understand the purpose of the research. The Medical Officer in Suratganj recommended the village of Basauli, where the village Chairman or Pradhan ('Thakur Sahib') was a prominent politician who spoke English and also had a good sense of humour. The village chosen was Basauli, which is located on the road from Barabanki to Suratganj, with (in 1982) four or five buses daily to Lucknow most of the year (see map).

Apart from its roadside location, Basauli proved much less of an 'interior' village than was initially thought. There are villages in the terai belt to the north of Basauli which are cut off from the main road by one or two medium-sized rivers and also by floods in the rainy season. It would be more accurate to describe Basauli as somewhere which was an interior village until recently, when the road was made pacca and communications to the outside opened up considerably. As an inhabitant of one of the 'true interior' villages of the terai correctly pointed out, in comparison to them, Basauli was a 'qasbah' (market village or small township).

A village in eastern or central UP was preferred to one in western UP because the former are generally considered to be more 'feudal' and less socially developed and so the effect of the social factors on health might be expected to be so much greater in central or eastern districts. On the other hand, it was subsequently found that the range of incomes seemed rather less than in the average village (mainly because the village was so relatively poor) and this narrowness of range of income also adds to the severity of testing of the hypotheses on the relative influence of economic and sociocultural factors on health. In other words, it is possible that the sociocultural factors have been given a greater chance of preponderating over the economic factors by choosing a relatively 'feudal' village with a somewhat narrower income range than may be normal in UP.

The village has one very unusual characteristic, which almost certainly has some relevance to health. The area devoted to village housing is unusually large and the houses are mostly very much more dispersed than is usual. This carries the obvious implication that infectious diseases are much less likely to spread than in a village with a more nucleated and concentrated layout of housing.

Language

The researcher entered the village on 15 November 1981 with some knowledge of Punjabi. This helped him somewhat in communicating with villagers but was not of much assistance in understanding their rapid-fire Avadhi which is the local, now mainly rural, dialect of Hindi spoken in central UP (in what used to be the kingdom of Avadh or Oudh). Interviews were conducted in Avadhi and by the time he left the village on 11 April, he had made some progress. The Pradhan spoke excellent English and, when he was available (which was not very often during the day and by no means invariably even in the evenings) he was able to interpret and explain at length. After leaving the village, the researcher continued learning Hindi and, whilst the research assistant was helping with data analysis in Lucknow from June to March, all conversation was in Hindi, interspersed with a few English words. Much of the more general information on the village was gained during this later period. The village was also visited for eight days in August and for one day in September 1982.

Sources of Data and Sampling

There were seven main sources of data:

1 A general listing of households in the gaon sabha with details of age, sex, marital status, landownership, occupation and infant mortality. This was done in December 1981. The gaon sabha is the 'village assembly' or local government unit which consisted, in this case, of two revenue villages.

2 Interviews of 102 (nearly 40%) of the household heads in the gaon sabha. The sampling fraction was 50% of those with the most and least land and 33% of those of medium landownership. Landownership was at this stage used as a proxy for income. Because of the existence of other income apart from agricultural, this was obviously not entirely satisfactory and the sample selected may not exactly fit the distribution of income categories that was originally desired. The interviews were deliberately completed within the shortest possible time from 21 January to 23 February 1982, with some help from the local research assistant in the later stages. The reason for the haste was that a major section of the schedule was concerned with illness since 1 January 1981 and it was felt desirable to keep the time period as similar as possible for all respondents, both in length and seasons covered. Respondents could have been asked exclusively about illness in 1981 to overcome this problem and to maintain consistency, but it seemed a pity to neglect the current period in early 1982, especially since people would remember this much better and be likely to be most forthcoming and accurate about current illness. However, it does mean that there is a difference of 32 days between the coverage of the first and last interview. This needs to be borne in mind when comparing the length of illness of different households. Each interview lasted from 30 to 90 minutes, depending usually upon the size of the household. Information on a further seven households was collected in December 1981 as part of pilot testing of a series of schedules.

3 Interviews of medical practitioners, traditional and modern, most of whom were used by one or more residents of Basauli. These were conducted in March and early April of 1982.

4 The records of the Primary Health Centre, Suratganj.

5 General observations made whilst the researcher was living in the village, mainly from 15 November 1981 to 11 April 1982. Altogether, the researcher was resident in the village for 100 days.

6 Discussions at length on many topics related to the village, with the research assistant who came from the village to Lucknow and helped on the data analysis and tabulation intermittently from June 1982 to March 1983.

7 The keeping of cuttings from the Lucknow and national English language press.

The Institute of Public Administration provided three successive research assistants who each came from the University of Lucknow for a week's stay in the village and who helped with 'labour peaks', such as the listing of households and the interviewing of doctors. Two claimed never to have stayed overnight in a village before. The Institute also provided funds for the employment of a recent graduate in Political Science, Hindi and Arab Culture from Lucknow University who had lived in the village all his life. He had an intimate knowledge of village affairs. He proved invaluable both as an interviewer, occasional interpreter, data processor and, above all, as a key informant, when writing up in Lucknow. The employment of a local person as research assistant arose mainly because the Institute had no member of staff who was either available or willing to spend long periods in a village. As things turned out, this alternative, fallback arrangement had many advantages and the local recruit proved a careful, discreet and inevitably well-informed assistant. He was recommended originally by the Pradhan as someone who was 'neutral' in village politics and experience proved that he was acceptable to all sections of the village, even though he came from a prominent Thakur family. His use as such a key informant does raise some important issues, including possible bias (intentional or otherwise) and anonymity of sources. Confidentiality has proved much more delicate in the case of the second most important informant, who was Thakur Sahib himself and who forms the main subject of the fifth chapter. The researcher has taken particular care to be as balanced and accurate as is humanly possible and the inclusion of considerable personal and family detail has been justified on the grounds that Thakur Sahib is a public figure, whose private life was much more open than that of the average villager and various aspects of his domestic matters were rather more widely known than in the case of other people in the village.

The Village and its Location

The village of Basauli is in Barabanki district and is situated 66 kilometres north-east of Lucknow, the state capital with a population of more than one million in 1981. Basauli is the name of the larger of two revenue villages within the gaon sabha local government unit, which is also called Basauli. For simplicity, this unit will be usually referred to as 'the village'. It could be reached from Lucknow by car in one and a half hours and by bus in three to four hours. Many buses, leaving from Kaiserbagh bus station, near the old Residency in Lucknow, go through Barabanki (with a population of over 43,000 in 1971 and nearing 62,000 in 1981) on their way to Faizabad and other eastern towns and four or five per day leave the main road and go all the way to Suratganj. The cost of the bus fare varied from seven to eight rupees, depending on whether a change of bus was necessary. The road to Barabanki was becoming increasingly built up and it would not be so long before the full length of this 27 kilometre stretch was a continuous ribbon of development linking Lucknow and Barabanki. In regional planning terms, the contrast between the high investment on the side of the main road and the lack of industry or other investment only a few miles into the interior is very striking. The residential colonies of Lucknow end after six kilometres and, after about 12 kilometres, few cyclists can still be seen commuting to Lucknow. The bus takes a fork from the main Faizabad road and halts at Barabanki bus station, where it is usually invaded by noisy hawkers with peanuts, mint sweets, magazines and pens. The bus then eventually continues and passes some of what little industry there is in Barabanki -an old sugar mill, redolent with the smell of molasses, and the Somaiya Chemical Works, partly financed by French capital. After 12 kilometres the bus stops briefly at Dewa Sharif, where there is a famous Sufi shrine and an important annual fair is held in October which attracts some poets and musicians of national reputation. Dewa is one of the few places of pilgrimage or tourist importance in Barabanki district. After a further 16 kilometres one reaches Fatehpur, designated officially as a Class IV town. The bus then has to negotiate its way through the narrow main bazaar which runs for nearly a kilometre and serves as the only thoroughfare until one day Fatehpur may eventually win its much-needed bypass. There now remain only eleven kilometres to Basauli and, if the particular bus is going no further than Fatehpur, then it is usually possible to take a horse and trap (kharkhara) for a rupee or so. In emergencies, richer villages may even hire a cycle rickshaw and this will cost eight rupees or more. Part of this stretch of the road becomes flooded during the rainy season and may become impassable to vehicles for up to four days each year. This section of the road, between Fatehpur and Ramnagar, was completed only in 1979 and it now enables buses to reach Suratganj. After nine more kilometres, there is a right-hand bend and many people descend to go to Mohammadpur and two other large villages which closely adjoin it. A tea shop and one or two stalls, including the inevitable pan stall, form the embryo of a bazaar here. After two more kilometres the bus passes through the small village of Imlipur, which forms part of Basauli gaon sabha. Imlipur village looks richer than Basauli because there are several brick houses, including the very large, new roadside house of a Lodh. It is now possible to see above the trees the tip of the tall temple in Basauli. The village lies to the right of the road and the nearest, kacha house stands about 60 metres from the road. The bus continues for another four kilometres, terminating on the outskirts of the block headquarters at Suratganj. The first bus from Lucknow leaves about 7 am and the last bus to Lucknow, about 4 pm.

The main impressions gained on such a journey are of much building of cold stores, factories and houses on the roadside as far as Barabanki and very little beyond there and of a sharp decline in the use of brick as distance from Lucknow increases. The crops in the fields remain broadly the same. In January, the wheat fields are illuminated with yellow sarson flowers, since sarson (mustard oil) is usually intercultured with wheat. Otherwise there are the tall, bushy plants of arhar, which produce the commonest form of dal and the even taller plantations of sugarcane. In August, one sees mainly bright green paddy and also sugarcane.

Barabanki District

Barabanki district lies to the east of Lucknow and both districts form part of the zone which is officially designated as Central UP. It is a fairly well-irrigated district, famed for its opium production, and, in terms of net domestic output per capita in 1976-7, it ranked twenty-second out of 56 districts. It is therefore well above average in economic terms but is generally considered to have lagged behind in social development. To some extent, it lies in the 'development shadow' of Lucknow city (which itself has suffered lack of industrial growth at the expense of over-development and serious over-urbanisation in Kanpur, 80 kilometres to the south-west). Barabanki district used to form part of the kingdom of Oudh and has retained some of the 'feudal', social characteristics of that kingdom, even after the abolition of Zamindari. This is not meant to indicate that production is also necessarily 'feudal' or even 'semi-feudal'. (For a discussion on whether the feudal mode of production survives now or even lasted until 1947 in India, see Alavi 1975.) Though nearer to Lucknow, Barabanki district is administered as part of Faizabad Division.

The district had a population of two million in 1981 and 92% of these lived in the rural areas. The district is divided into four tahsils, with their total population ranging from 351,000 to 631,000. Fatehpur tahsil, which includes Suratganj block, had a population of 519,000 in 1981 and only 5% of these lived in Fatehpur, the only urban area in the tahsil. The table shows that the tahsil had broadly similar characteristics to those of the whole district in 1981, except that it had a slightly smaller ratio of urban population (in what is a very unurbanised district), a slightly smaller ratio of agricultural labourers to total main workers and a much higher percentage of main workers employed for less than 183 days in a year.

Barabanki was regarded as one of the more developed districts even when the first district gazetteer was written in 1903. As the figures show, it had a net domestic output per capita slightly above the UP average in 1976-7. This was mainly due to an above average ratio of irrigated land (59%) and to agricultural productivity which moved above the UP average during the 1970s. Industrial development has been below average and in fact 85% of all workers were agricultural in 1981. Furthermore, 59% of total area was cultivated by small farmers, with less than 5 acres. Industrial productivity, in terms of value added per industrial worker, was less than half the state average. Roughly a third of villages were electrified, but consumption of electricity per capita was only 36% of the UP average and 23% of the consumption of neighbouring Lucknow district, with the very high electricity consumption in the state capital. Population density in Barabanki district was high, at 457 persons per square kilometre, in 1981 and this was 21% above the state average.

BARABANKI DISTRICT AND UTTAR PRADESH, 1970-81 PERIOD

	BARABANKI	UP
Rs NET DOMESTIC OUTPUT PC 1976-7	554	520
Rs AGRIC OUTPUT PER ACRE 1970-1	547	562
Rs GROSS OUTPUT VALUE PER HA NET SOWN 1976-7	2,941	2,703
Rs GROSS OUTPUT VALUE PER AGRIC WORKER 1976-7	1,858	2,220
Rs VALUE ADDED PER INDUSTRIAL WORKER 1967-7	4,846	9,857
NET IRRIGATED AS % NET CROPPED 1979-80	59%	45%
PERCENTAGE CROPPING INTENSITY	150%	139%
AREA SMALL AND MARGINAL HOLDINGS AS % TOTAL 1976-7	59%	46%
HA NET SOWN AREA PER CAPITA 1979-80	0.14	0.15
AGRIC WORKERS AS % TOTAL WORKERS 1981	85%	74%
KG FERTILISER PER HECTARE 1980-1	48	47
MANUFACTURING OUTPUT AS % TOTAL NET OUTPUT 1976-7	16%	15%
ELECTRIFIED AS % TOTAL VILLAGES 1981	30%	34%
KW-HOURS ELECTRICITY PER CAPITA 1978-9	32	89
PERSONS PER SQUARE KM 1981	457	377
1981 POPULATION AS % 1971 POPULATION	123%	126%
URBAN AS % TOTAL POPULATION	9%	18%
% VILLAGES WITHIN 3 KM OF ALLOPATHIC HOSPITAL 1978-9	12.9%	12.5%
POPULATION PER HOSPITAL BED 1979-80	5,000	1,961
POPULATION PER HIGHER SECONDARY SCHOOL	47,619	21,277
LITERATES AS PERCENTAGE POPULATION	20%	27%

Small and marginal holdings refer to those under 5 and 2.5 acres respectively.
Source: State Planning Institute, Uttar Pradesh (1982).

BARABANKI DISTRICT AND FATEHPUR TAHSIL 1981

	BARABANKI DISTRICT	FATEHPUR TAHSIL
THOUSAND POPULATION	2,013	519
RURAL AS % OF TOTAL POPULATION	91.2%	95.2%
MALES AS % TOTAL POPULATION	53.8%	54.5%
LITERATES AS % TOTAL POPULATION	19.5%	18.4%
MALE LITERATES AS % TOTAL MALES	29.3%	27.5%
FEMALE LITERATES AS % TOTAL FEMALES	8.2%	7.4%
AGRIC LABOURERS AS % TOTAL MAIN WORKERS	12.1%	9.1%
FEMALE AS % TOTAL AGRIC LABOURERS	26.5%	18.6%
HH INDUSTRY, MANUF., PROCESSING, SERVICES AS % TOTAL MAIN WORKERS	4.6%	4.7%
EMPLOYED LESS THAN 183 DAYS PA ie 'MARGINAL' WORKERS AS % TOTAL MAIN WORKERS	14.8%	37.1%
FEMALE AS % TOTAL MARGINAL WORKERS	57.5%	60.4%

Source: Census of India, 1981, Series 22 Uttar Pradesh Papers of 1981 Supplement. Provisional Population Totals, June 1981: 200-1.

CASTE POPULATION, BARABANKI DISTRICT, CENSUS 1901

CASTE OR CATEGORY		RELIGION	NUMBER	% OF TOTAL
BRAHMIN			85,579	7.3
SEYED		Muslim	7,407	0.6
BHAT		(1,000+ M) H (+M)	5,000+	0.4+
MUGHAL		Muslim	1,000+	0.1
SHEIKH		Muslim	34,225	2.9
THAKUR (43 'TRIBES')			41,210	3.5
Amethia			(3,989)	
Bais			(11,962)	(1.0)
Raikwar			(2,518)	
Surajbansi			(3,163)	
Panwar			(1,895)	
Chauhan			(2,893)	
Bisen			(1,663)	
Kalhans			(1,222)	
THAKUR		Muslim	6,958	0.6
BANIA			14,598	1.2
KAYASTH			13,000+	1.1
SONAR	Goldsmith		5,000+	0.4
KURMI			162,370	13.8
MURAO	Market gardener		21,455	1.8
AHIR			139,814	11.9
LODH			36,878	3.1
KORI	Farmer - Weaver		24,606	2.1
KALWAR			5,000+	0.4
FAQIR		Hindu	5,000+	0.4
FAQIR		Muslim	11,829	1.0
PATHAN		Muslim	12,622	10.7
KAHAR	Water-carrier		22,554	1.9
MALI				
BELWAR	Grain-dealer and farmer			
KUMHAR	Potter	(1,000+ M) M and H	2,000+	0.2
BARHAI	Carpenter			
LOHAR	Smith		5,000+	0.4
DHOBI	Washerman	Muslim + H	2,000+	0.2
DARZI		Muslim	6,768	0.6
QASSAB	Butcher	Muslim	2,000+	0.2
MANIHAR	Bangle maker	Muslim	2,000+	0.2
HALWAI	Sweet maker	Muslim	6,297	0.5
NAI	Barber	Muslim	11,686+	1.0
JULAHA	Weaver	Muslim	31,448	2.7
TELI	Oilpresser	Muslim	11,246+	1.0
DAFALI		Muslim	1,000+	0.1
TAWAIF		Muslim	1,000+	0.1
BHARBHUNJA		(1,000+) M and H	1,000+	0.1
MALLAH	Boatman			
KABARIA	Market gardener		182	<0.1
GUJAR		Muslim	2,000+	0.2
GADDI			1,000+	0.1
NAU-MUSLIM		Muslim	1,000+	0.1
KUNJRAS		Muslim	9,300	0.8
CHAMAR			91,967	7.8
PASI			134,736	11.4
DOM				
BANSPHOR	Bamboo worker		4,316	0.4
TAMBOLI				
DALERA	Basket maker itinerant			
Vaishnavite		Hindu		8.9
Sunni		Muslim		97.6
Shia		Muslim		2.2
HINDU			978,604	83.0
MUSLIM			199,474	16.9
JAIN			972	0.1
OTHERS			273	<0.1
TOTAL (49 out of about 76+ castes)			1,179,323	100.0
HIGH CASTE				18.1
MEDIUM CASTE				55.6
SCHEDULED				19.6

Barabanki district was represented by two Members of Parliament (one of whose constituency overlaps into Bahraich district) and six Members of the Legislative Assembly. One of the MPs was Congress (I) and the allegiance of the other, whose constituency includes Barabanki town, was not ascertained. Four of the Members of the Legislative Assembly (MLAs) were Congress (I) and included one Brahmin, two Thakurs and one Muslim. The remaining two MLAs were both members of the Lok Dal (People's Party). One was a woman from the Yadav caste and the other was a Pasi, a member of a scheduled caste. He was elected for Fatehpur constituency, which is reserved for a scheduled member. Congress (I) may be said to have been dominant without holding a monopoly of power in the district. (In the state elections of March 1985 Congress (I) lost three of its seats in Barabanki district.) No other party except the Lok Dal had much influence in the district and there was little sign of either socialist or communist parties. Broadly, the Congress (I) party has been dominated alternately by either Brahmins or Thakurs but currently was said to be more under the influence of Thakurs. (The MLA for Ramnagar constituency, which includes both Ramnagar and Suratganj blocks, was a Thakur.) The Congress (I) was also supported by a majority of Muslims and the scheduled castes. The Lok Dal was supported by important 'backward' castes, such as the Yadavs and Kurmis, (respectively 12% and almost 14% of population in 1901). The political affiliation of the Lodhs, another fairly numerous caste (3%), appeared to be less clear cut.

Fatehpur (with a population of 12,601 in 1971) is the headquarters for the tahsil in which Basauli is located. By 1981 it had a population of over 17,000, a large bazaar of at least 250 shops and a weaving industry which produces Kaleens (cotton mats laid on charpoys in winter) and darris (carpets and rugs). The majority of workers are Muslim Julahas and in fact Muslims form a very much higher proportion (58% in 1971) of the urban and semi-urban population than they do in most of the villages or even in Barabanki town (36% in 1971). Fatehpur has very little other industry, though a small sodium silicate factory was opened in May 1981. The town has an inter-college which provides education up to intermediate (12th class) level for about a thousand boys but no girls. Its principal was a Thakur who had quite close links with the Pradhan of Basauli. Four boys from Basauli were attending the college in 1982, including one temporary resident. There is a Primary Health Centre (PHC) with two doctors in post, and a large number of private doctors, including six with an MBBS qualification. There was at least one lady doctor, with some training but no MBBS.

From Basauli, Suratganj is the nearest qasbah or large market village and it is situated four kilometres to the east. The population in 1971 was 2,636 persons, most of whom were farmers and with a large Muslim minority. There were at least 70 small shops run mainly by Banias, and a market is held on Mondays and Fridays. The government has built an extensive complex of offices and residential quarters for the staff of the block headquarters and this is located on the eastern outskirts of the settlement. The campus of the block headquarters includes the office of the Block Development Officer (BDO), the various buildings for the Primary Health Centre, a sawmill and industrial unit for producing 'Dunlop' oxcarts, so named because of their inflatable tyres. However, about half the buildings consist of residential quarters for the staff of the block. The PHC had effectively one Medical Officer (MO) in post but there was establishment for three. A Thakur MBBS was appointed in 1980 but he was a 'royal man' who had good connections with the Health Directorate and rarely attended. There were at least six unqualified practitioners in Suratganj. There were eight or nine schools but none taught beyond high school (10th class) level. There was a police post (chauki) and two policemen.

The most senior officer of the block is the BDO and he is supported by eight Assistant Development Officers (ADOs), including those for agriculture, cooperatives, plant protection, panchayats and minor irrigation. The BDO was a Shukla Brahmin, aged 45 years, and not considered to be as interested in development as in maintaining good relations with the local (Thakur) MLA and other powers. As a Brahmin, this was difficult. He occasionally visited the Pradhan of Basauli and, as often happens, was able to mix official and personal work. For example, in mid-December 1981 he visited the Pradhan on his scooter and discussed the supply of labour for a kacha road and also a possible candidate

SURATGANJ BLOCK, 1980 and 1981

	1980	1981
HOUSES	19,437	20,184
TARGET COUPLES	20,503	20,080
POPULATION PER HOUSE	5.36	5.85
TOTAL POPULATION	104,182	118,076
HAMLETS	355	354
REVENUE VILLAGES	140	186
GRAM SABHAS	132	124
NYAYA PANCHAYATS	12	12
MARKETS	5	8
POST OFFICES		8
PRIMARY SCHOOLS	84	86
JUNIOR HIGH SCHOOLS	5	5
DRINKING WELLS	1,517	1,537
COMMUNITY HEALTH VOLUNTEERS		117
ALLOPATHIC DISPENSARIES	2	2
AYURVEDIC DISPENSARIES	2	2
VETERINARY HOSPITAL	1	1

Source: PHC, Suratganj, records.

as groom for the Pradhan's daughter. A new Veterinary Officer had arrived in the block and it was thought that his younger brother might be a suitable person. The BDO had an MA in Hindi, probably from Lucknow University. It was said that he was not very 'development-minded' and one pradhan contrasted him with the three previous incumbents, who had all been 'educated men, of some learning, good field workers and men with excellent connections'. The first was a Kayastha, the second a Muslim and the third a Shukla Brahmin (like the current BDO).

The table shows that the population of Suratganj block in 1981 was over 118,000. (The figures from the PHC show an increase of over 14,000 from 1980 and this remains unexplained.) The average population per household in 1981 was 5.85 persons. The population was distributed over 124 gram sabhas and the average gram (or gaon) sabha consisted of 1.5 revenue villages or 2.85 villages and hamlets. The average population of a gram sabha was 952 persons and the average number of recorded drinking wells per gram sabha was roughly 12 (up to 79 persons per well). Less than half the revenue villages contained primary schools and there were five junior high schools (to 8th class) in the block. Medical facilities registered by the MO included two allopathic and two ayurvedic dispensaries and nearly every gram sabha also had a Community Health Volunteer (CHV).

One of the most important places within the block is Mohammadpur, which really consists of three fairly large revenue villages and separate gram sabhas which form a single, moreorless continuous settlement. The British built a large police station (thana) to the west at Mohammadpur in 1908 and at that time Mohammadpur was presumably more important than Suratganj. The area covered by the thana is actually not congruent with block boundaries which is a nuisance, in planning terms, as the thana and block headquarters are separated, if only by five kilometres. Mohammadpur is only one kilometre from the main settlement in Basauli and it is visited for its shops, twice weekly market and also for the medical services of six unqualified practitioners. The thana staff consisted of 20 policemen, including a Station Officer (SO), a Sub-Inspector, two Assistant Sub-Inspectors and 16 constables. The SO was thought to be of Bhurji (ie. 'backward') caste and was not on good terms with the Pradhan of Basauli. He was replaced by a Thakur in late 1982, in a routine transfer.

The Landlord Class

There were two Rajas who used to live within ten kilometres of Basauli. The more important was the Raja of Mahmoodabad whose estate lay mainly in Sitapur district, to the north. He was a Shia Muslim, whilst the remaining one, who still lives at Ramnagar, is a Raikwar Thakur. The latter's estate has mainly been dispersed and in the old days he had a palatial two-storeyed residence at Suratganj, the substantial ruins of which still stand. The Raja of Ramnagar was more important for Basauli.

The landlord class in Ramnagar and Suratganj blocks consisted mainly of Thakurs and Brahmins, though the landownership and power of Kurmis had also been increasing. In some areas there were three-cornered fights between these three major castes of Barabanki district. Only the two most prosperous landlords could afford jeeps but between 100 and 200 had motorcycles or, less prestigiously, scooters. Even if a landlord could afford Rs 80,000 or more for a new car or jeep, the cost of petrol (Rs 6.50 per litre) was too high for most of them. (Since the rate of exchange in December 1982 was about Rs 15.50 per pound sterling, the price of petrol was similar to that of the UK but, relative to incomes, much dearer, of course.). Landlords' sons and especially those who were pursuing higher studies of some kind, were particularly fond of motorcycles and, driven in a fearless Thakur manner, these had become a new health risk in the locality. In February 1982 there were 23 Thakur Pradhans out of a total of 118 sitting Pradhans in Suratganj block. These Pradhans were usually interested in finding out how 'Thakur-minded' a particular district officer might be and in maintaining Thakurwadi or 'Thakurism'.

The Member of the Legislative Assembly for the constituency which embraces Ramnagar and Suratganj blocks, was GS Chandel, a Thakur landlord who lived in Ramnagar block and owned at least 250 kacha bighas (50 acres) of land. The Pradhan of Basauli said that he enjoyed only lukewarm relations with his MLA and, among other things, he was not very grateful for the MLA 'poking his nose' into his local affairs and securing the appointment of several of his men to the posts of chairmen of various cooperative associations. In the pending election for Block Pramukh (Chairman), the MLA was reported to be 'in a quandary' since he was trying to please both the Pradhan and another Thakur, who was said to be threatening to join the contest and who would split the Thakur vote.

The Pradhan claimed that the MLA had more trouble with the Ramnagar half of his constituency, which is Thakur-dominated, than he did with Suratganj, which used to be dominated by Kurmis. Nowadays the contest for power in the block had become more of a three-cornered fight (Thakur, Brahmin and Kurmi), with the Thakurs allegedly coming into the ascendency. The Pradhan found the MLA 'reasonably active as MLAs go', and he approved of his habit of living part of the time in his village and of his ability to keep contact with the rural people. He strongly disapproved of the kind of MLA who remained in the town, except on election day.

In mid-February, the Pradhan was invited to the MLA's village to attend a chhedana marriage ceremony for GS's son. However, the Pradhan said that the main purpose of the gathering was political and there would be various political figures there, including the District Magistrate and possibly one or two ministers from the state council of ministers. GS was said to speak very little English. The Pradhan planned to travel there on the back of a Thakur friend's scooter, though he disliked travelling on both motorcycles and scooters.

In the election of 1980, GS was opposed by an Awasthi Brahmin, who came from an 'interior village', near the Ghagra river and who had become very rich in Lucknow. He was now the most powerful person in Suratganj block but, even after a rumoured expenditure of Rs 40,000 on the election, he was unsuccessful in defeating GS in the constituency as a whole.

Basauli Gaon Sabha

Basauli Gaon Sabha consists of two revenue villages, Basauli and Imlipur, with a total of about 1,015 acres, at least half of which was irrigable. Imlipur is a smaller settlement, and includes numerous richer villagers, especially Kurmis, who have built brick houses. The second richest settlement was the core of Basauli, which is itself divided into two parts (tolas), which were sometimes loosely referred to as mohallas. The western mohalla was dominated by the Thakur Pradhan and, apart from one Dube Brahmin household, most of this mohalla were from Sudra castes. The main castes in the eastern mohalla were Brahmin, Mahabrahmin, Thakur and Chamar. The third richest settlement was Kiratpur hamlet which is about half a kilometre to the east of the core settlement. Kiratpur immediately adjoins Burhanapur, another (almost twin) hamlet which forms part of the neighbouring revenue village and gaon sabha of Karanpur. Only a cart track separates these two hamlets with similar caste composition and there was said to be some kin relationships between the two populations. Finally, there is a small hamlet (called Purwa or hamlet) on the north side of the road. The inhabitants of Purwa were mostly of lower middle and scheduled castes and it was visibly the poorest part of the gaon sabha.

A general listing and census of all households in the gaon sabha was conducted in December 1981 and this revealed a population of 1,425 persons

The number of households emerged as 263 and the average size was 5.42 persons. Household was defined in terms of those who shared the same cooking facilities and it needs to be stressed that this is only one of several criteria which may be used to determine household composition. In addition, it should be mentioned that the information was not always collected from door to door, mainly because of time shortage, and key informants had to be used for several localities. There is, therefore, likely to be some degree of error, apart from already known gaps in information.

BASAULI GAON SAB

	POND	CH	CHAMAR	PA	PATHAN
O	DRINKING WELL	DH	DHOBE	PATH	PATHARKOT
H	HANDPUMP (15)	K	KURMI	RA	RADHIKA
	DOOR FROM HOUSE OR YARD	KAB	KABARIA	SH	SHUKLA BRAHMIN
	PACCA HOUSE	LOH	LOHAR	T	TELI
A	AHIR	LON	LONIYA		
B	BHURJI	MAH	MAHABRAHMIN		
BA	BASPHOD	P	PASI		

TO MOHAMMADPUR VILLAGE & THANA

6 KABARIA HOUSES + WELL

R H LODH

TO FATEHPUR

LODH MISRA

LODH

PASI

P P K

H K

WOOD

KABARIA

LODH

R. LODH

LODH

LODH MISRA

K KURMI

H H H

MISRA K

BANIA

1·5 Kilometres

Bholapur (Grove)

KURMI

Imlipur

DUBE PRIEST

Foreshortened Scale (c 150 metres)

AHIR

LODH H

DHOBE

H

NAI

CK

LODH

LOH

KAHAR

LOH

LOHAR

PATHARKOT

GOVT. WELL

KAB BA

DHOBE DH

DH

PATH

RADHIKA

RA

TS EX-ZAMIND

PRADI

H

BAIS THAKUR

Wester

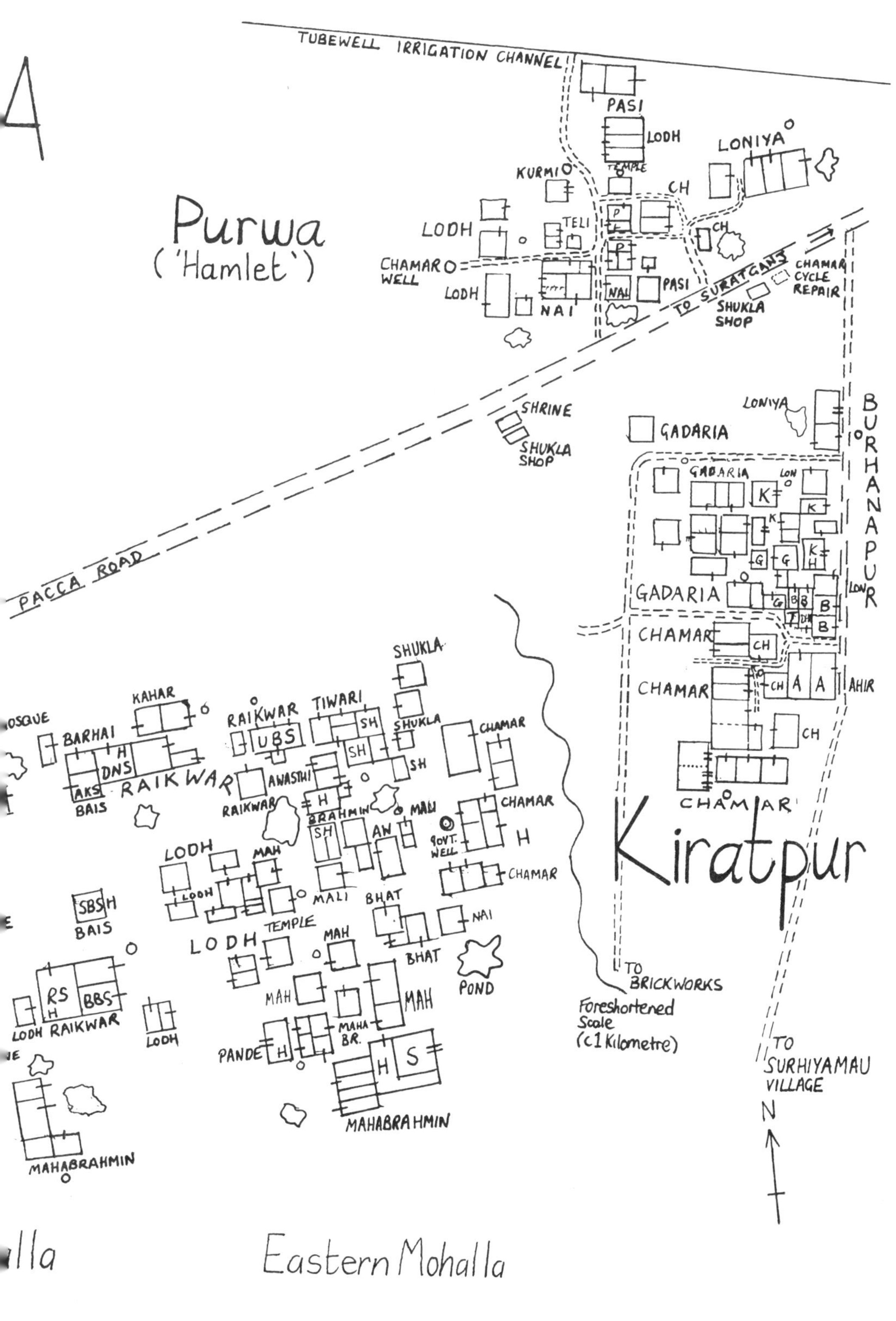
TUBEWELL IRRIGATION CHANNEL
Purwa
('Hamlet')
PASI
LODH
LONIYA
TEMPLE
KURMI
CH
LODH
TELI
CHAMAR WELL
LODH
NAI
PASI
TO SURATGANJ
CHAMAR CYCLE REPAIR
SHUKLA SHOP
SHRINE
SHUKLA SHOP
PACCA ROAD
LONIYA
GADARIA
BURHANAPUR
GADARIA
GADARIA
CHAMAR
CHAMAR
AHIR
CHAMAR
Kiratpur
TO BRICKWORKS
Foreshortened Scale (c1 Kilometre)
TO SURHIYAMAU VILLAGE
N
SHUKLA
KAHAR
RAIKWAR
TIWARI
SHUKLA
CHAMAR
BARHAI
RAIKWAR
AWASTHI
BRAHMIN
MALI
CHAMAR
BAIS
RAIKWAR
GOVT. WELL
LODH
MAH
CHAMAR
MALI
BHAT
NAI
SBS
BAIS
TEMPLE
LODH
MAH
BHAT
POND
RAIKWAR
LODH
MAH
MAH
MAHA BR.
PANDE
MAHABRAHMIN
MAHABRAHMIN
Eastern Mohalla

CASTE AND POPULATION, BASAULI GAON SABHA DECEMBER 1981

CASTE	SUBCASTE	PERSONS	HHS	PERSONS PER HH	MUSLIM	TRADITIONAL OCCUPATION	% OF TOTAL PERSONS
Upper Castes							
BRAHMIN	Shukla	40	8	5.0		Priest	2.8
	Awasthi	18	6	3.0			1.3
	Misra	47	9	5.2			3.3
	Tiwari	12	3	4.0			0.8
	Dwivedi	6	1	6.0			0.4
	Pande	8	1	8.0			0.6
BRAHMIN	TOTAL	(138)	(28)	(4.7)		Priest	9.2
MAHABRAHMIN	Misra	88	11	8.0		Funeral Priest	6.2
	Pande	26	5	5.2			1.8
MAHABRAHMIN	TOTAL	(114)	(16)	(7.1)		Funeral Priest	8.0
THAKUR	Bais	21	3	7.0		Warrior	1.5
	Raikwar	58	10	5.8			4.1
THAKUR	TOTAL	(79)	(13)	(6.6)			5.5
'PUNJABI'		10	1	10.0			0.7
Middle Castes							
BHAT		17	3	5.7			1.2
BANIA		1	1	1.0		Trader	
PATHAN		103	17	6.1	M		7.2
KURMI (VERMA)		115	18	6.4			8.1
AHIR (YADAV)		54	8	6.8		Herdsman	3.8
LODH		199	34	5.8			14.0
MALI		12	3	4.0		Gardener	0.8
BARHAI		11	2	5.5		Carpenter	0.8
LOHAR		18	3	6.0		Blacksmith	1.3
KAHAR		17	3	5.7		Water-carrier	1.2
DHOBE		35	7	5.0	M	Washerman	2.5
NAI		23	5	4.6	M	Barber	1.6
BHURJI		24	4	6.0	M + H	Grain-parcher	1.7
TELI		12	3	4.0	M	Oilpresser	0.8
GADARIA		71	17	4.2		Shepherd	5.0
LONIYA		58	12	4.8			4.1
KABARIA		29	8	3.6	M	Vegetable seller	2.0

CASTE AND POPULATION, BASAULI GAON SABHA DECEMBER 1981 (continued)

CASTE	SUBCASTE	PERSONS	HHS	PERSONS PER HH	MUSLIM	TRADITIONAL OCCUPATION	% OF TOTAL PERSONS
Scheduled Castes							
CHAMAR		131	27	4.8		Leather worker	9.2
PASI		73	13	5.6			5.1
BASPHOD		5	1	5.0			0.4
Scheduled 'Tribes'							
PATHARKOT		28	4	7.0		Stonecutter	2.0
RADHIKA		55	12	4.5			3.9
HIGH CASTE		334	58	5.76			23.4
MIDDLE CASTE		799	148	5.40			56.1
SCHEDULED CASTE		292	57	5.12			20.5
TOTAL		1425	263	5.42	220		100.0

Household listing done in December 1981.

M and H indicate that there are both Muslims and Hindus in the Bhurji caste.

There were approximately 220 Muslims or 15.5% of total persons present, ie. similar to the ratio for the UP.

The ratios of scheduled castes and scheduled tribes to total UP population in 1981 were 21.2% and 0.21% respectively. The ratios in Barabanki district were 27.7% scheduled caste and only 162 members of scheduled tribes, ie. a negligible percentage. Since part of the scheduled tribe population has always been itinerant, though less so now, the percentages in particular districts and even the total proportion in UP are open to question.

CASTE, POPULATION AND SETTLEMENT, BASAULI GAON SABHA 1981

CASTE	WEST BASAULI	EAST BASAULI	MAIN BASAULI	KIRAT-PUR	PURWA	TOTAL BASAULI	HHS BASAULI	IMLI-PUR	HHS IMLIPUR	BASAULI G S	TOTAL HHS
SHUKLA		40	40			40	8			40	8
MISRA								47	9	47	9
AWASTHI		18	18			18	6			18	6
TIWARI		12	12			12	3			12	3
DUBE	6		6			6	1			6	1
PANDE		8	8			8	1			8	1
BRAHMIN TOTAL	(6)	(78)	(84)			(84)	(19)	(47)	(9)	(131)	(28)
MISRA MAHABR		88	88			88	11			88	11
PANDE MAHABR		26	26			26	5			26	5
THAKUR	10	69	79			79	13			79	13
PUNJABI		10	10			10	1			10	1
BHAT		17	17			17	3			17	3
BANIA								1	1	1	1
PATHAN	103		103			103	17			103	17
KURMI				35	1	36	7	79	11	115	18
AHIR	49		49	5		54	8			54	8
LODH	39	42	81		34	115	21	84	13	199	34
MALI		12	12			12	3			12	3
BARHAI		11	11			11	2			11	2
LOHAR	18		18			18	3			18	3
KAHAR	12	5	17			17	3			17	3
DHOBE	32		32	3		35	7			35	7
NAI	3	3	6		17	23	5			23	5
BHURJI				24		24	4			24	4
TELI				4	8	12	3			12	3
GADARIA				71		71	17			71	17
LONIYA				38	20	58	12			58	12
KABARIA	2		2			2	1	27	7	29	8
CHAMAR		58	58	60	13	131	27			131	27
PASI					42	42	6	31	7	73	13
BASPHOD	5		5			5	1			5	1
PATHARKOT	28		28			28	4			28	4
RADHIKA	55		55			55	12			55	12
TOTAL PERSONS	362	419	781	240	135	1156	215	269	48	1425	263
NO HHS	62	76	138	53	24	215	215		48		263
AV PERSON PER HH	5.84	5.51	5.66	4.53	5.62	5.38		5.60		5.42	
HIGH	16	271	287			287	49	47	9	334	58
MEDIUM	258	90	348	180	80	608	116	191	32	799	148
SCHEDULED	88	58	146	60	55	261	50	31	7	292	57

AGE AND SEX, 102 SAMPLE HOUSEHOLDS, BASAULI GAON SABHA 1982

AGE	MALE	FEMALE	TOTAL	MALE AS % TOTAL ALL AGES	FEMALE AS % TOTAL ALL AGES	% TOTAL	MALE AS % TOTAL IN AGE COHORT
0 - 5	41	43	84	7.1	7.5	14.6	48.8
6 - 10	44	43	87	7.6	7.5	15.1	50.6
11 - 15	45	29	74	7.8	5.0	12.8	60.8
16 - 20	31	25	56	5.3	4.3	9.7	55.4
21 - 30	51	48	99	8.8	8.3	17.2	51.2
31 - 40	35	32	67	6.1	5.5	11.6	52.2
41 - 50	20	13	33	3.5	2.3	5.7	60.6
51 - 60	22	17	39	3.8	2.9	6.8	56.4
61+	19	19	38	3.3	3.3	6.6	50.0
TOTAL	308	269	577	53.4	46.6	100.0	53.3

Source: Income and Health Survey, January-February 1982

SEX AND STATUS IN HOUSEHOLD, 102 HOUSEHOLDS

	MALE	FEMALE	TOTAL
HOUSEHOLD HEAD	95	7	102
HOUSEHOLD HEAD'S WIFE	-	78	78
OTHER ADULTS	83	69	152
CHILDREN (0 - 15)	130	115	245
TOTAL	308	269	577
AV. PER HOUSEHOLD	3.02	2.64	5.66

Clearly, definition of household affects the sample frame and ultimate choice of sample whilst allocation of persons to household affects the calculation of the level of per capita income within the household. The 1971 census of Basauli revenue village indicated only 197 households and a total population of 979 persons. This implies an average household size of only 4.97 persons. The ratio of males was 56.7 percent, higher than in two other nearby villages, Baraiya and Suratganj. Assuming that the village population had grown at the same rate as that of UP, ie. 26 percent during the decade, the Basauli population in 1981 would be 1,234 persons. The household listing of December 1981 shows a somewhat smaller total, 1,156 persons in 215 households, which indicates a decennial growth of 18.1 percent.

There were 577 persons living in the 102 sample households, or an average of 5.66 persons per household. Over 42 percent of the sample population was aged under 16, including 14.6 percent aged five or less. The numbers aged 0 to 5 and 6 to 10 were more or less equal and this suggests either higher child mortality or reduced fertility in the last five years. The latter is perhaps the more likely.

Whereas children under 10 comprised nearly 30 percent of the population, those aged 11 to 15 formed only 12.8 percent and this does suggest a higher child mortality in the past (or, less likely, a lower fertility rate). The 16 to 20 cohort was even smaller (9.7%) and might seem to suggest a similar pattern of higher mortality. However, by this age, considerable out-migration of females occurs (as indeed it does to a lesser extent even from the 11 to 15 cohort) and so changes in mortality and/or fertility can only explain part of the story. However, one would expect an equivalent number marrying in. Those in their twenties were roughly in the same proportion as for late teens, but there is a sharp drop in the proportion of those in their thirties and sharper still for the forties and, for some odd reason, slightly less so for the fifties. Only 6.6 percent were aged 61 or more, compared with 12 percent or more in developed countries. In terms of sex balance, males amounted to 53.3 percent of the sample. The greatest imbalances were in the 11 to 15 and 41 to 50 age categories, where males predominated (nearly 61 percent in each case). Males comprised over 55 percent of the 16 to 20 year olds and over 56 percent of the 51 to 60 year olds. This suggests a higher female mortality in infancy and/or childhood among those born up to about 1971 and also possibly a higher female mortality in the childbearing ages for those women who have reached the age of 40 and above.

Of the adults, 95 were male household heads and seven were female household heads since their husbands had died and their sons were minors. Seventy-eight women were wives of household heads and there were also 83 other male adults and 69 other female adults. Comparison of the age and sex structure of the sample population in Basauli with that in the total population of Palanpur in 1974-5 shows considerable similarity (Bliss and Stern 1982:16).

There were 26 castes and comparable groups in the village, such as the two scheduled tribes represented. Certain upper castes were divided into subcastes and these included Brahmins (with six subcastes), Mahabrahmins (2), and Thakurs (2). The castes have been organised into three strata according to their varna status and/or social ranking in the village. Four castes are defined as 'high', though the case of the 'Punjabis' is far from clear cut. They were Punjabi Sikhs who had migrated recently to Basauli. When asked their caste, they quite seriously replied 'Thakur', which prompted smiles from the research assistant, himself a Thakur. There is not much difficulty in assigning 17 castes to the middle (and most numerous) stratum, though some may question the omission of Bhat and Bania from the high category. Finally, three castes and two tribes comprise the scheduled category.

The table shows that the village consisted of 23.4 percent high caste, 56.1 percent middle caste (including 15.5% Muslim) and 20.5 percent scheduled caste and tribes. The most important castes, in terms of numbers, were Lodh (14.0 percent of the total), Brahmin and Chamar (both 9.2%), Kurmi (8.1%), Mahabrahmin (8.0%), Pathan (7.3%), Thakur (5.6%) and Pasi (5.1%). Household size increased with rise in caste stratum. The average household size was only 5.12 in the lowest (scheduled) category and increased to 5.40 and 5.76 in the middle and high castes respectively. The number of children born per mother increased with level of caste stratum and it is also likely that higher caste households are more able to afford to incorporate older dependents. In addition, people from the higher castes have been more successful in obtaining service and other jobs outside the village and so the household data understated the actual difference in family size. Six groups had an average household size of seven or more and these were Punjabi (10.0), Pande Brahmin (8.0), Mahabrahmin (7.1), Bais Thakur and Patharkot (each 7.0). Four of the six groups with large households belonged to the high caste category. The largest household consisted of 26 Mahabrahmins where the families of three brothers lived together jointly. Two other households of middle caste contained 17 persons each.

Comparison of Basauli with Chinaura village in Lucknow district shows that in the latter there was a negligible proportion of high caste people and 35 percent were from the scheduled castes (Cf. 21% in Basauli). The average household size was 5.56 persons (only slightly higher than in Basauli) and there was no appreciable difference between middle and scheduled castes. The largest groups were Muslim (32% of the total population), Pasi (19%), Ahir and Chamar (both 12%) and Lodh (8%). The largest landowning castes were the Ahirs (26 percent of total land owned), Lodhs (15%) and Pasis (16%). Literacy differences in Chinaura were considerable, with 30 percent literacy among medium castes and only 3 percent among scheduled castes. A much higher proportion of medium caste households had a regular milk supply and, in the case of the Ahirs, it was 100 percent.

In Senapur village of Jaunpur district, which has been studied by numerous researchers as part of a long-term project organised by Cornell University, the dominant caste was Thakur and the members were descended from a Zamindar who had ruled 26 villages and who still owned 108 acres in other villages, even in 1955. Within their own village, Thakurs, forming less than 25 percent of the total population, owned 70 percent of the land and most of the trees, wells and animals. They were the best educated group and had the most people working outside the village in government, business and industry (Hopper 1957). Simon, in a re-study of Senapur, found that the most numerous castes were Chamar (34%), Thakur (20%), Noniya (12%), Brahmin and Ahir (9% each) and Lohar (4%). Other castes represented in the village included Kahar, Teli, Hela, Kalvar and Dhobe.

MAIN CHARACTERISTICS OF CASTES, BASAULI GAON SABHA

CASTE	NO. OF ELECTORS 1979	POPN AS % TOTAL	AVERAGE BIGHAS PER PERSON	AVERAGE IRRIG BIGHAS PER PERSON	AVERAGE YEARS SCHOOL HHH	PAID LABOUR AS % TOTAL INCOME	LAGAN AS % TOTAL PAID BY KNOWN RESIDENT OWNERS	% HHS SUPPORT PRADHAN
SHUKLA	25	2.8	1.09	0.40	3.4	-	1.1	43
AWASTHI	17	1.3	2.67	0.22	-	9	0.9	-
MISRA	18	3.3	1.04	0.77	0.6	22	0.8	-
TIWARI	NA	0.8	0.88	-	1.3	59	0.8	33
DUBE	4	0.4	3.33	1.33	4.0	-	0.9	NK
PANDE	NA	0.6	5.00	1.50	12.0	-	1.5	-
TOTAL BRAHMIN	(69)	(9.2)	(1.61)	(0.58)		20	(6.0)	15
MISRA		6.2	3.18	1.75	2.9	3	6.5	-
PANDE		1.8	3.15	1.35	0.7	18	1.9	40
TOTAL MAHABRAHMIN	53	(8.0)	(3.17)	(1.67)		4	(8.4)	12
BAIS	15	1.5	7.19	5.29	8.7	-		100
RAIKWAR	32	4.1	6.29	5.00	7.7	-		30
TOTAL THAKUR	(47)	(5.6)	(6.53)	(5.08)		-	23.9	46
PUNJABI	(5)	0.7	13.00	13.00	NK	-	3.4	NR
BHAT	7	1.2	1.29	-	2.3	-	0.4	-
BANIA	(1)	*	6.00	-	5.0	-	0.2	NV
PATHAN	60	7.2	1.15	0.64	-	21	5.3	100
KURMI	55	8.1	4.51	4.25	3.6	2	12.0	24
AHIR	15	3.4	2.78	-	1.6	10	1.6	-
LODH	123	14.0	1.89	1.25	1.1	13	12.2	41
MALI	7	0.8	0.83	-	-	80	0.2	33
BARHAI	2	0.8	0.64	0.18	-		0.2	-
LOHAR	10	1.3	1.17	0.61	-		0.7	33
KAHAR	9	1.2	1.24	0.47	-	39	0.7	66
DHOBE	17	2.5	1.23	0.14	-	19	1.1	100
NAI	13	1.6	0.48	0.09	-		0.4	20
BHURJI	11	1.7	1.08	-	-	26	0.2	NK
TELI	11	0.8	2.04	1.83	-	50	0.2	-
GADARIA	33	5.0	1.82	1.39	0.8	14	2.3	88
LONIYA	20	4.1	2.06	0.62	-	28	1.5	8
KABARIA	10	2.0	0.35	0.07	-	67	0.2	88
CHAMAR	55	9.2	1.74	0.48	-	46	6.6	25
PASI	39	5.1	2.04	0.72	1.1	38	3.0	78
BASPHOD	4	0.3	0.40	-	-	28	0.4	100
PATHARKOT	15	2.0	0.36	-	-	-	1.3	100
RADHIKA	28	3.9	0.56	-	-	-	1.9	100
NUMBER OF HOUSEHOLDS		263	263	263	263	102	263	263
TOTAL	731	100%	2.28	1.37	1.4	17	94%	46%
HIGH	169							
MEDIUM	403							
LOW	141							

NK = Not known
NR = Not registered to vote
NV = Nonvoter

CASTE, NET PER CAPITA INCOME AND WEIGHTED NET PER CAPITA INCOME, BASAULI GAON SABHA

CASTE	PCI Rs 810 AND BELOW AS PERCENTAGE TOTAL HHS		WPCI Rs 810 AND BELOW AS PERCENTAGE TOTAL HHS	IMPROVED STANDARD OF LIVING 1971-81 AS % TOTAL	WPCI Rs 1101+ AS % OF TOTAL	PCI		WPCI
						AVERAGE Rs NET		
POPN.	ALL HHS	SAMPLE	SAMPLE	SAMPLE	SAMPLE	ALL HHS	SAMPLE	
SHUKLA						954	934	1000
AWASTHI						834	819	894
MISRA						756	837	1011
TIWARI						828	812	902
DUBE						1000	*	*
PANDE						1074	1074	1306
TOTAL BRAHMIN	39	46	31	23	38	865	(870)	(1003)
MISRA						983	1198	1435
PANDE						733	652	778
TOTAL MAHABRAHMIN	50	29	14	29	57	926	(1129)	(1351)
BAIS						1233	1380	1590
RAIKWAR						1246	1399	1603
TOTAL THAKUR	-	-	-	75	100	1243	(1394)	(1600)
PUNJABI	-	*	*	(100)	(100)	2000	*	*
BHAT	66	-	-		100	837	955	1102
BANIA	-	-	-	-	-	1035	1035	1035
PATHAN	65	33	33	33	50	725	780	1006
KURMI	16	11	11	11	78	1102	1146	1472
AHIR	50	33	-	33	33	792	809	1040
LODH	41	50	25	67	33	984	1091	1290
MALI	100	100	50	-	-	620	605	793
BARHAI	100	*	*			682	*	*
LOHAR	66	*	*			806	*	*
KAHAR	-	-	-	100	-	1025	917	1056
DHOBE	86	80	60	60	-	684	664	791
NAI	100	*	*			674	*	*
BHURJI	100	100	50	-	-	657	661	773
TELI	100	100	50	-	-	632	655	706
GADARIA	41	40	40	40	40	780	745	887
LONIYA	67	50	25	25	25	745	815	926
KABARIA	75	67	33	33	-	657	791	875
CHAMAR	82	79	50	21	7	716	727	859
PASI	77	75	50	-	-	705	665	782
BASPHOD	100	100	100	-	-	633	633	783
PATHARKOT	100	100	-	-	-	610	572	820
RADHIKA	100	100	100	-	-	545	417	564
TOTAL	56	51	32	30	32	853	903	1088
HIGH	33	33	21	33	54	1009	1061	1241
MEDIUM	54	46	29	36	34	854	933	1136
SCHEDULED	86	82	55	14	5	672	677	819
NUMBER OF HHS	263	102	102	102	102	263	102	102

* Not included in sample

DIFFERENCES BETWEEN CASTE STRATA, BASAULI 1982

	ACTUAL					INDEX (AV = 100)		
	NO. OF HHS	CASTE STRATUM HIGH	MEDIUM	SCHEDULED	AV	CASTE STRATUM HIGH	MEDIUM	SCHEDULED
% OF TOTAL LAND	263	37.7	49.4	13.0				
% OF IRRIGATED LAND	263	40.9	50.7	8.4				
AV BIGHAS PER HOUSEHOLD	263	21.0	10.8	7.4	12.3	171	88	60
AV IRRIG BIGHAS PER HOUSEHOLD	263	13.7	6.7	2.9	7.4	185	90	39
AV BIGHAS PER CAPITA	263	3.6	2.0	1.4	2.3	160	88	63
AV IRRIG BIGHAS PER CAPITA	263	2.4	1.2	0.6	1.4	174	91	41
% OF TOTAL LAND REVENUE		41.7	39.4	13.2				
% OF LAND REVENUE PAID BY RESIDENTS OF GAON SABHA		44.2	41.8	14.0				
AV BIGHAS CROPPED PER HOUSEHOLD	102	22.4	17.0	12.2	17.2	130	99	71
AV BIGHAS OWNED PER HOUSEHOLD	102	14.8	9.5	8.8	10.6	140	90	83
AV IRRIG BIGHAS OWNED PER HOUSEHOLD	102	8.5	4.8	2.0	5.1	166	94	39
AV NON-IRRIG BIGHAS OWNED PER HOUSEHOLD	102	6.2	4.7	6.8	5.5	113	85	124
NO HHS TOTAL GAON SABHA	263	58	148	57				
NO HHS SAMPLE	102	24	56	22				
NO PERSONS	263	334	799	292				
% OF TOTAL POPULATION	263	23.4	56.1	20.5				
AV Rs NET PCI	263	1009	854	672	853	118	100	79
AV Rs NET INCOME PER HH	263	5811	4582	3384	4624	126	99	73
% OF TOTAL NET INCOME G S	263	27.7	56.2	16.1				
PCI Rs 810 AND BELOW AS % TOTAL	263	33	54	86	56			
WPCI Rs 810 AND BELOW AS % TOTAL	102	21	29	55	32			
IMPROVED S.O.L. AS % TOTAL	102	33	36	14	30			
AV YEARS SCHOOL HOUSEHOLD HEAD	263	3.5	1.0	0.4	1.4	250	71	29
AV YEARS SCHOOL SON 1 OF HH HEAD	263	6.4	2.6	0.8	2.9	221	90	28
CHILDREN AGED 5+ AT SCHOOL AS % TOTAL	263	72.8	22.6	17.9	30.2	241	75	59
WHEAT AS % TOTAL AREA 1981	102	27.5	27.3	37.1	29			
PADDY AS % TOTAL AREA	102	26.1	24.0	16.9	24			
ARHAR AND GRAM AS % TOTAL AREA	102	25.1	22.2	25.3	24			
POTATOES AND VEG AS % TOTAL AREA	102	4.7	6.6	1.4	5			
SUGARCANE AS % TOTAL AREA	102	3.0	7.2	2.6	5			
OILSEEDS AS % TOTAL AREA	102	1.6	1.3	0.6	1			
OTHER CROPS AS % TOTAL AREA	102	10.5	7.1	4.4	8			
EMPTY AS % TOTAL AREA	102	1.6	4.2	11.7	5			
QUINTALS WHEAT PER BIGHA 1981	102	1.7	1.7	1.3	1.6	106	106	81
QUINTALS PADDY PER BIGHA 1981	102	1.6	1.2	1.0	1.4	114	86	71

CASTE AND VOTING, BASAULI GAON SABHA 1982

CASTE	NO. HHS	BASAULI ELECTORS 1979		IMLIPUR ELECTORS 1979		GAON SABHA ELECTORS 1979			% HHS SUPPORT TS 1982
		M	F	M	F	M	F	TOTAL	
SHUKLA	8	13	12			13	12	25	43
AWASTHI	6	8	9			8	9	17	-
MISRA	9			7	11	7	11	18	-
TIWARI	3							NA	33
DUBE	1	3	1			3	1	4	NK
PANDE	1							NA	-
TOTAL BRAHMIN	(28)	(29)	(22)	(7)	(11)	(36)	(33)	(69)	15
MISRA MAHABR.	11							NA	-
PANDE MAHABR.	5							NA	40
TOTAL MAHABR.	(16)	25	28			25	28	53	12
BAIS	3	7	8			7	8	15	100
RAIKWAR	10	15	17			15	17	32	30
TOTAL THAKUR	(13)	(22)	(25)			(22)	(25)	(47)	46
PUNJABI	1	(3)	(2)			(3)	(2)	(5)	NOT REGISTERED
BHAT	3	3	4			3	4	7	-
BANIA	1	(1)				(1)		(1)	NV
PATHAN	17	28	32			28	32	60	100
KURMI	18	13	14	14	14	27	28	55	-
AHIR	8	8	7			8	7	15	-
LODH	34	40	38	21	24	61	62	123	41
MALI	3	3	4			3	4	7	33
BARHAI	2	1	1			1	1	2	-
LOHAR	3	5	5			5	5	10	33
KAHAR	3	3	6			3	9	9	66
DHOBE	7	8	9			8	9	17	100
NAI	5	7	6			7	6	13	20
BHURJI	4	5	6			5	6	11	NK
TELI	3	5	6			5	6	11	-
GADARIA	17	16	17			16	17	33	88
LONIYA	12	10	10			10	10	20	8
KABARIA	8			5	5	5	5	10	88
CHAMAR	27	33	22			33	22	55	25
PASI	13	8	8	14	9	22	17	39	78
BASPHOD	1	3	1			3	1	4	100
PATHARKOT	4	6	9			6	9	15	100
RADHIKA	12	16	12			16	12	28	100
TOTAL	263	297	292	70	72	367	364	731	46
HIGH	58	76	75	7	11	83	86	169	
MEDIUM	148	155	165	40	43	195	208	403	
LOW	57	66	52	14	9	80	61	141	

NK = Not known NR = Not registered to vote NV = Nonvoter

THE MAIN CASTES

The following section gives brief background information on the 26 castes which were represented in the permanent resident population of the gaon sabha, ie. this excludes the 'Reza' Adivasis and other 'temporary' residents, who were employed at the brick works. The various, main castes will be described in approximate descending order of social status, where status is accorded by varna and local social rank, according to the research assistant. (It should be borne in mind that he was a Thakur, though this does not appear to have led him to place Thakurs above their proper station.) No doubt different villagers from different castes might disagree about the rank order and, in any case, it is usually more difficult to allocate precise rank order in the middle range of the hierarchy (which usually and also in this population constitutes the majority). The most controversial allocations of rank order may be those of the 'Punjabis' whose caste remained undetermined; the Bhat, who are arguably a low form of Brahmin; the Bania, who are arguably higher caste; and the Pathan and other castes who are Muslim and, in theory, perhaps unplaceable in a hierarchical framework based initially on the Hindu varnas. The Pathans have been placed as 'upper middle' because of their being in a loose sense the Muslim analogue of the Thakur warriors and because their numbers gave them more power than their lack of wealth might suggest.

Time prevented a detailed analysis of interdining. Normally, there was interdining between Bhurji, Barhai, Teli and other castes of lower Sudra status, but members of these castes could not eat with upper Sudras such as the Kurmi, Ahir and Lodh.

Brahmins

Brahmins constituted over 9 percent of the population of the gaon sabha and six subcastes were represented. These, in descending order of social status were Shukla, Awasthi, Misra, Tiwari, Dube (or Dwivedi) and Pande. The most important numerically were the Misra and the Shukla. The Shuklas owned an average of only 1.1 bighas per person. However, they had above average education and seven of the 16 or so migrant workers from Basauli were Shuklas, as were two of the seven shopkeepers. Thanks to the income from these, Shukla per capita income (Rs 954) was above average, both for Brahmins and in general. The Shuklas included two households which enjoyed the higher status of Kanyakubjas. These two households were divided by conflict between father's brother and nephew and also as a group the Shuklas were politically divided. Another Shukla was a part time worker in the Home Guard which mainly assists the police in crowd control at fairs and other public meetings. Consequently, even though the Shukla Brahmins constituted part of the core of the opposition faction, three of the seven households supported the Pradhan's faction in 1982 and earlier. The Awasthis included one quite rich household, whose head worked for a Bania in Suratganj. The Misras of Imlipur were the poorest of the

Brahmins and at least one labourer had no house of his own. The Tiwaris were the second poorest Brahmins and actually earned 59 percent of their total net income from labouring. One household supported the sitting Pradhan in the 1982 election but this was unusual and for purely contingent reasons. (A son had abducted a girl and the father needed protection from the police who were, quite wrongly, treating the father as an accomplice.) There was only one Dube household and they were the only Brahmins to live in the western mohalla. They had been the family priests to the Zamindar over several generations and they had, until February 1982, supported the ruling faction. Indeed, the priest had been Deputy Pradhan since 1971 but, after the latter's involvement in a brawl with a carpenter, the Pradhan (Thakur Sahib) suggested that he should not contest the April elections. It was thought that the Dubes may have then voted against Thakur Sahib. The household owned above average land and its income was also above average. Finally, the Pandes owned most land per person and were the richest Brahmin subcaste, in terms of average per capita income. The group included the village family priest (purohit) and also a shopkeeper. None of its members was active in village politics.

Overall, the Brahmins owned less land and much less irrigated land than the average per capita. Their educational level was well above average in three of the subcastes. However, the largest subcaste, the Misra, was both the poorest and almost the least educated. Thirty-nine percent of households were below the poverty line and weighting for age and sex reduced the proportion only marginally. On the other hand, 38 percent of all Brahmin households belonged in the richest category. Their average per capita income was Rs 865 which was just above the average income in the gaon sabha. Only 23 percent of Brahmin households in the sample considered that their standard of living had improved in the period from 1971 to 1981 (Cf. an average of 30%).

Though it is frequently and rightly stressed that high ritual status may be combined with labouring and poverty, it is still quite surprising that in an area where many Brahmins owned considerable land and are the dominant caste in the north of the block (and also in the nearby village of Rammandai), the Brahmins of Basauli were so relatively impoverished. To some extent, the Brahmins of Basauli had been greater victims of Zamindari Abolition than the Thakurs. Before 1952, the Zamindars used to employ full time private guards who did no farm work but protected the persons and property of their Zamindar (especially against other Thakurs) and also performed various odd jobs for their employer. For example, the family of TS had employed sixteen such 'policemen' and three or four other Thakur families in the village also hired four 'policemen' each. Most of these men were Brahmins, though there was no exclusive rule about this and in fact the Zamindari 'police' also included at least one Bhat, one Mahabrahmin and one Pathan. Generally the position was hereditary but not invariably. Some Brahmins were also cooks or family priests (purohits) for the Zamindars. When Zamindari estates were abolished, the Zamindars no longer had either the need or the means to support such feudal retainers. Consequently, in 1952 many Brahmin families who had failed to acquire land and had shown little interest in what land they possessed, found themselves impoverished and without the traditional capacity for agriculture, which many of the lowest castes possessed.

The Brahmins, despite some educational improvement, remained a socially very conservative group, which was still very concerned about pollution and caste differences, even though the dominant values, both outside and possibly even within the village, were turning against such separation. Thakur Sahib, for instance, claimed that he could not behave as liberally towards the lower castes nor so freely in other respects as he would have liked, mainly because of possible disapproval from some Brahmins. Thakur Sahib, as a good politician, would shake hands and embrace persons of all castes (especially at Holi milan). When a Brahmin protested about his embracing Chamars at the Holi festival, Thakur Sahib told him that he only objected because it was a man: "If you are prepared to embrace their wives or their daughters, why not then the men themselves?" (It was rumoured that the Brahmin had illicit relations with a lower caste woman.) One old woman from the Awasthi subcaste was said to be a particularly fanatical pujari (sayer of prayers) and she was an extreme case of avoidance of physical contact with persons of scheduled castes. She was said to be an exception, though other elderly Brahmins also would not shake hands with them. No Brahmin would take food from scheduled persons nor would they have them in their houses. Nor would they allow them near their wells. However, Brahmins would accept pacca khana from higher caste non-Brahmins. Pacca khana refers to puris and tarkari cooked in ghee or oil. Brahmins would not accept kacha khana (the ordinary everyday food, consisting of chapatis, dal and/or vegetables cooked mainly in water), from Thakurs or even from a religious person such as BP Kurmi, who had built a temple within his house.

The danger of pollution from eating and drinking vessels remained a serious issue for at least 20 percent of village households and was of some concern to a wider number of households. Most of those in the 20 percent were Brahmins, but there were also a few Lodhs who held 'old fashioned' views on this, and, indeed, on many other matters. The Lodh position derived partly from their illiteracy and traditionally above average orthodoxy and also from their desire for upward mobility.

Some Brahmins still drew a (metaphorical) line round their kitchens, and, if a lower caste person put 'even a toe' across that line, then everything within had to be thrown away. Thakur Sahib (TS) claimed that he was the only villager who was prepared to provide food for a foreigner in his own vessels and that he would be criticised in some quarters for doing so. He said that, for a Brahmin host, the polluted vessel would have to be treated afterwards in some way: "heated in some flame and God knows what other special treatment". Though TS expressed a willingness to feed people of all castes, in practice he exercised considerable care in this matter, because he feared that people of high caste who threatened not to take food or tea from his house might carry out their threats. It was not clear whether TS found this a convenient rationalisation for continuation of some exclusiveness, but, given his natural caution towards social change, this may have been partly the case. Certainly, he steered a path of compromise between political open-handedness and consideration of the views of the conservatives. Some of the more old-fashioned Brahmins would insist on tea, say, from TS's house being served in a metal 'glass' rather than in an earthenware cup. TS laughed at this and observed that they believe there is less pollution from metal. He added that in fact an earthenware cup absorbed no more moisture than a metal receptacle and was just as easily cleaned.

Thakur Sahib still thought that Brahmins in Basauli were less concerned about ritual pollution than in most surrounding villages and this may have been partly because of their relatively low economic and political status in a Thakur-dominated village. The Brahmins were stagnating partly because of their own inherent social characteristics, partly because of lack of land and partly because, as a 'Forward' caste, they were not entitled to any government help, even though it was clear that, for instance, several Misra households in Imlipur deserved some assistance, because they had no land at all.

Politically, the Brahmins were divided by subcaste, gotra, class and other differences, but they were still fairly unanimous in their opposition to the ruling faction. However, even in 1982 when Thakur Sahib was elected Pradhan by the narrowest of majorities, still 15 percent of Brahmin households somehow continued to support him. The Shuklas were the main, active Brahmin politicians and even they were divided in their factional allegiance. Overall, the Brahmins of Basauli seemed to represent a case of a 'backward' Forward caste and they illustrate the dangers of adopting policies of positive economic discrimination based on caste and other broad social categories rather than basing them on the incomes of individual households.

The division within the Brahmin ranks is well illustrated by a fairly serious dispute between D. Awasthi and BP Shukla. The former had been financially successful and had built a new, pacca house next to his neighbour, BP Shukla. The latter was much less successful but had a large and aggressive family, which was too strong for D, whose household was weak in numbers. In addition, BP had married into a Misra Brahmin family of Rammandai, a 'notorious', neighbouring village. BP could rely on further support from his susral (affines). The focus of the dispute in February 1982 was the Shukla blocking of the Awasthi's right of way to his well and even another well nearby. The Shuklas refused to allow the Awasthis to walk across land overlooked by their house but not actually owned by the Shuklas.

Initially, D. Awasthi had extended his house in such a way that other people could not bring their bullock carts to their houses. The extension had also led to his entrance being moved to the western end of the house so that he now had to cross this land overlooked by the Shukla family. When access was refused, the dispute had come to the village panchayat, presided over by TS in about October 1981. He had tried to settle it by offering D a five feet wide lane to provide access. D, for some unknown reason, had insisted on a width of 8.25 feet. Since there was no intention to wall in the passageway, the discussion of the width of the passageway appears to have been mainly metaphysical. Thc panchayat failed to achieve a compromise and the matter then went to the court of the Civil Judge, Barabanki. The Shuklas won the case at this first round, but the litigation was continuing and was thought to be costing each side about Rs 50 per month. TS commented that the case had become a matter of prestige and of power and the Shuklas, in particular, were not amenable to reason on this, or, usually, on other matters. Their blocking of access to the second well was sufficient illustration of this. TS expressed lack of sympathy with either party, because "neither family had shown any interest in the problems of others and had behaved in a selfish way". Both families were also, incidentally, members of the opposition faction and the Shukla family included core members. TS said that BP Shukla and his 'mischievous' son, RN Shukla, were bent on power and were keen to provoke trouble among various sections of the society.

When asked why the Awasthi did not install a hand-pump within his household if he was fairly well off, TS explained that this would not end the dispute. The access to water supply was merely the pretext for confrontation and, if that problem was solved, the Shuklas would soon find another excuse. However, the Awasthi family has since installed a hand pump.

At 7.30 pm one night in late February, the wife of D. Awasthi came, very sorrowfully, to TS and poured out her troubles to him. TS, who was sitting on the southern verandah with his tappa (bonfire group) associates, listened in total silence and with almost palpable lack of sympathy, occasionally exchanging sidelong glances with his supporters, who were equally silent. The woman gave her story, standing in the yard below, with TS seated on the verandah. She mentioned the possibility of murder, though so far no injuries had been sustained. TS also thought that the dispute might be brewing up into a bloody encounter and he later said that most people wanted to keep out of it. He felt that the village panchayat was useless for people who were not amenable to reason and who wished to rely on numerical strength and lathis for power. This was particularly true of the eastern mohalla, where the Brahmins were politically mischievous but hopelessly disunited. CK Pathan later observed, laconically and sarcastically: 'Sangathan' ('Unity'). Apparently, the Brahmins had resolved to organise themselves but, as TS later said, their only organisation so far has been to fight among themselves. After a long pause, TS told the woman (who had broken into tears during her story) that there were only two solutions, the court or the lathi. The woman left, having received very little sympathy and no help. TS appeared a little uneasy about this afterwards and harked back nostalgically to the days when everyone in the village cared about and helped each other.

TS added that BP Shukla had earlier been keen to try his strength against AS, the brother-in-law of DNS Thakur, but TS had happened to be present when the Shuklas had paraded with their lathis. TS had immediately summoned the Pathan, Lodh and other lower caste 'militia' from his mohalla and the Shukla forces had dispersed. TS was aware that the Shuklas were keen to challenge 'even his authority', by threatening to use the strength of their relatives in Rammandai.

Mahabrahmins

The Mahabrahmins were regarded as a distinctly inferior kind of Brahmin and, apart from their main occupation of farming, they were mainly concerned with rituals after the cremation of the dead. The most important ritual was peformed at Daswan, the tenth day after the cremation. The second son of Thakur Sahib (not an extremely unbiassed observer, it is true) described the social status of Mahabrahmins as 'quite low' and he claimed that in the past they had been 'hated' for deriving profit from the deaths of fellow villagers. However, he thought that they had since developed a 'public touch' and people were now less hostile. (It may also have been the case that they were decreasingly dependent upon such income, though no households showed any sign of giving up their funeral work which was still quite lucrative.)

There were two subcastes, Misra and Pande. The Misras were much more numerous and also richer, though the land owned per capita was more or less the same. The Misras owned slightly more irrigated land per capita and also had other income from business, shopkeeping and other activities. They were also more educated. Misra income from labouring formed a negligible proportion of their total income, whereas Pandes derived nearly a fifth of their income from this source. The net per capita income of the Misras was Rs 983 and this was Rs 250 higher than the Pandes, who were well below the poverty line. The Pande Mahabrahmins settled in the village in 1952 and this may have some bearing on their poverty. They came from Rae Bareli district to claim land inherited from their nanihal (mother's family), rather as did Thakur Sahib about the same time. However, there was no connection between these two events. Two Pande households voted for him in 1982 and this reflected gratitude for land received under land reforms and also was a result of a dispute within the subcaste over land.

Overall, the Mahabrahmins comprised 8 percent of total population and their landownership was above average. Despite this, 50 percent of households were below the poverty line but this falls to a mere 14 percent when age and sex composition are allowed for in a weighted PCI. Only 4 percent of total income was earned by labouring. Fifty-seven percent of sample households received a net weighted per capita income (WPCI) of over Rs 1,100 and 29 percent of sample households reported an improvement in standard of living since 1971. One of the most dramatic rises in income had been that of S. Misra. Conversely, one of the poorest Mahabrahmins was S. Pande and his standard of living had deteriorated extremely as a result of filaria from 1978. Earlier, he was comfortably above the poverty line, deriving considerable income as a woodcutter. The average PCI for the whole caste was Rs 926. The Mahabrahmins formed the second largest upper caste group which was opposed to the ruling faction, but, even so, two of the sixteen households supported the latter.

The most important Mahabrahmin family was that of S. Misra who had risen from being a poor dependent of Thakur Sahib's family to a prosperous farmer and businessman. The family holding had increased from 8 acres to 25 acres in one generation. The conflict between the two families was central to the politics of the whole gaon sabha. Insofar as the conflict encompassed divisions between two individuals with strong personalities, between two families with large resources (by village standards), between the two richest upper castes and also between two elements of the upper class, with contrasting traditions and culture, the schism may be said to have been profound and growing deeper. The conflict may be seen particularly as one between a declining, feudal leader and a rising, capitalist farmer and businessman. Interestingly, the Mahabrahmins felt their social class inferiority keenly and, in an example of 'false consciousness', frequently identified themselves with the village poor. (So did Thakur Sahib, but only in political, not social or economic, terms.) Two of the youngest Mahabrahmins, including the nephew of S, were active in the Communist Party of India (Marxist). The nephew was secretary of the tahsil branch of the party and went to Delhi for a month's training in February 1983. The CPI (M) had very little following in Barabanki district and it was suggested by R. Thakur that the CPI (M) was chosen by them because it would be a small party, opposed to Thakur Sahib's party, in which it would be relatively easy to secure some form of official post. The nephew of S ran a small agency which sold pumpsets in Fatehpur but he expressed dissatisfaction with this job.

The personal and financial aspects of the conflict took on a more bitter dimension after a 'bomb' attack on the youngest son of Thakur Sahib in March 1981, by the elder son of S who was his contemporary and rival at the intermediate college in Fatehpur. Apart from having become richer than Thakur Sahib (at least in terms of capital and total household income, if not in per capita income), S. Mahabrahmin also headed a joint household, consisting of 26 members. This was the largest household in the gaon sabha and nearly three times as big as that of Thakur Sahib. S had built a fairly large, brick house on the south-east corner of the village. He had also installed two tubewells and a flourmill just beyond the abadi and he had connected electricity to his flourmill and also to his house - the only domestic connection in the whole gaon sabha. His electricity bill was roughly Rs 250 per month. S had also bought a machine to cut fodder, which was driven by a diesel engine.

S and his father had worked for Thakur Sahib and his Zamindar forebears. It was a matter of some bitterness to Thakur Sahib that his earlier assistance to the family of S was being rewarded by such violent opposition and personal animus. He accused S of being namak haram, ie. of having eaten his salt and then abused his hospitality and kindness. The second son of Thakur Sahib characterised S as a very cunning man who, he claimed, had accumulated part of his new wealth through smuggling, especially opium, but added that he also owed part of his enrichment to tobacco production and a profitable milling enterprise. It should also be said that all the adult males in the Mahabrahmin household worked hard on the farm or in the business and this contrasted with Thakur Sahib's situation, where he spent much of his time on politics or reading books, three of his sons were engaged in higher studies and relatively little family labour was expended on immediately productive activity.

Thakurs

The Thakurs have been the dominant caste in the gaon sabha and they were all Zamindars before abolition in 1952. Though they have lost ground economically, both because of abolition and also through their own inertia (especially in agriculture), they remained more or less dominant and had retained much of the social status of Zamindars. There were said to be at least 36 subcastes of Thakur (or Rajput, as they are called in Rajasthan, whence they are said to have come). In Barabanki district the majority subcaste was Bais and others included Suryabansi, Kalhans and Janwar. In Ramnagar and Haidergarh blocks, to the south of Suratganj block, the majority subcaste was Suryabansi and in Suratganj block the Raikwar were the most numerous. In neighbouring Gonda district, Bishen predominated and in Rae Bareli district Bais was the most common subcaste. It was alleged that the Raikwar expelled the Bhar (another Thakur subcaste) from Basauli at least 180 years ago. R. Thakur had a personal experience which brought home to him the history of the village. He was once travelling on a train and got into conversation with another young man, who turned out to be a fellow Thakur of Bhar subcaste. It transpired that his ancestors came from Basauli and he was now farming near Kanpur, some 120 kilometres away. R was relieved to meet no residual bitterness and they chatted amicably enough. When the train stopped at a station and there were cries of 'Chai, garam Chai', he offered to buy the Bhar a cup of tea. He politely declined, saying that his ancestors had sworn an oath never to accept anything from a Raikwar Thakur.

Apart from the ten Raikwar households, there were also three Bais households, including that of Thakur Sahib, the Pradhan. He and his father had come from Rae Bareli district to Basauli in order to take possession of property inherited from their Raikwar nanihal and two other households had also migrated from other districts. One, SBS, had also come from Rae Bareli and also to inherit uterine property. He came in 1957, more than ten years after Thakur Sahib and quite independently. The other, AKS, had come from Sitapur in 1980 to get away from a violent dispute with Pasis of his village. He had bought land in Basauli but his father and brothers remained in their own village.

The Bais owned more than three times the average area of land per capita and nearly four times the irrigated area per capita. Their educational level was the highest in the village and the household heads had an average of nearly nine years schooling, compared with the overall average of 1.4 years. The average net PCI was Rs 1,233, the third highest for any subcaste or caste in the village. Both the other households supported Thakur Sahib and the ruling faction, though SBS had sometimes grown closer to the opposing Thakur faction. This was despite the fact that Thakur Sahib had earlier helped him to take possession of his inheritance and to secure government service as a primary teacher. The Raikwar owned almost as much land per capita as the Bais and were almost as well educated. The average net PCI was Rs 1,246 and the second highest in the village. It is highly significant, though not so surprising, that only 30 percent of the Raikwar households supported Thakur Sahib in the 1982 election. The dynamics of factions within the Thakur caste involved some changes in allegiance over the years, but normally a majority of Thakurs had opposed the current Pradhan. In 1956, a Raikwar from an opposing faction had been elected Pradhan, but he had been less dominant than Thakur Sahib was able to be later.

There were no Thakurs below the poverty line in the sample, but there was one case of a Thakur occasionally working as a labourer for his chacha (father's brother). This was an unusual case, where the father was a migrant, who had disappeared without trace, the son gambled and his family had become relatively poor. (Another case was mentioned of a Thakur in Rammandai who worked as a labourer for various contractors outside his village and it was thought that, though very unusual, the incidence of Thakur labourers was on the increase.) All the Thakurs in the sample had a net PCI of more than Rs 1,100 and three of the four sample household heads said that they had improved their standard of living. The fourth was a tragic case of high expenditure on drinking, sale of land, wife's suicide and absenteeism from work by the household head.

One Thakur, UBS, had waived caste exclusiveness in relation to pollution. All can touch the family's vessels, at least in theory. In practice, the occasion to invite members of the scheduled castes to meals does not arise. R. Thakur said that he also was ready to get rid of all such restrictions in a similar fashion but he was opposed by his father's mother (daddi) who was aged 75 years and hardly likely to revise her orthodox views. Thakurs have been selling land over the past 30 years. They had sold about 400 bighas or 30 percent of their total land. There was said to be no resentment of the Lodhs, Punjabis and other lower castes for purchasing land from them. Still, quite a few Thakurs preferred to depend on government service and use agriculture as a mainly supplementary source of income. However, government jobs were becoming increasingly difficult for the younger generation to secure, whether they had contacts or not. Given that the sons of the rural middle class were competing with the sons of urban professionals and others who have much greater influence and access to information about jobs and how to secure them, there was a greater need for the younger generation of Thakurs to take farming seriously. The sons of larger Thakur owners could swallow this pill rather more easily if they felt that their entry into farming could be combined with investment in modern machinery, such as a tractor. The example of R and his desire to purchase a 20 horse power tractor was a case in point.

R predicted that the pre-existing trends in caste mobility would be sustained so long as other parts of the economic system remained the same, but if the Thakurs and other higher caste farmers began to invest in tractors and started to reap their potential, then the gap between them and the lower castes would begin to widen again and quite markedly. At present, the relative lack of economic inequality is partly explained by quite serious Thakur decline and partial apathy to farming and partly by a moderate rise in the incomes of some medium castes and of the 'upper' scheduled castes, especially the Chamars.

Punjabis

There was only one household of Punjabis and they had migrated to buy land in Basauli in 1978. There were a number of Punjabis in the central and eastern districts of UP who had sold their land at high rates in the Punjab and then bought more land at cheaper rates in UP. Many of them had then further consolidated this profitable exchange by progressive farming. The Punjabis were Sikhs and the men wore the traditional turban. However, their caste status was something of a mystery, and they claimed to be Thakurs.

Given the insecurity prevailing in rural UP, it might be thought that there would be considerable risk to Punjabis, especially isolated individual families, settling in alien villages without biraderi support. However, movement to a new village, by a Punjabi or by anyone else, requires no official notification or permission from the Pradhan or gram panchayat. In one important respect the Punjabis behave rather differently from the way a local landlord might behave in relation to his production. Punjabis were said to be usually 'progressive' and they, therefore, all used banks. When they had harvested their crop, then they normally sold the surplus immediately. This obviously entailed a loss, since prices are usually at their lowest in the post-harvest glut. The loss in income was compensated for by the much reduced risk of dacoity or theft and the greatly enhanced feeling of security.

The Punjabis had bought 130 bighas, including 60 bighas from the cousin of Thakur Sahib who had settled in neighbouring Bahraich district. The Thakur land was bought cheaply for only Rs 600 per bigha. The joint household consisted of ten members and therefore owned 13 bighas per person, all irrigated. In per capita terms, the Punjabi immigrants had become the largest landowners in the village and were becoming richer, through progressive farming, further land purchase, mortgage and other activities. Given that the villagers were prone to jealousy, it is surprising that the Punjabis appeared to be arousing very little jealousy or antagonism. Indeed, there was said to be no serious problem of Punjabi immigrants in UP as a whole. However, there had been a Thakur-Punjabi conflict in a nearby terai village which had led to the murder of a Thakur and the jailing of two Punjabis. The Punjabis in Basauli appeared to keep very much to themselves. As was frequently the necessity (as well as probably the preference), they had built their house on their farm land, outside the village. This increased the security risk but enabled greater contact with and better management of their farm. Their net PCI was estimated to be Rs 2,000 and this made them the richest household in the village. As part of their policy of minimum interference in the public life of the village, it is perhaps significant that, four years after settling in the village, they had still not been registered on the list of voters and, though they have made no public declaration of their political neutrality, it was implicit and generally known. Neither faction appears to have made any attempt to enlist their support.

Pathans

Pathans were the largest Muslim group and they all lived in the western mohalla, near to the house of Thakur Sahib. Seventeen out of 42 Muslim households were Pathan and the leader of the Pathans was also leader of the Muslims and of the mosque. With over 7 percent of the total population, the Pathans were the third largest group among the middle-ranking castes. They owned about half the average land per capita and less than half the average for irrigated land. All household heads in the sample were illiterate and generally the level of education was very low. CK ('Khalipha'), the leader of the Pathans, had nominal schooling but there was a Pathan shopkeeper with four years education. The son of CK had the highest level of education, with seven years of Islamic teaching at the Muslim School in Sikohna. He was literate in Urdu and Arabic and could read the Koran. There was also one Pathan boy who was reading in seventh class.

Sixty-five percent of households were below the poverty line. However, Pathan fertility was fairly high and there were many children in most households. Consequently, when weighting for age and sex is applied, the population below the poverty line falls to 33 percent, comparable to the Brahmins. Numerous Pathans worked at the local brickworks (owned by a Pathan from outside) and 21 percent of net income of sample households came from labouring of various kinds, but mainly at the brickworks. Three of the six Pathan households in the sample had a WPCI of over Rs 1,100 and in two cases this was partly because of (untypically) small household size. The sample proportion of rich households was nothing like 50 percent in the caste population as a whole. A third of the sample households reported improvement in their standard of living over the past ten years and one household, that of CK, has benefited particularly from his close association with SS, the absentee cousin of Thakur Sahib. He had worked for SS in Bahraich for a while and had been his sharecropper and manager ('Munijar') of his estate until SS had recently sold most of it. The average net PCI of all Pathan households was only Rs 725 and this was 10 percent below the poverty line and 15 percent below the village average.

The Pathans were solidly behind Thakur Sahib, who was sympathetic to Muslim interests, both from party political, village political and from a personal and intellectual point of view. The Pathans comprised by far the largest caste group which gave a hundred percent support to the ruling faction. As a large group with a big population of young (and not-so-young) aggressive males, low literacy and high loyalty to the leader of their mohalla and village faction, the Pathans represented the main 'militia' of Thakur Sahib. Brahmins and Mahabrahmins could offer little appeal to devout Muslims and the aggression of the Pathans towards the opposition faction sometimes needed to be tactfully restrained by Thakur Sahib. However, even the Pathans had quarrelled with Thakur Sahib in 1975 and for one year they had moved to give close support to the Thakurs, who were then all (including the other Bais households) in opposition to Thakur Sahib.

There has been a longstanding conflict between the Pathans and the Ahirs, who live in an adjacent part of the same mohalla. The main cause of dissension was land for housing and this was exacerbated by the high growth of population among the Pathans. Ironically, there was no general shortage of abadi, far from it, but the Pathans had refused Thakur Sahib's offer to settle some households on land to the east of the temple. Thakur Sahib was keen to reduce the divisions within his own mohalla (which probably explained the total lack of Ahir support for him in the 1982 election) and the Pathans were concerned to expand their housing near their immediate relatives. In fact, a lathi fight between Pathans and Ahirs occurred only an hour or so after the researcher, accompanied by the District Magistrate, had made his first visit to Basauli. The police were called from Mohammadpur and various persons, mostly Pathans (including CK), were charged under Section 107. For the following four months or so, the accused had the botheration of having to walk or cycle to Fatehpur to appear before the Sub-Divisional Magistrate (SDM), a Thakur. Postponement of a case and renewal of bail is used as a device to punish quarrelsome villagers and to deter any further aggression. At each appearance, their bail was renewed and eventually some kind of settlement was reached. The Pathans claimed that the police in Mohammadpur were biassed in favour of the Ahirs. Apart from the time factor, each visit would normally involve the expenditure of about Rs 12 to hire a lawyer.

Kurmis

Kurmis were generally given the more polite title of Verma and the change in name betokens the desired and actual upward mobility of the caste, both in Basauli, in the block and indeed over much of UP. The Kurmis were given the stereotype of being solid, fairly unimaginative, hard workers who attached less importance to social niceties and much more to the pressing practicalities of good farm management and building a durable (preferably brick) house of sensibly modest, utilitarian dimensions. In fact, they may be said to have a stereotype which is almost the opposite of the Thakur ideal and this contrast in stereotypes may owe at least some of its strength to the likelihood that Thakurs have been more active than most castes in propagating both stereotypes. In practice, of course, there were cautious, economical Thakurs and lavish, hospitable Kurmis but they were perhaps a minority. The Kurmis were said to belong to two different subcastes, but little importance seems to be attached to these divisions.

Kurmis have acquired a large amount of land, owning twice the average per capita. Five Kurmi farmers have each invested in a pumpset and the average area of irrigated land per capita was 4.25 bighas. This was three times the average and was exceeded only by the Thakurs and Punjabis. Their level of education was also quite high and much higher than that of any other large group in the middle range of castes. Only 16 percent of Kurmi households were below the poverty line and only 11 percent in terms of WPCI. Income from labouring was negligible. Seventy-eight percent of households had a net PCI in excess of Rs 1,100, yet only 11 percent in the sample admitted to having improved their standard of living in the period since 1971. This may partly reflect the fact that Kurmi prosperity dates back well before Zamindari Abolition and owes only a relatively small amount to this reform. Their prosperity is derived mainly from hard work and less from government help. However, in more recent years the Kurmis have been beneficiaries of government programmes in a wider and more indirect sense. They have benefited insofar as the innovations associated with the so-called 'Green Revolution' have been of a nature and scale which were within their capacity to adopt. As a consequence, the Kurmis of Barabanki district, as elsewhere in UP, have been more dynamic than most other farming castes. They have also sometimes been successful in challenging Thakur and Brahmin political supremacy. The previous MLA for Ramnagar had been a Kurmi and, for example, he had been able to provide considerable benefits to the nearby rich village of Baraiya. The block Pramukh was still a Kurmi in 1982, though it looked rather unlikely that he would win at the next election, since he had even lost his seat as Pradhan in the April election. He duly lost in May 1983.

Ahirs (or Yadavs)

The Ahirs have been traditionally herdsmen and they still had a higher ratio of animals and milk production than other castes of equivalent status. They preferred to be called Yadav and in many parts of UP the Yadav caste has become relatively highly mobilised in the political arena, thanks mainly to Choudhuri Charan Singh and the greater appeal of his Lok Dal party to the Backward castes. In eastern UP, where the Lok Dal presents a moderately serious challenge to the Congress (I) in certain districts, some Yadavs believed (or had been led to believe) that Charan Singh was a Yadav. (He was in fact a Jat.) The Yadavs are the only other middle caste from whose ranks politicians have risen to become Chief Minister of UP. This happened initially during the Janata interlude and in fact this Yadav was fairly quickly replaced within the Janata party by a Bania.

Judging by newspaper reports, there also seemed to be a disproportionate number of Yadavs as both leaders and members of various gangs of dacoits within UP. Conversations with district-level politicians, especially Brahmins and Thakurs within Congress (I), indicated that many members of the ruling class and party tend to dismiss all Yadavs as dacoits, criminals and trouble makers.

In Basauli, the Yadavs appeared to play a fairly important role in village politics. They were all open supporters of the opposition and, as a relatively large caste group, this bore some political significance in itself. They also voted for the Lok Dal. However, the Yadavs gave the impression of being more concerned with their economic advancement and with their domestic affairs. They were one of the most 'private' caste groups in the village and it was particularly noticeable that their womenfolk observed a stricter purdah than the Muslim women, some of whom were remarkably free in their movements and activities, probably because of poverty. Yadav women very rarely stirred outside their courtyards (which were surrounded by a high brick wall) and the open space in front of their houses was rarely used by the female members of the household. In the exercise to gather heights and weights, almost no Yadav woman could be persuaded to volunteer and the response rate was the most negative of any caste group in the village.

The Ahirs comprised 3.4 percent of total population and they owned slightly more than average land per capita. Their main problem was that they owned no irrigated land. Their education level was low but around the average. Fifty percent of households were below the poverty line but none of those in the sample had WPCIs below this threshold. A tenth of the net income of sample households was earned from labouring and 34 percent was gained from milk production. One of the three sample households had a WPCI above Rs 1,100 but the average PCI of all households was only Rs 792, just below the poverty line. One sample household (33%) reported an improvement in their standard of living. No households supported the ruling faction in the 1982 election but by August the Ahirs had switched their support to Thakur Sahib. This arose after a Lodh youth had beaten a Dhobe youth. The Dhobe complained to Thakur Sahib who sent his two youngest sons who abused the Lodh and also beat him. Thakur Sahib came later and also abused him, for good measure. This led the Lodhs of the western mohalla to transfer their allegiance to the opposition faction. Since disputes over abadi have made the Lodhs and Ahirs even more deadly enemies than the Pathans and Ahirs, and because the two castes were always members of opposing factions, it was assumed that, if the Lodhs moved to the opposition, then the Ahirs must automatically become supporters of the ruling faction.

This was not made public by any declaration or move by either the Ahirs or Thakur Sahib, but it was taken for granted by all. The realignment became explicit when the Ahirs came to Thakur Sahib about a piece of their land which the Lodhs had seized a year or so before. At that time, Thakur Sahib, in the presence of the lekhpal (revenue accountant), had inspected the land, which was surrounded by plots owned by Lodhs. Thakur Sahib had given judgement in favour of the Lodhs, who were then his supporters. This time, when the Ahirs came to him (as putative, indeed certain, supporters of him), Thakur Sahib reversed his earlier judgement and awarded in favour of the Ahirs.

Lodhs

The Lodhs formed the largest caste group in the village, with 14 percent of total population. They were also the group which was most widely spread across all the various settlements, except Kiratpur. They have been the most active in buying land in recent years from the upper castes, especially from the Thakurs. The Lodhs have been even more dynamic than the Kurmis in Basauli. Whereas only three or four Kurmi households in Imlipur had been really expanding their area, a large number of Lodhs have saved from the fruits of their hard labour and expanded their smallholdings to a modest, but significant, degree. One, R, has become the second largest farmer in the gaon sabha. However, the Lodhs started from a small base and they still have slightly less than the average per capita area of land, irrigated and unirrigated. Their educational level was below average and generally Lodhs tended to hold very traditional values in relation to religious, caste and social matters. Forty-one percent of households were below the poverty line but only 25 percent of the sample households fell below this level, using WPCI as the index. They gained 13 percent of their total net income from labouring and two poor Lodhs worked as biannual labourers for a Thakur and Mahabrahmin respectively. Two-thirds of the Lodhs in the sample considered that their standard of living had undergone some improvement and a third had a WPCI of over Rs 1,100. The average PCI was as high as Rs 984 (ie. 15 percent above average) and this was somewhat surprising. Such a relatively high average income level was mainly explained by the presence of three or four richer farmers, two of whose family members had migrated to good jobs outside and also the son of R had become a schoolteacher. Only 41 percent of the Lodhs supported the ruling faction in April 1982 and this included all the Lodhs in the western mohalla. As already described, subsequent events led to the latter deserting to the opposition and in early 1983 only about 20 percent of all Lodhs supported Thakur Sahib. If the dispute had occurred before April 1982, then it is certain that Thakur Sahib would have lost the election.

Gadarias

The Gadarias were a fairly small group (5 percent of total population) who constituted a large component of the population of Kiratpur. They owned below average total land but average amounts of irrigated land. Educational levels were low and not helped by the distance of Kiratpur from the primary school in Basauli and the need for children to help herd the sheep and goats, which was the traditional specialism of Gadarias. About 40 percent of households were below the poverty line and the use of the WPCI made no difference to this ratio in the case of the sample households, at least. Their proportion of income from labouring was similar to that of the Lodh (14 percent). Forty percent of sample households had a WPCI over Rs 1,100 and as many as 40 percent reported improved living standards. Average PCI was only Rs 780 and they were therefore hovering just below the poverty line. The majority (88 percent) supported the ruling faction.

Chamars (or Kureel or Raidas)

Chamars were the second largest caste group in the gaon sabha, with the same population size as the Brahmins and 9.2 percent of total population. They were the main scheduled caste in the village. Thanks partly to minor land distribution, mainly from the gram sabha, the Chamars owned some land and their area per capita was in fact 76 percent of the average. Much of this land was of poor quality and mostly unirrigable. Their irrigated land per capita was only 35 percent of the average. The Chamars benefited only slightly from Zamindari Abolition, because virtually all were mainly labourers at that time and it was only

Asamis (tenants) who received higher rights of ownership. However, the Chamar servants owned some mafi land given to them by their Zamindar employers and this tenure became sirdari or bhumidhari, according to its previous status when under Thakur ownership. More recently, some Chamars have benefited from modest land distribution and from various special government programmes which invariably offer a higher subsidy component than to non-scheduled categories. Despite this help, 82 percent of all Chamar households remained below the poverty line and 50 percent of sample households were still below this level, when the WPCI measure was used. Their partly newly acquired land yielded 40 percent of their total net income, but labouring still provided 46 percent of their income. No other major caste relied so much on labouring for their income and only three minor castes exceeded the Chamars in this respect. (They were the Malis, Kabarias and Telis, with 80 percent, 67 percent and 50 percent respectively.) Only three of the fourteen households in the sample considered that their standard of living had improved and only one, M, had an income of over Rs 1,100. This household included a labourer in the Public Works Department and they also hired out their Dunlop cart. M had been the first villager to purchase a Dunlop and had bought it with his own capital earned from farming. Since then the government had enabled scheduled persons to buy such carts with a 50 percent subsidy, under the Integrated Rural Development Scheme. One other, non-sample Chamar household also had a high income on paper, but they had other troubles and were deeply in debt so their net income belied their actual standard of living, which was quite low. Overall, the average net PCI of Chamars was only Rs 716, which was nearly 16 percent below the average and nearly 12 percent below the poverty line. Though both factions championed the cause of the poor and of the lowest castes, in practice only 25 percent of the Chamars supported the ruling faction. They all voted for Congress (I) in other elections, irrespective of their factional support in village politics. One Chamar was a member of the gram panchayat in 1971 but he was not selected by Thakur Sahib as a candidate in 1982.

The Chamars were followers of Narain Das, a seventeenth century Chamar saint whose shrine was in a village ten kilometres away from Basauli. He had exerted influence in at least four districts. The main effect on Chamar behaviour had been some abandonment of meat and alcohol consumption. However, half of the Chamars still ate meat occasionally and drank when they could afford to. The caste gave up the processing of animal skins and production of leather in 1977. This was to some extent involuntary insofar as the Janata government effectively 'nationalised' leather processing. The work was taken away from Chamars and put out on contract in each block. The single Chamar household in Basauli who had been doing this work did not offer a tender, because of lack of capital and management capacity, and the contract for Suratganj block was won by a Muslim. He was a Pathan butcher from Lalpur and he employed tribals from Ranchi rather than Chamars. The Chamar from Basauli had earned about Rs 700 per year, roughly 20 percent of his net income, from this work, but there was no loss to other Chamar households in the village. Indeed, the Chamar community as a whole welcomed the change as beneficial to their mild efforts to raise their status. No caste interdined with Chamars and there was no sharing of a well with them either, in Basauli. It was thought that in Burhanapur some lower middle castes (Teli, Gadaria and Dhobe) shared a well because of their close proximity.

Even now the Chamars could not use the wells of the high caste and in the past they had to use a dirty well, into which flood water seeped during the rains, or else ask some high caste person to be kind enough to draw a bucketful for them from a high caste well. TS still did not allow his Chamar labourers to touch the buckets used for human water supply and they were only allowed to draw water for the animals with the buckets used for the animals. This contradictory standpoint was paraphrased by TS in the Hindi saying, "I do not eat gur but I eat the stuff which is prepared from it", ie. "I do something but pretend that I do not". In theory, his well was reserved only for Thakurs and Brahmins (of which there were only two households in the mohalla) but in practice members of other castes, especially his Pathan supporters, used the well for drinking, bathing and washing their clothes. If TS's Chamar labourer wished to drink water, then he would ask someone, usually L. Kahar, to draw some water for him. If he were asked to draw a bucket for the researcher, B. Chamar either refused or ignored the request, without giving any explanation. On one occasion, the son of B. Radhika said that he was not allowed to, but nevertheless he drew a bucket when no one was watching.

Pasis

Pasis comprised 5.1 percent of total population and were the second largest scheduled caste. They owned only slightly less than average land per capita and their share of irrigated land was over half the average per capita. They had increased their holdings in recent years but less so than the Chamars. Their educational level was low but not much lower than the average. Seventy-seven percent of households were below the poverty line and generally their economic level was similar to that of the Chamars. However, there was one rich Pasi household whose head worked as a chuprasi (orderly) in the tahsildar's office. None of the four Pasis in the sample reported any improvement. Seventy-eight percent of households supported the ruling faction and in 1982 two Pasis were elected to the gram panchayat. One lived in Purwa and was educated to tenth class. He subsequently secured a part-time job as an assistant operator of the government tubewell for Rs 150 per month. In Imlipur another Pasi was educated to eighth class and was quite a key person in its politics. Overall, the Pasis were an important, lower caste, component in the ruling faction and they have benefited from government grants and loans.

Patharkots

The Patharkots were previously itinerant stone-cutters who had settled in Basauli in about 1950. The villagers referred to them as tribals (adivasis) but it was not certain that they were officially classified as tribal. The villagers' main criterion for defining a group as 'tribal' seemed to be whether they were itinerant. However, it was clear that the Patharkots were scheduled, whether as a caste or as a tribe. They occupied very simple huts on the western edge of the western mohalla. They were considered of particularly low status because, not only did they eat meat but also ate the flesh of wild animals such as rabbit, jackal, fox and pig, which they hunted with the help of fierce dogs. They also kept about a dozen hens and sold most of their eggs. For their stone-cutting business, each year they would buy a truck-load of 400 stones which had been machine-cut and brought from Shankergarh. This cost around Rs 3,000 or about Rs 15 per pair of stones. There were two other groups of Patharkot in the tahsil, both related to the largest group in Basauli. Consequently, the four households in Basauli would need to raise about Rs 1,000 to pay for the stones, which was always done on delivery. Part of this capital was usually borrowed from S. Kurmi of Imlipur. After fashioning the stones by hand, they toured the villages, by cycle or with yokes, to sell the grindstones (chakkis) for Rs 35 to Rs 50 per pair. They also sold stone slabs (silwats) for grinding spices and these cost Rs 15. Though there were two milling machines in Basauli and several others in nearby villages, there was no immediate danger of the Patharkots losing their trade in grindstones, because these were still needed to remove the shell from pulses and for a variety of other domestic tasks which the milling machinery cannot fulfil. A chakki is also needed for emergencies, when power cuts or other contingencies put the machines out of action.

The Patharkots were only 2 percent of the total population and have been described here mainly because of their interesting occupation and social status. They owned very little land and none was irrigated. All adults were illiterate and only one child attended school. All households were below the poverty line, by both measures, but no income was derived from labouring. The Patharkots were in fact an example of 'businessmen' who were truly impoverished. Their average PCI was estimated to be only Rs 610 (25% below the poverty line), but it should be stressed that their income from hunting and other possible sources was difficult to assess. Their housing and general visible standard of living tended to confirm the estimate of income. However, they were able to find enough money to enjoy the occasional bottle of desi sharab (local wine) at Rs 7 per bottle and, even more rarely, the shop-bought sharab at Rs 20 per bottle. The Patharkots were dependent on Thakur Sahib and, as such, there was hardly any question of supporting any other faction. In the summer of 1983 TS Thakur, Pramukh of Suratganj block, secured sanction for a kachchi colony of eight rooms for the Patharkots, as part of the government's Harijan Avas and Gramin Rojgar Yojana. These houses were completed some time before July 1984.

Radhikas (or Khatiks)

The Radhikas constituted 3.9 percent of the total population and, as the main musician and dancing group, they were the most colourful and unusual caste in the village. They first came to Basauli in 1950, left in 1958 and then returned in 1975. As another erstwhile itinerant group, they were also referred to as Adivasis by villagers, but the official census of 1981 lists the Khatiks as a scheduled caste, not tribe. The name Radhika was more often used by villagers. They earned their living by singing and dancing at weddings, religious festivals and a variety of other social functions, where some form of tamasha was required. The men and boys dressed as women for their dancing and the women themselves did not participate. The Radhikas also received some income (about 25%) from begging. One day in August 1982, one of the Radhika became possessed by a spirit and performed the annual ritual of appeasing the village deity. (In some years this ritual was also performed by persons from other middle or lower castes such as Ahir, Lodh, Chamar or Pasi and it was not an exclusively Radhika duty.)

The Radhikas owned very little land and none was irrigated. Only one household had taken to farming and its head had learned to farm as a biannual labourer elsewhere. The rest of the caste scorned the manual labour of farming as 'too hard' for them and Thakur Sahib claimed that, when he had offered to provide land for them from the gram samaj, they had actually refused the offer. They rejected it both because agriculture did not interest them and also because they feared that lagan (land tax), which had been waived for small owners since 1976, might be reintroduced and they would have to pay lagan for any land given to them. No other group has refused land in this way. Hardly any Radhikas did labouring work either. All adults were illiterate and no children attended school. All were below the poverty line and their average net PCI was estimated to be only Rs 545, which was 33 percent below the poverty threshold. Their housing consisted of the crudest of shelters and their lack of possessions was still more consistent with that of an itinerant caste, albeit in the process of sedentarisation.

The Radhikas and the Patharkots tended to be treated as in a different category from other villagers. Even members of a quite low caste like Dhobe (which is sometimes treated as a 'quasi-untouchable' caste) could behave in a quite discriminatory way towards the members of these two lowest groups. For example, a fairly new, quite carefully designed (though uncovered) well had been built near the blacksmith's housing. It had been financed mainly by funds from the block, plus a small contribution from a Dhobe family. The Radhikas and Patharkots lived within 50 to 150 metres of this well and when they started using it, the Dhobes, who are Muslims, objected on the grounds that members of both these scheduled tribes ate pork. TS told the Dhobes that it was a public well, not built purely with Dhobe funds, but he would ask the scheduled tribes not to wash utensils used for pork at the well. However, in return the Dhobes should not bring utensils which had contained beef. Later, TS had secured further funds from the block to build a separate well for the scheduled tribes, to avoid any further trouble. This well was smaller and less well designed than the earlier one but was near the scheduled housing. The Radhikas and Patharkots seemed fairly well satisfied with it.

The Village Power Structure

The village was still dominated by Thakurs and particularly by the Pradhan who was the uterine descendent and heir of the Zamindar family which had dominated Basauli and its region for at least a century. The dominance of the Thakurs and of its leading family was becoming increasingly shaky, for several reasons. Firstly, the Thakurs were disunited and the Pradhan, as an immigrant who had inherited his father's mother's mother's property perhaps had even more difficulty in commanding their support than might have a locally born Thakur. Secondly, Zamindari Abolition had weakened the Thakurs and forced them to change from landlords to ordinary farmers, with resources not so much greater than richer farmers of other castes and considerably less than those of four or five such farmers. Land reform had particularly weakened the economic strength of the Pradhan's family, both through loss of land revenue and costs of litigation with pattidars, but the Pradhan's political power had declined less quickly, partly because he had become the chairman of the block committee of Congress (I). Thirdly, other castes had become wealthier and were opposed to the Pradhan. In their opposition, they were prepared to ally with those Thakurs who also currently opposed the Pradhan. By 1982 the same man had been Pradhan for over 20 years and it seemed that perhaps his power was beginning to decline. In 1983 the Thakur Pradhan was elected Pramukh (Chairman) of the block committee and this precipitated an election for a new Pradhan. In this election the Mahabrahmin defeated a new Thakur candidate.

Caste Panchayats (or Jawars)

Some castes, none of them upper caste, still held caste societies (panchayats). These included the Lodh, Mali, Kahar, Gadaria, Pasi, Chamar, Patharkot and Radhika castes. It is possible that the Dhobes also had a 'society'. The Kurmis used to have one of the members of the society, from a village or a group of neighbouring villages, elected as chairman or president, but no longer hold panchayats. Meetings were held ad hoc and were most often called to regulate marriages and to adjudicate in disputes arising from marriage or from extra-marital relations. Penalties in the form of fines might be imposed and, at least in theory, members could be 'outcasted' if the penalty were not paid. No case of permanent outcasting was known of in the village and it is possible that none has occurred in the past 30 years or so, except for temporary periods. The caste societies have some lateral links between societies and if a member of one society were to defy that particular institution, and if, for example, intermarriage with members of his family was forbidden to members, then it would not be possible to secure a marriage among members of a neighbouring, or indeed a distant, society. The societies also regulated interdining and food and drink behaviour.

Thakurs and Brahmins were said never to have had such societies. It may be that Thakurs are too individualist to submit to the regulation of such bodies and it may also be that they felt less need of such collective organisation.

In Basauli there were three Lodh panchayats whose membership corresponded to neither residential nor kinship boundaries. Generally, new panchayats may be formed if a panchayat leader 'becomes a dictator or if he fines and punishes people unjustly or if he does other wrong work'. The new leader is usually a 'maldar aadmi', ie. one of the richer members. The leader of Lodh, Kurmi and most caste panchayats was called the Mahtaw and the Chamars called their panchayat leader Choudhuri. The splitting of panchayat membership may sometimes have some political significance but the main functions of the panchayat seemed to be social.

Religion

Nearly 85 percent of the village population was Hindu and the rest, except for one family of Sikh immigrants, were Muslims. There were two Siva temples and at least two other temples, one attached to the house of a Dube Brahmin and the other within that of a Kurmi. The Muslims had already completed a new mosque of fairly modest size and design. This had cost at least Rs 10,000 and they had been helped by contributions of about Rs 1,000 from Muslims in other villages. Its design had not, so far, incorporated a hand-pump for washing before prayers. A pre-existing, nearby well was being used for this purpose.

The main temple in the village was built in about 1890 by the paternal grandmother of Thakur Sahib, who had no sons and disposed of some of her wealth in building. It was dedicated to Siva and was thus known as the Shivala temple. The building was unusually beautiful for a village temple, and had a tall spire, at least 30 metres high, which stood out as a landmark above the trees of Basauli. Thakur Sahib claimed that it was the highest building in the block and it was a reminder of the more opulent days of Zamindari. The lower walls and interior incorporated some fine sculptures and craftsmen had been brought from as far as Allahabad to decorate the temple. There was hardly space for six persons to stand inside the temple and the yard around the octagonal base of the building was not of a shape and size to lend itself to collective worship. If ever large numbers did gather for religious activity (which was very rare), then they normally stood in the open space at the foot of the temple steps. Normally, the only person who worshipped there was the Dube Brahmin priest whose family had been the temple priest for Thakur Sahib's family over several generations. He had four years education and cultivated a medium-sized farm. He usually sounded the temple bell at 12.30 and 7.30 pm, after the prayers. The temple was kept locked by the priest because earlier some furnishings had been stolen from inside by an unknown person. Thakur Sahib said puja in the temple only four or five times a year and these occasions were more according to his mood or family needs than on particular Hindu festival days. He bemoaned the modern trend towards greed and selfishness and he thought that people now looked more to their own salvation. This had meant that the rich, including Zamindar families like his own, had built personal temples for their families and had not built for the mass of the people. They had also prayed on their own rather than collectively. He added that in south India temple designs were more conducive to collective worship.

The other temple, also called Shivala, was in the eastern mohalla. It seemed older than that of TS and had been built in the late nineteenth century by a goldsmith whose family has died out. Ownership of this temple had been transferred to N, father's brother of S. Mahabrahmin when N was given all the goldsmith's other property. The temple was now in poor repair and even lacked a door. TS had earlier suggested to the people of the eastern mohalla that they might collect Rs 600 or so and do the necessary repairs, including the fitting of a new door. He claimed that the Thakurs and Brahmins had not done so, simply because it was he who had made the suggestion. He then urged them to do it on their own account and not to mind him. He suggested that a committee of two or three persons be formed for this purpose and that they should collect a percentage of the grain harvest so that most householders contributed 5 or 10 kilograms. He said that, on this basis, it would cost him at least two quintals which would be worth nearly Rs 300. In the meantime a Tiwari Brahmin from the village who had migrated to South Africa returned for a holiday in 1979 and during this time visited a nephew in the eastern mohalla. The South African Brahmin was distressed by the disrepair and had donated Rs 300 towards the costs of refurbishment, and offered to provide another Rs 100 or 200, if necessary. This money was alleged to have been 'eaten' and the temple still awaited its repairs.

In Purwa, one relatively rich, bachelor Kurmi had built a pacca house and half of it he had made into a place of worship, with the god Ram in the usual altar-place and columns, just like a temple. In north India, at least, temples within domestic houses (Thakurdwara) are said to be always dedicated to Ram, the Thakur warrior-king. The temple was visited by people of other castes, including Brahmins.

Thakur Sahib, who was more interested in the theological and philosophical aspects of Hinduism, would sometimes complain that villagers paid too much attention to rituals and to the form rather than the substance of their faith. He also felt that interest in Hinduism was declining. However, the large Brahmin population still observed many aspects of their faith and a wide variety of people showed keen interest in Akhund Ramayana (recitations of the most popular text in northern India). These recitations of the Ramayana were the most lively manifestations of the continued strength of Hinduism and there were about a dozen organised each year. They might be in celebration of a household event or to compete with a neighbour who had earlier held a recitation. A variety of lower caste households with some literacy, including Lodhs and Carpenters, were among those who sponsored such readings. Usually, nowadays, the recitation is expected to be amplified and this entails the hire of loudspeakers from Mohammadpur for about Rs 30 and other expenditure. The competitiveness of recitation and its amplification has meant that the peace of the village and also the sleep of its inhabitants may be fairly frequently disturbed by readings, which were not always very harmonious, but so far villagers have not become opposed to loudspeakers in the way some towndwellers have. Thakur Sahib sometimes lamented over the introduction of loudspeakers into villages and made disapproving noises about some of the 'howling', religious or secular, which they transmitted.

TS discounted the suggestion that there are certain Hindu gods specifically related to health. His view was that all deities were so related since all are beneficent in some way or other. He cited the instance of Lakshmi for wealth and Saraswati for education. However, Sitala Mata (the smallpox goddess) was still worshipped even now, and people still prayed to be spared from smallpox even though certainly in theory and almost certainly in practice the virus has been eliminated.

Manifestations of religiosity were by no means infrequent but they were sometimes, perhaps increasingly, capable of evoking a humorous response. For example, an elderly Brahmin was walking barefoot past the tiny, unused house built for the pujari near, but not actually contiguous with, the Shivala temple. In passing this entirely nondescript building, he felt it reverentially, touched his forehead with the forefingers of his right hand and bowed slightly, before passing quickly on his way. A young Thakur and others sat watching this performance and laughed. The Dube priest of the Shivala temple was among the company and he also grinned. This very small building was earlier used by Thakur Sahib's father and a Brahmin from Mosundi for a homeopathic dispensary from about 1958 to 1970 when the Brahmin died. TS's father had acted as patron of the clinic.

Muslims seemed more active in their daily worship and usually about 25 males attended for Friday prayers. For other prayer times the number ranged from one to ten. The total Muslim population was about 220. The leader of the Muslims was CK Pathan (nicknamed 'Khalipha') who had worked for the cousin of Thakur Sahib and was a key member of the core of Thakur Sahib's faction. He had also been a member of the gaon panchayat until April 1982 when Thakur Sahib recommended that CK's son should take his place. CK was an aggressive Pathan who rose each day at 5.30 to say his prayers. He was also a singer of qawwalis and ghazals and was able to recite poetry at great length. When he was in a proselytising mood, he tended to be listened to in a tolerant, slightly bemused silence and sometimes he was laughed at in a good natured way, especially by the sons of Thakur Sahib, or sideways glances were exchanged. Occasionally, his more extreme pronouncements of fundamentalism were challenged. Very often the Dube Brahmin priest was present but he very rarely entered into debate with CK who was much more articulate as well as being more aggressive in his faith. CK said that he had not migrated to Pakistan because Pakistani Muslims were 'beiman' (without faith) and that Islam exists in all countries, not just in Pakistan. He and nearly all the Muslims supported Thakur Sahib on most issues, especially since the latter was clearly more sympathetic and was at pains to express his interest in and sympathy with Islam much more than the mainly Brahmin opposition. The Muslims were also keen supporters of Congress (I), both because Muslims normally support this party and also because of their close allegiance to Thakur Sahib. A division within the ranks of his own supporters between Pathans and Ahirs led Thakur Sahib to drop CK from his list of candidates for the gaon panchayat elections.

Development in the Village

Though situated on the roadside, Basauli cannot be described as a very developed village. In any case, the road had only been surfaced in 1978 and before that there was only a sandy and broken track which was difficult for both carts and kharkharas to use. The main signs of development were a government tubewell and over 20 private pumpsets. The tubewell was capable of irrigating 100 acres or so, including some land in neighbouring Karanpur, but lack of electricity supply, voltage fluctuations and breakdowns reduced its usefulness to 25 percent or less of its potential capacity. Electricity was rarely available for more than eight hours on any one day, whereas in Lucknow city it was available for at least 22 hours per day and after March 1982 usually for a full 24 hours. Apart from being supplied for only about a quarter of the total day, its arrival was unpredictable and, even if foreseeable, it usually came at the least convenient times, especially after dark and frequently after 9 pm. In times of drought or other rural crises, the government would give orders for the rural supply to be increased temporarily to ten or twelve hours per day. This appeared to have no effect on supply in Basauli and the announcements were either merely for political effect or were implemented selectively according to region. There were frequent complaints about the laziness of the government contractor who looked after the state tubewells and, partly because of him, farmers were obliged to irrigate during the night in November 1982. The main grid line from Fatehpur to Suratganj runs through Basauli, near the south-east corner of the main settlement. Thanks to this, S. Mahabrahmin and Thakur Sahib had electricity connected to their tubewells and installed flourmills and S also had the only domestic connection in the village.

Housing was very poor in Basauli, where only about six houses were even partially pacca. There were more pacca houses in Imlipur and housing standards there were generally somewhat better. The worst was in Purwa.

There was a primary school in Basauli, with a headmaster, two teachers and about 120 pupils on the rolls. The headmaster was a cheerful, moustachioed Kayastha (of Srivastava subcaste), aged about 50 years who came (usually rather late) from his home in Raipur. He also ran the sub-post office in Basauli and would sit at a table in the open, performing both roles at the same time. Post Office officials had asked him to resign in September 1981 because the holding of two government posts was not permissible. Inertia in the system left him still in their employment in March 1983.

Another teacher, a Thakur, came from Mohammadpur and he was about 40 years. The youngest teacher, a Brahmin from Rammandai, was the most enthusiastic of the three and was also active in the politics of his own village. In winter, the school was supposed to meet from 10 am to 12.30 pm and from 1.30 to 4 pm. In summer the hours were only from 7.30 to 11 am. Attendance ranged from 40 to 80 children, depending upon the weather and other factors and the average number was 55, including at least a dozen girls. Attendance was lower from Kiratpur and some people in Kiratpur thought that there should be a school in their hamlet, to avoid the necessity of walking a kilometre to the school in Basauli. The teachers were sometimes assisted by two teenage girls as monitors, one Brahmin and one Mahabrahmin. They seemed to have the most direct interaction with the children. Much of the time, the children were assigned copying and reading tasks and were left to work on their own, with little direct instruction. Even though there were three teachers and ample space, the children were often seated together in one place instead of being divided into separate classes and positioned out of earshot of each other.

The current school buildings were constructed in two phases. The first part was built in 1968 and the contractor was TS, who succeeded in making a reasonable profit from the work. The building, however, remained incomplete and to this day the verandah and other finishing touches have not been applied, even though there was an inspection by a Junior Engineer who was paid by TS. There was the addition of another room in 1977 and this time TS did not apply for the contract, not because of any odium arising from non-completion of the earlier building, but simply because he lacked the capital to undertake the work. The contractor this time came from Lucknow.

There were two largish rooms in the rather dingy, brick schoolhouse but these were only used in very hot or wet weather. There was ample space outside the schoolhouse for dispersed groups. There was little attempt at attractive presentation of visual materials inside the school and there were various maps and other display materials, in various stages of decay, in a cupboard at the back of the room. The children brought their own slates and pens, ink and (mostly very tatty) text books. If teachers were asked to perform some other assignment, such as a census of school-age children or to attend a meeting, then school would be terminated early.

There were no official fees, but the teachers were said to charge five rupees for those children taking examinations in fourth and fifth class and a rupee for class one examinations. They also required Katha (literally 'story') for buying sweets for puja (there are five stories which, according to the Brahmins, each provide a particular benefit to the giver). The cost of Katha amounts to only about one rupee, plus some wheat or other gift in kind. All parents paid up at examination time and they did not complain in case they might find that their children had failed the examination. The Katha has religious associations and the money is used by the teachers to buy sweets which are shared with the children. It was, therefore, seen less as corruption and more as a means of acquiring merit. In addition, the government sometimes allotted money for teachers for the purchase of sweets to celebrate Republic Day or Independence Day, though this money was not always used for this purpose.

Some children also walk the kilometre to Mohammadpur, where there is a government middle school and a private secondary school. In 1982, five or six children from Basauli were attending the middle school.

The village was visited periodically by the Gram Sevak (Village Level Worker) who was responsible for about 12 villages altogether. The name Gram Sevak was changed to Gram Vikas Adhikari (Village Development Officer) in early 1981 and this more grandiose title somehow symbolised a very distinct change in the role of the VLW which had already taken place. The VLW has become more of a roving, junior bureaucrat and less of a community development worker, still less someone who actually worked at village level. In fact, the VLW for Basauli lived in Fatehpur where he was busy building a house in early 1982. He had also suffered from a swollen face after a tooth extraction and was not to be seen much in Basauli in the first two months of 1982. The Pradhan said that he would not complain about his absence, partly because he had no wish to cause trouble to someone with whom he was able to work quite satisfactorily and partly because the transfer of the VLW might bring someone less easy to deal with. The VLW was an intelligent Brahmin who still wore the choti (the strand of hair kept at the back of the head by orthodox Hindus and said to be used to pull people up to heaven). He travelled to Basauli either on his motorcycle or, less frequently, by cycle. He was a cheerful, extrovert and practical type of person and much of his time was spent in bringing a seemingly endless supply of forms to applicants for grants, subsidies and loans to either sign or apply a thumbprint.

It was generally assumed that he would expect Rs 100 or 200 from a grant involving Rs 3,000 or more, ie. at least 3 percent. There were frequent complaints both from the would-be recipients (who were often lower caste) and also from the funding banks, that the BDOs, VLWs and other medium-level officials who act as brokers in the system of dispensation of patronage were taking both an illegal and unfair share of the grants and subsidies intended mainly for the so-called 'weaker sections'. This problem was discussed with a BDO in another district, a keen development worker, and his view was that there were certainly cases of VLWs exploiting their clients but that very often the farmer who wanted government aid was too busy, lazy or just too apathetic to see to all the paper work involved and so he delegated this to the VLW. In such cases the VLW was fully justified in charging something for a service, without which the farmer would have little hope of getting his money from the government fund. In addition, most farmers were ignorant of the full details of the schemes, including legitimate fees which had to be paid as part of the general routine of Indian, bureaucratic procedures and so very often jumped to the wrong conclusion that they were being cheated.

5 The Pradhan and his family

Since the Pradhan plays such a key role in the political life of both the gaon sabha and the block, it is necessary to describe him and his family in some detail. The Pradhan was a 54-year old Thakur who had been educated to matriculation or tenth class level. Though three of his sons had proceeded further than him in their education, they lacked his intelligence and sophistication. Their father had been educated in the English medium and had also developed his mastery of English to a high level after leaving school, whereas his sons were of a new generation in UP who were educated mainly through the medium of Hindi. The Pradhan had left his native village in Rae Bareli district, which adjoins Barabanki district to the south, in 1944, to come with his father to claim the land and other property of his father's nanni (maternal grandmother), who received land revenues from about 16 villages. He said that "sometimes, in order to earn one's living, one has to leave one's home district". The Pradhan was the younger son and he and his father came to settle in Basauli permanently in 1952, leaving the elder brother to manage the property in Rae Bareli. The Pradhan's father was a Gandhian social worker and a homeopath and he remained in Basauli until his death in about 1971. Most people knew the Pradhan as 'Thakur Sahib' or by his popular nickname (especially among non-villagers) of 'Bacha Singh' ('Baby Lion') and many, even of his close acquaintances, were unaware of his actual name. Some villagers, particularly women, called him Daddaji. Thakur Sahib had been chairman of the Congress committee for Suratganj block since about 1965 and, as such, was known to most people even in the remote corners of a block which has some fairly inaccessible places. He sometimes toured the block on his cycle, especially during election periods, and many people would greet him with a namaskar, placing hands together and diagonally upwards, in front of the chest. Others would shout Jai Ram or Jai Shankar (Hindu greetings) and some, if he stopped, would come forward and touch the upper portion of both feet or his knees, as a mark of respect to a superior, and, in this case, a 'feudal' dignitary. Thakur Sahib was never embarrassed by this and would claim that he did not insist on, or even ask for, such marks of respect. He claimed that, for him, a simple namaskar was enough. However, it is more likely that, as his power might be beginning to decline, he was somewhat gratified by the continued display of feudal respect. For example, a Lodh member of the gaon panchayat, who supported Thakur Sahib, had trained his grandson, aged under five, to come to touch the feet of Thakur Sahib. This never failed to please and Thakur Sahib would make a great fuss of the child. He emphasised that people showed such respect to him, not because of his caste, but because of favours rendered in the past.

TS still felt keenly the fact that, as younger brother, he had been obliged to move from his native district of Rae Bareli to the less congenial atmosphere of Barabanki. He pointed out that there had been no big Talukdars in Barabanki district, whereas Rae Bareli was dominated by distinguished families from the feudal aristocracy. He also pointed out that military recruitment was low in Barabanki because "people are cowards and bullies who will only attack if someone is asleep but not otherwise". On the other hand, Rae Bareli, along with other districts, like Unnao and Ballia, provide many recruits for the armed services. Even when TS was a child, there had been members of the scheduled castes attending school with him and he claimed that Rae Bareli had always been more socially advanced than Barabanki. Since then, and especially recently, Rae Bareli had caught up with Barabanki in economic terms, largely due to the patronage of Mrs Gandhi, who used to be one of the MPs for the district.

The father's father of Thakur Sahib came from Jaunpur district at the age of 23 years when TS's father was aged only three. The father of Thakur Sahib had been a strong moralist who had built a temple in his village. He had also been chairman of the Cooperative Federation in Rae Bareli, as well as a member of the Talukdars Association at Lucknow and the Kshetriya Mahasabha at Agra. He was said to have approved of Zamindari Abolition but this was debatable. However, he had lived very simply, even before Abolition. Before Independence, he had sheltered Congress activists and revolutionaries, including one who had hidden in an outbuilding for six months. As a relative and neighbour of Rana Sahib Kajurgaon, who had British connections, the family was protected from harassment. Thakur Sahib considered that his father had been 'too mild' for the new environment of Basauli. He came from a conservative and cultured family and he never resorted to abuse. Because of his mildness, his father had been given less respect than his position warranted. Thakur Sahib, who originally came to Basauli in 1944 at the age of 16 years, had never even smoked in front of his father. He was shocked by the behaviour in Basauli, which included drinking, abusing and the dishonouring of women, and he set out to change all this from at least 1952. He claimed that in three or four years he saw 'some improvement' but he was still not entirely satisfied, even in 1982. His father had rebuked Thakur Sahib for resorting to abusive language and harsh behaviour towards villagers. Thakur Sahib admitted, sadly, that he had become 'habituated' to the poor social atmosphere of Barabanki and that it had even corrupted him to some extent. When his father was insulted by JS and other rival Thakurs, his son took action and threatened 'to break the bones' of anyone in the family of JS who even came out of their house. He claimed that they were so frightened by this that they stayed inside the house for six days, even excreting within their courtyard.

Thakur Sahib was highly articulate, both in Hindi and English. In characteristically humorous vein, he would point to a small protuberance on his face and say that this was the source of his eloquence. Thakur Sahib laughed frequently and he was adept at using his good humour and wit to disarm opponents, to defuse tension or to ridicule people who might be bothering him with demands which he considered irrelevant or unworthy of consideration. Educationally and culturally, Thakur Sahib was a mixture of sophistication and irrationality, even naivety. However, there are many more in India and indeed elsewhere who have been educated to much higher levels than tenth class who combine such qualities. From fourth class onwards, Thakur Sahib attended school in Lucknow, where he lived for seven years. He remembered it as a quiet, uncrowded city in the late 1930s and early 1940s but he said that he felt strange when visiting it now. In Lucknow, he first attended the Queen's High School, Qaiserbagh and then the Kanyakubja College, Charbagh which his father's brother and other agnates had attended. In 1944 his father's brother died and he was obliged to leave school to begin to learn the management of the estate in Rae Bareli, which then consisted of about 110 acres, from the munshi. His fluency in English far exceeded that of the average young graduate and he attributed his command of the language to wide reading of English books and to watching English language films (of which there are now usually only two being shown in the 28 or so cinemas in Lucknow). In the beginning, he found Tarzan pictures particularly useful because there was much action and very little dialogue. As evidence of his 'progressiveness' he pointed out, rather touchingly, that he had been to see James Bond and similar films.

Thakur Sahib had often taken a regular newspaper. In the past this had been most frequently the Swatantra Bharat but he also sometimes had bought the Nava Jeewan. In late 1982, he was buying Amrit Prabhat, from the same press as the Northern India Patrika. If he was not taking a newspaper each day in the village, because of supply difficulty or parsimony, then he usually managed to read either a Hindi or an English language newspaper during his peregrinations in the bazaars of Suratganj and Mohammadpur. He also listened fairly regularly to the radio news in Hindi from Akashvani at 8.45 pm. The radio news gave long, detailed and often very boring facts, mainly from government sources, and lively or controversial material, which might be in the newspapers, was strictly excluded from radio news. Thakur Sahib, as a government supporter, grudgingly conceded that the radio news had only limited value.

For all his native intelligence, TS still remained only partially educated and he lacked the coherent rationality of a disciplined, fully trained mind. For example, TS showed keen interest in astrology and was frequently to be seen consulting his astrological tables, though he tended to play down their importance when asked about them. He also wore a rather distinctive copper ring with strange symbols on it which he sometimes tied onto his holy thread. He claimed that the ring had no religious or other significance. Rings are commonly worn by men in India and some of the 'flashier' politicians may have four or even more rings, some with stones, on their fingers.

Thakur Sahib was an avid reader and there were usually Hindi and English books, plus his reading spectacles, by his charpoy and he would read in quiet moments during the day and also by lamplight until 10 pm or even later. Among the books he had read in English were biblical and epic novels (such as 'The Big Fisherman', some novels of Sir Walter Scott and some works on English history). He was very interested in tracing back the ancestry of his subcaste of Thakurs. He also bought various Hindi and other magazines, including Hindustan Weekly and Manohar Kahanion. He had seen such films as 'Ben Hur', 'The Robe' and 'Quo Vadis'.

Thakur Sahib showed a keen interest in religion, indeed in all religions, and had a distinctly eclectic approach to the subject without detracting from his Hindu identity. He showed much interest in the theological and intellectual aspects of religion but was no more devout in the ritual sense than the average villager. He usually joined in recitations of the Ramayana for only a brief, seemingly token period and seemed self-conscious when he was part of collective chanting or singing. It was not clear whether this was because of his higher status or not. Thakur Sahib was convinced that God exists because even those who do not believe in God could only not believe because the idea of God existed in the first instance. Like most members of 'twice-born' castes, he wore a holy thread, a double thread made of white cotton which ran diagonally from his left shoulder to his right waist. For ablutions, he wound the thread round his left ear so that it was raised from any danger of being soiled whilst squatting.

Capital

Thakur Sahib's grandfather had owned over 120 acres in Musapur when he died. By 1927, the estate had been reduced slightly to 110 acres. His father's original inheritance in Basauli had been about 70 acres and his father's cousin had also inherited another 70 acres. They each lost about 15 acres when the Adhivasi Act of 1954 transferred asli tenure to shikmis (sharecroppers).

Most of the ancestral land was in Basauli but there was also some in five neighbouring villages including Banmau, Mamtamau and Jigni. Since then Thakur Sahib had sold some land, especially that in other villages which he could not supervise and thus found unprofitable. By 1982, he estimated that he had only 28 acres, which was five acres less than the full limit allowed to a family under the land reforms. This land included 14.5 acres of irrigable land and four acres of grove land. Thakur Sahib valued the land at Rs 200,000. Most of the land was worth Rs 1,000 to 1,200 per bigha, but a few bighas were worth Rs 1,500 each.

His father also inherited rights to collect land revenue (malguzari), as Zamindar, from about 1,000 acres in 16 villages and this yielded him an annual income of about Rs 10,000, which was a very large sum in 1950. Given that agricultural wholesale prices have more than trebled and consumer prices for the working class had more than quadrupled since 1950, the malguzari income would have been worth between Rs 30,000 and Rs 50,000 at 1982 prices. This far exceeds Thakur Sahib's current income from all sources. He lost all this income after Zamindari Abolition but he received some compensation in stages over about five years. The deteriorating condition of the Zamindar's house provided a conventional symbol of the family's worsening economic situation, even though they remained at least one of the ten richest households in the gaon sabha.

In 1944 Thakur Sahib came to supervise his late pernanni's estate in Basauli, which he found in considerable disarray. The mama (mother's brother) of Thakur Sahib had been in service as 'Munijar' to the pernanni and had leased out most of the land. There had been neglect and Thakur Sahib set about gathering together lost property. The relative became handicapped and returned to Kaisarganj tahsil in Bahraich district. TS went back to his home village because the joint property there was being divided. He returned to Basauli in 1952 and assumed the role of Zamindar. In order to retain the family's right to the land, he was obliged to go and live in Basauli, since absenteeism would have led to expropriation. His father, Lalan Sahib, joined him after a few months. The same year the Zamindari Abolition Act was passed and from 1953 to 1961 Thakur Sahib took a seasonal job as supervisor of sugarcane purchase near Colonelganj, not far from his first wife's village in Gonda district. For this he was paid over Rs 150 per month in the crushing season and Rs 75 per month in the off-season, as a retaining fee. Since then he had lived permanently in Basauli and had taken no other jobs outside, apart from a brief period as a Naib Tahsildar in Gonda district.

The Zamindar ancestors of TS had built a large, 20-roomed house in Ayodhya which was known as the Basauli mandir (temple). The house was said to be still in fairly good condition and TS had no immediate intention of selling it, even though its value had increased considerably and he was short of funds. In 1982 it was occupied by the elder son of the Dube Brahmin priest in the village and by the three younger sons of TS intermittently during term-time. The rest of the house was rented to students for nominal amounts. Other occupants included a Thakur friend of the second son who hailed from a village near Basauli and a Brahmin friend from Raipur village. The priest was said to earn a bare subsistence most of the year, but earned a little more at key festivals, such as Ram Naumi in March and Parikrama in November. It was claimed that at least 100 persons would go to stay in the house at the time of Ram Naumi each year, but only two or three went from Basauli in 1982. For the Parikrama festival, only ten or twelve villagers usually visited Ayodhya.

In 1981 the gross value of Thakur Sahib's output from his farm was about Rs 18,000 in what was not a very good year. Assuming that net value of output was 75 percent of gross value, then his net agricultural output would be about Rs 13,500. His son entered service as a revenue accountant in July 1981 and earned Rs 450 per month for six months of that year. Therefore, total net household income would be at least Rs 16,200 in 1981. The cash component of this amounted to over Rs 11,000. Thakur Sahib claimed that in 'a good year' his household income would normally be Rs 28,000 but this appears to have been an exaggeration.

Thakur Sahib was able to employ two full-time and one part-time biannual labourers, plus a number of casual daily labourers but rarely more than a total of five labourers in any one day. None of his family worked on the land regularly, though all the sons carried fodder to the animals and looked after them generally, if labourers were not in attendance. The youngest son also worked in the fields occasionally.

In November 1981 TS owned two pairs of oxen, one buffalo, its calf and one cow. Since the birth of a grandson in 1980 he had felt the need of more cow's milk, because buffalo milk is considered fatty and heavy for infants and his cow was only producing one to one and a half kilograms of milk per day. (Buffalo milk contains up to 9 percent fat whereas cow's milk has only 4 or 5 percent.) In December he bought an additional cow from a Yadav in Banmau village for Rs 1,050 and the cow calved in January 1982. Apart from S. Mahabrahmin, who had a household of 26 members, TS owned the largest number of bovines.

The family was confidently predicting a daily output of 4 kilograms from the new cow but it turned out to be a very awkward beast to milk (a 'badmash') and in fact produced barely 2 kilograms per day, in its first few months. The animals were usually milked by RS Kahar or his elder son at about 7.30 am and at 7 pm and they could get an average of 3 or 4 kilograms of milk from the buffalo each day. After wintry rain, this output would fall to only 2.5 kilograms per day. An average daily production of 5 kilograms had to satisfy family needs as well as the demands of a constant stream of guests, many of whom had to be given tea, which contained a quarter milk. There were eleven members of the household in 1982, including one young affine who later joined his family in Lucknow.

In 1982 TS sowed the RR-21 variety of wheat on 21 November which was slightly late. The best seed in terms of production and price was Shonakalyan but TS, unusually, preferred the taste of RR-21. His labourers ploughed the land three times only. The seed rate was 10 kilograms per bigha or roughly 50 kilograms per acre. Other Thakurs tended to be rather critical of TS as a farmer. He wanted to be taken seriously in this role but the general view seemed to be that he neglected his farm because of his politicking and his sons were either absent or, with the possible exception of the eldest son, lacking the necessary detailed knowledge to achieve high production. Even TS's labourer, G. Nai - no great farmer himself, commented that TS's black mustard was a poor crop because TS had not put mehnut (hard work) into it.

Though TS used, until 1980, to have electricity supplied to a flourmill and tubewell, he had never had any such supply to his house. There were several reasons for this. The first was that his house was located at least 250 metres from the nearest pole and it would have cost him several hundred rupees to connect. The line from the main grid would cost over Rs 2,500 and there were no rich residents in his mohalla who could share the cost. Secondly, much of his house was kacha and there were dangers of rain seeping in and causing short circuits. Thirdly, he was currently short of money. Fourthly, he was in dispute with the electricity department over a large, unpaid bill for energy consumed by his grain mill and tubewell. TS claimed that the reason for the disconnection of his tubewell was that he wished to transfer the name of ownership to his four sons, because the land on which it was situated had become their property. He also said that he would have been to Barabanki to complete this transaction had it not been for the election campaign for block Pramukh. He added that S. Mahabrahmin and family had been 'a thorn in his flesh' because he had a connection to their double pole with a transformer on it. They had been in the habit of pushing a pole up against his line to disconnect it or to short-circuit it. He felt that, apart from general hostility, they were trying to sabotage his milling machine because it was more popular than theirs. (The two of them comprised the main rivals for milling custom in the village, though some people went to mills in other villages.)

Thakur Sahib had a household income which was at least four or five times that of the average villager, but he lived a fairly simple life. He inhabited a large, partly pacca house but it was old and rambling and not in the best of repair. (The part owned by his absent 'cousin's brother' was in better condition. He had extended it with three brick rooms inside the courtyard, but the outer rooms, built before 1900, had thick kacha walls and large doorways with beautiful carved frames made of sheesham which are no longer purchaseable.) Thakur Sahib slept all the year on the verandah, even on cold winter nights, or, if the weather was very hot and airless and there was no rain, then he slept in the yard (duara) in front of his verandah. Here he could keep an ear cocked to his cattle which were tethered in the yard and could also be ready for attack by thieves, dacoits or his political enemies. Usually, a sharp spear, a halbard (ie. an axe-head on a long pole called a farsha) and a few lathis (heavy bamboo sticks) were stored under the charpoys in case of attack. During the period of research, no attacks in fact occurred, though on three separate occasions in November and December Thakur Sahib roused people when noise of gunshots and bomb explosions was heard within a mile of his verandah. On such occasions, he would call for his pistol, an Italian Biretta, to be brought from within the house, about 80 metres away. He also owned three long-barrelled guns, including one double-barrelled, one single and an old topedar, which used gunpowder and shot. Thakur Sahib owned four of the six licensed guns in Basauli. There were said to be some unlicensed weapons, including about 15 country pistols (katta) owned by people of various castes.

There was a traditional taboo among Thakurs in the locality against building in brick, which was said to bring misfortune. TS told the story of his cousin's brother's desire to extend his portion of the house and of his fear of using brick and especially of laying the first brick, a task which was traditionally expected of the household head. Thakur Sahib told him not to worry and that he would lay the first brick for him and so no harm would come to his cousin's brother. TS advised him to extend the house by building outwards but he ignored his advice. Instead he consulted Brahmin astrologers and others as to what would be the most auspicious design and then extended within the inner courtyard. By doing this, he reduced the area of open garden space which made the housing seem very cramped. He spent about Rs 40,000 on the extension but left for Bahraich within 15 days. He had intended to return to live in Basauli but then changed his mind.

Women

Thakur Sahib had married a second time after his first wife died in 1951 when he was only 23 years. His first wife was a Bishen Thakur from near Colonelganj in Gonda district and her brother was elected as a Congress (I) MLA for a constituency in Gonda district in 1980. The first wife produced one daughter but died of septicemia after the birth of a second child which died two months later. Thakur Sahib then married another Bishen Thakur, this time from Ramkola, a small town in the far eastern district of Deoria. The second wife produced four sons and a daughter. All the women of the household observed purdah and they rarely emerged from their large, inner courtyard (angan) except when going to other villages. They used a shawl (chadr) rather than burqah. No males except close relatives, trusted servants and workers, with permission, were allowed into the inner courtyard and the researcher was never allowed into this inner area. Thakur Sahib admitted that 'purdah had its inconveniences' but it was also quite useful for him in some ways. Very often his verandah and the outer yard below his verandah were thronged with villagers and outsiders waiting to see him on political, legal, social, medical or other business. In order to preserve his privacy and his family life, it was probably very necessary that even someone as gregarious and patient as Thakur Sahib should have an inner retreat which was inaccessible to the general public. He also maintained that his high social status made it necessary for his women to be secluded.

TS claimed that the idea that Hindu women are subjugated arose from a misinterpretation of the scriptures. He had never abused his wife, not to talk of beating her. If he were to go inside the house and his wife should happen to not be in a good mood, then he would merely take one cup of tea and then return outside and wait for her mood to change. He invariably avoided disagreement or conflict. He pointed out that in the marriage rites (to which, he claimed, most people paid little serious attention), the bride had the opportunity to question the groom on how he would treat her. The groom usually replied that, just as the sun shines, so he will look after her. She then asks what about the time when the sun goes down, and he then swears by the moon and stars as well. TS conceded that he and his wife led separate lives and he claimed that, as a result of this, they were the more affectionate towards each other. TS was indeed sometimes absent, not only from his wife, but from his family, for several days at a time, because of political and social work and also, incidentally, because of family duties such as trying to arrange his daughter's marriage in quite distant districts.

One of the campaigns which had made TS very unpopular with the higher castes, especially the Thakurs but also some Brahmins, had been his strong opposition to any disrespect shown to women ('the ladies') and, more particularly to any extra-marital or pre-marital relationships. Most of all, he had come down heavily against higher caste exploitation of their caste status in seducing, abducting or simply assaulting lower caste women. This had brought him into conflict particularly with the family of JS Thakur. He claimed that the Thakurs in Rae Bareli district had higher standards and that his own father had instilled in his sons very high standards of sexual morality. He found that the Thakurs of Basauli had been used to drinking, drugs, gambling, wenching and other vices and his first duty, as leader of the village, was to put a stop to this. He alleged that their political opposition to him stemmed mostly from his having, to a large extent, though not completely, stopped their fun.

Partly because TS was known to be a stickler for purdah, the village women took care to cover their heads, faces or mouths (according to their age, status and temperament) when they passed him in the village. TS was gratified that their fear of him was such that, one day, when Muslim women who were quarrelling saw him coming, they quickly went indoors. However, he added wryly that they resumed their dispute when he passed out of sight.

TS was very worried that the western mohalla would be 'contaminated' by the alleged immorality of the eastern tola which had already 'spread' to Purwa. He had, in the past, expelled three or four persons from the village, including a Pathan, a Pasi and an Ahir. One of these had died 'in exile' in a village five kilometres away. TS cited the case of a 'black woman' of the eastern ward who was 'used' by both Brahmins and Thakurs and this had even been done in the open, which was particularly offensive to Indian culture. He had forbidden the woman to come near his house or in the mohalla and she normally went to shop in Mohammadpur by the road or along the track, past the Patharkot quarter. He also mentioned the case of one young girl who was virtually kidnapped and raped by some Brahmins and others and that he had taken action against the Brahmins. He said that it was intolerable that a young girl should have to run away from the village because of such happenings.

Social Attitudes

Thakur Sahib, like all the other Thakurs in the village, used to eat meat (except beef) and fish but in 1978 he, alone in his family, gave them up before going on pilgrimage to Gaya in the neighbouring state of Bihar. The pilgrimage had connections with a Vaishnavite cult and marked for him the beginning of the third (Banaprasta) stage in the Hindu life cycle, when a man gradually starts to sever family ties and to retreat from the world. (This forms the prelude to the final stage of Sanyas.) TS said that in the past people used to bring him fish quite frequently, but this happened more rarely now that only his family members ate fish.

TS insisted, paradoxically and probably misleadingly, that he had not become a vegetarian for religious reasons and that the main reason was gastric trouble. He found it increasingly difficult to digest meat. This was probably only part of the explanation, since TS also observed that meat was now so expensive (Rs 14 per kilogram), that the cost of meat for all the family (including his very carnivorous sons) would be Rs 28 and the whole meal might cost Rs 35 or 40. He compared this with a mere Rs 3 to 5 for a vegetable curry and said that he obviously could not afford meat every day, at such prices. In any case, the meat which was available in the village was usually very bony and of the lowest quality, whilst the best meat was taken to the cities.

TS admitted that he sometimes missed the occasional change in diet which meat had previously provided him and he also felt weaker as a result of the loss of this food. The rest of his family, including (unusually) his womenfolk, continued to eat fish and, more rarely, meat, mainly as a change in diet. (In 1982, the potato production had been good and the pulse crop poor, so potatoes proved to be a very useful but somewhat repetitive element in the household diet.) In cases where the diet within the household differed, it was more common for the wife to be vegetarian and the husband a meat-eater. The fish tended to be more often gifts from friends or relations of TS and was usually only bought if a son was returning from college or if there was some other special celebration. The youngest son of TS earned the disapproval of his father by making himself sick by consuming too much fish on one occasion.

TS usually bought his meat from a Pathan of Sikohna village who had worked as a butcher in Calcutta. He knew how to cut the meat well and, though he charged slightly more, TS normally bought from him. TS recalled that his maternal great grandfather, Lalan Singh, had kept a hundred goats in the old days and was said to have eaten 1.25 kilograms of meat every day. TS said that it is not an easy matter to digest such a large amount of meat, cooked in black mustard oil (not in modern Vanaspati) and therefore so much more greasy and heavy for the stomach. Lalan Singh ate little rice or chapatis and was a very strong man of mild temperament.

TS had no inhibitions about providing food to non-Hindus, including Christians. He was criticised by orthodox Hindus for giving food to a Christian friend from Barabanki town but he asked them what harm there was in this and where precisely a prohibition was written in the Hindu scriptures. No one could answer him on this. TS added that he was chairman of the block Congress (I) committee and therefore nobody dared disagree with him. However, TS was characteristically Congress (I) in his gradualist and Fabian philosophy. He said that he did not believe in caste discrimination himself and received tea from lower caste people in restaurants outside. He did not care at all about interdining restrictions nor which caste milked his buffalo and cows but others in the village would object and that might make it difficult for him to live in the village. All the time, the accent was not on leadership from the front (and from his privileged social and political position) but on a very cautious concern for what would be the reaction of the majority of villagers to his behaviour. The fact that the majority of the village are lower caste and might conceivably approve does not seem to be valid and it is of course quite possible that the backward castes might take an even more narrow-minded view of complete freedom of caste restrictions than might the Brahmins (including the so-called communist Mahabrahmins). TS summarised his attitude to change by two metaphors. Firstly, change could not be forced and it is better to lead a horse to water ..... Secondly, if the cart were made to turn the corner too fast, then it would surely overturn and everything would be spoiled. He quoted some Sanskrit verses to support his theory. TS claimed that the villagers, especially (but not only) the higher castes, would not follow him if he tried to change things any faster. Given the extreme caution of the leadership at all levels and the conservatism of the led, an equilibrium of 'social stalemate' had arrived. Part of the dominant class was aware of the need for some change and favoured it. However, it feared chaos if the change was embarked upon too quickly, especially since the lower caste leaders were seen as uneducated, unsophisticated and, in some cases, brutish. They were not regarded as ready to replace a Thakur/Brahmin hegemony.

Thakur Sahib was a loyal, but nevertheless critical, member of the Congress (I) who prided himself on being able to stand up to officials and ask pertinent questions in meetings which included them. He attended the political rally held in Lucknow in December 1981 when Mrs Gandhi addressed her supporters. Thakur Sahib was accompanied by over 30 people from Basauli, including DNS Thakur, DPS Thakur (a member of the opposition faction in the village), AK Thakur (sister's husband of DNS), CK Pathan and B. Lodh. Others who went were mainly Thakurs, Pathans, Lodhs, Pasis and Gadarias.

As a political and social worker, TS was an extremely energetic person for a man of 54 years and he was frequently gone from the village at 6 am, before taking tea or other refreshment. Sometimes he would not return until 9 or 10 pm. On his rounds he was occasionally asked to settle disputes in surrounding villages. On his return he might then also find a knot of people sitting in his yard (or, if they were important, on his verandah) waiting to talk with him. For example, he once returned at 5 pm after a full day, settling disputes in four different villages, only to find that a plank (sarawan) had been stolen and he was expected to deal with the problem. TS claimed to be ready to go at any time to help villagers, even at 10 or 12 at night.

TS was opposed to the manner and methods of the rural police but, as a shrewd politician, he recognised the necessity of preserving reasonably good relations with them. His general policy was to resist firmly any police encroachment on his territory or authority, to avoid referring cases to them whenever possible and never to ask them to do anything illegitimate. For this, he had earned the respect, if not the close cordiality, of the local police. He would talk of his defence of villagers against the rural police and he cited the case of the 16-year old nephew of CK Pathan who was once arrested by a policeman, simply for carrying a stick. At the time TS was carrying a lota, in preparation for going to the latrine. He remonstrated with the policeman, saying that the boy was not a badmash (villain). TS went to the latrine and then cycled to Mohammadpur to rescue the youth from the police.

The Male Relatives of Thakur Sahib

Thakur Sahib's elder brother was a graduate in Physics, Chemistry and Biology and, as Thakur Sahib observed, he had a very different kind of personality and behaviour. He was physically large whereas Thakur Sahib was tall and thin. He was said to be less gregarious and more selfish in nature and he did not meet with villagers very much. He had come and tried to live in Basauli but could not tolerate its backwardness. The elder brother "considered it beneath his dignity to come and live in this ilaqa". Thakur Sahib had "certain differences with his brother and preferred to live separately from him" to avoid dispute. For this reason and also because of his seniority, it had been agreed that the elder brother would inherit the Rae Bareli property and live there. According to Thakur Sahib, his elder brother had invested wisely and had accumulated. He was said to own land worth Rs 450,000 in 1982 and this was more than twice the value of the land owned by his younger brother in Basauli. The elder brother had bought some very good quality land in Mirzapur district which was said to be worth Rs 3,000 per bigha.

Half of the old Zamindar residence in Basauli was the property of Thakur Sahib's 'cousin' (mausera bhai in fact, though usually he was loosely referred to as chacha zat bhai). His cousin had an MSc in Commerce and had become an accountant in the Bahraich branch of the Punjab National Bank and his family also lived in Bahraich. Thakur Sahib used one of his cousin's kacha rooms as a storeroom, one was normally empty (and occupied by the researcher during his stay), and a third was used to house animals in bad weather. The brick portion inside the courtyard was mainly unused, except as a place to store foodgrain and other crops produced by the cousin's sharecropper and munshi, CK Pathan. Thakur Sahib was critical of the new building and had advised him to build outside so that the inner courtyard would remain an open, uncramped space. Recently, the cousin had sold his remaining land, about 70 bighas. At one time, CK had lived with the cousin in Bahraich and managed his land there. The cousin visited the village once, on his scooter, during 1982 but he stayed only for a few hours.

Thakur Sahib had four sons, two of whom had already married, and two daughters, of whom the elder was married to an accountant in the Bank of Baroda. The eldest son had two children and the wife of the second son gave birth to a stillborn daughter in September 1982. Earlier, in August 1981, the family suffered a more grave tragedy, from which they were still trying to recover a year later. The wife of the eldest son, who was particularly liked within the family, vomited three times in quick succession after lunch and died within a matter of five or six hours. TS described it as 'cholera' but the MO of the PHC, who examined her after death, thought it was a case of severe food poisoning. TS had not thought it serious until he was called to examine her again about 7 pm and he then called for Dr S. Kurmi, an unqualified doctor from Mohammadpur, because he was the nearest. TS gave her a homeopathic injection but he feared that it was too late and that she had already the colour, skin texture and perspiration of one near to death. He described, very movingly, how she had observed purdah from him until the end and how he told her in her dying moments that she was like a daughter to him and that she should remove her veil to allow him to treat her effectively. The dead wife left a daughter aged 4 years and a baby boy aged 10 months who were then looked after by the wife of the second son. At 13 months, the boy was still not weaned of milk and looked very chubby. He would lick dal and biscuit crumbs from his grandfather's fingers.

The eldest son of TS, aged 27 years, had failed his matriculation three times and was the only son not to have entered higher education. With the help of his father-in-law, he and his brother-in-law were both somehow able to obtain certificates of matriculation and thereby be sent for training as lekhpals (revenue accountants). He joined service in July 1981. In March 1982 he was forced to resign his job because, ostensibly, he refused to be posted to another district. By March 1983, he had still not succeeded in being reinstated and it was rumoured that a further problem, that of the false certification, was adding to his problems. He looked the most like a traditional Thakur, with long moustaches, fierce eyes and the harshest tongue for recalcitrant labourers. He was also the only son who really understood the farm work properly and he would most often bring fodder for the animals when labourers were not available. He spent much of his time away from the village, seeking a groom for his younger sister.

TS was most concerned about his eldest son whom he regarded as the most considerate to him and as the one who was the most vulnerable because of his lack of education. However, he once confided that he did not really see why he should bother himself about what would happen to his sons after his death. It was then up to them to make their own lives. In practice, TS must have been worried about the future. It was alleged that, despite some attempts to boost the productivity of the family farm, Thakur Sahib's production and general economic position had grown steadily worse each year since about 1975. His prolonged inability to settle the marriage of his younger daughter and the demands for a large dowry added a further crushing potential burden which hampered his economic manoeuvrability in any other direction. TS complained that some of the families he approached were asking over Rs 20,000 and he claimed that his own capacity was only for Rs 10,000. Some, who took a more pessimistic view of his family fortunes, suspected that even this was an exaggeration. However, in January 1983, TS settled the marriage of his daughter, with a dowry of Rs 10,000 and the wedding ceremonies were completed in May.

On 22 January 1982, about five months after his wife's death, the eldest son journeyed to Allahabad, scene of the Kumbh Mela, to do pilgrimage and also to dip his wife's ashes in the holy waters of the Sangam on the festival of Amawasya, when millions bathe in the Ganges. He travelled by bus to Lucknow and then by train to Allahabad, a journey of about nine hours altogether. For this sad duty he wore smart grey flannel trousers and a bright blue pullover with a fair isle pattern on the midriff. His luggage consisted of a medium-sized suitcase, with green cloth round it and a green bedroll which cost about Rs 75. TS also took his father's ashes on a similar journey in 1974, but this coincided with a different Hindu festival.

TS said that it would be possible for his son to remarry, but not before they had found a husband for his daughter. In fact, TS thought it might be considered more 'scandalous' for the son to remain without a wife than to remarry. He remarried in May 1985.

The second son, aged 24 years, was shorter in stature and much milder than his elder brother. He had had a long but not particularly distinguished academic career and had succeeded, somehow, in eventually passing various examinations, including his BA at Lucknow University and he passed his final LLB examinations from Saket Degree College, Avadh University, Faizabad in August 1982. His examinations took place after those of his two younger brothers partly because the postgraduate law course had been delayed by political and other problems. He at first had intended joining a family friend in Barabanki and trying to begin to make his way as a trainee lawyer in this small district town. This would not be easy because competition, even at this low level, is fairly intense and there were many lawyers to be seen in their black frock coats and white two-tailed, clerical ties. He later took entrance examinations to become a trainee kanungo (revenue official). There were about 50,000 candidates from all over UP for 90 posts. Some time before July 1984 he had entered into a legal practice.

Part of the ancestral property of TS's uterine family included a large house (with temple attached) in Ayodhya, birthplace of Rama, the city of many temples to which pilgrims come from all over India. This house, though now dilapidated, had at least 20 rooms and was used by the sons when they were studying at the degree college. However, none of the sons ever attended the college full-time, either because of trouble within the University, or because of farm, family or political duties in the village, or simply through illness and/or homesickness. They would take foodgrain and other subsistence materials from the farm and these they would cook for themselves in Ayodhya. Their pleasure at returning to their family and to their mother's cooking (usually more elaborate on their return and just before their departure) was almost tangible. The life of a student at Avadh University, even if a son of an ex-Zamindar, was not an easy one.

If the second son had become established with his family in Barabanki, then he had planned to take in his young niece so that she would be able to study at a reasonably good school there.

The third son, aged 20 years, took his BA final examinations in March 1982, and heard that he had passed by August. His subjects were Economics, Sociology and Military Science and it seemed both possible and fitting that he should become a military officer. However, competition for entry into this profession is extremely tough and he suffered the acute disadvantage, like all four brothers and many other students from the 'Hindi belt' of northern India, that he had been educated almost entirely in the medium of Hindi and would find both entry to, and courses in, military college quite difficult. However, he seemed otherwise very suited in caste, physique and personality for the army. None of his near relatives had entered military service, though TS was friendly with another Thakur who used to be in the Indian Air Force.

The third son said that the Avadh University had acquired a bad reputation three or four years ago and had also been closed frequently in 1980-1. The current year had been quiet and he said that, when lecturers turned up, he usually received three or four lectures per week. He was both worried and very annoyed that some of his examinations had been timed so that they coincided with the Ram Naumi festival in Ayodhya. The implication of this was that his period of revision and actual examination would be disturbed by the large inrush of pilgrims and the very loud amplification of religious music on most street corners. The examinees had protested and asked for an earlier date for the examination. All the sons preferred to work at their house rather than in the library, because they found the library atmosphere 'too serious' and insufficiently relaxed.

The third son decided in October, rather belatedly, to enrol for an MA in Sociology at Lucknow University. Though he applied late, he was successful in being admitted. Unfortunately, news of admission is only given through lists on the notice-board in the University and so, living in the village, he received news of his admission too late to meet the deadline for payment of admission fees. The university authorities are particularly strict in insisting on the prompt payment of this first instalment of fees and no reasons for non-payment are acceptable other than on medical grounds. Rural residence was not an acceptable justification for ignorance and failure to meet the deadline. Consequently, the third son was obliged to go to a Medical Officer and ask him to provide a letter certifying that he had been suffering from typhoid fever. This satisfied the registration authorities and he deposited Rs 168 as the first instalment of what would be total fees of about Rs 1,000 for the whole session. Many of the lectures for the MA in Sociology are given in English and this was clearly going to be a problem for him, though it was one that he himself dismissed as of minor importance.

Having been admitted late to the course at Lucknow University, it was even more difficult to secure a hostel place than for those with early admissions. It was assumed that a hostel place was dependent upon sofarish (patronage) and on establishing some caste, or other connection, however remote, with those in charge of allocations. The son was said to have a '20 percent chance'. In the meantime, he had other options, which he would explore. One was to live with his elder brother's late wife's brother, AKS, in Daliganj (adjacent to the campus) but he did not even consider this, as AKS had no spare space and, anyway, 'there were other objections'. He and R. Thakur agreed that it was not a good area.

He could go and live in the attic flat of his sister's husband's house but this was a long way from the university, nine kilometres to the south-west of the campus. A third possibility was to try to rent privately and he said that he was prepared to spend up to Rs 75 per month on rent. However, the most suitable places, in the better parts of Daliganj, cost Rs 150 per month and so he could only afford to do this if he shared with one or two others. The problem was that he would only share with Thakurs or Brahmins from his locality and he was not willing to contemplate sharing with complete strangers, particularly not people of lower castes, whose ritual status, living standards and behaviour were likely to be below his. Sharing with someone from a scheduled caste need not even be considered, because, even if he were willing, 'his society', including his parents, would not allow it. So the usual device used by western students, the notice on the departmental or union board, was not favoured by most students at Lucknow University. R. Thakur suggested that he could share with NK Shukla from Basauli who had recently shifted to a new room but was not satisfied with it, because of the distance from his work in the Telephone Department. The son raised his eyebrows at the mention of Shukla (whose family members are regarded as the main political opponents and 'trouble makers' in the village) but R assured him that NK had no connection with RN Shukla and was not the least interested in village politics. R also suggested that for Rs 100 per month, NK might be willing to do the cooking and other chores. Eventually, the third son's dilemma was resolved by his sister's husband being transferred from Jaipur to a bank in an eastern district of UP and this meant that his sister resumed residence in their Lucknow house and her brother was able to live with her. In July 1984 he was waiting for the results of his final examinations for the MA in Sociology.

The youngest son of TS was only 18 years and he took his BA Previous (ie. first year) examinations in April 1982. He was the least studious of the three and rarely stayed in Ayodhya for very long, ostensibly because 'the water did not suit him' and he became weak or even ill from its effect. His attempts at study in the village were spasmodic and not helped by the general environment, including his need to supervise the farm work, in the absence of his father, who neglected the farm in preference for politicking. He was also distracted by the village youths, much of whose culture and interests he shared far more than did the other brothers. It was almost certain that he could only pass this and earlier examinations by copying. His study technique consisted of writing out large chunks from the Hindi textbooks. His subjects included Economics, Sociology and Political Science. He openly admitted to having only passed an earlier English examination by copying, as had also the third son.

He was the most aggressive, least mature but also, in many ways, the most independent of the sons. He showed the keenest interest in following his father in a political career but he could be rash as well as brave. He had narrowly survived an attack on his life in March 1981 when a Mahabrahmin youth threw a small bomb at him in Fatehpur when he was returning from college. The assault arose out of a petty quarrel at the inter-college in Fatehpur, but was part of the much wider and deeper conflict between TS and the Mahabrahmin/

Brahmin opposition in the village. Since then, the youngest son had been normally accompanied by an armed bodyguard if he visited the fields or went out of the village, especially if he visited Fatehpur.

TS dismissed the attack as one 'by a dull youth', incited by criminals and crop-cutters from Rammandai, a nearby village, dominated by Brahmins. After the attack, about 300 men gathered in the night and were all in favour of attacking and destroying the house of the youth's father. TS restrained them and told them that they could be charged with theft and dacoity. He would try to sort matters out in the morning. Next morning he went early to Fatehpur and on his return, his kharkhara crossed with that of S. Mahabrahmin who was on his way to Fatehpur. The two Thakur youths accompanying TS forced S to descend from his kharkhara and he was 'persuaded' to return with them to the village, where a large meeting was called. TS declared that he wanted no revenge and he only asked the family concerned to either live peaceably in the village or else to name a date for a fight and they would then see who was the stronger. TS neither wished to kill S nor to break his bones and only desired that he should live in harmony, not only with TS but with the whole village.

TS concluded his reminiscence of this encounter by noting that he was still not on favourable terms with the family but that they were living peaceably. The youngest son (and his brothers and indeed also the father) swore that they would avenge both the attack and also the insult implied by such an attack. Even before this provocation, TS had invariably carried his pistol and a band of bullets round his shoulder and under his waistcoat whenever he went out of the village. He claimed never to have used it and that he wore it purely as a psychological and preventive device.

The youngest son was a great admirer of Subhash Chandra Bose, the revolutionary freedom fighter who had liaised with both the Germans and the Japanese against the British during the Second World War. Bose was a much more radical nationalist than most, believing in violent methods, and, according to some, dabbling in fascist ideology. The son related, in all seriousness, rumours that Bose was still alive and that he was living, incognito, in Ayodhya. He spoke of a lonely old man who had been visited by the CID. It seemed that other such 'mystery stories' were circulating about Bose's survival of the air crash and his continued (strangely silent) presence. The third son also admired Bose but was slightly less credulous about his having survived. The existence of such stories illustrates both the popularity of Bose among some Thakur and other semi-educated youths and also the credulity with which such rumours are greeted even by relatively educated sections of rural society. It also possibly hints at the search for a 'brave saviour' who can lead people out of their current misfortunes. Though Bose was not a Thakur, his qualities were those which many Thakurs admire.

In March 1983, it seemed likely that the third and fourth sons would secure clerical employment with the help of TS's MLA brother-in-law and of his local MLA. The first son intended to begin contracting work and the second son to try legal practice in Barabanki. To raise capital for the first son's business, TS intended to sell 25 trees on his garden land, which would raise at least Rs 15,000. (One of the key aims of the government's 20-point programme was the planting of trees and cutting them down without permission was illegal. It was estimated that the timber contractor would need to pay at least Rs 5,000 in bribes to the police to facilitate the logging. In Mausandi, a Brahmin had sold his trees but local Thakurs and others informed the District Magistrate and were able to save the trees.)

The Younger Daughter of Thakur Sahib

By early 1982, TS was beginning to be seriously worried about finding a suitable husband for his younger daughter who was now 23 years old. He said that he had approached so many people and his eldest son had recently used his holiday to visit a family in Lucknow, without success. TS complained that some 'were not in a mood' to get married yet, some were finishing their education and others were wishing to secure employment first: "The most troublesome bit is that I have to settle it in certain Thakur subcastes including Rathaur, Kushwaha, Chauhan, Bhadoria and Tomar" and he claimed that they were 'few in number' in this locality. (Bais was the majority subcaste of Thakur in Barabanki district.)

TS claimed that some families were asking for a dowry of Rs 18,000 to Rs 24,000 and this would imply total marriage costs for him of Rs 40,000. He 'did not appreciate' the dowry system of his society, but he had to take something for his sons in order to balance the cost of his daughter's marriage. He wanted her to marry into 'a decent family of good behaviour and culture' who would treat her well. He did not want her to marry among the rich, "who are often sharks who live off the blood of others". He said that his daughter, though only educated to matriculation standard, read newspapers, listened to the radio news and was familiar with outside world events: "She has been brought up in a good society". He thought too little attention these days was being given to personality and too much to looks. TS repeated that Rs 40,000 was beyond his capacity. He was prepared to marry her into 'a very ordinary family', provided that he could have 'proper relations' with them. Asked why he did not consider marriage outside the caste, he replied that "he had to live in the society". He quoted the example of a Brahmin boy in Mohammadpur who had married an Agarwal (Bania) and had then been rejected as an outcaste by his family. In his attempt to find a suitable groom, Thakur Sahib had travelled to many districts in UP, including Etawah, Kanpur, Hardoi, Lucknow, Barabanki, Unnao, Mainpuri, Shahjahanpur and Sitapur. The rule among Thakurs, not always followed, was that the girl should come from somewhere to the east of the groom's village. He had arranged a match with a family in Sitapur in 1980 but then the father of the groom, a lieutenant colonel, had died of a heart attack and the family had called off the marriage. He had later arranged another groom from within Barabanki district, but in April 1982 the marriage was postponed, and this was usually a tactful indication that the family was no longer interested. In early 1983, a marriage was arranged with a Chauhan Thakur, who had a diploma in electrical engineering. TS was relieved that at last this worry seemed over, though he was ill with low blood pressure in February, which he partly attributed to the hassle of making the marriage arrangements. However, he was pleased that the dowry demanded was Rs 10,000, much less than the Rs 16,000 agreed during the earlier engagement. One family member commented that the boy's family lived simply but 'behaved more like Kurmis'.

Other Relations

Finally, AKS, the eldest brother of the late wife of the first son, needs to be mentioned since he had remained a close family friend and was a frequent visitor to the village. Indeed, as an aggressive Thakur with strong views, he acted as a prominent member of Thakur Sahib's dominant faction who would speak at public meetings in the village and offer his advice on other occasions. AKS came from the interior village of Daulatpur, on the eastern bank of the river Samli, where his father was a respected landlord of the Janwar subcaste. The family owned about 80 acres. AKS was setting up a business as a building contractor and rented a very modest house in the Daliganj quarter of Lucknow, just behind the university. For this extravagant move, he was much criticised by Thakur Sahib. He was educated to tenth class but tended to combine a 'middle class' irritation with the Indian masses and a combative, Thakur spirit, displayed in his large, prominent moustache. In 1982, AKS was building the headquarters for a Flood Control Officer who was due to take up his new post in Suratganj. The elder son of AKS lived with Thakur Sahib because this enabled him to attend the intermediate college in Fatehpur. In July 1982, he left Basauli to join his parents in Lucknow to continue his schooling there.

Finally, the domestic staff of Thakur Sahib should be mentioned. TS employed the elder sister of G. Nai, a Muslim girl aged about 17 years, as domestic labour. Her duties were mainly to look after the grandchildren and also to clean the dishes and do other household jobs. If there was extra work, her mother would come and help with cooking and other tasks, whilst her younger sister quite often helped look after one of the two children. There was no fixed monetary payment and remuneration was in the form mainly of food, old clothing and ad hoc help to the family, when necessary.

Most evenings, any time from about 5 pm onwards, a few people from the mohalla (and sometimes beyond) would gather on the verandah and in winter a fire (tappa) would be lit there. The membership of the tappa group varied within an evening, because of domestic and other calls to duty, and it also varied over a longer period because of absence from the village, individual divergences of interest, completion of common business or because of some, often mild, disagreement. In January 1982, the tappa group included TS and his sons (when not in Ayodhya), the younger brother of his late daughter-in-law, the Dube Brahmin priest and his younger son, CK Pathan (who also slept on the southern verandah in winter), CK's brother, S. Pathan, N. Dhobe (friend and confidant of the eldest son), TS's servant and labourer, L. Kahar, 'Gomalu' Nai and three or four Pathan youths. Sometimes he would also be joined by DNS Thakur or SBS Thakur. The former was a large farmer who usually came if he had some specific business in mind, but SBS was a teacher who came less purposefully and tended to call on days he had been to Mohammadpur to see his son and also to buy vegetables.

This long digression on the most powerful person in the village illustrates several points. Firstly, there was one family which continued to exercise much of the power and influence of the traditional Zamindar, even though its resources were now much more limited and to some extent dwindling. However, the economic decline of the family should not be exaggerated. Part of Thakur Sahib's financial difficulties was a result of Zamindari Abolition but they were also due to his own mismanagement and apparent relative lack of interest in his farm and other economic affairs. He was experiencing an unusual squeeze on his resources because his household was at the stage in the development cycle when three of his sons were still undergoing (relatively) expensive higher education and were not contributing much, if anything, to the income of the household.

Secondly, the dominant leader in the village had a complex personality, whose main characteristic was a moderate conservatism but who combined autocracy with some liberal and self-critical values. He was neither a full-blooded 'feudal' leader nor was he a fully persuaded democrat. Thirdly, his immigrant status and his inability to command the support of even the small minority of Thakurs in Basauli meant, that, like many a Congress (I) leader, he was obliged to cultivate the support of the Muslims and lower castes. He was successful in winning Muslim backing but not many Chamars and some lower castes were divided in their support. In fact, both the dominant faction and the opposition, led by Mahabrahmins, Brahmins and Thakurs, claimed to represent, and have the major support of, the poorer and lower castes.

The Major Conflict in Basauli

The major conflict in Basauli was between the declining 'feudal' Thakur family of TS and the rising, entrepreneurial, Mahabrahmin family of S. The second son of TS claimed that there had never been any intercaste fighting in the village but that there was fighting between families (but not between biradaris). His father was more forthright and feared that the nature of conflict in the village was changing from factionalism within the Thakur caste to intercaste struggle. TS, like many Congress (I) politicians, blamed Charan Singh of the Lok Dal party for the increase in casteism (jatwadi) since he had espoused the cause of the backward castes and classes, including Jats, Ahirs, Kurmis amd Gujars.

TS observed that there was growing conflict between Thakurs and Brahmins in Basauli and he emphasised that he was particularly anxious to avoid this type of conflict. In fact the conflict was by no means fully intercaste and it reflected more the growing opposition of the Brahmins and other residents of the eastern mohalla to the hegemony of TS, family and supporters. Insofar as nearly half the

Thakurs were on the side of the Brahmins and all Thakurs but TS lived in the eastern mohalla, the conflict groups did not coincide with caste groups so very closely. As TS himself pointed out, Thakur and Brahmin households numbered only 10 and 100 (sic) respectively, so neither caste could win an election without the votes of the other castes. TS knew that his one-time staunch supporter, S. Mahabrahmin, wanted to challenge him now that S had become rich, but TS would never demean himself by standing for election when there was only S as his opponent. If S were to stand, then TS would depute a supporter to contest him so that S could not be considered as his equal in an electoral battle. In this way, TS concluded, "he may be crushed psychologically".

Elections for Pradhan of Basauli Gaon Panchayat

The first election for Pradhan occurred in 1949. At that time TS was only 21 years old and had been resident in the village for less than three years. (Now there is a minimum age requirement of 30 years for candidates for Pradhan.) The constituency of the gaon sabha at that time contained five villages, including Burhanapur and two other villages to the east. TS was opposed by a Kurmi from Satmohli. The election consisted of a show of hands and TS defeated his Kurmi rival. He was elected unanimously in Basauli proper, by all except one Kurmi voter in Kiratpur, and he even gained a majority in the village of his Kurmi opponent.

The next election was held in 1956. In the meantime Zamindari Abolition had upset TS's position and, in order to recoup costs of litigation and other serious losses, he had been obliged to take a job as a sugarcane purchasing contractor at Sarju procuring centre for Jarwal sugar mill in Bahraich district. He claimed that he was in loss from this enterprise and for two years he became a Naib Tahsildar. Since TS was busy elsewhere in 1956, he proposed the name of another Thakur, JS Raikwar, who was elected unopposed. TS said that he wanted JS to show his true colours and to destroy himself politically. However, some villagers feared that the brothers of JS might encourage him to abuse his power and so they made sure that the eight others who were elected unopposed as members should keep an eye on the new Pradhan. It so happened that the latter was able to facilitate the sale of some village land to the south of Kiratpur, to a Muslim from Fatehpur, who wished to start a brick kiln. He also helped someone else secure a house site. For these services, some money was extracted. He then informed the beneficiaries that the land was now being allocated to others and he thus tried to extract more money. TS, who was not a member, ensured that a motion of no confidence was passed at a gaon samiti meeting in 1957. The Pradhan swore on an oath of the temple of TS's family that he would accept any punishment of the village if he were to misbehave in future. Moved by this, his opponents compromised and he was allowed to complete his term.

TS had had to adjust his political ideas from those of a feudal autocrat (albeit united to some extent in the past with the lower classes against occupation by a foreign power) to a democrat in a society which at national level claimed to be secular, democratic and socialist (usually in that order). TS said that democracy had its problems and 'lacunae' and that the average Pradhan was elected on the basis of caste majority and then acted according to his whims and necessities (plus those of his caste). Such men usually did not understand the needs of their village. He once quoted Plato's view that democracy was the rule of fools.

In 1961, TS again expressed his unwillingness to contest but he claimed that he was pressed to do so by Thakurs, Brahmins and others because they were now in fear of the brothers of JS, who had promised to secure the latter's re-election, even if they had to do it with lathis. TS was duly elected and had remained in this office for the past 21 years. He claimed that he had been brought down to the level of the villagers and, in order to survive, he had been obliged to contest for the not very elevated post of Pradhan. He regarded most Pradhans as people "of little consequence, who could be pushed around by the rural police".

JS subsequently left the village in 1965 to become a sadhu and vaid in a village about eight kilometres from Basauli. More recently, he had moved to Naumish in Sitapur district and, when in October 1982 his relatives went to call him to the funeral of one of his brothers, they found that he had gone to the famous religious pilgrimage centre of Rishikesh in Dehra Dun district.

The election in 1971 caught TS at a time when he was very busy arranging his eldest son's marriage and also when his wife was severely ill. He claimed that he did not devote even a single hour to canvassing and that those candidates for members' posts who supported him did his canvassing for him. He won by 320 votes to 207. There was no further election until 1982.

TS attributed his success to the fact that people deemed him to be of 'a courageous heart' and ready to resist police or other officers who tried 'bad work' or to impose unpopular programmes within the village. He denied that he won because of caste and he pointed out (as politicians invariably do when rebutting accusations of casteism) that Thakurs constitute a minority in the village. He stressed that, although he may have come from a Zamindari family, his father was a Gandhian who disapproved of Thakurs and Brahmins maltreating the lower castes. His father apparently used to reprove TS when, partly out of rashness of youth and partly because he was less mild than his father, he spoke harshly to the lower castes.

TS was confident of Muslim support. He received 100 percent of the votes from Pathans, the main Muslim caste, in 1982 but none of the Telis and not all the Nais or Muslim Bhurjis voted for him. TS said that Muslims were 'very touchy' about their religion and he was known to be sympathetic to religious freedom of Muslims, particularly to their rights to prayer. He said that, wherever Brahmins and Thakurs co-existed in the same village, there was competition between them and therefore he had had to rely on the support of the lower castes.

TS claimed that he deliberately 'did not press' the lower castes and, as result, he thought that he received better cooperation and reciprocity and good relations in the village. He considered that he now got more from the lower castes by this policy than his grandfather gained through pressing the lower castes. It was significant that his aim was similar and only the method differed in being more subtle. (Others differed on the degree to which he was so gentle towards the lower castes and it was said that in the recent past, when no elections were in the offing, his behaviour towards the lower castes could be harsh and rude.) TS also claimed to benefit from his having come from outside and that he received more respect than local Thakurs who were mostly dissolute. Little children would come to touch his feet and he said they did this out of familial affection and not just because he was Pradhan. Villagers would come to greet him on his verandah by touching his knees or feet and then putting their hands together in front of their chests up to three times. TS maintained that, even when he abused the villagers, they still appreciated that he was working for their benefit. He said that he sometimes abused them out of temper and sometimes merely as a stratagem.

One of TS's closest associates in the 1982 election was S, a tall Muslim Kabaria from Burhanapur hamlet who was alleged to have been involved in at least half a dozen murders. Hitherto, S had sought the help of TS when he had been in trouble with the police and sometimes TS had been willing to help, at least up to a point. His entry into politics was something of a surprise but TS quickly formed an alliance with him, as a Muslim, as a long standing dependent and as the opponent of his political rival in the neighbouring constituency of Karanpur. S normally wore a green blazer, grey trousers and patched, black leather shoes. Usually he came on a cycle and, during the pre-election month, he visited TS almost every evening to report on the campaign and to seek TS's advice on various problems. He would come and touch TS's knees deferentially and then squat on the ground at the feet of TS. The latter seemed to enjoy coaching a younger man in the wiles of politics and he confided that S seemed very inexperienced. When asked how he could form an association with someone having such a reputation for criminal violence, TS affirmed, somewhat piously, that he hoped that the responsibilities of office might have a steadying influence upon S (who subsequently won his seat).

A relatively new ally for TS in the 1982 election was DNS Thakur. TS said that his 'mentality' was very similar to that of the old Thakurs and, until a year ago, he had been a member of the opposition faction. However, he had since quarrelled with part of the opposition and also needed the help of TS in arranging his daughter's marriage to a Bais Thakur whom TS knew and so DNS had started 'coming to his side' (ie. both spatially and politically). It was widely predicted that DNS would become Deputy Pradhan (as indeed he did) and that, in the event of Thakur Sahib being elected Block Pramukh at a later date, then he would become his successor as Pradhan. TS also commented that two years ago SBS Thakur, who had relied heavily on TS for patronage, earlier 'had tried to sail in both boats'. He had 'gone to both sides'. TS had not objected openly and he merely waited for some friction to develop when the other Thakur faction would inevitably misbehave, which they did. Someone slapped the brother of SBS and gave SBS the verbal equivalent of a 'square cut' to the jaw. SBS had since rejoined TS though he was less politically active or influential than DNS Thakur.

RS WPCI AND PERCENTAGE SUPPORT FOR TS IN ELECTION OF PRADHAN 1982

RS WPCI	SUPPORTED TS	NOT VOTED	NOT KNOWN	TOTAL HHS	% VOTE TS EXCL. NV + NK
401 - 700	3		1	8	43
701 - 810	13		2	25	52
811 - 950	11			20	55
951 - 1100	6	1		16	40
1101+	15	1		33	47
TOTAL	48	2	3	102	49

THE 12 MEMBERS OF THE GAON PANCHAYAT, BASAULI 1971 AND 1982

1971 NAME	CASTE	AGE IN 1971	YEARS SCHOOL	BIGHAS OWNED IN 1982	LOCALITY	FACTION	OTHER
RUDR NARAYAN SINGH	Bais Thakur	43	10	125	W Basauli	TS	Pradhan
RAM PADARATH	Dube Brahmin	50	4	20	W Basauli	TS	Deputy-Pradhan
CHEDU KHAN (CK)	Pathan	50	1	6	W Basauli	TS	Muslim head
KALIKA	Lodh	50	0	10	W Basauli	TS	
RETIPAL SINGH	Raikwar Thakur	40	7	24	E Basauli	TS	
RAM NAND	Awasthi Brahmin	45	1	15	E Basauli	TS	
RAM ADHIN	Gadaria	60	0	15	Kiratpur	TS	
NANHOO	Chamar	60	0	7	Kiratpur	TS	Scheduled
BISHEMBER	Pasi	60	0	10	Purwa	TS	Scheduled
RAMESUR	Kurmi	50	5	21	Imlipur	TS	
RAM PRASAD	Lodh	65	0	18	Imlipur		Died before 1982
KULLU	Mahabrahmin	64	4	10	E Basauli	TS	Died before 1982
AVERAGE		53	2.7	23			
MAXIMUM		65	10	125			
MINIMUM		40	0	6			

1982 NAME	CASTE	AGE IN 1982	YEARS SCHOOL	BIGHAS OWNED	LOCALITY	FACTION	OTHER
RUDR NARAYAN SINGH	Bais Thakur	54	10	125	W Basauli	TS	Pradhan
DEEP NARAYAN SINGH	Raikwar Thakur	34	12	39	E Basauli	TS	Deputy
DUJENDRA PRATAP S	Raikwar Thakur	32	9	10	E Basauli		Unopposed
RAJ NARAIN	Shukla Brahmin	28	9	7	E Basauli		Unopposed
RAISH KHAN	Pathan	25	3	6	W Basauli	TS	Son of CK
RAM NARESH	Kurmi	28	9	50	Imlipur		
FATEH BAHADUR	Lodh	26	4	10	W Basauli	TS	
RAGHUNATH	Lodh	30	9	30	Purwa	TS	
RAM ADHIN	Gadaria	71	0	15	Kiratpur	TS	
RAM CHANDRA	Pasi	32	8	16	Imlipur	TS	
MURLI DHAR	Pasi	32	10	10	Purwa	TS	
HIRAI	Chamar	50	0	11	E Basauli		
AVERAGE		37	6.9	27			
MAXIMUM		70	12	125			
MINIMUM		25	0	6			

R. Thakur was asked to indicate which candidate he thought the various sample households had supported in the election of Pradhan. In all but five cases he felt confident that he knew the direction of the allegiance and, in these five cases, two households had not voted and three had not declared their position. The result is interesting because it suggests that only 48 households supported TS, the winning candidate, as compared with 49 for the opposition candidate. (The possibility of split voting within households was said to be very unlikely, but certainly cannot be ruled out altogether.)

The victory of TS (by a narrow margin of 34 votes) is explained by both the larger number of voters in the households supporting him (including the Muslims) and also manipulation of the electoral roll so that under-age supporters of TS were prematurely enfranchised and adult, opposition electors were summarily disenfranchised.

The table confirms the claims of both the rival candidates, namely that they each represented the poorer villagers and that they were supported by a wide cross-section of villagers. Support for TS was highest among those just above the poverty line. The figures confirm what was already apparent: the contest for Pradhan did not represent a conflict between class groups (see table, p.171).

In terms of caste, Thakur Sahib received the most solid support from Pathans, Dhobes, the Patharkots and Radhikas, Gadarias, Kabarias and Pasis, as well as his own Bais Thakurs. The main castes which opposed him included 70 percent of the Raikwar Thakur households, 88 percent of the Mahabrahmins, 85 percent of the Brahmins, all the Ahirs (until August 1982) and all the Barhais and Telis.

Comparison of the successful candidates in 1971 and 1982 shows almost total change in personnel and some changes in the social but none in the economic characteristics of members. The only continuity in membership was the Pradhan who had been in office since 1961 and who probably would not have survived in the 1982 election, but for the use of his powers of office to do some electoral gerrymandering. Such a wholesale change of members partly reflects the prolonged interval between elections (during which time two members 'left for their heavenly abode', to use the Indian newspaper idiom) and also suggests a fluidity in village politics. Above all, it shows the powers of the Pradhan to call on more or less whomever he pleased from his own faction and he said that his choice of new candidates for members arose because he felt there was a need for younger, better educated members. At least three of the older members in his faction had involved themselves in either conflict with the Pradhan or in public controversy or even brawls or in conspicuous drinking and drunkenness. The 1971 panchayat achieved a remarkable spread of castes, with 12 members representing 11 castes. These included five high, five middle and two scheduled caste members. This should not lead one to conclude that the panchayat was an example of rural democracy. The wide range of castes was probably a reflection of the usefulness of having candidates from the larger castes to maximise voting power. All members were from groups with at least 70 members, with the exception of the Pradhan himself. In terms of the population distribution (of 1982), the 1971 membership had an excessive number of high caste members, mainly at the expense of middle castes. Given that less than 14 percent of the sample population of 1982 was aged over 50 years, the elderly were grossly over-represented in the 1971 committee. Nine members were aged 50 years or more and the average age was 53 years. The youngest member was a 40 year old Raikwar and choice of very old men was particularly frequent in the lower castes. There was no woman member nor indeed candidate in 1971. Five members had no schooling, two only one year and the average education was only 2.7 years. (This was still nearly twice the average for the sample household heads.) The Thakur member and the Pradhan had seven and ten years education respectively. The average landownership was 23 bighas or over twice the average area owned per household and a third more than the average area cropped per farm in the sample. The Pradhan owned 125 bighas and the next largest holding was 24 bighas, owned by the other Thakur member. The smallest owner was a Pathan with six bighas. Four members came from west Basauli, three from east, two each from Kiratpur and Imlipur and one from Purwa. This gave slight over-representation to west Basauli, home of the Pradhan and a core area for his support, but in fact the residential distribution of members was remarkably similar to the population distribution in the five parts of the gaon sabha. Finally, there was only one Muslim member and this was only half what their numbers might suggest. However, the Pradhan was also sensitive to Muslim interests and voting support and so this was perhaps not such a serious under-representation. In any case, as already suggested, balanced numerical distribution on any criterion was not so important since many of the members had probably been puppets of the Pradhan. In 1971 all but one member was said to have been in the Pradhan's faction, at least when originally elected, but this requires rather deeper investigation.

By 1982, the Pradhan appeared to be declining and becoming slightly beleaguered. The 1982 committee reflects this decline in power and the new composition of the panchayat, with both ruling and opposition members, indicates some change in social background. There were now only four from the high castes (including two opposition members), five from the middle castes and three from scheduled (including two young Pasi supporters of the Pradhan). Nine castes were represented, compared with 11 earlier. Average age was down, remarkably, from 53 years in 1971 to 37 years in 1982. Two of the new members were in fact sons of members elected in 1971 and dropped by the Pradhan in 1982. This was a very young committee, especially when one bears in mind that the rules forbid candidates aged under 30 years from competing for the post of Pradhan. The sharp fall in average age was parallelled by an even greater improvement in the level of education. The average length of schooling actually increased from 2.7 years to 6.9 years and the only illiterates were the Gadaria and Chamar members. Eight members had at least eight years education, including the Deputy Pradhan with 12 years. The average size of landholding was slightly, but not significantly, higher. Only three members owned less than the average household in the sample. Three members came from west Basauli, four from east, two each from Imlipur and Purwa and one from Kiratpur. This redressed the imbalance in representation between the west and the east of main Basauli but over-represented Purwa at the expense of Kiratpur. The opposition faction now had four members, three of whom came from east Basauli, including two who were elected unopposed. There was again one Muslim member, the son of CK Pathan, the leader of the Muslims who was elected in 1971. The Pradhan dropped the latter from his team in 1982, partly because CK Pathan was currently involved in various controversies, including litigation with Yadavs, and also perhaps because of some disagreement with the Pradhan in the fairly recent past and partly out of genuine desire for new and younger blood.

The Election for Block Pramukh

The UP government fixed the election date of the Block Pramukh for 14 February and later postponed this to 22 February 1982. There were four candidates in Suratganj block. The first was TS who represented Congress (I), though officially the contest was not fought on party lines. TS began canvassing the electorate (118 gaon sabha Pradhans, dispersed all over the block) and visited nearly all of them on his cycle. Each night he sat round the tappa with his Basauli cronies and worked out how many Pradhans he thought were certain to, and how many might, vote for him. From these detailed calculations, he grew daily more confident. He was being assisted by the Muslim from Burhanapur in his talks with Muslim Pradhans and he also sent CK Pathan to visit them since he was related to at least one. TS was confident of the Muslim vote but still sent canvassers to show that he cared about them.

The second candidate was C, the sitting Pramukh, a Kurmi from Dafarpur, a village eight kilometres to the south of Basauli. The Kurmi was richer than TS, but older, less educated and less sophisticated. TS described him as coming from a 'hardworking' family (the Kurmi stereotype) that had risen economically. TS alleged that C had gone into a 'second grade trade' which was tantamount to black marketing and he had dealt in kerosene, sugar and other scarce commodities. TS considered that his rival had helped the rich during his previous period of office up to 1976 and "he could not get even one bag of fertiliser for the poor". He had also helped his own family. Since he was not very well educated, C could not read those letters sent from the district offices which were written in English. (However, very few circulars are in English these days.) Both TS and the Pramukh were on the Governors' Council of the degree college in Ramnagar. TS complained that, whereas he had opposed the transfer of funds from Suratganj block to the degree college in the adjacent block, at least until an intermediate college was built in Suratganj, his rival acquiesced silently in such inequities because he was in awe of the District Magistrate who was in the chair. TS pointed out that currently students from the Suratganj catchment area (including Basauli) had to travel 11 or more kilometres to Fatehpur for intermediate level education. Because the Kurmi Pramukh had no education, he was 'putty in the hands' of the BDO and of the assistant directors of development. C. Kurmi had supported the Janata and Lok Dal parties in recent years.

The remaining two candidates were both Brahmin lawyers from Barabanki town. One was a Dikshit Brahmin who came originally from Chandura village and he was a supporter of the Bharatiya Janata Party (BJP). The other was a Dwivedi (or Dube) from Mahar village and he was independent from any party affiliation. TS was puzzled as to why they had entered the contest but he was not entirely displeased, because he hoped they might have the effect of splitting the Brahmin vote, much of which TS, as a Thakur, probably could not have relied on anyway. When TS visited the northern parts - which he termed 'the Brahmin-infested areas', he discovered that the Dube's motivation for contesting was simply to oppose the Dikshit and TS was delighted to find that the two Brahmins were in fact fighting each other as he had hoped they would.

It became apparent that the BDO was to some extent supporting TS. On 16 January the BDO arrived fairly late at night (about 8.30 pm) in his jeep accompanied by RL Tiwari, a Congress (I) worker. He and TS soon fell into an earnest and hushed conversation. It centred around the need to correct the voters' list, which still included one Pradhan who had died and one who had been dismissed two years before. TS asserted later that, if these mistakes were not corrected before the election, then the opposition could bring a petition against the successful candidate. Asked if the BDO was supporting him, he replied that the BDO disliked him because he asked awkward questions but they had a common purpose insofar as TS was the officially approved candidate of the ruling party. TS felt it necessary to further justify his favoured treatment and he pointed out that he was the only candidate who had been democratically chosen by his party. By this he meant that he had been elected chairman of the Block Committee of Congress (I), not that he had been specifically elected to contest for Pramukh. All the other candidates were either independent or had simply adopted the label of some party or other, without due process of election or even nomination. However, TS did mutter something about the declining integrity of Congress (I) and expressed private reservations about its malafide.

TS was not at all put out by the postponement of the election to 22 February and indeed claimed to welcome it, as giving him more time to campaign. Most of the Pradhans were known to him personally, and when he arrived in a village, he would send a message to the fields and they would come to greet him. He gave the instance of the (completely illiterate) Loniya Pradhan who was actually working in his fields when TS arrived but this was not unusual for a Pradhan. TS sent word that he should not be disturbed and he would call on him on his way: "We had an ordinary discussion". TS was well aware that it was a much more difficult exercise than a gaon sabha election, where there might be 700 or 800 voters in one or two adjacent villages. In the block election, a candidate had to make contact with only 100 to 150 Pradhans, but these were dispersed over a large area and might well be out when he called. TS pointed out that, psychologically, people are not impressed if a candidate comes on his own and it is best to have a large number of camp followers, preferably from a variety of castes. He had noted that his opponents were usually accompanied only by their own castemates. He was very pleased with his canvassing technique which was relatively subtle and did not involve pressing the voters to support him and he particularly avoided trying to extract explicit promises of support from them. He was clever enough to realise that this antagonised the undecided and was worthless from those who had already decided not to support him. TS contented himself with appealing to them on the basis of his work record and his personality (which he said was inseparable from his policies). He ended by merely asking them to think it over. He considered that caste, working capacity and method or style of working were, in that order, the three most important factors which would decide the election.

At first, TS had said that he did not mind the possibility of postponement, since he needed to keep in touch with his constituency anyway. He had clearly been exhilarated by his campaign tours and seemed very satisfied with the amount of support, both promised and apparently latent. He had journeyed to the interior, including the area between the rivers Samli and Ghagra, which constituted the least developed part of a relatively undeveloped block. He felt that people in this backward, interfluvial area expected him to do more for their problems than the other candidates. At first, he was not even expecting the election to be postponed because he thought that there was an ambiguity in the newspaper announcement. His initial interpretation was that there would be no election of members of the Block Development Committee, but that there would be an election for Chairman. He pointed out that elections for Pradhans would not be possible until the voters' lists were completed in 1983. (In fact, these elections for Pradhans were held between April and June all over UP and were held on 10 April 1982 in Suratganj block.)

TS had been keen to ensure that he won by at least 20 votes so that he would not have to rely on the votes of the 15 nominated members of the Block Development Committee for a final majority. He pointed out that, though the nominated members were originally intended to be the impartial choice of the Governor of UP, in practice they were invariably chosen by the 'ruling class' (by which he meant the ruling party).

On 22 January he went for a meeting of the BDC (which had been reactivated three months before, to prepare for elections) and he expected to have the position clarified on whether and when the elections would now be held. Only 36 Pradhans attended the meeting, though these included some from quite remote villages (who possibly were keener to exchange political gossip than those more centrally located). One of the people absent was C. Kurmi, the sitting Chairman, who was either too busy electioneering or thought that his absence might be a good psychological ploy. The meeting required a chairman and so TS proposed AS Thakur, a gentle Pradhan, to whom no one could raise an objection. This was seconded and passed. TS had also, earlier and without his knowledge or consent, nominated AS for the post of chairman of the Surhiyamau Cooperative Association. AS had been happy to receive a letter from the block saying that he was appointed. AS was described by TS as 'a loyal member of the party'.

The meeting proceeded 'in a calm and friendly way' and TS came away pleased that he had scored at least three points. Firstly, his choice of chairman had been accepted, nem. con. Secondly, when the subject of waterlogging was raised, he was able to name all the main places affected. Other Pradhans asked TS how he had such detailed knowledge of the subject and he was quick to point out that his election tour had not been simply to canvass votes. TS felt that this was a telling, psychological blow against his opponents, none of whom was present at the meeting. Thirdly, he found that those present were already raising problems to him as if he were by now elected Pramukh, and he said that people had been growing into the habit of doing this. It was TS who normally made a précis of details of particular problems for the minutes of the committee proceedings.

TS was already very confident of winning. His main worry was that, as chairman of the BDC, he would not be able to talk as much as he normally did. He intended to use Pradhans to raise points which needed discussion and action. He also noted that Pradhans were tired of meetings and of the red tape associated with such meetings and this partly explained the low attendance.

TS claimed that two of the main reasons why he wished to become Pramukh were in order to secure a state tubewell for the south-eastern section of the village (which would benefit some of the poorest villagers, including those in Purwa) and also to pursue analogous interests of the poor in the underprivileged north-west of the block, where he had just been touring. Both he and his Kurmi rival travelled by cycle and in fact the Kurmi candidate had begun canvassing 15 to 20 days before TS. The latter felt that cycling brought him into closer and better touch with the people but he thought he might have a 'final round' by motorcycle on the eve of the election.

TS calculated that there were 35 Brahmin Pradhans, 32 Kurmis, 23 Thakurs, 10 Muslims, 8 Yadavs, 2 Muraus, 2 Pasis, 1 Barhai, 1 Loniya, 1 Kayastha (of Srivastava subcaste) and 1 Teli. Altogether there should be 126 Pradhans voting in the election. However, since the last elections in 1971, seven had died (including one who had been murdered) and one had been dismissed by the District Magistrate. There were thus 118 Pradhans remaining to be canvassed. TS said that the average age of these was also higher than would normally be the case, because of the long lapse of time between elections. TS considered that Pradhans normally tended "to look behind to see what their electorate thought and to be reluctant to take unpopular initiatives". This election might be even more conservative than usual. TS then expatiated on a favourite theme, the disadvantages of democracy. TS felt confident that he would secure some of the Kurmi votes and that he would command the support of all Thakurs. However, he stressed that he deplored caste voting and that his own appeal was multi-caste, because he wanted educational development and more resources for the poor.

His second son had compiled a list of the Pradhans on 18 January and he ticked off those which TS had visited and those they were confident would support him. When TS was not away on tour, he spent much of the evenings checking the amount of support and going over the names seemingly endlessly with CK Pathan, his son and other members of his inner circle. On 22 January, his count showed a guaranteed vote of at least 52 Pradhans out of 118 including 18 to 20

Thakurs (out of 23), 8 to 10 Kurmis (out of 32), 7 Muslims (with three more to see), at least 7 and possibly a majority of the 35 Brahmins, at least 3 Yadavs (4 more to see), 2 Pasis (including one yet to be visited) and one each from the Barhai, Loniya, Kayastha, Murau (one to see) and Teli castes.

Prominent among the tiny minority of Thakurs who, TS claimed, were opposing him was the member of a powerful family in a village 18 kilometres to the east. This Thakur was unpopular because he had been associated with some 'mismanagement' of the sugar and kerosene rations and it was also felt by some that he was seeking to use the party label for his own ends and was really not very loyal to Congress (I). TS avowed to have very little respect for his fellow Thakurs and he seemed to derive least pleasure from extracting their votes. He felt that the Thakur Pradhans would mainly vote for him because they knew that he could command a majority of votes from the other castes, especially the lower castes. TS reminisced, with some amusement, how a young Raikwar Thakur had wished to contest for Block Pramukh and had approached a Pradhan, also a Raikwar, on the subject. The Pradhan had told the young man to go and study the problems and needs of the block and had then reported the young man's ambitions to TS, who had laughed. (This possible threat to TS in the form of splitting of the Thakur votes was removed when he was later killed because of a personal enmity with a Brahmin.)

Another Thakur who did not support TS was RS of Banarki village, about seven kilometres from Basauli. TS described him as someone who was able to provide 'some profit' (unspecified) to the MLA whereas TS could only provide him with votes. TS particularly resented RS's lack of commitment to Congress (I) in 1980 and the fact that he had made his support clear only five days before the polling date. Indeed, the uncle of RS had supported an opposition party, possibly the Lok Dal. RS then was a nominal supporter of Congress (I), whose commitment was regarded as highly suspect. TS slightly feared that in January 1982, RS was seeking to take the post of block Pramukh 'by force'. Even so, he felt that in the end RS would not actually stand and that he was raising the possibility with the MLA in order to waive his right to stand and thus claim some other post or benefit.

The news of the postponement of the election to 1983 was brought on 18 January, by the son of the MLA for Ramnagar, RL Tiwari (a private, unqualified, allopathic practitioner in Suratganj) and three other young men who came on a scooter and a motorcycle. The news was announced cheerfully enough and it was received quite phlegmatically by the second son of TS. (TS himself had been absent for two nights on an election tour of distant villages by cycle and was still away.) The second son said that it was government policy and the government had not given a reason. In no way did his words or manner suggest that a reason need be given. The new position was accepted immediately with quiet passivity and apparent fatalism. The fact that his father and his confidants had spent the previous two or three weeks touring and campaigning seemed not to bother him at all. The son said he did not know what was happening in other states, with regard to block elections. In fact, when his father returned, he continued his campaign, waiting for more definite news of what was going to happen.

By 26 January, the motives and strategy of one of the Brahmins became clearer. The Dikshit approached TS for a compromise whereby either one of them would support the other for Pramukh and this person, having been so elected, would then use his influence within the BDC to persuade the members to appoint the other as the nominated representative on the Zila Parishad (District Council). In this way, both of them would hope to ensure a place on the District Council, the Pramukh ex officio and the other, through the Pramukh's pressure on his block committee. It therefore emerged that the Dikshit (and also no doubt his fellow Brahmin rival) were somewhat less than fully interested in the block committee, just as TS had suspected. In his reply to the offered 'deal', TS told the Dikshit that he was not in a position to promise a seat on the Zila Parishad and the choice of the nominated member was a matter for his party, not something that could be settled between individuals. He suggested that it would be better to let the democratic process run its course and see what happened. (TS was, by then, confident of victory.)

By at least 11 February the postponement of the election was finally confirmed. TS said the main reason was that there was opposition within the Congress (I) and so Mrs Gandhi had intervened to stop the disputes over who should receive the nominated posts (whose existence TS opposed in principle anyway, on democratic grounds). He also said that Congress (I) feared that it would win control of only 40 percent of the blocks in UP. He also repeated that he had not wished to win through the support of nominated members. The new arrangement, which sounded more logical, was to hold elections for new Pradhans from April to June and then the Pramukh elections in September. TS was very careful not to be annoyed by the postponement and he had clearly received both refreshment and a morale boost from his touring. He repeated that in his canvassing he never led up to a direct demand for a vote before leaving a Pradhan. He would merely say, "Think it over. You have plenty of time. If you think I am a suitable person to look after the affairs of the block, vote for me and otherwise not".

TS expected the new elections for Pradhans to be held in June. They would be held in several 'rounds' of two Nyaya Panchayat areas at each round (ie. about 18 gaon sabhas). In this way the government could save on the manpower required for administering the elections. Each time they would have available about 60 block staff, 45 police and home guards, plus 20 or so schoolteachers.

It was the policy of TS to try to ignore and avoid bitterness in politics and, even when there had been violent opposition to him in Basauli (with support to that opposition from the Brahmin Pradhan of Rammandai), he claimed that he had said nothing. (This was not quite true, but it was the case that TS resisted the temptation to retaliate.) He considered that this policy had paid off because, for instance, the Pandit of the family temple had heard that the Brahmin Pradhan of Rammandai was actually thinking of supporting TS in the coming election for BDC Chairman. This was because he 'did not appreciate' the two Brahmin candidates and he doubted very much whether either, if elected, would be available locally to do the necessary work. It was likely that, like TS, the Brahmin Pradhan suspected that they were wishing to use their position as Block Chairman as a qualification for membership of the much more powerful and prestigious Zila Parishad.

TS emphasised further that he always tried to preserve good relations, even with his political opponents. At the last general election in January 1980, he had gone by jeep to visit a Kurmi Pradhan who told him frankly that he would be supporting the Janata party. He still gave TS tea, dal mot (spiced savouries) and crisps. Soon after, TS was greeted by another Kurmi (an enemy of the first) and he had provided TS and his companions with puris to eat on the way because they were in a hurry. At the coming election, TS thought that the first Kurmi might well vote for him this time. The main point of his story was the possibility and indeed desirability of rival politicians observing the norms of politeness and hospitality.

TS still gave the traditional respect to Brahmins. One winter evening on 28 January, Lalla, a Pandit, who was a family friend from a nearby village, arrived along with AKS, the brother of the late wife of TS's eldest son and one or two others. The Pandit was a rough, well-built man with a muffler, khadi jacket (like that of TS), dhoti and black, modern style shoes. He was given the only chair and there he sat, above the rest of the assembly squatting on their bricks around the tappa, barefoot, cross-legged, occasionally hiccupping and spitting on the ground. AKS, who had a robust, joking relationship with the Brahmin, said sarcastically: "Wah! India government baithe hai", which provoked some laughter. The assembly became both very lively and very good-humoured, with frequent jokes, especially between the two main visitors. TS mentioned a bribe of Rs 700 which had been paid to the chairman of a cooperative and there was also lengthy discussion of the approaching election for block Pramukh. When the son of AKS came, he touched his father's feet and TS's third son went to touch the knees of the Pandit. The sons were, as usual, responsible for bringing the mandatory mugs of tea.

The Pandit stayed the night and in the morning he and his aide sat opposite TS on a takhat (wooden platform) and they talked and joked while a breakfast of tea and biscuits was brought by the eldest son. A servant (or confidant) of the Brahmin stood in attendance behind him. The Pandit was wearing a woolly, balaclava-like hat, that fitted very snugly over the ears and head so that it looked like a wig, and occasionally he would spit. After a fairly jolly discussion, they wheeled their cycles eastwards out of the village, towards Suratganj, with the servant carrying Panditji's bulging, leather briefcase which acted as his overnight bag.

TS subsequently explained that his visit was related to a 'small election' of cooperative society administrators. There were four candidates and the successful ones would become ex officio members of the BDC and thus eligible to vote in the election of Pramukh. TS said that he had nothing to fear from the 15 nominated and ex officio members of the BDC, because most would be Congress

(I) supporters who would follow him.

Postscript

In early June 1983, TS wrote, indicating that he had been "extremely busy in the arrangement of my daughter's marriage and election campaign of Chairman Block Development Committee (Block Pramukh). The marriage of my daughter Poornema was solemnised on 24th May and the marriage party left on 26th morning. I was too busy for a week and could not look after the election work till 26th. The nomination papers were filed on 27th. Among six contesting candidates [for Block Pramukh] three were Thakurs, two were Brahmins and one was Verma [ie. Kurmi]. The votes were polled on 29th May from 9 am to 17 pm (sic) and counting of votes was completed at about 18.15 pm. The votes polled according to caste system were 40 Brahmins, 30 Thakurs, 30 Verma, 13 Muslims, 9 Scheduled caste and 20 other backward class [ie. a total of 142]. I was declared elected by a margin of 13 votes. The voting system was on basis of preference and 14 voters in their zeal wrote my name in place of marking first preference in my name's column. These votes were cancelled, otherwise I would have been able to secure the majority by the margin of 27 votes. I am happy enough to get the support of all the castes and am not handicapped by caste opposition". For the marriage TS received help from R. Thakur and from R. Lodh of Imlipur and his sons. In addition, "the local MLA also stayed here for two days and thus the gathering became political up to some extent".

The success of TS in the election for Block Pramukh meant that the post of gram Pradhan fell vacant in Basauli and an election was held on 4 September 1983. DNS Thakur was supported by TS and the other candidate was RP Misra Mahabrahmin, nephew of SN Misra. The Mahabrahmin won by a narrow majority of only 6 votes, mainly because 70 percent of the Pathans (including CK 'Khalipha') and all the Lodhs of west Basauli supported him.

In 1984, some time before September, TS resigned from the Presidency of the Block Congress (I) committee but remained in the party. The reason for the resignation was reported to be a dispute with the MLA, Gajendra Singh (also a Thakur).

6 The economy of the village

This chapter examines the economy of Basauli and how this affects the level and distribution of incomes in the gaon sabha. The economy of the village was based mainly on agriculture, about half of which was irrigated, a brickworks, and a small amount of income from service employment in the tahsil headquarters, plus rather more income from a fairly small number of migrants.

Land

Basauli and Imlipur are two distinct revenue villages with separate records kept by the same revenue accountant (lekhpal). The records show that the gaon sabha included 899 acres on which land revenue (lagan or malguzari) was payable. There were also at least a further 116 acres of abadi and non-cultivable land, making a total area of about 1,015 acres. The area of abadi for Basauli itself was exceptionally large and accounted for nearly 15 percent of its total area. There were 640 landholders (khatedars), owning an average of 1.59 acres each. The rates for land revenue were Rs 12.5 for an irrigated pacca bigha (ie. Rs 20.8 per acre) and rates varying from Rs 2.5 to 6.25 for a pacca bigha of unirrigated land. In Basauli, one pacca bigha is equal to 0.6 acres or three kacha bighas. One kacha bigha is therefore equal to 0.2 acres. The size of a kacha bigha varies in different parts of UP. For instance, in Moradabad district, in western UP, a bigha is equal to 0.156 acres (Bliss and Stern 1982). In this study bigha will be used to refer to a kacha bigha and this unit will be used wherever possible. If a pacca bigha is intended, then this will be written in full. When the area for which land revenue was payable is compared with the area reported as owned in the household listing, the latter amounts to 252 acres less than the former. Part of

LAND IN BASAULI AND IMLIPUR REVENUE VILLAGES

		BASAULI	IMLIPUR	TOTAL
ACRES	Sankar Manya (Full Bhumidari)	555		
	Asankar Manya (new distribution to Harijans)	93		
TOTAL	for which Lagan paid	649	250	899
ACRES	irrigated	221		
	unirrigated	253		
ACRES	reported as irrigated in household listing			390
TOTAL	cultivated	474		
	cropped twice	237		
ACRES	Abadi (residential) and other	(111?)	5	(116?)
TOTAL ACRES		760	255?	1015?
NUMBER of Khatedars (landholders)		461	179?	640?
AVERAGE ACRES per landholder		1.65	1.40	1.59
AVERAGE Rs Lagan per acre		11.8	8.4	10.8
Rs TOTAL Lagan payable 1981-2		7646	2103	9749
Rs Lagan payable by non-residents and caste unknown				NA
Rs Lagan payable per acre irrigated				20.8
Rs Lagan payable per acre unirrigated				4.2 to 10.4
Rs Lagan Sankar Manya		6827		
Rs Lagan Asankar Manya		804		
ACRES reported as owned in household listing				647
ACRES owned outside the Gaon Sabha				
AVERAGE Rs Lagan per acre Sankar Manya		12.3		NA
AVERAGE Rs Lagan per acre Asankar Manya		8.6		

Lagan rate per acre: Irrigated Rs 20.8
Non-irrigated Rs 4.2 to 10.4

Source: Records of Lekhpal 1982

the difference is explained in terms of ownership by non-residents and by those whose caste or other identity was untraceable and the remainder may be due to under-reporting of landownership in the listing.

The District Census Handbook for 1971 gives a total area of 1,027 acres (761 in Basauli and 266 in Imlipur):

VILLAGE	TOTAL ACRES	SCHOOL	COMMS.	CROPS	TOTAL ACRES IRRIG.	CANAL ACRES IRRIG.	WELL ACRES IRRIG.	TANK ACRES IRRIG.	NON IRRIG. ACRES	CULTI VABLE WASTE	NA FOR CULTI- VATION
BASAULI	761	Junr.	Kacha	Wheat	(11)	-	-	11	580	76	94
IMLIPUR	266	Basic	Road	+ Rice	(74)	16	32	26	123	36	33
TOTAL	1027				(85)	16	32	37	703	112	127

Source: GOI 1972:44-5

Taking each of the revenue villages separately, rather more detail was collected on Basauli. Altogether, 555 acres were sankar manya which implied full bhumidhari rights. A further 93 acres (14%) were designated as asankar manya and this land, having recently been distributed to the scheduled, included no rights of sale. (This was intended to protect the scheduled castes against exploitation rather than to discriminate against them by offering them an inferior tenure.) Insofar as 14 percent of the land was thus withdrawn from the market, the price of sellable land might have appreciated a little. However, most of the scheduled asankar manya land is inferior and so the price of the good land would hardly be affected.

The average amount of land revenue paid per acre was 43 percent higher on the sankar manya land than on the asankar manya land. This tends to confirm the reports that land distributed to the scheduled was of an inferior quality. The area recorded as irrigated was 221 acres (47%), which is considerably lower than the 60 percent reported in the household listing (for the gaon sabha) but is almost exactly the same as the ratio of 48 percent given by respondents in the sample.

The area of Imlipur, for which lagan was payable, amounted to 250 acres or only 39 percent of the area of Basauli revenue village. The area of land per khatedar was also slightly smaller and the average land revenue paid per acre was only Rs 8.4 compared with Rs 11.8 in Basauli. This suggests a lower degree of irrigated land in Imlipur. (It is also likely that in both revenue villages irrigated land was under-reported to the lekhpal, to minimise the amount of land revenue payable.)

The system of settlement (sansodhan) of land revenue rates changed in 1980. Previously, the land had been taxed according to the various qualities of soil. In 1980, after a long period of unchanged rates, the UP government increased the land revenue and used only two categories, irrigated and non-irrigated. To give an idea of the increase, the malguzari of R. Thakur shot up from Rs 177 to Rs 276, a rise of 56 percent. (It should have been more, but the assessor registered one plot as non-irrigated when it should have been assessed as irrigated.) However, this large increase in land revenue was probably fairly typical of what happened to other owners, who would mostly own less land and less irrigated

SOILS IN BASAULI

TYPE	% TOTAL AREA	APPROX Rs PER BIGHA SALE PRICE	QUALITY	CROPS
MATHIARA	20	800		RICE WHEAT GRAM
MUTH 1		1000+		POTATOES VEGETABLES
MUTH 2		1000+		POTATOES VEGETABLES
BALAWEE		400	SANDY	BAJRA ARHAR GROUNDNUTS

Soils according to the Amin (assistant to the Revenue Accountant)

1 GWEND AWAL - best
2 KACHIANA
3 GWEND DO
4 MATHIARA AWAL
5 MATHIARA DOM
6 MAJAR AWAL
7 BHUR
8 PALO
9 MATHIARA DO MUTH

land. There had been no further increase between 1980 and 1982 and legislation would be necessary before the rates could be increased again.

The total lagan payable by owners of land in the revenue villages of Basauli and Imlipur was Rs 10,186, of which 72 percent was payable for Basauli. It should be noticed that the lagan totals calculated from the detailed lists of the lekhpal do not correspond very closely with the other totals supplied by the lekhpal. This is particularly true in the case of Imlipur, where there is a discrepancy of Rs 783. No immediate explanation of the differences can be suggested. A large proportion of the land revenue (25.5%) was payable by owners who lived in neither of the villages. This included Rs 1,531 (53%) of the Imlipur lagan and Rs 1,065 (14.6%) of the Basauli lagan. The residents of the gaon sabha paid a total of Rs 7,590, an average of Rs 5.3 per person. The average lagan per person was Rs 5.0 in Imlipur and Rs 5.4 in Basauli. Within Basauli, the averages were over Rs 6.0 in main Basauli, over Rs 2.3 in Kiratpur and over Rs 4.2 per person in Purwa. (The exact amount for each settlement cannot be determined because Rs 404 were untraceable to household, caste or settlement.) The low figure for Kiratpur does not signify less land owned per person than in Purwa, since additional lagan would be paid for land owned in other, neighbouring villages, especially in Karanpur. It should not be deduced that this necessarily indicates 'absentee' ownership on any major scale. Most of the non-resident owners of Basauli land came from the nearby villages of Burhanapur, Parvatpur and Marocha. It was estimated that Imlipur residents owned about 20 acres in Raipur and Basauli residents about 10 acres each in Burhanapur, Parvatpur and Marocha.

CASTE AND LANDOWNERSHIP, ALL HOUSEHOLDS, BASAULI

CASTE OR SUBCASTE	TOTAL BIGHAS OWNED	IRRIG. BIGHAS OWNED	AV. BIGHAS OWNED PER HH	AV. IRRIG. BIGHAS OWNED PER HH	TOTAL WTED BIGHAS OWNED	AV. WTED BIGHAS PER HH	BIGHAS OWNED PER PERSON	IRRIG. BIGHAS OWNED PER PERSON
BRAHMIN								
SHUKLA	44	16	5.44	2.06	76	9.56	1.09	0.40
AWASTHI	48	4	8.00	0.66	56	9.33	2.67	0.22
MISRA	49	36	5.44	4.00	121	13.44	1.04	0.77
TIWARI	10	0	3.50	0	10	3.50	0.88	-
DUBE	20	8	20.00	8.00	36	36.00	3.33	1.33
PANDE	40	12	40.00	12.00	64	64.00	5.00	1.50
TOTAL BRAHMIN	211	76	7.54	2.73	364	13.00	1.61	0.58
MAHABRAHMIN								
MISRA	280	155	25.41	14.05	588	53.50	3.18	1.75
PANDE	82	35	16.40	7.00	152	30.40	3.15	1.35
TOTAL MAHABRAHMIN	362	190	22.59	11.84	740	46.28	3.17	1.67
THAKUR								
BAIS	151	111	50.33	37.00	373	124.33	7.19	5.29
RAIKWAR	365	290	36.50	29.00	945	94.50	6.29	5.00
TOTAL THAKUR	516	401	36.69	30.85	1318	101.38	6.53	5.08
PUNJABI	130	130	130.00	130.00	390	390.00	13.00	13.00
BHAT	22	0	7.33	0	22	7.33	1.29	-
BANIA	6	0	6.00	0	6	6.00	6.00	-
PATHAN	118	66	6.94	3.88	250	14.71	1.15	0.64
KURMI	519	489	28.83	27.17	1497	83.17	4.51	4.25
AHIR	136	0	17.00	0	136	17.00	2.52	-
LODH	374	247	10.99	7.26	867	25.51	1.89	1.25
MALI	10	0	3.33	0	10	3.33	0.83	-
BARHAI	7	2	3.50	1.00	11	5.50	0.64	0.18
LOHAR	21	11	7.00	3.67	43	14.33	1.17	0.61
KAHAR	21	8	7.00	2.67	37	12.33	1.24	0.47
DHOBE	43	5	6.14	0.71	53	7.57	1.23	0.14
NAI	11	2	2.20	0.40	15	3.00	0.48	0.09
BHURJI	26	0	6.50	0	26	6.50	1.08	-
TELI	24	22	8.17	7.17	56	18.50	2.04	1.83
GADARIA	130	99	7.62	5.82	328	19.26	1.82	1.39
LONIYA	120	36	9.96	3.00	192	15.96	2.06	0.62
KABARIA	10	2	1.28	0.28	15	1.84	0.35	0.07

CASTE AND LANDOWNERSHIP, ALL HOUSEHOLDS (contd.)

CASTE OR SUBCASTE	TOTAL BIGHAS OWNED	IRRIG. BIGHAS OWNED	AV. BIGHAS OWNED PER HH	AV. IRRIG. BIGHAS OWNED PER HH	TOTAL WTED BIGHAS OWNED	AV. WTED BIGHAS PER HH	BIGHAS OWNED PER PERSON	IRRIG. BIGHAS OWNED PER PERSON
CHAMAR	227	63	8.42	2.32	354	13.11	1.74	0.48
PASI	149	101	11.44	7.77	352	27.06	2.04	0.72
BASPHOD	2	0	2.00	0	2	2.00	0.40	-
PATHARKOT	10	0	2.50	0	10	2.50	0.36	-
RADHIKA	31	0	2.58	0	31	2.58	0.56	-
HIGH CASTE	1218	797	21.00	13.74	2812	48.48	3.65	2.39
MIDDLE CASTE	1597	989	10.79	6.68	3563	24.07	2.01	1.25
SCHEDULED CASTE	419	164	7.35	2.86	749	13.12	1.43	0.56
GRAND TOTAL	3235	1950	12.30	7.41	7124	27.09	2.27	1.37
% OF TOTAL	100%	60%						

STRATUM	%	%	INDEX	INDEX	%	INDEX	INDEX	INDEX
HIGH	37.7	40.9	171	185	39.5	179	160	174
MIDDLE	49.4	50.7	88	90	50.0	89	88	91
SCHEDULED	13.0	8.4	60	39	10.5	48	63	41
GRAND TOTAL	100%	100%	100	100	100%	100	100	100

NB 1) 1 irrigable bigha is weighted to equal 3 non-irrigable bighas

2) Percentage of Total Population: High 23.5% Medium 55.9% Scheduled 20.6%

CASTE, SETTLEMENT AND RUPEES LAND REVENUE, 1981-2

CASTE	IMLIPUR	BASAULI	KIRATPUR	PURWA	BASAULI TOTAL	IMLIPUR AND BASAULI	% OF TOTAL TAX OF RESIDENTS	% OF RESIDENT POPULATION
			RUPEES LAND REVENUE					
SHUKLA		82			82	82	1.1	2.8
MISRA	70					70	0.9	3.3
AWASTHI		61			61	61	0.8	1.3
TIWARI		64			64	64	0.8	0.8
DUBE		65			65	65	0.9	0.4
PANDE		112			112	112	1.5	0.6
TOTAL BRAHMIN	(70)	(384)			(384)	(454)	(6.0)	(9.2)
MISRA MAHABRAHMIN		495			495	495	6.5	6.2
PANDE MAHABRAHMIN		146			146	146	1.9	1.8
THAKUR		1815			1815	1815	23.9	5.6
PUNJABI		255			255	255	3.4	0.7
BHAT		32			32	32	0.4	1.2
BANIA	12					12	0.2	*
PATHAN		400			400	400	5.3	7.2
KURMI	780		68	64	132	912	12.0	8.1
AHIR		108	18		126	126	1.6	3.4
LODH	363	332		231	564	927	12.2	14.0
MALI		19			19	19	0.2	0.8
BARHAI		17			17	17	0.2	0.8
LOHAR		51			51	51	0.7	1.3
KAHAR		56			56	56	0.7	1.2
DHOBE		83	NA		83	83	1.1	2.5
NAI		10		18	28	28	0.4	1.6
BHURJI			16		16	16	0.2	1.7
TELI			NA	12	12	12	0.2	0.8
GADARIA			175		175	175	2.3	5.0
LONIYA			84	32	116	116	1.5	4.1
KABARIA	15	NA			NA	15	0.2	2.0
CHAMAR		237	194	73	504	504	6.6	9.2
PASI	92			136	136	228	3.0	5.1
BASPHOD		28			28	28	0.4	0.3
PATHARKOT		97			97	97	1.3	2.0
RADHIKA		145			145	145	1.9	3.9
TOTAL CASTE KNOWN	1334	4709	555	566	5830	7164	94.4	
RESIDENT, CASTE NOT KNOWN	22	NA	NA	NA	404	426	5.6	
TOTAL RESIDENT	1356	4709+	555+	566+	6234	7590	100	100
NON RESIDENT	1531				1065	2596	25.5	
GRAND TOTAL	2886	4709+	555+	566+	7299	10186	100	

Shown to nearest rupee. The lekhpal's records showed Rs 2102 as total lagan for Imlipur and Rs 7646 for Basauli. The records indicate who are non-residents.
The Malguzari year starts with Rabi and coincides with the financial year.

Caste, Revenue Payment and Landownership

Of those whose caste was traceable, the main resident payers of lagan in Imlipur were Kurmis (58%), Lodhs (27%) and Pasis (7%). In the main settlement of Basauli, the chief resident payers of lagan, whose caste was traceable, were Thakurs (38.5%), Mahabrahmins (13.6%), Brahmins (8.2%), Lodhs (7%),Punjabis (5.4%) and Chamars (5%). In Kiratpur, where there were no higher caste households, the main amounts were paid by Chamars (35%), Gadarias (31.5%) and Kurmis (12.2%). In Purwa, where there were also no higher castes represented, the largest amounts of lagan were payable by Lodhs (41%), Pasis (24%), Chamars (13%) and Kurmis (11%). Taking the gaon sabha as a whole, the largest amounts of lagan were due from Thakurs (25.3%), Lodhs (12.9%), Kurmis (12.7%), Mahabrahmins (8.9%), Chamars (7%) and Brahmins (6.3%). The single Punjabi household was also liable for 3.6 percent of the total. It should be noted that the above analysis of lagan is based on amounts that owners were liable for up to 1976. Just before the UP state election in 1977, the government waived the lagan payments from owners with less than 6.25 acres and this arrangement continued to 1982. However, many kisans assumed that lagan would be reimposed on small owners and some worried that they would have to pay back tax or that non-payment of lagan meant less security of title.

There was a fairly close association between caste status and total land owned per capita. This was particularly true of caste strata. The high castes owned an average of 3.65 bighas per person, the middle castes 2.01 bighas and the scheduled castes only 1.43 bighas. Of the castes above the Lodh caste rank, all but three groups, the Brahmins, Bhat and Pathans, owned above average area per capita, whilst none below the Lodh owned above average. There were in fact only two lower caste groups, the Teli and Loniya, who owned more than two bighas per person. The overall average was 12.3 bighas per household, including 7.4 bighas irrigated, and the average per person was 2.3 bighas.

The Punjabis and Thakurs had the highest average per capita (13.0 and 6.5 bighas respectively) and these were followed by the Banias (6.0) and Kurmis (4.5). The lowest amounts owned were those of the Basphods, Patharkots and Kabarias with 0.4 bighas per person. The high castes, with only 23.5 percent of total population, owned 37.7 percent of the land. The share of the middle castes was almost proportional to their numbers but the scheduled groups, with 20.6 percent of total population, owned only 13 percent of all land.

The differences between strata were even greater in the case of irrigated land, the scheduled castes owning only 8.4 percent of the irrigated area. The high caste ownership of land per household was 71 percent above average, whilst the middle and scheduled castes were 12 percent and 40 percent respectively below average. The implication of these figures is that, in the highly unlikely hypothetical event of equalisation of land holding per household, then the high castes would have to lose nearly 42 percent of their land so that the middle castes increased their share by 13 percent and the scheduled castes by 67 percent. The index of irrigated land per household shows the superiority of the higher castes slightly accentuated and the inferiority of scheduled castes much more sharply defined. The scheduled groups owned 60 percent of the total land owned by an average household but only 39 percent of the average irrigated area. This supports the contentions of the villagers that an increase in irrigation facilities for poorer farmers had the greatest potential for removing inequalities of income.

Finally, these figures give no indication of the variations in quality. Much of the land owned by the lower castes was not only unirrigated but was also of poor quality. The lack of irrigation facilities partly stemmed from the poor quality of land in the general area in which lower caste land was situated. Some of the land had been granted in the 1970s to the scheduled categories from the gram samaj pool of land. It is reasonable to suppose that this land would not have been uncultivated by the higher caste powers if the land were of any great value, nor that it would have been granted to the lower castes.

BIGHAS OWNED PER CAPITA, INCLUDING CHILDREN, ALL HOUSEHOLDS

CASTE	BASAULI 1981	PALANPUR 1974-5
Thakur	6.53	3.41
Gadaria	1.82	1.97
Dhobe	1.23	2.06
Teli	2.04	0.98
Chamar	1.74	1.62
Pasi	2.04	1.34
TOTAL	2.28	2.56

Note that, because there were 6.4 bighas to the acre in Palanpur, the original figures have been converted into bighas as used in Basauli, where there are 5 kacha bighas to the acre.
Source: Bliss and Stern 1982:21.

When intercaste differences of landownership in Basauli in 1981 are compared with those in Palanpur village, Moradabad district, in 1974-5, it can be seen that there was greater intercaste inequality in Basauli.

Apart from the data on landownership in the list of all households in Basauli, the 102 household heads in the sample were also asked about landownership. The data broadly corresponds but the sample understates the Thakur area and slightly overstates that of the average Chamar household. Taking the sample data and examining differences in average area cropped per household (including non-farming households), one can see that the differences between the caste strata are somewhat reduced. The average area cropped per sample household was 17.2 bighas and the medium caste area almost exactly coincides with this. The high castes cropped 30 percent more than the average, thanks mainly to their superior irrigation facilities but also due to higher landownership. The scheduled castes cropped 29 percent below the average area. The highest area cropped was that of the Mahabrahmins and this was 226 percent of the average. However, the level was inflated by the large, joint household in the sample. Second were the Kurmis, with 217 percent of the average, followed by Thakurs (154%) and Lodhs (135%). A few lower castes, such as the Malis, Bhurjis, Kabarias, Basphods and Patharkots, cropped less than 25 percent of the average area in the sample and most of these could not survive purely on their farm income.

In absolute terms the differences in landownership between the sample caste strata are minuscule indeed. However, in relative terms, the range for individual castes is very wide, varying from 219 percent of the average in the case of Thakurs to almost nil in the case of the Radhikas. The range of difference in ownership is naturally smaller between caste strata. The high castes owned 140 percent of the average owned per household, medium castes 90 percent and scheduled castes 83 percent. The average area of ownership per household was 10.6 bighas or just over two acres. The ceiling under the current land reform legislation was from 18 to 33 acres, depending on various allowances and exemptions. The differences are even greater when the irrigated component is compared. High castes owned an average of 8.5 bighas, medium castes 4.8 and scheduled castes only 2.0 bighas per household. The differences in the average area of non-irrigable land were relatively slight and in fact the scheduled castes owned marginally more non-irrigable land than the high castes and appreciably more than the medium castes. It has to be borne in mind that the upper caste advantage in terms of greater ownership of irrigable land is partly reduced by the difficulties of getting electricity, diesel oil and other vital inputs for irrigation. Thus the area which is potentially irrigable may only be watered once or twice rather than the five or six times desirable for the best of the HYVs and in very bad years may actually remain entirely unirrigated. This reduces the comparative advantage of the upper castes (and of some members of lower castes) to some extent. Conversely, the fact that the scheduled castes owned the largest average area of non-irrigable land is obviously double-edged, because this includes a large proportion of very poor quality, marginal land or land which is of medium quality, but much reduced productivity, until it can be linked to an irrigation source.

In order to allow for the differences in the value and productivity of irrigable and non-irrigable land, irrigable land was weighted to be equivalent to three non-irrigable units and thus a weighted total area was calculated. When this weighted area owned is compared for the three caste strata, the distribution by area owned appears remarkably similar, especially in the case of high and medium castes. Even the scheduled caste difference lies mainly in a smaller proportion of those owning 16 or more bighas and a higher proportion owning 11 to 15 bighas, ie. the ratio of very small and small owners is similar across the caste strata. The main difference exists in the percentage of irrigable land. For high castes, 57 percent of their land was irrigable whilst the comparable figures for medium and scheduled castes were 51 percent and 23 percent respectively.

CASTE AND AVERAGE BIGHAS CROPPED, 102 HOUSEHOLDS

CASTE	TOTAL BIGHAS OWNED	TOTAL BIGHAS IRRIGATED	AVERAGE* BIGHAS CROPPED PER HH	INDEX BIGHAS CROPPED PER HH
BRAHMIN	91	39	12.2	71
MAHABRAHMIN	171	85	39.0	226**
THAKUR	93	81	26.5	154
BHAT	13	7	20.0	116
BANIA	6	6	12.0	70
PATHAN	27	15	8.5	49
KURMI	179	106	37.4	217
AHIR	33	9	18.0	105
LODH	162	74	23.2	135
MALI	7	5	3.5	20
KAHAR	8	8	16.0	93
DHOBE	19	11	7.8	45
BHURJI	3	0	1.5	9
TELI	16	0	13.5	78
GADARIA	33	14	9.6	56
LONIYA	20	12	13.8	80
KABARIA	4	2	1.3	8
CHAMAR	152	34	15.0	87
PASI	34	9	13.0	76
BASPHOD	4	0	4.0	23
PATHARKOT	3	0	3.0	17
RADHIKA	-	-	-	-
TOTAL	1078	517	17.2	100
HIGH	355	205	22.4	130
MEDIUM	530	269	17.0	99
SCHEDULED	193	43	12.2	71
AVERAGE PER HOUSEHOLD	10.6	5.1	17.2	100

* Includes non-farming households

** Mahabrahmin average boosted by presence of Surnarayan, a large owner and farmer.

CASTE AND BIGHAS OWNED PER HOUSEHOLD, 102 HOUSEHOLDS

	NO OF HHS	AV TOT BIGHAS OWNED	AV BIGHAS IRRIG OWNED	AV BIGHAS NON-IRRIG OWNED	BIGHAS AS % AV TOTAL	WEIGHTED BIGHAS 0-5	6-10	11-15	16+	16+ WTED BIGHAS AS % TOT HHS
BRAHMIN	13	7.0	3.0	4.0	66	6	2	2	3	23
MAHABRAHMIN	7	24.4	12.1	12.3	230	1	1	1	4	57
THAKUR	4	23.2	20.2	3.0	219	-	-	-	4	100
BHAT	1	13.0	7.0	6.0	123	-	-	-	1	100
BANIA	1	6.0	6.0	-	57	-	-	-	1	100
PATHAN	6	4.5	2.5	2.0	42	3	1	-	2	33
KURMI	9	19.9	11.8	8.1	188	2	-	-	7	78
AHIR	3	11.0	3.0	8.0	104	-	1	-	2	67
LODH	12	13.5	6.2	7.3	127	1	4	2	5	42
MALI	2	3.5	2.5	1.0	33	1	-	1	-	0
KAHAR	1	8.0	8.0	-	75	-	-	-	1	100
DHOBE	5	3.8	2.2	1.6	36	4	-	-	1	20
BHURJI	2	1.5	-	1.5	14	2	-	-	-	0
TELI	2	8.0	-	8.0	75	1	-	1	-	0
GADARIA	5	6.6	2.8	3.8	62	2	-	2	1	20
LONIYA	4	5.0	3.0	2.0	47	1	1	-	2	50
KABARIA	3	1.3	0.7	0.7	12	2	1	-	-	0
CHAMAR	14	10.8	2.4	8.4	102	3	2	5	4	29
PASI	4	8.5	2.2	6.2	80	-	2	-	2	50
BASPHOD	1	4.0	-	4.0	38	1	-	-	-	0
PATHARKOT	1	3.0	-	3.0	28	1	-	-	-	0
RADHIKA	2	0	-	-	-	2	-	-	-	0
TOTAL	102	10.6	5.1	5.5	100	33	15	14	40	39
HIGH	24	14.8	8.5	6.2	140	7	3	3	11	46
MEDIUM	56	9.5	4.8	4.7	90	19	8	6	23	41
SCHEDULED	22	8.8	2.0	6.8	83	7	4	5	6	27

	PERCENTAGE WITH WEIGHTED BIGHAS 0-5	6-10	11-15	16+	TOTAL NUMBER	TOTAL %
HIGH	29	12½	12½	46	24	100
MEDIUM	34	14	11	41	56	100
SCHEDULED	32	18	23	27	22	100
TOTAL	32	15	14	39	102	100

NB Those selected for the sample lead to an understatement of Thakur area owned and an overstatement of Chamar ownership.

Distribution of Main Capital

Main capital here refers to land, animals, irrigation and other farm equipment, including carts, plus buildings. Details of the value of pumpsets and borings were collected in the survey but the omission of more traditional irrigation facilities serves to show a slightly greater inequality of capital ownership than actually existed. Thirty-four percent of households reported ownership of assets worth Rs 15,000 or more and 28 percent owned assets under Rs 5,000:

HOUSEHOLDS OWNING CAPITAL WORTH Rs:

0-4,999	5,000 -9,999	10,000 -14,999	15,000 -29,999	30,000+	TOTAL HHs
29	19	19	17	18	102

The government in 1982 considered that aid of Rs 4,000 to 5,000 was the minimum necessary to raise many poor households above the poverty line.

Gross Household Income

Gross household income refers to gross output value (GOV) of crops, income from animals, from hire of labour to farmers or to other employers and income from other sources, such as from social and religious functions. Since much of the agricultural production was not sold, approximate 'average prices' for crops in the year 1981 were ascertained from villagers and used to calculate the gross output value of crops. The figures may slightly understate the actual GOV, because time prevented an exhaustive inventory of very minor crops.

Net Household Income

Net household income from crops has been calculated by deducting a standard 50 percent from the gross output value of land cultivated by share-croppers, to allow for the cost of rent. In the case of all farmers, it was assumed that cultivation costs, excluding the farm household's own labour, accounted for 25 percent of total gross output value (minus the 50 percent rent just mentioned, where relevant). The resulting net output value of crops was added to other sources of income to produce net household income. The estimate of 25 percent expenditure on cultivation costs was based on villagers' calculations but it is clearly somewhat arbitrary. It was likely that some richer farmers spent more than 25 percent and some poor farmers considerably less than this ratio of GOV minus rent. It is arguable that the ratio should be fixed higher than 25 percent in the case of sharecroppers because they had to pay for all seed, most labour and, in theory, all manure, whereas the landlord only paid a half share for chemical fertiliser, harvest labour, water hire and pesticides. In practice, the sharecropper paid nothing towards the cost of manure unless it was matched by a contribution from the landlord. In fact few sharecroppers applied manure.

When the data from the questionnaires were checked by the research assistant, he found some major omissions and other errors in the statements of income by certain household heads and these were corrected to the best of his fairly detailed, local knowledge. He also made an estimate of the total net household income for the 161 households which were not included in the sample. This latter estimate was made to the nearest thousand rupees and does not pretend to be more than a rough indication. The final data on household income remain, inevitably, imperfect and are only the best that could be managed with the resources available. They are likely to be more reliable as a guide to relative ranking of income than to absolute values.

The figures suggest that households selected for the sample were slightly richer than the average. Sample households constituted 38.5 percent of total households and had 44.1 percent of total net income. The average net household income for the sample was Rs 5,168, which was nearly 12% above the overall average.

It was originally intended to collect only relatively brief details of income from crop value, labour and rent so as to arrange the households in broad income categories. However, it so happened that the research assistant remained available to help in the data processing in Lucknow. The data were checked for obvious inaccuracies and omissions and revised figures, based on his more detailed and considered knowledge of the households were compiled. This was really essential since many farmers had given only their own share of produce from rented land instead of total production, as was intended. The effect of the revision was to change the original values of PCI by at least 10 percent in the case of 50 percent of the households (including a change of at least 25 percent in the case of 16 households) and altogether, the resulting changes were as follows:

DIFFERENCES FROM ORIGINAL NET PCI DATA

Increase			No Change	Decrease			TOTAL HHs
25%	10-24%	1-9%	0	1-9%	10-24%	25+%	
(9	18	20)	5	(26	17	7)	102
47			5	50			

The table shows that the number of increases and decreases was roughly equal.

This procedure of 'retrospective adjustment' is clearly open to criticism and its utility and reliability obviously depends much on the knowledge and objectivity of the research assistant. He had a good, detailed knowledge of crop production since his family had a 16 acre farm and he had lived in the village all his life. In cases where he was unsure, he declined to guess and he also displayed unusual neutrality and objectivity towards different groups in what was a highly factionalised village situation. This inside information, with the attendant risks of use of a 'key informant', enabled details of income from milk sales and animals, of milk consumption within the household, income from jajmani (both economic and social income) and also, in a very few cases, some guesstimates of income from such sources as theft to be also added.

Net Household Income Per Capita

Net household income per capita was calculated by dividing the total net household income by the number of persons resident for at least six months during the calendar year 1981. The table shows a fairly wide range of net per capita incomes, with 51 percent of sample households and 56 percent of all households having a net PCI below the poverty line (estimated at Rs 810 or less):

Rs NET INCOME PER CAPITA, SAMPLE AND TOTAL HOUSEHOLDS

	Percentage of households							
	VERY POOR	POOR	LOWER MEDIUM	UPPER MEDIUM	FAIRLY RICH	RICH	TOTAL	BELOW POVERTY LINE
Rs net PCI	401 -600	601 -700	701 -810	811 -950	951 -1100	1101+	No. Hhs.	810 and Below as % Total
Sample	17.6	14.7	18.6	20.6	11.8	16.7	102	51%
All Hhs.	15.8	19.6	20.8	17.7	12.5	13.6	263	56%

The main differences between the sample and all households are that the sample had 5 percentage points less of those below the poverty line, slightly more very poor and nearly 4 percentage points more of the relatively rich. The highest PCI was over five times that of the lowest and shows a relatively high degree of inequality for such a poor village.

CASTE AND RS NET INCOME PER CAPITA, 102 HOUSEHOLDS

	Rs NET INCOME PER CAPITA								
CASTE	401 -600	601 -700	701 -810	811 -950	951 -1100	1101+	TOTAL HHS	Rs 810 AND BELOW AS % TOT 102 HHS	263 HHS
	NUMBER OF HOUSEHOLDS								
BRAHMIN	2	1	3	3	3	1	13	46	39
MAHABRAHMIN		1	1	1	1	3	7	29	50
THAKUR						4	4	-	-
BHAT					1		1	-	66
BANIA					1		1	-	-
PATHAN	2			2	1	1	6	33	65
KURMI	1			4		4	9	11	16
AHIR		1		1	1		3	33	50
LODH	1		5	3	1	2	12	50	41
MALI	1	1					2	100	100
KAHAR				1			1	-	-
DHOBE	3	1		1			5	80	86
BHURJI		2					2	100	100
TELI	1		1				2	100	100
GADARIA		2		1	1	1	5	40	41
LONIYA			2	1	1		4	50	67
KABARIA			2	1			3	67	75
CHAMAR	3	4	4	2		1	14	79	82
PASI	1	1	1		1		4	75	77
BASPHOD		1					1	100	100
PATHARKOT	1						1	100	100
RADHIKA	2						2	100	100
TOTAL	18	15	19	21	12	17	102	51	56
HIGH	2	2	4	4	4	8	24	33	33
MEDIUM	9	7	10	15	7	8	56	46	54
SCHEDULED	7	6	5	2	1	1	22	82	86

Sample Average Net PCI = Rs 913

PER CAPITA NET INCOME, AT CURRENT PRICES IN RUPEES 1976-82

	1976-7	1977-8	1978-9	1979-80	1980-1	1981	1981-2
INDIA	1082	1198	1250	1316	1537		
INDIA (1970-1 PRICES)	653	695	715	661	696		
INDIA POVERTY LINE		720				810E	
UTTARPRADESH	834	952	977	994	1287		1309E
UTTAR PRADESH (1970-1 PRICES)	487	519	530	436	526		
BARABANKI DT (NET DOMESTIC OUTPUT PC)	554		615		(683?)	(721?)	(758?)
BASAULI, 102 SAMPLE HOUSEHOLDS						913	
BASAULI GAON SABHA, 263 HOUSEHOLDS						853	

N.B. The 1980-81 figure is an extrapolation of the trend in the previous two years, ie. at 11% growth in two years. The extrapolated figures for Barabanki district in 1980-1 onwards are expressed at 1978-9 prices. All others are at current prices. If one assumes that prices increased by 20% between 1978-9 and 1980-1 (ie. average 10% per annum), then the Barabanki PCI in 1981 should be Rs 820 in 1980-1 and say Rs 861 in 1981 calendar year. In that case, if these assumptions are correct, then PCI in Basauli almost exactly corresponds with the district average (especially if one allows for the overstatement of income caused by overpricing of sugarcane in the sample).
The average WPCI for the 102 Basauli sample households in 1981 was Rs 1088.

Sources: Draft Annual Plan 1983-4 (1982); Pioneer, 11 February 1983:1.

The average net income per capita was Rs 913 in the sample and Rs 853 from the less precise estimates for the whole gaon sabha. The former represented 59 percent and 71 percent of the PCI for India and UP respectively in 1980-1 and the percentages would be slightly lower for the calendar year 1981. No figure for Barabanki district's net domestic output was available beyond 1978-9 but an extrapolation of the trend from the earlier figures, assuming a continuation of the earlier growth rate, suggests that PCI in 1980-1 might be Rs 683 at 1978-9 prices. Even if annual inflation was 10 percent for the next two years, the PCI for Barabanki in 1980-1 at current prices would still only be Rs 820 and in calendar year 1981 at current prices it would be Rs 861. From this it appears as if Basauli had a PCI slightly higher than the district average. Assuming that the poverty line for 1981 has in fact been correctly estimated here at Rs 810 per capita, then the Basauli sample average was only 13 percent above this level and the average for all households was only 5 percent above. Fifty-one percent of the sample and 56 percent of all households in Basauli were below the poverty line in 1981, compared with 50 percent for UP and 51 percent for India in 1977-8.

Per Capita Income weighted in terms of adult male equivalent consumption units

It is clearly misleading to compare simple per capita incomes for households with varying ratios of children and of other categories of person with lower food consumption. Consequently, the number of adult male equivalent consumption units (AMECUs) was calculated for each household, using the coefficients devised by the Indian Council of Medical Research which are given in Rajalakshmi (1981: 44):

ADULT MALE EQUIVALENT CONSUMPTION UNITS (AMECUs)

SEX	AGE RANGE	CONSUMPTION UNITS AS % OF MALE aged 20+
Male	16-19	125
Male	13-15	104
Male	20+	100
Female	13-19	92
M + F	11-12	88
Female	20+	79
M + F	7-10	75
M + F	5-6	62
M + F	0-4	50

Source: Rajalakshmi 1981:44, based on Indian Council of Medical Research (Cf. Smucker 1980:324, with 100% for adult males, 83% for adult females and 50% for children)

The values fixed for these coefficients are clearly open to dispute but they at least provide a more refined measure of the burden of consumption needs in each household. As a result, most but not all households had AMECUs lower than the actual number of household members and, when the total net household incomes were divided by the AMECU, the results for weighted PCI were almost invariably higher than for the simple PCI. For some of the very poorest, such weighting raises their PCI level to a point where their sheer survival becomes somewhat more credible and possible than would be the case from their unweighted PCI level. The weighted per capita income (WPCI) has not been calculated for individual non-sample households, because the original figures for total income are not sufficiently accurate to justify their use in a more sophisticated form. Weighting converts the average PCI of Rs 853 (for all households) to Rs 1,030, ie. 27 percent above the estimated poverty line for 1981.

Factors influencing Income

A major influence on income was obviously land ownership. There is an almost uniform trend from a high rate of impoverishment (75%) among the landless to a minority of poor (24%) among those owning over ten bighas. When the area is weighted for irrigated land, the relationship is even more clear-cut. This confirms a reasonable assumption and a firm impression that non-agricultural income was of minor importance in the village. Despite having 26 or more weighted bighas, two households still languished just below the poverty line. These households were both Chamars and their land was very poor quality, mostly granted to them by the gram samaj.

Change in Standard of Living

Household heads were asked whether their standard of living had changed over the ten years from 1971 and, if so, to what extent and in what ways. It is fairly certain that a few responses to this question were either false or misleading, but the overall pattern of replies seems reasonably reliable and are of some interest. The research assistant considered that at least five replies were clearly wrong.

EDUCATION OF HHH AND REPORTED CHANGE IN STANDARD OF LIVING, 1971-81

YRS EDUC OF HHH	BIG IMPROVEMENT	SMALL IMPROVEMENT	NO CHANGE	SMALL DECLINE	BIG DECLINE	TOTAL	IMPROVED AS % TOTAL		
0	2	16	29	22	6	75	24)		
1-2		2	2	1		5	40)	25)	33
3-4	1		2		1	4	25)	)	
5-6	1	4	2	2		9	56)	56	
7+	2	3	2	2		9	56)		
TOTAL	6	25	37	27	7	102	30		

Only six household heads claimed a big improvement in their standard of living, but a further 25 thought that there had been some. The largest category (37) reported no change and the rest alleged that there had been either decline (27) or serious decline (7). Altogether, 30 percent of household heads said that they had raised their standard of living and 33 percent had seen it fall. R. Thakur thought that nearer 40 percent had in fact improved their conditions and he was not usually given to making over-optimistic assessments of development in the village.

Most of the improvement in living standards appeared to derive from purchase of land or development of the existing holding. Indeed, a relatively small proportion of those who had received land in government distribution reported any improvement. Six households had been awarded one or two bighas and only one of these reported some improvement. Two of them actually reported a big decline. Nineteen households had received three or more bighas and in this category 37 percent thought that some increase in economic welfare had occurred. Even in this category, four households reported some deterioration.

REPORTED CHANGE IN STANDARD OF LIVING, 102 HOUSEHOLDS 1971-81

	NUMBER				%		
	RISE	NO CHANGE	FALL	TOTAL	RISE	NO CHANGE	FALL
HIGH CASTE	8	7	9	24	33	29	38
MEDIUM CASTE	20	20	16	56	36	36	29
SCHEDULED CASTE	3	10	9	22	14	45	41
TOTAL	31	37	34	102	30	36	33
OWNERS OF PUMPSETS/BORINGS	11	2	3	16	69	12	19
NO SCHOOLING	18	29	28	75	24	39	37
1-4 YEARS SCHOOLING	3	4	2	9	33	44	22
5+ YEARS SCHOOLING	10	4	4	18	56	22	22
Rs 0 to 10,600 MAIN CAPITAL	11	23	18	52	21	44	35
Rs 10,601+ MAIN CAPITAL	22	13	15	50	44	26	30
Rs WPCI 513-700	-	7	1	8	-	88	12
701-810	8	7	10	25	32	28	40
811-950	5	11	4	20	25	55	20
951-1100	4	6	6	16	25	38	38
1101+	16	6	11	33	48	18	33
TOTAL	33	37	32	102	32	36	31
POVERTY Rs 513-810	8	14	11	33	24	42	33
ABOVE POVERTY LINE Rs 811+	25	23	21	69	36	33	30
% HOUSEHOLD HEADS ILL FOR 31+ DAYS IN 1981				38	41	28	46

CASTE AND REPORTED CHANGE IN STANDARD OF LIVING, 102 HOUSEHOLDS 1971-81

CASTE	BIG	SOME	NO	DECLINE	SERIOUS	TOTAL	IMPROVED	COMMENTS
	IMPROVEMENT		CHANGE		DECLINE	HHS	AS % TOTAL	
BRAHMIN		3	6	3	1	13	23	
MAHABRAHMIN	2		1	4		7	29	
THAKUR	1	2		1		4	75	SBS government work Land dev & purchase
BHAT			1			1	-	
BANIA			1			1	-	
PATHAN		2		4		6	33	
KURMI	1		3	4	1	9	11	Should be 40%
AHIR	1		1	1		3	33	
LODH		8	1	1	2	12	67	Land dev & purchase
MALI			2			2	-	
KAHAR		1				1	100	Land dev & reform
DHOBE	1	2	2			5	60	Land dev & reform
BHURJI			1		1	2	-	
TELI			2			2	-	
GADARIA		2	2	1		5	40	
LONIYA		1	2	1		4	25	Should be higher (50%)
KABARIA		1	2			3	33	
CHAMAR		3	7	4		14	21	Should be higher (40%)
PASI			1	2	1	4	-	Should be higher (30%)
BASPHOD				1		1	-	
PATHARKOT			1			1	-	
RADHIKA			1		1	2	-	
TOTAL	6	25	37	27	7	102	30	Should be higher (40%)
HIGH	3	5	7	8	1	24	33	OK
MEDIUM	3	17	20	12	4	56	36	Should be higher (45%)
SCHEDULED	0	3	10	7	2	22	14	Should be higher (33%)

There was some positive relationship between education and reported change in standard of living. Only 24 percent of the 75 household heads without schooling reported any improvement and six of the seven reporting serious decline belonged to this category. The proportion was still only 33 percent for those who had been to school for four years or less. In contrast, 56 percent of those educated to fifth class or beyond reported some improvement in their standard of living over the past ten years.

Caste and Per Capita Income

The table on page 256 shows major differences in income distribution both between caste strata and individual castes. The incidence of poverty in the high, medium and scheduled categories was 33 percent, 46 percent and 82 percent, using the sample data, and 33 percent, 54 percent and 86 percent, using the estimates for all households. Perhaps the only slightly surprising aspect of these figures is that 33 percent of the high caste households were below the poverty line. Looking at the figures for individual castes, no Thakur households were poor and high caste poverty occurred only in the Brahmin and Mahabrahmin groups. The Pathan households sampled were richer than in the caste as a whole. Only one out of nine Kurmi households were poor and the cause in this case was slightly unusual but by no means unique. (The family belonged to a lower subcaste of Kurmi and was unable, partly for this reason and partly because it was not very prosperous, to secure wives for the three sons without paying money to the girls' families. Such a 'marriage' is called 'ghar baithna' or 'sitting at home' and the marriage payments are in the reverse direction to the more usual marriage transactions. No marriage feast was held. In this particular case the expenditure was further enhanced because two of the wives thus obtained subsequently ran away and replacements had to be found, again with payment. In all, the family had had to sell about 12 bighas, worth about Rs 15,000, and were now in a poor financial position but all the sons currently had wives. Apparently, there was a greater risk of the wife leaving in such marriages.)

In the case of the other main castes of upper sudra status, the Ahirs and Lodhs, the incidence of poverty was 50 percent or less. For the remaining castes below them the proportion of impoverished households was at least 67 percent, except in the case of the Gadarias and Loniyas (40 percent and 50 percent respectively). A few Chamars and Pasis were above the poverty line, around 20 percent, but all the other scheduled households were not only below the line, but well below it.

The differences in actual PCI were rather less than the incidence of poverty. The table shows that the averages for the high, medium and scheduled strata of all households were Rs 1,009, Rs 854 and Rs 672 respectively. In other words, high caste income was about 18 percent above the average PCI for all households, the medium caste income virtually coincided with the average and the scheduled categories were 21 percent below the average. The average household income per stratum ranged from Rs 5,811 in the high castes, Rs 4,582 in the middle castes to Rs 3,384 in the lowest.

Caste and Weighted Per Capita Income

When the sample data is weighted to give the average income per adult male equivalent, then the incidence of poverty decreases in many castes, at least statistically. Overall the proportion falls by roughly a third. The incidence for high, medium and scheduled castes was 21%, 29% and 55% respectively.

Caste and Sources of Income

There were major differences between caste strata in their pattern of sources of income. Net income from crops accounted for over half the total net income of high and medium castes, whereas it comprised only a third of scheduled caste income. The proportion of total income derived from agricultural labouring increased by doubling between the strata, rising from 7 percent in high castes to 13 percent in medium castes to 27 percent in the case of the scheduled castes. High and medium strata earned a negligible share of their income from labouring at the brickworks, whereas 12 percent of scheduled caste income came from this

CASTE, NET HOUSEHOLD INCOME AND PER CAPITA INCOME, ALL HOUSEHOLDS

CASTE	Rs TOTAL NET HH INCOME	NO. OF PERSONS	AV Rs NET PCI	PCI AS % AV	NO. HHS	AV Rs PER HH
SHUKLA	38,170	40	954	112	8	4771
AWASTHI	15,011	18	834	104	6	2502
MISRA	35,554	47	756	89	9	3950
TIWARI	9935	12	828	97	3	3312
DUBE	6000	6	1000	117	1	6000
PANDE	8592	8	1074	126	1	8592
TOTAL BRAHMIN	113,262	131	865	101	28	4045
MISRA	86,526	88	983	115	11	7866
PANDE	19,064	26	733	86	5	3813
TOTAL MAHABRAHMIN	105,590	114	926	109	16	6599
BAIS	25,900	21	1233	145	3	8633
RAIKWAR	72,278	58	1246	146	10	7228
TOTAL THAKUR	98,178	79	1243	146	13	7552
PUNJABI	20,000	10	2000	234	1	20,000
BHAT	14,229	17	837	98	3	4743
BANIA	1035	1	1035	121	1	1035
PATHAN	74,678	103	725	85	17	4393
KURMI	126,777	115	1102	129	18	7043
AHIR	42,792	54	792	93	8	5349
LODH	195,899	190	984	115	34	5762
MALI	7446	12	620	73	3	2482
BARHAI	7500	11	682	80	2	3750
LOHAR	14,500	18	806	94	3	4833
KAHAR	17,421	17	1025	120	3	5807
DHOBE	23,938	35	684	80	7	3420
NAI	15,500	23	674	79	5	3100
BHURJI	15,770	24	657	77	4	3942
TELI	7588	12	632	74	3	2529
GADARIA	55,387	71	780	91	17	3258
LONIYA	43,220	58	745	87	12	3602
KABARIA	19,039	29	657	77	8	2380
CHAMAR	94,551	131	716	84	27	3502
PASI	51,491	73	705	83	13	3961
BASPHOD	3165	5	633	74	1	3165
PATHARKOT	17,075	28	610	71	4	4269
RADHIKA	30,000	55	545	64	12	2500
TOTAL	1,216,031	1425	853	100	263	4624
HIGH	337,030	334	1009	118	58	5811
MEDIUM	682,719	799	854	100	149	4582
SCHEDULED	196,282	292	672	79	58	3384

The Poverty Line is assumed to be Rs 810 PC or, assuming an average 5.42 persons per household, Rs 4390 per household.

CASTE, AVERAGE RS PCI AND WPCI, 102 HOUSEHOLDS

CASTE	TOTAL NET INCOME	PERSONS	PCI	ADULT MALE EQUIVALENT PERSONS	WEIGHTED PCI
SHUKLA	4670	5	934	4.67	1000
AWASTHI	9011	11	819	10.08	894
MISRA	19,254	23	837	19.05	1011
TIWARI	8935	11	812	9.91	902
PANDE	8592	8	1074	6.58	1306
TOTAL BRAHMIN	(50,462)	(58)	870	(50.29)	1003
MISRA	57,526	48	1198	40.08	1435
PANDE	4564	7	652	5.87	778
TOTAL MAHABRAHMIN	(62,090)	(55)	1129	(45.95)	1351
BAIS	6900	5	1380	4.34	1590
RAIKWAR	23,778	17	1399	14.83	1603
TOTAL THAKUR	(30,678)	(22)	1394	(19.17)	1600
BHAT	5729	6	955	5.20	1102
BANIA	1035	1	1035	1.00	1035
PATHAN	24,178	31	780	24.04	1006
KURMI	85,985	75	1146	58.40	1472
AHIR	17,792	22	809	17.11	1040
LODH	83,999	77	1091	65.11	1290
MALI	5446	9	605	6.87	793
KAHAR	6421	7	917	6.08	1056
DHOBE	13,938	21	664	17.63	791
BHURJI	7270	11	661	9.41	773
TELI	4588	7	655	6.50	706
GADARIA	17,887	24	745	20.16	887
LONIYA	12,220	15	815	13.20	926
KABARIA	5539	7	791	6.33	875
CHAMAR	65,401	90	727	76.13	859
PASI	13,291	20	665	17.00	782
BASPHOD	3165	5	633	4.04	783
PATHARKOT	4575	8	572	5.58	820
RADHIKA	5000	12	417	8.86	564
TOTAL	526,689	583	903	484.06	1088
HIGH	143,230	135	1061	115.41	1241
MEDIUM	292,027	313	933	257.04	1136
SCHEDULED	91,432	135	677	111.61	819

CASTE AND RS WEIGHTED NET INCOME PER CAPITA, 102 HOUSEHOLDS

CASTE	Rs NET INCOME PER CAPITA 401 -700	701 -810	811 -950	951 -1100	1101+	TOTAL	Rs 810 AND BELOW AS % TOTAL WPCI	PCI
	NUMBER OF HOUSEHOLDS							
BRAHMIN	1	3	3	1	5	13	31	46
MAHABRAHMIN		1	1	1	4	7	14	29
THAKUR					4	4	-	-
BHAT					1	1	-	-
BANIA				1		1	-	-
PATHAN		2		1	3	6	33	33
KURMI	1			1	7	9	11	11
AHIR			1	1	1	3	-	33
LODH	1	2	1	4	4	12	25	50
MALI		1	1			2	50	100
KAHAR				1		1	-	-
DHOBE	1	2	1	1		5	60	80
BHURJI		1	1			2	50	100
TELI	1		1			2	50	100
GADARIA		2	1		2	5	40	40
LONIYA		1	1	1	1	4	25	50
KABARIA		1	2			3	33	67
CHAMAR	1	6	4	2	1	14	50	79
PASI		2	1	1		4	50	75
BASPHOD		1				1	100	100
PATHARKOT			1			1	-	100
RADHIKA	2					2	100	100
TOTAL	8	25	20	16	33	102	32	51
HIGH	1	4	4	2	13	24	21	33
MEDIUM	4	12	10	11	19	56	29	46
SCHEDULED	3	9	6	3	1	22	55	82

CASTE AND SOURCES OF INCOME AS PERCENTAGE OF TOTAL NET INCOME, 102 HOUSEHOLDS

	PERCENTAGE OF TOTAL NET INCOME										Rs
CASTE	NET FROM CROPS	AG LAB	BRICK LAB	TOTAL LAB	GOVT AND OUTSIDE SERVICE	MILK	BUSINESS	ANIMALS	SOCIAL INCL JAJMANI	OTHER	TOTAL NET INCOME
BRAHMIN											
SHUKLA	61	-	-	-	-	39	-	-	-	-	4670
AWASTHI	56	9	-	9	-	15	-	-	-	20	9011
MISRA	59	22	-	22	-	5	14	-	-	-	19,254
TIWARI	11	26	17	59**	-	30	-	-	-	-	8935
PANDE	15	-	-	-	63	13	5	-	5	-	8592
MAHABRAHMIN											
MISRA	60	3	-	3**	7	9	16	*	2	2	57,526
PANDE	40	18	-	18	-	35	-	-	7	-	4564
THAKUR											
BAIS	22	-	-	-	78	-	-	-	-	-	6900
RAIKWAR	55	-	-	-	35	8	-	-	2	-	23,778
BHAT	30	-	-	-	-	-	-	-	-	70	5729
BANIA	100	-	-	-	-	-	-	-	-	-	1035
PATHAN	36	11	10	21	-	17	15	10	-	2	24,178
KURMI	68	2	-	2	-	11	-	-	-	20	85,985
AHIR	40	10	-	10	-	34	-	8	-	7	17,792
LODH	64	12	2	13	9	13	1	*	-	-	83,999
MALI	14	80	-	80	-	-	-	-	6	-	5446
KAHAR	29	30	9	39	-	13	-	-	16	4	6421
DHOBE	36	19	-	19	-	8	-	11	26	-	13,938
BHURJI	12	11	15	26	-	25	21	11	-	6	7270
TELI	43	50	-	50	-	-	-	7	-	-	4588
GADARIA	47	9	6	14	8	14	-	16	-	-	17,887
LONIYA	62	28	-	28	-	9	-	-	-	-	12,220
KABARIA	21	67	-	67	-	5	-	6	-	-	5539
CHAMAR	40	29	16	46	3	3	-	6	-	3	65,401
PASI	37	38	-	38	-	-	-	5	-	20	13,291
BASPHOD	-	28	-	28	-	17	-	16	39	-	3165
PATHARKOT	2	-	-	-	-	-	61	15	-	22	4575
RADHIKA	-	-	-	-	-	-	36	32	-	32	5000
TOTAL	49.6	13.5	3.5	17.4	6.5	10.7	4.3	3.4	1.6	6.4	526,689
HIGH CASTE	51	7	1	9	16	11	8	**	2	2	143,230
MEDIUM CASTE	54	13	2	15	3	13	2	3	2	8	292,027
SCHEDULED CASTE	34	27	12	39	2	3	5	8	1	8	91,432

* Less than 1%

** Includes income from labour other than agricultural and brickwork labour.

source. The importance of labouring in total income varied inversely with caste status, as one would expect. Indeed, the high caste proportion was only 9 percent compared with 39 percent in the case of scheduled castes. The converse was true for government and other service outside the village, with the difference that, for this category of income, the medium castes resembled the scheduled more than the high castes. High caste households earned a sixth of their total income from such service whereas other castes earned only 2 or 3 percent.

The pattern for income from milk was analogous to that from crop income. Milk, both consumed and sold, accounted for 11 percent of high caste and 13 percent of medium caste income, whereas scheduled caste households earned only 3 percent of total net income from milk. Most scheduled caste people were too poor to own milk animals and most of those who owned animals had to sell their milk production. It is noticeable that, both for crops and for animal husbandry, the medium castes earned the largest share of their income from these sources. The pattern for business income is slightly surprising. It is predictable that the upper castes would earn most from business but it is unexpected that the scheduled castes were second and closer to the proportion of the upper than of the medium castes. This was because the stonecutters were, technically, in business. Keeping of smaller animals, such as goats, sheep and pigs represented a very negligible portion of upper caste income, 3 percent of medium caste income and 8 percent of that of the scheduled castes. High castes earned 2 percent of their income from social services within the village and this is explained almost entirely in terms of the funeral services provided by Mahabrahmins and the various ritual services supplied by Brahmins. The ratio was the same for medium castes and this related to the jajmani services of the Dhobes and the social income of the Mali and Kahar castes. Given their status as ex-untouchables, it is hardly surprising that the social services of the scheduled castes were not in great demand and they earned only 1 percent of their income from such sources. This income related exclusively to the drumming of the Basphod and the midwifery performed by his wife. Finally, other income refers to a mixed bag of sources, including income from land belonging to relatives, especially affines, from cultivation of water chestnuts (singhare) in ponds, from parching of grain (eg. making popcorn), from hiring out Dunlop carts, from hunting, music and theft. From this residual and very heterogeneous category, the medium and scheduled castes earned equal proportions and the high castes a nominal amount, but less significance can be attached to this difference because the category includes such a wide range of activities of differing prestige, though most were of lower prestige.

When the income sources of individual castes are examined, even greater differences are discernible than those between caste strata. For example, one can see the very high percentage of Thakur and Pande Brahmin income from service occupations; of Mahabrahmin and Misra Brahmin income from crops and business; of Pathan and Bhurji income from the greatest variety of sources in relatively equal shares (except for crops, much the largest share in the case of Pathans); of Kurmi, Lodh and Loniya income from crops and milk (especially from crops); of Ahir income from milk production, their traditional occupation; of Mali, Teli, Chamar, Pasi and Basphod income from agricultural labour; of Dhobe income from washing; of Gadaria income from keeping sheep, again a traditional occupation; of Patharkot income from their petty business as makers of grindstones; of Radhika income from petty business, keeping animals and providing music at religious and social functions. One remarkable feature was the unwillingness of the members of the two scheduled 'tribes', Patharkot and Radhika, to engage in either agricultural production or labouring of any kind. There was one exception, a Radhika who was a biannual labourer turned farmer who also did labouring for TS. TS complained that in general the Radhikas were unwilling to indulge in the hard labour of farming, even when he had offered to provide them with gaon sabha land.

A few castes derived a relatively high share of their total income from brickworks labour, notably the Chamars (16%) and Pathans (10%). Other castes, with fewer households in the sample, also had high shares: Tiwari Brahmin 17%, Bhurji 15%, Kahar 9% and Gadaria 6%.

Caste and Change in Standard of Living 1971-1981

Similar proportions of high and medium caste household heads reported some improvement in their standard of living and in fact the medium castes (36%) marginally exceeded the high castes (33%) in this respect. However, there were only three scheduled caste heads (14%) who acknowledged any improvement. An impartially minded Thakur informant considered that the high caste replies in the sample reflected reality, but that nearer 45 percent of middle caste households and nearer 33 percent of scheduled caste households in the village as a whole had in fact achieved some improvement. Looking at individual castes, he considered the reported 11 percent improvement among Kurmis much too low and that it was actually nearer 40 percent. Loniyas (25%), Chamars (21%) and Pasis (nil) had also each under-reported improvement and the true figures for these castes were probably nearer to 50 percent, 40 percent and 30 percent respectively.

The proportion of households reporting a big improvement in standard of living increased with stratum level. No members of the scheduled castes reported such a happy trend and only one person of high caste (a Brahmin) admitted to serious decline. Thakurs (75%), Lodhs (67%), Dhobes (60%) and Gadarias (40%) were the individual castes within which the highest proportion of households reported some improvement.

Caste and Education

Whilst the high castes as a whole had started with an advantage in landownership, the hierarchical differences become much more sharp when the education level of adults in the three strata is compared. In the case of all household heads, the average education was abysmally low (1.4 years).

CASTE AND AVERAGE YEARS EDUCATION OF ADULTS (16+ YEARS), ALL HOUSEHOLDS

CASTE	NO. HHS	HHH	WIFE OF HHH	S1	WIFE OF S1	S2	S3	D1 + D2	OTHER MALES	OTHER FEMALES
BRAHMIN										
SHUKLA	8	3.4	0	6.8	0	6.5	10.0	5.0	7.0	0
AWASTHI	6	0	0	2.0	0	3.0	0	0	0	0
MISRA	9	0.6	0	7.0	0	0	7.0	0	0	0
TIWARI	3	1.3	0	0		2.0	0	0	0	0
DUBE	1	4.0	0	8.0	0	12.0	0	0	0	0
PANDE	1	12.0							5.0	
TOTAL BRAHMIN	28	1.9	0	4.8	0	6.0	4.2	1.7	6.0	0
MISRA	11	2.9	0	8.5	1.0	5.0	0	4.3	4.9	3.5
PANDE	5	0.7	0					5.0		
TOTAL MAHABRAHMIN	16	2.2	0	8.5	1.0	5.0	0	4.5	4.9	3.5
BAIS	3	8.7	4.4	10.0	0	17.0	14.0	9.0	11.5	7.5
RAIKWAR	10	7.7	0.8	8.5	6.0	12.0	8.0	6.0	8.8	1.9
TOTAL THAKUR	13	7.9	1.8	8.8	6.0	13.7	11.0	7.2	9.7	2.8
PUNJABI	1	NA	NA	NA	NA	NA	NA			
BHAT	3	2.3							5.0	
BANIA	1	5.0								
PATHAN	17	0	0	1.4		0				
KURMI	18	3.6	0.3	6.5	0	9.0	8.0	0	5.6	0.4
AHIR	8	1.6	0	3.2		2.0				
LODH	34	1.1	0	3.5	0	2.0	3.0	0	1.6	0
MALI	3	0	0						3.0	
BARHAI	2	0	0	0	0	0				
LOHAR	3	0	0	6.5					0	0
KAHAR	3	0	0	0	0	0				
DHOBE	7	0	0	0					0	0
NAI	5	0	0	0	0	0	0			0
BHURJI	4	0	0			0			0	0
TELI	3	0	0	0	0	0				
GADARIA	17	0.8	0	1.9		2.2		0	0	0
LONIYA	12	0	0	1.6	0	3.0	0	0	1.2	0
KABARIA	8	0	0	0	0				0	
CHAMAR	27	0	0	0.6	0	2.3	0	0	0	0
PASI	13	1.1	0	2.5	0	3.3	0	0	0	0
BASPHOD	1	0	0							
PATHARKOT	4	0	0						0	0
RADHIKA	12	0	0	0	0	0	0		0	0
HIGH CASTE	58	3.5	0.4	6.4	2.1	8.4	6.5	4.9	6.1	2.9
MIDDLE CASTE	148	1.0	0.04	2.6	0	1.7	1.8	0	2.1	0.1
SCHEDULED	57	0.4	0	0.8	0	2.1	0	0	0	0
TOTAL	263	1.4	0.1	2.9	0.3	3.2	2.8	3.0	2.8	0.9
TOTAL ADULTS (855)		259	208	97	55	42	19	20	63	96
INDEX										
HIGH		250	400	221	700	262	232	(163)	240	440
MIDDLE		71	4	90	0	53	64	0	84	20
SCHEDULED		29	0	28	0	66	0	0	0	0

CASTE AND AVERAGE YEARS EDUCATION OF CHILDREN AGED 5+, ALL HOUSEHOLDS

CASTE	NUMBER OF PUPILS AT SCHOOL	NUMBER NOT AT SCHOOL	AGE 5	6	7	8	9	10	11	12	13	14	15
BRAHMIN	23	16	0.4	0.5	0.7	1.6		1.6	0	3.5	4.0	7.0	6.3
MAHABRAHMIN	21	6	0.2	1.0	1.5	2.7	2.7	3.5	3.0	3.6	2.0	5.0	
THAKUR	15	-	1.0	2.0	2.0	3.5	4.5	6.0	4.0				8.5
PATHAN	2	22	0	0	0	0	0	0		1.6		0	1.8
KURMI	14	18	0.2	0	0.7	0	3.2	2.0	2.5	2.7		0	5.0
LODH	18	37	0	0.3	0	0.8	0	1.8	0	2.8	2.2	3.7	2.0
CHAMAR	2	32	0	0	0	0	0	0.8	0	0	2.0	0	0
HIGH	59	22	0.5	1.0	1.3	2.2	3.4	2.8	1.4	3.5	3.3	6.3	7.2
MEDIUM	47	161	<0.1	0.1	0.2	0.4	1.3	1.3	0.8	1.3	1.7	1.2	2.4
SCHEDULED	5	23	0	0	0	0.6	0	0.5	0	0	1.6	0	0
TOTAL	111	206	0.2	0.2	0.5	0.9	1.7	1.3	0.7	1.6	1.9	2.6	2.8
NO PERSONS	111	206	8	6	7	17	8	18	6	15	6	8	12
HIGH CASTE AS PERCENTAGE OF AVERAGE			250	500	260	244	200	215	200	219	174	242	257

However, the high caste heads had achieved 250 percent of the average compared with 71 percent for middle and 29 percent for scheduled heads of households. The ratios were similar for first and third sons and also for other adult males in the households but in the case of second sons, the middle castes had relatively less education than in the case of other adult males and the scheduled castes actually had a higher level than the middle castes. The inter-stratum differences increased extremely sharply in the case of adult women. This was particularly true of the wives of the first son of the household head, where the high caste women had an average of 2.1 years schooling and the rest had none at all. Looking at individual castes, really the only ones with even moderately good standards of male education were the Shukla, Misra and Dube Brahmins, Mahabrahmins, Thakurs (especially Bais) and Kurmis.

The same hierarchical differences were still being reproduced in the younger generation. The average years schooling of the high caste 15-year olds was 257 percent of the overall average and this was at least the same for high caste 5 to 7-year olds. The education of middle caste children remained below the average (for all except 10 and 11-year olds) and the trend was worsening. In all but three years, the scheduled caste children had no education. Here there was no trend towards an improved level of schooling. It was said of village leaders that, whilst there had been no active discouragement to educate lower caste children, there had also been no positive encouragement for them to attend school either. Inwardly, the upper caste were probably mainly pleased to see no lower caste improvement in education because such a development could mean competition for government and other jobs, greater scarcity of labour and less opportunity to exploit the illiteracy and ignorance of the lower orders. The Pradhan had done nothing to motivate the Chamars and others to send more children to school. The teachers had tried a little but this was probably mainly in response to government orders.

However, perhaps too much can be made of the intercaste differences. What was equally striking was the extremely low level of education in almost all castes. This is best illustrated by the figures for 15-year olds, where the average number of years schooling was only 2.8.

Zamindars

Before Zamindari Abolition, the main Zamindar castes in the block were Thakur and Brahmin but Kurmis and Banias also had a little Zamindari. The Banias became Zamindars through malguzari mortgaged to them by Thakur and Brahmin Zamindars, which was later unredeemable and had to be sold to the Banias. There were two types of ownership right, Bhumidhari and Sirdari. Bhumidhar rights included income from the malguzari or lagan. The tenants (asamis) paid anything from Rs 12 to Rs 25 per bigha to the Zamindars who kept about 80% of this land revenue (malguzari).

LANDOWNERSHIP AND PER CAPITA INCOME

BIGHAS OWNED	% OF HOUSEHOLDS Rs 433-810	Rs 811-950	Rs 951-2000	TOTAL HHs
0	75%	-	25%	8
1-7	61%	23%	27%	44
8+	38%	22%	40%	50
TOTAL	50%	22%	28%	102
WEIGHTED BIGHAS OWNED				
0	75%	-	25%	8
1-12	46%	27%	27%	48
13+	13%	13%	74%	46
TOTAL	32%	21%	48%	102

Land Reforms

In 1952 all the asamis (occupancy tenants) became full owners and they were thus no longer liable to pay the malguzari to the Zamindars. They now only paid malguzari to the government and this amounted to only about 25 percent of the sums previously paid to the Zamindars. The two castes which benefited most from Zamindari Abolition in Basauli were said to be the Kurmis and Lodhs, simply because they were taking most interest in agriculture and were the main cultivators. The Lodhs benefited less because many were still migrating, doing mainly labouring and other work at that time. In fact Zamindari Abolition may have acted as an incentive to some of the Lodhs and other migratory groups to settle down on newly acquired land. (By 1982 only about 10 percent of Lodhs were migratory and some from Basauli had shifted to Kotwa village on the road between Fatehpur and Dewa Sharif. Lodhs, however, were mainly migrating into Basauli because there was relatively more land available in Basauli.) The Brahmins in Basauli fared badly from the Abolition because at that time most of them were functionaries of the Zamindars or employed outside farming. Since they were not asamis, they were not in a position to be awarded full ownership rights. Equally, the Chamars also benefited relatively little because most of them in 1952 were agricultural labourers rather than tenants, though most households owned about five bighas of mafi land, which might have been Bhumidhari or Sirdari or both. Those mafi tenants who now owned their Sirdari could convert this into Bhumidhari by paying ten times (or, later, 20 times) the lagan, and, later still, all has become Bhumidhari without payment being necessary.

It was estimated that only about 200 bighas had been given by the gram samaj during the land distribution after Consolidation in the 1970s and the chief beneficiaries had been Chamars, Pasis and Dhobes. Thakur Sahib claimed that 97 persons(!) had received small amounts of land from the gram samaj. He usually phrased this in terms of 'I gave so-and-so x number of bighas', as if the gram samaj land were his personal property. Thakur Sahib had lost relatively little of his own land through earlier land redistribution under the Adhivasi Acts and the only landlord in Basauli who subsequently lost any land under the ceiling acts was his cousin, SS, who had 11 bighas confiscated, with no compensation, in 1976.

One of the recipients of this land of SS Thakur was K. Chamar. The land was taken from the Thakur during the Emergency period and four bighas were given to K by the lekhpal as a reward for having a vasectomy and helping him fill his quota. K was the only example of anyone in Basauli being so rewarded for sterilisation. He then took a loan of Rs 1,500 from the Land Development Bank (Bhumi Vikas Bank) for a boring. In the end, he neither did a boring nor bought oxen and he owed Rs 1,500, of which bank employees had 'eaten' Rs 500 earlier. At the same time, R. Thakur, by whom he was employed as a biannual labourer, had lent him Rs 500 to help towards the purchase of two oxen. Ultimately, K never bought oxen and did not get round to making a serious attempt at farming and he sold the land, unofficially, to the Punjabis for Rs 3,200. The sale had to be unofficial and unrecorded because property transferred to the scheduled through land reforms could not be alienated. This measure was meant to protect the interests of the poor and lower castes. There was no agreement with the Punjabis that would allow the Chamar to re-purchase the land, if he should ever raise the money (which was highly unlikely anyway). K could probably still have reclaimed it if he had gone to the government, because he would have the law on his side. There was no village hostility towards the Punjabis over this transaction, and the fact that they were relatively recent immigrants appears to have made no difference to people's general indifference to such a transaction.

K died soon after, from 'general weakness' and it seems that his economic 'opportunity' came too late in life (though he was only 50 years old when he died). His son then came to the family of R. Thakur, seeking employment as a monthly labourer, but they refused. This was not because they expected him to be a bad worker, but because they had already employed a Lodh and also they now preferred not to employ a Chamar or other scheduled caste person, which could cause complications in relation to loans. It is more or less inevitable that a farmer will have to make loans to a biannual labourer and, if he should renege, it is highly likely that the government will support the labourer. However, this is but one consideration in the decision concerning whom to employ and it is still unlikely to be the major factor. The son of K was now a casual labourer and had also started a cycle repair 'shop' on the roadside. He lacked the necessary capital and later he gave this up to go and work at the brick kiln.

The position of the Thakur Zamindars in Basauli had worsened, partly through loss of the malguzari income and partly through mismanagement and internal divisions. At least two Thakur household heads in 1982 were imprisoned against payment of their own malguzari. In March 1982 the Sub-Divisional Magistrate (a Thakur), accompanied by a police sub-inspector (a Yadav) and the Amin, came to Basauli to recover unpaid malguzari. Two Thakurs owed Rs 1,200 and Rs 800 respectively for the past two years but one was said to be not present in the village and his door was locked. The SDM and party stormed into the courtyard of a relative and there they made enquiries about their whereabouts. The son of the larger Thakur debtor was very incensed at the intrusion into private houses without a warrant and he spoke up strongly against this. His objections were based on a number of grounds, including entrance without a warrant, invasion of privacy, and breaking of purdah prohibition. He told the SDM that he had no right to enter the house without a warrant. The SDM replied that he could easily get one. The son accepted this and said that he would then be free to enter people's houses but not until. The SI became angry and said that he would arrest the son as the next of kin of the defaulter. The son retorted that he was not the debtor and they had no complaint against him. He maintained that, though he lived with his father, he was quite independent of him and that he derived no benefit from his father's land (which was untrue). The SI took him and brought him to TS's verandah where the SDM and SI were given tea. The threat to arrest and detain the son was subsequently dropped, because they had no right to do so. However, they demanded the payment of the debt. The son said that he could raise Rs 1,200 but they would need to give him a week. They replied that he must raise half immediately and pay the other half the following day. The son said that he could only raise Rs 200 or so immediately and the matter was dropped for the moment.

As luck would have it, his father then appeared, returning from the fields towards evening. No one had gone to inform him of the presence of the officials. Still no problem need have arisen for him, since the police had no idea what he looked like. However, a Pasi enemy of the family informed the police of his appearance and so he, along with the other Thakur and a Mahabrahmin, were taken to Fatehpur and put in the police lock-up (havaldad). The father was released the following day when his family, by various means, succeeded in raising the necessary money. The father bore the authorities no grudge because 'he had been a defaulter all his life' and had so far managed to escape without detention. His younger son said that his defaulting was due more to his mismanagement than to any other factor.

The story arose from a general discussion on how many Indians tend to be so subservient to their superiors and how this emboldened senior officers and the upper class generally to take advantage of the lower class. The son claimed that he would have taken the same stand even if the SDM had been a non-Thakur or if he had been a less reasonable man. His position all along was that if the law empowered officials to invade people's courtyards or to arrest them, then they were free to do so but, if not, then not. However, the son conceded that the SDM could have arrested him on the charge of abusing him (even if he had not) and so his resistance was more than a little risky.

The other Thakur and the Mahabrahmin remained in the havaldad for 14 days. The law then requires a detainee to be released but he is usually only allowed to go just a few paces before he may be arrested for a further 14 days. After a total of 28 days he has to be released and then, if he still does not pay up, his property may be confiscated (neelam) or his land auctioned. In the case of the second Thakur he had no land of his own left but his son owned 21 bighas in his own name. Therefore there was really only one remaining strategy for the government to reclaim the Rs 800 of (very old) debt to them and that was to dock part of his salary as a government employee. So far they had not resorted to this extreme course. Inmates of the havaldad can either be brought food by their family or else they may have food brought from the bazaar, which would cost them about four rupees per meal. The other Thakur was neither bitter nor angry over his detention and merely accepted it as part of his fate. Such a detention does involve a loss of status but he well appreciated that in his case, as a drunkard, he had no respect now and he tried to console himself and raise his status by doing puja.

Consolidation

Consolidation (chakbandi) took place in 1968 and it was felt by TS's family to have been a success. TS allocated himself an L-shaped block of nine acres to the north of the road and three more acres of paddy land further to the north. As Pradhan, TS had the power to decide who his farming neighbours would be and he decided that, if he had good farmers around his land, then there would be less nuisance and also, psychologically, he would be encouraged to produce more. He chose R. Lodh as his main neighbour because he rightly regarded R and his four sons as 'very laborious' and highly capable farmers.

Renting of Land

Renting of land was, strictly speaking, illegal and the legislation was designed to protect lower caste tenants from exploitation. In practice, there was some renting, mostly sharecropping (batai), but hardly any renting for cash. The rate of batai was normally 50 percent, both on irrigated and unirrigated land, with the landlord being expected to pay 50 percent of the costs of water, fertiliser, pesticide and harvest labour. On unirrigated land, the sharecropper bore all the costs of cultivation.

In the sample, the amount of land owned had little relationship to whether an owner rented in, up to holdings of ten bighas, but 14 percent of owners of 11 or more bighas rented in, compared to 27 percent of all owners. Altogether, 28 household heads reported some renting in but only seven admitted renting out. This may have been partly because it was technically illegal, though most people did not seem all that nervous about the topic. Bliss and Stern mention how landowners in Palanpur feared that sharecroppers (bataidars) might claim ownership rights, especially if they were allowed to cultivate the same land for more than one season. They also found that there were 'more lettings from higher to lower castes' (1982:25).

In fact there is a law which gives a bataidar the right to claim ownership of rented land if he cultivates it for more than six crop seasons but there were no examples of sharecroppers claiming ownership and it also depended on the cooperation and diligent recording of the lekhpal, who was more likely to take the part of the maliks and was also somewhat careless about recording such matters. The lower reporting of renting out in the present study is more likely to have been a result of the way the questionnaire was framed.

LAND OWNED AND LAND RENTED IN AND OUT

BIGHAS OWNED	BIGHAS RENTED IN 0	1-2	3-4	5-6	7+	TOTAL	RENTERS IN AS % TOTAL
0	5				3	8	38
1-3	15	3	2	1		21	29
4-7	15	3	1		4	23	35
8-10	14	3	1	1	2	21	33
11+	25	1	1	1	1	29	14
TOTAL HHS	74	10	5	3	10	102	27

BIGHAS OWNED	BIGHAS RENTED OUT 0	1-2	3-4	5-6	7+	TOTAL	RENTERS IN AS % TOTAL
1-3	18	1	2			21	14
4-7	22	1				23	4
8-10	20				1	21	5
11+	27				2	29	7
TOTAL HHS	87	2	2	-	3	94	7

Irrigation

Irrigation was provided by one electrically driven, government tubewell, 21 private, mostly diesel-run tubewells, and also a few traditional wells, using Persian wheel (rahat), gravity slope (purahi) or lift (dhenkuli) methods. There was also a channel which ran from a canal south-west of Basauli and this supplied some farmers with water in Imlipur. The sample survey indicated that 60% of the total area owned was irrigated, but the records of the revenue accountant indicated that only 47% was irrigable in Basauli revenue village out of the total cultivated area. Irrigable area was also rather greater than the area actually irrigated, mainly because of brief and erratic supplies of electricity in the rural areas and because of breakdowns in farmers' diesel engines, some of which

OWNERS OF PUMPSETS AND BORINGS

NAME OF FARMER	CASTE	TYPE OF PUMP	HORSE POWER	DATE INSTALLED	Rs COST		NUMBER OF BORINGS	Rs COST OF BORINGS	BIGHAS IRRIG	TOTAL Rs COST
DEEP NARAYAN SINGH	THAKUR RAIKWAR	MAYURE	6½	1974	4000		2	2000	30	6000
UDAI BHAN SINGH	RAIKWAR	FIELD MARSHAL	8	1978	5000		1	1500	12	6500
SATYADEO SINGH	RAIKWAR	BHARAT SHAKTI	9	1979	5000		1	1200	20	6200
SURYANARAIN	MAHABR)	HARVEST	6½	1974	4000					
	MISRA)		8	1981	5000		4	4000	80	13,000
GIRISH CHANDRA	MAHABR MISRA	FIELD MARSHAL	8	1980	5500		2	3000	25	8500
LIAQAT KHAN	PATHAN	COOPER	6½	1979	3000	S/H?	1	1200		4200
SASHIDA SINGH/ CHEDU KHAN	BAIS PATHAN	MAYURE	6½	1981	2000	S/H	1	1200		3200
RAM PRASAD	KURMI	USHA	6½	1977	4400		2	2000		6400
BAJNATH	KURMI		6½	NK	NK		2	NK		
RAMESUR	KURMI		6½							
RAM KHELAWAN	KURMI	KISHAN	6½	1970	3500		1	500		4000
RAM NARESH	KURMI	MINRWA	6½	1978	4400		2	2000		6400
RAMESUR	LODH	RUSTON	6½	1975	3000		2	2000	32	5000
RAM SAGAR	LODH	USHA	6½	1981	4000		2	2000		6000
DURBIJE	LODH	RUSTON	6½	1979	2500	S/H	1	1000		3500
TULSI RAM	LODH	SWARAJ	9	1981	5500		1	1500		7000
SAMBHU	LODH	SWARAJ	9	1981	5500		1	1500	8	7000
MANGAT	DHOBE	COOPER	6½	1980	2000	S/H	1	1000		3000
BHALLAR	CHAMAR	BSA	6½	1979	4500		1	1500	21?	6000
BIRJAP	PASI	FIELD MARSHAL	8	1980	5000		1	2000	12	7000
RUDR NARAYAN	THAKUR		)	1960						
SINGH	BAIS		)	1970			2			
RAMCHANDRA	THAKUR		)	1975						
SINGH	RAIKWAR		)	1977			2			
RATIPAL SINGH	RAIKWAR						1			
RAGHURAJ SINGH	RAIKWAR						1			
BEJNATH	AHIR						1			
GAYAPRASAD	PANDE			1982			1			
ABDUL KARIM	PATHAN						1			
TOTAL		21 pumpsets			77,800		38 borings			108,900
AVERAGE					4095					

S/H = Second-hand

were bought second-hand. Except on rare occasions (such as emergency situations arising from extreme drought), electricity was only available for five to eight hours per 24 hours and this was usually after 7 pm, sometimes only after 9 pm. The one farmer with a domestic electricity supply in Basauli kept a bulb permanently switched on outside his house to give the earliest possible warning of the arrival of the electricity supply, so that he could start his engine immediately.

In 1971 the question of the location of the first government tubewell 700 metres to the east of the village, on the land of M. Chamar, arose because of some manoeuvring by SDS Thakur, a member of the opposition faction of Thakurs. TS was temporarily absent from the village and SDS, who had some relationship with the engineers, invited them to come and choose a site. They insisted on the Pradhan being present and so SDS persuaded the Pradhan of neighbouring Burhanapur (a Kurmi and political foe of TS) to masquerade as the Pradhan of Basauli. The Kurmi cooperated because the proposed site was also next to his own village and could benefit people in his constituency as well as his own land. TS was angry when he returned because the siting was sub-optimal both for him and, he claimed, also 'for those who needed it most'. The engineers were apologetic but had by then half finished the boring.

One of the most important decisions made by TS during his tenure as Pradhan had been his refusal to accept a second state tubewell in the village, because its location, according to him, was also unsuitable, especially as it would not supply water to certain poor farmers whose land was most urgently in need of irrigation. TS had applied for the government tubewell to be built on the south-eastern side of the village. This would have provided water to both the dry land of the south-east and also the sandy soil of the south-west. However, again whilst TS was away from the village in early 1980, the engineers came and chose a location north of the roadside and west of Purwa, partly because this was most convenient and cheapest for them and partly because a member of the Mahabrahmin, opposition faction had given them the impression that this was where it was desired by the villagers. TS was furious on his return and he refused to accept a tubewell on this site, both because he considered that it was ridiculous to install it where there were already irrigation facilities and partly because the water could not flow uphill to reach the land of Chamars and other poorer farmers who he thought should benefit most from any new irrigation capacity. TS added that his stand over this was one of the first issues which brought him into conflict with his new MLA, who failed to support him. TS would have preferred to have had the tubewell located on the Punjabis' land, ie. south-east of the house of S. Mahabrahmin. This would also have benefited TS the most. The second possible location and possibly the optimal one from nearly everyone's point of view, was midway between the tubewell of TS and S. Mahabrahmin, but further south. As it turned out, neither faction succeeded and it was generally thought that the chance of a tubewell had been passed to village Richhla.

The site chosen, incidentally, had been on the land of DNS Thakur. He already had adequate irrigation facilities of his own and he did not want to lose valuable land for the construction of the well-head, even though he would receive compensation. He, therefore, filed an application against its location there.

The state tubewells were all 15 horse power and the water depth in Basauli was about 25 metres. The Irrigation Department charged all farmers about Rs 10 per bigha per watering from state tubewells. The rate was fixed in relation to the area cultivated and was also affected by the amount of electricity used. The rate was not affected by the crop. A typical farmer might irrigate his wheat twice and thus his water costs would be about Rs 20 per bigha. The water rate was paid six months in arrears to the Amin. In 1979 the government charged a small command area tax to all in the proximity of the state tubewell, as well as a rate for waterings. This was to encourage such farmers to use the tubewells more but it was both ineffective and unpopular.

There were 20 owners of pumpsets and one of these, S. Mahabrahmin, owned two engines. The owners of pumpsets included five Kurmis, five Lodhs, four Thakurs, two Mahabrahmins, and one each from the Pathan, Dhobe, Chamar and Pasi castes. It is noticeable that no Brahmin owned a pumpset. In addition, four Thakurs, one Ahir, one Brahmin and a Pathan owned a total of nine tubewell borings but were lacking pumpsets. The Pathan used the engine bought by SS Thakur who worked in Bahraich and who may have given the engine to his ex-manager. Thakur Sahib owned two borings but could not use his electric motor because the UP State Electricity Board had cut off his supply. RS Thakur had sold his second-hand diesel engine after damaging it by overloading it with threshing work and he hoped to buy another engine if his wheat and coriander crops of 1983 proved satisfactory. The diesel engines and pumps were often mounted on wheeled trolleys which allowed them to be moved between owners' borings or indeed to be hired to farmers with borings but no engine. Fourteen of the engines were 6.5 horse power, four were of 8 horse power and three of 9 horse power.

The first pumpset was said to have been introduced in 1963 by TS. The oldest, surviving pumpset was 12-years old and belonged to a Kurmi. The second oldest pumpsets still working in 1982 were 8-years old and belonged to S. Mahabrahmin and DNS Thakur respectively, two of the best farmers in the village. Of the remainder, fourteen pumpsets had been purchased from 1978 to 1981, an indication of a recent rise in prosperity. Two of the three Thakur pumpsets were among these recent purchases, two of the three Mahabrahmin, only one of the five Kurmi engines and all the pumpsets of the lower castes except that of R, the richest Lodh. This suggests that the capacity of a very small number of lower caste farmers to purchase modern irrigation machinery had arisen only within the last four years.

The cost of a pumpset varied from Rs 2,000 for a second-hand model bought by a Dhobe to Rs 5,500 for new 9 horse power machines, invested in by two Lodhs and one Mahabrahmin. The engine and pump were separate and the pump was driven by a belt on the larger models, with the engine costing Rs 4,500 and the pump Rs 1,000. The smaller engines were linked to the pump by a coupling and the two items could both be transported on one trolley. The water output of smaller and larger engines was the same and the advantage of larger engines was mainly their capacity to do threshing and other work. There were as many as 11 different makes and the average pumpset cost Rs 4,095 (Rs 4,553 for new ones only). The buyers of cheaper, second-hand ones were two Thakurs, a Lodh and a Dhobe. Nine of the farmers had two borings per engine and S. Mahabrahmin had four borings. Two Thakurs each had two borings but currently no power. The borings had cost from Rs 500 to Rs 1,500, partly depending upon how recently the work had been done. Each pumpset, regardless of size, was capable of irrigating about 10 bighas per day. A pumpset could irrigate roughly 0.75 bighas in an hour, using one litre of diesel oil which cost Rs 3.15 in 1982. Some farmers hired out their pumpsets and the normal charge for this was Rs 12 per hour.

One purchaser of a second-hand pumpset had been R. Thakur. His elder brother had found a second-hand 6.5 horse power model and its owner had demanded Rs 2,300 for this. R then visited the owner without declaring his connection with his elder brother and, after dissecting the engine and pointing out its faults, he succeeded in buying it for Rs 1,500. Repairs cost a further Rs 500. As it happened, the engine only lasted the family three years, mainly because they overworked it by using it to thresh wheat in 1981. The damage done was repairable but the family decided to buy a larger engine, selling the old one for Rs 800.

In 1975, S. Chamar was given 21 bighas of good land by the gram samaj. In 1979, S took a loan of Rs 5,000 from the Land Development Bank to buy a pumpset. The eldest son of S was B, who worked for TS as a part-time, biannual labourer. When they proposed to buy a second-hand engine and set up a milling machine as well, TS advised them against this because he (rightly) considered it was beyond their capacity. The family ignored his advice and one son also borrowed Rs 2,000 from his employer at a brick works. They bought a pumpset from an unscrupulous agent in Fatehpur and then had to sell this at a loss when it soon went wrong. They now had to work for nothing at the brickworks to repay the debt and monthly interest of 3 percent upon it. To add to their misfortune, they sold the engine for Rs 3,000 to a Kurmi in Chhandol and he offered to deposit the money with the LDB on their behalf. The Kurmi connived with the bank clerks to forge an official receipt and this was given to the Chamars. The Kurmi was a business partner of the brickworks owner and also, incidentally, of a nephew of S. Mahabrahmin. As a result of all this, the Chamar family was unable to repay the loan and so the government auctioned nine bighas of their land. No one in Basauli was willing to buy it and the purchaser was S. Kurmi, a private allopath from Mohammadpur. It was claimed that the auction was not conducted properly, the matter was under litigation and in 1982 the Chamars still had possession of the land, for the moment at least. The doctor from Mohammadpur bought the land on behalf of the nephew of S. Mahabrahmin (the CPI-M official) and later sold him the land for Rs 8,000, the same price as he had paid. The Mahabrahmin could not take possession because of the protection afforded by TS so long as B remained in his employment. However, they were now involved in two court cases, one over the auction of the land and the other over the bank fraud. Altogether, it was alleged that they had been cheated by three separate sets of people, the owner of the brick kiln, the engine agent and the three partners who were depositors of the debt repayment (plus their bank clerk friends).

Three Lodh farmers still used five dhenkulis, the lever-system of lifting a bucket of water on the end of a long bamboo pole counterweighted at the other end by a large stone or, more commonly, a large dollop of earth tied onto the pole. This is a very ancient and laborious method of irrigation, but it is a cheap and feasible one where the water table is only two to four metres below the surface. This was the case in terai and by the roadside. There was also one Persian well still surviving until 1980 and also one well where the water was lifted by bullocks descending a slope. A Dhobe farmer had replaced the Persian well with a pumpset and boring (ie. pipe) placed within the well. In fact, S. Lodh had completed digging a new kacha well which would use the dhenkuli system, near the roadside in 1981. The cost of digging this was only Rs 50 because it was kacha and a pacca well would have cost Rs 2,000. He had also installed a boring in another dhenkuli. For this the Lodh had hired a timber derrick, rotating clamp (operated manually) and pipes. Another set was available from the block and could be borrowed free, on payment of a deposit of Rs 50. Another interesting development was the digging of a kacha dhenkuli in 1982 by BP Shukla, whose son was a leader of the opposition faction. This was only the second Brahmin investment in irrigation and it arose because of a dispute over irrigation channels from the state tubewell. The dispute was with his brother and others.

Tractorisation

In contrast to the proliferation of pumpsets, no one in the village yet owned a tractor but about five farmers sometimes hired one from outside. A Misra Brahmin of Mohammadpur had a tractor and used it to cultivate some land which he owned in Imlipur. At least three Thakur farmers were interested in buying a tractor: TS, DNS, and RS Thakur.

R. Thakur asked my advice about going into partnership with TS for the purchase of a tractor. TS was currently very keen to buy one and R, who had 45 bighas of sudh matiyar on the north side of the village which was too heavy for ox ploughing, was also very interested but R hesitated to go into partnership with TS, partly because of past quarrels and partly because he realised that it would be an unequal partnership, in which his usually mild-mannered and unpolitical father would always take second turn. R had tentatively agreed with DNS Thakur that they would go into such a partnership, but DNS would not be ready to purchase for at least one or two more years. R considered that his family had more political pull than the more prosperous DNS. Since R had been unable to find permanent employment, he felt the desire to go into farming. He claimed to be knowledgable about machines, especially pumpsets, and was also interested in machinery - unusually so for an arts graduate. TS was not willing to go into partnership with DNS because he feared that he was a 'narrow-minded' person who would cause trouble.

R was interested in buying a 20 horse power Eicher tractor which cost about Rs 58,000 and used a litre of diesel (Rs 3.15) per hour. He would really have preferred to buy individually but such a tractor required a deposit of Rs 15,000. He claimed that, with difficulty, he would be able to raise this amount but clearly it would be easier and in some ways less risky if he could share the cost of the deposit. He thought that, taking just the 45 bighas of matiyar, he could increase the average paddy production from 15 to 100 quintals and the average wheat production from zero to 60 quintals (given also the purchase of a pumpset to complement the already installed boring). This would represent an increase in the gross value of production by Rs 18,890 (using 1982 procurement prices). He claimed that the land was very heavy and became very hard after rains so that ox ploughing could really only scratch the surface. R had four choices in relation to this matiyar. He could either plough it himself with oxen; or rent it out in two to three bigha plots to bataidars; or hire a tractor each season to break it up; or purchase a tractor. Currently, he was renting the land to ten sharecroppers who mostly took little interest in it, merely touching the topsoil and securing very low paddy production (about 30 kg per bigha). One Ahir sharecropper of his from another village was producing two quintals (200 kg) per bigha and generally farmers from other villages tended to be better tenants for Basauli landlords because the 'land surplus' said to prevail in Basauli was non-existent elsewhere. Small owners from other villages took more pains with their rented land, perforce. Use of oxen on such heavy land was liable to cause damage to the animals out of all proportion to the marginal increase in production. The hiring of a tractor was not a very attractive option because there were only about 60 tractors in the whole block and it was extremely difficult to find an owner and driver who would be prepared either to bring a heavy plough or to plough the land carefully, whether with a light or heavy attachment. In addition the rates were expensive, Rs 10 per bigha and, in his sister's area in Lucknow district, the charge was actually Rs 35 per hour. It was also extremely difficult to secure the hire at the precise time when needed. Currently, R used a tractor sometimes and in 1981-2 he hired the tractor of a Kurmi in village Jeoli. (He also noted that in Badholi, a village near Barabanki, there was an absurd surplus of tractors, since at least 30 farmers (mostly Kurmis), many of them owning only five or six acres of land each, had all bought tractors, partly for reasons of prestige. They were such small farmers that many of them did not even have room in front of their houses to stand the tractors and so they had to be parked together in a public, open space.)

R claimed that if he bought a tractor, he would have the knowledge and skill to maintain it and that, in any case, there were adequate facilities at Fatehpur. Usually the mechanics would be able to come to the village within two days. He also had no qualms about villagers not paying their debts for hiring the tractor, since he claimed that social pressures (and not the danda) would be sufficient to ensure this. In cases of hire to persons in another village, then the custom was to insist on payment immediately after the ploughing. However, there was little that a tractor owner could do, if the farmer said he had no money to pay. If the tractor owner had any reason to doubt the farmer's capacity or willingness to pay, he might insist on payment before the work began. R also realised that a fairly sharp increase in the price of diesel oil in the medium term was almost inevitable. R would really have preferred to purchase a second-hand tractor and he quoted the case of someone he knew who went to the Punjab and bought a second-hand model for about Rs 18,000 and then spent Rs 5,000 on its repair. He had brought it to Lucknow by train, which cost a further Rs 400 or so.

R regarded the labour hire situation as difficult and it was becoming more so. Labourers, say from the Pathan caste, preferred to work at the brickworks or, when the brickworks was closed in the rainy season, they sought work with various building and other contractors. It was suggested to R that one possible solution was to increase the wage payment to agricultural labourers and to this he offered no reply. It is possible that large owners might be prepared to do this, if they felt confident that the labour was of a higher quality. As it was, many labourers were considered either weak, unskilled or lacking in commitment to the work.

R was emphatic that a cooperative solution to the lack of a tractor in the village was not only impossible, but unthinkable. He characterised the village as being full of various jealousies. With two or three tractors in the village and good management, he claimed that production could be increased by 40 percent. He thought that it was likely that S. Mahabrahmin and DNS Thakur would purchase tractors first and that there would be five or six in the village within the next ten years. In fact, by July 1984 TS had purchased a 35 horse power tractor, with the financial help of the State Bank of India. R. Thakur complained that he was not being given access to use of this tractor. In January 1984 R. Thakur faced up to the virtual impossibility of securing a white collar job, especially if he remained unwilling to offer a bribe. He tried to buy a mini tractor costing Rs 54,000 but the bank could only lend him 50 percent of this. He thought that he could raise only Rs 16,000 towards the required Rs 27,000 and this by sale of jewelry (Rs 12,000) and of gram (Rs 4,000). He was seriously considering the alternative possibility of buying a second-hand tractor for 25,000 to 30,000 rupees, thus saving the interest on a loan from the bank. He claimed to have some mechanical knowledge to enable him to maintain a second-hand machine.

Agricultural Equipment

There were no farmers who used a seed-drill and indeed no such thing existed in the village. The general view was that sowing (buwai) in this manner took too long and the sowing of the wheat was a rushed business in 1982 in any case, because of the late sowing of the paddy earlier. For those farmers employing labour to sow the seed, then a slow method was seen as particularly expensive and unattractive. However, R was worried to see windy weather in October 1982 because broadcast sowing is difficult in such conditions. R was intending to begin farming and to develop the technical side. He had bought the thresher of UBS Thakur for Rs 700. There were seven threshers in the village, owned by three Thakurs, two Lodhs, one Mahabrahmin and one Kurmi. Thakur Sahib had also bought a new thresher for about Rs 2,000 but, because his electricity supply was cut off, he had to employ young boys and bullocks to thresh his wheat. All the paddy had to be threshed by bullocks. The village could probably manage with a maximum of ten threshers, if used fully. In addition, S. Mahabrahmin bought a gobar gas plant privately for Rs 4,000 and this was almost fully installed by March 1983. There were at least three sizes available: capacity for 60, 75 and 90 kilograms of manure provided by at least two, three and four buffaloes respectively. S owned three buffaloes and had purchased the smallest size plant.

Credit

Details of as many of the loans and grants of Rs 1,000 or more since 1975 as could be ascertained were recorded. The list shown is unlikely to be exhaustive but should be fairly complete. It shows that a total of Rs 157,400 was given to 41 villagers, not all of whom were heads of households. Nearly 39 percent of this was in the form of grants and over 61 percent was as loans.

CASTE AND GOVERNMENT GRANTS AND LOANS, 1975-82

CASTE	NO. OF RECIPIENT PERSONS	Rs GRANTS AND LOANS	AVER Rs PER HH	% OF TOTAL GRANTS AND LOANS	% OF POPN	5 AS % OF 6
1	2	3	4	5	6	7
CHAMAR	9	35,500	3944	22.6	9.2	246
MAHABRAHMIN	4	28,000	7000	17.8	8.0	222
LODH	6	25,700	4283	16.3	14.0	116
THAKUR	8	25,000	3125	15.9	5.6	284
PASI	6	23,000	3833	14.6	5.1	286
PATHAN	4	12,500	3125	7.9	7.2	110
LONIYA	1	3,000	3000	1.9	4.1	46
SHUKLA BR.	2	2,500	1250	1.6	2.8	57
DHOBE	1	2,200	2200	1.4	2.5	56
TOTAL	41	157,400	3839	100	100	100

The average grant component, loan component and total amount per recipient was Rs 1,483, Rs 2,356 and Rs 3,839 respectively. The table shows that Chamars received Rs 35,500 or nearly 23 percent of the total and almost two and a half times their share of the total population. The Mahabrahmins received the second largest amount and their proportion was well over twice their share of population. The Lodhs were third but their share was more in proportion with their population. Thakurs received Rs 25,000 and Pasis Rs 23,000 so that both had shares which were nearly three times their respective ratios of population. Pathans were the recipients of the fifth largest total but their share only exceeded their population ratio by a nominal amount. The remaining three groups (Loniya, Shukla Brahmin and Dhobe) each contained one or two households which had received one to three thousand rupees and their share of funds was in each case around half their population fraction. The figures show that the Pasis did best (286%), presumably because of positive discrimination to a scheduled caste, in which 78 percent of households supported the Pradhan. The Thakurs fared next best (284%), as the dominant caste, with many creditworthy, larger farmers who had no shortage of ideas needing credit, including some which were clearly fraudulent and different from the intended real use of the money. Next came the Chamars (246%) as the largest scheduled caste entitled to positive discrimination. Perhaps their share might have been even higher had not their support of the Pradhan been as low as 25 percent of the households. The Mahabrahmins received proportionately the fourth largest share and this was perhaps a function of their position as the second most powerful caste group. The amounts received by them were particularly large, averaging Rs 7,000 per household. The largest amount was Rs 10,000 of Taccavi provided to a nephew of S. Mahabrahmin to start a fertiliser agency. Thus the largest amount went to the biggest household with the most capital and net income (though not the highest PCI). The other average amounts per household which were above the overall mean were those of the Lodhs (Rs 4,283) and Chamars (Rs 3,944). The share of the supporters of the Pradhan was nearly 57 percent, while opposition households received 42 percent and the factional support of one Chamar household is untraceable.

The grant component averaged 39 percent of the total overall and for five of the non-scheduled castes it was the standard 33 percent. The grant element was higher in the case of Pasis (50%), Chamars (43%) and, because of one Antayodhaya award, even Thakurs (36%). It was noticeable that at least five Chamar households had not received 50 percent of their money from the Land Development Bank in the form of grants, but only 33 percent.

Most of the money was received in 1981 (39%) and 1982 (35%). The relatively small amounts recorded for earlier years, especially before 1980, may be mainly due to lower reporting, though one might conclude that there had been some acceleration in payments, especially to the scheduled castes, since Congress (I) returned to power in early 1980. However, these figures show that the scheduled castes received less than 28 percent of the total amount in 1981 and 1982, compared with over 37 percent for the whole period. This rather suggests that government aid was relatively more important to the lower castes and that they therefore had a fuller recall of such aid, even going back as far as 1975 in the case of one Chamar.

The table shows that 13 of the 41 recipients were in the richest income category. Among these, three Thakur households, including that of the Pradhan, had received aid for at least two separate projects. Ten recipients were from the upper medium income (from a variety of castes) and ten from the very poorest category, consisting of five Chamars, four Pasis and one Mahabrahmin. Five came from the lower medium category and only three from the fairly rich category. Predictably, the average aid to the richest households was Rs 6,670, which was 61 percent above the overall average of Rs 4,142 per household. The three households containing two separate recipients received an average of Rs 11,000 per household. The largest aid of all consisted of Rs 10,000 for a fertiliser agency and Rs 8,000 for a pumpset to the nephew and younger brother of S. Mahabrahmin who were both members of his large joint household. This both confirms that the largest government aid went to the household with the largest income and also that leadership of the opposition faction did not prevent the wealthy from access to generous amounts of help from the government.

PER CAPITA INCOME, CASTE, AID AND TYPE OF INVESTMENT (AID IN THOUSAND Rs)

Rs PCI	PUMPSET AND/OR BORING	DUNLOP CART	SHOP OR AGENCY	OXEN	HORSE AND KHARKHARA OR CART	BUFFALO	OTHER	TOTAL AID THOU Rs
401-700	5.5 CH; 7 PASI; 2(Boring) CH	5 CH; 5 PASI	2 MAHABRAHMIN	2 CH; 3,3 PASI	5 CHAMAR			39.5
701-810	5 CH; 1.5(Boring) CHAMAR			2.2 DHOBE		3 LODH; 3 PASI		14.7
811-950			2.5,3 PATHAN; 2 LODH	2.5 CH; 2 PASI	4,3 PATH; 3 LONIYA	1.5 TH; 3 LODH		26.5
951-1100	8 MAHABRAHMIN		1.5 SHUKLA				0.5(NA) THAKUR	10.0
1101+	4 THAK; 8 MAH; 8,8 LODH	7 CH; 4,4,4 THAKUR	1 SHUKLA; 10 MAH Agency	1.7 LODH		3 THAKUR	4 (Tobacco Industry)	66.7
THAKUR								
TOTAL. THOU RUPEES	60.5 + 3.5 = 64.0 Borings	22.0	22.0	16.4	15.0	13.5	4.5	157.4
NO. OF RECIP-IENTS	9 + 2 = 11 Borings	5	7	7	4	5	2	41
AVERAGE THOUSAND Rs PER RECIPIENT	6.72 pumpset; 1.75 boring	4.40	2.0 Shop; 10.0 Agency	2.34	3.75	2.70	2.25	3.84

CH = Chamar; MAH = Mahabrahmin; PATH = Pathan; TH or THAK = Thakur

PER CAPITA INCOME, TOTAL AID, AVERAGE AID PER HOUSEHOLD AND RELATIVE SHARE OF AID

Rs PCI	THOU Rs TOTAL AID	THOU Rs GRANT AID	NUMBER OF RECIPIENT HOUSE-HOLDS	AVERAGE Rs PER HOUSE-HOLD	HHS AS % OF SAMPLE TOTAL	Rs TOTAL AID AS % TOTAL	Rs GRANT AID AS % TOTAL	NUMBER RECIPIENTS AS % TOTAL
401-700	39.5	19.0	10	3950	32.4	25.1	31.2	26.3
701-810	14.7	6.1	5	2940	18.6	9.3	10.0	13.2
811-950	26.5	9.6	10	2650	20.6	16.8	15.7	26.3
951-1100	10.0	3.3	3	3333	11.8	6.4	5.4	7.9
1101+	66.7	22.8	10*	6670	16.7	42.4	37.5	26.3
TOTAL	157.4	60.8	38	4142	100	100	100	100

* Includes three distinct provisions of aid to separate individuals within one household.
Data based on a non-random, retrospective survey which was meant to be exhaustive but is unlikely to have traced all aid received.

The table shows the distribution of government help to different kinds of project and the per capita income and caste of recipients of the various types of project. It should be stressed that these heads are misleading since quite a few recipients of aid (especially rich Thakurs) spent their money on projects other than those specified in their application or used it for current consumer expenditure. The largest share of aid went on irrigation (nearly 41 percent, including over 38 percent for pumpsets for mainly the richest households, but also to three households below the poverty line and 2 percent for borings for poor Chamars). There were eleven recipients and the average aid for a pumpset was Rs 6,720 and Rs 1,750 for a boring. The second most popular project was Dunlop carts (14%) and these were asked for by three rich Thakurs (in two households) and a very poor Chamar and Pasi. There were five recipients and the average aid for a Dunlop cart was Rs 4,400. Aid to begin or expand shops or agencies also accounted for 14 percent of the total and six of the seven recipients were above the poverty line. The average aid for a shop was Rs 2,000 and the government provided Rs 10,000 to enable a fertiliser agency to be established. Help in buying oxen comprised over 10 percent of the total aid and went mainly to poorer and medium farmers. There were seven recipients and the average amount was Rs 2,340. By 1982, four people had been assisted in buying a horse and kharkhara (cart) and, in view of this, it was slightly odd that none was plying from Basauli until early 1983 and even then the kharkhara owned by one of the Pathan recipients was alone. Kharkharas accounted for nearly 10 percent of the total and the average amount provided for a horse and kharkhara was Rs 3,750. The other Pathan had bought a horse which he intended to train and sell for a profit, but he had left its training late and it appeared as if he would have to spend a considerable sum on special training to make the horse at all saleable. Nearly 9 percent of the total aid went on buffalo purchase. There were five recipients, including four in the poor or medium income categories. Nearly 3 percent went on other projects including over 2.5 percent on a Thakur project for a 'tobacco industry'. It is not clear what was meant by this but in any case half of this was actually spent on buying a buffalo and the other half on consumption, including a few 'luxuries' for the wife.

At least 50 households had received loans, grants or subsidies from the government under one scheme or another. Moneylending by professional mahajans had become rare and there were very few villagers who lent money on any scale. In the past, private moneylending had been very common and one of the biggest moneylenders was C, the rich Brahmin lamberdar of Rammandai. The decline of private moneylending in the ilaqa was said to be partly an indication of the improvement in people's conditions and it also reflected the increasing availability of government aid and credit. Poor people in urgent need of cash usually mortgaged their jewelry, mainly in Suratganj, where there were numerous Bania jewellers, metal dealers and other traders.

Within the village, at least four persons were said to lend medium amounts of money. The main one was S. Kurmi of Imlipur. Apart from him, DNS Thakur, DPS Thakur and S. Mahabrahmin were also prepared to make loans, but most of their credit was extended as a device to secure agricultural labour on a medium term basis.

Some Thakurs incurred large debts, partly because of the difference between their current income and their traditional lifestyle. It was estimated that one Thakur had accumulated debts to government departments which totalled at least Rs 23,000. The largest was Rs 8,000 owed to the UP State Electricity Board. He had paid his bills in time for the first two years or so and had then been disconnected. An illegal connection was later discovered and an estimated bill was prepared on the basis of average consumption by a machine such as his. The consumer tried to have the connection restored in the name of his second son, but that ploy had failed. Currently, the case was proceeding in a court in Barabanki. The same Thakur had also succeeded in obtaining Rs 5,000 from the Antayodhaya scheme, in the name of his second son to buy oxen. The scheme was intended to help the very poorest villagers and the only justification he might conceivably make was that his son was currently a married and poor student. He had also earlier borrowed a further Rs 5,000 from the Land Development Bank for a pumpset, but had only repaid part of this.

He had also been trying in late 1982 to secure two separate loans of Rs 5,000 each from the Gramin Bank in Mohammadpur, to help him in his current financial difficulties. The ostensible purpose of the loans was to buy a Dunlop cart and kharkhara, though in fact he had no intention of buying either. The manager and inspector came from the bank to discuss the possibility of the loans, and they agreed to the cart (even though they knew he already owned such a cart) but they suggested that the kharkhara was "not a project that would appear appropriate to his status". They proposed that he should forward such an application in the name of some lower caste villager. He agreed and his son's confidant, N. Dhobe, persuaded his brother M to apply. After further consideration of the full implications, the Dhobe then changed his mind. He had appreciated that, in the event of the Thakur not repaying the loan (which was virtually inevitable), then he would be responsible for the debt. N remained neutral on the matter, but the Thakur was very annoyed. He then asked M. Pathan, an elderly, none-too-bright and very faithful Pathan, who sometimes worked for him. M agreed in the evening but returned the following morning to express his regrets. The Thakur then moved further down the social hierarchy and persuaded L. Radhika, the harmonium player, to apply. He was the third choice and was actually on his way to Fatehpur with the Thakur to have his photograph taken (as part of the lending procedure) and had reached the Mohammadpur 'crossing' when he too had second thoughts and declined.

Another Thakur family was frequently in debt. In March, before the wheat had been harvested and sold, the family's finances were at a low ebb and they owed about Rs 2,000. The two sons differed in education and personality and tended to operate separately within the joint household, Not only did they go their individual ways but they tended to keep communication and questioning on each other's business to the minimum, presumably as a means of avoiding conflict. Many people expressed amazement that the joint arrangement had survived and some attributed it to the tolerance of the younger son. The elder brother borrowed from people in his entirely separate social network and, though he informed the younger brother of any success in getting loans, he neither volunteered nor was he asked for further details. The younger brother borrowed about Rs 600 from the family of a Bania old school friend who ran a jewelry shop in Fatehpur. He seemed somewhat embarrassed at admitting to having borrowed from a personal friend and he said that the interest charged was only 3 percent per month, considerably lower than the usual rate. He claimed that he would find difficulty in borrowing from a professional moneylender (mahajan), because they disliked lending to people from higher castes. They usually tried to avoid loans to the upper castes because they feared that such people would not repay them and the power of upper caste persons would enable them to resist attempts to realise the debt. Apart from Banias and members of other castes who acted as moneylenders, there were also a few Thakur mahajans, but even these would feel less than confident about reclaiming loans from higher caste borrowers. Consequently, moneylenders preferred, from many points of view, to deal with members of the lower castes, who were also usually more naive about usurious rates of interest. He stressed that these high rates of interest did not deter most higher caste borrowers either. If members of the lower castes were to renege, then the moneylenders could press them to repay the loan through manual labour or other services. In some cases the person seeking a loan would deposit jewelry and other property (effectively pawning his belongings) but this again was more common among the lower castes. In fact, the lower castes increasingly had a larger share of their capital in the form of jewelry than the upper castes who had been quicker to appreciate the security risk involved in owning and still more in wearing expensive jewelry in a time of apparently increasing crime and dacoity. Women of lower caste households who sought to raise their status by a display of fine silver ornaments on various appointed parts of the body were exposing themselves to some risk of being robbed as well as of physical injury, should they resist.

The elder brother was also successful in getting a loan of about Rs 4,000 from the Land Development Bank in December 1982. The younger brother was very annoyed when he found that his elder brother had already frittered away Rs 2,000 on inconsequential items such as new clothing for his wife. When the younger brother was offered part of the loan, he firmly refused and deliberately kept himself from being involved in it. His elder brother intended to use the remaining money to buy a buffalo, which he would hand to a Gadaria to look after and the two of them would later sell it and share the profit.

Another source of credit was from mortgaging land (girvi). In the past mortgages were written officially in the lekhpal's records, but this had more or less ceased, mainly because people could not afford to pay up to Rs 200 or sometimes even more to keep the lekhpal happy. Some mortgagees took the land on mortgage mainly for the benefit of rent-free cultivation and few expected to eventually take possession of the land. Legal protection of the mortgageor made such possession a far from easy matter. Thakur Sahib nevertheless commented that the Punjabi and so many others gave mortgage loans in the hope of taking possession but this was not simple and it was also socially disapproved of by some villagers. Usually, the amount loaned was from Rs 100 to 150 per bigha. Though this was not normally recorded officially, R. Thakur knew of only one case where this lack of registration had been exploited. In this case, the mortgageor had been richer than the mortgagee. BBS Thakur had mortgaged six bighas to R. Misra of Imlipur for Rs 800 in 1979. R. Misra had wished to extend his area of cultivation. Later BBS returned only Rs 400, and then sold 26 bighas of land, including the six bighas he had mortgaged, for Rs 30,000 in 1981. R. Misra then complained and asked for the return of the remaining Rs 400. The land was bought by L and BL, two Lodh brothers of Imlipur, and L occupied the mortgaged land immediately. His brother, BL, was in the CID department of the Lucknow police and this did not exactly strengthen R. Misra's position. He was powerless and BBS merely argued that, since R. Misra had had the benefit of cultivating the land for four seasons and had earned more than Rs 400 from this, BBS no longer owed him anything. R. Misra was a member of the opposition faction in the village and so did not feel able to come to Thakur Sahib for help against BBS (who was opposition candidate in the 1982 election for Pradhan). However, even if R. Misra had been a member of the ruling faction there would have been nothing that Thakur Sahib could have done to help him in this matter.

As the above case illustrates, mortgage of land was just as likely to occur from rich to fairly poor as the reverse. This was possible because the loans advanced were not so large as to be beyond the means of medium income villagers and also because the poor were keen to increase their area of cultivation. Where rich villagers were mortgaging land to poorer, weaker persons, the need to register the mortgage officially was less urgent and could be dispensed with. In this particular instance, the lack of registration was exploited by the mortgageor rather than the mortgagee.

Consumer Goods

Among the new consumer goods owned by an increasing number of households were watches, torches, radios and cycles. There was estimated to be an average of one wrist-watch per household, though many men did not normally wear their watches. Most watches cost from Rs 150 to 200 and most people had bought their watches in the past ten years. A Pathan shopkeeper had been on Haj and had brought back a few foreign watches with him. There were about 100 cycles in the village and the average value in the sample was about Rs 230. A new cycle cost from Rs 370 to 450, depending on the make and the number of accessories. A second-hand model usually cost anything from Rs 150 upwards.

Farm Area

The average farm area, including uncultivable and uncultivated owned land of all sample households, cultivating and noncultivating, was 15.3 bighas or just over three acres. The average area sown was at least 14.6 bighas and probably at least 15 bighas, because of some under-reporting of pulses, oilseeds and other minor crops. The average area cropped was 17.2 bighas. The largest average sown area was of wheat (4.4 bighas), followed by paddy, arhar and gram (each 3.6 bighas), potatoes and vegetables (0.8 bighas), sugarcane (0.8 bighas) and 1.2 bighas of other crops. Since a few sample households (about 15) did little or no farming, the actual average area of cultivation per household in the sample which actually farmed would be somewhat higher, say 6 percent, above the figures given.

Cropping Pattern

Sample households were asked about the crops grown on the land owned and rented in. Wheat accounted for 29 percent of total area, followed by paddy (24%), gram (12%), arhar and urad (12%), sugarcane (5%), maize (2%), oilseeds (over 1%), potatoes (over 1%), tomatoes (1%) and vegetables (nearly 1%). Arhar is red gram and was the most common pulse eaten in the village. Urad is the black or green gram, which has a high vitamin content. Another pulse grown was masoor. The oilseeds were mainly black mustard (sarson), which was usually intercultured with wheat, and lahi. The cultivation of tomatoes had increased since 1978, when the road was made pacca and marketing became easier. The vegetables grown included brinjal (aubergine), lowki and other gourds, jackfruit, torail, radish, spinach and peas. Fruits grown in the village on a small scale included mangoes, guavas, jackfruit and custard apples (sherifa). Other crops included groundnuts, grown on very poor land. According to sample responses, only 5 percent of the total area was uncultivated. In view of the large area of uneven and uncultivated land between the settlements of Basauli and Kiratpur and small patches elsewhere, it is likely that there was considerable understatement of the uncultivated area.

The area of wheat exceeded that of paddy but it was estimated that the village imported no wheat and actually exported 20 percent of its paddy.

Caste and Cropping Pattern

There were variations in the cropping pattern of the different castes and of different caste strata, but these were less than might be expected, given the caste differences in ownership of land, irrigation and other basic resources. Taking first of all the caste strata, one immediately sees that the scheduled castes devoted a much larger part of their sown area to wheat than did the medium and high castes and that wheat constituted 37 percent of the total area cropped by the scheduled castes. Conversely, the latter grew a much smaller proportion of paddy than members of other castes and this reflects the location and low quality of their land. The proportion of pulses was similar for all three categories. The difference for potatoes and vegetables was sharp. The medium castes grew the most and this was mainly because these crops require very intensive labour and such castes as Kurmi and Lodh were sufficiently hard-working to undertake such a demanding workload. In addition, the upper castes had more cash to enable them to purchase vegetables from the market.

However, too much emphasis should not be made of this latter factor, because observation suggested that all households (except those containing salaried members) were invariably short of ready cash and no farmer liked the idea of buying food.

CASTE AND PERCENTAGE CROPPING PATTERN, 102 HOUSEHOLDS

	PERCENTAGE OF TOTAL AREA CROPPED, PLUS UNCULTIVATED									
CASTE	WHEAT	RICE	ARHAR + GRAM	POTATO + VEGS	SUGAR CANE	OIL SEED	OTHER CROPS**	EMPTY	TOTAL CROPPED	TOTAL BIGHAS***
BRAHMIN										
SHUKLA	14	14	36				36			14.0
AWASTHI	11	32	41				16			37.0
MISRA	31	23	23	11			6	7		71.0
TIWARI	27	27	43							7.2
PANDE	21	21	18		6		27	6		33.0
MAHABRAHMIN										
MISRA	33	29	16	7	5	3	7			174.5
PANDE	24	32	32				12			12.5
THAKUR										
BAIS	38	19	10		24	5	5			10.5
RAIKWAR	25	25	37	2		2	9			91.0
BHAT	30		19		4	6	41			13.3
BANIA	33						17	50		12.0
PATHAN	35	35	22	5	*		3			48.1
KURMI	29	22	17	7	13	*	8	4		271.0
AHIR	23	39	24		5		2	6		51.2
LODH	23	26	23	11	4	2	8	3		292.0
MALI	42		50				8			6.0
KAHAR	35	24	24		12	6				8.5
DHOBE	25	25	35	7	*	2	5			36.7
BHURJI	33		77							3.0
TELI	11	33	41		9		7			23.0
GADARIA	30	22	20		11		2	15		47.0
LONIYA	39	14	28		5	5	6	4		53.5
KABARIA			11	33	56					4.5
CHAMAR	36	16	26	1	3	*	3	14		193.4
PASI	43	24	17	2	1	*	13			42.2
BASPHOD										-
PATHARKOT			100							3.0
RADHIKA										-
PERCENTAGE OF CULTIVATED AREA PLUS OWNED UNCULTIVATED AREA										
	29	24	24	5	5	1	8	5	1487.1	1487.1
PERCENTAGE OF CROPPED AREA ONLY										
	30.2	24.7	24.7	5.5	5.5	1.3	8.1	-	100	1487.1
HIGH CASTE	27.5	26.1	25.1	4.7	3.0	1.6	10.5	1.6	100	450.7
MIDDLE CASTE	27.3	24.0	22.2	6.6	7.2	1.3	7.1	4.2	100	870.8
SCHEDULED	37.1	16.9	25.3	1.4	2.6	0.6	4.4	11.7	100	238.6
TOTAL BIGHAS	449.8	367.0	267.1	81.5	82.5	20.0	120.2	72.0	100	1560.1

* = Less than 1% of the total

** includes urad (black or green gram), maize, masoor, mung, bajra, jowar.

*** Total Bighas includes uncultivated land.

Even the relatively very rich Thakurs would put up with a fairly repetitive diet of potato curry and/or dal rather than purchase a more varied diet from the bazaar. The low ratio of potatoes and vegetables grown on farms of the scheduled castes again reflects the poor quality and non-irrigability of much of their land. The same applies for sugarcane, though to a less marked degree. However, the difference between medium and high castes was greater in the case of sugarcane than in that of potatoes and vegetables. It is difficult to pinpoint a reason for this, except that again sugarcane is a fairly labour intensive crop, especially in the final stages, when the gur is being manufactured. (Only three or four farmers, mostly Thakur, sold their cane to the factory at Burhwal and many farmers reduced their acreage three or four years ago when a glut led to a sharp fall in prices and to the factory failing to buy their cane. In 1981-2 there was also a glut but this hardly affected farmers in Basauli, because many had reduced their area of sugarcane or stopped growing it altogether.) The scheduled castes grew much less oilseeds than other castes though probably rather more than the figures show. Farmers' responses tended to give more priority to sarson and any other oilseed grown separately and less attention was given to any sarson which was intercultured with wheat or gram. The scheduled castes were the most likely to grow oilseed in this way because they lacked surplus land for such a (relatively) 'luxury' item. The proportion of cropped area devoted to 'other crops' increases with caste status, whereas the proportion uncultivated decreases with the rise in status. High caste farmers left hardly any land empty whilst the scheduled castes, with considerable banjar land issued to them as part of land distribution, were able to grow nothing at all on at least a ninth of their total area.

Wheat

By 1981 wheat was the main foodgrain in the village but this was a relatively recent development. Traditionally, paddy had been the major source of grain and the area of wheat had expanded only in the past fifteen years or so. There were at least six varieties grown in Basauli, but RR-21 (RR-Ekees) accounted for 90 percent of the total area of wheat. This variety was introduced into the village in about 1972 and it had become the most popular because it required 20 percent of the fertiliser and from 20 to 33 percent of the water necessary for successful cultivation of higher yielding and better tasting varieties such as Shonakalyan and UP-265. The average yield of RR-21 was said to be 2.5 quintals per bigha, and this was only 20 percent less than that of HD-1982 and Shonakalyan, which both required much more fertiliser and irrigation. Apart from being much more profitable, RR-21 was also liked because it produced a longer straw and therefore more fodder. Its main disadvantage was taste, which was ranked by most villagers as the least attractive of the six varieties. Because of this, its average harvest price reached only Rs 136 per quintal in 1981, which was 9 percent below that of Kanpur-68, the variety with the most popular taste. However, the second largest area (8%) was devoted to HD-1982, mainly by richer farmers, because of its higher yield. Kanpur-68 only averaged about two quintals per bigha and its area amounted to only 1 percent of the total area of wheat. The average yields for wheat shown in the table are rather high. The average yield reported by sample farmers in 1981 was only 1.6 quintals per bigha but the 1981 crop was partially damaged by unseasonal, late rain and some earlier hail and the crop was well below average. The average yield in UP as a whole that year was 1.3 quintals per bigha.

VARIETIES OF WHEAT

NAME	APPROX % TOTAL AREA	APPROX DATE INTRO IN VILLAGE	FERTILISERS REQUIRED	KG FERT REQD PER BIGHA	NUMBER WATERINGS NECESSARY	AVERAGE QUINTALS PER BIGHA	STRAW	TASTE RANKING (1=BEST)	RS/QUINTAL HARVEST TIME
RR-21	90	1972	UREA, INCL NITROGEN. GOBAR NOT ESSENTIAL	10	1	2.5	LONG	6	136
HD-1982	8	1977	PHOSPHATE + POTASH MIXTURE PLUS ZINC SULPHATE	50	3 TO 5	3.0	SHORT	5	136
KANPUR 68 (K-68)	1	1968	UREA	10		2.0	LONGEST	1	160
SHONAKALYAN	½	1968)	PHOSPHATE + POTASH	50		3.0		4	145
UP-315	¼	1978)	MIXTURE PLUS ZINC	50		3.0		3	145
UP-265	¼	1978)	SULPHATE	50		3.0		2	145

VARIETIES OF PADDY

NAME	APPROX % TOTAL AREA	APPROX DATE INTRO IN VILLAGE	FERTILISERS REQUIRED	NUMBER WATERINGS NECESSARY	DAYS TO MATURE	AVERAGE QUINTALS PER BIGHA	STRAW	TASTE RANKING AND COOKING QUALITY	GRAIN
NEW									
SAKET-4	50	1976	UREA		90	2.0	DWARF	GOOD, BETTER THAN JAYA	LONG THIN
JAYA	40	1974			120	3.0 MAX 4.5	DWARF	ONLY AVERAGE	VERY FAT
IR-8	5	1974			120	3.0	DWARF	ONLY AVERAGE	VERY FAT
GC-98		1970			95	1.5	LONG		
NAGINA 22		DESI		VERY LITTLE	80	1.0			
BISHUN PARAG		DESI			100	1.5	LONG	BEST	
FARAM		DESI			100	2.0	LONG		V. LONG
SUGUND RAY		DESI		VERY LITTLE	80?	1.0			
LAL MUTHI		DESI			95	1.0	GOOD		
USHA		1974			100	2.0	POOR		V. HARD

Paddy

Though paddy occupied a smaller area than wheat, it was still grown on nearly 25 percent of total cropped area. No single variety of paddy was quite as dominant as RR-21 was for wheat, but 50 percent of the paddy was Saket-4, a new and widely popular variety in UP. A further 40 percent of paddy area was given to Jaya, 5 percent to IR-8 and the rest to GC-98 (also a new variety) and at least five desi varieties. Saket-4 was liked because of its short maturation (90 days), moderate yield (two quintals per bigha), its long thin grain and good cookability and taste. Jaya and IR-8 both produced considerably higher yields but needed 120 days and had very fat grains which were rated only average in terms of cookability and taste. Some of the desi varieties needed very little water and two matured in 80 days. They were also mostly considered good in taste, especially Bishun Parag, but only two had average yields as good as Saket-4. Bishun Parag was easily damaged by bacteria called gundhi and one of the higher yielding desi varieties, Faram, had a very hard grain and was considered to have a poor taste.

The paddy crop had been adversely affected by the weather in at least the last three years. The crop was said to have been roughly 75 percent of normal in 1980 and only about 50 percent in 1981, when average productivity in the sample was 1.4 quintals per bigha. Nearly half the paddy grown in the sample that year failed to achieve even one quintal per bigha and only 12 percent exceeded two quintals. In 1980 there was heavy rain but the yield was also reduced by dryness in the later stages of growth. In 1981 and 1982 the heavy rain was serious, causing damage to houses as well as crops. There was also a very late monsoon in 1982, but the yields for that year proved much higher than was initially feared, roughly two quintals per bigha. The paddy crop in 1984 was reported to have been good.

Caste and Foodgrain Productivity

Despite the differences in land owned, in capital and in education there was no difference between high and middle caste productivity of wheat in 1981 (1.7 quintals per bigha) and even the scheduled caste productivity (1.3) was only about 18 percent below the average. The highest productivity in the sample was that of the Ahirs, Banias, Kahars and Kurmis. The Kurmi productivity is the most noteworthy because this group had eight households producing wheat. The Gadarias and Mahabrahmins also achieved high productivity and even the Brahmin farmers did better than the Thakurs (who only achieved 1.4 quintals per bigha). The lowest productivity belonged to the Pasis, Telis, Malis and Bhats.

Paddy productivity in 1981 was lower overall than that of wheat but still the differences between caste strata exceeded those for wheat. High castes produced an average of 1.6 quintals, middle castes 1.2 and scheduled castes 1.0 quintals per bigha. However, the proportion of farmers with very high productivity of paddy varied inversely with the status of the caste strata. For paddy, Thakurs excelled, followed by Mahabrahmins and Pathans. In 1982, the most successful paddy growers were S. Mahabrahmin, DNS Thakur and two brothers, T. and L. Lodh, all of whom achieved a production of at least 3.5 quintals per bigha. The Lodh brothers have become successful farmers through hard work, skill and use of new inputs. All these farmers sowed Jaya.

CASTE AND QUINTALS PER BIGHA, WHEAT 1981

	QUINTALS PER BIGHA						
CASTE	0-1.0	1.1-1.5	1.6-2.0	2.1+	TOTAL	AVERAGE QUINTALS PER BIGHA	2.1+ AS % OF ROW TOTAL
	NO. OF FARMS						
BRAHMIN		6	2	1	9	1.6	11
MAHABRAHMIN	1	1	4	1	7	1.8	14
THAKUR	1	2			3	1.4	-
BHAT	1				1	1.0	-
BANIA					1	2.0	-
PATHAN	1	2	1	1	5	1.4	20
KURMI	1	2	1	4	8	2.0	50
AHIR			2	1	3	2.1	33
LODH	4		5	1	10	1.6	10
MALI	1	1			2	1.0	-
KAHAR			1		1	2.0	-
DHOBE	1	1	1		3	1.1	-
BHURJI		1			1	1.5	-
TELI	2				2	1.0	-
GADARIA		2	1	2	5	1.9	40
LONIYA	1		1	1	3	1.4	33
CHAMAR	5	2	2	2	11	1.3	18
PASI	3			1	4	1.2	25
HIGH CASTE	2	9	6	2	19	1.7	11
MIDDLE CASTE	12	9	14	10	45	1.7	22
SCHEDULED CASTE	8	2	2	3	15	1.3	20
TOTAL	22	20	22	15	79	1.6	19

NB Compare Basauli's 1.6 with 1.138 Q/Bigha in Palanpur, Moradabad District. There 6.4 bighas = 1 acre, so the output per acre would be 7.28 quintals in 1974-5, compared with 8.0 quintals in Basauli (see Bliss and Stern 1982).

The Ahir percentage of high productivity is too low and should really be near to the Kurmi level.

CASTE AND QUINTALS PER BIGHA, PADDY 1981

	QUINTALS PER BIGHA						
CASTE	0-1.0	1.1-1.5	1.6-2.0	2.1+	TOTAL	AVERAGE QUINTALS PER BIGHA	2.1+ AS % OF ROW TOTAL
	NO. OF FARMS						
BRAHMIN	4	1	2	1	8	1.2	12
MAHABRAHMIN	1	2	2		5	1.7	
THAKUR		1	2		3	2.0*	
PATHAN	2	1		2	5	1.6	40
KURMI	3	2	1	1	7	1.3	14
AHIR	2	1			3	0.8	
LODH	3	1	4	1	9	1.3	11
KAHAR	1				1	1.0	
DHOBE	2		1		3	0.8	
TELI	2				2	0.4	
GADARIA	2	1	2		5	1.4	
LONIYA	1		1	1	3	1.5	33
CHAMAR	5	1	1	1	8	0.9	12
PASI	2			1	3	1.5	33
HIGH CASTE	5	4	6	1	16	1.6	6
MIDDLE CASTE	18	6	9	5	38	1.2	13
SCHEDULED CASTE	7	1	1	2	11	1.0	18
TOTAL	30	11	16	8	65	1.4	12

* Actually 1.96. The distribution between productivity categories is correct. The area involved in the 1.1 to 1.5 Q/B category was very small.

NB Compare Basauli's 1.4 with 1.024 Q/Bigha in Palanpur, Moradabad District. This would be 6.55 Q/Acre in Palanpur, compared with 7.0 for Basauli in 1981.

Pulses

The third major component in the villagers' diet was pulses. The national production of pulses had not kept pace with population growth as well as in the case of foodgrains and there was a national shortage of pulses and especially dal, which was reflected in the very high price. Consequently, dal had changed from a food symbolic of a poor man's diet to one which is increasingly difficult for the poor to afford. Therefore, poorer farmers whose crop of pulses failed found themselves unable to afford a normal diet of dal. The three main pulses grown in Basauli were red gram (arhar), gram (chana) and black or green gram (urad). Arhar was the most popular in eastern UP, but gram was preferred in Punjab and is generally acknowledged to be more nutritious. The local preference for arhar was said to be because of its ability to be cooked and made tasty without being complemented with expensive cooking oils and spices.

About 200 bighas of gram were sown late in 1981 and much of this was seriously damaged by rain in February 1982. The gram on the terai land, with its poorer drainage, suffered the worst and the rest on the inferior, sandier soils to the south of the village was largely unaffected. Some farmers, including Thakur Sahib and R. Thakur, estimated that they each lost as much as Rs 5,000 because of the failure of their gram crop. This represented over a quarter of their gross annual household income.

Potatoes

Potatoes began to be introduced into Basauli on a fairly large scale from about 1971. Two of the more nutritious varieties were C-1 and C-40. The main varieties grown in Basauli were 'Pahari' (60 percent of total area), C-1 (20%), C-40 (10%), 'Lal Pahari' (5%) and 'Satha' (5%). They were all sown at the beginning of October, except the quicker-maturing 'Satha' which was sown in September. There had been something of a 'potato revolution' in UP and overproduction had occurred in at least two recent years, 1979 and 1982, when there was a shortage of railway wagons to transport the surplus to the ports and also a lack of cold storage space. Consequently, potatoes, which normally offered a high income, higher than most vegetables in Basauli, fetched very low prices for much of 1982. In January 1982 they were selling for one rupee per 2.5 kilograms and by March the price had dropped still further to 30 paisas per kilogram - some said even to 20 paisas. G. Nai, an agricultural labourer, commented on what a benefit it was for the poor that potatoes had become so cheap. The completion of the pacca road enabled farmers to market potatoes much more easily. For example, R. Lodh sold five bags of potatoes in Fatehpur in early December 1981. For many other farmers and villagers, the glut of potatoes helped compensate for the underproduction of pulses.

Sugarcane

Though sugarcane accounted for only 82.5 bighas (5.5 percent of cropped area) in the sample, it was nevertheless a fairly important crop which provided a cash income for a minority of farmers in Basauli. As already indicated, sugarcane is a controversial issue in its many aspects, economic, nutritional and political. Sugarcane has been grown in Basauli since at least 1935, when the sugar mills at Burhwal and Barabanki (and also Jarwal in Bahraich district) were being opened. As a village which was about 23 kilometres from Burhwal, the nearest sugar mill near Ramnagar, and therefore on the outer periphery in terms of delivery distance, Basauli had not become dependent on sugarcane in the way that many UP villages, especially the poorer ones of the eastern and central zones, have done. Thakurs in Basauli and a few other, local villages had only recently begun the self-cultivation of sugarcane and before 1979 they avoided it because of a purely local belief that Thakurs who ate sugar they had grown themselves 'would die'. Many farmers of various castes in Basauli have been content to grow enough sugarcane to supply their domestic needs plus seed and any cultivation beyond that level has been influenced as much by the chances of selling to the overworked mills as by the price itself. In any case prices are invariably announced too late by the government to influence cropping decisions. Since the mills have become old and uneconomic in size, their capacity and desire to crush all the cane in their area had been weakened, both in mechanical and in financial terms. Those farmers who produce a surplus and cannot sell to the mill may find that, instead of receiving Rs 20.5 per quintal (the price paid at delivery centres in 1981-2), they can only secure Rs 8 per quintal from kandsari or gur processing units. (The price paid at the mill was Rs 21.5 in 1981-2 but this was irrelevant for Basauli farmers, because their transport costs to the mill would have far exceeded the extra rupee received per quintal. Farmers delivered cartloads, containing about 20 quintals, to the delivery centre one kilometre away where the cane was loaded onto a lorry from a ramp. It would have cost the farmers at least Rs 60 to take the cane to the mill by bullock-cart, apart from the time involved.) High production costs in the mill and low government prices for the levy sugar (the large percentage, usually over 60 percent of sugar production, which had to be sold at a lower price, fixed by the government) have meant that most sugar mills were unprofitable and usually had to pay cane producers in arrears. In Basauli, farmers who were lucky enough to be issued purchis (tickets) to sell some or all of their quota in the first month of crushing (normally December) usually received their money within two months, though not without big bureaucratic botheration. Farmers who were behind in the queue and supplied in the later months of crushing (often May and occasionally June) might have to wait until the next November, just before crushing re-commenced and the mill's liquidity position improved. Farmers were only given a purchi for one cartload on any one day.

The area and production of sugarcane appeared to have fluctuated sharply. In 1980-1 there was a glut and many farmers were unable to sell their cane to the mill. Consequently, in 1981-2 many of these farmers reduced the area to supply only their own needs and in fact some cut their production so drastically that they had to buy some gur, especially to pay their labourers. In 1982-3 the price was fixed at the same level as in 1981-2, though this cannot have influenced areas grown, because the central and state government prices were not announced until November, whilst the sugarcane is usually sown from March onwards. The UP government told farmers that their delivery quotas would be based on the amount delivered in the previous year. This threw those farmers who, for some reason, had not supplied any cane the year before and wished to do so in 1982-3. There were said to be 15 farmers in Basauli alone who fell into this category and only one of these, R. Thakur, was able to secure a cane union pass card and be allocated a quota of 100 quintals. Even his case was treated as a favour and the exception was only made in response to a gratuity of forty rupees to the sugarcane supervisor. A sum of Rs 100 was demanded but ten minutes bargaining reduced this to forty. Government announcements on many other policies, apart from cane quotas, are invariably ad hoc, often quite complicated and sometimes either internally contradictory and/or inconsistent with previous statements or simply incomprehensible, especially in the form they are reported in the press. Policies on sugarcane, with so many vested interests locked in very intricate patterns of combat, were usually more complex than most. One statement in late January 1983 laid down that quotas would be based on average deliveries in the previous three years but that years of non-delivery would not count towards the average. There also appeared to be different policies (and slightly different prices) governing various zones of UP. The last minute statements on quotas seemed to ignore the fact that officials of the cane union, the cane supervisors, had gone round each village in about October to assess the production quotas of cane growers. The latest announcements appeared to make their work entirely redundant. A further change in UP government policy in March 1983 discriminated against new suppliers for the next season. Briefly, new suppliers would only be allowed half the quota of old suppliers and the quota of the latter would continue to be based on the average weight sold in the previous three years.

Thakur Sahib used to be the cane union delegate from Basauli. The delegates elect the cane union directors who, he maintained, had become the pawns of the management, whether mills were government owned or capitalist owned. The three mills in this area were all 'sick units' and, as such, were taken into state government ownership in about 1962. Thakur Sahib said that the whole business of sugarcane had become very complicated. As delegate he had proposed that they should stop cane supplies in the cane union to extract better prices. Unfortunately, after a week's withdrawal the mill started to get supplies from the other cane union supplying Burhwal mill and this union was able to double the amount that it sold and so the strike of growers failed. TS also said that he had proposed at a district level meeting of the Congress (I) party, plus some officials, that, to reduce the over-dependence on the mills and to minimise the problem of over-supply, the government should help each group of four or five villages to set up small-scale canecrushers to make gur. These should use diesel or electric motors to drive the crushers. TS was not in favour of relying on traditional canecrushers which he said required much more labour than was usually available in the village from January onwards and which were not very efficient in extracting the juice. He said that such machines were all very well in the past when there had been no alternative.

TS also said that he found it difficult to persuade labourers to accept roasted or fried gram in the mornings instead of gur. The labourers always grumbled, if given gram. As a result of the hunger for gur, he had had to make large purchases of gur from the market in 1981-2. The increase of his area of sugarcane in 1982-3 had been made partly in order to meet this insatiable demand of labourers. Broadly, he seemed to agree that other crops would be more beneficial than sugarcane.

Certain smaller farmers in Basauli, including some Lodhs and their neighbours in the western mohalla, organised the processing of each other's gur on a cooperative basis. Village crushing usually began in mid-January and continued until at least the end of April.

Total Gaon Sabha Income

The total annual net income of the gaon sabha in 1981 is estimated to have been roughly Rs 1.2 million or about Rs 853 per person. It is possible that the income or remittances from some migrants may have been missed and so the actual income may be slightly in excess of the above figure. Since the total number of migrants from the gaon sabha was in any case relatively small, the discrepancy on that score is unlikely to be very substantial. It is worth noting that a village, with a roadside location only 66 kilometres from the state capital, with about 50 percent of its land irrigable, a brickworks and nearly a quarter of its population from the high castes, still barely achieved an average net income per capita above the poverty line.

Seasonality of Income

Apart from the difficulties raised by the small total annual income, most households were also bothered by the seasonal variation in income, especially in cash income. Seasonality of income affected nearly all households except perhaps the minority of households which included one or more salary earners who received a moreorless regular monthly pay. However, the season of lowest income differed for various economic categories and individuals. For example, the worst time for agricultural labourers was said to be late August and early September and also, to a lesser extent, January. For farmers, especially smaller and poorer ones, the most difficult month was March, before the harvest and/or sale of the wheat, the main foodgrain of virtually every household. September could also be difficult, before the paddy harvest, but much less so than March.

MONTHLY PRODUCTION, INCOME AND EXPENDITURE, HOUSEHOLD OF R.S. THAKUR

MONTH	CROP OR OTHER ITEM	QUINTALS PRODUCED	RS VALUE TOTAL	RS VALUE SOLD	ITEM OF EXPENDITURE	RS EXPEND	RS EXPEND SUBSISTENCE INCLUDING PAYMENTS TO MONTHLY LABOURER (Rs 60)	RS NET CHANGE IN CASH STOCKS	RS CASH STOCK	RS CHANGE IN CAPITAL	CUMU-LATIVE TOTAL CAP.
1981											
MARCH	CASH AND CROPS STORED IN HOUSE								600		3000
APRIL	WHEAT	30	3750								
	GRAM	10	2500								
	MASOOR	2	450	350							
	SARSON	0.5	200				INCL. 400 CASH				
	TOTAL	42.5	6900	350			1000	-50	550	+5900	8900
MAY	ARHAR	5	1250	700	LAND TAX	300	1000	0	550	-50	8850
JUNE	MELONS		400	300	HAND PUMP	1100					
	WHEAT			1200	MARRIAGE,S2	NET 1500					
	WHEAT STRAW			300							
	GRAM			1500							
	TOTAL		400	3300		2600	1000	+300	850	-3200	5650
JULY	WHEAT			600	ADVANCE TO AGRICULTURAL LABOURER	600	1000	-400	450	-1600	4050
AUGUST							1000	-400	50	-1000	3050
SEPT	GREEN + BLACK GRAM	0.5	200				1000	-200	-150	-800	2250
OCT	PADDY	12	1440				1000	-400	-550	+440	2690
NOV	GRAM			900	WHEAT SEED	200					
	WHEAT			650							
	SALE OF PUMPSET ENGINE			800*							
	TOTAL			2350		200	1000	1750	1200	+400	3090
DEC					LABOURERS	200	1000	-600	600	-1200	1890

MONTHLY PRODUCTION, INCOME AND EXPENDITURE, HOUSEHOLD OF R.S. THAKUR (Contd.)

MONTH	CROP OR OTHER ITEM	QUINTALS PRODUCED	RS VALUE TOTAL	RS VALUE SOLD	ITEM OF EXPENDITURE	RS EXPEND	RS EXPEND SUBSISTENCE INCLUDING PAYMENTS TO MONTHLY LABOURER (Rs 60)	RS NET CHANGE IN CASH STOCKS	RS CASH STOCK	RS CHANGE IN CAPITAL	CUMU-LATIVE TOTAL CAP.
DEC								-600	600	-1200	1890
1982											
JAN							1000	-400	200	-1000	890
FEB	BLACK MUSTARD OIL	1	400				1000	-400	-200	-600	290
MARCH	POTATOES	2	150		LAND TAX	800	1000				
	RESEARCH			500				-700	-900	-1150	-860
APRIL	MASOOR	2	420	310	IRRIGATION	300					
	GUR	1	200								
	RESEARCH		-	285							
	TOTAL		620	595		300	1000	-105	-1005	-395	-1255
MAY	WHEAT	28	3920								
	ARHAR	3	900								
	GRAM	1	300								
	SARSON	0.1	50								
	TOTAL	32.1	5170				1000	-400	-1405	+4170	2915
JUNE	WHEAT			2500							
	ARHAR			300							
	WHEAT STRAW			150							
	RESEARCH	FOOD	210	210?							
	TOTAL		210	3160			1000	2760	1355	-580	2335
JULY					AGRICULTURAL LABOURERS	200	1000	-600	755	-1200	1135
AUGUST	RESEARCH			130			1000	-270	485	-870	265

MONTHLY PRODUCTION, INCOME AND EXPENDITURE, HOUSEHOLD OF R.S. THAKUR (Contd.)

MONTH	CROP OR OTHER ITEM	QUINTALS PRODUCED	RS VALUE TOTAL	RS VALUE SOLD	ITEM OF EXPENDITURE	RS EXPEND	RS EXPEND SUBSISTENCE INCLUDING PAYMENTS TO MONTHLY LABOURER (Rs 60)	RS NET CHANGE IN CASH STOCKS	RS CASH STOCK	RS CHANGE IN CAPITAL	CUMULATIVE TOTAL CAP.
<u>1982</u>											
AUGUST								-270	485	-870	265
SEPT					FERTILISER	250					
					LABOURERS ETC						
					HOUSE REPAIR	150	1000	-800	-315	-1400	-1135
OCT	RESEARCH		630	630	FRAUD	1200	1000	-970	-1285	-940	-2075
NOV	PADDY APPROX	15	1800				1000	-190	-1560**	+1220	-855
	RESEARCH		210	210							
DEC	RESEARCH		210	210			1000	-190	-1750	-790	-1645
<u>1983</u>											
JAN	RECOVERY OF ADVANCE			1200			1000	+5400	3650	+4800	3155
	GOVERNMENT LOAN			4600							

		JAN	FEB	MAR	APR	MAY	JUN	JUL	AUG	SEP	OCT	NOV	DEC
CASH	81			600	550	550	850	450	50	-150	-550	1200	600
	82	200	-200	-900	-1005	-1405	1355	755	485	-315	-1285	-1560	-1750
	83	3650											
CAPITAL	81			3000	8900	8850	5650	4050	3050	2250	2690	3090	1890
	82	890	290	-860	-1255	2915	2335	1135	265	-1135	-2075	-855	-1645
	83	3155											

* The engine, a Kisan 6 hp, went wrong during the threshing of the wheat in 1981. The work put excessive load on the engine.

** Probably actually about Rs 400 in Nov 1982 if the Rs 1200 temporarily lost through fraud is added, then the record seems to tally. R was cheated of Rs 1200 in October 1982. His brother secured its return, through threats in December-January. Total income from research, up to December 1982 was Rs 2800. A further Rs 800 or so likely to be paid January-March 1983 = Rs 3600?

Labourers never had any surplus food in store and so in times of low employment they were forced to live on one meal per day and/or be pushed into debt. It hardly needs to be added that in late August and early September the risk of disease is also higher than at other seasons of the year. Common problems at this time were gastro-intestinal and skin diseases.

The case of a Thakur illustrates the fluctuation in current capital (cash plus crops) and in available cash from March 1981 to February 1983. The Thakur was a small ex-Zamindar who owned about 80 bighas and had a per capita income of Rs 1,222 in 1981. In March 1981 the joint household possessed crops worth about Rs 2,400 and also had Rs 600 in cash. The table shows the production, crop sales and other income, as well as items of major expenditure. The Thakur estimated that the household used an average of Rs 1,000 of current capital on subsistence each month, including an average of Rs 400 in cash. This cash expenditure includes the Rs 60 needed to pay the cash component of the monthly wages of the biannual labourer. The final four columns show the flow and stock of cash only and the same for current capital, in terms of cash plus unsold crops. The figures are only approximate because only major items of over about Rs 100 have been included in the balance sheet and there is also a possibly quite large component of income about which there is some uncertainty. In particular, the income of an elder son who may have been earning a little from smuggling and other enterprises has not been included.

In March 1981 the family was well in surplus and presumably had been saving to meet the forthcoming expenditure on the younger son's marriage. The gram crop is worth noting and comparing with the very nominal gram output in 1982. The sale of gram in June actually provided the largest cash inflow of the whole year (Rs 1,500). By the time the harvest was over at the end of April, cumulative capital amounted to Rs 8,900 and this was the happiest situation during the whole two years which are recorded. In May over half of the arhar was sold and Rs 300 was paid out of about Rs 1,500 on land tax, which was outstanding. A hand-pump was installed in the courtyard of their house and this cost Rs 1,100. The marriage cost a net Rs 1,500 but this conceals a two-way flow of money, including purchases of jewelry, clothes and other gifts to the bride. The dowry paid was worth about Rs 10,000, including Rs 7,000 in cash. The capital situation remained in a healthy position until March 1982, but there were problems with cash as early as September 1982 when the family was Rs 150 in the red. The cash position worsened to a debt of Rs 550 in October but was then resolved by the sale of gram, wheat and a pumpset in November. All this yielded Rs 2,350 in cash and the family now had Rs 1,200 in cash and over Rs 3,000 in cash and kind. There was no further cash income until March 1982 when the younger son secured temporary employment. Even with this unexpected 'windfall' income, the household's position was considerably worse than that of March 1981. Instead of having Rs 600 in cash, they were Rs 900 in deficit. This was mainly because the authorities came to insist on payment of Rs 1,200 for some land revenue which was two years overdue. Instead of a reserve of Rs 3,000 in cash and crops, as in 1981, they were actually in deficit by Rs 860 in March 1982. The sale of some masoor, plus further payment of salary stabilised the cash situation, but there was a further depletion of food supplies. In May, the harvest was complete and capital stocks stood at Rs 2,915. The cash stocks plummeted to a new low (minus Rs 1,405) but this also was resolved by sale of wheat and arhar. The cash position moved from over Rs 1,400 deficit to a surplus nearly as large. However, they were later to have regrets about having been obliged to sell their wheat so early in the year, because wheat prices reached nearly Rs 300 per quintal in January 1983, ie. more than double the price that they had received earlier. In October a severe blow to the cash situation occurred when a son paid an advance of Rs 1,200 to a Pradhan of another village who promised to get him a cheap, second-hand pumpset engine but instead just held onto the money. This money came from a loan from the Gramin Bank to the elder son. Originally, no hope was entertained of recovering the money, since the Pradhan concerned was subsequently discovered to be a fairly well-known 'Char-so-vees' ('420' or con man) who owed a larger sum to others. However, possibly more by luck than by terror, the elder son continued to badger him and was able to arrange a buyer for some land belonging to the Pradhan and he was then able to repay all he owed in January 1983. In November the cash position was a deficit of Rs 1,560. On checking with one son, he said, without knowing the amounts calculated in the table, that the family had debts of around Rs 400 and so, counting the Rs 1,200 temporarily lost through fraud, the record tallied with the real position.

What emerges from the detail of these figures from month to month is that even a relatively very rich villager rarely handles cash worth more than Rs 1,500, except if he succeeds in 'landing' a government loan such as the elder son managed to do in October 1982. Secondly, the cash stock ranged from a maximum surplus of about Rs 1,400 to a deficit of a similar amount. The worst months were normally the pre-harvest months, March and September, as people had said. The best months were June and November. Thirdly, the figures show how a farmer whose approximate total net household income was only about Rs 11,000 could move from a surplus of cash and crops valued at Rs 8,900 to a deficit of over Rs 2,900 within thirteen months, when failure of an important crop, repayment of debts and other contingencies arose, such as purchase of a hand-pump and marriage of a son.

Agricultural Labour

Agricultural labourers may be employed on an annual, biannual or casual, daily basis. There were two Chamar annual labourers in Basauli in 1982, one working for S. Mahabrahmin and one for a Thakur. It was becoming increasingly difficult to get annual or biannual labourers, especially suitable ones. Most labourers preferred the greater freedom of working on a casual, daily basis even though they might still sometimes work for one large farmer for a fairly prolonged period. In 1982 there were only 11 biannual labourers and these were mostly Chamar, Lodh and Pasi plus one Kahar. Their employers were five Thakurs, one

Mahabrahmin, two Kurmis and one Lodh. S. Mahabrahmin employed two such labourers, at varying rates of payment. Annual and biannual rates of payment might differ from daily rates but there was no way of predicting which would be the greater. Annual contracts began in mid-June and were verbal. If the labourer broke the contract, then the labourer would have to start paying interest on any cash loan still outstanding from his employer. If a labourer remained in employment over the full year or for longer, he paid no interest on such loans from his employer. It was very difficult for an annual labourer to break contract before the end of the Kharif season and likewise for a biannual labourer before the end of the crop season for which he had contracted. R. Thakur released his Lodh labourer mid-year without penalty but this occurred because it was mutually beneficial, since R was short of cash to pay the labourer. It was likely that he would re-employ him later.

There were said to be several causes of the decline in the number of labourers willing to work on a biannual basis. Differences in remuneration were said to be not a cause, since the rate of payment for daily and biannual work usually worked out to be roughly the same. Firstly, most lower caste households now had a small amount of their own land and it was difficult for a biannual labourer to cultivate this for more than seven days per month without creating tensions with his employer. Secondly, there had been a gradual increase in sharecropping in recent years and so lower caste households which owned only a small amount of land had additional work on their rented plots. Thirdly, the brickworks provided an alternative source of employment from October to June and mostly for earnings higher than those from agricultural labour.

The ownership of small plots by the lower castes was nothing new but had been expanded to include the majority of the lower caste poor, as a result of the land distribution. These had not achieved any major redistribution of capital ownership in the village but had helped to make marginal changes in the occupational and class status of some lower caste poor. The willingness of owners to rent out some of their land on batai, even though this was technically illegal, served to raise the class status of erstwhile labourers a little further. It is arguable that larger owners of land were behaving irrationally by renting out land and thus making their labour supply situation worse. Indeed, they were creating a malevolent circular process whereby renting out reduced the supply of labourers which in turn led to a need to increase the area rented out, because of the lack of labour. However, in the absence of any concerted action on the part of the larger owners, which seemed unlikely, the problem of labour shortage was probably going to become worse. It was exacerbated by the fact that some medium owners who rented out land were hardly interested in hiring labourers at all and so felt no constraint in renting out. Others, such as R. Thakur, had a fairly large area of land which was currently difficult to cultivate without heavy ploughing by a tractor and such farmers rented out because the land was not considered worth self-cultivation. R had the 'double bind' of receiving nominal amounts of rent for such land, which was not cultivated seriously by most of the various small sharecroppers, and of having to face the problem of labour shortage.

LABOURERS OF TS, NOVEMBER 1981 TO AUGUST 1982

NAME	CASTE	AGE	WORK	Rs MONTHLY	OTHER PAYMENTS
<u>NOVEMBER 1981</u>					
PHUL CHAND	RADHIKA	22	PLOUGHING AND HEAVY WORK		
BUDALOO	CHAMAR	30	PART-TIME FEEDING ANIMALS AND DUNG COLLECTION	30+ 1.5 BIGHAS	GUR 1 BIGHA
LAKHAN	KAHAR	20	PLOUGHING AND GENERAL DUTIES INCLUDING INSIDE HOUSE	60?	GUR 2 MEALS
MADAN	KAHAR	22	MILK BUFFALO AND COW	-	
RAM SEVAK	KAHAR	42	MILK BUFFALO AND COW	-	
'GOMALU' KAMALA DIN	NAI	17	CASUAL ('FREELANCE')	DAILY	
NOT KNOWN	2 BRAHMIN BROTHERS	14 +16	WEEDING POTATOES	DAILY 3.0	
	DHOBE	28	WEEDING POTATOES	DAILY 3.0	
MANUWAR	PATHAN	25	PLOUGHING AND SOWING WHEAT		
BICHU	RADHIKA	45	PLOUGHING AND FODDER CUTTING		
(FEB) BHAGWAN	LODH				
<u>APRIL 1982</u>					
BUDALOO	CHAMAR	30		30	1.5 BIGHAS PRO TEM, RENT FREE
SHERIF	PATHAN		PLOUGHING AND HEAVY WORK	45 or 60	2 MEALS
ISAR	CHAMAR		SUBSTITUTE FOR SICK BROTHER		
<u>AUGUST 1982</u>					
MAJID	PATHAN PATHAN	15			
MADAN	KAHAR	22	MILKING BUFFALO AND TWO COWS		

TS says he pays Lakhan Rs 60 per month and 2 meals per day (clothing optional on TS's choice).

TS claimed it was not an easy matter to cook meals for everyone - but his familiy cooks for Lakhan and Sherif.

The richer Thakur farmers were still able to hire biannual labourers, though with some difficulty. The labourer might not be their first choice and, if he were a good worker, he might stay for a shorter time than could have been expected in the past. Some Kurmi farmers and also S. Mahabrahmin wanted biannual labourers but were finding greater difficulty in securing them, partly because of their caste. Even two Thakur farmers had been unable to hire such labourers. The richer Kurmi farmers had the capacity to employ labour and were even prepared to pay higher rates than the Thakurs but, with the exception of the three richest Kurmis in Imlipur, none of them was able to get hold of such labour. Whilst it is likely that higher wages would bring expectations of a higher workload, it was alleged that the reluctance of lower caste labourers to work for Kurmi (and other middle caste farmers) did not stem from fear of being overworked or of ill-treatment. On the contrary, even a Thakur informant said that the labourers would be likely to receive more polite treatment from Kurmis than from farmers of his own caste. The reluctance was said to boil down to the traditional mentality of labourers towards caste and their concern over status. It was simply considered less prestigious to work for a Kurmi than for a Thakur. However, the Kurmis of Imlipur were paying their labourers Rs 75 to Rs 100 per month, plus food, and this was more than the Rs 30 to 60, plus food, which was being paid by Thakur Sahib and others of his caste. R. Thakur felt that such differences were bound to lead soon to economic factors outweighing the importance of traditional social attitudes. This was one more reason why the richest Thakur farmers were beginning to think in terms of buying tractors. In two cases, Thakurs had loaned one or two bighas of average quality land to their labourers and in one case the labourer chose the plot he wished to have. This practice of land loans has become more common to try to attract labour, but only two labourers were thus benefiting in 1982. The employers considered this system more expensive than payment exclusively in cash and kind.

Though the government of UP had fixed the legal minimum wage at seven rupees per day for the central zone in January 1981, the rates being paid during 1982 in Basauli ranged from only two to five rupees per day, always with breakfast and usually with lunch. Young boys or women doing weeding or other 'light' work were paid two rupees and no food and a labourer doing ploughing or heavy digging work might be paid five rupees per day plus food. The normal hours of work were usually from 8 am to 12 noon and from 2 to 5 pm in winter and from 7 am to 12 noon and 4 to 7 pm in summer. If the employer provided lunch, then in winter the afternoon session would start at 1 pm. Work traditionally ends at sunset, around 6 to 7 pm. At harvest time, labourers were invariably paid in kind and this was valued at 10 to 12 rupees per day. The farmer normally took twelve measures and the labourers the thirteenth of what was harvested. It was said that no one would accept cash wages at harvest time. However, labourers who did not work throughout the whole harvest period but who came for only odd days usually had to accept cash wages, even though this form of payment was unpopular. The traditional payments of ser and bhata, with their allowances for subsistence, have been abolished. Thakur Sahib claimed that this old, feudal system of payment had provided labourers with a higher income than now.

Wage rates were said to vary with the season as well as the task. This seemed to be the case though inter-seasonal comparisons are made more difficult when the crops, and tasks associated with the crops, are not quite the same in different months. Apart from harvest time, the highest wage rate was said to be paid in July, when paddy was being transplanted, among other tasks, and wages were four or five rupees, plus breakfast and lunch. Assuming that breakfast cost about 50 paisas and lunch at least one rupee, then wages in July were worth a total cash equivalent of at least 5.5 to 6.5 rupees, ie. not so far short of the legal minimum. However, the July rate was said to be about 50% more than the average normally paid in Basauli and in other villages the July rate even rose 60 or 70% above their average rates. August was said to be the slackest month for labour demand but in months of low demand the rate did not usually go below the standard, normal rates.

Apart from cash, most labourers were given 250 grams of gur, usually in the morning, two hours after work started. In February 1982 gur was cheap at Rs 1.5 per kilogram and so the 'breakfast' cost only 38 paisas. However, gur could cost up to three rupees per kilogram and breakfast might be worth 75 paisas. In November 1982 the price of gur had risen to two rupees per kilogram. Sometimes, if gur prices were very high or if a farmer had run out or was running short of gur, he might substitute gram or some other food to chew (chabena). Thakur Sahib said that such substitution was unpopular with many labourers and might even be refused by some, even though gram was usually worth more in money terms. It was clear that labourers mostly had a sweet tooth and, according to Thakur Sahib (from his somewhat biassed position), some labourers would eat more gur than was good for their health. An additional consideration may be that few labourers had enough irrigated land to enable them to produce sugarcane of their own, whereas some might produce their own gram. However, from the point of view of the employers, the supply of gur or indeed of gram had its advantages over cash payments, since it gave the labourer more energy to perform manual work. In summer, labourers were brought a drink of sharbat, made of rab (molasses) and water. Thakur Sahib remembered one labourer who could drink two lotas (brass-pots) full of sharbat. On one occasion the labourer had asked for a third pot but Thakur Sahib refused, saying that it would be his employer's responsibility if the labourer 'died of cholera' from such excess. It was clear that labourers derived considerable enjoyment from their gur. In January 1982 G. Nai was brought a large lump of gur wrapped in old newspaper, at about 1 pm by his elder sister who worked in Thakur Sahib's household. He ate part of it with relish, saved some (which he wrapped in a dirty piece of copy paper, salvaged from the floor of the front yard). He then whistled for his three dogs who came flying to him and ate up the fallen crumbs of gur.

The second son of Thakur Sahib claimed that wage rates did not vary with supply and demand for labour. He argued that in the village economics does not apply ('gaon men economics nahin chalta'). Though this may be partly true, the fact remains that harvest wages were higher and there were other seasonal fluctuations. There were also the differences in the rates paid by Kurmi employers, as already noted.

There was no vestige of a trade union or other association to represent and protect the interests of labourers - nor, for that matter, of sharecroppers and other farmers. Thakur Sahib thought that labourers were less well protected than sharecroppers by legislation. He confirmed the widely held impression that the government was unable to enforce its legislation on minimum wages. In regions where agrarian capitalism is more advanced, such as the western districts, changes in the relative position of village caste groups had been more radical and lower castes (forming a larger proportion of the total population in some south-western districts) had become much more aware of their rights. This had led to bitter conflicts and bloody fights in some districts. In the south-western districts the class conflict was interwoven with conflict between police and criminals, especially dacoits. Some claimed that the dacoity problem was purely a question of class conflict. Whether this was true or not, the fact remains that dacoity cannot be regarded as a new problem, especially in these areas, and it had been a threat to the stability of many areas of north and central India long before the development of agrarian capitalism.

Despite the view of Thakur Sahib's son, it seemed that each village was left to settle its own equilibrium price, according to supply and need for labour. There was said to have been no significant recent increase in real agricultural wages in Basauli. However, Thakur Sahib claimed that one important change was that labourers could no longer be 'pressed' to accept a particular wage by his employer. He also argued that the strict enforcement of the minimum wage laws would rebound to the disadvantage of labourers, because poorer farmers would be incapable of employing them at higher rates. Three boys aged 13 or 14 years had spent the whole of that day in fairly hot sun weeding his potatoes and he had paid them each two rupees plus breakfast. He pointed out that they had taken home six rupees which would not otherwise have been available to them, if wage rates were fixed higher. (He did not expound on which member of his family would have done the weeding, if no labour was employed for this task.)

Some of the Chamars in Basauli were asked why they accepted wages below the official minimum rate and at first they were silent. They then shrugged their shoulders and asked what else could they do, in the present circumstances. The older Chamars seemed resigned to the situation, but the younger ones rather less so. A young son of S. Mahabrahmin, whose father was a major employer of labour (including at least one Chamar), was acting as interpreter and interlocutor and he pointed out that farmers would only be able to afford higher wages if they in turn were paid higher prices for their crops. The Chamars feared unemployment if wage rates were raised and also anticipated hostility from other villagers - with minimum protection from the government. Enforcement of minimum rates might lead to much harsher working hours and conditions and loss of minor benefits of food, drink, bidis, clothing and so forth.

TS claimed that the main disputes over wage payments in the area had occurred between farmers from the 'backward' castes and labourers from the scheduled castes. The most serious recent dispute had been between Kurmi farmers and Chamar labourers at harvest time in a village about four kilometres from Basauli. The Chamars had refused to harvest the Kurmis' crops until the wage rate was raised and, in retaliation, the Kurmis prevented the Chamars harvesting on the land they had leased to them. There was a stalemate which threatened to lead to the crop being wasted or to violence. TS was called to mediate and it took him three days of hard diplomacy to achieve a 'compromise'. He urged the labourers to finish their contracted period of labour which was due to expire within a month and then a new contract could be re-negotiated. He pointed out that the Kurmis had been providing "a good breakfast and also lunch, tobacco and whatever else the labourers required". The 'compromise' amounted to the Chamars finishing the harvest at the previous rate and the Kurmis allowing them to harvest the fields leased to them. TS admitted that the strategy of the higher caste farmers was to provide incremental improvements of the benefits in kind rather than to countenance any serious shift in the cash component of the payment. Most poor farmers have a serious shortage of ready cash (until harvest at least and often even after harvest) but may have some surplus of consumable commodities. TS pointed out that the Chamars had been encouraged by an educated castefellow from Fatehpur or some other urban area but they were unable to raise sufficient funds to pursue the dispute at court. The episode illustrates how a mediator was selected from the employing class and, though Thakur rather than Kurmi by caste, he was almost inevitably going to support the employers. The fact that a powerful leader like Thakur Sahib was likely to come down openly on the side of the Kurmis, if the Chamars continued to press their claim, was probably sufficient to break their opposition to the Kurmis.

Conflict between TS and his Chamar labourer

TS claimed to be dissatisfied with B. Chamar, who fed the animals, gathered up the manure and did some ploughing and other tasks. The major objection to B was that he was only willing to come from about 8 am to 12 noon and for a brief period in the evening to feed the animals. B was quite adamant against working full-time and so TS had been willing to pay him only Rs 30 per month, plus the use of a plot of land in lieu of meals, compared with Rs 45 per month paid to his Lodh predecessor. TS allotted B two bighas initially, then reduced his allocation to one bigha, and currently B was actually occupying 1.5 bighas. Though B had a father and two younger brothers able to work on the joint family farm of 21 bighas, he insisted on working there part of the time and he also made it clear that he valued some leisure time. TS was especially bitter because B had refused to help with irrigation, particularly at night, and that, as a result of this, TS and his sons had had to water their crops during the night "whilst B sat at home smiling and doing God knows what". TS subsequently felt impelled to terminate the services of B but the latter prayed to remain in his employment even though

TS reassured him that, "if you leave my service, I will not abuse you, nor will I beat you". B succeeded in staying on and TS observed that 'no one' sympathised with B who owed money to so many people in the village that, if B were to lose his job and the protection of his employer, many people would 'pounce' on him and his family for repayment of debts. TS gave an example of his protection of B. The latter had bought seven sacks of potato seed at an extortionate price, some Rs 20 per bag above the going rate. When the seller came to TS to complain that B owed him money, TS gave him no support because he had overcharged the Chamars and also because he said that he should not have extended so much credit to such a poor family. TS had also been instrumental in awarding 21 bighas of gram samaj land to the family in 1975 to attract their labour and without this the family 'would not have been able to remain in the village'. In March, B was ill with eczema and other problems and so his younger brother deputised for him in looking after TS's animals.

TS affected to be unwilling to trust B in ploughing because he did not work hard. He said that he could trust B. Radhika because, "though he may take an hour off, he works hard and is able to use his own initiative". TS resented the fact that B. Chamar cherished his leisure and insisted on being able to do whatever he wished in the evening. He claimed, wrongly, that B returned home about 4 pm. TS pointed out that other farmers were paying Rs 60 per month but required their labourers to work from 7 am until sunset. Not only that but most farmers were working alongside their labourers and so the question of 'taking it easy' did not arise. TS emphasised that he did not 'press' his labourers and preferred to leave them to their own devices as much as possible. Others viewed the position somewhat differently.

On the evening of 19 January, there was a major row between the eldest son of TS and the labourers, with most of the abuse directed at B. Chamar, about whom TS and his sons complained most. On this occasion the substance of the complaint concerned tardiness in arrival to attend to the fodder for the animals, both in the morning and also that afternoon. Usually in the morning very little was said in the yard by anyone, except politicians and those coming to see TS on business. Disputes, whether between labourers or between employer and labourers, were more usual from 4 pm onwards when they were often tired and tempers frayed. Frequently the row was over cutting fodder. The eldest son shouted in a very deep and loud voice and his brother, M, provided his characteristic support by adding mildly sarcastic comments and questions, punctuated by his giggle, which added force to the complaint whilst at the same time helping to keep down the temperature of the dispute.

TS had a high turnover of labourers, possibly because he paid them such low wages. In fact, it was alleged that TS had encouraged B to give up his work at the brick kiln, where he owed money to his employer and he attracted B to his employ by large grants of gram samaj land. TS seemed to think that many members of the lower castes were prepared to work for him below the going rate, partly for the 'honour' of working for him and partly for the hidden benefits, such as political protection and security, from creditors, the police and others, which being in his employment might provide. TS also received some casual labour from persons who were seeking political or other favours from him. For example, two men whom TS was helping over some litigation were set to work chopping up a large tree trunk.

Sometimes TS had a small task which required many hands but hardly justified the employment of a hired force. A good example was the topping and tailing of some spring onions which TS intended to plant. Early one morning he gathered six of his dependents from the mohalla and the job was completed within an hour. The 'volunteers' included B. Lodh, three Dhobes and two Kahars, including the elder brother of TS's biannual labourer. There was no payment, except that the onion cutters retained the onion tops which could be shredded and used in making pakore.

During the early mornings in winter, when G. Nai was sometimes working for TS, the latter would shout for him to get up, if he were showing no signs of rising from his straw bed on the southern verandah. TS would then follow his sharp command of 'Uttao' with his characteristic chuckle to humour G out of bed.

It was clear that Thakurs and other richer farmers were having some difficulty in obtaining labourers, especially permanent labour paid on a monthly basis. TS was a particularly conspicuous example, both because of his large holding size and because none of his family members normally worked in the fields. In 1974, the father of G. Nai died when his son was aged about 8 years and it was left to TS to support the family by employing the mother and the two sisters in his house. TS had also managed to secure the family two or three bighas from the gram samaj, some of it of moderately good quality, which G. Nai rented out on batai because, he said, he had no oxen. TS commented, affectionately, that 'this young swine' was not willing to work on his own land nor, for that matter, was he prepared to work on a biannual basis for TS. As it was, G probably worked for TS about 15 days per month, when he was needed most and when he needed the cash, but he preserved some degree of independence.

On the first of February, a fight occurred between G. Nai and M. Kahar (another non-permanent labourer of TS) because G. Nai expressed an unwillingness to go and help him cut black mustard. G. Nai was worsted in the scuffle and he complained to TS. The latter burst out loudly to ask why G. Nai had waited until M. Kahar had gone before raising the matter. Earlier G had given TS a leg massage, whilst he lay in the straw with a shawl over his body.

Apart from hire of human labour, there was also hire of bullock labour. However, this was not very common and only three or four of the poorer farmers resorted to this, charging Rs 10 per bigha for their own and their animals' labour. As Bliss and Stern (1982) point out, Thakurs are not willing to hire their bullocks because this entails either hiring out their own labour, most likely to a lower caste farmer, or entrusting valuable animals to a poor farmer who may have less than average experience and competence in handling bullocks.

Non-agricultural Labour

The main sources of non-agricultural employment were the Public Works Department, road building and other schemes organised by the block, three private brickworks nearby and private building. The most important sources for men in Basauli were the brickworks in the village itself and also the canal maintenance for the Irrigation department.

The land for a brickworks was purchased by a Muslim from Fatehpur in the late 1950s. Since about 1965 he had built one brick furnace and a large yard with very rudimentary, low-slung accommodation for workers. He was in the process of completing a medium-sized, two-storey house for his manager in 1982. The total investment to date was estimated to be Rs 400,000. The brickworks was in operation from late October to June, ie. in all but the rainy sesson. At its peak it provided employment for over a hundred persons, including at least 20 from the western mohalla of Basauli (mostly Pathans but also a few Lodhs and others) and five from Kiratpur. Other workers came from Sikohna and other nearby villages. The labour force also consisted of at least 20 tribal people from Ranchi district in Bihar. These included about 12 women, mostly married, and three children (two of them girls) who carried the mud bricks on their heads to be stacked in the furnace for baking later. They were to be seen carrying usually either eight or sometimes more bricks on their heads at a time, moving at a semi-run, partly because of the weight and partly because they were paid on a piecework basis. After each pile of bricks had been unloaded from their heads by the men (villagers) who stacked them ready for firing, the women quickly collected a token from a munshi who sat at a table in the well of the furnace and then rushed back for more bricks. They were paid 2 paisas for each load of eight bricks and 3 paisas for a larger load of 12 bricks. They tucked the tokens into a pouch or pocket in their clothing. The women earned an average of Rs 8 per day, whilst the men stacking were paid Rs 5 per day. The range of the women's pay was from Rs 6 to 12. In order to earn Rs 8 a woman had to carry 3,200 bricks a day and make 267 trips, carrying 12 bricks at a time. Assuming an average of two minutes per trip, a woman would need to work nearly nine hours to earn eight rupees. The use of wheelbarrows appeared called for, but they are not very much used in India.

Those who prepared the clay and moulded the bricks usually worked in pairs and they were the highest paid workers. The rate in 1981 was Rs 15 per 1,000 bricks, (increased to Rs 20 in early 1983) and there were one or two villagers, including M, an intelligent young Pathan, who could achieve this level of productivity. The average daily output per worker was probably nearer 660 bricks (Rs 10) per day and the range was between 500 and 1,200 bricks. The price of best quality bricks was Rs 230 per thousand in 1981 and this was increased to Rs 260 in early 1983.There was clearly a major difference between the wage paid to the average brick worker and the average agricultural labourer and this helped to explain why farmers of Thakur and other castes were complaining of an increasing shortage of agricultural labour and of the increasing desirability of investment in a tractor. The difference in the respective wage rates was explained purely in terms of the much greater work required for brick making. The clay had to be dug and was usually very hard indeed.

The brickworks seemed well organised and laid out in a tidy manner. The business also seemed to be run on sound but very harsh capitalist lines, with a rational division of labour. The owner lived in Fatehpur but was usually on the site, along with two or three munshis, who supervised operations. Altogether, the works employed a maximum of 130 people but some days there were only about 70 persons working. These included 16 making the mud bricks, with hand moulds; 22 coolies carrying bricks to the furnace - these were mostly tribal women and children though there was also one man with a horse; seven men stacking the mud bricks in the kiln, four shifting the ash and five actually baking bricks in a small part of the furnace which was working; seven unloading logs from carts and splitting them, ready to fuel the furnace; and three loading fired bricks onto a lorry.

In March 1982 a major dispute arose between the tribal workers and Haji Sahib, the owner of the brickworks. One of the Lodh men, who was also employed at the brickworks, had been having illicit relations with a married tribal woman, with her permission, and she had been unfortunate enough to become pregnant. It was not particularly unusual for there to be a sexual relationship, especially as the husbands of some of the women were elsewhere, but she was now five months pregnant and her condition had become public knowledge. The tribals were incensed and demanded that Haji Sahib should dismiss the Lodh and bar him from being allowed to return. (There were up to 15 other Lodhs working at the brickworks from time to time, but they were not implicated in the discussion.) Haji Sahib refused to dismiss him and so the tribals packed up their cooking pots and other belongings and departed. They had reached Fatehpur before their employer relented and agreed to ban the Lodh from further work. Subsequently, in the late afternoon the tribals returned and their women were to be seen in silhouette on the horizon against the evening sky, carrying their pots on their heads.

It may be added that the problems of the Lodh worker were not over. His caste mates called a panchayat to discipline him for bringing the caste into disrepute and pollution. The final decision on his penalty was that he should provide two meals, one pacca and one kacha, to his caste fellows. This would be likely to set him back about Rs 300. Usually the two meals were given on a single day with the pacca meal in the evening.

During the rainy season when the brickworks had to close down, some of the tribal workers returned to Ranchi district whilst the rest worked as agricultural or general labourers for Haji Sahib. They were mostly paid Rs 150 per month, with no food. This wage was quite high, but they were expected to be available at all hours, whenever work presented itself. The main tasks were sowing, weeding and harvesting of paddy. The only other people in Basauli who paid such high wage rates were one or two Kurmi farmers to their biannual labourers and occasionally the Punjabi farmer paid five rupees per day to his labourers.

Other employers of labour were the Irrigation and Public Works departments, which normally hired about a dozen workers in winter to dig and maintain irrigation channels from a canal to the south-west of Basauli. In 1981-2 the numbers employed were usually large and at times as many as fifty workers were hired to widen and clean a new channel. The work was considered very strenuous and, as with the brickworks, most of the labourers were young. No particular caste was associated with this work. Normally work was paid according to the cubic capacity of earth shifted but in this case payment was by the day. (All over India, small, neatly dug pits with a central pillar of earth left standing may be seen. These enable the inspecting official to calculate the amount of earth which has been shifted. The pits also store rain-water and provide excellent breeding-places for mosquitoes and other insects. They are a good example of one government department creating problems for another.)

The PWD workers were supposed to be paid Rs 7 per day. In November 1981 a boy came to Thakur Sahib to complain that the contractor was only prepared to pay Rs 6 per day to those who wished to be given their money each evening. Labourers who could wait until the end of the week would be paid the full Rs 7. Thakur Sahib promised to have a word with the contractor and was confident that the labourers would receive their full entitlement.

Some villagers found jobs as labourers for builders from time to time. Often these jobs were secured through higher caste patrons and leaders in the village who either had relatives who were building contractors or who had the official contacts or knowledge of where building was going on. For example, G. Nai worked as a frequent casual labourer for Thakur Sahib and he was able to get a job on the building site of AKS Thakur, the brother of the late daughter-in-law of TS. AKS was required to pay his labourers Rs 7 per day, as part of the government contract. However, he openly admitted to paying only Rs 5 per day and said that, if he were to pay the minimum stipulated by the government, it would be impossible to make a profit. This was mainly because his profit was pre-empted by the bribes and other expenses necessary to secure the contract and facilitate the construction. In effect, the government officials were taking part of the wages of the building labourers, though this is not to assume that building contractors would necessarily pay up the full wage even if they did not have to budget for illegal expenditure. It was said that labourers on urban building sites were paid Rs 10 to 12 in Lucknow. By way of comparison, a poor villager who migrated to the city and hired a cycle rickshaw for five to seven rupees per day might earn from three to fifteen rupees net per day. In 1979 a Mali from Basauli did this work for one year in Lucknow and claimed to average Rs 15 per day and sometimes to earn Rs 20.

Bonded Labour (Bandhua Mazdoor)

No cases of bonded labour were mentioned in the area. In the past a farmer might lend a labourer from Rs 300 to 500 and then make him work off the debt at three percent interest per month whilst paying him a pittance per day. There were frequent newspaper reports of bonded labourers in UP, Madhya Pradesh, Bihar and Orissa and also of their being recruited from these poor states to go and work in brickworks and other industries or agriculture in the rich states of Punjab and Haryana. The owner of the brickworks in Basauli employed tribal labourers from Bihar but there was no suggestion that they were bonded. It was thought that there might be a few, fairly isolated cases in the terai interior area, beyond Daulatpur, but it was not thought to be a serious problem in Barabanki District.

Students

There were at least six students at the tertiary level in the village. Four of these were Thakurs and three of them were the sons of Thakur Sahib. There was also a Shukla Brahmin who had done six years of a Sanskrit course, the Prathama Purb Madhyama Shastri. He had attended courses at Ayodhya for four years, studied privately in the village for two years and then had finally given up the course, partly because it offered very little hope of employment. It was also thought that he would not be able to pass without cheating, which was rife in such institutions which were even more loosely regulated than the more formal sectors of higher education. He was currently the Community Health Volunteer and also a core member of the opposition faction. The younger son of the Dube Brahmin priest was also a private student of BA in Political Science, Sanskrit and Sociology at the Avadh University in Ayodhya. His studies had to be fitted around his farming and priestly duties, especially after his father was injured in a serious assault and could not perform the twice daily puja at Thakur Sahib's Siva temple. He stayed with the sons of Thakur Sahib when visiting Ayodhya for admission, for examination or for other purposes related to his studies. He passed his first year examination in 1982 and was due to take his finals in 1983.

Whilst attending classes at the Avadh University in Ayodhya, the three sons of Thakur Sahib stayed at the family house, the Basauli Mandir. One or two other Thakur and Brahmin student friends from the tahsil also stayed there, rent free.

None of the sons remained in Ayodhya for the full academic session and it was very rare for all three to be in residence together. They would return to the village on various pretexts, including illness, elections, the need to supervise labour peaks on the farm or because there were strikes, disruption or simply inactivity in the college. When due to return to the college, they invariably postponed their departure by a day or two, because of the weather or delay in milling their foodgrain or on some other excuse. Normally, they would travel to Barabanki by bus for four rupees and then catch a passenger train to Ayodhya. Passenger trains took four hours compared with two hours by 'express' train to travel the sixty or so miles to Ayodhya. However, the cost was only five rupees, which was cheaper than the 'express' (Rs 8) and the UP State Road Transport Corporation bus (Rs 10.75) and also normally much less crowded. This latter consideration was important, since they travelled laden with both ordinary luggage and about 100 kilograms of basic food items for their subsistence.

COST OF STUDY PER STUDENT PER MONTH

ITEM	KG PER MONTH	Rs COST PER SESSION	APPROX Rs COST PER MONTH
SUBSISTENCE (excluding food brought from own farm)			200
FOOD BROUGHT FROM FARM			
WHEAT	25		38
RICE	15		30
PULSES (mainly arhar, also gram)	7		35
GHEE	0.5		17
COOKING OIL	1+		16
TOTAL			(136)
ADMISSION FEES FOR BA *		50	4
TUITION FEES FOR BA **		300	25
OTHER CONTINGENCIES			
NOTEBOOKS AND BOOKS			10
MEDICINE			5
TRANSPORT			10
FILMS			5
OTHER			5
TOTAL CONTINGENCIES			35
GRAND TOTAL			400

* Rs 100 had to be paid initially and this included Rs 50 returnable indemnity against any charges of indiscipline.

** The third son claimed that fees are payable even for May and June when the college was closed and that fees are payable for all months, whether the student is in residence or not.

The third son of Thakur Sahib estimated that the monthly cost of his studies in Ayodhya was Rs 400 and the cost was similar for each of the three brothers. This cost included the value of subsistence items brought from their own farm. He considered that it was possible for students to survive on less and some certainly were doing so in Ayodhya. On the other hand, most other students had the expense of rent, which could vary from Rs 40 to 100 per month. These figures imply that a student who was in residence for six to nine months each year would need to find a total of Rs 2,400 to Rs 3,600 per year. If his father were not a farmer and produced no food, then this would be a cash requirement. It is clear that a family would normally need to earn a net annual, household income of at least Rs 8,000 and preferably Rs 10,000 in order to afford to send a child to university. In the case of the sons of Thakur Sahib, the second son was doing the final year of his LLB in law and attended for a maximum of only four months of the 1981-2 session. The third son was doing his BA finals in

Economics, Sociology and Military Science and was in Ayodhya for six months. He returned in April, looking tired and drawn and seemed to have worked the hardest. The youngest son only attended for two months and he passed his BA Previous (ie. first year) with the help of some copying. He then became a private student for the final year. Assuming that the three sons were in Ayodhya for a total of twelve man-months, then the total annual cost would be at least Rs 4,800, including about Rs 3,200 in cash.

There was also one graduate in the village. R. Thakur, aged 22, had studied Political Science, Hindi and Arab Culture at Jal Narain Degree College, Lucknow which was affiliated to the university. The choice of Arab Culture was interesting and there had been some vague thoughts of migrating for work in the Middle East. TS said, laughingly, that R chose this subject "because he wanted to become a Hafiz". TS had previously been on bad terms with R's family and he once described R's father as "being of a quarrelsome nature". However, good relations had been restored fairly recently and it was in fact TS who recommended that R should be asked to assist with the research. R had graduated in November 1980 and, except for a brief, temporary post as a surveyor's assistant, he had been unemployed since then. He said that he had applied for only about a dozen jobs hitherto, mainly because the application process was both expensive (about Rs 40 or 50 per application, in most cases) and very time-consuming. Another important reason was that an unsponsored villager was unlikely to succeed against competitors who had powerful patrons, such as MLAs or Ministers. The final reason was that neither his father nor his elder brother were in perfect health and so much of the more strenuous work on the farm that was not done by the biannual labourer, plus much of the supervision, had to be done by R.

Migrant Workers

It was claimed that there had been only about 30 villagers who had migrated for work outside in the past thirty years. Details were collected of sixteen such migrants, who still had ties with the village, and these included seven Shukla Brahmins, one Pande Brahmin, one Dube Brahmin, three Misra Mahabrahmins, two Lodhs and one Kahar. There was, surprisingly, only one Thakur migrant, though a few had service occupations which involved daily commuting from the village. The Shukla Brahmins owned less than half the average area of land per capita and less than a third of the average irrigated area per capita. The influence of migrants was not significant in the prominent role played by the Shuklas in opposition to the Pradhan.

Four of the migrants were currently aged over forty, five were in their thirties and the rest in their twenties. Their current average age was 33 years. Three, all in the least skilled and lower paid category, had left the village before the age of 20 years. Four had gone between the age of 20 and 24 years, six between 25 and 29 years and three had been aged 30 years or more when they left. The average age at migration was 25 years. The earliest migrants who still had links with the village went in 1955 and 1958 and both of these were still working within Barabanki district. The one migrant recorded for the 1960s was a Village Development Officer in a neighbouring district. There were three migrants who left between 1970 and 1974 and again only one had gone out of the district. He was employed as a junior electrician in Lucknow's Post and Telegraph Department. Seven of the 14 migrants left Basauli from 1975 onwards and this suggests some recent acceleration of out-migration, probably more as a reflection of rising educational standards than of any other factor. Four of these later migrants were educated to tenth or twelfth class and all but the youngest of these was earning at least Rs 700 per month. All the migrants except one were educated to at least fourth class and the average was at least seventh class.

Only one of the migrants was working in a factory, the nearby sugar mill at Burhwal. Seven were in government service, including one in central government, six for the UP government and one for Barabanki Municipal Corporation. Only two migrants worked for a private company and three were self-employed. The jobs included one Village Development Officer, one policeman, one clerk, three electricians, one tubewell operator, two drivers, one boilerman, one petrol-pump attendant, one small restaurant owner, one betel shop owner, a sweet vendor, a sweet maker and a temple priest. Seven were still working within Barabanki district, one in Sitapur district, five in Lucknow city, two in other districts of UP and only one person had migrated beyond UP, to Ludhiana in Punjab. Eight of the migrants were earning between Rs 700 and 900 per month and the other eight earned Rs 400 to 700. The lowest monthly earnings were those of the employee in the private sector, the petrol-pump attendant, who received only Rs 350 per month. The average monthly earnings were Rs 611 or an average of over Rs 20 per day.

Only two migrants had taken their family to stay with them and both of these lived in Barabanki town, where housing and other costs were rather cheaper than in Lucknow. Of the remainder, one migrant sometimes had his family with him in Lucknow, but space was limited there and they lived mainly in the village. The family of another was living with the wife's parents. Ten had their families in the village and two were unmarried. One Lodh was working about 65 kilometres away in the south of the district. It took him about four hours to travel by bus via Barabanki and he usually came home after about 14 days. He had applied for a transfer to Barabanki or Fatehpur but without success. He acted as a leader in some Hindu festivals and processions and was referred to as munshi, because he had earlier been a temporary teacher. On one occasion, he had an impromptu debate with Thakur Sahib on socialism, from which the latter returned in some irritation. He dismissed the Lodh's arguments as having been 'irrelevant and of a highly generalised nature'. The Thakur migrant had not been seen or heard of since 1972 when he had come to the village for his mother's funeral. He was last known to have been a UPSRTC bus driver in the remote hill district of Pithoragarh but his wife and children did not know whether he was still alive. They lived off their land and help from their agnates and the children were nearing an age to be able to do thc cultivation themselves.

There was also the possibility of one female Thakur becoming a migrant worker. R's brother reported that his wife had been offered the post of social worker in the Anganbari Child Welfare Scheme. (Anganbari means literally courtyard park and it conveys the idea of turning a yard into a park by planting flowers, ie. children, in it.) R stressed that the appointment would be for a post in the eastern districts where there was greater social work activity than in Barabanki district. By chance it was quite likely that the post might be in Basti district, which happened to be the wife's native district and there was even a possibility that the department might allow her to work from her home village, which was only about four kilometres from a block headquarters. She had seven years education and hitherto no experience of such work. She was also of a fairly shy, quiet disposition and so would find the work particularly challenging, especially if she in fact had to work away from her parental village. The work involved going from door-to-door, giving health education advice and organising meetings at which children play and mothers discuss their health problems. The salary would only be about Rs 250 per month and so would hardly cover subsistence expenditure. She had two children, five and three years old, who would be able to attend the Anganbari, since the age range is roughly 3 to 12 years. R was not all that enthusiastic about the job because of the low pay and the disturbance to the family.

There were also about five villagers who worked away from Basauli for less than six months in a year. These were usually lower caste labourers, who went to do seasonal work in local brickworks or to crush sugarcane. Apart from the brickworks in Basauli, there were others at Banjaria (Thakur-owned), Naurangabad (Kurmi) and a new one at Mohammadpur (Brahmin). The seasonal migrants in 1982 included a young Radhika who had previously worked as a biannual labourer for Thakur Sahib, a Pasi and a Gadaria, who worked at a sugar-crushing machine near Mahadewa, in Ramnagar block.

There were also villagers who commuted daily to work outside the village. A Thakur was employed by the Education Department as a Primary School teacher. He had had tragic family problems and possibly, either as a cause or result of these, he had taken to drinking when he could afford it. His attendance at the village school to the south of Basauli sank to only about four times per month and, since he was the only teacher there, the parents were particularly vocal in their complaints. He was therefore transferred to a larger school at Mohammadpur but after a time he was again transferred back to the original school. At this the villagers rebelled, abusing him and refusing to accept his return. He had then been transferred yet again, but still had not been dismissed. He had sold nearly all his land and was therefore highly dependent upon the income from his salary. His remaining land, 21 bighas, had been registered in the name of his seventeen year old son. The son had failed his High School examination in four successive years.

Another Thakur worked as a clerical supernumerary in the tahsildar's office in Fatehpur and he was deputed, on a casual, daily basis, to go and help the lekhpals and other revenue staff when they faced an excess load of work. He was paid

Rs 8 to 10 per day and sometimes earned Rs 300 per month. It was alleged that he was also able to earn further amounts in the form of gratuities and perquisites.

Shops

There were currently eight small shops in the gaon sabha. There were four in west and three in east Basauli and also a small shop, selling mainly pan, on the roadside opposite Purwa. All the shops had been started since 1970 and six since 1975 or later. The average value of stock was estimated to be Rs 528 per shop, ranging from Rs 300 to Rs 1,000. Partly because of the relatively low amount of capital required to start a shop, entry into this occupation was fairly easy and the impression given was that there had been a fairly high rate of entry and exit from shopkeeping. Three of the shopkeepers were Brahmin, including two Shuklas, and a fourth was Mahabrahmin. The remainder included two Pathans and two Lodhs, all in west Basauli. The average value of sales per day was estimated to be Rs 14 worth of goods and the value ranged from Rs 10 to 30.

SHOPS IN BASAULI

NAME	CASTE	DATE BEGUN	STOCK VALUE Rs	DAILY SALES Rs	AV NUMBER CUSTOMERS PER DAY	AV SALES PAISAS PER CUSTOMER	MAIN COMMODITY	LOCATION
PARMANAND	SHUKLA	1970	200	12	20	60	BIDI	EAST BASAULI
RAJ NARAIN	SHUKLA	1975	300	20	30	67	BIDI	ROADSIDE OPPOSITE PURWA
BENIRAM	MAHABRAHMIN MISRA	1976	300	10	15	67	BIDI	EAST BASAULI
GAYAPRASAD	PANDE	1976	400	10	15	67	BIDI	EAST BASAULI
DURBIJE	LODH	1980	500	8	10	80	BIDI	WEST BASAULI
BISOSHAR	LODH	1979	1000	30	50	60	BIDI	WEST BASAULI
LIAQAT	PATHAN	1977	1000	10	15	67	BIDI	WEST BASAULI
TOTAL			3700	100	155	468		
AVERAGE			528	14	22	67		
ABDUL KARIM	PATHAN							WEST BASAULI

The shop with the largest turnover was run by a Lodh who had been disabled after customers had broken his leg when he ran his shop in east Basauli. The estimated number of customers averaged 22 per day and ranged from 10 to 30. This means that the average customer spent only 67 paisas per day. The main commodity purchased was bidis.

Caste and Main Occupations of Household Heads

There were clear differences in the occupational structure of the three caste strata. Four of the 24 high caste household heads in the sample had service jobs outside the village and ten were exclusively farmers. However, six earned more from their labouring than from their own farm. In the medium stratum the proportion in service jobs was less but the ratio of farmers was slightly higher.

There were also five heads who were exclusively labourers. In the scheduled category, only four household heads were exclusively farmers out of 22 and the largest category was farmers who also did some labouring. Eight household heads were engaged in other activities and these were either musicians or stonecutters.

CASTE AND MAIN OCCUPATION OF HHH, 102 HOUSEHOLDS

CASTE STRATUM	OUTSIDE SERVICE OR SHOP	FARMER	FARMER AND LABOURER	LABOURER AND FARMER	AGRICULTURAL LABOURER	BRICK LABOURER	OTHER INCLUDING MENIAL SERVICES	RETIRED	TOTAL
HIGH	4	10	2	6			1	1	24
MEDIUM	3	26	10	8	3	2	3	1	56
SCHEDULED		4	8	4	2		4		22
TOTAL HHHs	7	40	20	18	5	2	8	2	102

Main Occupation of Household Head and Weighted Per Capita Income

MAIN OCCUPATION OF HHH AND RS WEIGHTED PER CAPITA INCOME

OCCUPATION	401 -700	701 -810	811 -950	951 -1100	1101+	TOTAL	810 AND BELOW AS % TOTAL
OUTSIDE SERVICE OR SHOP					7	7	-
FARMER	1	4	5	8	22	40	12
FARMER AND LABOURER	2	9	2	5	2	20	55
LABOURER AND FARMER	2	6	7	2	1	18	45
AGRICULTURAL LABOURER		2	2	1		5	40
BRICK LABOURER		1	1			2	50
OTHER, INCL. MENIAL	3	2	3			8	62
RETIRED		1			1	2	50
TOTAL HHHs	8	25	20	16	33	102	32

The seven households which were engaged in service outside the village or shopkeeping within the village were all in the richest category. The largest category of household heads (40) consisted of those who were exclusively farmers (ie. with no labouring) and out of these only 12 percent had a WPCI below the poverty line and over half were in the richest category. There were a further 20 household heads who combined farming with some labouring and, of these, 55 percent were below the poverty line. Surprisingly, the percentage of household heads who earned more from labouring than from farming and who were below the poverty line was less than for farmer-labourers. This may suggest that those who do mainly labouring earn more than some small farmers who supplement their farm income with only a little labouring. One of the two household heads who had retired, but none of those who were in service or running a shop, had an income below the poverty line. One of the two brickworks labourers fell below the threshold and five of the eight household heads in other, mainly menial and artisan service occupations also had a WPCI of Rs 810 or less.

7 Health of villagers

This chapter presents some (by no means entirely satisfactory) data on the nutrition and health of villagers in Basauli. The assessment is based on information derived from the random sample survey of 102 households and the 'census' of all 263 households within the Gaon Sabha; the outpatient registers of the Primary Health Centre at nearby Suratganj; and the nonrandom sample survey of 50 rural medical practitioners who constituted a majority of the seventy or so RMPs practising within about a 12 kilometre radius of Basauli.

NUTRITION

Rich villagers in particular considered that nutrition had improved generally in the village. The cultivated area, production and consumption of wheat had increased since about 1967, ie. not much later than western UP. The area of paddy had hardly increased but average productivity had risen from 4 to 20 quintals per hectare. Vegetable quantity and variety had increased, especially thanks to potatoes and also to tomatoes, introduced in 1977. On the other hand, the area of wheat had expanded at the expense of pulses, which had become very expensive: dal had changed from being a poor man's staple to a richer man's food. Apart from pulses, consumption of oilseeds, milk, meat and fish, as well as less prestigious foods such as barley, jowar, bajra, sawan and kodo, was said to have declined. Four impoverished Patharkot households kept a few chickens but sold the eggs to Thakur and other rich households. S. Mahabrahmin installed electric milling machinery in 1970 and TS had followed suit. This lightened the workload of many women (especially richer ones) but, despite TS claiming to have removed only the inedible chaff, there had been some reduction in the nutritional value of rice. Despite gram (chana) being regarded as more nourishing than arhar and despite the soil being no more suited to arhar than gram, local farmers grew mainly arhar because they preferred its taste.

There was said to be a growing shortage of milk. Most bovines produced only one or two kilograms per day. From 1978 to 1980 a lorry from a Lucknow dairy had collected about 40 kilograms of milk per day, paying on average Rs 2.1 per kilogram. The lorry collected from a 100-mile radius of Lucknow and RP, a nephew of S. Mahabrahmin, had organised the milk collection within Basauli. Sales from Basauli reached a maximum of 50 kilograms per day and the price ranged from Rs 1.8 to 2.7 per kilogram. Altogether, the local collecting centre purchased from 40 to 200 kilograms per day, averaging about 75 kilograms daily. When the sweetsellers (halwais) of Mohammadpur raised their purchase price from Rs 2.0 to 2.5 per kilogram, the Basauli supply to the dairy fell to only 15 kilograms per day and the collecting centre was eventually closed down.

One less nutritious but nevertheless subsidised food which aroused immense public interest was sugar and in December 1981 people in Purwa were angry with the BDO, the VLW and the lekhpal for failing to supply them with the ration cards to enable them to collect cheap supplies of sugar and kerosene. TS and other employers complained that their labourers insisted on being partly paid in, and thus consumed too much, gur. TS even claimed that excessive consumption of gur had given his Chamar labourers eczema.

The data on household food expenditure proved very unreliable and in many instances the estimates exceeded those for total income. Comparing nine average-sized households, from the poorest to the relatively very rich, there was a range of daily consumption: wheat (1.5 to 3.3 kg); rice (1.0 to 3.3 kg); gram (0 to 1.0 kg); potatoes (0.75 to 2.0 kg); vegetables (0 to 1.0 kg); tomatoes (0 to 0.4 kg, mostly in richer households); milk (0 to 2.0 kg); gur (0.2 to 0.7 kg); shukur (0 to 0.5 kg); meat (0 to 0.4 kg, but including four vegetarian households in the upper income range); and fish (0.2 kg in the only household buying fish). Monthly expenditure varied: ghee (Rs 0 to 7.5); tel or oil (Rs 2.5 to 32); spices (Rs 15 to 50); tea (mostly none but some and up to Rs 16 per month in richer households); tobacco (Rs 2 to 40); alcohol (probably over Rs 100 in the only household of the nine that imbibed); and meat, fish and eggs (Rs 0 to 160).

Most Hindus in the past ate no meat but the slow decline in vegetarianism means that a majority (54%) of household heads in the sample were non-vegetarian. Meat was eaten occasionally by Muslims, by most Thakurs and by various lower castes, including the scheduled. TS claimed that the best quality meat was reserved for city people, leaving villagers to chew on the gristle. Prices were also lower in the villages and goat meat sold for Rs 14 per kg in Mohammadpur, compared with Rs 22 in Lucknow. The scheduled, especially the Patharkots, also ate pig and various wild animals, including rabbits and foxes. The Loniyas were sometimes employed by farmers as rat-catchers, at the rate of Rs 2 per rat, and Loniyas were said to eat the rats they caught. More chickens would be kept if it were not for disease, village dogs and also the possibility of really quite serious inter-household disputes arising from petty infringement, especially if the chickens ate the grain drying outside a neighbour's house. The government provides aid for chicken-rearing projects, but the minimum investment had to be 200 chickens or about Rs 2,000. Uncooked eggs cost 60 paisas each (50 paisas in summer) and boiled eggs were 90 to 100 paisas. Uncooked eggs were frequently exposed to the hot sun in the bazaar. However, the meat consumption of most non-vegetarians was not very high and the health implications of the really fairly minor dietary differences between vegetarians and most non-vegetarians could well be quite small.

Certain days are designated for fasting (vrat) and on other days only certain types of food are permitted. For example, Shivratri on 22 February 1982 was a day when only fruits and vegetables should be consumed and TS observed this 'fast'. Many Hindu women fast on Tuesdays or on other days on behalf of their husbands.

Malnourishment was frequently expressed as lack of 'ghee dud' (clarified butter and milk), ie. in terms of lack of protein.

Apart from food, there was also considerable consumption of and expenditure on non-medicinal drugs. These included bidis in particular and also cigarettes, tobacco (both for smoking and for chewing), pan and betel nut, marihuana (either smoked as ganja or imbibed as bhang), alcohol and opium (afim). Only 17 household heads in the sample spent nothing on such drugs. Thirty-eight spent up to 50 paisas per day and 47 exceeded this, including 25 (mostly richer heads) who spent over 75 paisas per day (or over Rs 274 per year).

Bidis are very small, brown cigarellas, made of tobacco and tendu leaf, measuring about 6 centimetres in length. They were usually sold in small, cone-shaped packets of 25 and their price rose from 55 to 60 paisas per packet in February 1982. (Given the replies concerning daily expenditure on drugs, it would appear that the marketing agents have probably fixed the quantity and price per packet about right for the average villager.) Some villagers, especially children and youths, bought in smaller quantities: the smallest Indian coin in 1982 was a paisa. However, a plurality of household heads (43 percent) did not smoke bidis. A further 19 percent spent less than 50 paisas per day and only 5 percent averaged one packet per day. Bidis perform the function of dampening the appetite and are therefore particularly useful for the poor. They break the monotony of the diet, of long periods of no food and of the daily routine and also provide a cheap and instant instrument and symbol of hospitality in a culture which places very high religious and social value on receiving guests in the proper manner. Bidis were smoked by youths and they and others sometimes gave bidis to boys aged eight or even younger (see Nath 1985 on the risks to health).

There were also at least seven villagers, including three Thakurs and two Mahabrahmins, who were using or had used opium. The poppies have been grown locally for a long time and the opium product was still being processed under licence in the district. It was no longer grown commercially in Basauli, probably because producers in the village had broken the government regulations on the amount produced and/or on sale to the government and thus had found their licences revoked. Opium was still being smuggled out of Barabanki district, to Assam, Calcutta, Bombay and elsewhere and the price was said to be expensive (Rs 1,000 per processed kilogram). Partly because of the cost, the smoking of opium has been mainly a habit of the richer and upper castes, especially the Thakurs, who had previously possessed licences to cultivate it in Basauli. In the village the opium was either eaten direct or else the poppy heads were soaked in water for twelve hours and then the mixture drunk. In Barabanki district opium smuggling was said to be controlled mainly by Muslims and to be based in the village of Jikra.

The main types of alcohol consumed were Santra and Malta (both manufactured from oranges by the large Mohan Meakin brewery in Lucknow) which cost Rs 22 per bottle; 'desi', a local concoction made from the mahua fruit (Rs 10); tharra, a strong and manufactured spirit (Rs 16); and toddy (tari) which was made locally and sold for Rs 3 per bottle. Consumption of the first three types was roughly equal, whilst toddy was drunk in smaller quantities, partly because of its seasonal availability. The main consumers of alcohol had been Thakurs until recently, but in 1982 they also included Brahmins, Lodhs and the scheduled. Drunkenness was said to have declined and occurred mainly on pay days, at weddings and on festival days, especially Holi.

Height and Weight

Heights and weights of 483 villagers were measured in the first two weeks of August 1982. It should be noted that August is a difficult time for agricultural labourers and so the weights of some of the poorer villagers may have been slightly lower than at certain other times of year. Heights were measured, using a bamboo stave (lathi) which was graduated specially into inches. The lathi is more usually an instrument of defence - and offence, in village fighting and it was chosen deliberately as a familiar rustic object which might occasion some laughter and thus help remove any residual inhibitions to undergoing the somewhat bureaucratic and/or medicalising experience of 'being measured' by the postcolonial anthropologist. There may, however, have been some slight loss of accuracy, in the absence of the proper instrument for the job. Bathroom scales were used to weigh people and this unfamiliar object prompted some hesitation, especially among the women (who 'volunteered' in significantly smaller numbers anyway). Even some of those women who did volunteer needed a certain amount of cajoling to undergo 'ordeal by bathroom scales'. The result was a distinctly non-random sample of 34 percent of the total population of the Gaon Sabha and there was under-representation, notably of female villagers, especially adults and more particularly of upper caste, adult females. The table shows that for certain ages, including teenage girls, the numbers were very small. Average heights for men and women aged 21 and over were 164.7 and 150.8 centimetres respectively, indicating that the average man was over 9 percent taller than the average woman. Perhaps partly because of misreporting of ages and also because of small numbers in some age categories, there are inconsistencies and anomalies in the data: average height does not always increase with age and for some ages girls were taller than boys.

Male adults weighed very significantly (19%) more than female adults. The average weights for men and women aged 21 and over were 46.8 and 39.3 kilograms respectively. Comparison with a sample of British children shows that 12 year old boys and girls in Basauli had average weights which were about 65 percent and 61 percent respectively of the British average for both sexes.

The above figures inevitably lead to the Basauli male weight for height (.284) exceeding the female weight for height (.261) by nearly nine percent. Note that female weights for heights are higher than male in eight out of 20 comparisons of those aged under 21.

AVERAGE WEIGHT, HEIGHT AND WEIGHT FOR HEIGHT, BY AGE, SEX AND CASTE STRATUM, AUGUST 1982

YEARS	MALE				FEMALE				UK SAMPLE BOTH SEXES		BEFORE 1981
AGE	NO.	AV.KG WEIGHT	AV.CM HEIGHT	AV.WT FOR HT x 1000	NO.	AV.KG WEIGHT	AV.CM HEIGHT	AV.WT FOR HT x 1000	AV.KG WEIGHT	AV.CM HEIGHT	AV.WT FOR HT x 1000
0									3.8	55	73
1	6	6.8	68	101	6	4.4	62	71	10.0	77	121
2	3	6.3	71	90	1	5.0	69	73	12.5	87	149
3	5	9.0	79	114	5	7.5	76	99	15.0	95	158
4	7	10.3	90	114	6	10.9	91	119	17.0	102	167
5	11	13.1	100	130	2	14.2	112	127	18.8	109	174
6	8	12.9	102	127	6	13.9	105	133	21.0	114	184
7	12	17.2	114	151	8	16.1	113	143	23.0	119	193
8	21	18.9	120	158	16	18.4	118	155	26.0	126	206
9	12	19.5	123	159	5	19.7	125	157	29.0	132	219
10	10	20.6	126	164	9	19.6	122	161	32.0	137	234
11	12	23.9	132	181	4	24.5	136	181	35.0	142	246
12	14	24.7	134	184	8	23.0	131	176	38.0	148	257
13	10	26.4	139	190	4	32.0	142	225		154	
14	10	33.6	152	221	3	32.0	146	218		160	
15	17	35.7	150	238	5	32.8	144	228		168	
16	6	35.0	154	228	2	37.5	147	255		173	
17	4	39.8	159	250	2	37.5	121	309		174	
18	12	45.7	167	273	4	41.5	137	303		175	
19	2	42.0	160	262	1	40.0	152	262		175	
20	10	45.2	164	275	6	36.8	149	248			
21+	129	46.8	165	284	59	39.3	151	261			
18+	153	46.5	165	282	70	39.8	152	260			
TOTAL	321	33.6			162						
CASTE STRATUM											
HIGH		48.9	167	292		40.5	149	272			
MEDIUM		45.5	161	282		38.7	146	265			
SCHEDULED		46.7	164	285		38.7	154	252			

Sources: Basauli survey; Jolly 1981:219.

MORTALITY

No direct and systematic data was collected on the overall crude death rate in 1982. However, R. Thakur was able to recall at least 12 deaths which had occurred between August 1982 and February 1983. Nine were aged 50 or more and two were infants, including one who died from diarrhea and liver trouble and also the granddaughter of TS who died at birth. The average age at death was 48 years (57 for adults). Some approximation of the annual crude death rate can be derived from the figure of 12 deaths out of a population of 1425 in a period of seven months: the annual rate per thousand persons would be roughly 12x(12÷7)x(1,000÷1,425) = 14.4 deaths per thousand population. This obviously rather rough estimate is likely to be on the low side, mainly because deaths of other infants may have been unknown to a young male informant. (The CDRs for rural UP and rural India in 1979 were 17.0 and 13.9 respectively, according to the Indian Express, 30 November 1981).

Hindus have a saying that, if a person dies within a five-day period in the month (a period known as Pochuk), then five more persons will die immediately afterwards. R thought that about 90% of villagers believed in it, including TS who believed in it wholly and his third son who more than half believed in it. Indeed, TS had gone so far as to ask the relatives of UBS Thakur to delay his cremation for two days until the Pochuk period had expired, but this would have created other difficulties for the family and so they were unable to oblige. It was not clear whether the shifting of attention to the date of cremation from the date of actual death was a subterfuge or whether the latter is really the more crucial. Certainly, it appears to be quite common to try to delay cremation in such cases, though in summer this is clearly very difficult to do.

Apparently, five deaths had followed Pochuk death and this sequence had happened twice in the previous three months. Understandably, when the second Pochuk death occurred people were extra nervous and taking precautions. The multiple death sequence may well have been a likely possibility in the past, when infectious diseases were frequently mortal. R claimed that the succession of deaths in late 1982 were of those old or who had been ill for a long time (such as K. Ahir with cancer) and so might have been expected to die anyway.

Stillbirths and Infant and Child Deaths

The 'census' of all 263 households and 309 mothers accidentally (or rather crucially) omitted a question on deaths of children and this information had to be collected from key informants and neighbours at a later date. Not surprisingly, the data proved incomplete: whereas the average mother in the 'census' was reported to have had 3.5 live births and 0.8 child deaths, the average household in the sample of 102 households had 5.3 live births and 2.4 child deaths, including stillbirths. (This included deaths of children belonging to other mothers in the household, apart from the wife of the household head. The average number of child deaths for the latter was 2.0 per wife.)

% OF TOTAL STILLBIRTHS, INFANT AND CHILD DEATHS, 102 HOUSEHOLDS

	DATE OF DEATH	M	F	T	No.
	1941-50	63%	37%	100%	24
	1951-60	63%	37%	100%	57
	1961-70	53%	47%	100%	63
	1971-80	43%	56%	100%	48
TOTAL	1931-82	54%	46%	100%	204
	1961-80	49%	51%	100%	111

NB These show number and % of deaths, not rates. In fact female mortality under 5 was 24% higher than male, especially in the period up to 1965 (41% higher).

The census data implied an overall very high under-five death rate of 229 deaths per 1000 births while the sample rate was even higher, at 331 per 1000. This is almost certainly higher than in reality, partly because of the omission of some adult children (especially females) who were alive, married and, in many cases, resident elsewhere. From the dates of birth (which were unlikely to be very accurate) and the age at which children had died, a rough chronology of deaths and changing annual rates has been calculated:

CHILD DEATHS AGED 0 TO 5, BY SEX AND QUINQUENNIUM, 102 HHs, BASAULI 1931-81

YEARS	1931 -40	1941 -45	1946 -50	1951 -55	1956 -60	1961 -65	1966 -70	1971 -75	1976 -80	1981	TOTAL 1941-81
MALE	(3)	10	5	19	17	17	16?	12	9	1	106
FEMALE	(2)	3	6	8	11	13	17?	13	13	4	91
TOTAL	(5)	13	11	27	28	30	33*	25	22	5	199
AV.PER YEAR	(0.5)	2.6	2.2	5.4	5.6	6.0	6.6	5.0	4.4	5.0	4.9

* Includes two whose gender is not known.

The table shows changes in mortality rates for males and females in the sample households. Out of 501 children recorded as ever born to 98 sample mothers, only 272 (54%) were still alive in 1982. Actual survival rates were higher than this and the mortality is overstated because of the serious initial design fault in the questionnaire which led to omission of some adult children, especially married daughters, who had left the household and even the village. This is probably the main explanation for the much lower number of female births recorded (195 as against 293 males) and the correspondingly higher mortality rates for females, especially in the period before 1965. After that time birth cohorts become increasingly too young to have left the household but recorded births for females only equalise from 1975 onwards. This differential in reporting of females inevitably reduces the accuracy and usefulness of the data and must impose a very strong upward bias on female mortality rates, as can be seen from the absurdly high postneonatal and infant mortality rates to 1964 (see p.324).

Given the imperfections in the Basauli data, it is instructive to compare it with similar data collected from a larger population in two adjacent villages in Bijnor, western UP in 1985 (see Jeffery 1989). The ratio of children who had survived to the age of five was much higher: 74%, compared with only 57% in Basauli, with its highly inflated female mortality rates. However, the mortality rates for the first week and first month of life are very comparable. Apart from the flaws in the Basauli data, the comparison suggests that the higher stillbirth rate may be due to inferior health care in Basauli and the very much higher postneonatal rate may be due to the lower income and development in the central UP village. The fact that the Jefferys conducted their survey three years later could also make a small difference, too.

CHILD MORTALITY IN BASAULI 1982 AND JHAKRI-DHARMNAGRI VILLAGES 1985

VILLAGE	DATE	DISTRICT	LOCATION	NO. OF HOUSE-HOLDS	EVER MARRIED WOMEN	AV. AGE	EVER BORN CHILDREN TO 1982 OR 1985	TO 1977 OR 1980	NUMBER SURVIVED TO AGE 5	%
BASAULI	1982	Barabanki	Central UP	102	98	41	501	c454	295	57%
JHAKRI+ DHARMNAGRI	1985	Bijnor	Western UP	180	236	38	1210	725	980	74%

MORTALITY RATES	STILLBIRTH RATE	FIRST WEEK RATE	PERINATAL RATE	NEONATAL RATE	POST NEONATAL RATE	IMR
BASAULI	62	28	88	70	136	206
JHAKRI+DHARMNAGRI (JD)	30	33	62	63	45	108
B as % of JD	207%	85%	142%	111%	302%	191%

** Live born to 1980 ie. this excludes some of the 36 stillbirths to 1985, most of them presumably having occurred up to 1980

Sources: Basauli Survey; Jeffery 1989.

Age of child and mortality

The table shows the age distribution of mortality and the probability of stillbirth or death.

AGE	STILL BIRTH	1-6 DAYS	7-30 DAYS	31-180 DAYS	181-365 DAYS	1-365 DAYS	1-4 YEARS	5-15 YEARS	16+ YEARS	NOT KNOWN	TOTAL
% of total stillbirths or deaths	14	5	9	28		42	30	7	5	3	100
Probability of stillbirth of death per time period	1.06	.03	.04	.07	.08	.21	.18	.05	.04	-	
% Probability of stillbirth or death per day	6.0	.5	.17	.047	.043	.058	.016	NEGLIGIBLE			

Incidence of death was most frequent in the 1 to 4 age category, followed by the neonatal period and at birth. However, the highest risk of dying *per day* was actually at birth (ie. stillbirth) or in the first six days of life. After this the probability of dying declined sharply.

Stillbirths

The term for stillbirth was 'turand', literally sudden. Thirty-one stillbirths were reported for 98 mothers and 14% of all stillbirths and deaths of ever born were due to stillbirth. The accumulated rate was 62 per 1000 total births, double the rate in the Bijnor villages and about ten times the rate in the UK during 1984. The male rate was about 20% higher than the female, both in Basauli and Bijnor, but the male rate in Basauli had declined, especially from 1970, while the female rate had not. From 1966 onwards the rate for both sexes had fallen by at least 40% in both Basauli and Bijnor.

Other Perinatal Deaths

Thirteen babies had died in the first six days. Numbers are too small to yield meaningful rates: the rate actually increased from 16 pre-1965 to 42 thereafter. Improvement in the stillbirth rate could possibly lead to an increase in deaths in the first week. Female deaths exceeded male and had increased much more than male.

Neonatal Mortality

Thirty-three babies had died in the first month. The neonatal rate was 70 and had increased from 66 pre-1965 to 88 thereafter. The ratio of neonatal to total infant deaths increased from 26% pre-1965 to 44% in the later period. This is consistent with the usual trend as societies become more developed and in fact in a country like Sweden neonatal deaths account for 80% of total infant deaths. Neonatal rates in Basauli were virtually the same for males and females.

Neonatal mortality was still slightly (11%) higher than in Bijnor (63) but the respective rates were closer than for any of these mortality indicators. Basauli and Bijnor both had very slightly higher rates for males but Bijnor differed in that there was only a very minor increase in the proportion of neonatal deaths to total infant deaths.

Postneonatal Mortality

The postneonatal rate was 136 but the male rate had fallen sharply from 200 per 1000 live births in the 1940s to 100 by 1970-74. The female rate, biased upwards by incomplete numbers of births, averaged 179 for the whole period and started to decline from 1965. The postneonatal rate in Bijnor was very much lower (45), the female rate exceeded the male by much more even than in

Basauli and the trend for both sexes was even more sharply downward than in Basauli.

Infant Mortality

Infant deaths totalled 97 and the cumulative rate was very high (206). IMR had declined from 257 pre-1965 to 200 thereafter. The female far exceeded the male rate but was very unreliable, especially for the period before 1965. The male IMR had virtually halved from 259 in 1950-54 to 133 in 1975-79.

The IMR in Bijnor was 108, almost half that of Basauli but there was an identical gender difference. The female rate exceeded the male by about 33%. Bijnor's IMR fell by 41%, from 147 pre-1966 to 86 later and this decrease compares very favourably with the rather modest decrease of 22% in Basauli (from 257 to 200). Reservations have already been expressed about the Basauli data, which are almost certainly inflated but the figures should increase in accuracy for the later period. The records should be very accurate for the period from 1970 to 1982 (when no children, female or not, should have married or have been missed). The IMR for Basauli in this period was 164, very similar to the average for rural UP during the 12 years 1970-76, 1978 and 1980-83, which was 177:

INFANT MORTALITY IN RURAL UP, BASAULI AND TWO BIJNOR VILLAGES

PERIOD	RURAL UTTAR PRADESH	BASAULI GAON SABHA, CENTRAL UP			TWO BIJNOR VILLAGES, WESTERN UP
	T	M	F	T	T
Up to 1964 or 1965	250+?	220	504**	278	147
1965-9	(c220?)*	229	(333)	272	
1970-4	182	180	86	141	
1975-9	184	133	258	197	
1980-2	160	(0)	250	154	
1970-82 or 83	177 (1970-83)	153	176 (1970-82)	164	
1965-82	(c186?)	180	224	200	
1966-85					86
Up to 1982 or 1985	(c218+?)	187	250	229	108

* The average IMR for all UP in 1961-70 was 235 and so an estimate of 220 for rural UP in the late 1960s seems reasonable.
** Obviously inflated by under-recording of births, especially of females.
Sources: Visaria 1985:1353; Jeffery 1989:242.

Child Mortality

Sixty-nine children died between the ages of one and five. Mortality of male children has been lower and fell from 238 per 1000 live births in the 1950s to 112 in the 1970s. The female rate fell even more and almost converged with the male rate by the 1970s.

REPORTED AGE OF MOTHER AND NUMBER OF CHILDREN STILLBORN, DEAD AND STILL LIVING, PER MOTHER, BASAULI

REPORTED AGE OF MOTHER	NO. OF MOTHERS	AVER. NO. OF CHILDREN STILL-BORN OR DIED	AVER. NO. OF CHILDREN STILL ALIVE	AVER. NO. OF CHILDREN STILLBORN + BORN ALIVE	NO. OF MOTHERS	AVER. STILL BORN+ DEAD	AVER. ALIVE	AVER. TOTAL EVER BORN	BIJNOR AVER. TOTAL EVER BORN
						AGE 15-24			
18	1	0.0	2.0	2.0					
20	3	0.3	1.0	1.3	5	0.2	1.2	1.4	1.3
24	1	0.0	1.0	1.0		14%	86%	100%	(N=50)
						AGE 25-34			
25	9	1.3	1.3	2.7					
26	3	1.3	1.7	3.0					
27	1	0.0	3.0	3.0					
28	2	1.5	2.5	4.0	25	1.2	2.2	3.5	3.9
30	8	1.4	3.0	4.4		34%	63%	100%	(N=65)
32	1	0.0	2.0	2.0					
33	1	1.0	5.0	6.0					
						AGE 35-44			
35	11	2.0	3.3	5.3					
38	2	1.0	4.5	5.5					
40	13	3.2	3.0	6.2	28	2.4	3.2	5.8	6.4
41	1	2.0	4.0	6.0		41%	55%	100%	(N=45)
42	1	2.0	3.0	5.0					
						AGE 45+			
45	9	3.8	3.7	7.6					
48	1	2.0	6.0	8.0					
50	6	4.3	2.8	7.2					
55	9	3.8	3.2	7.0					
56	1	NA	3.0+	NA					
60	5	3.0	4.2	7.2	37	3.4+	3.2+	6.6+	7.8
65	1	1.0+	2.0	3.0+		52%	48%	100%	(N=76)
70	2	3.0	2.5	5.5					
75	1	6.0	3.0	9.0					
80	2	1.0	0.0	1.0					
NK	1	1.0+	1.0	2.0+					
TOTAL	96	2.4+	2.8+	5.3+	95	2.4+	2.8+	5.3+	5.1
AV. AGE	41								38

Notes

1. The age heaping is very noticeable. The percentage of ages between 23 and 62 ending with 0 and 5 is 82%, giving a Whipple's Index of 412 ie. indicating extremely rough data on age (see Newell 1988:24).
2. The apparent anomaly of a slightly higher average number of children in Basauli than in Bijnor, despite higher figures for Bijnor in the disaggregated age categories, is explained by differing age distribution and a higher average age of the Basauli mothers.

Source: Jeffery 1989:241 for data on two villages in Bijnor district.

The table shows the age of sample mothers and the number of children ever born, dead and still alive. The household heads gave even more approximate answers for their wives' ages than for themselves and the age data are obviously as rough as can be. The data show that the average married woman had at least 5.3 ever born children and at least 2.4 (45%) of these had either been stillborn or died, leaving at least 2.8 living children. The proportion of dead predictably increased with the age and parity of the mother, rising sharply from 14% in those aged under 25 to 34% in those aged 25 to 34. There were further smaller increases to 41% and 52% respectively in the two older age categories. The average numbers ever born rose to a maximum average of at least 6.6 children in the oldest age category. The numbers ever born for three age categories were 10 to 16% lower than the equivalents in the two Bijnor villages, the exception being the youngest category. On the other hand, the Basauli fertility data for 5-year age categories were all higher than for all-India. The excess increased from 8% in the case of the 20 to 24 year olds to 53% for the 45 to 49 year olds.

AVERAGE NO. OF CHILDREN EVER BORN PER WOMAN, INDIA 1972 + BASAULI 1982

	INDIA			BASAULI SAMPLE	
Age of Women	1972	1981	% Change	1982	As % India 1981
15-19	0.23	0.17	-26	(2.00)	
20-24	1.28	1.13	-12	1.22	108
25-29	2.73	2.41	-12	2.95	122
30-34	3.94	3.46	-12	4.32	125
35-39	4.74	4.26	-10	5.33	125
40-44	5.08	4.71	-7	6.11	130
45-49	5.07	4.99	-2	7.64	153
Av. age of woman at marriage	17.8	18.7	+5	NA	

Source: Dyson 1984:4.

Because of age heaping it is not possible to be sure of the precise number of stillbirths, infant and child deaths experienced by mothers at each successive age. An estimate has been attempted by plotting the existing known (heaped) data on a graph and then reading off the numbers for all ages. The following figures are based on this procedure and its possibly dangerous assumption that the number of stillbirths and deaths shows a continuous linear increase.

ESTIMATED AVERAGE NUMBER OF STILLBIRTHS, INFANT AND CHILD DEATHS PER MOTHER, RELATED TO AGE OF MOTHER, 102 HOUSEHOLDS

Age	18	19	20	21	22	23	24	25	26	27	28	29
No. of stillbirths + deaths per mother	0.0	0.2	0.3	0.4	0.6	0.8	0.9	1.1	1.2	1.3	1.5	1.6
Age			30	31	32	33	34	35	36	37	38	39
No.of stillbirths + deaths per mother			1.7	1.8	2.0	2.2	2.3	2.5	2.5	2.6	2.6	2.6
Age			40	41	42	43	44	45	46	47	48	49
No.of stillbirths + deaths per mother			2.7	2.8	2.9	3.3	3.6	3.8	3.8	3.8	3.7	3.7

Source: Basauli survey data, plotted on and then read off a graph.

Adult Mortality

Eleven out of 102 household heads were widows and one man had experienced the loss of two successive wives. Eight of the wives had died at the age of 50 or younger and one had died aged 26. Three had died of TB and three from fever, including two at delivery, when their babies had died with them. One wife had thrown herself and her two young children into the well, allegedly because of family problems associated with fairly heavy drinking by the husband.

Household heads were asked the age of their parents. The majority of both their fathers and mothers were dead, though 31 mothers still survived, compared with only five fathers. There was little difference in the average age of fathers and mothers still alive, and the average ages at death for fathers and mothers were 71 and 68 years respectively. Looking at the distribution of age at death, there are only minor differences between fathers and mothers. More mothers had died up to the age of 60 and more fathers were alleged to have survived beyond 80.

Given that ages of old people were probably not known with any great accuracy, this gender difference might seem insignificant. However, 31 mothers were still alive and already had an average age of 65 years, and so it was most likely that average longevity of all the mothers would ultimately exceed that of all the fathers.

AGE OF PARENTS OF HOUSEHOLD HEADS

	% OF TOTAL								
	REPORTED AGE AT DEATH								
	35-60	61-70	71-80	81+	NK	TOTAL No.	Av.Age at Death	No. still Alive	Av. Age of those still Alive
FATHER	23%	26%	27%	21%	4%	97	71	5	63
MOTHER	28%	25%	24%	17%	6%	71	68	31	65
TOTAL	25%	26%	26%	19%	5%	168	70	36	65

MORBIDITY

Household heads (or, in a few cases, their proxies) were asked about illnesses that household members had experienced between January 1981 and the day of the interview. The interviews were conducted from early January to 23 February 1982 and so the maximum number of days of illness was about 420. On the interview schedule there was a separate page for each household member, with space for details of relationship to the household head, age, education, marital status, job, days of, and income from, labouring, and consumption of bidis, cigarettes and other drugs.

The main section was on bouts of illness, the date they began and ended, the various 'doctors' consulted, the places, numbers of visits, treatments, costs and the effect of the treatments. Finally, briefer details of 'serious' illness which had occurred before 1981 were recorded. Respondents were quite often helped with examples of 'serious' illness (such as malaria, smallpox, cholera and typhoid) but otherwise the interviewees were left to define 'serious' illness as they saw fit. In fact relatively few of them included trivial types of illness but no doubt respondents varied considerably in the extent to which they included intermediate types of illness such as some fevers and some gastric complaints. The replies on the dates when illness during 1981-2 began and ended were not always very precise, usually referring to Vikram samvat months rather than to actual dates. Mostly the number of days of illness was asked but in some cases there is only information on the month and in these instances the length of illness cannot be expected to be very accurate. The general effect of this has almost certainly been to give an upward bias to duration of illness during the 14 months, perhaps especially of those illnesses which lasted for more than about 14 days. On the other hand, a number of illnesses had begun before January 1981 and these had either recurred some time during 1981-2 or had merely continued to be an ongoing source of ill-health. In addition, there were cases of people who had become ill during 1981-2 and whose illness was still continuing when the survey ended in February 1982. In other words, the biases of error are not all upwards, even though the net effect is likely to be some overstatement of overall morbidity.

Categorisation of Illness

Villagers, when asked about illness, obviously do not resort to the WHO international classification of diseases. Though the local, popular and vernacular terms they used are instructive about rural perceptions and categorisation of illness and disease, they are often vague and inevitably frustrating to a medical expert. Where the villager has used a technical medical term, this has been translated but for many complaints the researcher has had no alternative but to use the local term, unsatisfactory and confusing as this may sometimes be. This was partly because the researcher himself lacked the medical (and sometimes also the linguistic) knowledge and indeed the researcher's background in certain medical matters may sometimes have been inferior to that of a respondent! It should also be stressed that, even when a respondent used a technical term, referring to a specific disease, this does not by any means guarantee that the diagnosis was always necessarily any more reliable than those implied in the vaguer, folk terms.

Persons who were healthy were described as khushti (strong, robust) or pelwan. Those who were unhealthy were referred to as kamzoor (weak), sast ('lazy', weak) or bimar (ill). Having serious illness was referred to by one respondent as being 'bahut tagri bimari'. One aspect of causation of ill-health was choreae, arising from 'gelut kam' ('wrong work' or wrongdoing).

Aggregate Days of Illness

Aggregate or total days of illness refers to the duration of one or more bouts of a single illness or two or more different illnesses. The table shows the detailed breakdown of illness, complaints and symptoms, organised under six main broad headings or types and 71 less, but still fairly, aggregated illness categories. These general headings are no more satisfactory than some of the individual categories and the types are not always completely mutually exclusive. They represent an attempt to aggregate to allow some analysis, however unsatisfactory.

Overall, the relative incidence and average duration of the main broad categories of illness are shown in the next table.

The largest proportion of days of illness was due to gastro-intestinal problems (nearly 27%). Skin problems were the next most important, accounting for nearly 16% of total days of illness. The remaining categories each comprised about 14% of days of illness: aches, pains and fractures; colds, coughs and pulmonary

% INCIDENCE AND DURATION OF TYPES AND CATEGORIES OF ALL ILLNESS 1981-2 AND % INCIDENCE OF SERIOUS ILLNESS BEFORE 1981, 102 HOUSEHOLDS

TYPE AND LOCAL NAME/CATEGORY OF ILLNESS	% OF TOTAL DAYS ILL	% OF TOTAL BOUTS OF ILLNESS	AVER. DAYS ILLNESS PER BOUT	% OF TOTAL CASES SERIOUS ILLNESS
	FROM JAN. 1981 TO FEB. 1982			BEFORE 1981
GASTRO-INTESTINAL PROBLEMS				
PETH KA TAKLIF (or SHIKAYAT) Stomach trouble	17.0	7.6	135	5.5
PECHISH Dysentery	4.9	2.4	125	1.7
JIGAR Liver trouble	1.8	0.8	137	0.7
ANAU BATI Liver trouble + Diarrhea	0.9	0.3	215	0.3
PESHAB (Urination) Trouble	0.8	0.3	180	
SUKKA ROG (or BIMARI) Dehydration?	0.4	0.3	90	1.4
'CHOLERA' Mainly Dysentery, sometimes Diarrhea	0.3	2.4	7	8.7
PALTI Vomiting + sickness	0.3	0.5	31	0.7
Digestive problem	0.3	0.3	60	
DAST Diarrhea	0.1	1.0	6	
PETH KA KEERA Stomach worms	0.1	0.3	15	
GAS in stomach	*	0.3	7	
MUHA Mouthache; stomatitis?; mouth ulcers	0.1	0.5	20	0.3
SANGRHNI Sprue				0.3
% TOTAL GASTRO-INTESTINAL PROBLEMS	26.9	16.8	97	19.7
No. of Days + Cases	6181	64	97	57
SKIN PROBLEMS				
KHAJULI Scabies	3.8	1.3	176	
DANE Eczema; rash; pimples	3.8	1.3	175	
CHERUM ROG Skin disease	2.6	0.5	300	
KUSHT BIMARI (or ROG) Leprosy	1.8	0.3	420	0.3
PHOORA Boils, ulcers, abscesses	1.6	3.7	32	2.1
ADANGI (?) Brown + white blotches	0.8	0.3	180	0.3
PHOORA (Ulcers) on leg or foot	0.7	1.6	28	
PHOORA + swollen Knee (Filaria?)	0.4	0.5	48	0.3
Body or face PUKGEA (swollen)	0.1	0.3	30	0.3
% TOTAL SKIN PROBLEMS	15.8	9.7	98	3.5
No. of Days + Cases	3626	37	98	10
ACHES, PAINS + FRACTURES				
Arm, elbow, hand or finger	3.9	1.0	225	0.3
Leg, knee, foot or toe	3.7	1.3	171	1.7
BAI, SERDI HAWA (cold wind), Ache, including rheumatic	2.7	0.5	309	1.4
SHEENA, SINE (chest) or ribs	2.2	1.0	170	0.3
Chest + legs	1.8	0.3	42	
Teeth	0.1	0.3	16	1.4
Back, jaw, skull, incl. fractured skull				1.7
% TOTAL ACHES, PAINS + FRACTURES	14.4	4.4	195	6.9
No. of Days + Cases	3318	17	195	20

COLDS, COUGHS + PULMONARY PROBLEMS	% OF TOTAL DAYS ILL	% OF TOTAL BOUTS OF ILLNESS	AV.DAYS ILLNESS PER BOUT	% OF SERIOUS ILLNESS
KHANSI-ZUKHAM Cough-cold	2.8	3.7	46	1.0
TB	2.8	0.5	223	1.0
SERDI-ZUKHAM cold-cold	1.9	9.4	12	1.4
KHANSI Cough	1.4	2.6	35	1.0
DAMA Asthma	0.8	0.5	90	0.7
KHANSI-BUKHAR Cough-fever	0.8	1.0	44	1.0
ZUKHAM Cold	0.7	1.6	25	
PURANA (or DAMA) KHANSI (Old Cough) Bronchitis	0.6	0.3	135	0.7
SERDI-BUKHAR Cold-fever	0.6	2.4	15	0.7
SUANS Breathlessness; bronchitis?	0.5	0.5	60	
JAKRA Influenza or pneumonia	0.4	1.6	14	1.4
KALI KHANSI (Empty cough) Whooping Cough	0.4	1.0	21	
Pneumonia	0.3	0.3	60	2.1
SERDI or THANDA or JOORI Cold	0.2	0.8	16	1.4
NAJLA or NAZLA Influenza	0.2	0.8	18	
% TOTAL COLDS, COUGHS + PULMONARY PROBLEMS	14.1	27.0	33	12.5
No. of Days + Cases	3254	103	33	36
FEVERS AND INFECTIONS				
BUKHAR Fever	9.2	21.2	26	16.3
BUKHAR-ZUKHAM Fever-cold	1.1	4.2	16	1.0
CHOTI CHECHUK Measles	11	2.4	26	0.3
PIL PAU Filaria	0.8	1.0	48	1.4
ROGI BUKHAR (?)	0.7	0.3	150	
Phylorea (?)	0.4	0.3	87	
JOORI BUKHAR (Cold fever) Malaria	0.3	1.8	10	2.1
ALAMANDI (?) A kind of fever	0.3	0.3	60	
KANWAR Jaundice	0.1	0.3	30	0.3
MYADI BUKHAR or MOTI JHARA B. Typhoid	0.1	0.3	30	4.2
CHECHUK Smallpox (to 1974); Chickenpox; measles				11.4
Diphtheria				0.7
JADI BUKHAR Ague				0.3
JAMOGO Tetanus				0.3
MAHEEN BUKHAR Postpuerperal fever				0.3
% TOTAL FEVERS AND INFECTIONS	14.0	31.9	26	38.8
No. of Days + Cases	3220	122	26	112
OTHER ILLNESSES				
ANKH (Eye) problems, including blindness	4.8	2.9	101	2.4
KHUN KI KHARABI Bad blood; anemia	2.0	1.3	94	2.1
DIL KA BIMARI Illness of the heart	1.8	0.3	420	0.7
Pain in bottom	1.8	0.3	420	
DHAT (or SUGAR) KI BIMARI Diabetes	1.6	0.3	365	
Ear problems, including deafness	0.8	0.5	90	0.7
Menstrual problems	0.5	0.3	120	0.3
CHOT (Injury),fall or cut,incl.from assault	0.5	2.1	15	2.8
Burns	0.4	0.3	90	2.1
General Weakness	0.3	0.3	75	
Psychological,incl. possession by ghost	0.1	0.3	15	1.4
Other, including DAURA or MIRGI (Epilepsy) + pregnancy problem	0.1	1.6	3	5.9
% TOTAL OTHER ILLNESS	14.8	10.2	87	18.7
No. of Days + Cases	3402	39	87	54
GRAND TOTAL ILLNESS: DAYS + CASES	23,001	382	60	289

complaints; and fevers and infections. The residual category, including eye, blood and heart problems, explained the remaining 15% of days of 'other illness'.

The distribution of bouts of illness was different from that for days of illness. The commonest type of illness was fever and infections (nearly 32%), followed by colds, coughs and pulmonary complaints (27%), gastro-intestinal troubles (17%), skin problems (10%), aches and pains and fractures (over 4%) and other illness (10%).

The most frequently reported serious illness which occurred before 1981 was fevers and infections (nearly 39%) followed by gastro-intestinal problems (nearly 20%), 'other illness' (nearly 19%), colds, coughs and pulmonary problems (12.5%), aches, pains and fractures (nearly 7%) and skin problems (3.5%). The reported incidence before 1981 was almost double for 'other illness', much higher for aches, pains and fractures and appreciably higher for fevers and infections and gastro-intestinal problems (especially 'cholera'). There was much less reporting of colds, coughs and pulmonary problems, a category which includes less serious episodes.

Moving from the broad types to the more disaggregated categories, the lower table on page 333 shows the distribution of days of illness, in descending order of illness category. Four categories of illness account for over 43% of total days of illness, including stomach complaints (nearly 18%), fevers (over 11%), colds, coughs and sore throat (over 9%) and diarrhea, dysentery and 'cholera' (over 5%).

% DISTRIBUTION OF TYPES OF ILLNESS, 102 HHS 1981-2 AND BEFORE 1981

	1981-2			BEFORE 1981
Type of illness and symptoms	% of total days illness	% of total illness bouts	Av.days illness per bout	% of total serious illness
Gastro-intestinal	26.9	16.8	97	19.7
Skin Problems	15.8	9.7	98	3.5
Aches, Pains and Fractures	14.4	4.4	195	6.9
Colds, Coughs & Pulmonary	14.1	27.0	33	12.5
Fevers and Infections	14.0	31.9	26	38.8
Other, including eye, blood and heart problems	14.8	10.2	87	18.7
TOTAL %	100%	100%	60	100%
TOTAL NO.	23,001	382	60	289

% OF TOTAL DAYS ILLNESS, 102 HHs JANUARY 1981 TO FEBRUARY 1982

ILLNESS OR COMPLAINT	% OF TOTAL DAYS ILLNESS	ILLNESS OR COMPLAINT	% OF TOTAL DAYS ILLNESS
Stomach problems	17.6	Measles	1.0
Fever (Bukhar)	11.2	Other fever	0.9
Cold, cough, sore throat	9.4	Filaria	0.8
Diarrhea, dysentery, 'cholera'	5.3	Flu, pneumonia	0.8
Eye complaints	4.8	Blotchy skin (Adangi)	0.8
Chest & leg complaints	4.0	Asthma	0.8
Arm, elbow, hand	3.9	Ear problems	0.8
Scabies (Khajuli)	3.8	Urinary troubles	0.8
Eczema, rashes, pimples (Dane)	3.8	Other gastric trouble	0.5
Leg, knee, foot	3.7	Whooping cough, other pulmonary	0.4
TB	2.8	Toothache	*
Boils, ulcers (Phoora)	2.8	Other skin troubles	*
Liver complaints	2.7	Other illness	1.9
Bone aches and pains (Bai)	2.7	TOTAL	100.0
Skin disease (Cherum Rog)	2.6	TOTAL DAYS ILLNESS	23,001
Blood complaints	2.0		
Other fevers	1.9		
Heart complaints	1.8		
Leprosy	1.8		
Diabetes	1.6		

* Less than 0.1%

Gastro-intestinal problems

More than a quarter of all days and a sixth of all illness bouts were put down to gastro-intestinal problems, especially 'stomach trouble' (peth ka taklif or shikayat). Other forms of gastric problem included dysentery (pechish or penchees), liver (jigar) trouble (including anao bati), problems with urination (peshab), dehydration (sukka rog or bimari) and nine cases of so-called 'cholera', a term often used loosely to refer to dysentery or diarrhea. The remaining cases were vomiting and sickness (palti), diarrhea (dast), stomach worms (peth ka keera), wind ('gas') and mouth ulcers, possibly stomatitis (muha). The number of cases described specifically as diarrhea seems obviously too low and raises questions about under-reporting, particularly for women and children. The average duration of a gastro-intestinal problem was surprisingly long: 97 days. The most commonly mentioned forms of serious gastric problem which occurred before 1981 were 'cholera' and 'stomach trouble'.

Skin problems

About a sixth of illness days and a tenth of illness bouts were due to skin problems, especially phoora (boils, ulcers or abscesses), scabies and skin rashes ('dane', possibly eczema?). The single case of leprosy in the sample was probably one of two in the village, though the stigma and fear of leprosy obviously affects reporting. Other problems included brown and white blotches (adangi), phoora in conjunction with a swollen knee (locally diagnosed as filaria) and being 'cooked' (pukgea, probably also phoora). Skin problems lasted an average of 98 days per bout but scabies, dane, cherum rog, leprosy and adangi lasted much longer. Very few household heads mentioned skin problems as a serious illness afflicting household members before 1981 but this was probably partly because most were not regarded as a serious illness.

Aches, pains and fractures

About a seventh of illness days but only about 4% of illness bouts arose from aches, pains and fractures. In other words, these ailments lasted a very long time and the average was 195 days, longer than for any illness category. Bai or serdi hawa (cold wind, presumably rheumatism) continued for an average of 309 days and problems affecting parts of the upper limb lasted 225 days. Nearly 7% of previous illness reported involved aches, pains and fractures, including one fractured skull.

Colds, coughs and pulmonary problems

About a seventh of illness days and over a quarter of illness bouts arose from colds, coughs and pulmonary problems. The table shows that there was a bewildering variety of terms, including khansi (cough), serdi or zukham (cold) and these terms were sometimes suffixed with bukhar (fever). The reporting of this category was certainly inflated by the timing of the survey in January and February, a time of year when it can be bitterly cold, especially at night and when poverty and/or ignorance and carelessness lead many villagers (and especially children) to be very underprotected against the cold. The average duration of a bout in this category was relatively short (33 days) but the two cases of TB and the one case of bronchitis lasted 223 and 135 days respectively. The most frequent sub-category was serdi-zukham, the common cold which lasted for the shortest time (12 days). Complaints involving a cough lasted for nearly three times as long, or even longer. Asthma and pneumonia lasted 90 and 60 days respectively.

Whereas colds, coughs and pulmonary problems were the most commonly reported forms of illness for 1981-2 (with 27% of total bouts), they comprised only 12.5% of previous illness: mostly pneumonia, jakra (influenza or pneumonia) and common cold.

Fevers and infections

None of the broad categories are very mutually exclusive and this applies particularly to fevers and infections. About a seventh of illness days and nearly a third of illness bouts fell into that category. Bukhar accounted for 66% of both days and of illness within this section and the rest were mostly 'fever-cold', choti chechuk (measles or chicken pox), pil pau (filaria) or joori bukhar (malaria). These illnesses were relatively shortlived, averaging only 26 days each. The commonest earlier serious illnesses were 42% for bukhar and 29% for chechuk (smallpox up to its eradication in India by about 1974 and also used to refer to measles and chicken pox thereafter).

Other illness

Remaining forms of illness refer to only 15% of illness days and 10% of bouts. The commonest cases were eye problems (including blindness), anemia, heart disease, diabetes, ear problems (including deafness), menstrual problems (certainly under-investigated and under-reported) and injuries (involving a fall, a cut or damage from physical assault). Very few psychological problems were reported but again these were not investigated with much vigour. They include one case of possession by a ghost (15 days) and cases of daura or mirg (hysteria, fits or epilepsy).

Total Incidence of Illness

Altogether, taking the 582 members of the 102 households, 382 bouts of illness were reported for 338 persons (58%), who had experienced illness in the previous 13 or 14 months (maximum 420 days). A total of 23,001 days of illness were reported, implying an average of about 39 days per household member or 68 days per member who had been ill. There was an average of 0.66 illness bouts per household member and 1.1 bouts per sick member.

Incidence of Illness among PHC Patients

The table shows incidence of illness for those who attended the government outpatient clinic at Suratganj Primary Health Centre, four kilometres south of Basauli, between April 1981 and March 1982. Many members of the Basauli sample frequented this PHC (inter alia) and there is thus some overlap, albeit small because the Basauli sample comprised a very small fraction of total patients who travelled from within a fairly wide area to use the PHC. The table on page 338 compares the distribution of types of morbidity between the two populations but differences in terminology serve to obscure the comparison. The PHC doctor, a fully qualified MBBS, (or sometimes his compounder assistant) used official medical terms in the register. They were often working under pressure, seeing many patients in quick succession and there was a tendency to write a rapid diagnosis (sometimes illegible), which included such standard and oft-repeated terms as URTI ('Upper Respiratory Tract Infection'), fever and PUO ('Pyrexia of Unknown Origin'). Without impugning the competence of PHC doctors in India, it has to be said that some diagnoses couched in such terms (especially the more ritualised rigmarole such as the above) are not necessarily any more reliable than those of mature and experienced villagers.

The PHC registers showed that there had been 16,024 patient-visits during 1981-2. At least 1,772 (11%) of these visits involved patients with more than one illness or set of symptoms. The total number of patients (as distinct from patient-visits) cannot be calculated because the copies made from the registers concentrated on age, sex and diagnosis. Without names it is impossible to monitor return visits and, even with the original registers, the similarity of names and also illegibility would make the task less than easy. By far the commonest categories were bronchitis and pneumonia (including URTI) which accounted for nearly 23% of visits. Colds, coughs and sore throats involved a further 17% and no other category included more than a tenth (diarrhea 9% and fever 9%).

Comparison with the village sample reveals a much higher reference to the vague term fever in Basauli. The proportion of colds, coughs and sore throats in the village was somewhat higher than that for URTI in the PHC. Stomach pain, wind and vomiting was reported nearly twice as often by the village sample but combination of this category with diarrhea and 'cholera' makes the difference between Basauli and Suratganj much smaller. Pain in limb or back was much more common in Basauli, as were boils, ulcers and abscesses. The proportions of eye or ear trouble, dysentery, skin diseases and cuts and wounds were almost identical in Basauli and Suratganj. Filaria was mentioned much more often in the village, raising questions about villagers' diagnosis of the disease. The incidence of anemia or other blood troubles was lower in Basauli and this probably reflects the lack of interviewing of women and also lower consciousness of this problem

DISEASES + SYMPTOMS OF PATIENTS ATTENDING PHC, SURATGANJ, APRIL 1981-MARCH 1982

DISEASE OR SYMPTOM	NO. OF PATIENT VISITS	% OF TOTAL	OTHER ILLNESS OR SYMPTOM	NO. OF PATIENT VISITS	% OF TOTAL
ACUTE BRONCHITIS	4015	22.6	JAUNDICE	41	0.2
UPPER RESPIRATORY TRACT INFECTION	3074	17.3	WHOOPING COUGH	40	0.2
DIARRHEA (Dast)	1666	9.4	BACKACHE	33	0.2
FEVER	990	5.6	PREGNANCY	29	0.2
PYREXIA OF UNKNOWN ORIGIN (PUO)	524	2.9	PEPTIC ULCER	28	0.2
ANEMIA	503	2.8	SCIATICA	25	0.1
ABSCESS	447	2.5	LEUCORRHEA	24	0.1
DYSENTERY (Penchees)	430	2.4	PAIN IN LEG	23	0.1
OTITIS MEDIA	336	1.9	DOG BITE	22	0.1
OTHER DIGESTIVE DISEASES	327	1.8	PAIN IN CHEST	22	0.1
CONJUNCTIVITIS	297	1.7	BURNS	20	0.1
DERMATITIS	268	1.5	BLEEDING	19	0.1
INJURY	254	1.4	HEPATITIS	19	0.1
PAIN IN ABDOMEN	227	1.3	ECZEMA	17	0.1
TOOTH CARIES, TOOTHACHE OR LOOSE TOOTH	207	1.2	OTALGIA	17	0.1
TB IN LUNG	176	1.0	STOMATITIS	17	0.1
MULTIPLE ABSCESS	167	1.0	GLANDULAR TROUBLE	15	0.1
OTHER ILLNESS OR SYMPTOM (see below)	2356	13.2	TB IN ABDOMEN	14	0.1
SECONDARY ILLNESS OR SYMPTOM 1	1033	5.8	ESNOFILIA	12	0.1
SECONDARY ILLNESS OR SYMPTOM 2	269	1.5	PILES	12	0.1
ENTRY IN REGISTER ILLEGIBLE	230	1.3	PLEURISY	11	0.1
TOTAL ILLNESSES + SYMPTOMS	17,796	100	URETHRITIS	11	0.1
			SNAKEBITE	10	0.1
TOTAL PATIENT-VISITS	16,024		DYSPEPSIA	9	*
PATIENT-VISITS WITH 2+ SYMPTOMS	1772		DEHYDRATION	8	*
TOTAL PATIENTS	NK		HYPERTENSION	8	*
			MEASLES	8	*
DETAILS OF OTHER ILLNESSES OR SYMPTOMS			NEPHRITIS	8	*
ASTHMA	135	0.8	GENERAL WEAKNESS	7	*
ARTHRITIS	119	0.7	PAIN IN HAND	7	*
HEADACHE	113	0.6	HYPERACIDITY	5	*
FILARIA	77	0.4	NAUSEA	5	*
MEDICAL LEGAL CASE	72	0.4	PHLEBITIS	5	*
ASCARIASIS	64	0.4	MENTAL DISTURBANCE	4	*
GLOSSITIS	64	0.4	RINGWORM	4	*
WOUND	63	0.3	WORM	4	*
TONSILITIS	62	0.3	SWELLING	3	*
INDIGESTION	60	0.3	CHICKEN POX	2	*
BODYACHE	58	0.3	LEPROSY	2	*
PNEUMONIA	57	O.3	ULCER	2	*
PAIN	55	0.3	CHOLERA	1	*
VOMITING	53	0.3	TB IN GLAND	1	*
ENTERIC FEVER	47	0.3			
SCABIES	45	0.3			
TYPHOID	45	0.3	TOTAL OTHER ILLNESS	2356	13.2
NEURITIS	42	0.2			

* Less than 0.1% of total.

NB May 1982 substituted for missing May 1981 data.

% REPORTED ILLNESS, BASAULI AND PATIENT-VISITS, SURATGANJ PHC 1981-2

ILLNESS	% OF TOTAL ILLNESS BOUTS BASAULI	% OF PATIENT -VISITS SURATGANJ	% OF TOTAL ILLNESS BOUTS HHHs BASAULI	AV. DAYS ILLNESS TO DATE PER BOUT, HHHs
FEVER	25.5	9.4	26.7	3 to 32
COLD, COUGH OR SORE THROAT	23.9	17.3(URTI)	16.4	14
STOMACH PAIN, WIND OR VOMITING	9.3	4.8*	11.2	618
BOILS, ULCERS OR ABSCESSES	5.9	3.5*	5.2	39
DYSENTERY	3.0	2.4	2.6	728?
EYE OR EAR TROUBLE	3.0	3.7	3.4	168
CUTS + WOUNDS	2.7	1.8	1.7	12
'CHOLERA'	2.3	5.2	8	
DIARRHEA	2.3	9.4*	5.2	233
PAIN IN LIMB OR BACK	1.8	0.3	6.0	177 to 335
CHEST OR RIB TROUBLE	1.6	1.0	1.7	374
MEASLES	1.6	Under 0.1		
FILARIA	1.4	0.4	2.6	53
MALARIA	1.4			
BRONCHITIS OR PNEUMONIA	1.1	22.9*		(135)
RHEUMATISM	1.1		0.9	365
SCABIES	1.1	0.3		
OTHER SKIN DISEASES	0.9	2.1	2.6	854 to 3468
VOMITING	(0.9)	(0.3)	(60?)	
ANEMIA OR BLOOD TROUBLE	0.5	2.8	1.7	70
HEART TROUBLE	0.5		1.7	157
OTHER ILLNESS	9.1	17.9*	5.2	
TOTAL ILLNESS	100%	100%	100%	
TOTAL ILLNESS BOUTS OR VISITS	439	17,796 VISITS	116	
TOTAL PERSONS	577	NA	102	
AV. BOUTS PER TOTAL PERSONS	0.76	NA	1.14	
NO. OF PERSONS WITH NO ILLNESS	245		19	
% PERSONS WITH NO ILLNESS	42%		19%	
AV. BOUTS PER SICK PERSON	1.32		1.40	

The Basauli sample survey was done in Jan-Feb 1982 and refers to illness between 1 January 1981 and Jan-Feb. 1982.
The data on Suratganj PHC refers to outpatients who were registered as having visited between 1 April 1981 and 31 March 1982. (May 1982 data has been used as a substitute for May 1981, since the register for May 1981 was missing.)
URTI Upper Respiratory Tract Infection.

in the village than in medical circles. The incidence of bronchitis was reported to be only 1.1% of total illness in the sample households, compared with 22.9% in the PHC. Clearly, these two diseases and especially the more common bronchitis were being reported in other less specific terms such as fever and cold, cough and sore throat. Malaria comprised 1.4% of village illness and was not listed at all in Suratganj. No doubt some was disguised under the reporting of 'fever'. Measles amounted to 1.6% in Basauli, even though the MO himself had commented that the village's unusually dispersed physical layout was not conducive to the rapid spread of infectious diseases. In fact few cases of measles cropped up at Suratganj. Similarly, rheumatism amounted to 1.1% of illness in the village but none is mentioned in the PHC records.

The comparison reveals considerable discrepancy between disease distribution in the two populations. These cannot be fully explained but contributory factors include the relative affluence and possibly better health of a roadside village like Basauli, its dispersed layout of housing, the possible selection of the PHC for treatment of certain types of symptoms and the preference of private and/or traditional medical practitioners for others. One would expect a higher proportion of more serious illness in the PHC profile and the strikingly higher reporting of bronchitis or pneumonia (23% at Suratganj compared with only 1% in Basauli) provides a rather extreme confirmation of this. The differences remain a worry.

Position in Household and Duration of Total Illness

STATUS IN HOUSEHOLD AND AVERAGE AGGREGATE DAYS OF ILLNESS PER PERSON, 102 HHs JAN. 1981 - FEB.1982

AGGREGATE DAYS ILL	HH HEADS		WIVES OF HHHs	ADULT SONS 1+2	MINOR SONS 1+2	MINOR DAUGHTER 1	OTHER MALES	OTHER FEMALES	OTHER MALES	OTHER FEMALES INCL. DAUGHTER 2	TOTAL HOUSEHOLD	
	M	F	F	M	M	F	M	F	M	F	No.	%
AGE	16+	16+	16+	16+	0-15	0-15	0-15	0-15	16+	16+		
					APPROXIMATE % OF COLUMN TOTAL							
0	20		37	40	46	46	59	53	50	46	245	42
1-7	7		11	9	17	22	11	19	9	10	71	12
8-14	17		11	23	10	5	11	4	12	9	65	11
15-30	17	38	17	15	16	16	15	15	9	14	91	16
31-90	12	25	9	6	5	3	5	5	12	13	48	8
91-365	15	12	11	4	5	3		3	6	5	37	6
366-420	13	25	4	4	2	5		1		3	25	4
31+	(39)	(62)	(24)	(13)	(11)	(11)	(5)	(9)	(19)	(21)	(110)	(19)
TOTAL NO. OF HH MEMBERS	95	8	75	53	63	37	66	75	32	78	582	100
TOTAL DAYS ILL	8765	1215	3416	1565	1422	1317	502	1296	676	2429	22603	
AV.DAYS ILL PER PERSON	92	152	46	30	23	36	8	17	21	31	T 39 M 42 F 36	
RANK ORDER OF AV. DAYS ILL	2	1	3	6	7	4	10	9	8	5		

The table shows the distribution of aggregate days of illness(es) per person for different age, sex and kin categories. About 42% of all household members in the sample had not been ill in the previous 14 months and 12% had only been ill for up to 7 days. A further 11% had been ill for 8 to 14 days and 16% for 15 to 30 days. Altogether, nearly 19% of the sample had been ill for more than 30 days, including 8% for 31 to 90 days, 6% for 91 to 365 days and 4% for 366 to the maximum of 420 days. The average duration per person was 39 days. The highest average duration was 152 days in the case of eight female household heads, who were mostly elderly widows. The next highest was 92 days, for the 92 male household heads. Average duration of illness was much shorter for other categories in the household which were, in descending order: wives of household heads (average 46 days), minor daughters (36), other adult females (31), first and second adult sons (30), first and second minor sons (23), other adult males (21), other female minors (17) and other male minors (8).

The next table shows that, though the overall average duration for male illness exceeded that for female by 20%, comparison of males and females of similar age and status within the household reveals a very different picture.

AVERAGE DAYS AGGREGATE ILLNESS PER PERSON, BY STATUS IN HOUSEHOLD

SEX	HH HEAD	WIFE OF HHH	ADULT SONS 1+2	OTHER ADULTS	ADULT SONS + OTHER ADULTS	ALL ADULTS 16+	MINOR SONS 1+2 OR DAUGHTERS	OTHER MINORS	TOTAL MINORS	TOTAL HH MEMBERS
M	92	-	30	21	(26)	(61)	23	8	(15)	42
F	152	46	-	31	(31)	(44)	36	17	(23)	35
T	97	46	30	28	(29)	(53)	27	13	(19)	29
NO. OF PERSONS	103	75	53	110	(163)	(341)	100	141	(241)	582
FEMALE AS % OF MALE	165	50		148	(119)	(72)	157	212	(151)	83
FEMALE 101+% OF MALE	*			*	*		*	*	*	

For persons of roughly equivalent status within the household, females experienced greater average length of illness: 19 percent longer for other adults, 51 percent longer for all minors and 112 percent longer for other minors (ie. excluding the first two sons and all daughters of the household head). The crucial difference which produces an apparent overall excess of morbidity among males is the much greater duration of illness reported by household heads for themselves, compared with what they mentioned for their wives. This is likely to reflect both their own (male) self-centredness, design faults in the questionnaire (which also did not directly address or seek out specifically female illnesses) and the probable reluctance or embarrassment of most male household heads to discuss gynaecological, menstrual and other 'women's problems' with male interviewers.

To allow a very rough comparison with morbidity in England and Wales, Townsend (1988:64) has used OPCS data which shows that working males were absent from work due to illness or injury for an average of 9.1 days in 1971 and 8.4 days in 1972. The highest absence from work was by the lowest category, the unskilled manual workers (18.4 days in 1971). Male adults in Basauli were reported to have had an average of 61 days illness in up to 14 months and thus an equivalent of about 52 days in a 12-month period. On some (probably many?) of these days Basauli males would have had to do some work. The poorer household heads reported an average of 97 days of illness, implying about 83 days in a 12-month period. Even assuming that poorer household heads worked on at least half the days they were ill, their rate of sickness absence in 1981-2 would still be more than double that of the unskilled manual worker in England and Wales in 1971. There is no indication whether Basauli had experienced untypical morbidity during 1981-2 (though there is no evidence of any widespread epidemics).

The table shows the distribution of population and of illness days between six broad demographic categories, based on age and sex. The index of incidence of illness shows how proportionate the share of illness was to the share in total population. For example, males over 60 comprised 3.1% of the sample population but endured 7.1 percent of total illness days. This gives them a Total Illness Incidence Index of 229, the highest. Older men were ill for 90 days, more than twice the average:

POPN. CATEGORY	OLD MEN	OLD WOMEN	MEN	WOMEN	GIRLS	BOYS	TOTAL
ILLNESS INDEX 1981-2	229	203	142	115	54	38	100
AV. DAYS ILL 1981-2	90	80	57	46	21	15	40
SERIOUS ILLNESS INDEX,PRE-1981	197	187	141	89	46	85	100
AV. SERIOUS ILLNESSES, PRE-1981	1.00	0.94	0.72	0.45	0.23	0.43	0.51

TYPE OF ILLNESS, AGE + SEX: PERCENTAGE DISTRIBUTION, INDEX OF INCIDENCE AND AVERAGE DAYS ILLNESS PER PERSON, 102 HHS, BASAULI 1981-2

TYPE OF ILLNESS	MALE 0-15	FEMALE 0-15	MALE 16-60	FEMALE 16-60	MALE 61+	FEMALE 61+	TOTAL %	TOTAL PERSONS
% OF POPULATION	21.7	19.9	27.6	24.6	3.1	3.1	100	577
DAYS ILLNESS AS % OF TOTAL DAYS IN ILLNESS CATEGORY								DAYS
GASTRIC	1.6	13.7	53.7	19.9	8.7	2.5	100	5934
ACHES	1.3		19.4	69.1	10.2		100	4108
OTHER	15.2	5.5	49.6	10.5	0.9	18.4	100	3344
COLDS, COUGHS	10.7	13.8	22.7	33.6	0.9	18.3	100	3317
SKIN	14.3	10.6	44.4	14.9		15.7	100	3258
FEVERS	13.7	22.2	39.5	18.4	3.8	2.4	100	2912
TOTAL 1981-2	8.2	10.7	39.3	28.4	7.1	6.3		22,873
(TOTAL PRE-1981 SERIOUS ILLNESS)	(18.4)	(9.2)	(38.8)	(21.8)	(6.1)	(5.8)		294 Cases of illness

TYPE OF ILLNESS, AGE + SEX: PERCENTAGE DISTRIBUTION, INDEX OF INCIDENCE AND AVERAGE DAYS ILLNESS PER PERSON, 102 HHS, BASAULI 1981-2 (continued)

TYPE OF ILLNESS	MALE 0-15	FEMALE 0-15	MALE 16-60	FEMALE 16-60	MALE 61+	FEMALE 61+	TOTAL %	TOTAL
INDEX OF INCIDENCE OF ILLNESS								
% OF TOTAL DAYS ILL IN ILLNESS CATEGORY AS % OF POPULATION SHARE. 100 = illness incidence proportionate to population share								
GASTRIC	7	69	195	81	281	80	100	
ACHES	6		70	281	329		100	
OTHER	70	28	180	43	29		100	
COLDS, COUGHS	49	69	82	137	29	594	100	
SKIN	66	53	161	61	506	590	100	
FEVERS	63	112	143	75	123	77	100	
TOTAL	38	54	142	115	229	203	100	
RANKING OF INDEX	6	5	3	4	1	2		
DAYS TOTAL ILLNESS	1872	2445	8995	6505	1611	1440		22,873
NO. OF PERSONS	125	115	159	142	18	18		577 Persons
AVERAGE DAYS ILLNESS PER PERSON								DAYS
TOTAL	15.0	21.3	56.6	45.8	89.5	80.0		39.6
GASTRIC	0.7	7.1	20.0	8.3	28.6	8.3		10.3
ACHES	0.4	0.0	5.0	20.0	23.3	0.0		7.1
OTHER	4.1	1.6	10.4	2.5	1.7	34.1		5.8
COLDS, COUGHS	2.8	4.0	4.7	7.8	1.7	33.7		5.7
SKIN	3.7	3.0	9.3	3.4	28.3	0.0		5.6
FEVERS	3.2	5.6	7.2	3.8	6.2	3.8		5.0

The likelihood of inflated or disproportionately full reporting of their own illness by household heads needs to be borne in mind and this has almost certainly led to relative overstatement of illness among adult males. In view of this, the fact that indices for certain categories of illness among adult males fall below 100 is of enhanced interest. Absence of data on some 'female illnesses' must deflate total illness among women but should not affect most of the indices for illness categories very much. The highest index for boys was in the case of 'other illness' (70), which includes accidents, injuries, bites and burns, ie. events to which the more active young male is usually more susceptible. The highest index is 594, for colds, coughs and pulmonary problems among old women. Boys had relatively high incidence of other illness, skin problems and fevers, considering their general lack of morbidity. Girls were relatively prone to fevers, gastric problems and colds, coughs and pulmonary problems. Men had high indices for all categories of illness except colds, coughs and pulmonary problems but the indices for gastric problems and 'other illness' were their highest. For women, only the indices for aches and pains (281) and for colds, coughs and pulmonary problems exceeded 100. Indices ranged very widely for both old men and old women, partly reflecting the small numbers involved.

The patterns for cases of serious illness before 1981 show the same rank order of demographic categories, except that previous serious illness of boys was almost twice that of girls. This was true for all categories of illness: the index for boys was highest for colds, coughs and pulmonary problems but the boy-girl differential was most marked for gastric problems (the very opposite of the pattern for 1981-2).

Method Problems in studying Morbidity

Morbidity is notoriously more difficult to study even than mortality, especially in LDCs. The survey conducted in Basauli has many flaws, some inevitable, others, in retrospect, distinctly avoidable. These include: (1) the choice of an excessively long period (up to 14 months) to record incidence of illness, imposing an unrealistic burden on respondents' memory and time; (2) no guidance on deciding criteria for the duration of illness eg. in terms of days off work, in bed or incapacitated, in pain, 'under the doctor' or whatever; (3) by no means consistent prompting on what constitutes 'serious' illness, in the question on earlier illness, before 1981; (4) usually much more detail and incidence of illness reported by household heads (or, in a few cases, 'proxies' for them) on their own health problems than on those of other household members; (5) insufficient attention to the definition of household and the criteria for deciding on membership of particular households (see Jeffery 1989). (This could have quite a serious effect on inter-household comparison of health but is not likely to have so much effect on health differences between income and class categories.); (6) the relative absence of information on illness which is exclusive to women, which is mainly explained by the two interviewers and most of the interviewees being men; (7) the length of the period varies from 365 to 420 days, because of the timing of the interviews over the first two months of 1982. No attempt has been made to adjust for this up to nearly 15 percent difference, mainly because the average difference is likely to be 7 percent and the survey is not expecting to operate to such fine limits of accuracy on length of illness; and (8) overstating of winter illness (especially colds, coughs and sore throats) because of the timing of interviews in January and February.

Just as the PCI data needed to be weighted to allow for difference in age and sex composition of the household, so the data on days illness in the household really should have a similar adjustment. This need to allow for variation in composition is indeed greater, because of the obvious fact that respondents (who were nearly all male household heads) were usually more forthcoming about their own illnesses than about those of their household members, perhaps particularly their female relatives.

SEASONALITY OF ILLNESS

The northern Gangetic plain is the home to three seasons with very contrasting climates:

1. JARA Winter: usually from October to March.
2. GURUMI or GARMI Summer: April to searing June, when temperatures occasionally reach around 45°C or 113°F.
   A very hot and unpleasant wind called the loo blows in March and April.
3. BARSAAT The rainy season or Monsoon: from mid-June or early July to September.

The sharp differences in weather help generate major seasonal variations in some types of illness and, without falling into an environmental determinist or 'tropical' reductionist theory of disease, it has to be recognised that India's sometimes harsh and extreme climate must inevitably play a mediating role in the relationship between nongeographical factors and ill health. A key question then is whether, for example, seasonal peaking of illness in the wet season (especially in wettest July and August) serves to increase or decrease social and economic gradients of illness.

Sample respondents named the Vikram samvat month when illness began for 364 out of the 439 episodes of sickness reported. Since Vikram samvat months overlap two English months, for consistency of conversion it has been assumed that onset occurred in the first half of the Indian month. This is obviously an unrealistic assumption and data will be more reliable for two adjacent months than for single months.

Onsets of ill health in the Basauli sample peaked in Sawan, ie. from the second half of July through to the first half of August. The highest attendance and highest number of symptoms diagnosed and treated at the nearest health centre was in August. The trough for onsets was February 1981 and for PHC treatment was January - February 1982. (The relatively high onsets in January -February 1982 was due to the timing of the survey and included mainly minor illness anyway. Comparing the January - February figures for 1982 with those for 1981, there was a 55 percent increase in reporting of illness for 1982 and most of this excess was for coughs, colds and other pulmonary problems and the rest was for 'other illness'.)

The daily registers of outpatient visits to Suratganj PHC provide more accurate and reliable data on month of treatment of 17,796 symptoms or illnesses diagnosed during 16,024 visits by patients from April 1981 to March 1982. Though the PHC data are more reliable than the sample survey, the monthly and seasonal distribution will still be distorted if certain individual patients made a disproportionate or 'unreasonable' number of visits to the PHC. Thus an apparent peak of 9 visits in March out of an annual total of 17 eczema patient-visits could refer to a single patient and give an entirely misleading impression of seasonality.

% DISTRIBUTION OF MONTH OF ONSET OF ILLNESS, 102 HOUSEHOLDS, JANUARY 1981 TO 23 FEBRUARY 1982

ENGLISH MONTH 1981	J	F	M	A	M	J	JY	A	S	O	N	D	1982 J	F	MONTH TOTAL	TOTAL NO. OF OF ONSETS OF ILL-NESS
	JARA I			GURUMI I			BARSAAT I			JARA I						
APPROXIMATE VIKRAM SAMVAT MONTH	MAGH	PHAGUN	CHETH	VAISAKH	JETH	ASAR	SAWAN	BHADON	KUAR	KHATIK	AGAHAN	PUSH	MAGH	PHAGUN	NK	
ILLNESS	APPROX % OF ROW TOTAL															
Stomach problems	9		9	9	4	4	17	13		9	4	4	4	9	4	23
Dysentery + Diarrhea	3	10	3	10	10	7	14	14	7	3	3	7	3		3	29
TOTAL GASTRIC	5	7	5	9	9	5	19	12	3	5	3	5	3	3	5	58
TOTAL ACHES + PAINS	12	12			12	12	12						25		12	8
Khansi-Zukham	10		3		3			7		10	14	14	17		21	29
Serdi-Zukham	7		2	2		5	5	5	7	7	14	2	17	12	14	42
Khansi-Zukham + Bukhar-Serdi		5		5		5	14	5	5	9	14	9	18	9	5	22
Jakra, Najla	18		9			9			9	18	9		9		18	11
TOTAL PULMONARY	8	1	3	2	1	4	4	5	5	10	12	6	19	6	14	113
Khajuli (Scabies)									100							6
Phoora (Boils)	8		4	8	8	8	4	25		8		8	4	8	4	24
TOTAL SKIN	10		3	5	5	11	3	16	18	5	5	5	5	5	3	38
Bukhar, incl. Bukhar-Zukham	2	3	4	5	3	1	16	11	10	13	12	4	3		12	93
Choti Chechuk	33					22			33	11						9
Joori Bukhar (Malaria)				43		14			29		14					7
TOTAL FEVER	4	3	3	7	3	3	14	9	12	12	12	3	3		10	116
Eye problems	14						14					29		43		7
Blood problems				25			25		25	25						4
Injury				11		11		11			11	11	11	33		9
TOTAL OTHER ILLNESS	6			10	3	6	13	3	3	6	3	10	6	23	6	31
% TOTAL ILLNESS	6	2	3	5	4	5	10	9	8	9	9	5	9	5	10	364
No.OF ILLNESS BOUTS	24	9	11	20	13	18	38	31	30	32	33	19	33	18	35	364
% OF AV. BOUTS IN AV. MONTH (329÷14 = AV.23.5 ILLNESSES PER MONTH)	INDEX 102 *	38	47	85	55	77	162 * *	132 *	128 *	136 *	140 *	81 *	140	(77)	-	100 (23.5)

% OF AV.VISITS IN AV. MONTH SURATGANJ PHC	J	F	M	A	M	J	JY	A	S	O	N	D	J	F	M	
	NA INDEX	NA	NA	99	(93) see note**	104	118	154	107	112	85	100	65	68	81	16,024 patient-visits

**The Suratganj PHC % for May refers to May 1982 because the register for May 1981 was missing.

MONTHLY VARIATION IN PATIENT SYMPTOMS FOR COMMON ILLNESSES, PRIMARY HEALTH CENTRE SURATGANJ, 1981-2

ILLNESS AS % OF MONTHLY TOTAL SYMPTOMS														
		1981									1982			% OF YEAR
ENGLISH MONTH		A	M(1982)	J	Jy	A	S	O	N	D	J	F	M	TOTAL
VIKRAM SAMVAT MONTH		CHETH		JETH		SAWAN		KUAR		AGAHAN		MAGH		
			VAISAKH		ASAR		BHADON		KHATIK		PUSH		PHAGUN	
SYMPTOMS ILLNESS	TOTAL NO. WITH SYMPTOMS													
ACUTE BRONCHITIS	4015	22	15	24	20	29	21	24	24	29	19	29	10	23
UPPER RESPIRATORY TRACT INFECTION	3074	24	15	12	13	14	10	16	16	23	28	21	22	17
DIARRHEA	1666	10	20	9	8	7	8	9	8	7	10	7	9	9
FEVER	990	4	9	4	2	5	5	6	7	7	5	5	9	6
PYREXIA OF UNKNOWN ORIGIN	524	1	2	2	2	4	4	3	4	3	2	4	3	3
ANEMIA	503	2	2	3	6	4	3	4	2	2	1	1	2	3
ABSCESS	447	2	3	2	5	2	3	2	2	2	2	2	3	2
DYSENTERY	430	1	2	3	4	2	4	3	2	2	1	2	2	2
OTITIS MEDIA	336	2	1	2	2	2	4	2	1	1	2	2	2	2
OTHER DIGESTIVE	327	2	2	1	1	1	2	2	2	2	4	3	2	2
CONJUNCTIVITIS	297	1	1	2	5	4	2	*	1	1	*	*	1	2
DERMATITIS	268	1	1	2	4	2	1	1	2	1	*	2	1	2
INJURY	254	1	1	2	3	1	*	1	1	1	1	2	3	1
PAIN IN ABDOMEN	227	1	2	2	1	2	1	1	1	1	2	1	2	1
TOOTH PROBLEMS	227	1	1	1	1	1	1	2	2	1	2	1	2	1
TB LUNG	176	1	2	1	2	1	1	1	1	*	1	1	1	1
MULTIPLE ABSCESS	167	*	1	1	2	1	2	1	*	*	*	*	*	1
TOTAL	(13,928)													
OTHER ASSOCIATED SYMPTOM 1		5	6	5	6	6	5	6	8	6	6	5	6	6
OTHER ASSOCIATED SYMPTOM 2		1	2	2	2	1	1	2	2	1	1	2	2	2
% TOTAL SYMPTOMS		100	100	100	100	100	100	100	100	100	100	100	100	100
TOTAL NO. OF SYMPTOMS		1456	1627	1557	1774	2308	1586	1369	1358	1536	987	1016	1222	17,796
TOTAL PATIENT VISITS		1318	1431	1395	1571	2052	1426	NA	1141	1330	871	914	1076	16,024
PATIENTS WITH 2+ SYMPTOMS		138	196	162	203	256	160	NA	217	206	116	102	146	1772
TOTAL SYMPTOMS AS % MONTHLY AVERAGE INDEX (1483)		98	110	105	120 **	156 ** PEAK	107	92	92	104	67	69	82	100

* 0.5% or less

The next table shows which diseases or symptoms peaked in each successive month. It refers to *onset* of illness for Basauli and symptoms currently identified and treated at Suratganj. This table is meant to show as clearly as possible when different forms of illness peak rather than to demonstrate month by month incidence of every disease or symptom (which is shown in the earlier tables, for Basauli and for the nearby PHC). Distribution of onsets and/or incidence may give a misleading impression of cumulative illness and/or prevalence, especially if many episodes of illness last beyond the initial month.

There was daily variation in attendance of new and old patients at Suratganj PHC. This reveals considerable fluctuation within particular months, with a range from 35 to 127 patients in the busiest month of August. The average number per day from April 1981 to March 1982 was 44.5 but the patient load exceeded 100 on at least 9 days in the July - September peak period. The month with the highest daily average was August (66) and the lowest averages were January (34) and February (33).

Apart from monthly variation, there was also daily variation:

DAY	Av.Mon -Sat	Mon.	Tues.	Wed.	Thurs.	Fri.	Sat.	Sun.	Total
AV. PATIENTS DAILY APR.1981-MAR.1982	51	53	48	50	49	62 *	46	4	44.5
Comment		Market day				Market day	Half day	Emerg- encies only	

Fridays produced 21 percent more patients than the average working day (51 patients) because this was the main market day in Suratganj. Monday was also a market day and attracted slightly more than an average working day. There were least patients on Saturdays, when the MO usually left at lunch-time to go and join his family who lived in Lucknow. The PHC was normally closed on Sundays but a few emergency and other cases were seen either by the MO's assistant or by the MO, if his family had come to stay the weekend with him (in winter). Closer examination of the daily pattern reveals some anomalies, including some low attendances on Fridays and unusually high numbers on other days. These abnormalities are mostly attributable to variations in the weather, absence of the MO and/or his assistant and events in Suratganj which is the administrative headquarters for the block as well as being a market centre.

The number of outpatient cases seen at Suratganj had risen sharply since 1976:

		1976	1977	1978	1979	1980	Apr. 1981- Mar. 1982
OPD Cases	M	2326	4130	7184	7497	8246	
	F	2299	4202	5959	3387	4217	
	T	4625	8332	13,143	10,884	12,463	16,024
	%F	49.7	50.4	45.3	31.1	33.8	

Much of the increase appears to have been male patients and the female ratio seems, inexplicably, to have fallen from a half to a third of the total.

Overall, seasonal factors obviously do play an important part in illness causation and variation, especially for infectious, communicable and gastric complaints.

MONTHS WHEN GENERAL AND PARTICULAR ILLNESS ONSET OR TREATMENT PEAKED, BASAULI + SURATGANJ PHC 1981-2

ENGLISH + VIKRAM SAMVAT MONTH	% TOTAL ONSETS OF ILLNESS + ILLNESS ONSET INDEX, BASAULI AV. MONTH = 100	NO. OF ONSETS OF ILLNESS, BASAULI		SYMPTOMS FREQUENCY FOR COMMONEST DISEASES, PATIENTS AT SURATGANJ PHC		PHC SYMPTOMS AS % OF AV. MONTH, PLUS COMMENTS
1981 Jan. Light Rain				No information (see Jan. 1982)		NA
11. MAGH	6% 102	COLDS + COUGHS Measles Influenza	6 3 2			
Feb.				No information (see Feb. 1982)		NA HEALTHIEST MONTH?
12. PHAGUN	2% 38	Fevers	3			
Mar.				No information (see Mar. 1982		NA
1. CHETH	3%	FEVERS	4			
April Gurumi or hot season	47			UPPER RESPIRATORY TRACT INFECTION (URTI) ACUTE BRONCHITIS DIARRHEA Other Digestive Diseases SCABIES Leucorrhea Stomatitis	349 327 143 37 10 10 5	98
2. VAISAKH or TAPAN	5% 85	FEVERS Malaria	5 3			
May				FEVER DIARRHEA URTI Abscess Pain in Abdomen VOMITING	142 329 249 48 25 11	110 PHC data is for May 1982
3. JETH	4% 55	Fevers	3			
June				ACUTE BRONCHITIS Diarhhea 143; Anemia Dysentery 50; Dermatitis Conjunctivitis Pain in Abdomen Allergic Disorder Ascariasis	380 53 35 26 25 17 10	105
4. ASAR Barsaat or Monsoon Rains	5% 77	Varied				
July				ACUTE BRONCHITIS Diarrhea 144; ANEMIA ABSCESS 85; DYSENTERY CONJUNCTIVITIS DERMATITIS	364 98 73 81 68	120 SECOND MOST UNHEALTHY MONTH
5. SAWAN	10% 162	FEVERS GASTRIC	13 8			

Cont.

ENGLISH + VIKRAM SAMVAT MONTH	% + INDEX	No. OF ILLNESS ONSETS BASAULI	SYMPTOMS, SURATGANJ	% OF AV. MONTH
5. SAWAN			INJURY 46; OTITIS MEDIA 39 MULTIPLE ABSCESS 33 SNAKEBITE 8	
Aug.			ACUTE BRONCHITIS 661 URTI 329; DIARRHEA 165 FEVER 113; ANEMIA 89 CONJUNCTIVITIS 90; PUO 9 ABSCESS 51; DYSENTERY 46 Dermatitis 41 INJURY 33; Otitis Media 39 ASTHMA 27 Ascariasis 13; GLOSSITIS 12; JAUNDICE 9 Pneumonia 9; HEPATITIS 7	156 MOST UNHEALTHY MONTH
6. BHADON	9% 132	FEVERS 10 GASTRIC 7 BOILS + ABSCESSES 6 COLDS + COUGHS 5		
Sept.			ACUTE BRONCHITIS 336 Fever 83; OTITIS MEDIA 57 Pyrexia of Unknown Origin 69 DYSENTERY 62; Anemia 54 Abscess 49; ASTHMA 25 Multiple Abscess 35 Conjunctivitis 25 Scabies 9; Enteric Fever 8 ASCARIASIS 18; Filaria 11	107
7. KUAR Jara or winter	8% 128	FEVERS 8 SKIN DISEASES 7 Measles 3 Colds + Coughs 4		
Oct.			ACUTE BRONCHITIS 323 Anemia 52 Pyrexia of Unknown Origin 46 Otitis Media 32 ESNOFILIA 9 FILARIA 8	92 10 days Dashahra festival in Suratganj
8. KHATIK	9% 136	FEVERS 12 COLDS + COUGHS 8 Flu or Pneumonia 2		
Nov.			ACUTE BRONCHITIS 323 Fever 94 Pyrexia of Unknown Origin 48 Dermatitis 27 HEADACHE 14	92
9. AGAHAN	9% 140	COLDS + COUGHS 13 FEVERS 9		
Dec.			ACUTE BRONCHITIS 441 URTI 359 Fever 108 Pyrexia of Unknown Origin 44 Other Digestive Diseases 37 JAUNDICE 12	104
10. PUSH	5% 81	COLDS + COUGHS 7 Fevers 4 Eyes 2		
1982 Jan.			UPPER RESPIRATORY TRACT INFECTIONS (URTI) 277 OTHER DIGESTIVE DISEASES 39	67 HEALTHY except colds
11. MAGH	(9%) (140)	COLDS + COUGHS 16 WHOOPING COUGH 4 Fever 3		
Feb.			ACUTE BRONCHITIS 299 Other Digestive Diseases 34 Pneumonia 8	69 HEALTHIEST MONTH
12. PHAGUN	(5+%) (77+1)	COLDS + COUGHS 7 Eyes 3		
Mar.			FILARIA 15 URTI 268; Fever 110 INJURY 39; HEADACHE 18 PNEUMONIA 10 Bodyache 14; ECZEMA 9 Whooping Cough 7; Scabies 6	82
1. CHETH	NA NA			
TOTAL	100%	Episodes 364	Symptoms 17,796	100

N.B. Names of diseases in capitals indicate a very common disease in the month and/or a disease that peaks in that month (regardless of its relative incidence).

The most dangerous month, August, had around 60 percent more illness than the average month and about twice the morbidity of the healthiest months, February and January. Acknowledgement of the importance of seasonality should not be an excuse for downplaying social and economic factors: the poorer villagers are more vulnerable, inter alia, to seasonal hunger and malnutrition, to outdoor work in inclement weather, to contamination of well water, to lack of clothing and bedding in cold weather and to destruction or damage to housing by heavy rain. Finally, partly because of seasonal severities, the north Indian climate is in aggregate a tough regime for the human body and some of India's deficit in terms of life expectancy is no doubt attributable to the cumulative effect of years of harsh climate in an environment which is difficult anyway.

CONCLUSION

Mortality in Basauli over the past 40 years or so has been very high and it was higher for almost every indicator than for two villages in western UP. The infant mortality for the period from about 1941 to 1982 was at least 206 and even higher for females. Under-enumeration of female survivors can explain only part of this very high rate (nearly double that of the IMR in two villages in western UP). The IMR had fallen from 1965 onwards and was continuing to fall but in fact the divergence from western UP had actually increased. This is particularly significant, since the more recent data is much more reliable. For the period from 1970 to 1982 the IMR was still 164, slightly lower than the average for rural UP. The under 5 child mortality rate in Basauli was a cumulative 344 per 1000 total births for the 1941-82 period. Births per women aged 45 and over averaged at least 6.6 and was 7.6 for women aged 45 to 49. An average of over 3.7 of these children had died in stillbirth, child or adult death. Only 6.2 percent of the sample were aged 61 or more.

Villagers reported an average of 0.66 bouts of illness per person in the previous 13 or 14 months. Each bout lasted an average of 60 days and the average number of days illness per person was 39. However, 42 percent had experienced no illness and it was the remainder who averaged 1.1 bouts of illness and 68 days of ill health. Altogether, 23,001 days of illness were reported or the equivalent of 63 years of sickness. The most common illnesses were fevers and infections (32% of total bouts) followed by colds, coughs and pulmonary problems (27%), gastro-intestinal problems (17%), other illnesses (10%), skin problems (10%) and aches, pains and fractures (4%). In terms of days of sickness, gastro-intestinal problems accounted for by far the largest share (27% of total sickness days). The remaining five categories of illness each accounted for around 15 percent of total days of illness. Male adult morbidity was probably at least five times as high as that of working males in Britain. Persons over 60 suffered most illness (average 85 days), followed by males aged 16 to 60 (57 days), females aged 16 to 60 (46 days), then girls (21 days) and boys (15 days). Overall *reported* female morbidity was only 83 percent of that of males. It is possible that overall morbidity has been overstated but female morbidity somewhat underreported. About half the sample had experienced a serious illness before 1981.

8 Health inequalities in the village

This chapter examines the social distribution of mortality, physical size, morbidity, health expenditure and health care relative to need, between caste strata, income categories and classes, as well as between males and females. The analysis will focus on raw data for selected health indicators, indices relative to average performance and on gradients of inequality between socioeconomic categories. Patricia and Roger Jeffery, with Andrew Lyon, studied women and childbearing in two villages, Jhakri and Dharmnagri (JD) in Bijnor district, western UP, between 1982 and 1986. Jeffery (1989) provides valuable data, especially on child mortality, and thus allows some partial comparison and cross-checking with the Basauli data.

The table on pages 352-3 summarises the health standards of four caste strata and six income categories, in terms of indices for 12 indicators of nutrition, morbidity and mortality. Scores above 100 indicate below average performance and vice versa. Thus, rich high caste males, who have an index of 93 in deficiency of weight for weight, scored 7 percent above average. Approximate raw scores can be calculated by referring to the averages for actual measurements which are provided in the notes of this table and bottom rows of subsequent tables. The aggregate health index (in row 8 of each listing of indicators) is the average of the first seven indicators (and thus excludes male and female weights and heights).

The table on pages 354-5 shows *indices* of under 5 mortality for all babies born alive in the Basauli sample up to 1977, as well as disaggregations for the two periods, up to and after 1965. The average *rate* for the whole period was 371 deaths of children under the age of 5 per 1000 live births. The data show that the highest mortality index for the whole period occurred among Muslim females

(150), Muslims of both sexes (130), middle caste females (119) and Muslim males (116). The lowest were high caste males (80), followed by scheduled males (81), the scheduled of both sexes (87), middle caste males (92) and the high caste of both sexes (90). In the earlier period, scheduled females had the highest mortality index (158), followed by Muslim females (127) and middle

CASTE STRATUM, WEIGHTED PER CAPITA INCOME + MAJOR INDICES OF NUTRITION, MORTALITY + MORBIDITY (AV. = 100)

	RICH		F. RICH		UPPER MEDIUM		LOWER MEDIUM		POOR		VERY POOR		TOTAL		RICHER	POORER	P AS % OF R
Rs WTED PCI	1401-2500		1101-1400		951-1100		811-950		701-810		401-700				951+	401-950	R
HIGH CASTE	No.	Index	No.	Index	No.	Index	No.	Index	No.	Index	No.	Index	No.	Index	Index	Index	
INDICES ABOVE 100 INDICATE BELOW AVERAGE PERFORMANCE																	
MALE WT/HT*	8	93	18	98	7	92	5	108	7	101	1	110	46	98	96	104	109
FEMALE WT/HT	4	59	11	106	2	113	4	94	6	89			27	94	96	91	95
ALL WT/HT	26	98	5	96	8	98	6	102	5	101	1	110	51	99	98	102	104
CHILD DEATHS	42	82	22	154	11	145	21	66	22	93	0	0	118	100	112	80	71
DAYS ILL HHH	8	17	5	189	2	41	4	200	4	35	1	0	24	88	78	104	134
DAYS ILL WIFE	6	71	2	0	1	27	2	2	3	147	1	0	15	59	50	74	148
DAYS ILL ALL	59	115	25	102	11	52	17	115	19	52	4	5	135	95	104	74	71
HHs/AGGREGATE HEALTH INDEX	8	76	5	106	2	81	4	98	4	88	1	38	24	90	87	87	100
MALE WT	8	88	18	93	7	92	5	108	7	98	1	113	46	95	92	103	112
MALE HT	8	97	19	99	7	98	5	101	7	98	1	105	47	99	98	100	102
FEMALE WT	4	71	11	106	2	109	4	86	6	95			27	96	98	91	93
FEMALE HT	4	111	11	100	2	96	4	94	6	103			27	101	102	99	97
MIDDLE CASTE																	
MALE WT/HT	7	98	7	102	12	104	12	101	5	100	5	106	48	102	102	102	100
FEMALE WT/HT	1	106	5	105	8	105	4	95	2	101	2	106	22	103	105	99	94
ALL WT/HT	15	91	8	99	6	98	12	104	6	100	4	104	51	98	95	103	108
CHILD DEATHS	37	72	52	109	36	89	25	109	42	109	9	100	201	98	92	108	117
DAYS ILL HHH	8	122	8	72	9	100	5	23	7	78	2	285	39	94	98	88	90
DAYS ILL WIFE	5	186	6	174	7	180	5	49	5	22	2	0	30	120	180	30	16
DAYS ILL ALL	67	82	49	88	44	118	27	42	38	75	15	140	240	88	94	76	81
HHs/AGGREGATE HEALTH INDEX	8	108	8	107	9	113	5	75	7	84	2	120	39	100	109	86	79
MALE WT	7	95	7	100	12	103	13	109	4	102	5	105	48	105	100	107	107
MALE HT	7	98	7	100	12	100	13	102	4	102	5	101	48	101	99	102	103
FEMALE WT	1	103	4	106	8	103	4	98	2	102	2	107	21	103	104	101	97
FEMALE HT	1	97	5	99	8	97	4	103	2	101	2	102	22	99	98	102	104
MUSLIM																	
MALE WT/HT			3	97	3	95	8	96	5	113	4	106	23	101	96	103	108
FEMALE WT/HT			1	103			2	106	2	117	5	96	10	103	(103)	103	(100)
ALL WT/HT			4	98	3	109	1	115	14	105	2	115	24	106	103	106	104
CHILD DEATHS			15	152	11	123	18	139	30	98	11	123	85	123	140	115	82
DAYS ILL HHH			3	43	2	16	5	114	5	234	2	250	17	142	32	187	583
DAYS ILL WIFE			3	45	2	424	4	18	4	220	1	0	14	137	197	106	54
DAYS ILL ALL			13	150	9	135	18	110	24	165	7	185	71	148	144	148	103
HHs/AGGREGATE HEALTH INDEX			3	98	2	150	5	100	5	150	2	125	17	123	119	125	105
MALE WT			3	92	3	97	8	94	5	114	4	107	23	101	94	103	110
MALE HT			3	97	3	103	8	99	5	103	4	102	23	101	100	101	101
FEMALE WT			1	105			2	105	2	117	5	93	10	101	(105)	103	(98)
FEMALE HT			2	101			2	101	2	100	5	97	11	99	(101)	99	(98)
SCHEDULED CASTE																	
MALE WT/HT			2	107	1	86	8	96	14	103	8	99	33	100	100	100	100
FEMALE WT/HT			1	107	1	107	1	117	3	97	6	107	12	105	107	105	98
ALL WT/HT			1	111	3	98	3	95	9	108	5	93	21	101	101	101	100
CHILD DEATHS			(3+	NA)	14	98	28	57	61	89	19	120	122	8	98	86	88
DAYS ILL HHH			1	0	3	7	6	157	9	83	3	105	22	92	(5)	111	(2227)
DAYS ILL WIFE					2	0	5	73	7	100	2	12	16	69	(0)	78	
DAYS ILL ALL			6	220	16	72	30	142	64	82	17	55	133	98	112	86	77

Cont.

CASTE STRATUM, WEIGHTED PER CAPITA INCOME + MAJOR INDICES OF NUTRITION, MORTALITY + MORBIDITY (AV. = 100)

	RICH		F. RICH		UPPER MEDIUM		LOWER MEDIUM		POOR		VERY POOR		TOTAL		RICHER	POORER	P AS % OF R
Rs WTED PCI	1401-2500		1101-1400		951-1100		811-950		701-810		401-700				951+	401-950	R
	No.	Index	No.	Index	No.	Index	No.	Index	No.	Index	No.	Index	No.	Index	Index	Index	
HHs/AGGREGATE HEALTH INDEX			1	109	3	67	6	105	9	95	3	84	22	93	78	96	124
MALE WT			2	106	1	83	8	92	14	104	8	98	33	99	98	99	101
MALE HT			2	100	1	98	8	98	14	102	8	100	33	100	99	100	101
FEMALE WT			1	108	1	103	1	113	3	91	6	107	12	103	106	103	97
FEMALE HT			1	102	1	97	1	97	3	95	6	101	12	99	100	99	99
TOTAL 102 HOUSEHOLDS																	
MALE WT/HT	15	95	30	99	23	98	33	100	31	104	18	103	150	100	98	102	104
FEMALE WT/HT	5	68	18	106	11	107	11	98	13	97	13	103	71	100	101	99	98
ALL WT/HT	41	96	18	98	20	100	22	102	34	104	12	102	147	100	97	103	106
CHILD DEATHS	79	77	89	127	72	104	92	89	152	98	39	116	523	100	104	98	94
DAYS ILL HHH	16	70	17	98	16	65	20	121	25	103	8	173	102	100	78	120	154
DAYS ILL WIFE	11	122	11	108	12	178	16	43	19	112	6	4	75	100	137	69	51
DAYS ILL ALL	126	98	93	110	80	102	92	102	145	90	43	101	579	100	108	96	89
HHs/AGGREGATE HEALTH INDEX	16	89	17	107	16	108	20	94	25	101	8	100	102	100	101	98	97
MALE WT	15	91	30	99	23	98	34	101	30	104	18	103	150	100	97	103	106
MALE HT	15	98	31	99	23	100	34	100	30	102	18	101	151	100	99	101	102
FEMALE WT	5	77	17	106	11	104	11	96	13	98	13	102	70	100	101	99	98
FEMALE HT	5	108	19	100	11	97	11	99	13	101	13	100	72	100	100	100	100

Notes:

1. All indices are expressed as a % of the overall average and scores over 100 indicate worse performance, eg. a score of 105 indicates 5% below the average weight for height.
2. The indicators in full are:

   MALE WT/HT Average deficiency in weight for height (kg per cm) Males aged 18+ (overall av. = .283) non-random sample.

   FEMALE WT/HT Average deficiency in weight for ht. (kg per cm), allowing for age. Females aged 18+ (overall av. = .263) non-random sample.

   ALL WT/HT Average deficiency in wt. for ht. (kg per cm), allowing for age. Members of sample 102 hhs only, all ages (overall av. = 100).

   CHILD DEATHS % of children of sample household heads who had died, all ages plus stillbirths (overall av. 44% of total born).

   DAYS ILL HHH Average days illness experienced by sample household heads between 1 Jan. 1981 and 23 Feb. 1982 (overall av. 86 days).

   DAYS ILL WIFE Average days illness experienced by wives of sample household heads Jan. 1981-Feb. 1982 (overall av. 51 days).

   DAYS ILL ALL Average days illness experienced by all members of sample households (overall av. 32 days).

   HHs/AGGREGATE HEALTH INDEX No. of households and the average of the above seven indices.

   MALE WT Deficiency in av. male weight (overall av. 46.1 kg).
   MALE HT Deficiency in av. male height (overall av. 165 cm).
   FEMALE WT Deficiency in av. female weight (overall av. 39.1 kg).
   FEMALE HT Deficiency in av. female height (overall av. 149.8 cm).

CASTE STRATUM, GENDER AND INDICES OF UNDER 5 MORTALITY PER 1000 LIVE BIRTHS, 102 HHs, BASAULI
(Av for each period = 100)

	BORN UP TO 1965			BORN 1966-77			ALL BORN UP TO 1977		
SEX	RICHER	POORER	TOTAL	RICHER	POORER	TOTAL	RICHER	POORER	TOTAL
HIGH CASTE (24 HHs)									
M	126	18	84	67	71	68	108	37	80
No. of live births (LB)	(19)	(12)	(31)	(16)	(10)	(26)	(35)	(22)	(57)
F	84	(155)	109	118	71	97	97	111	103
No. LB	(13)	(7)	(20)	(12)	(10)	(22)	(25)	(17)	(42)
T	109	69	94	89	71	81	103	69	90
No. LB	(32)	(19)	(51)	(28)	(20)	(48)	(60)	(39)	(99)
MIDDLE CASTE (39 HHs)									
M	52	137	90	110	37	86	73	120	92
No. LB	(42)	(35)	(77)	(39)	(19)	(58)	(81)	(54)	(135)
F	93	167	122	108	130	115	98	157	119
No. LB	(21)	(13)	(34)	(23)	(11)	(34)	(44)	(24)	(68)
T	72	145	100	109	71	97	82	131	101
No. LB	(63)	(48)	(111)	(62)	(30)	(92)	(125)	(78)	(203)
CASTE HINDU ie. High plus Middle Caste (63 HHs)									
M	75	103	88	97	49	80	84	96	88
No. LB	(61)	(47)	(108)	(55)	(29)	(84)	(116)	(76)	(192)
F	90	163	117	112	102	108	98	138	113
No. LB	(34)	(20)	(54)	(35)	(21)	(56)	(69)	(41)	(110)
T	80	123	98	103	71	91	89	111	97
No. LB	(95)	(67)	(162)	(90)	(50)	(140)	(185)	(117)	(302)

CASTE STRATUM, GENDER AND INDICES OF UNDER 5 MORTALITY PER 1000 LIVE BIRTHS, 102 HHs, BASAULI (contd.)
(Av for each period = 100)

	BORN UP TO 1965			BORN 1966-77			ALL BORN UP TO 1977		
SEX	RICHER	POORER	TOTAL	RICHER	POORER	TOTAL	RICHER	POORER	TOTAL
MUSLIM (17 HHs)									
M	(72)	115	109	(178)	110	12	(116)	117	116
No. LB	(3)	(17)	(20)	(4)	(13)	(17)	(7)	(30)	(37)
F	(217)	118	127	(305)	(89)	190	(236)	113	150
No. LB	(1)	(11)	(12)	(7)	(8)	(15)	(8)	(19)	(27)
T	(109)	116	115	259	102	156	180	116	130
No. LB	(4)	(28)	(32)	(11)	(21)	(32)	(15)	(49)	(64)
SCHEDULED (22 HHs)									
M	(87)	54	62	(178)	107	113	(116)	75	81
No. LB	(5)	(16)	(21)	(2)	(20)	(22)	(7)	(36)	(43)
F	(217)	152	158	(71)	71	71	(90)	92	92
No. LB	(1)	(10)	(11)	(5)	(25)	(30)	(6)	(35)	(41)
T	(109)	92	95	(102)	87	89	104	84	87
No. LB	(6)	(26)	(32)	(7)	(45)	(52)	(13)	(71)	(84)
TOTAL (102 HHs)									
M	76	98	88	105	80	93	87	95	91
No. LB	(69)	(80)	(149)	(61)	(62)	(123)	(130)	(142)	(272)
F	97	148	124	136	86	109	111	116	113
No. LB	(36)	(41)	(77)	(47)	(54)	(101)	(83)	(95)	(178)
T	83	115	100	118	83	100	96	104	100
No. LB	(105)	(121)	(226)	(108)	(116)	(224)	(213)	(237)	(450)
Actual Mortality Rate per 1000 live births	381	529	460	333	233	281	357	384	371

NB Indices are in parentheses if the number of live births (LB) was small.

INDICES OF UNDER 5 MORTALITY PER 1000 LIVE BIRTHS, 180 HHs, JHAKRI + DHARMNAGRI VILLAGES, BIJNOR DISTRICT

	BORN UP TO 1965			BORN 1966-80			ALL BORN UP TO 1980		
SEX	RICH+ MIDDLE PEASANT (89 HHs)	POOR PEASANT & LANDLESS (91 HHs)	TOTAL (180 HHs)	RICH + MIDDLE PEASANT	POOR PEASANT & LANDLESS	TOTAL	RICH + MIDDLE PEASANT	POOR PEASANT & LANDLESS	TOTAL
	INDICES EXPRESSED AS A % OF THE TOTAL AVERAGE (=100) IN EACH PERIOD (*)								
CASTE HINDU (71 HHs)									
M	39	119	75	60	54	57	46	104	71
No. of live births	(57)	(46)	(103)	(66)	(48)	(114)	(123)	(94)	(217)
F	91	97	94	65	38	52	81	81	81
No. LB	(43)	(43)	(86)	(52)	(43)	(95)	(95)	(86)	(181)
T	61	109	84	62	47	54	62	93	76
No. LB	(100)	(89)	(189)	(118)	(91)	(209)	(218)	(180)	(398)
MUSLIM (63 HHs)									
M	72	122	94	125	179	143	93	147	113
No. LB.	(39)	(34)	(73)	(83)	(42)	(125)	(122)	(76)	(198)
F	125	147	135	136	228	169	124	181	148
No. LB	(38)	(36)	(74)	(67)	(36)	(103)	(105)	(72)	(177)
T	97	135	115	130	202	155	107	164	130
No. LB	(77)	(70)	(147)	(150)	(78)	(228)	(227)	(148)	(375)
SCHEDULED (46 HHs)									
M	102	91	96	114	54	85	100	85	92
No. LB	(19)	(30)	(49)	(34)	(30)	(64)	(53)	(60)	(113)
F	116	133	126	103	38	65	116	100	107
No. LB	(19)	(25)	(44)	(21)	(29)	(50)	(40)	(54)	(94)
T	109	111	110	109	46	76	107	92	99
No. LB	(38)	(55)	(93)	(55)	(59)	(114)	(93)	(114)	(207)
TOTAL (180 HHs)									
M	61	114	86	98	98	98	73	112	90
No. LB	(115)	(110)	(225)	(183)	(120)	(303)	(298)	(230)	(528)
F	108	122	116	103	103	103	104	120	112
No. LB	(100)	(104)	(204)	(140)	(108)	(248)	(240)	(212)	(452)

INDICES OF UNDER 5 MORTALITY PER 1000 LIVE BIRTHS, 180 HHs JHAKRI + DHARMNAGRI VILLAGES (Contd.)

	BORN UP TO 1965			BORN 1966-80			ALL BORN UP TO 1980		
SEX	RICH+ MIDDLE PEASANT (89 HHs)	POOR PEASANT & LANDLESS (91 HHs)	TOTAL (180 HHs)	RICH + MIDDLE PEASANT	POOR PEASANT & LANDLESS	TOTAL	RICH + MIDDLE PEASANT	POOR PEASANT & LANDLESS	TOTAL
	INDICES EXPRESSED AS A % OF THE TOTAL AVERAGE (=100) IN EACH PERIOD (*)								
T	83	118	100*	100	101	100*	87	116	100*
No. LB	(215)	(214)	(429)	(323)	(228)	(551)	(538)	(443)	(980)
Actual Mortality Rate per 1000 live births	298	425	361	184	185	184	226	300	259

Source: Jeffery 1989:243, plus further calculation. * Average for total births in period.

CASTE STRATUM, CLASS, WEIGHTED PCI AND INDEX OF MORTALITY, ALL AGES, PLUS STILLBIRTHS, PROGENY OF HHHs, BASAULI

	RICH		F. RICH		UPPER MEDIUM		LOWER MEDIUM		POOR		VERY POOR		TOTAL	
% OF CHILDREN OF HHHs STILLBORN OR DEAD, ALL AGES (AV. 44% OF TOTAL BORN)														
CASTE AND CLASS	NO.OF TOTAL BIRTHS	INDEX	NO.OF TOTAL BIRTHS	INDEX	NO.OF TOTAL BIRTHS	INDEX	NO.OF TOTAL BIRTHS	INDEX	NO.OF TOTAL BIRTHS	INDEX	NO.OF TOTAL BIRTHS	INDEX	NO. OF TOTAL BIRTHS	INDEX OF % OF AV. MORT.
HIGH CASTE														
HIGH CLASS	42	82	15	136									57	95
MEDIUM			7	195	11	145	9	100	6	39			33	123
LOW							12	39	16	114			28	82
TOTAL	42	82	22	154	11	145	21	66	22	93			118	100
MIDDLE CASTE														
HIGH CLASS	37	72	25	100	1	0							63	82
MEDIUM			16	114	23	89	21	130	10	23			70	98
LOW			11	125	12	95	4	0	32	134	9	100	68	114
TOTAL	37	72	52	109	36	89	25	109	42	109	9	100	201	98
MUSLIM														
MEDIUM CLASS			11	145	7	130							18	139
LOW			4	170	4	114	18	139	30	98	11	123	67	118
TOTAL			15	152	11	123	18	139	30	98	11	123	85	123
SCHEDULED														
MEDIUM CLASS	79	77	40	114	1	0							120	89
LOW			(3+	NA)	14	98	20	68	47	97	19	120	100	95
TOTAL			(3+	NA)	14	98	28	57	61	89	19	120	122	88
ALL HHs														
HIGH CLASS	79	77	40	114	1	0							120	89
MEDIUM			34	141	41	111	38	102	30	45			143	102
LOW			15	136	30	98	54	80	125	111	39	116	263	104
TOTAL	79	77	89	127	72	104	92	89	155	97	39	116	526	100

caste females (122). Scheduled males experienced the lowest mortality (62), along with high caste males (84). In the later period Muslim females had the highest mortality (190), with Muslims of both sexes (156) and Muslim males (126) having the next highest. High caste males (68) and scheduled females (71) enjoyed the lowest mortality after 1965.

The table on page 357 summarises indices of mortality of progeny of household heads, by caste stratum, class and income in Basauli.

The table on pages 356-7 shows child mortality indices based on survival rates for Jhakri and Dharmnagri. The data are fairly comparable except that high and middle castes are aggregated and, instead of income categories, the Jefferys used five 'classes' based on acreage owned per able-bodied adult. Live births were studied up to 1980 rather than the 1977 cut-off in Basauli. The number of births was also more than twice as large as that in Basauli. The average mortality rate was 259 deaths of children under 5 per 1000 live births ie. 30 percent lower than in Basauli. Bijnor is a richer, western district but my under-recording of female births and other data imperfections may also partly explain the higher mortality figure for Basauli.

CASTE, CLASS COMPOSITION + FERTILITY BY AGE, JHAKRI + DHARMNAGRI VILLAGES, BIJNOR DISTRICT, WESTERN UP 1985

CLASS		1 LAND-LORDS	2 RICH PEASANTS	3 MIDDLE PEASANTS	4 POOR PEASANTS	5 LAND-LESS	TOTAL
Av. acres owned per able-bodied adult male		100+?	5.1 to nearly 18	1.1. to 5.0	0.1 to 1.0	0	0 to 100+
NO. OF HOUSEHOLDS	Caste Hindu	1	7	27	17	19	71
	Muslim		5	32	6	20	63
	Scheduled		1	16	16	13	46
	TOTAL HHs	1	13	75**	39	52	180
	TOTAL POPN	5	98	474	214	252	1043
% of POPN	Caste Hindu	1.2	15.2	42.1	20.8	20.8	100
	Muslim		9.0	54.2**	9.3	27.5	100
	Scheduled		1.1	38.6	35.6	24.7	100
	TOTAL HHs	*	9	46	21	24	100
AV. STILL AND LIVE BORN TO EVER-MARRIED WOMEN							
Age of Woman	15-24		1.2	1.4	1.2	1.3	1.3
	25-34		4.3	4.3	3.8	3.3	3.9
	35-44		7.2**	6.5	5.7	5.6	6.4
	45+		7.5	8.4**	7.9	7.2	7.8
	ALL		5.4**	5.4**	5.0	4.5	5.1
Average Age of Women			38	37	39	37	38

Source: Jeffery 1989:239 + 241. * Less than 0.5% ** Worth noting

The table above shows the social composition and average fertility of classes (based on landownership) in the two Bijnor villages.

The Bijnor data show that Muslims had the highest mortality index (130), whilst both the scheduled (99) and the caste Hindus (76) were below average. In the earlier period, when mortality was nearly double that of the latter period, differences between caste strata were smaller: Muslims still had the highest mortality index (115), but the scheduled (110) exceeded the average and only caste Hindus (84) were below average. For those children born between 1966 and 1980, inter-strata differences were large: Muslims 155, the scheduled 76 and caste Hindus 54. In other words, Muslim under 5 mortality was treble that of middle and high caste Hindus. Inequalities in mortality were greater for females and scheduled females fared worse than their brothers. This applied particularly to the earlier period when the mortality of the female scheduled was almost as high as that of the female Muslims. In the later period (when the gender difference in mortality had fallen to a low level), Muslim female children still fared worse than males but the opposite was true for the scheduled. All this suggests that from 1966 scheduled females reduced their relative mortality most, followed by caste Hindu females, then caste Hindu males, with only a slight decrease for scheduled males. Muslim females scored worst of all in the later period and also suffered higher mortality than earlier but Muslim males experienced the worst deterioration in their relative mortality: the Muslim male mortality index rose from 94 (ie. below average) in the earlier to 143 in the later period.

The table on page 360 juxtaposes the under 5 mortality indices for the two samples, those of Basauli and JD and this is probably the most interesting table. Despite the differences in location, level of development and overall mortality *rates*, there are nevertheless some quite striking and interesting similarities in mortality *indices* for certain categories in the two 'villages'. Particularly noticeable are the indices for Muslims which are 130 in both populations, and also the relative indices for Muslim males and females (116 and 150 in Basauli; 113 and 148 in JD). Excess child mortality among Muslims is thus consistently 30 percent whilst being nearly 50 percent among female Muslims. This excess is one of the greatest for any major hierarchical category, over the whole period. Both male and female caste Hindus in Basauli fared relatively worse than in JD but the differential was higher for females (whose mortality exceeded the Basauli average). The reverse was true for the scheduled, but less so for females. The data seem to suggest that the scheduled suffer (or perhaps report?) lower under 5 mortality than caste Hindus in Basauli. This may be because the scheduled are less disadvantaged in central UP than in western UP where more of them are likely to be landless labourers, including immigrants from the impoverished eastern sector of UP.

In the earlier period, the relative mortality of caste Hindus was more similar in the two populations than later, when caste Hindus in JD improved much more than in Basauli. Almost as dramatic was the fall in the index for the scheduled in JD (from 110 earlier to 76 later), compared with a nominal decrease in Basauli. The Muslim indices were almost identical for the two populations in both periods, despite rising from 115 to about 155, as both groups of Muslims became relatively more disadvantaged on this point. This coincidence in deterioration in both areas may be of some significance. For males in the earlier period, the scheduled in Basauli had the lowest index whilst in JD the scheduled and the Muslims both had appreciably higher mortality than caste Hindus even though all males were below the overall average. In the later period, both the indices (and the ranking) of caste strata were more similar in the two villages, even though the inter-strata gradient was much steeper in JD. Turning to females in the earlier period, indices were universally higher in both populations but the ranking similar to that for males, except that scheduled females in Basauli had by far the highest index (Cf. the lowest for males). The indices for Muslim females and for caste Hindu males were the most similar in the two areas.

INDICES OF UNDER 5 MORTALITY PER 1000 LIVE BIRTHS, BASAULI TO 1977 + JHAKRI-DHARMNAGRI VILLAGES TO 1980

SEX	BORN TO 1965				BORN 1966-77 or 1966-80				ALL BORN UP TO 1977 or 1980			
VILLAGE	RICHER RMP	POORER PPL	TOTAL	POOR AS % RICH	RICHER RMP	POORER PPL	TOTAL	POOR AS % RICH	RICHER RMP	POORER PPL	TOTAL	POOR AS % RICH
CASTE HINDU				GRADIENT				GRADIENT				GRADIENT
(B 63 HHs; JD 71 HHs)												
M B	75	103	88	137	97	49	80	51	84	96	88	114
JD	39	119	75	305	60	54	57	90	46	104	71	226
F B	90	163	117	181	112	102	108	91	98	138	113	141
JD	91	97	94	107	65	38	52	58	81	81	81	100
T B	80	123	98	154	103	71	91	69	89	111	97	125
JD	61	109	84	179	62	47	54	76	62	93	76	150
MUSLIM (B 17 HHs; JD 63 HHs)												
M B	72	115	109	160	(178)	110	126	(62)	(116)	117	116	(101)
JD	72	122	94	169	125	179	143	143	93	147	113	158
F B	(217)	118	127	(54)	(305)	(89)	190	(29)	(236)	113	150	(48)
JD	125	147	135	118	136	228	169	168	124	181	148	146
T B	(109)	116	115	(106)	259	102	156	39	180	116	130	64
JD	97	135	115	139	130	202	155	155	107	164	130	153
SCHEDULED (B 22 HHs; JD 46 HHs)												
M B	(87)	54	62	(62)	(178)	107	113	(60)	(116)	75	81	65
JD	102	91	96	89	114	54	85	47	100	85	92	85
F B	(217)	152	158	(70)	(71)	71	71	(100)	(90)	92	92	(102)
JD	116	133	126	115	103	38	65	37	116	100	107	86
T B	(109)	92	95	(84)	(102)	87	89	(85)	104	84	87	81
JD	109	111	110	102	109	46	76	42	107	92	99	86
TOTAL (B 102 HHs; JD 180 HHs)												
M B	76	98	88	129	105	80	93	76	87	95	91	109
JD	61	114	86	187	98	98	98	100	73	112	90	153
F B	97	148	124	153	136	86	109	63	111	116	113	104
JD	108	122	116	113	103	103	103	100	104	120	112	115
T B	83	115	100	139	118	83	100	70	96	104	100	108
JD	83	118	100	142	100	101	100	101	87	116	100	133
ACTUAL MORTALITY RATE PER 1000 LIVE BIRTHS												
T B	381	529	460		333	233	281		357	384	371	
JD	298	425	361		184	185	184		226	300	259	
Basauli as % of Jhakri-Dharmnagri	128%	124%	127%		181%	126%	153%		158%	128%	143%	
NO. OF LIVE BIRTHS												
T B	105	121	226		108	116	224		213	237	450	
JD	215	214	429		323	228	551		538	442	980	

B = Basauli; JD = Jhakri Dharmnagri; RMP = Rich and Middle Peasant; PPL = Poor Peasant and Landless.
Sources: Basauli Survey; Jeffery 1989:243

The patterns for females in the later period were also strikingly alike, except that caste Hindu females improved much more in JD: their index of 52 was the lowest for any gender or stratum. The relative disadvantage of Muslim females increased more in Basauli in the later period.

INDEX OF UNDER FIVE MORTALITY - BASAULI HINDUS

	TO 1965			1966-77			TOTAL TO 1977		
	RICHER	POORER	P AS % R	RICHER	POORER	P AS % R	RICHER	POORER	P AS % R
High Caste	109	69	61	89	71	80	103	69	67
Middle Caste	72	145	201	109	71	65	82	131	160
Non-Scheduled	80	123	154	103	71	69	89	111	125
Scheduled	109	92	84	102	87	85	104	84	81

The table below compares percentage survival and mortality of children in Basauli and Jhakri-Dharmnagri, related to six income categories in Basauli and to two classes in JD.

NO. OF LIVE AND STILL BIRTHS, PERCENTAGE SURVIVING AND MORTALITY RATES, BY CLASS, JHAKRI-DHARMNAGRI AND BY WPCI, BASAULI

	JHAKRI-DHARMNAGRI				BASAULI							
	RICH + MIDDLE PEASANT RMP	POOR PEASANT + LANDLESS PPL	TOTAL	PPL AS % OF RMP	RICH	FAIRLY RICH	UPPER MEDIUM	LOWER MEDIUM	VERY POOR	POOR	TOTAL	POORER AS % OF RICHER
NO. OF HOUSEHOLDS	89	91	180		16	17	16	20	25	8	102	
NO. OF MOTHERS	121	115	236		16	17	16	18	24	8	99	
AV. AGE OF MOTHERS	37	38	38		42	43	36	42	42	41	41	105%
STILL + LIVE BIRTHS	663	547	1210		79	91	76	92	138	39	515	
STILLBIRTHS	19	17	36		5	10	4	2	11	1	33	
LIVE BIRTHS	644	530	1174		74	81	72	90	127	38	482	
LIVE BIRTHS PER MOTHER	5.3	4.6	5.0		4.6	4.8	4.5	5.0	5.3	4.8	4.9	
AV. APPROX. YEARS BETWEEN BIRTHS INC. STILLBIRTHS					4.4	2.5	3.8	4.3	4.2	2.9	4.3	114%
% SURVIVING												
STILL + LIVE BIRTHS	100	100	100		100	100	100	100	100	100	100	
BORN ALIVE	97	97	97		94	89	95	98	92	97	94	
ALIVE ON DAY 8	94	94	94		92	89	92	96	90	90	92	
ALIVE ON DAY 29	90	92	91		91	86	84	95	86	85	87	
ALIVE ON DAY 366	85	88	87		80	75	72	84	72	64	75	
BORN UP TO 1980 OR 1977	538	442	980									
ALIVE 5TH BIRTHDAY	77	70	74		76	52	62	67	60	54	62	
ALIVE 15TH BIRTHDAY					73	47	58	66	57	51	58	
% DEAD BY 1982					34%	55%	46%	39%	45%	51%	45%	96%
ALIVE IN 1985 OR 1982			NK		66	45	54	61	55	49	55	104%
MORTALITY RATES PER 1000 BIRTHS												
STILLBIRTH/ TOTAL BIRTHS	29	31	30	107%	63	110	53	22	80	26	64	68%
PERINATAL/TOTAL	65	60	62	92%	76	110	79	43	101	103	85	90%
DEATHS IN WEEK 1/ LIVE BIRTHS	36	30	33	83%	13	0	26	22	22	76	21	250%
DEATHS, WEEKS 2,3+4/ LIVE	40	17	30	42%	14	37	97	11	47	53	41	73%
NEONATAL/LIVE	76	47	63	62%	27	37	125	33	71	132	64	108%
POST NEONATAL/LIVE	48	42	45	88%	122	123	139	111	150	184	135	110%
INFANT/LIVE	124	89	108	72%	149	160	264	144	220	316	199	110%
STILLBIRTH, INFANT + CHILD (0-4)/TOTAL	236	300	259	133%	240	480	380	330	400	460	380	105%
% OF INFANT DEATHS												
NEONATAL	61%	53%	58%		18%	23%	47%	23%	32%	38%	33%	
POST NEONATAL	39%	47%	42%		82%	77%	53%	72%	68%	62%	67%	
TOTAL	100%	100%	100%		100%	100%	100%	100%	100%	100%	100%	

	RICH + MIDDLE PEASANT RMP	POOR PEASANT + LANDLESS PPL	TOTAL	PPL AS % OF RMP	RICH	FAIRLY RICH	UPPER MEDIUM	LOWER MEDIUM	VERY POOR	POOR	TOTAL	POORER AS % OF RICHER
POSTNEONATAL RATE	90	91	103	82	111	136	100(135)		95	104	110	
INFANT M. RATE	75	80	133	72	111	159	100(199)		95	104	110	
STILLBIRTH AND CHILD (0-5) RATE	63	12	100	87	105	121	100(380)		96	101	105	
CHILD MR, 0-5	59	122	105	90	103	137	100(344)				108	
CHILD MR, ANY AGE	76	122	102	87	100	113	100(450)				94	

	RICH	FAIRLY RICH	UPPER MEDIUM	LOWER MEDIUM	POOR	VERY POOR	TOTAL (ACTUAL RATE PER 1000 IN BRACKETS)	RICHER	POORER	POORER AS % OF RICHER
MORTALITY INDICATOR, BASAULI										
TOTAL NO. OF BIRTH	(79)	(91)	(76)	(92)	(138)	(39)	(515)	(246)	(269)	
	INDICES AS % OF AVERAGE (=100) : ABOVE 100 = WORSE									
STILLBIRTH RATE	98	172	83	34	125	41	100 (64)	120	81	68
UNDER ONE WEEK RATE	62	0	124	105	105	362	100 (21)	56	143	255
PERINATAL RATE	89	129	93	51	119	121	100 (85)	106	95	90
WEEKS 2 TO 4	34	90	237	27	115	129	100 (41)	73		
NEONATAL RATE	42	58	195	52	111	206	100 (64)	97	105	108

WEIGHTED PER CAPITA INCOME + INDICES OF PARENTS' AGES AT DEATH

INDEX OF AV. DEFICIT IN AGE OF PARENT OF HHH AT DEATH (% OF AV.)	RICHEST	UPPER MEDIUM	LOWER MEDIUM	POOR	VERY POOR	AV.(NO.)
FATHERS	99	97	100	101	101	100 (71)
MOTHERS	101	100	103	103	87	100 (68)
INDEX OF % OF PARENTS WHO DIED AGED BETWEEN 35 + 60						
FATHERS (N=15)	71	79	117	121	158	100 (24)
MOTHERS (N=20)	107	103	150	67	57	100 (30)
NO. OF HHs	17	16	20	25	8	102

Nutrition

The table on page 363 shows indices of deficiency in weight for height, related to class as well as caste stratum and income. The data relate to those 147 (30%) of the 483 villagers measured who were traced to be members of the sample households (for whom more precise information on income was available). This advantage is partly cancelled out by discrepancies and uncertainties over the age of some of the children measured; by small numbers in some categories; by lower weights and heights for some older women; and by the non-randomness of the sample measured. There was an excess proportion of rich, high caste and male persons. This presumably distorts the averages (mostly upwards?) and thus probably serves to accentuate the deficiency in weight for height of the poor. The next anomalous result is the low deficiency in weight for height (93) of the five very poor, low class scheduled. These were all members of the Radhika caste who ate meat, including some carrion, and also begged for food.

The most impressive weights for height were achieved by rich, high class members of middle castes:

CATEGORY	INDEX OF DEFICIENCY IN WT/HT	NO.
Rich, high class and middle caste	91	15
Very poor, low class and scheduled	93	5
Rich, high class and high caste	98	26
Poor, low class and Muslim	104	13
Lower medium income, low class and middle caste	107	7
Poor, low class and scheduled	109	7

CASTE STRATUM, CLASS, WEIGHTED PER CAPITA INCOME + INDICES OF DEFICIENCY IN WEIGHT FOR HEIGHT, SAMPLE HHs, ALL AGES

CASTE AND CLASS	RICH		F. RICH		UPPER MEDIUM		LOWER MEDIUM		POOR		VERY POOR		TOTAL		RICHER		POORER		POORER AS % OF RICHER
	NO.	INDEX	NO.	INDEX	NO.	INDEX	NO.	INDEX	NO.	INDEX	NO.	INDEX	NO.	INDEX	NO.	INDEX	NO.	INDEX	
HIGH CASTE																			INEQUALITY GRADIENT
HIGH CLASS	26	98	2	86									28	97	28	97			
MEDIUM			3	102	8	98	4	106	3	99			18	100	11	99	7	102	103%
LOW							2	95	2	104	1	110	5	102			5	102	
TOTAL	26	98	5	96	8	98	6	102	5	101	1	110	51	99	39	98	12	102	104%
MIDDLE CASTE																			
HIGH CLASS	15	91	7	99									22	93	22	93			
MEDIUM			1	97	5	94	5	99					11	97	5	94	5	99	105%
LOW					1	119	7	107	6	100	4	104	18	105	1	119	17	104	(87%)
TOTAL	15	91	8	99	6	98	12	104	6	100	4	104	51	98	29	95	22	103	108%
MUSLIM																			
MEDIUM CLASS			3	99	2	114			1	114			6	106	5	105	1	114	(109%)
LOW			1	96	1	99	1	115	13	104	2	115	18	105	2	98	16	106	(108%)
TOTAL			4	98	3	109	1	115	14	105	2	115	24	106	7	103	17	107	104%
SCHEDULED																			
MEDIUM CLASS									2	104			2	104			2	104	
LOW			1	111	3	98	3	95	7	109	5	93	19	101	4	101	15	101	100%
TOTAL			1	111	3	98	3	95	9	108	5	93	21	101	4	101	17	101	100%
ALL HHs																			
HIGH CLASS	41	95	9	96										50	95	50	95		
MEDIUM			7	100	15	99	9	102	6	103			37	100	22	99	15	102	103%
LOW			2	104	5	102	13	103	28	104	12	102	60	103	7	103	53	103	100%
GD. TOTAL	41	95	18	98	20	100	22	102	34	104	12	102	147	100	79	97	68	102	106%

NB Gradients based on small numbers are in parentheses

Morbidity

The tables show indices of length of illness for various members of the sample households, organised by caste stratum, class and weighted per capita income.

CASTE STRATUM, CLASS, WEIGHTED PCI + INDEX OF AV. DAYS ILLNESS, HHHs, WIVES OF HHHs AND TOTAL HH

CASTE AND CLASS	RICH		F. RICH		UPPER MEDIUM		LOWER MEDIUM		POOR		VERY POOR		TOTAL		RICHER		POORER		POORER AS % OF RICHER
	NO.	INDEX	NO.	INDEX	NO.	INDEX	NO.	INDEX	NO.	INDEX	NO.	INDEX	NO.	INDEX	NO.	INDEX	NO.	INDEX	
INDEX OF AV. DAYS ILLNESS, HOUSEHOLD HEADS (MAX. 420, AV. 86 DAYS)																			
HIGH CASTE																			
HIGH CLASS	8	17	3	174									11	60					
MEDIUM			2	214	2	41	1	488	1	70			6	178					
LOW							3	105	3	22	1	0	7	55					
TOTAL	8	17	5	189	2	41	4	200	4	35	1	0	24	88					
MIDDLE CASTE																			
HIGH CLASS	7	137	4	26	1	244							12	109					
MEDIUM	1	17	2	70	4	121	3	35	2	9			12	63					
LOW			2	165	4	44	2	5	5	106	2	285	15	107					
TOTAL	8	122	8	72	9	100	5	23	7	78	2	285	39	94					
MUSLIM																			
MEDIUM CLASS			2	24	1	21							3	24					
LOW			1	81	1	12	5	114	5	234	2	250	14	167					
TOTAL			3	43	2	16	5	114	5	234	2	250	17	142					
SCHEDULED																			
MEDIUM CLASS							1	5	2	105			3	71					
LOW			1	0	3	7	5	187	7	77	3	105	19	95					
TOTAL			1	0	3	7	6	157	9	83	3	105	22	92					
TOTAL HHHs																			
HIGH CLASS	15	73	7	90	1	244							23	86					
MEDIUM	1	17	6	102	7	84	5	120	5	59			24	88					
LOW			4	103	8	26	15	122	20	115	8	173	55	112					
GD. TOTAL	16	70	17	98	16	65	20	121	25	103	8	173	102	100		78		121	155%
Aggregated	16	70	33		81		45			112	8	173	102	100					

CASTE AND CLASS	RICH		F. RICH		UPPER MEDIUM		LOWER MEDIUM		POOR		VERY POOR		TOTAL		RICHER		POORER		POORER AS % OF RICHER
	NO.	INDEX	NO.	INDEX	NO.	INDEX	NO.	INDEX	NO.	INDEX	NO.	INDEX	NO.	INDEX	NO.	INDEX	NO.	INDEX	
INDEX OF AV. DAYS ILLNESS OF WIVES OF HHHs (AV. 51 DAYS)																			
HIGH CASTE																			
HIGH CLASS	6	71	1	0									7	59	7	59			
MEDIUM			1	0	1	27	1	2	1	0			4	8	2	14	2	1	(7%)
LOW							1	0	2	222	1	0	4	110			4	110	
TOTAL	6	71	2	0	1	27	2	2	3	147	1	0	15	59	9	50	6	74	148%
MIDDLE CASTE																			
HIGH CLASS	5	186	3	341	1	20							9	220	9	220			
MEDIUM			2	16	3	337	3	71	2	16			10	129	5	74	5	49	66%
LOW			1	0	3	78	2	18	3	27	2	0	11	31	4	58	7	17	29%
TOTAL	5	186	6	174	7	180	5	49	5	22	2	0	30	120	18	180	12	20	11%
MUSLIM																			
MEDIUM CLASS			2	55	1	824							3	310	3	310			
LOW			1	27	1	24	4	18	4	220	1	0	11	90	2	25	9	106	(424%)
TOTAL			3	45	2	424	4	18	4	220	1	0	14	137	5	197	9	106	54%
SCHEDULED																			
MEDIUM CLASS							1	8	2	16			3	12			3	12	
LOW					2	0	4	88	5	133	2	12	13	80	2	0	11	95	(0%)
TOTAL					2	0	5	73	7	100	2	12	16	69	2	0	14	78	(0%)
TOTAL WIVES OF HHHs																			
HIGH CLASS	11	122	4	255	1	20							16	149	16	149			
MEDIUM			5	27	5	373	5	45	5	12			20	114	10	200	10	28	14%
LOW			2	14	6	43	11	41	14	149	6	4	39	73	8	36	31	83	229%
GD. TOTAL	11	122	11	108	12	178	16	43	19	112	6	4	75	100	34	137	41	69	51%
INDEX OF AV. DAYS ILLNESS, ALL HOUSEHOLD MEMBERS (MAX 420, AV. 40 DAYS)																			
HIGH CASTE																			
HIGH CLASS	59	115	17	90									76	110					
MEDIUM			8	132	11	52	5	272	7	22			31	92					
LOW							12	72	12	70	4	5	28	62					
TOTAL	59	115	25	102	11	52	17	115	19	52	4	5	135	95					
MIDDLE CASTE																			
HIGH CLASS	66	85	34	92	5	112							105	88					
MEDIUM	1	38	10	42	22	118	13	75	12	110			58	92					
LOW			5	148	17	120	14	12	26	60	15	140	77	85					
TOTAL	67	82	49	88	44	118	27	42	38	75	15	140	240	88					
MUSLIM																			
MEDIUM			10	175	5	225							15	192					
LOW			3	70	4	22	18	110	24	65	7	185	56	135					
TOTAL			13	150	9	135	18	110	24	65	7	185	71	148					
SCHEDULED																			
MEDIUM							4	10	24	35			28	32					
LOW			6	220	16	72	26	162	40	112	17	55	105	115					
TOTAL			6	220	16	72	30	142	64	82	17	55	133	98					
TOTAL HH MEMBERS																			
HIGH CLASS	125	98	51	92	5	112							181	97					
MEDIUM	1	38	28	116	38	113	22	96	43	54			132	91					
LOW			14	162	37	89	70	104	102	106	43	101	266	105					
GD. TOTAL	126	98	93	110	80	102	92	102	145	90	43	101	579	100		103		96	93%

NB Gradients based on small numbers are in parentheses

CASTE, WEIGHTED PCI + INDEX OF DAYS ILLNESS, OTHER HOUSEHOLD MEMBERS

	RICH		F. RICH		UPPER MEDIUM		LOWER MEDIUM		POOR		VERY POOR		TOTAL		RICHER		POORER		POORER AS % OF RICHER
INDEX OF AV. DAYS ILLNESS, WIVES OF HHHs (MAX. 420, AV. 51 DAYS)																			
HIGH CASTE	6	71	2	0	1	27	2	2	3	147	1	0	15	59					
MIDDLE	5	186	6	174	7	180	5	49	5	22	2	0	30	120					
MUSLIM			3	45	2	424	4	18	4	220	1	0	14	137					
SCHEDULED					2	0	5	73	7	100	2	12	16	69					
TOTAL	11	122	11	108	12	178	16	43	19	112	6	4	75	100					
INDEX OF AV. DAYS ILLNESS, SONS 1 + 2 OF HHHs, AGED 0-15 (MAX 420, AV. 22 DAYS)																			
HIGH CASTE	8	64	3	9	1	0	2	0	3	0			17	32					
MIDDLE			2	18	8	45	5	36	4	27	1	0	20	32					
MUSLIM			1	0	4	27	3	9	5	91	2	14	15	41					
SCHEDULED					1	36	6	473	3	541	2	0	12	373					
TOTAL	8	64	6	9	14	36	16	191	15	145	5	5	64	100		38		146	384%
INDEX OF AV. DAYS ILLNESS, SONS 1 + 2 OF HHHs, AGED 16+ (MAX. 420, AV. 32 DAYS)																			
HIGH CASTE	3	463	1	0	1	0	2	19					7	203					
MIDDLE	8	28	5	6	2	0	4	28	6	56	2	234	27	44					
MUSLIM			1	25			2	256	1	0	1	62	5	119					
SCHEDULED			2	678	1	25	1	34	6	50	2	25	12	147					
TOTAL	11	147	9	156	4	6	9	78	13	50	5	116	51	100		127		72	57%

The Aggregate Health Index

The mean scores of the first seven indices in the earlier table have been averaged to give an (unweighted) aggregate health index. This index is meant to be indicative rather than definitive and to clarify broad differences between caste strata and income categories, given that there are considerable differences in distributional patterns between individual indicators and indices. The aggregate health index does reveal some differences but these should clearly be treated with some caution. For example, the indicators themselves involve some overlap or repetition: days illness of both household heads and their wives are included in days illness of all household members and is repeated mainly because a) the accuracy and reliability of data on household heads probably exceeds that on other household members and b) the ill health of the household head is arguably more important for the family than that of, say, a young child. There is poor correlation between some constituent indicators of the AHI.

The aggregate health index suggests that richer scheduled caste households were healthiest and poorer Muslims the least healthy.

AVER. OR ABOVE AVER. AGGREGATE HEALTH INDEX			BELOW AVERAGE AHI		
CATEGORY	NO. HHs	AGGREGATE HEALTH INDEX	CATEGORY	NO. HHs	AGGREGATE HEALTH INDEX
Richer scheduled	4	78	RICHER	49	101
Poorer middle caste	14	86	Richer middle caste	25	109
Richer high caste	15	87	Richer Muslim	5	119
Poorer high caste	9	87	MUSLIM	17	123
HIGH CASTE	24	90	Poorer Muslim	12	125
SCHEDULED CASTE	22	93			
Poorer scheduled	18	96			
POORER	53	98			
MIDDLE CASTE	39	100	TOTAL	102	100

The results are not quite what might be expected, with poorer performing slightly better than richer and scheduled castes better than middle castes. The highest performance by the richer scheduled is interesting but the number of households involved was only four. The ranking for caste strata is, first, high caste healthiest (90), then scheduled (93), middle caste (100) and Muslim by far the least healthy (123). The inferiority of the Muslims is the most clear-cut but the superiority of the scheduled over the middle castes is sufficiently large to be worth taking seriously. The poor performance of the middle castes is entirely due to very significantly worse health of richer middle caste households. This may raise some questions about the alleged rise of the middle castes and/or of the effect of the Green Revolution on the health of the ostensibly 'rising middle castes'. (Reference to the earlier table, showing basic data in the households, reveals that, out of 25 richer households of middle caste, 9 reported downward economic mobility, 9 claimed an improvement in standard of living during the 1970s whilst 7 remained the same.)

The differences between richer and poorer households within caste strata are also interesting. The largest gradient is for the scheduled caste (with poorer scoring 124 percent of that for richer), followed by Muslims (105%). There was no difference within the high caste stratum (100%) and there was even a negative gradient (79%) within the middle caste stratum. Overall the gradient between richer and poorer households of all caste strata was also negative (97%), indicating slightly worse health among the richer. Disaggregating into the six income categories, the richest had the healthiest index and the next two richer categories the worst indices.

Rs WTED PCI	RICH 1401-2500	F. RICH 1101-1400	UPPER MEDIUM 951-1100	LOWER MEDIUM 811-950	POOR 701-810	V. POOR 401-700	TOTAL
AGGREGATE HEALTH INDEX	89	107	108	94	101	100	100

Disaggregating further to income categories within caste strata, expectations are confirmed, with the healthiest category emerging as the richest high caste households, with poor Muslims as the lowest. Ignoring most categories with small numbers, the ranking is as follows:

ABOVE AVERAGE HEALTH			BELOW AVERAGE HEALTH		
CATEGORY	NO. OF HHs.	INDEX	CATEGORY	NO. OF HHs.	INDEX
Rich high caste	8	76	Fairly rich middle caste	8	107
Poor middle caste	7	84	Rich middle caste	8	108
Poor scheduled	9	95	Upper medium income middle caste	9	113
			Very poor Muslim	2	125
			Poor Muslim	5	150

The degree of inferiority of the most unhealthy category (poor Muslims) exceeds the degree of superiority of the healthiest category (rich high castes) by a factor of two. However, the overall usefulness of the AHI, given problems of selection of indicators and of weighting, is very much open to question.

Health Care

The table on page 367 shows variations in expenditure on treating illnesses of household heads, by caste stratum, class and weighted per capita income. The lower table on page 372 shows variations in expenditure per household and per household member.

CASTE STRATUM, CLASS, Rs WPCI AND INDEX OF AV. EXPENDITURE ON HEALTH, HH HEADS JAN 1981-FEB 1982

	RICH	FAIRLY RICH	UPPER MEDIUM	LOWER MEDIUM	POOR	VERY POOR	TOTAL	RICHER	POORER	POORER AS % OF RICHER
HIGH CASTE										
HIGH CLASS	287*	114					240	240		
MEDIUM		216	12	58	197		119	114	127	111
LOW				31	76	0	53		53	
TOTAL	287	154	12	38	106	0	160	206	72	35
MIDDLE CASTE										
HIGH CLASS	495**	27	1087***				388	388		
MEDIUM	1	16	9	5	3		7	9	4	44
LOW		12	52	5	39	94	41	38	44	116
TOTAL	433	20	147	5	29	94	138	161	30	19
MUSLIM										
MEDIUM		8	20				12	12		
LOW		7	15	6	91	32	41	11	46	409
TOTAL		8	18	6	91	32	36	12	46	383
SCHEDULED										
MEDIUM				92	2		32		32	
LOW		0	2	32	26	36	24	2	30	1500
TOTAL		0	2	42	21	36	25	2	30	1500
TOTAL HHHs										
HIGH CLASS	384	64					256	317		
MEDIUM	1	80	11	33	42		39	40	37	92
LOW	10	29	20	53	45	37	26	39	150	
GRAND TOTAL	360	57	87	23	50	45	100	166	39	24
AV. Rs H. EXP.	586	92	142	37	82	73	163	270	64	24
NO. OF HHHs	16	17	16	20	25	8	102	49	53	

* The total expenditure of Rs 3740 includes one Thakur HHH who spent Rs 3700 on dysentery and stomach disorder.

** The total expenditure of Rs 5636 included Rs 3000 and Rs 2050 respectively by 2 of the 7 HHHs. *** One HHH only.

Having provided some data on differences in health and health care, it is now possible to examine the differences in health between caste strata, individual castes, income categories, classes and genders. The next sections will consider these in turn.

CASTE STRATUM AND HEALTH

In this section Muslims will be treated as a 'caste stratum' insofar as the term Muslim represents an aggregation of caste categories.

Mortality

The seven male household heads who had died included 4 middle caste, 2 high caste and 1 Muslim. Twelve out of 95 household heads who had married were widowers by 1982 and the proportion of dead wives was 21 percent among high castes, 14 percent among scheduled, 12 percent among Muslim and only 5 percent for middle castes.

The data on the population and on the sample produce conflicting results on under 5 mortality. For the total population (with less reliable data), the scheduled had the highest mortality index (126), followed by Muslims (118), high castes (109) and middle castes particularly low (65). The index of mortality per mother (rather than per total births) was worst for high castes (150), followed by Muslim and scheduled (125) and with middle castes again very low (62). The table on caste stratum and gender (pages 354-5) shows sample data with Muslim under 5 mortality 30 percent above average, compared with much lower Hindu indices: middle castes 101, high castes 90, scheduled 87 and all Hindus 95. Inter-strata differentiation increased in the period after 1965 when mortality fell by 39 percent overall. The Muslim excess above average increased from 15 percent earlier to 56 percent in the later period. The high caste index fell from 94 to 81 (ie. 19 percent below average mortality). The high increase in the Muslim index (to 156) in the later period seems to have been wholly due to deaths (especially female) in richer households (index 259). More generally, differentiation between caste strata was greater among richer households, especially in the later period.

In the Bijnor villages, under five mortality of Muslim children has been 30 percent above average and that of caste Hindus 24 percent below average. The differences in mortality between strata were very much smaller for those born up to 1965 (and thus potential deaths analysed up to 1970). The range in indices widens from 31 points in the earlier period to 101 points in the period of births from 1966 to 1980 (and thus of potential under 5 deaths up to 1985). In this second period, the Muslim-caste Hindu gradient of child mortality has doubled from 137 percent to 287 percent. Earlier, there was an almost negligible difference between Muslims and the scheduled but in the recent period the gradient was actually 204 percent. (This adds support to the frequently heard complaints of Muslims in Basauli that they were losing out at the expense of both the scheduled and 'backward', ie. middle castes.) In short, as the overall child mortality rate halved, the inter-strata differences had doubled or almost tripled. These differences are all the more important because Muslims accounted for over a third of households in JD and also had in some ways a somewhat better class composition than the scheduled or all Hindu castes: 63 percent of Muslim households were middle or rich peasants, compared with only 55 percent of total households.

Stillbirths in Basauli occurred most among high castes (index 167), nearer the average among both the scheduled (110) and middle castes (82), and least among Muslims (39). The index for fairly rich, high class Hindus was actually 541 and one such Brahmin reported four male stillbirths in the 1940s (plus a daughter who died of tetanus at six months).

One Pasi (scheduled) household reported five stillbirths (as well as two miscarriages and six surviving children). The husband was sterilised in about 1975. Even in the later period, from 1966 to 1981 when the ratio of stillbirths to total births fell from 7.8 to 5.1 percent, high castes retained the highest index (151), followed by scheduled (106) and with seemingly none among middle castes and Muslims.

Indices have also been calculated for the percentage of progeny of sample household heads who had died at any age, ie. not just up to the age of 5. The scheduled had the lowest mortality (index 89), followed by middle castes (98) and high castes (100). Muslim progeny mortality was again by far the worst (123).

The table shows changes in the caste stratum and gender distribution of stillbirths and under 5 deaths for successive quinquennia between 1941 and 1980.

CASTE STRATUM, GENDER + QUINQUENNIA: STILLBIRTHS + UNDER 5 DEATHS, BASAULI 1931-82

STILLBIRTHS AND UNDER FIVE DEATHS	HIGH CASTE		MIDDLE		MUSLIM		SCHEDULED		TOTAL		
DATE OF DEATH	M	F	M	F	M	F	M	F	M	F	T
1931-40	1	1	3						4	1	5
1941-5	3	1	2		3	1	1	1	9	3	12
1946-50	1	2		3	1	2	3		5	7	12
% of Row	8	17		25	8	17	25		42	58	100
1951-55	2	4	14	2	1		2	2	19	8	27
% of Row	7	15	52	7	4		7	7	70	30	100
1956-60	3	4	10	2	2	3	2	2	17	11	28
% of Row	11	14	36	7	7	11	7	7	61	39	100
1961-65	2	1	8	5	7	1	1	6	18	13	31
% of Row	6	3	26	16	23	3	3	19	58	42	100
1966-70	3	3	6	7	4	3	4	4	17	17	34
% of Row	9	9	18	21	12	9	12	12	50	50	100
1971-75	2	2	7	2	3	3	4	2	16	9	25
% of Row	8	8	28	8	12	12	16	8	64	36	100
1976-80	2	3	5	4	1	3	2	5	10	15	25
% of Row	8	12	20	16	4	12	8	20	40	60	100
1981 + 1982		2	1			1		1	1	4	5
% of Row									20	8	100
Date not known				2						2	2
TOTAL	19	23	56	27	22	17	19	23	116	90	206
% of Row	9	11	27	13	11	8	9	11	56	44	100
TOTAL BIRTHS	68	49	139	68	39	27	47	45	293	189	482
DEATH RATE PER 1000 TOTAL BIRTHS	279	469	403	397	564	630	404	511	396	476	427

* Note the lower reporting of female births, probably mainly married daughters no longer in the household.

Nutrition

The high caste males aged 18 and over had 5 percent greater weight than average and middle castes 5 percent below average (indices 95 and 105 respectively: see the earlier table on the 12 health indicators). The scheduled males were slightly above and Muslims slightly below average. Differences in height were smaller, with the high castes only 1 percent above and middle and Muslim castes 1 percent below average. Consequently, high castes performed best on weight for height (index 98), scheduled were average and Muslims (101) and middle castes (102) did worst.

Fewer women were measured for weight and height. High caste females again enjoyed a superiority in weight (4 percent above average compared with 5 percent for males), whilst Muslims and other strata were 1 percent and 3 percent respectively below average. Conversely, high caste women (who included several old women with stoops) were 1 percent below average height and other strata were 1 percent above average. Consequently, high caste women end up with weight for height 6 percent above average, scheduled 5 percent below and other strata 3 percent below. Female inequalities in weight for height thus far exceeded those for men in different caste strata. Comparison of sample household members, including children (with some fairly large age discrepancies) produced the following ranking of weight for height: middle caste heaviest (98), high caste (99), scheduled (101) and Muslim worst (106).

Sample data on page 375 also show that the scheduled had the highest fertility index (107), followed by Muslims (104), high castes (96) and middle castes (94).

Morbidity

Inter-strata differences in morbidity (ie. days of illness) existed but these were not uniform for all types of kin status within the household. For household heads, indices for Hindu strata ranged between 88 and 94, with Muslims much higher (index 142 and 56 percent higher than the average Hindu).

The ranking of wives is the same as for household heads but the range rather wider. High caste wives (index 59) and scheduled wives (69) were healthier, both absolutely and relatively, than wives of middle (120) and Muslim castes (137). The position of middle caste wives was significantly worse than that of middle caste household heads. This tends to confirm the suggestion of Jeffery (1989) that women in middle caste medium to large acreage farms suffered greater stress and ill health because of greater workloads on the farm, particularly more outwork and looking after more animals and being exposed to diseases (such as tetanus) transmitted by or through animals. The index of morbidity for 18 richer middle caste wives of household heads in Basauli is as high as 180.

Excess illness was particularly high among lower class, poor Muslim wives and among upper class, richer middle caste wives but numbers are small and may easily be distorted by a single person reporting maximum length of illness (420 days).

For all members of the household, differences between Hindu castes were relatively small, compared with the gap between all Hindus and Muslims (index 148). Middle castes (88) had the lowest morbidity, followed by high castes (95) and then the scheduled (98).

For first and second sons of the household head, aged 0 to 15, there was relatively little difference among the non-scheduled castes, though Muslims had a slightly higher index (41 compared with 32 for the high and middle castes). The scheduled had almost four times the average amount of illness (373).

For first and second sons of the household head, aged 16 plus, the pattern differed from that for minor sons. Differences were large, though numbers rather small. The high castes had the longest illness (index 203), followed by the scheduled (147) and Muslims (119) whilst the middle castes were in a distinctly lower category (44).

Aggregate Health

On the basis of the aggregate health index (combining 7 indicators of weight for height, child mortality and days illness), the high castes emerge as the healthiest with an index of 90. They were followed by the scheduled (93) and the middle castes (100), with the Muslims again clearly differentiated with an index of 123. If the high castes are compared with all other strata, then the gradient of inequality is a modest 114 percent.

If the performance of the high castes is compared with that of other strata, including Muslims, then by far the highest gradient of inequality was for days illness of wives of household head (187%).

INDICES OF HEALTH (Av = 100)

	MALE WT/HT	FEMALE WT/HT	ALL WT/HT	CHILD DEATHS	DAYS ILL,HHH	DAYS ILL,WIFE	DAYS ILL, ALL	AGGREGATE HEALTH INDEX
High Caste	98	94	99	100	88	59	95	90
Others	101	104	101	101	104	110	101	103
GRADIENT Others as % of High Caste	103	110 *	102	101	118 *	187 **	106	114

Unlike in the case of gradients based on per capita income, the inter-strata gradients are all positive and there is no indicator where the high castes performed worse than the lower castes. The relatively high gradient for female weight for height is particularly noticeable (and almost certainly suspect).

Health Care

Probably the most reliable data on health expenditure related to treatment of illnesses of household heads (see table on page 367). The average during the 14 months was Rs 163 or about 3.5 percent out of an average net household income of Rs 4,624. The high caste index was 160 percent of the average, followed by middle castes (138%), Muslims (36%) and scheduled (25%). When these differences in expenditure are related to indices of days of illness (ie. 'use-need') the inter-stratum disparity increases:

INDEX	HIGH	MIDDLE	MUSLIM	SCHEDULED
Days ill HHH	88	94	142	92
Health Expend. HHH	160	138	36	25
Health Expend. as % of Days ill	182	147	25	27

Taking total health expenditure for all household members, the medium castes spent most (index 148), followed by the high castes (109), Muslims (48) and the scheduled (45). The high expenditure by medium castes applies only to their richer households (index 208) and especially the richest (413). The income difference is sharpest for medium castes and was relatively small for Muslims and the scheduled.

CASTE STRATUM, Rs WPCI AND INDEX OF HOUSEHOLD EXPENDITURE ON HEALTH (TOTAL AND PER CAPITA)

INDEX OF TOTAL HEALTH EXPENDITURE PER HOUSEHOLD

CASTE STRATUM	RICH	FAIRLY RICH	UPPER MEDIUM	LOWER MEDIUM	POOR	VERY POOR	TOTAL	RICHER	POORER	POORER AS % OF RICHER
HIGH	207	100	12	36		69	109	146	47	32
MEDIUM	413	151	77	18	29	142	148	208	41	20
MUSLIM		72	45	8	89	17	48	61	43	70
SCHEDULED	54	28	63	35	26	45	54	43	80	
TOTAL	310	117	60	33	49	50	100	161	43	27
Rs TOTAL EXPENDITURE	1204	453	234	127	192	194	388	625	167	27

INDEX OF AVERAGE HEALTH EXPENDITURE PER HOUSEHOLD MEMBER

CASTE STRATUM	RICH	FAIRLY RICH	UPPER MEDIUM	LOWER MEDIUM	POOR	VERY POOR	TOTAL	RICHER	POORER	POORER AS % OF RICHER
HIGH	181	152	11	59	73	6	116	149	60	40
MEDIUM	219	262	94	22	39	117	136	187	44	24
MUSLIM		81	66	12	81	22	53	76	43	57
SCHEDULED	55	44	112	31	30	56	46	58	126	
TOTAL	200	186	70	45	50	47	100	153	51	33
Rs AVERAGE EXPENDITURE	128	119	45	29	32	30	64	98	33	33

NB The averages for health expenditure per HH member are unweighted.

Calculation of unweighted averages per household member serves to reduce inter-stratum differences a little and to level the gradient between lowest and highest slightly from 30 percent to 39 percent. Again the medium castes were the biggest spenders in total and per household member and it was only in the case of expenditure on household heads that high castes led the field. Whereas the highest expenditure in total was by rich households of medium caste (index 413), the highest expenditure per capita was by the fairly rich of medium caste (index 262). The eight fairly rich medium caste households included 2 Kurmis, 2 Lodhs, 1 Bhat, 1 Ahir, 1 Gadaria and 1 Loniya and the figures suggest, almost certainly wrongly, that in aggregate they had spent 10 percent of total income on medical treatment.

CASTE + INDICES OF DEFICIENCY IN WEIGHT, HEIGHT + WEIGHT FOR HEIGHT, MEN + WOMEN AGED 21 PLUS, BASAULI

CASTE		NO. OF MEN	INDEX OF DEFICIENCY WEIGHT	HEIGHT	WEIGHT FOR HEIGHT	NO OF WOMEN	INDEX OF DEFICIENCY WEIGHT	HEIGHT	WEIGHT FOR HEIGHT
BRAHMIN	Shukla	7	99	100	100	4	77	98	80
	Misra	5	94	101	93	2	112	101	112
	Other subcastes	5	92	99	92	4	98	99	99
TOTAL BRAHMIN		17	95	100	95	10	91	99	92
MAHABRAHMIN		10	100	98	101	4	93	95	98
THAKUR		10	93	98	95	7	107	108	99
PUNJABI (Sikh)		1	82	91	93				
TOTAL HIGH CASTES		38	96	99	97	21	97	101	96
KURMI		6	100	100	100	7	101	97	104
AHIR		6	109	105	104	1	124	104	119?
LODH		17	99	99	101	6	107	100	107
MALI						2	105	102	103
LOHAR		4	104	99	105	1	93	102	92
KAHAR		1	102	106	95	1	86	102	84
BHURJI		3	107	102	105	1	98	101	97
GADARIA		4	108	101	107	1	96	104	92
LONIYA		1	121	111	112				
TOTAL MIDDLE CASTES		42	103	101	102	20	103	100	103
PATHAN		7	90	98	92	3	103	101	102
DHOBE		5	105	100	105	1	116	101	115
NAI		6	114	104	111	1	119	102	118
TELI		3	103	100	104	3	81	98	84
KABARIA						1	106	97	108
TOTAL MUSLIM		21	103	101	102	9	99	100	100
CHAMAR		7	99	100	99	8	102	98	104
PASI		5	104	101	104				
PATHARKOT		3	93	103	90	1	101	101	100
BASPHOD		2	105	99	105				
RADHIKA		11	100	100	100				
TOTAL SCHEDULED		28	100	101	100	9	102	98	103
GRAND TOTAL, INDEX		129	100	100	100	59	100	100	100
GRAND TOTAL, ACTUAL		129	46.8 kg	164.7 cm	.284 kg/cm	59	39.3 kg	150.8 cm	.261 kg/cm

CASTE AND HEALTH

Nutrition

The table shows detailed indices for members of individual castes, aged 21 and over. Comparing the average for the four strata, all are within 4 percent of the overall average for all those measured. For men, the high castes were above average in height and especially in weight. The scheduled were about equal to the average and the middle castes and the Muslims were slightly below average, especially in weight. The pattern was similar for women except that Muslim women were at least equal to the overall average and scheduled women were underweight. Numbers measured for particular castes were in some cases very small and results are also biassed by differing age distributions within different caste samples. Among men, a Punjabi, Pathans, Thakurs, Patharkots and Brahmins were the heaviest and Muslim Nais and some middle Hindus were the lightest. There was less variation in height, with a Punjabi, Mahabrahmins, Thakurs and Pathans enjoying a slight superiority. The weight for height of a Loniya, Nais and Gadarias was particularly low. In the case of women, caste numbers are even smaller than for men and the patterns are similar. Female weight for height exceeded that of males in the case of Shukla Brahmins and Telis. The highest female weights for height occurred among Telis, Brahmins and Mahabrahmins and the lowest were Lodhs and Kurmis (excluding castes with very small numbers measured).

Fertility and mortality

The table shows indices of fertility for individual castes in both the total population and also in the sample. The data on the whole population are less reliable and clearly understate average fertility with a figure of 3.5 births per mother, compared with 5.4 births in the sample. Assuming that the sample data are certainly more accurate and indeed may be reasonably accurate, then this is an underestimate of about 35 percent. In the whole population, the fertility of the more numerous castes, in descending order was Nai (highest, with an index of 149), Mahabrahmin 146, Thakur 120, Pasi 117, and Brahmin and Loniya and Pathan each 114. Below average were Radhika 97, Lodh 91, Kabaria 89, Kurmi 86, Chamar and Gadaria both 74, and Ahir lowest with an index of 69. The sample data differed considerably and only for Mahabrahmin (111), Pasi (204), Loniya (126), Kurmi (89), Chamar (89) and Ahir (93) was there much similarity either in absolute indices or in relative ranking.

The discrepancies appear to illustrate the possible risks and unreliability of 'quick and dirty' censuses of the total population and the need to investigate samples in greater depth. Though the data on the sample may be far from perfect, they are likely to be a more reliable guide to inter-caste variations.

In the total population, the highest indices of mortality for children under the age of five were, in descending order, Nai 210, Radhika 167, Mahabrahmin 154, Dhobe 145, Pasi 128, Chamar 117 and Thakur 114. The lowest mortality indices were those of the Loniya and Pathan (87), Kabaria (85), Lodh (68), Gadaria (67), Brahmin (66), Ahir (55) and Kurmi (44). The indices for the sample were also discrepant (except in the case of Ahir) and the sequence was Kabaria 163, Loniya 117, Radhika 113, Brahmin and Pathan 109 and Dhobe 108. The lowest indices included Thakur (92), Kurmi (84), Chamar (80) and Ahir (60).

CASTE + INDICES OF AVERAGE FERTILITY + CHILD MORTALITY PER MOTHER, TOTAL + SAMPLE POPULATION

	TOTAL POPN. 263 HOUSEHOLDS					SAMPLE 102 HOUSEHOLDS				
		INDEX OF AVERAGE PER MOTHER			INDEX OF UNDER 5 MORTALITY		INDEX OF AVERAGE PER MOTHER			INDEX OF MORTALITY ALL AGES
CASTE	NO. OF MOTHERS	BORN	DIED	ALIVE	PER 1000	NO. OF MOTHERS	BORN	DIED	ALIVE	PER 1000
BRAHMIN	27	114	75	122	66	11	91	100	83	109
MAHABRAHMIN	24	146	225	122	154	7	111	100	120	91
THAKUR	15	120	138	115	114	5	81	75	87	92
PUNJABI	2	NA	NA	93	NA					
HIGH CASTE	68	126	150	119	109	23	96	96	97	100
BANIA	1	29	0	37	(0)	1	74	125	33	(169)
BHAT	4	143	250	111	175	1	19	42	0	(226)
KURMI	19	86	38	100	44	9	89	75	100	84
AHIR	13	69	38	78	55	3	93	54	123	60
LODH	42	91	63	100	68	12	111	117	107	103
MALI	3	143	125	148	(87)	2	83	62	100	(75)
BARHAI	2	157	188	148	(118)					
LOHAR	5	109	75	119	69					
KAHAR	4	80	25	93	31	1	93	83	100	(90)
BHURJI (H+M)	5*	109*	0*	141*	0*	Hindu: 1	93	83	100	(90)
GADARIA	19	74	50	81	67	4	111	117	107	103
LONIYA	13	114	100	119	87	4	126	146	107	117
MIDDLE CASTE	130	91	62	100	65	38	94	96	93	103
PATHAN	18	114	100	119	87	6	96	104	90	109
DHOBE	7	77	112	70	145	5	85	92	80	108
NAI	6	149	312	100	210					
TELI	3	86	125	74	(145)	2	102	146	67	(144)
KABARIA	8	89	75	93	85	3	111	179	57	163
BHURJI (M)	See BHURJI (Hindu and Muslim) above					1	37	0	67	(0)
MUSLIM	42	106	125	100	118	17	104	112	97	109
CHAMAR	37	74	88	70	117	13	89	71	103	80
PASI	15	117	150	107	128	2	204	208	200	(103)
BASPHOD	1	86	0	111	(0)	1	93	83	100	(90)
PATHARKOT	5	143	175	133	122	1	111	42	167	(38)
RADHIKA	11	97	162	78	167	2	148	167	133	(113)
SCHEDULED	69	91	112	85	126	19	107	96	120	87
TOTAL INDEX	309	100	100	100	100	97	100	100	100	100
TOTAL ACTUAL	309	3.5	0.8	2.7	229	97	5.4	2.4	3.0	443

* Bhurjis, both Hindu and Muslim
Indices in parentheses are based on small numbers

PER CAPITA INCOME AND HEALTH

This section examines the relation between per capita income and health indicators. For male and female adult weight, height and weight for height, unweighted PCI is used because those measured were a non-random sample whose PCI was estimated by a key local informant. For the remaining indicators, including weight for height of all household members (in the random sample), weighted PCI is available and can be used.

Nutrition

The table on page 353 shows indices for male and female deficiencies in weight for height. Apart from minor blips, there is a smooth trend towards greater weight of males aged 18 plus, as PCI increases. However, the inequality gradient between poorer and richer households was only a modest 106 percent. The trend was similar for male height and again the poor performed worse than the very poor. The gradient between poorer and richer was only 102 percent. Apart from the fairly rich, there is a smooth trend towards greater weight for height, as PCI increases. The gradient between poorer and richer is 104 percent.

WEIGHTED PER CAPITA INCOME AND INDICES OF HEALTH, BASAULI 1981-2

HEALTH INDEX AS % OF BASAULI AVERAGE (=100)	RICH	FAIRLY RICH	UPPER MEDIUM	LOWER MEDIUM	POOR	VERY POOR	TOTAL BASAULI	POORER AS % OF RICHER
		RICHER			POORER		ACTUAL	INEQUALITY GRADIENT
MAX Rs WPCI	2500	1400	1100	950	810	700	2500	
MIN Rs WPCI	1401	1101	951	811	701	401	401	
AV. Rs WPCI	1664	1242	1032	877	762	619	1037	(167)
WEIGHT FOR HEIGHT DEFICIENCY INDEX						Rs 601-700 401-600		
MALES, 18+		98		99	101	102 103	.282 Kg per cm	104
FEMALES, 18+		97		106	97	102 102	.260 Kg per cm	98
STILL + LIVE BIRTHS PER WIFE OF HHH	100	102	91	96	109	92	5.3 total births	

The trend was less smooth in the case of females aged 18 and over. The richest category was heaviest but otherwise overall the richer women were slightly lighter than the poorer, including even the poorest. The gradient was very small, smaller than for males, but in the reverse direction from that for males. The richest category had the lowest heights but again there was no difference overall between richer and poorer women. The five richest women had much greater weight for height than the rest but the trend was far from smooth. The average weights for height of the fairly rich and upper medium incomes were 6 percent and 7 percent respectively below the overall average and in aggregate richer women performed slightly worse than poorer women. The gradient was 98 percent, ie. in the opposite direction from that of male weight for height.

Taking members of sample households, both sexes and all ages, weight for height increased steadily and uniformly with weighted PCI, except for the poor (who performed worse than the very poor). The gradient between poorer and richer was 106 percent, higher than for male adults, but the discrepancies on some children's ages make these results less reliable. The income gradient is non-existent among low class households and only 103 percent among the medium class.

Mortality

The table on pages 361-2 shows the number of live and stillbirths, percentage surviving and actual mortality rates for (landownership) classes in JD and for weighted per capita income categories in Basauli. This also provides indices of mortality levels for six income categories in Basauli, plus indices of ages of those parents of household heads who had died by February 1982.

The table below shows that stillbirth rates were higher in the period before 1966 and, for both periods, among males and in richer households.

INDICES OF STILLBIRTH RATES PER 1000 TOTAL BIRTHS (AV=100)

	TOTAL BIRTHS TO 1965			TOTAL BIRTHS 1966-77			TOTAL BIRTHS TO 1977		
SEX	RICHER	POORER	TOTAL	RICHER	POORER	TOTAL	RICHER	POORER	TOTAL
M	185	129	156	100	26	63	147	85	116
F	85	76	79	97	58	76	92	64	77
T	153	111	131	98	40	69	126	77	100

NB The average rate of stillbirths per 1000 total births was 62 (30 out of 480 total births to 1977). There were also at least two stillbirths after 1977.

The stillbirth rate nearly halved in the second period, after 1965.

Seventeen of the 32 recorded stillbirths occurred in high caste households, 8 were scheduled, 4 were middle caste and only 2 were Muslim. The highest stillbirth rates per 1000 total births were as follows:

Male, high caste and rich, before 1966	240
Male or female, high caste and rich, 1966-77	200
Female, scheduled and poor, before 1966	167
Male, scheduled and poor, before 1966	158
Female, high caste and rich, before 1966	133
Male, Muslim and poor, before 1966	105
Male, high caste and poor, before 1966	77
Female, scheduled and poor, 1976-77	74
Male, middle caste and rich, before 1966	67
Male, scheduled and poor, 1966-77	48
Male, middle caste and poor, before 1966	28

Obviously, these rates need to be treated with great caution, given the small numbers in each cell.

The stillbirth rate was higher in richer households (under 120) than in poorer ones (81). The highest *index* was among the fairly rich (161), followed by the poor (118) and the rich (103). Taking just the 12 stillbirths occurring between 1966 and 1981, seven of these were in rich or fairly rich (mainly Kurmi) households and the remaining five were in poor (scheduled) households. This evidence is particularly important (though almost certainly incomplete) insofar as it relates to a recent period when a) the stillbirth rate appears to have fallen by about a third; and b) the data on WPCI in 1981-2 are more relevant. The disparity actually increased quite sharply in the later period when the stillbirth rate almost halved. The excess of stillbirths among the richer was greater for males overall and was particularly marked after 1965. The negative gradient increased sharply from 70 percent to 26 percent (see pages 361-2 and 377).

Overall, poorer households (index 104) had a higher rate of under 5 mortality than richer households (96). However, the pattern has changed from much greater excess mortality among the poor for births before 1966 to almost exactly the reverse in the subsequent period of births up to 1977:

	BORN UP TO 1965		BORN 1966-77		TOTAL BORN TO 1977	
	RICHER	POORER	RICHER	POORER	RICHER	POORER
INDEX	83	115	118	83	96	104

Among high castes, the richer households experienced higher mortality, though less so in the later period. The income difference in mortality among the middle castes (the largest category) was greater, with a gradient of 160 percent. However, even here there was a switch from a very high positive gradient of 201 percent in the earlier period to a fairly high negative gradient of 65 percent in the later period. Muslims, like both the high and the scheduled castes, suffered higher mortality among richer households and this was mainly because of a very high negative gradient (39%) during the later period. However, the number of Muslim live births after 1965 was small (32). Overall, it is clear that the slight positive gradient between poorer and richer households is entirely attributable to excess mortality among the poorer from middle castes who accounted for 203 out of the total 450 live births. Even the middle castes had a negative gradient in the later period (as did all caste strata) and the overall slightly higher mortality of the poorer during the whole period (gradient 108%) is almost entirely attributable to the huge difference within middle castes (richer index 72, poorer 145 and a gradient of 201%) in the earlier period. The implication is that, as child mortality has fallen from the extremely high 460 to the still very high 281 deaths per 1000 live births, the reported rates have fallen more rapidly among the poorer households, despite fewer of the poorer households reporting an improvement in income and living standards during the 1970s (see table). The 1970s represent roughly 25 percent of the total time period during which this apparent improvement in mortality had occurred. The trend towards a lower per capita income gradient for child mortality in this single Indian village is in distinct contrast to what seem to be mainly increasing class gradients for various health indicators in Britain over a similar time period (Townsend 1988).

WEIGHTED PER CAPITA INCOME AND REPORTED CHANGE IN STANDARD OF LIVING OF HOUSEHOLD, 1971-81

NUMBER OF HHs	RICH	FAIRLY RICH	UPPER MEDIUM	LOWER MEDIUM	POOR	VERY POOR	TOTAL NO.	RICHER	POORER
IMPROVEMENT	7	8	3	5	6	0	29	18	11
NO CHANGE	3	4	8	10	10	6	41	15	26
DETERIORATION	6	5	5	5	9	2	32	16	16
TOTAL	16	17	16	20	25	8	102	49	53
% of HHs									
IMPROVEMENT	44	47	19	25	24	0	28	37	21
NO CHANGE	19	24	50	50	40	75	40	31	49
DETERIORATION	38	29	31	25	36	25	31	33	30
TOTAL	100	100	100	100	100	100	100	100	100

Comparison of Basauli and Jhakri-Dharmnagri

Patterns of under 5 mortality for landownership categories in JD (Bijnor) will now be compared with those for income categories in Basauli. The reasons for not comparing them with the class categories in Basauli are: a) that the JD classes are based on acres per able-bodied adult male and do not appear to facilitate calculation of land owned per household; b) the analysis on Basauli devotes more attention to income than landowning/class categories; and c) the JD classes are perhaps to some extent proxies for income anyway.

Under 5 mortality was lower among the richer in Basauli and the more landed in Jhakri-Dharmnagri but the class difference in JD far exceeded the income difference in Basauli (see table on page 360). The indices for richer and poorer in Basauli were 96 and 104, giving a gentle inequality gradient of only 108 percent. The equivalents in JD were 87 and 116, with a steeper gradient (133%). However, the indices were amazingly similar for the period up to 1965 and the gradient for Basauli (139%) was virtually the same as that for JD (142%). The difference in the respective gradients for the whole period derive from the sharply contrasting trend in child deaths among those born after 1965. Whereas the mortality index for 1966-77 in Basauli was higher for the richer, giving a negative gradient of 70 percent, mortality indices for upper and lower peasants in JD (1966-80) more or less equalised to a non-gradient of 101 percent.

For the whole period, the income or class gradient for males was steeper than for females in both samples, but much more sharply so in JD (male 153 percent and female 115 percent). In the earlier period, the male gradient in Basauli (129%) was much less steep than in JD (187%) whilst the reverse was true for female gradients (Basauli 153 percent and JD only 113 percent). The highest indices were for poorer females in both populations (Basauli 148 and JD 122) and the lowest were for richer males (76 in Basauli and 61 in JD). In the later period, the relative mortality of the richer worsened and the relative rate for the poorer improved, especially in Basauli. The reversal of the relative rates for richer and poorer in Basauli was particularly dramatic in the case of females (and may owe something to lower reliability of the earlier data on females in Basauli?) whereas in JD the change in the female gradient was from moderate to complete equality.

Income gradients of child mortality differed for the constituent caste strata. For caste Hindus, the gradient was high in both samples, especially so for males in JD (226%) and to a lesser extent for females in Basauli (141%). The higher gradient in JD derived mainly from the earlier period. In the later period the gradients fell sharply in both areas and also became very similar between the two areas. In the case of Muslims, the patterns for the two areas differed very sharply and this was because of a surprising and unusual negative gradient of 64 percent in Basauli, which arose out of a particularly high mortality index (259) for richer Muslims in the later period. This high rate was due to an extremely high mortality index (305) for a few richer female Muslims in the latest period. Muslim gradients contrasted tremendously between Basauli and JD in the later period (B 39% and JD 155%). The mortality indices for the scheduled were similar in the two areas, except for the poorer being very low in the later period in JD (46). In JD only the Muslims had a positive income gradient in the later period but the negative gradient for the scheduled was far steeper than that of the caste Hindus. The data shows that the gradient was most negative for scheduled females in JD in the later period and that the gradient was only positive for scheduled females in JD in the earlier period, ie. there was a major change in gradient between the two periods (just as there was a comparable smaller change for scheduled males in JD).

In Basauli the richest had the lowest rate of child deaths of any age, including adulthood, and the poorest had the second highest but otherwise there was no trend in relation to income. The fairly rich had by far the highest index (122). The gradient was actually perverse (94%), with richer households reporting more child deaths than poorer households. This could be partly explained by better memory and fuller reporting by richer households, who would be both better educated and arguably more likely to remember such events.

The ages reported for parents who had died were, like other ages, not very accurate. For what they are worth, they reveal no significant income differences for fathers of household heads and only one difference for mothers of the poorest household heads. This difference - 77 years, compared with an overall average of 68, could be due to illiteracy and exaggeration of ages of the old. However, if this were the full explanation, then similar greater longevity might be expected for fathers as well as mothers of the poorest.....

Morbidity

The richest and poorest household heads had respectively the least and most days of illness but again the trend with weighted PCI is not smooth. The lower medium income category reported the second highest morbidity. A smooth trend can be elicited by re-aggregating the income categories as follows:

Rs Wted PCI	1401-2500		951-1400		701-950		401-700		TOTAL	
	NO.	INDEX	NO.	INDEX	NO.	INDEX	NO.	INDEX	NO.	INDEX
Index of Days Illness	16	70	33	81	45	112	8	173	102	100

The overall difference between richer and poorer households is very clear and the gradient high (155%). This income inequality is the highest for any of the major health indicators used. If the morbidity of the richest and the poorest only are compared then the gradient becomes even higher (247%), much higher than the 151 percent gradient for child deaths of the poorest and richest.

Upper medium income wives had the longest illness, followed by the richest and the poor. There was no regular trend with weighted PCI. Overall, the richer wives had much longer illness than the poorer ones and the inequality gradient was 51 percent. In other words, the trend, albeit irregular, was in the opposite direction from that for household heads and the inequality was considerably greater. Numbers were smaller and data almost certainly less reliable than for household heads but this cannot explain the very strong difference in results. Part of the explanation may perhaps be found in the claim by Jeffery (1989) that women in richer agricultural households faced greater workloads (especially looking after animals) and greater non-domestic responsibilities and stress than those in poorer households, with fewer or no animals to look after.

Taking all household members, the fairly rich had the highest morbidity and the poor the lowest. The rest were near to average. Overall the richer had 8 percent above average, the poorer had 4 percent below average number of days of illness and the gradient of inequality was 89 percent.

The table shows the percentage distribution of days of various types of illness by income, gender and age. Given the percentage of the population in various categories of income gender and age, it is possible to ascertain how proportionate the distribution of days of illness was to relative population size. For example, 22 percent of the sample were rich, they endured only 20 percent of total morbidity but 37 percent of 'other illness' and only 5 percent of skin complaints. 'Other illness' was particularly disproportionate (and high) for rich males aged between 16 and 60. Rich women aged 16 to 60 experienced more colds and coughs, as well as aches. Older men had double their quota of total illness.

The fairly rich reported a disproportionately high amount of total morbidity, 'other illness' and also of fevers and even skin complaints. Fairly rich boys had very little illness though a very high incidence of colds and coughs. Fairly rich girls experienced over six times their share of fevers. Adult males suffered particularly from skin complaints and adult females from aches and also gastric problems. Older females suffered seven times their due share of illness, especially 'other illness' and colds and coughs.

INDEX OF TOTAL DAYS ILLNESS, BY TYPE OF ILLNESS, AGE, SEX AND INCOME, 102 HHs

TYPE OF ILLNESS + INCOME	% OF TOTAL DAYS ILLNESS AS A % OF POPULATION SHARE						TOTAL
	MALE 0-15	FEMALE 0-15	MALE 16-60	FEMALE 16-60	MALE 61+	FEMALE 61+	
RICH							
% OF POPN.	4.2	5.5	5.9	5.2	0.3	0.9	22.0
GASTRIC	24	132	75	56	633	222	87
ACHES			173	196			93
OTHER	300	24	308	69	300		166
COUGHS, COLDS	69	55	34	262	133	200	107
SKIN	43		39	17			23
FEVERS	24	62	63	162		33	76
TOTAL	69	54	114	121	200	89	92
FAIRLY RICH							
% OF POPN.	3.6	2.2	4.3	4.5	0.3	0.3	15.4
GASTRIC		82	84	267			113
ACHES				353			103
OTHER	22		295	42		4200	182
COUGHS, COLDS	83	186	153	78		600	123
SKIN	8		365	102			140
FEVERS		655	251	60			181
TOTAL	17	132	172	171	33	700	135
UPPER MEDIUM							
% OF POPN.	3.8	2.6	3.6	3.1	0.2	0.3	13.7
GASTRIC	3		289	16			80
ACHES				329			74
OTHER	Neg			58			16
COUGHS, COLDS	37	192	94	148	200	4200	201
SKIN	24		78	119			29
FEVERS	66	35	164	16			72
TOTAL	18	31	119	97	Neg	633	79
LOWER MEDIUM							
% OF POPN.	3.1	2.9	4.5	3.6	1.2	0.5	15.9
GASTRIC		159	327	3	592		167
ACHES			204	589	85		255
OTHER		93	206	64			89
COUGHS, COLDS	Neg	17	36	39		360	35
SKIN	13		20	78	75		32
FEVERS	226	48	111	17	283	200	117
TOTAL	32	62	173	133	358	80	127
POOR							
8% OF POPN.	5.4	5.2	7.3	6.1	0.5	0.9	25.3
GASTRIC	7		182	26		56	63
ACHES	24			166			45
OTHER	33	19	67	148		600	55
COUGHS, COLDS	26	15	116	174			84
SKIN	200	204	111	103	2580		192
FEVERS	56	29	152	87	80	111	88
TOTAL	50	38	110	90	380	111	83

INDEX OF TOTAL DAYS ILLNESS, BY TYPE OF ILLNESS, AGE, SEX + INCOME, 102 HHs (Contd.)

	% OF TOTAL DAYS ILLNESS AS A % OF POPULATION SHARE						
TYPE OF ILLNESS + INCOME	MALE 0-15	FEMALE 0-15	MALE 16-60	FEMALE 16-60	MALE 61+	FEMALE 61+	TOTAL
VERY POOR							
% OF POPN.	1.6	1.4	1.9	2.1	0.5	0.2	7.6
GASTRIC		Neg	379	129			133
ACHES				71			20
OTHER		29	237				64
COUGHS, COLDS	112	36	32			Neg	41
SKIN			774		180		207
FEVERS	12	36	153	48			60
TOTAL	19	14	268	52	20	Neg	91
TOTAL SAMPLE POPULATION							
% OF POPN.	21.7	19.9	27.6	24.6	3.1	3.1	100%
							TOTAL DAYS ILLNESS
GASTRIC	7	69	195	81	281	80	5934
ACHES	6		70	281	329		4108
OTHER	70	28	180	43	29		3344
COUGHS, COLDS	49	69	82	137	29	594	3317
SKIN	66	53	161	61	506	590	3258
FEVERS	63	112	143	75	123	77	2912
TOTAL	38	54	142	115	229	203	22873
NO. OF DAYS OR PERSONS							
DAYS OF TOTAL ILLNESS	1872	2445	8995	6505	1611	1440	22873
NO. OF PERSONS	125	115	159	142	18	18	577
AV. DAYS ILLNESS PER PERSON							
TOTAL ILLNESS	15.0	21.3	56.6	45.8	89.5	80.0	39.6
GASTRIC	0.7	7.1	20.0	8.3	28.6	8.3	10.3
ACHES	0.4	0.0	5.0	20.0	23.3	0.0	7.1
OTHER	4.1	1.6	10.4	2.5	1.7	34.1	5.8
COUGHS, COLDS	2.8	4.0	4.7	7.8	1.7	33.7	5.7
SKIN	3.7	3.0	9.3	3.4	28.3	0.0	5.6
FEVERS	3.2	5.6	7.2	3.8	6.2	3.8	5.0

NB 100 indicates illness incidence proportionate with population share. For example, 4.2% of the total population were rich males aged 0-15. The index 24 for gastric indicates that rich boys had 1% of total gastric problems. Neg = Negligible, below 0.1%

INDEX OF TOTAL SERIOUS ILLNESS REPORTED BEFORE 1981, BY ILLNESS, AGE, SEX AND INCOME, 102 HHs

	% OF CASES OF ILLNESS AS % OF POPULATION SHARE						
REPORTED SERIOUS ILLNESS BEFORE 1981	MALE 0-15	FEMALE 0-15	MALE 16-60	FEMALE 16-60	MALE 61+	FEMALE 61+	TOTAL SERIOUS ILLNESS
RICH							
% OF POPN.	4.2	5.5	5.9	5.2	0.3	0.9	22.0
GASTRIC	95	36	153	212	1333	444	155
ACHES	119	91	390	173			186
OTHER	71		85	38			45
COUGHS, COLDS	310	55	169	154			150
SKIN			136	154		888	105
FEVERS	167	73	237	115		111	141
TOTAL	145	44	190	125	233	156	128
FAIRLY RICH							
% OF POPN.	3.6	2.2	4.3	4.5	0.3	0.3	15.4
GASTRIC	167		46	44		667	71
ACHES			326	111			117
OTHER	56		163	111	667	667	110
COUGHS, COLDS			116				32
SKIN		364	186				97
FEVERS	83	91	93	22	333		65
TOTAL	67	45	119	44	233	233	77
UPPER MEDIUM							
% OF POPN.	3.8	2.6	3.6	3.1	0.2	0.3	13.7
GASTRIC	105		111	65	1000	667	
ACHES			389	161		1667	168
OTHER	53		83	97		1667	102
COUGHS, COLDS	211	115	83		1000	109	
SKIN	211		222				109
FEVERS	105	115	222	129	131		
TOTAL	97	54	169	87	150	667	119
LOWER MEDIUM							
% OF POPN.	3.1	2.9	4.5	3.6	1.2	0.5	15.9
GASTRIC	189		89	222		400	107
OTHER	97		67	83	417		101
COUGHS, COLDS		103	111		250	6	3
FEVERS	32		89	83	83	200	57
TOTAL	54	10	76	8	142	140	69
POOR							
% OF POPN.	5.4	5.2	7.3	6.1	0.5	0.9	25.3
GASTRIC	37		82	148			67
ACHES	93		68				36
OTHER	93	58	192	82		333	123
COUGHS, COLDS	93	154	137	49			103
SKIN	148		205	131			123
FEVERS	37	115	96	82	800		95
TOTAL	63	79	121	84	280	78	93

INDEX OF TOTAL SERIOUS ILLNESS REPORTED BEFORE 1981, BY ILLNESS, AGE, SEX + INCOME, 102 HHs (Contd.)

REPORTED SERIOUS ILLNESS BEFORE 1981	% OF CASES OF ILLNESS AS % OF POPULATION SHARE						TOTAL SERIOUS ILLNESS
	MALE 0-15	FEMALE 0-15	MALE 16-60	FEMALE 16-60	MALE 61+	FEMALE 61+	
VERY POOR							
% OF POPN.	1.6	1.4	1.9	2.1	0.5	0.2	7.6
GASTRIC			211	95	400		105
ACHES			263	238			118
OTHER	188		158	95	600		158
COUGHS, COLDS			158	238		1500	132
SKIN				381	1600		197
FEVERS	62		316	48			92
TOTAL	62	0	216	114	280	150	121
TOTAL SAMPLE POPULATION							
% OF POPN.	21.7	19.9	27.6	24.6	3.1	3.1	100
							NO. OF CASES
GASTRIC	88	10	101	138	258	290	53
ACHES	41	25	214	93	161	22	
OTHER	88	15	130	85	323	323	58
COUGHS, COLDS	120	75	130	61	97	161	39
SKIN	69	40	138	93	258	258	13
FEVERS	78	75	152	73	194	64	109
TOTAL CASES OF ILLNESS, PRE-1981	85	46	141	89	197	187	294
NO. OF SERIOUS ILLNESSES	54	27	114	64	18	17	294
NO. OF PERSONS	125	115	159	142	18	18	577
AV. SERIOUS ILLNESS PER PERSON	0.43	0.23	0.72	0.45	1.00	0.94	0.51

Those with upper medium incomes had less than average morbidity but double their due share of colds and coughs and yet very few skin problems. Children experienced very little illness and only older women had disproportionately high morbidity.

Persons with lower medium incomes had more than average morbidity and especially aches and gastric problems. Children had few days of illness but adults, especially males and particularly older males, were often ill. Adults, especially women, suffered particularly from aches and men had nearly twice their due share of aches.

The poor had slightly less than their due share of total morbidity, even though they accounted for 49 percent of skin complaints. The only category of poor with significantly excess morbidity was older males, with roughly four times their expected share.

Finally, the very poor had very slightly less morbidity than their population share would lead one to expect. They had thrice their quota of skin complaints and also a high proportion of gastric problems but reported few colds, coughs and aches. Children had very few days of illness and the main category with excess morbidity was very poor household heads, with 268 percent of expected days of illness.

The table opposite shows comparable distribution for 'serious' illness experienced before 1981. The table of indices shows that the rich had the highest proportion of 'serious' illness, relative to their population and that the very poor and upper medium incomes also had a disproportionately high incidence. In the case of the rich, the excess was due mainly to a high share of aches, gastric problems, and coughs and colds. The fairly rich also reported a high incidence of aches, as well as 'other illness' and skin complaints. Upper middle income households also suffered from an excess of aches whilst lower medium incomes reported more gastric problems and 'other illness'. The poor encountered more skin complaints, 'other illness', coughs and fevers and the very poor also suffered most excess in skin complaints and 'other illness'.

When an index of relative morbidity is constructed, dividing the percentage of total days illness by the percentage of total population, the fairly rich and lower medium income categories emerge as having the longest illness:

	INDEX 1981-2	INDEX PRE-1981		INDEX 1981-2	INDEX PRE-1981
Fairly rich	135	77	Very poor	91	121
Lower medium	127	69	Poor	83	93
Rich	92	128	Upper medium	79	119

Health Care

The middle incomes had the most household heads who endured their illness without consulting a practitioner. The incidence of frequent visits (6 or more) was highest among the very poor (38%) and the richest (30%). The population travelling five or more kilometres to a practitioner increased with income but was only 20 percent of the 59 household heads who consulted a practitioner at all. More of the very poor went outside Basauli and slightly more of the richest used facilities at tahsil or district level.

WEIGHTED PER CAPITA INCOME AND HEALTH CARE

	RICH	FAIRLY RICH	UPPER MEDIUM	LOWER MEDIUM	POOR	VERY POOR	TOTAL NO.
% OF HOUSEHOLD HEADS							
NOT ILL	24		12	20	16	12	19
ILL BUT NO CONSULTATION	16		25	30	32	12	24
1-5 VISITS TO RMPs	30		38	30	28	38	32
6+ VISITS TO RMPs	30		25	20	24	38	27
TOTAL	100		100	100	100	100	102
% TYPE OF MEDICAL PRACTITIONER CONSULTED BY HHH FOR FIRST ILLNESS							
PRIVATE MBBS	5			10			2
PHC MBBS	32		30		8	17	11
LESS QUALIFIED ALLOPATH	47		60	50	62	33	30
VAID, UNANI (INCL HOMEOPATH)	16(5)		10	30	23(8)	33	12
OTHER				10	7	16	4
TOTAL	100		100	100	100	100	59
% TYPE OF MEDICAL PRACTITIONER PREFERRED BY HHH, ILL + NOT ILL							
PRIVATE MBBS	23		19	10		12	13
PHC MBBS	34		12	30	24		26
LESS QUALIFIED ALLOPATH	23		50	35	44	50	37
VAID, UNANI (INCL HOMEOPATH)	11		12	15	16(4)	25	14
OTHER	9		7	10	16	13	120
TOTAL	100		100	100	100	100	102
LOCATION OF MEDICAL PRACTITIONER CONSULTED, FIRST ILLNESS OF HHH							
% 5+ KILOMETRES	25			20	16		59

RMPs = Rural Medical Practitioners, including unqualified; MBBS = Qualified Allopathic Doctor; PHC = Primary Health Centre

Consultation of private MBBS doctors was minimal: one of the two household heads using them belonged to one of the richest households. Ironically, the MBBS doctors in the government Primary Health Centres were consulted more by richer household heads, followed by the poorest. Government policy presumably intends that the poor should use PHCs more, leaving the richer villagers to use private MBBS and other practitioners. In practice the poorest resorted to less qualified (private) allopaths most of all and their relative use tended to decrease as income rose. The poorest household heads also consulted traditional medical practitioners (including homeopaths) the most but even 16 percent of the richest used TMPs (including 5 percent who went to a homeopath). The poorest also used the district hospital the most.

Household heads were asked about which types of health practitioner they actually consulted, which they would prefer to consult and also about satisfaction with the care they received. The very poor expressed a clear preference for less qualified 'allopaths' (LQAs) and no desire to use the PHC but in practice used LQAs and traditional practitioners equally often, followed by PHCs (17%). The poor used LQAs much more than their stated preference, the traditional practitioners slightly more and the PHC much less than preferred. Those with medium income did not use the PHC, despite this being mentioned as their second favourite option. The rich expressed a low desire to use PHCs but resorted to them for 30 percent of their consultations. The rich professed low confidence in LQAs but used them 47 percent of times. Twenty-three percent of the richest preferred a private MBBS but only 5 percent actually consulted one. A third of the richest expressed a preference for the PHC and nearly a third actually visited one for their first illness.

Apart from preference for and use of the various types of RMP, heads were also asked about their satisfaction with the service they had used. More of the richer heads had consulted the PHC at Suratganj but the frequency of full satisfaction with its care was similar for richer and poorer. More of the richer heads had also consulted the more distant PHC at Fatehpur, though less frequently than Suratganj. Full satisfaction with the PHC at Fatehpur was slightly higher among richer heads than among poorer. The reverse was the case for traditional practitioners and, even more significant, 92 percent of poorer heads were fully satisfied with less qualified allopaths compared with only 74 percent of richer heads. All this suggests that the PHCs which are supposed to be designed for the poor are both being used less by the poorer households and also giving them slightly lower satisfaction. At the same time, and possibly partly in consequence, poorer people are making great use of less qualified private allopathic practitioners and deriving a correspondingly higher satisfaction from their services. A further factor may be the more critical attitude of richer heads.

As expected, the proportion of households spending the most (over Rs 50 per person) on health care increased with weighted PCI. There was a very marked difference between the richest two categories and the poorest but the proportion of households in three middle income categories were similar to each other and nearer to that of the poorest.

WEIGHTED PER CAPITA INCOME + HEALTH EXPENDITURE PER HHH, HH MEMBER + HOUSEHOLD

HOUSEHOLD HEADS	RICH	FAIRLY RICH	UPPER MEDIUM	LOWER MEDIUM	POOR	VERY POOR	TOTAL	TOTAL NO.
Rs AV. TOTAL HEALTH EXPENDITURE			% OF COLUMN TOTAL					
0	30		19	45	28	25	30	31
1-25	30		38	25	36	25	31	32
26-100	18		31	25	16	38	23	23
151+	21		12	5	20	12	16	16
TOTAL	100		100	100	100	100	100	102
AV. Rs. PER ILLNESS OF HHH								
ANY ILLNESS		186		39	82		129	102
GASTRO-INTESTINAL		602		51	130		335	28
FEVER		56		47	32		48	30
COLD, COUGH OR SORE THROAT		9		0	4		8	19
AV. Rs HEALTH EXPENDITURE PER HOUSEHOLD MEMBER					% DISTRIBUTION			
1-10	15		38	40	36	38	30	31
11-25	12		25	30	24	25	22	22
26-50	24		19	10	20	25	20	20
51+	48		19	20	20	12	28	29
TOTAL	100		100	100	100	100	100	102
AV. Rs TOTAL EXPENDITURE PER HOUSEHOLD					% DISTRIBUTION			
1-25	18		25	30	20	38	24	24
26-50	6		12	15	20	12	12	
51-100	3		19	20	24	25	16	16
101-250	24		19	15	12	12	18	18
251-500	6		19	20	20	12	15	15
501-1000	27				12	10	10	
1001+	15		6		4		7	7
TOTAL	100		100	100	100	100	100	100
NO. OF HHs SPENDING Rs 251+	48		25	20	24	25	31	102

The table on page 367 showed that rich household heads spent by far the most on treating their illness (360% of the average) but the trend was not entirely smooth: the fairly rich spent much less (index 57%), upper medium incomes 87 percent and lower medium incomes the lowest amount (23%). The poor and the very poor spent 50 percent and 45 percent respectively of the average. The poorer-richer gradient of unequal health expenditure was 424 percent and the poorest-richest gradient was 800 percent.

When expenditure indices are related to indices of days illness, then the disparity between the rich and the remainder (and especially the lower medium and the very poor) increases considerably to 894 percent.

The poorer-richer gradient for expenditure related to days ill is 677 percent and the poorest-richest gradient is a whopping 1,977 percent.

INDICES AS % OF AVERAGE (=100)

INDICATOR	RICH	FAIRLY RICH	UPPER MEDIUM	LOWER MEDIUM	VERY POOR	POOR
Days Ill	70	98	65	121	103	173
Health Expend.	360	57	87	23	50	45
Health Expenditure as % of Days Ill	514	58	134	19	49	26

Income differences in expenditure on the health of household heads was greatest in the low class (gradient 150%, compared with only 92 percent in the medium class). Among caste strata, the gradient was highest for the scheduled (1500%) and the Muslims (383%). Poorer scheduled and Muslims thus spent far more than their richer caste mates, whilst there was higher expenditure by richer household heads in the high and middle castes. The gradients there were negative (35% and 19% respectively).

Total household expenditure on health declined steadily as weighted per capita income fell, except for the two poorest categories (index 50%). The richest households spent over three times the average and the lower medium income category spent the least on health (index 33). Poorer households only paid 27 percent of what richer households expended on treating their illness. Per capita expenditure also declined with WPCI, though there was hardly any difference between the three poorest categories. Disparity between poorer and richer expenditure on health was slightly lower in per capita terms (33%) than for total household spending on health (27%).

CLASS AND HEALTH

Households are classified as high class if they included salaried workers or if they cropped at least 20 kacha bighas (at least 4 acres) of land that was owned by them. Medium class households are those which crop 10 to 19 owned kacha bighas (2 to 4 acres). Low class households include those cropping less than 10 owned kacha bighas (under 2 acres), tenant farmers, and/or those receiving income mainly from labouring, whether agricultural, at the nearby brick factory or elsewhere.

Nutrition

Weight for height was calculated for those members of the household sample who also happened to be included in the sample measured for height and weight (see upper table on page 363). Weight for height increased with class status and the gradient between low and high class was 108 percent.

Mortality

The table on page 357 shows that overall there was a lower index of child deaths (all ages) in high class households and that there was no significant difference between medium and low class households. The gradient of inequality between other and high classes is about 116 percent and between low and high class is 117 percent. The class differences are strongest in the scheduled caste stratum (gradient 183%) and the middle castes (gradient between high and other classes 129%). The gradient between other and high classes is less steep for the high castes (109%) but there is no smooth trend. In fact the medium class had the worst child death rate among high castes. For Muslims, the trend is actually perverse, with an index of 139 percent for the medium class - the highest of any subcategory, and the low-medium class gradient is thus, uniquely, negative (85%).

Morbidity

There was virtually no difference between high and medium classes (indices 86 and 88 respectively) but low class household heads had 112 percent of average days illness. The low class-high class gradient was thus 130 percent. The greatest inter-class differences occurred in Muslim households (gradient 696%) and these were also appreciable (gradient 134%) among the scheduled. However, there were few Muslims and scheduled in the medium class (and none at all in the high class). Large differences also existed between classes in high and medium castes but the pattern was irregular. For example, medium class household heads in the high castes had a morbidity index of 178, higher than any class-cum-caste category (including low class Muslims with an index of 167).

Low class households had the highest average length of illness per member (index 105), followed by the high class (97) and then the medium class (91). Within caste strata, morbidity decreased with rising class status only in the scheduled category. The high caste pattern is particularly interesting: illness was longest in the high class (index 110), then the medium class (92) and shortest in the low class (62). Similarly, in the (highest morbidity) Muslim category, the medium class had even more illness than the already long illness among low class Muslims. Differences between classes among the middle castes were very small and slightly irregular (see pages 363-4).

Health Care

There was a huge difference between the high class and the rest in terms of expenditure on treatment of household heads. When expenditure is related to days illness (ie. 'use-need'), the inter-class disparity increases slightly:

INDEX	HIGH	MEDIUM	LOW
Days Ill	86	88	112
Health Expenditure	256	39	37
Health Expend. as % of Days Ill	298	44	33

The medium class were close to the high class in morbidity but resembled the low class in health expenditure. The low class-high class gradient was 692 percent. The disparity between high and low class ratios of expenditure to illness or need is extremely high, with a gradient of 903 percent (see page 367).

GENDER AND HEALTH

The social, medical and other processes leading to gender inequalities of health in the rural sector of western Uttar Pradesh have been well documented by Jeffery (1989). This amply demonstrates the many problems (health and otherwise) faced by village women in northern India. Given that Basauli is almost certainly poorer, arguably less socially developed but with a significantly smaller Muslim minority than Jhakri-Dharmnagri, similar or perhaps even greater female inferiority may be expected in the Barabanki village. Much of this may not emerge, partly because the researchers in Basauli were all male and partly because the focus has been more on income than gender inequalities of health - not that the two are disconnected.

Nutrition

For those aged 18 and over, males weighed 17 percent more than females and were 10 percent taller than women. Male weight for height exceeded that of females by 8 percent. These women averaged only 39.1 kilograms in weight and only 149.8 centimetres in height, with a weight for height of .263. Smallness of females was itself in relation to males who were themselves short and light by international standards.

Mortality

In the period to 1965 the male rate for stillbirths was roughly double that of the female but this changed to a slight female excess from 1966, when the overall rate virtually halved. For the whole period, the male index (116) exceeded the female (77), giving a negative gradient of 66 percent.

The table on page 369 shows a higher percentage of under 5 deaths among boys than girls, probably mainly because of much higher reporting of male deaths in the period before 1961. This may be partly due to a design fault in the questionnaire. From 1961 the ratios of male and female deaths were more equal. For medium castes (and Muslims) males accounted for 60 percent of early deaths between 1931 and 1982 (Cf. 45 percent for other castes).

Whilst the reported number of deaths of male children was greater, the *rates* of mortality were almost universally higher for females. This was true of JD as well, though in some ways to a lesser extent than Basauli, especially for those born in the period after 1965. There are some striking similarities between gender gradients in the two 'villages', even though Basauli reported an overall mortality rate for the under 5s which was 43 percent higher than that of JD. Firstly, the gender indices and gender gradients for the whole period were virtually identical (124 percent, ie. the female death rate was 24 percent higher than the male). Secondly, the gradients for the earlier period were also quite similar (141 percent in Basauli and 135 percent in JD). Thirdly, the gender difference fell in the period after 1965, though it fell by slightly more percentage points in JD and to a level which was closely approaching gender equality (105%, compared with 117 percent in Basauli). Fourthly, the Muslim record was in most ways the worst in both areas. The Muslim gender gradient was 14 percent higher than the non-Muslim one in JD and though the Muslim gradient fell substantially, the decline was lower than for non-Muslims. The end result was a Muslim gender gradient of 118 percent in JD in the later period and only Muslim females by then still had a higher mortality than their male equivalents. The gender gradient for the scheduled actually swung from 131 percent to 76 percent between the two periods. The pattern for Basauli is not entirely the same as for JD. The gender gradient for Basauli Muslims over the whole period (129%) was as near as dammit the same as for JD Muslims (131%) but, curiously, the Basauli Muslim gradient was the lowest of any caste stratum in the earlier period (117%) and increased substantially, by 34 percentage points, to 151 percent in the post-1965 period. (This was parallelled to a much smaller extent by the high castes in Basauli.) Muslims in Basauli had the highest child mortality and the relatively low gender gradient for Muslims in the earlier period may be partly a reflection of a high mortality for Muslims of both sexes. Fifthly, the scheduled in both areas had the lowest gender gradient in the later period (B 63% and JD 76%) and also both achieved the highest reduction in gender gradient after 1965 of any stratum. The earlier gender gradient for the scheduled in Basauli was the highest for any category (255%). Finally, another important difference between Basauli and JD is the lack of change in the Basauli caste Hindu gender gradient between periods, compared with a drop of 34 percentage points in JD (from 125 percent to 91%). One further point needs to be made: a low or negative gender gradient may not necessarily indicate female 'progress': sometimes (as in the case of scheduled children born in Basauli after 1965) it may be more of an indication of a high mortality rate for both sexes and/or a worsening in male mortality. However, whereas scheduled male mortality in Basauli increased from an index of 62 to 113, the scheduled female index dropped by more percentage points, from 158 to 71. The example of caste Hindus in JD seems to indicate that, the lower the actual mortality rate, the lower the gender gradient. The scheduled record in Basauli was of the sharpest decline in the gender gradient, from 255 percent to 63 percent (see page 360).

CHANGE IN GENDER GRADIENT OF UNDER 5 MORTALITY, BASAULI AND JHAKRI-DHARMNAGRI

UNDER 5 MORTALITY OF FEMALES AS % OF MALES PERIOD WHEN BORN	HIGH CASTE	MEDIUM CASTE	CASTE HINDU	MUSLIM	SCHEDULED	TOTAL
BASAULI						
To 1965	130	136	133	117	255**	141
1966-77	143	134	135	151*	63	117
% POINTS CHANGE AFTER 1965	+13	-2	+2	+34**	-192**	-24
TOTAL TO 1977	129	129	128	129	114	124
ACTUAL MORTALITY RATE PER 1000 LIVE BIRTHS	344	375	360	482	323	371
JHAKRI-DHARMNAGRI						
To 1965			125	144**	131	135
1966-80			91	118	76	105
% POINTS CHANGE AFTER 1965			-34	-26	-55**	-30
TOTAL TO 1980			114	131**	116	124
ACTUAL MORTALITY RATE PER 1000 LIVE BIRTHS			197	337	256	259

* The gradient was actually 171 percent for those born in richer Muslim households but the number born was only 11. (The earlier gradient was 301 percent but for an even smaller number: 4 births.)

** High gradient or change.

INDEX OF DAYS ILLNESS AS % OF OVERALL AVERAGE, BY SEX AND AGE

	HH HEADS	WIVES OF HHHs	MINORS 0-15	OTHER ADULTS	TOTAL
Male	236		39	68	108
Female	390*	118	60	79	91
Female as % of Male	165	50**	154	116	84

* Only 8 women ** As % of Male HHHs.

STATUS WITHIN HOUSEHOLD AND Rs EXPENDITURE ON TREATMENT, JAN.1981- FEB. 1982

STATUS	HHH	WIFE OF HHH	ELDEST TWO SONS OF HHH	OTHER MEN	OTHER WOMEN	BOYS	GIRLS	OTHER HH MEMBERS	TOTAL	TOTAL NO.
Rs TOTAL EXPENDITURE ON TREATMENT				% OF COLUMN TOTALS						
0	30	47	46					57	8	254
1-25	31	15	31					28	27	144
26-150	23	25	19					11	17	89
151+	16	13	4					4	8	40
TOTAL NO.	102	75	114					236	527	527
26+	38	39	23*					15	24	129
AV. Rs PER CONSULTATION			% OF COLUMN TOTALS							
0-4	31	21		36	21	56	27		33	97
4.1-10	32	28		34	26	38	49		34	99
10.1-30	19	37		20	30	4	22		21	61
30.1+	19	13		10	22	2	3		12	35
TOTAL	100	100		100	100	100	100		100	100
TOTAL NO.	97	46		41	23	48	37		292	292
AV. Rs PER CONSULTATION	20.8	12.4		9.2	19.5	6.4	8.6		15.3	
INDEX OF Rs PER CONSULTATION	136	81		60	127	42	56		100	

INDEX OF AV. Rs PER CONSULTATION OR VISIT (AS % OF AVERAGE FOR ALL HH MEMBERS)

	HHH	WIFE OF HHH	ELDEST TWO SONS OF HHH	OTHER MEN	OTHER WOMEN	BOYS	GIRLS	OTHER HH MEMBERS	NO.	AV. Rs PER HH MEMBER
DISTRICT HOSPITAL	88	101		7	165				15	36.0
PHC	97	90		155	236	58	57		55	8.8
PRIVATE MBBS	227	81		81	43	46	46		30	21.7
LESS QUALIFIED ALLOPATH	146	75		38	114	66	66		122	13.5
VAID + UNANI	89	227		115	58	38	94		48	7.1
HOMEOPATH	61	128				66			6	8.5
OTHER, MAINLY DIHATI	91			174			102		8	4.3
COMMUNITY HEALTH VOLUNTEER		0			133	111			8	0.9
TOTAL	136	81		60	127	42	56		292	15.3
NO. CONSULTATIONS	97	46		41	23	48	37		292	
% OF TOTAL CONSULTATIONS	33	16		14	8	16	13		100	292
% OF SAMPLE POPN	18**	14		15	12	22	20		100	577 Persons

* 28% for the eldest son and 14% for the second son

** 16% male HHHs, 2% female

Av. about Rs 43 total cost of treatment per HH member (incl. non-consulters of RMPs). If PCI = Rs 853 for all HHs, then this would be about 4% of PCI.

Harriss (1986) suggests that higher death rates for girls in South Asia occur mainly because of delayed presentation for treatment, not because of higher morbidity.

Some gender differences in morbidity were presented briefly in Chapter 7. Reported days of illness for wives of household heads were only 50 percent of those of their husbands, though female household heads (mostly elderly widows) had the highest morbidity of all.

The table on page 394 shows differences in expenditure per consultation or visit for various male and female categories within the household. Household heads (including 8 females) spent 36 percent above average per visit to a medical practitioner and 'other females' in the household spent 27 percent above average. Wives of household heads (81 percent of average), other adult males (mostly sons, 60%), female minors (56%) and male minors (42%) all spent below average per visit. Higher expenses on household heads was partly associated with their higher average expenditure on more costly sources of care, particularly private MBBS doctors - 127 percent above average. They also spent 46 percent above average on less qualified allopathic doctors. Wives of household heads exceeded average expenditure on ayurvedic and unani consultations (also 127 percent above the mean) and on homeopathy (28 percent above). Significantly, these were cheaper types of treatment. The costs of other adult male members of the household (mainly sons) were 55 percent above average for PHC treatment and 15 percent above for ayurvedic and unani consultations. Expenditure on treatment of other adult females exceeded the average by 36 percent, ie. slightly less than for comparable males, at PHCs and by 14 percent at less qualified allopaths. Expenditure on children was mainly below average and was mostly identical for girls and boys except that costs associated with ayurvedic treatment of girls was much higher than for boys.

Overall, female physique, especially weight, was smaller and under 5 mortality was at least 24 percent higher for females. The gender gradient for child mortality declined from 141 percent to 117 percent in Basauli and in lower mortality JD the fall was even sharper, from 135 percent to 105 percent, ie. approaching equality. However, Basauli wives of household heads had half the morbidity reported for male household heads and the female stillbirth rate was two-thirds of the male rate. Expenditure on treatment of wives of household heads was 60 percent of that for male households heads and so the expenditure relative to morbidity was higher for females.

CONCLUSION

The tables summarise indices and gradients of inequality of indicators for physical deficiency, morbidity, mortality, health care expenditure and expenditure relative to morbidity. The data relate to caste strata, class and gender in Basauli and Jhakri-Dharmnagri 'villages' and also to weighted per capita income in Basauli.

CLASS, GENDER, HEALTH INDICES AND INEQUALITY GRADIENTS, BASAULI, BARABANKI AND JHAKRI-DHARMNAGRI, BIJNOR

HEALTH INDICATOR	HIGH CLASS	MEDIUM CLASS	LOW CLASS	LOW AS % OF HIGH	MALE	FEMALE	FEMALE AS % OF MALE
BASAULI							
KACHA BIGHAS CROPPED + OWNED	20+	10-19	0-9	(<20%)			
DEFICIENCY WT, 18+					92	108	117%
HT, 18+					95	105	110%
DEFICIENCY WT/HT, 18+ **	95	100	103	108%	96	104	108%
DAYS ILL, HHH	86	88	112	130%	95	157	165%
DAYS ILL, WIFE OF HHH	149	114	73	49%			
DAYS ILL, MALE HHH or WIFE					128	64	50%
DAYS ILL, ALL HH MEMBERS	97	91	105	108%	108	91	85%
DAYS ILL, HIGH CASTES, ALL HH MEMBERS	110	92	62	56%			
STILLBIRTH RATES					116	77	66%
UNDER 5 MORTALITY, MUSLIMS					116	150	129%
U5 MR, HIGH CASTE HINDUS					80	103	129%
UNDER 5 MORTALITY, TO 1965					88	124 OE	141%
1966-77					93	109	117%
UNDER 5 MORTALITY, TO 1977					91	113 OE	124%
UNDER 5 MORT., INCL. STILLBIRTHS					93	111	119%
JHAKRI + DHARMNAGRI, BIJNOR							
APPROX KACHA BIGHAS OWNED PER HH		9+ KB	0 TO 8 KB				
UNDER 5 MORTALITY, TO 1965		83	118	142%	86	116	135%
1966-80		100	101	100%	98	103	105%
TO 1980		87	116	133%	90	112	124%
BASAULI							
MORTALITY, ALL CHILDREN							
- OF HHHs, ALL AGES	89	102	104	117%			
- MUSLIMS ONLY		139	118	-			
- MUSLIMS ONLY, UNDER 5					116	150	129%
Rs H. EXP., HHHs	256	39	37	14%	136	81*	60%
Rs H. EXP. OTHERS, 16+					60	127	212%
MINORS, 0-15					42	56	133%
Rs H. EXP. ÷ DAYS ILL, HHHs	298	44	33	11%	106	127*	120%

OE Probably an overestimate because of under-recording of married females still alive.
* Wives of HHHs only
** For 3 classes, sample HHs only and includes both sexes.

CASTE STRATUM, WEIGHTED PCI, HEALTH INDICES AND INEQUALITY GRADIENTS, BASAULI, BARABANKI + JHAKRI-DHARMNAGRI, BIJNOR

HEALTH INDICATOR	INDEX AS % OF AVERAGE						POORER AS % OF RICHER 60%(167)
	HIGH CASTE	MIDDLE CASTE	MUSLIM	SCHEDULED	RICHER Rs 951-2500 Av. 1311	POORER Rs 401-950 Av. 784	
							INEQUALITY GRADIENT
A. NUTRITIONAL DEFICIENCY							
WEIGHT, MALE 18+	95	105	101	99	97	103	106%
HEIGHT, MALE 18+	99	101	101	100	99	101	102%
WEIGHT FOR HEIGHT, MALE 18+	98	102	101	100	98	102	104%
WEIGHT, FEMALE 18+	96	103	101	103	101	99	98%
HEIGHT, FEMALE 18+	101	99	99	99	100	100	100%
WEIGHT FOR HT., FEMALE 18+	94	103	103	105	101	100	98%
WEIGHT FOR HEIGHT, ALL (HH SAMPLE ONLY)	99	98	106	101	97	103	106%
AVERAGE OF ABOVE	97	102	102	101	99	101	102%
B. MORTALITY							
STILLBIRTHS PER 1000 TOTAL BIRTHS	167	82	39	110	120	81	68%
FIRST WEEK DEATHS PER 1000 LIVE BIRTHS					57	143	255%
PERINATAL PER 1000 TOTAL BIRTHS					106	95	90%
WEEKS 2 TO 4 PER 1000 LIVE BIRTHS					117	85	73%
NEONATAL PER 1000 LIVE BIRTHS					97	105	108%
POSTNEONATAL PER 1000 LIVE BIRTHS					95	104	110%
INFANT MORTALITY PER 1000 LIVE BIRTHS					95	104	110%
UNDER 5 RATE PER 1000 LIVE BIRTHS	90	101	130	87	96	104	108%
STILLBIRTH AND UNDER 5 RATE PER 1000 TOTAL BIRTHS					96	101	105%
CHILD DEATH RATE, ANY AGE, PER 1000 LIVE BIRTHS	99	97	122	88	104	98	94%
[UNDER 5 RATE PER 1000 LIVE BIRTHS, 263 HHs	109	65	118	126			]
UNDER 5 RATE PER 1000 LIVE BIRTHS							
BORN ALIVE TO 1965	94	100	115	95	83	115	139%
1966-77	81	97	156	89	118	83	70%
B. TOTAL BORN ALIVE TO 1977	90	101	130	87	96	104	108%
% OF HHHs WHO HAD DIED	121	149	86	0	119	83	70%
% OF WIVES OF HHHs WHO HAD DIED*	165	40	94	108	135	66	49%

JHAKRI + DHARMNAGRI VILLAGES, BINJOR					RICH + MIDDLE PEASANT	POOR PEASANT + LANDLESS	PPL AS % OF RMP
STILLBIRTHS PER 1000 TOTAL BIRTHS					97	103	107%
FIRST WEEK DEATHS PER 1000 LIVE BIRTHS					109	91	83%
PERINATAL PER 1000 TOTAL BIRTHS					105	97	92%
WEEKS 2,3 + 4 PER 1000 LIVE BIRTHS					133	57	43%
NEONATAL PER 1000 LIVE BIRTHS					121	75	62%
POST NEONATAL PER 1000 LIVE BIRTHS					107	93	87%
INFANT MORTALITY PER 1000 LIVE BIRTHS					115	82	72%
UNDER 5 PER 1000 LIVE BIRTHS					87	116	133%
STILLBIRTH + UNDER 5 PER 1000 TOTAL BIRTHS					87	116	133%
UNDER 5 RATE PER 1000 LIVE BIRTHS, JD							
BORN ALIVE TO 1965	84		115	110	83	118	142%
1966-80	54		155	76	100	101	100%
TOTAL BORN ALIVE TO 1980	76		130	99	87	116	133%

CASTE STRATUM, WEIGHTED PCI, HEALTH INDICES AND INEQUALITY GRADIENTS, BASAULI, BARABANKI + JHAKRI-DHARMNAGRI, BIJNOR (Contd.)

HEALTH INDICATOR	INDEX AS % OF AVERAGE						POORER AS % OF RICHER
	HIGH CASTE	MIDDLE CASTE	MUSLIM	SCHEDULED	RICHER	POORER	
							INEQUALITY GRADIENT
C. MORBIDITY (DAYS ILLNESS)							
HOUSEHOLD HEAD	88	94	142	92	78	120	154%
WIFE OF HOUSEHOLD HEAD	59	120**	137	69	137	69	51%
SONS 1 + 2 OF HHH, 0-15	32	32	41	373	38	146	384%
16+	203	44	119	47	127	72	57%
C. ALL MEMBERS OF HH*	95	88	148	98	108	96	89%
NO ILLNESS, HHH					90	109	121%
D. HEALTH CARE							
AV. Rs EXP., HHH	160	138	36	25	166	39	24%
AV. Rs EXP. PER HH	109	48	48	45	161	43	27%
AV. Rs EXP. PER HH MEMBER	116	136	53	56	153	51	33%
E. HEALTH CARE RELATED TO MORBIDITY							
AV. Rs H. EXP. HHH ÷ DAYS ILL	182	147	25	27	207	34	16% (625%)
AGGREGATE HEALTH							
A. NUTRITIONAL DEFICIENCY	97	102	102	101	99	101	102%
B. MORTALITY	90	101	130	87	96	104	108%
C. MORBIDITY	95	88	148	98	108	96	89%
AV. OF A, B + C	94	97	127	95	101	100	99%
AV. OF 7 SELECTED INDICATORS	90	100	123	93	101	98	97%
D. HEALTH CARE	116	136	53	56	153	51	33% (300%)***
E. H. EXP. RELATED TO NEED	182	147	25	27	207	34	16% (625%)

* 95 HHHs had been married

** For richer middle caste wives of HHHs, the index was 180

*** Where a negative gradient (ie. below 100%) is associated with worse performance by the poorer, then this is converted into a positive gradient and placed in parentheses. If the poorer have worse health, then this yields a positive gradient directly. If the poorer spend less on health care, then this yields, initially, a negative gradient which needs 'conversion'.

Data refer to 102 sample households in Basauli, unless stated otherwise.

Caste Stratum

The scheduled castes reported the least child mortality and Muslims by far the highest. The major difference was between Muslims and Hindus, with a particularly high differential in the period after 1965. In JD the caste Hindus had the lowest child mortality but the Muslim-Hindu gradient steepened even more sharply in the later period even than in Basauli. Inter-strata differences were inevitably much smaller for height and weight, especially of males. The middle castes, especially males, were the lightest and had the lowest index of weight for height, except for scheduled females. The high castes performed best and the differential between high castes and others was greater for females, especially in weight for height, but this was partly due to below average height among high caste females. Muslim weights and heights were near to average, except those measured who also were in the household sample and who had an index of weight for height which was 6 percent below the average. This could possibly indicate that Muslims selected in the household sample were less well nourished than Muslims as a whole in Basauli.

Muslim morbidity was by far the highest, 42 percent above average compared with 30 percent above for Muslim child mortality. Differences between Hindu strata were small, except for high morbidity (approaching Muslim levels) for middle caste wives. Expenditure on treatment was highest in the middle castes, though high caste household heads spent the most of all on themselves. However, the main difference was between caste Hindus and others (ie. Muslims and the scheduled). Caste Hindus spent about 230 percent of what the others spent. Expenditure related to morbidity was greatest among the high castes, still high in the middle castes and was equally very low among the rest. Overall, Muslims performed worst on every major indicator and the evidence of one very important criterion, under 5 mortality, suggests that Muslim excess mortality had increased from 15 percent to 56 percent after 1965. The evidence from JD (with lower mortality, higher incomes and a larger ratio of Muslims) is of an identical worsening of relative under 5 mortality of Muslims, particularly so in relation to the high castes. The average mortality rate for the under fives among the 17 Muslim households in Basauli was 541 per 1000 births and, within the Muslim category, the highest mortality rate (769) was for lower medium income labourers who also farmed a little. The second highest mortality rate (670) was for the five farming households, three of whom belonged in the richer category. The lowest under 5 mortality rate was among Muslims who worked as washermen (333) and as labourers at the brick factory (278).

Weighted Per Capita Income

Income had little effect on child mortality over the whole period. However, the gradient was 139 percent for births up to 1965, falling sharply to 70 percent thereafter. In JD division by landowning classes (ie. not by income per se) produced a bigger mortality differential for the whole period. For the earlier period, the class gradient for JD was nearly the same as the income gradient for Basauli. After 1965 mortality equalised between classes in JD and in Basauli child mortality of the poorer actually fell well below that of the richer. Income differences in weight and height were small, especially for women, and the largest gradient (106%) was for male weights. The income gradient of weight for height of both sexes probably ranged between 102 and 106 percent. Overall morbidity was slightly lower in poorer households but this may partly reflect differences in reporting. Morbidity was much higher for poorer household heads but much lower for their wives. Income correlated highly with expenditure on treatment, especially of household heads, and even more so with expenditure relative to their morbidity.

Class

Class was analysed in less detail. The pattern for child mortality in JD has already been discussed, showing a class gradient of 133 percent. In Basauli the class gradient in weight for height of adults (household sample members only) was 108 percent. The class gradient of morbidity of all household members was also 108 percent, unlike the negative gradient for income (89%), but the class gradients of morbidity for household heads and their wives were 130 percent and 49 percent respectively. Medium class morbidity was closer to high than low class. Conversely, medium class expenditure on medical treatment barely differed from low class and the class gradient was negative and very steep (14%). Given smaller class differences in morbidity, the expenditure-morbidity gradient was the steepest of any negative gradient (11%).

Gender

Under five mortality of females was 24 percent higher than male in both Basauli and JD for the whole period but after 1965 the earlier difference was reduced by at least 24 percentage points in both 'villages', producing near equality in JD (105%, compared with 117% in Basauli). Male physiques were larger, as is usual in all societies, with males achieving 17 percent more weight, 10 percent more height and 8 percent more weight for height. Gender ratios of morbidity varied with age and kinship status but female household heads (mostly elderly widows) had 65 percent longer illness than male heads. Wives of household heads had half as much morbidity as male household heads, 60 percent of what males spent on health and thus a 20 percent higher ratio between expenditure and morbidity. Overall the morbidity of all female household members was 15 percent less than male.

To summarise, the under five mortality is arguably the most serious indicator of health for which data was collected. The highest gradients of inequality of child mortality were for caste strata (Muslim-Hindu), then gender and income inequalities which were in fact slight. Muslim child mortality was 44 percent higher than high caste Hindu, indeed 93 percent higher in the period after 1965. Whereas income and gender gradients of child mortality were higher than the Muslim-high caste gradient until 1965, thereafter the income gradient halved to 70 percent, the gender gradient declined slightly to 117 percent but the Muslim-high caste gradient increased sharply from 122 percent to 193 percent. In JD the Muslim-high caste gradient of child mortality was also the largest, the class gradient was also big (significantly more than the income gradient in Basauli) and the gender gradient was exactly the same as in Basauli. Over time, the Muslim-high caste gradient in JD actually doubled whilst the class and gender gradients (both similar to the caste gradient up to 1965) fell to 100 percent and 105 percent respectively, ie. they reached or approached equality.

In the case of weight and height, the gender gradient was larger than the income and Muslim-high caste gradients for male weight and height.

Reported morbidity per household member varied more than physique but mostly less than child mortality. As with under five mortality, the Muslim-high caste gradient of days ill far exceeded the much smaller gradient for class and the slightly negative gradients for income and gender. However, the gradients of morbidity were much higher for household heads and their wives than for the average household member. In the case of household heads, the gender and Muslim-high caste gradients were both over 160 percent, followed by the income gradient (154%) and with the class gradient some way behind (130%). The pattern for morbidity of wives of household heads is as varied as it is confusing: the Muslim-high caste gradient was extremely high (232%) whilst the income and class gradients were both negative and very similar to each other, around 50 percent.

GRADIENTS OF INEQUALITY OF HEALTH, MAIN INDICATORS: HEALTH INDEX OF LOWER CATEGORY AS % OF INDEX OF HIGHER CASTE STRATUM, GENDER, INCOME AND CLASS

		CASTE STRATUM	GENDER	WEIGHTED PER CAPITA INCOME	LANDOWNING CLASS
INDICATOR		MUSLIM AS % OF HIGH CASTE	FEMALE AS % OF MALE	POORER AS % OF RICHER	LOW AS % OF HIGH
BASAULI					
UNDER 5 MORTALITY,	BORN TO 1965	122	141	139	
	BORN 1966-77	193	117	70	
	TOTAL BORN TO 1977	144	124	108	
JHAKRI-DHARMNAGRI		MUSLIM AS % OF CASTE HINDU			
UNDER 5 MORTALITY,	BORN TO 1965	137	135	(142)*	142
	BORN 1966-80	287	105	(100)*	100
	TOTAL BORN TO 1980	171	124	(133)*	133
BASAULI					
MALE WEIGHT		106	117	106	
MALE HEIGHT		102	110	102	
MALE WEIGHT FOR HEIGHT		103	108	104	(108)**
DAYS ILLNESS, HOUSEHOLD HEADS		161	(165)	154	130
	WIVES OF HHHs	232	-	51	49
	ALL HH MEMBERS	156	85	89	108
AV. GRADIENT OF HEALTH INEQUALITY		160	121	103	95
Rs HEALTH EXPEND., HH HEADS		22	60	24	14
	TOTAL HOUSEHOLD	44			27
	PER HH MEMBER	46			33
Rs H. EXPEND. ÷ DAYS ILLNESS, HHHs		14	120	16	11
AV. GRADIENT OF INEQUALITY OF HEALTH CARE		403	(125)	429	

* In parentheses because data does not actually refer to per capita income but rather to class (See next column). The JD data on class is still worth comparing with the Basauli data on WPCI.

** Those measured who were also in the household sample only, both sexes.

9 Conclusion and summary: Political economy and health inequalities

As incomes and health standards rise, there is the possibility or even the likelihood that some income and health inequalities increase. Modernisation of health care can help raise average levels of health but it requires political and economic changes to promote equalisation of wealth, incomes and health.

Measurement of Health Inequality

Measurement of health includes at least five different components:
(1) mortality; (2) nutrition and physical measures which are indicative of nutritional status; (3) morbidity, both acute and chronic; (4) health care; and (5) health care relative to morbidity, ie. 'use-need'.

Economic inequalities can be measured, using Lorenz curves, Gini coefficients and the like. Le Grand (1989) uses a modified Gini coefficient to show variations in age of death between individuals (ie. not between structural categories). The Black Report and other European studies measure gradients of health inequality. These show the health performance of lower categories expressed as a percentage of that of higher categories (whether based on social and occupational class, income, gender, race or other stratum). Where there are several classes or income categories, then various permutations of comparison are possible. The Black Report concentrates particularly on comparison of the lowest and highest two classes in a five or six class system. Obviously, comparison of extreme ends of the hierarchy may show greater inequality than merely comparing the upper and lower halves. This needs to be borne in mind when considering variations in gradient, from studies which concentrate on different fractiles or percentiles.

When the lowest two classes have a mortality rate which is 25 per cent higher than that of the two highest classes, then the lowest-highest class gradient of mortality may be said to be 125 percent. In describing the size of gradients of inequality, the following words, somewhat arbitrarily, have been used:

1% to 99% NEGATIVE GRADIENT, ie. the lower class or other category performs better than the higher.
100% COMPLETE EQUALITY, ie. absence of gradient.

POSITIVE GRADIENTS

101% to 150%	Low Inequality
151% to 250%	Medium Inequality
251% to 400%	High Inequality
401% to 800%	Very High Inequality
801% plus	Extremely High Inequality, ie. the rich have at least 8 times the income of the poor or the poor have at least times as much sickness as the rich.

This scale may be used to compare inequalities in a wide range of economic, social and medical indicators. Obviously for a single specific indicator (such as the class gradient of infant mortality) then a gradient of 250 percent is relatively very high, even though it is only medium compared, say, with international gradients of maternal mortality.

INTERNATIONAL INEQUALITIES IN HEALTH

International Gradients of Income

International gradients of per capita income have been extremely high and it is well known that they are increasing. The gradient between poor and rich countries increased from 5,338 percent in 1988 to 6,014 percent in 1991 (ie. 4.2% annually). The gradient between low and high development countries is less steep but this also increased from 2,417 percent in 1976 to 3,083 percent in 1987, ie. an average increase in inequality of 2.5 percent per year. Even the gradient for parity purchasing power, which allows for differing living costs, was 1,223 percent in 1987, ie. people in highly developed nations had an average of 12 times the purchasing power of those in low development countries.

International Gradients of Mortality

International gradients of mortality exceed intra-national ones and should accordingly be of greater concern. Though a less empirical indicator, life expectancy is rightly preferred to crude death rate, because LE is standardised for age and sex. Insofar as LE has a narrower relative range, internationally, from 40 to 79 years, than CDR (3 to 23 plus pcr 1,000), usc of LE as thc indicator understates international inequality. The high-low income gradient of life expectancy was 162 percent in 1960, around 145% in both 1965 and 1975 and had fallen substantially to 124 percent by 1991. If middle income countries are included to produce a higher-lower income gradient, then this fell from 124 percent in 1965 to 113 percent in 1988. Interestingly, since 1965 the gradient for male life expectancy has fallen significantly from 140 percent to 120 percent whereas the female gradient fell only slightly from 148 percent to 139 percent between 1965 and 1970 and remained at 138 percent in 1991 (but the World Bank data on low income nations may be wrong - see WB 1993:300).

INTERNATIONAL GRADIENTS OF INCOME AND MORTALITY, 1965-1991

INDICATOR	YEAR	HIGH INCOME	UPPER MEDIUM	LOWER MEDIUM	LOW INCOME	WORLD	LOW AS % OF HIGH INCOME GRADIENT
NO. OF COUNTRIES	1991	22	22	43	40	127	
MAX $ GNP PC	1988	27,500	5,909	2,199	545	27,500	(5046%)
	1991	33,610	7,910	2,520	635	33,610	(5293%)
MIN $ GNP PC	1988	6,000	2,200	546	100	100	(6000%)
	1991	7,911	2,521	636	80	80	(9889%)
AV $ GNP PC	1988	17,080	3,240	1,380	320	3,470	(5338%)
	1991	21,050	3,530	1,590	350	4,010	(6014%)
AV. LIFE EXPECTANCY	1960						(162%)
	1965						(144%)
	1975						(145%)
	1988						(127%)
	1991						(124%)
	1988	76	68	65	60	64	(127%)
	1991	77	69	67	62	66	(124%)
AV. MALE LE	1965	67	59	54	48	54	(140%)
	1970	68	59	57	53	57	(128%)
	1988	73	65	62	60	63	(122%)
	1991	73	65	64	61	64	(120%)
INCREASE 1965-91		+6	+6	+10	+13	+10	
AV. FEMALE LE	1965	74	62	57	50	57	(148%)
	1970	75	64	61	54	60	(139%)
	1988	79	70	67	60	65	(132%)
	1991	80	72	69	58	65	(138%)
INCREASE 1965-91		+6	+10	+12	+8	+8	
CRUDE DEATH RATE	1965	10	12	13	16	14	160%
	1970	10	10	12	14	13	140%
	1988	9	8	8	10	10	111%
	1991	9	8	8	10	9	111%
INFANT MORTALITY RATE	1965	25	82	107	124	97	496%
	1970	20	72	87	109	85	545%
	1988	9	42	57	72	57	800%
	1991	8	34	42	71	53	888%
UNDER 5 MORTALITY MALE	1988	12	55	75	97	77	808%
	1991	11	46	60	104	77	945%
UNDER 5 MORTALITY FEMALE	1988	10	46	64	89	69	890%
	1991	8	36	50	96	69	1200%
MATERNAL MORTALITY PER 100,000 LIVE BIRTHS	1980	11	107	246	564	278	5127%
	1988	Under 10	104	111	308	237	3080+%

NB The national composition of the four income categories has changed over the years and especially after the break up of the former USSR. Sources: WB 1988 and 1993.

International comparison also needs to take acount of the huge differences in population between countries and regions. Greater weight needs to be given to inequalities between the ten most populous nations, which accounted for 63 per cent of global population in 1990. Their population in millions was:

1.	China	1134	7.	Japan	124
2.	India	850	8.	Nigeria	115
3.	Former USSR	289	9.	Pakistan	112
4.	USA	250	10.	Bangladesh	107
5.	Indonesia	178	1 - 10	TOTAL	3309
6.	Brazil	150			
				WORLD	5284

A deficit in life expectancy matters much more, cumulatively, in a country like India. India's aggregate deficit in LE can be crudely calculated by multiplying the deficit (6 years below the global average in 1991) by population size (over 866 million). The resulting deficit is 5.2 billion years of life expectancy, far greater than the other major deficit countries, which were Bangladesh (1.6 B.), Nigeria (1.4 B.), Indonesia (1.1 B.) and Pakistan (0.8 B.).

Whereas the richer-poorer country gradient of life expectancy has fallen from 144 percent to 120 percent, the gradient for the crude death rate declined much more, from 160 percent in 1965 to 111 percent in 1991. Unfortunately, standardisation, to allow for the much younger age composition of poorer countries, is likely to make this equalisation of death rates look much less favourable. Regionally, Subsaharan Africa and South Asia have the highest CDRs. However, the India-rich nation gradient of CDR has fallen from 180 percent to only 111 percent since 1970. Even the established market economies - Subsaharan Africa gradient of life expectancy has improved slightly from 163 percent in 1960 to 151 percent in 1991.

International inequalities in infant mortality have greatly increased from being very high (496%) in 1965 to extremely high (888%) in 1991. The annual rate of unequalisation has been 3.0 percent, slightly faster than for PCI. The gradients for both male and female under five mortality have increased but the gradient for females is both much higher than the male and has increased much more, even between 1988 and 1991. A corollary of a marginal decrease in infant mortality in poor nations has been an increase in child mortality, both male and female.

Kent compares mortality rates in LDCs and MDCs. His data suggest that the gradients for both infant and child mortality almost doubled between 1950 and 1980 but were not projected to increase much further by the year 2000:

LDC-MDC GRADIENTS OF INFANT AND CHILD MORTALITY, 1950-2000

	LDC MORTALITY AS % OF MDC 1950	1980	2000(P)	1980 GRADIENT AS % OF 1950	2000(P) GRADIENT AS % OF 1980
IMR	294	511	536	174	105
UNDER 5 MR	351	645	725	184	112
U5 MR GRADIENT AS % OF IMR GRADIENT	119	126	135		

Source: Kent 1990:6

The gradient for child mortality was 19 percent higher than for infant mortality in 1950 and the differential has increased slightly

Maternal mortality fell quite dramatically in poor nations during the 1980s and so the gradient declined from over 5,000 percent to 3,000 percent or less, but this is still a huge differential.

A more sophisticated measure of the burden of disease is disability-adjusted life years (DALYs) which are lost through premature death and loss of healthy life through disability (see World Bank 1993:212-25). In 1990 India had by far the largest national burden of disease (292 million years), plus the largest national, and the second largest regional, burden per capita (0.34 years, 31% above the world average):

BURDEN OF DISEASE IN DISABILITY-ADJUSTED LIFE-YEARS (DALYs) PER CAPITA, REGIONS 1990

COUNTRY OR REGION	MILLION DISABILITY-ADJUSTED LIFE YEARS LOST (DALYs) 1990 M	F	T	M. POPN MID-1990	DALYs PER CAPITA	DALYs PER CAPITA AS % OF WORLD AV.
Subsaharan Africa	153	140	293	510	0.57	219%
India	145	147	292	850	0.34	131%
Middle East Crescent	74	70	144	503	0.29	112%
Other Asia & Islands	95	82	177	682	0.26	100%
Latin America and Caribbean	57	46	103	444	0.23	88%
China	103	98	201	1134	0.18	69%
Formerly Socialist Economies of Europe (FSEs)	33	25	58	346	0.17	65%
Established Market Economies (EMEs)	52	42	94	798	0.12	46%
FSEs & EMEs (MDCs)	85	67	152	1144	0.13	50%
Demographically developing (DD or LDCs)	628	582	1210	4123	0.29	112%
WORLD	713	649	1362	5267	0.26	100%
DD as % of FSE/EME	739%	869%	796%	360%	223%	223%

Source: WB 1993:212-25

Using World Bank data for 1990, it is possible to calculate rough estimates of the gradients of mortality between 'demographically developing' countries and established market economies plus former socialist economies for the ten main causes of death. These reveal that the highest LDC-MDC inequality was for measles, since there were virtually no measles deaths in MDCs. The other gradients, in descending order, were mostly positive: acute watery diarrhea, all ages (6,300%); TB, all ages (1,600%); perinatal (382%); lower respiratory infections, all ages (328%); peri-, endo- and myocarditis cardiomyopathy, all ages (250%); chronic obstructive pulmonary disease, all ages (135%). The only negative gradients (ie. for causes of death with higher mortality in MDCs) were: cerebrovascular disease, all ages (61%); ischaemic heart disease, all ages (26%); and cancer of the trachea, bronchus and lung, all ages (24%). These last three gradients would be somewhat higher, if children were excluded. In addition, gradients of male mortality exceed those of female mortality for all these major causes of death, except in the case of three (respiratory, pulmonary and TB disease). Where a cause of death affects both those aged under five and older persons, the gradient for under five mortality was much higher. For example, the gradients of mortality for lower respiratory infections were almost 1,818 percent (ages 0-4) and 125 percent (ages 5 plus).

Income Distribution and Mortality

Gini coefficients of income distribution were available for only 28 countries. These limited data show no relationship to either life expectancy or crude death rate.

The tables show that in the 56 countries with recent data on income distribution, on average the richest decile (10%) received 5.5 times the income (or consumption) of the poorest quintile (20%). Using this D1:Q5 ratio as a sensitive though selective indicator of income inequality, it seems that this form of inequality was lowest in rich nations (ratio 4.2), second lowest in poor nations (6.9) and highest in medium income nations (8.7 for lower and 13.9 for upper medium). The smallness of the upper medium sample and the inclusion of very unequal countries like Brazil and Botswana almost certainly overstates the inequality of upper medium countries in general.

When the D1:Q5 ratio is compared for countries with differing life expectancies, those with the highest LE (75 to 79) had the lowest average ratio (4.3). However, this is almost certainly a spurious relationship, since 19 of these countries with very high longevity were also rich nations. Indeed, average longevity of nations seems to correlate more with per capita income than with income equality. In other words, *international* income distribution seems more significant in determining relative life expectancies between nations than are intranational distributions of income or consumption. The D1:Q5 ratio does increase as life expectancy decreases to medium levels but it then falls. The three poorest (African) countries with the lowest LEs also have the lowest average inequality. All this tends to confirm the view that income inequality increases in the intermediate stages of income growth and development and then falls to its lowest level in rich, developed nations with progressive taxation and other policies, including perhaps some attempt at regulation of the worst effects of capitalism. The intermediate, transitional and medium income countries also tend to have life expectancies mainly in the range 60 to 74. This may reflect their average income levels as much as their income inequality.

PER CAPITA INCOME, INCOME INEQUALITY AND LIFE EXPECTANCY, 56 NATIONS 1981-91 PERIOD

INCOME SHARE OF RICHEST 10% (D1) ÷ SHARE OF POOREST 20% (Q5) = RATIO

LIFE EXPECTANCY	RICH NO. OF COUNTRIES	RICH AV. RATIO	UPPER MEDIUM NO. OF COUNTRIES	UPPER MEDIUM AV. RATIO	LOWER MEDIUM NO. OF COUNTRIES	LOWER MEDIUM AV. RATIO	POOR NO. OF COUNTRIES	POOR AV. RATIO	TOTAL NO. OF COUNTRIES	TOTAL AV. RATIO
79	Japan	2.6								
78	3	4.7								
	Hong Kong	5.8								
	Switzerland	5.7								
	Sweden	2.6								
77	7	4.0								
Incl.	Australia	5.9								
	Norway	3.4								
	Netherlands	3.3								
76	6	4.0								
Incl.	New Zealand	5.6			Costa Rica	8.5				
	Finland/Germany	3.4								
	Belgium	2.7								
75	2	4.0								
Incl.	UK	4.0								
75-79 VERY HIGH	19	4.1			1	8.5			20	4.3
70-74 HIGH	Singapore	6.6	4	5.9	5	10.0	1	8.8	11	8.1
			Mexico	9.6	Panama	21.0	Sri Lanka	8.8		
			Hungary	1.9	Poland	2.3				
60-69 MEDIUM			2	29.9	8	8.6	4	7.0	14	11.2
			Botswana	35.4	Guatemala	22.2	Honduras	17.7		
			Brazil	24.4	Domin.Rep.	9.4	China	3.8		
					Colombia	9.3	Indonesia	3.2		
							India	3.1		
50-59 LOW					1	3.7	7	8.4	8	7.8
					Côte d'Ivoire	3.7	Tanzania	19.4		
							Kenya	16.8		
							Pakistan	3.0		
							Nepal	2.7		
							Bangladesh	2.6		
40-49 VERY LOW							3	3.0	3	3.0
							Ethiopia	3.2		
							Uganda	3.2		
							Rwanda	2.5		
TOTAL	20	4.2	6	13.9	15	8.7	15	7.0	56	5.5

Source: World Bank 1993

INCOME DISTRIBUTION, LIFE EXPECTANCY AND INCOME, 56 NATIONS 1981-91 PERIOD

INCOME CATEGORY OR COUNTRY	LE 1991	CDR 1991	DATE FOR INCOME DISTRIB.	% SHARE OF INCOME/CONSUMPTION POOREST 20% Q5	Q4	QUINTILES Q3	Q2	Q1	RICHEST 10% D1	D1 ÷ Q5	$ GDP PC PARITY PP 1990	$ GDP PC 1991
LOW INCOME												
Sri Lanka	71	6	1985-6	4.9	8.4	12.4	18.2	56.2	43.0	8.8	2,650	500
MEDIUM LE (4 nations)	64	8		6.6	10.4	14.7	21.1	47.2	31.9	7.0	1,845	478
Incl: China	69	7	1990	6.4	11.0	16.4	24.4	41.8	24.6	3.8	1,680	370
India	60	10	1989-90	8.8	12.5	16.2	21.3	41.3	27.1	3.1	1,150	330
Indonesia	60	9	1990	8.7	12.1	15.9	21.1	42.3	27.9	3.2	2,730	610
LOW LE (7)	55	13		6.2	9.9	14.0	20.4	49.5	34.4	8.4	1,439	317
Incl: Pakistan	59	11	1991	8.4	12.9	16.9	22.2	39.7	25.2	3.0	1,970	400
Bangladesh	51	13	1988-9	9.5	13.4	17.0	21.6	38.6	24.6	2.6	1,160	220
VERY LOW LE (3)	47	19		8.9	12.6	16.4	21.4	40.7	26.4	3.0	723	187
ALL LOW INCOME (15)	57	12		6.8	10.4	14.6	20.6	47.6	32.7	6.9	1,485	345
LOWER MEDIUM INCOME												
Costa Rica	76	4	1989	4.0	9.1	14.3	21.9	50.8	34.1	8.5	5,100	1,850
HIGH LE (5)	72	7		5.1	9.0	13.5	20.2	52.2	36.6	10.0	5,508	1,996
Incl: Panama	73	5	1989	2.0	6.3	11.6	20.3	59.8	42.1	21.0	4,910	2,130
MEDIUM LE (8)	66	7		5.0	9.0	13.6	20.7	51.8	35.9	8.6	3,821	1,129
Côte d'Ivoire	52	14	1988	7.3	11.9	16.3	22.3	42.2	26.9	3.7	1,510	690
ALL LOWER MEDIUM (15)	68	7		5.1	9.2	13.8	20.7	51.2	35.4	8.7	4,315	1,437
UPPER MEDIUM INCOME												
HIGH LE (4)	71	8		6.3	10.7	15.2	21.9	46.0	30.2	5.9	6,204	(2,827)
MEDIUM LE (2)	67	6		1.8	4.8	9.1	17.5	67.0	50.4	29.9	4,965	2,735
Incl: Brazil	66	7	1989	2.1	4.9	8.9	16.8	67.5	51.3	24.4	5,240	2,940
ALL UPPER MEDIUM (6)	70	8		4.8	8.7	13.2	20.4	53.0	37.0	13.9	5,791	2,790
HIGH INCOME												
Japan	79	7	1979	8.7	13.2	17.5	23.1	37.5	22.4	2.6	19,390	26,930
HIGH LE (19)	76	9		6.0	11.9	17.3	23.9	40.7	30.2	4.3	17,309	19,556
Incl: Hong Kong	78	6	1980	5.4	10.8	15.2	21.6	47.0	31.3	5.8	18,520	13,430
Sweden	78	11	1981	8.0	13.2	17.4	24.5	36.9	20.8	2.6	17,490	25,110
USA	76	9	1985	4.7	11.0	17.4	25.0	41.9	25.0	5.3	22,130	22,240
UK	75	11	1979	5.8	11.5	18.2	25.0	39.5	23.3	4.0	16,340	16,550
Singapore	74	5	1982-3	5.1	9.9	14.6	21.4	48.9	33.5	6.6	15,760	14,210
ALL HIGH (20)	76	9		6.1	12.0	17.3	23.9	40.5	29.8	4.2	17,413	19,925
ALL (56 nations)	68	9		5.9	10.5	15.2	21.8	46.6	32.8	5.5	8,393	7,892

NB The averages are unweighted
Source: World Bank 1993:238, 290 + 296

The effect of average income level can be reduced by comparing inequality trends within the four categories, from rich to poor nations. The rich country with the highest LE was Japan (79) and its inequality ratio was very low (2.6). The average ratio for countries with LEs of 78, 77, 76 and 75 were very similar (4.7, 4.0, 4.0 and 4.0). The three countries with an LE of 78 had differing inequalities: Hong Kong 5.8, Switzerland 5.7 and Sweden 2.6. Only Belgium (LE 76, ratio 2.7) approached the very low inequality of Japan and Sweden, though the Netherlands, Norway, Finland and Germany also had low inequality. Singapore was the rich nation with the lowest LE (74) and it also had the highest inequality (6.6). In the upper medium income nations there was a huge difference in average inequality between high and medium LE countries but a sample of only 6 countries is too small to warrant jumping to conclusions. In lower medium income and poor nations, average inequality differed little with level of life expectancy, except that countries with the lowest LE in each income level had below average inequality.

Overall, there is no simple and clear conclusion on the relationship between national income inequality and life expectancy. The countries with the highest life expectancies are almost exclusively ones with below average inequality but they are also, except for Costa Rica, rich nations. The country with the highest LE also happens to have almost the lowest inequality ratio. On the other hand, countries with particularly high LE relative to income, such as Costa Rica and Sri Lanka, nevertheless have quite high inequality. Both these countries, and especially Costa Rica, have well developed welfare, social and medical infrastructure. Others, such as Mexico and particularly Panama, perform well on LE but badly on equality. Finally, countries with the worst LE in their income band, all in Africa, also have low inequality.

Countries with more equal income distribution actually had higher crude death rates. This is largely explained by rich nations having older populations.

Le Grand has done a regression of standardised absolute mean differences in mortality against the standardised mean age-at-death and other variables for 32 countries, mostly European. (The absolute mean difference is the Gini coefficient multiplied by the mean.) He found 'a significant positive relationship between mortality inequality and economic inequality and a significant negative relationship between GNP per head and mortality inequality, suggesting that richer and more equal countries economically are also more equal in terms of mortality. Perhaps more surprisingly, there was a positive significant relationship between mortality inequality and per capita medical expenditures' (1989:82-3). As Le Grand acknowledges, his measurement of inequality of mortality between *individuals* ignores structural inequalities such as those of class, income, gender or region and thus, arguably, offers less insight into the causal process.

Poverty incidence may affect health more than income distribution per se. Lower incidence of urban poverty (less than 30%) seems to have been associated with higher average life expectancy in 1988 and this was even truer if rural poverty were below 50 percent. Poverty incidence (especially urban) seemed less related to crude death rates.

Average 'Cost' Per Year of Average Life Expectancy

Out of 98 countries with life expectancy above the world average in 1988, 25 had a per capita income which was low or lower medium:

LIFE EXPECTANCY, GNP PER CAPITA AND AVERAGE 'COST' PER YEAR OF LIFE EXPECTANCY

YEARS AV. LE°	COUNTRY	$ GNP PC	AV. $ GNPPC PER YR. LE°	AV. LE°	COUNTRY	$ GNP PC	AV. $ GNPPC PER YR. LE°
76	CUBA	NA		69	Mexico	1760	26
75	Costa Rica	1690	22	68	Colombia	1180	17
74	Dominica	1680	23	67	Paraguay	1180	17
73	Jamaica	1070	15*	67	Botswana	1010	15*
72	Panama	2120	29	67	Mauritius	1800	27
72	Chile	1510	21	67	Belize	1500	22
72	POLAND	1860	26	66	Jordan	1500	23
72	BULGARIA	NA		66	Tunisia	1230	19
71	Sri Lanka	420	6*	66	Dominican Rep.	720	11*
71	Fiji	1520	21	66	Ecuador	1120	17
71	St. Lucia	1540	22	65	Syria	1680	26
70	Malaysia	1940	28	65	Thailand	1000	15*
70	CHINA	330	5*				
				64	WORLD	3470	54
				75	UK	12,810	171
				78	Japan	21,021	270

* Very low 'cost' per year of LE

The average 'cost' per year of life expectancy was particularly low in China, Sri Lanka and the Dominican Republic. Cuba and Costa Rica had the highest LE among the lower income countries. Apart from China, the only other country with a high population in this poorer category is Mexico. Eight are islands, including six in the Caribbean.

HEALTH INEQUALITIES WITHIN NATIONS

Townsend (1988) and Fox (1989) analyse health inequalities in Britain and in Europe respectively.

Class Gradients of Mortality

Apart from Britain, the class gradient of mortality has probably also increased particularly in the USA, Australia, Canada and Japan and also to a lesser extent in north and western Europe. The increase in the gradient has probably been due more to the higher classes giving up smoking and improving their diet, housing and lifestyles rather than to actual deterioration in health of the lower classes. Health promotion, the welfare State (including health care) and lifestyle changes all tend to reach the higher classes first. It is arguable that, the more health standards rise in rich nations, the greater the inequality in health, because richer people can change their behaviour and improve their welfare faster and earlier than poorer people. This trend can be compounded by strategies which accelerate economic growth at the expense of poverty alleviation, living standards and working conditions, as seems to have happened in the UK during the 1980s. Increase in health inequalities in the UK seems especially likely during the 1980s and may have also been mainly due to widening inequalities in income.

Changes in British Class Structure and Health

Economic growth has increased the size and importance of the British upper classes and has reduced the size of the unskilled and semi-skilled classes. There has been in fact some 'de-proletarianisation', even allowing for the growth of a large 'class' (??) of unemployed (over 3, or even 4, millions in the trough of the worst recessions). As middle class size and power has increased and traditional Labour party voters have become 'bourgeoisified' (socially as well as politically), new parties have competed for the centre ground and the capacity of the Labour party to win elections has been seriously eroded. In fact, the Labour party has now lost four elections in a row since 1979. The Conservative government has privatised State sectors and partly undermined local government finance and power, thus further reducing the number of public sector employees, who have traditionally been the core of Labour support, partly regardless of class. As support for the Labour party has declined, its leaders have felt obliged to softpedal on proposals of progressive taxation of wealth and income and other redistributive policies. They have also often tended to trap themselves within narrower debates over health care (and especially the NHS, its funding and management) rather than emphasising more basic issues of political economy and health.

Class Gradients of Health in Britain

Since about 1930 class gradients of most indicators of British mortality appear to have increased and perhaps peaked in the early 1960s, though some (such as infant and postneonatal mortality) have decreased or fluctuated slightly from year to year. Townsend (1988) and others point to the difficulties of intertemporal comparison because of changes in methods of collection and classification of data. Among the many formidable problems of method are the changing status and classification of occupations, and 'numerator-denominator bias', arising from differing reports on a person's occupation.

Class gradients of mortality are high in the early years (especially in infancy) and then tend to decrease as age increases. For example, in 1951 the gradient of mortality was 221 percent in the case of infants. This fell to 145 percent for men aged 25 to 34 and was nearing equality (112%) for those aged 55 to 64. For the period 1971-80 the mortality ratio of unskilled male workers to all employed men peaked at 136 percent for ages 35 to 39 and then declined steadily to 108 percent in ages 60 to 64 (Leclerc in Fox 1989:97). Between 1951 and 1971 class gradients for most ages had increased by about a quarter but the increment was rather more for those aged 25 to 34.

In the 1970s class gradients of morbidity (especially chronic sickness) tended to be up to three times higher than those for mortality. Class gradients of health care in the 1970s were much lower than those for morbidity and thus there was insufficient compensation to the unskilled for their very high excess morbidity, though the unskilled (especially male) did make relatively much higher use of hospital inpatient services (but relatively lower excess use of GP services) than the professional class. Blaxter argues that, as mortality has fallen in developed countries, 'morbidity or general health status are increasingly more important indicators of inequality' (1989:199). Gender differences in morbidity are almost always the reverse of those for mortality. In addition, women in Britain often show steeper social class gradients in morbidity than men.

Class gradients for various health indicators may be compared between the sexes to see whether class differences in health are greater among men or women. The British evidence up to about 1971 suggests that class differences between males were greater than between females in the case of mortality, acute morbidity, use of health care and use of GPs relative to restricted activity ('use-need'). The reverse was true for infant mortality (by a small amount), chronic and longstanding illness and especially use of hospital outpatients and GPs relative to chronic handicapping illness. Here the female class gradients were higher. As health standards rose and many class gradients (both male and female) increased, class inequality in mortality of male adults increased more rapidly than that of female adults, between 1971 and about 1981. This suggests that whatever changes were disadvantageing the lower classes were serving to worsen the relative mortality of lower class men slightly more than women. On the other hand, whilst lower class women had relatively worse chronic sickness than higher class women, compared with the smaller male inequalities between classes, this was not compensated for by higher relative use of health care by lower class women. In consequence, the comparative lack of use of hospital outpatients and GP services relative to chronic sickness by lower class women was very much greater than in the case of lower class men.

It should be added that feminist ideas have served to produce rather more sensitive and sophisticated analyses of class among women. Thus Arber (1989) is able to demonstrate class gradients as large for women as for men.

Hart (1989) claims that the male-female gender gradient of mortality has increased with industrialisation and urbanisation. For England and Wales, both in 1930 and still in 1970-2 the gender gradient of professionals exceeded those of the unskilled. Between 1970-72 and 1979-83 the gender gradient of the manual classes increased from about 180 percent to about 206 percent and the latter now outstripped the 188 percent for professionals in 1979-83. This change may be partly attributable to the class gradient in smoking.

National Per Capita Income and Income Gradients of Health Care

The World Bank (1993) compares rich-poor differences in access and use of health care within low and middle income countries and also within the former socialist economies. The authors do not elaborate a theory of increasing or decreasing income or class inequality as nations become richer or more or less socialist. However, they do point out that in low income countries the rich benefit more because government expenditure on health is heavily skewed toward high-cost and/or urban hospital services: 'In Indonesia, despite concerted government efforts in the 1980s to improve health services for the poor, government subsidies for the richest 10 per cent of households in 1990 were still almost three times the subsidies going to the poorest 10 per cent' (1993:4), ie. the income gradient of subsidised health care was nearly 300 percent. In middle income countries governments frequently subsidise health insurance (private or public) which usually only benefits the relatively rich and/or the industrial workers. The poor in a country like Peru may travel for an hour or more to reach primary health care which is both low quality and involves long waiting times, short consultations, poor diagnosis and inappropriate treatment, often requiring payment of cash. In former socialist countries like Romania and Hungary health care may be free in principle but the rich make under-the-table payments which can amount to 25 percent of total health costs. Transition to market-oriented economies has led to dramatic reduction in government expenditure on health, almost certainly harming the poor most. The World Bank does not discuss high income, more capitalist countries but reference to Britain and the Black Report enables four types of economy and health inequality to be compared, albeit superficially. There is obviously a need for a more ambitious theory of stages in the development of economies, of health and of health inequalities.

POLITICS AND HEALTH IN INDIA

So far the discussion of trends in health and health inequalities has been rather abstract, numerical (with all the perils of numbers) and mainly lacking in analysis of the political and economic changes allegedly underlying these trends. It is time to focus on a particular country, India, the second largest and the nineteenth poorest nation. India is seen by many as in a process of political deterioration, verging on a degree of 'nongovernability' which could threaten its democratic system. It has been achieving steady but unspectacular economic growth, and showing considerable resilience through global recessions. India has improved its health faster than many other LDCs and is now on the threshold of a medium level of life expectancy (60). Despite this, in 1990 India contained the largest national burden of disease, both in aggregate and per capita terms.

The Indian State is dominated by a loose coalition of classes, whose composition and configuration changes over time. Class formation and dissolution and other changes in the power of classes have been small and gradual. There has been differential change within classes, including within the upper class and also within the dominant, upper class and upper caste category. Zamindari Abolition in the 1950s transferred land revenue to the State and, ostensibly, 'feudal' landlords lost wealth and power mostly to (or these Zamindars turned into?) rich, capitalist landowners and farmers. These include very large and large owners with holdings of 20 or more acres and 10 to 20 acres respectively per household. Recently, the national business class, both industrial, commercial and financial, has lost some power and international business (multinationals, other foreign companies, international bankers and agencies as well as foreign governments) appear to have made greater inroads. Liberalisation and some privatisation serve to reduce the power of senior civil servants and of some professionals. The Congress party continues to rule most of the time but is no longer permanently dominant. The 'dynastic' continuity of the rule of the Nehru-Gandhi family has been broken partly fortuitously, but all except two of the ten Prime Ministers of India have been either Brahmin or Thakur. The two exceptions were a high caste Kayastha and a lower middle or backward caste Jat. Neither ruled for very long and Charan Singh's tenure was purely interim.

The middle class, middle caste category has become the most assertive, whether this refers to middle and small peasant farmers (including many Punjabi and Jat Sikh farmers) and/or the 'backward' castes. Medium owners hold 5 to 10 acres (ie. usually just above average) and small owners hold 2.5 to 5 acres. The rural middle class and castes have benefited from mild agrarian reforms and other government policies, including promotion of the Green Revolution and perhaps Mandal-inspired reservation and other affirmative policies. However, only one or two percent of total cultivated land has been transferred through land ceiling legislation. Much of the rise of the rural middle class seems to have been due more to non-government action, through economic growth, rural capitalism and the spread of 'market forces'. The middle ranks may have become more assertive but they have not gained power at the centre nor in many states and, even in states where they have achieved some power, that has not been for long. However, the electoral successes of Janata in 1977 and of the Janata Dal led 'National Front' in 1989 partly reflect this increased participation of the middle ranks, especially from the rural sector, in Indian politics.

The lower classes include marginal farmers (owning 1.25 to 2.5 acres), submarginal farmers (owning 0.1 to 1.25 acres) and the landless. The lower classes and castes benefited from some government schemes, especially from about 1975 onwards but not as much as the plethora of programmes, political rhetoric and propaganda might suggest. There has been differential change within the lower class and especially within the lower class, lower caste category.

The upshot has been that the upper classes and castes have retained their control of central power but, as Kohli (1991) documents so very well, popular and populist discontent has been increasing to such an extent that the 'governability' of India has come to depend more and more on devious, manipulative, corrupt and ultimately often self-defeating political stratagems (Cf. Bailey 1988). Mrs Gandhi was killed after she and the Congress party had played some dangerous political games, not least perhaps with factions within the Sikh party. Now the Bharatiya Janata Party has risen from decline and obscurity by exploiting mainly Hindu communalist susceptibilities and perhaps particularly the resentment of the middle and backward Hindu castes against what they see as preferential treatment of both Muslims and possibly also the scheduled (but still Hindu) castes.

The continued power of the property owning, and especially the landowning classes, has meant that policies have concentrated more on income and other transfers rather than on redistribution of land and other capital. These policies have included credit-based self-employment, especially through the Integrated Rural Development Programme; wage employment, through the National Rural Employment Programme, the Rural Landless Employment Guarantee Programme and the Maharashtra Employment Guarantee Scheme; a plethora of anti-poverty programmes, such as Antayodhaya; and area development, including watershed development, the Drought Prone Areas Programme and desert development. By 1988 the IRDP claimed to have benefited 25 percent of all rural households and thus, arguably, at least half of the rural poor (though the composition of this is constantly shifting as different households rise above and fall below the poverty line). Politicians and civil servants have displayed great virtuosity in inventing populist and well publicised programmes against poverty. Apart from their effect on income distribution, they have served to reduce the pressure for redistribution of land and other wealth.

Income distribution in India has become more equal between 1965 and 1989-90. The share of the richest quintile (Q1) has fallen from 48.9 percent to 41.3 percent and the poorest quintile (Q5) has increased its share from 6.7 percent to 8.8 percent. While the richest quintile has lost 16 percent of its share since 1965, the second, third, fourth and fifth quintiles have increased their shares by 9 percent, 13 percent, 19 percent and 31 percent respectively. The Q1:Q5 ratio has fallen from 2.8 in 1968 to 1.9 in 1989-90 and, if the World Bank data can be believed, then India now has a more equal income distribution than China. It has moved into the category of those more equal nations with a Q1:Q5 ratio of less than 2. Obviously, there are some doubts, given the liberalisation policies of the later 1980s and given the size of the black or parallel economy. Even so, the data for both 1983 and 1989-90 suggest similar and increasing trends toward equalisation which are not just the chance product of one year with good harvests and incomes for the poor. Rural income distribution is particularly susceptible to such annual fluctuations, especially in harvests and crop prices. For example, the rural Q1:Q5 fell from 2.14 in 1950-5 to 1.62 in 1973-4 but rose again to 1.86 in 1977-8.

Incidence of rural poverty peaked at 57 percent in the famine year of 1966-7 but had fallen to nearer 40 percent by 1984-5. Long-term trends may be obscured by volatile annual fluctuations but, whatever the trend, it has been slowly downward. Incidence of extreme rural poverty (ie. receiving less than 80 percent of poverty income) fell from 42 percent to 30 percent between 1972-3 and 1983. This actually signified a thirteen percent reduction in numbers of extremely poor and it is *numbers* which affect health, not percentages. There were still 160 million extremely poor, plus another 95 million ordinary poor, living in Indian villages in 1983.

Health and Health Inequalities in India

Between 1901 and 1991 life expectancy rose from 24 to 60 years, an increase of 155 percent. The crude death rate has fallen from 43 to 10 (a decrease of 77%) and even infant mortality has dropped from 295 to 90 or less (a reduction of at least 70%). Since 1901 life expectancy has been lengthening at an annual rate of 1.7 percent. The rate of increase peaked at 2.9 percent annually in the 1950s but was still 1.5 percent in the 1980s.

Two studies show that the poorest-richest gradients of low birthweight in New Delhi in 1969-70 and in Calcutta in 1976-7 were 152 percent and 157 percent respectively. (The poorest received under Rs 50 and Rs 70 respectively and the richest over Rs 200 and Rs 300 respectively.) Apart from the politics of class inequalities in health, there is also the question of the health of politicians and of the political élite. Politicians in LDCs have for a long time tended to lead very unhealthy lives, with populist attempts to 'square the circle' of trying to satisfy rising expectations and excessive popular demands with grossly inadequate resources; with long, stressful hours of work which is often poorly separated from domestic and private life; and with over-consumption, including of unhealthy, mass catering food, tobacco, pan and alcohol.

As politics has become more violent, and indeed partially criminalised, the risk of attack and even assassination has increased. Chief Ministers seem particularly prone to cardiovascular, cancer, throat and other health problems and it is especially noticeable how many have undergone double or triple bypass heart operations, often at considerable expense in the private hospitals of western countries.

India is the third largest producer of tobacco leaf. The growth in the manufacture and sales of tobacco, alcohol and other drugs poses a threat to the health of all Indians but perhaps particularly of the richer, more urban and most modernised. In addition, poor sex education, patriarchy, macho values, urban migration, changing sexual mores and large-scale prostitution (especially in Bombay) indicate that AIDS may soon begin to expand quite exponentially. A recent estimate suggests that there may already be one million who are HIV positive in India and there are fears that numbers could rise very rapidly up to 50 million. Policies are mostly weak on key issues such as drug use and prevention, health education, sex education, homosexuality and even on family planning itself. For example, homosexuality is illegal in India, the number of homosexuals may be as many as 50 million and, because there is a reluctance to even acknowledge the existence of a 'homosexual problem', there is hardly a programme to prevent AIDS among homosexuals. The income, class and gender distribution of AIDS and its implication for future health inequalities needs to be assessed.

There is more evidence on India's rural-urban and inter-state inequality than on income or class inequality of health. In 1978 the rural-urban gradient for the crude death rate was 163 percent.

There is ample evidence of health inequalities between India's 26 states. In 1986 Kerala had a life expectancy of over 65 whilst Uttar Pradesh and Bihar had very low life expectancy (46), comparable with those of some of the poorest African countries. Kerala's current LE is 73 for females and 67.5 for males. A regional gradient can be calculated by expressing average health levels in India's five most unhealthy states (UP, Bihar, Madhya Pradesh and Rajasthan, ie. the Hindi heartland, plus Orissa) as a percentage of those in Kerala. The gradients were highest for infant mortality (394% in 1984) and child mortality (336% in 1974-6) but somewhat lower for the crude death rate (222% in 1985) and life expectancy (135% in 1986). The Kerala-UP gradient for life expectancy was 142 percent, compared with 165 percent for the comparable international gradient between Japan and Ethiopia. The Kerala-UP gradients for urban and rural CDRs in 1979-81 were 160 percent and 250 percent respectively. In 1983 Kerala had a slightly higher income and slightly less poverty but its distribution of consumption was slightly more unequal than that of UP. During the 1970s Kerala ranked first in state health expenditure per capita and UP ranked among the lowest. By 1983 Kerala had slipped to ninth place and UP's expenditure on health seems to have been increasing rapidly.

A regional gradient which compares health levels in the three healthiest and the three unhealthiest states avoids the risk of overstating the inequality which arises from comparing Kerala with the worst one or five states. The healthiest 3 states - unhealthiest 3 states gradient for infant mortality in the 1960s was still 287 percent. This fell to 223 percent in the 1970s but rose again to 241 percent in the early 1980s.

Comparison of Kerala and the four states with the lowest life expectancy suggests that regional inequality in LE has increased as LE itself has risen. The Kerala-four states gradients for male and female life expectancy were only 106 percent and 114 percent respectively in 1951-60. These increased to 127 percent and 137 percent respectively in 1961-70 but had stabilised around 140 percent in both 1976 and 1986.

It may be tempting to explain the health inequalities between Kerala and the unhealthy Hindi belt (particularly UP itself) by reference to 'socialism' in Kerala and 'quasi-feudal' conservatism in UP. Some caution is required here because communist party policies in Kerala and elsewhere have been more reformist than socialist, as well as being intermittent. The CPI has been only the largest component in a broad Left Front coalition which has included various conservative forces, including Christians and Muslims. In any case the federal structure of power in India imposes certain constraints on the revolutionary zeal of any state government. Other states, notably West Bengal, have had longer and more stable socialist oriented Left Front administrations and have achieved significantly less improvement in health than their southern counterpart. Kerala, perhaps because of rapid change both from internal political pressures and also from the external pressures of migrant workers and their links with the Gulf, has demonstrated various signs of economic and social stress, in terms of inflation, unemployment, suicide and mental illness, and some problems such as these have arguably been less serious even in the less developed but perhaps more stable UP and Bihar. However, the CPI and the Left Front can claim credit for, among other things, modest agrarian reform; politicisation and mobilisation of labourers and subsequent substantial increases in payment; and improvement in the education, employment, income, health care, contraceptive services and overall rights and status of women, including female labourers.

POLITICS AND HEALTH IN UTTAR PRADESH

Uttar Pradesh had a population of about 144 million in 1993. If it were independent, it would be the world's seventh most populous nation. Of the major 17 states in India, UP competes with (and probably beats) Bihar for the unenviable position of being India's most unhealthy state. This is a particularly invidious status, given that India itself, despite some quite rapid recent improvements, continues to have a life expectancy of 60 (which is 9% below the world average) and to suffer the largest national burden of disease (see WB 1993:216-17). In short, Uttar Pradesh encompasses the largest concentration of ill health on the planet. Anyone who wishes to understand why this is so needs to study the politics and political history of UP.

Class in Uttar Pradesh

The great source on the politics of UP is Paul Brass and Chapter 3 attempted to summarise some of his important work on this subject. It appears that class has had less effect on politics in UP than in Kerala and that other influences, such as personal and family power, faction, caste, region and (now, increasingly) religion have also directed events. Class clearly is important both for politics and health in UP, but it has to be said that the class structure of rural UP (and India) is obscured to some degree by households (and even individuals within households) combining several class statuses. For example, many small (and some larger) landowners rent in some land and also do some labouring. In 1947 the majority of households were categorised as small peasants (63%, owning 5 acres or less). The next most frequent category was labourers (21%, owning no land), followed by medium to large owners or middle and fairly rich peasants (13%, owning 5 to 16 acres). The remainder were Zamindars (from grand Talukdars with large estates to more modest members of a locally dominant caste) and large owners or rich peasants (2%, owning 16 acres plus). Variation (and sometimes imprecision) in occupational and class categorisation make it difficult to compare past and present class structure. However, the ratio of labourers in 1977-8 remained about the same (23%) as in 1947 and these included 18 percent who were agricultural labourers.

The Zamindar class was mainly, though not exclusively, Brahmin and Thakur. From 1951 onwards the Zamindars became ex-Zamindars but they have retained much of their land and even more of their political power and social influence. They lost their income from collection of land revenue but many have used the compensation and other finance to change their class identity and become rich, capitalist farmers. Others, through age, personality or other factors, were less able to shake off their 'feudal' class characteristics but have still found it convenient to ally themselves with the richer peasants. Smaller ex-Zamindars may, similarly, join with the middle peasants and/or castes. Rich peasants (those with 10 or more acres) have benefited from Zamindari Abolition (slightly), rural capitalism, the Green Revolution (much more), and other development programmes, patronage and favours from the government. Middle peasants probably benefited rather more from Zamindari Abolition and subsequent (very modest) agrarian reforms. From about 1967 the Green Revolution began to benefit western UP in particular and contributed to the much vaunted 'rise of the middle peasants' and/or middle castes. These middle ranks of rural society in UP include the eastern Yadavs or Ahirs (probably about 8% of UP's population), western Jats (up to 1%), Kurmis (about 4%), Gujars, Koris and Muraos, all of which have provided some support to populist, pro-rural and anti-Congress political parties such as the Lok Dal.

Brass contends that, though the middle classes and castes clearly became more assertive and more electorally significant during the 1970s, the upper class and the élite castes (notably the Brahmins, Thakurs and Kayasthas, who dominate the Congress-I party) had retained much of their traditional dominance until at least 1980. The lower classes consist of the middle and small peasants, plus (mostly landless) labourers. These comprise over 80 percent of the rural population and at least half of them at any one time are likely to be below the poverty line. The lower classes have usually been particularly divided in their interests, aims, strategy and policies. Apart from being internally split by class itself (eg. between different holding and farm areas or between owners, tenants and labourers), caste, religion (increasingly so), region, political party, family, clan, sect, village and other locality are just a few of the other forces which serve to make such a large and heterogeneous lower class difficult to organise and unite. Caste and, particularly recently, communal conflicts have served to attenuate, or distract from, class conflict which has tended to be intermittent, localised and of low to moderate intensity. In contrast, intercaste conflicts (some admittedly involving a class component) have been intense and sometimes very violent, especially (but not solely) in the south-western, 'dacoit-infested' districts.

The lower classes have to choose between various key economic issues, which include distribution of wealth (especially land) and of income (especially farm incomes dependent on land revenue charges, supplies and prices of inputs and outputs, and wage rates and employment for labourers); and social issues such as caste discrimination (especially against the scheduled), jajmani disputes and compulsory labour (begar); and many other grievances. Right from 1947 the Kisan Sabha had wished to focus on the land distribution issue and to avoid being distracted by the many other agrarian issues. This obviously favoured the landless labourers and smaller peasants at the expense of the middle peasants and/or the bigger scheduled peasants. Partly because of failure on the crunch issue of land distribution and partly because of the diversity of agrarian interests and partly for other reasons, the power of the Kisan Sabha declined in the later 1970s, especially in the west, after an abortive campaign of 'land-grabbing' which peaked in 1971. The strongest rural class associations have been the sugarcane cooperative 'unions', especially in the west.

Overall, the failure of the lower classes to organise in UP has been a problem of identification, unification, mobilisation and choice of strategy. Many in the lower classes may be unsure of their own objective class position (which in any case is liable to change with their day-to-day struggle to survive); even those who are sure of their class identity are constrained from uniting with others of the same class, by caste and other horizontal divisions and by a host of vertical divisions, not least of which is the vast geographical distance between east and west; those who do unify can be discouraged or distracted from mobilisation by landlord and police terror or by being absorbed into multiclass coalitions within political parties led by upper and middle class persons; and those who succeed in mobilising may still be divided and diverted by the sheer multiplicity of agrarian and other issues which require firm decisions over priorities and strategy.

Given the relatively weak articulation of class conflict, it seems that caste conflict, communal conflict, factionalism and interpersonal conflict, and political (sometimes geriatric) egocentricity continue to thrive in UP.

Brass concludes that, because of conflicts between leading landowning castes, between such castes and also within the rich farmer category, 'these issues and conflicts intersect with each other in such a way as to prevent a polarisation of class conflict' (1981:28) in the western, more capitalist district of Meerut. This may be less true in eastern UP but cross-cutting ties seem to help reduce class consciousness and conflict across the breadth of UP. Politics in north India involves tactics of coalition, division and cooption of particular caste groups and their leaders rather than class-caste polarisation. (The candidate is usually not so much chosen to match the largest caste vote in the constituency but rather both to counterpoise the castes of the other candidates and also to maximise the appeal to an effective, if temporary, coalition of some of the larger caste segments in the electorate.) The lack of class mobilisation in UP may be compared with the situation in Kerala and in (the much more urbanised and industrialised) West Bengal. Arguably, much of the class conflict in UP has remained at the level of 'primitive rebels', banditry, dacoity and other crime (Cf. Hobsbawm 1954).

Political Parties in Uttar Pradesh

Political parties obviously appeal to class but in UP they continue to be based more on caste and, increasingly, religion, and especially the communalist susceptibilities of the Hindu majority. There is maximum focus on persons and personalities and many senior politicians come from privileged, upper class backgrounds in which, as children, they may have been indulged by family, servants and other dependents and more generally encouraged later to cultivate highly individualist, if not plain egocentric, and factious personas. These are not the most auspicious circumstances for building up disciplined organisation either of classes or of political parties. This partly explains the lesser attention to policies, including those on health. Weak social and political organisation of class is even more feebly articulated into political party formation and practice. Brass concludes that in 1980 'the landed castes continue to be politically dominant in the UP countryside and constitute the central core of support for all the leading political parties' (1981:34).

The Congress (I) party is still led by Brahmins, Thakurs, Bhumihars and Kayasthas, with traditional support from a majority of the other upper castes, which account for 20 percent of the population. Congress (I) has also usually been supported by the scheduled (23%, including 13% from the Chamar caste) and by most Muslims (16%). Congress has dominated, particularly up to 1967, and its success has been based on a multicaste and multiclass appeal to a 'consensus' on secularism, democracy and socialism. The Jats have led the backward castes to challenge upper caste Congress dominance through parties such as the Lok Dal. This has prompted the upper castes to close ranks within Congress (I) and has encouraged Brahmins to cooperate with and offer Thakurs a greater role within the party.

Various socialist parties opposed Congress, especially in the east, until the mid-1970s but the two communist parties (with CPI the stronger) have never commanded more than 5 percent of votes. The CPI in particular has been more prepared to cooperate with Congress (I) than the socialist parties, but it compromised itself particularly badly during the Emergency and is now in a state of national decline.

The socialist parties appealed to smaller peasants, (especially in the east), backward castes, high caste Bhumihars (ie. the opposition within the élite castes of eastern UP?) and landless labourers. The Praja Socialist Party called for a landownership ceiling of 20 acres in the 1962 election, suggesting a very moderate approach to land reform which would not, in theory, preclude support even by many rich peasants? By the late 1960s socialist parties were appealing increasingly to the backward castes on social issues rather than to the lower classes on economic issues.

From 1967 the Congress party began to decline and a Jat ex-Congresswala, Choudhuri Charan Singh, was able to mobilise the rich and middle peasants into a succession of populist, anti-Congress, non-socialist parties. This culminated in the formation of the Bharatiya Lok Dal in 1974, Janata victory in the 1977 elections and the setting up of the Lok Dal in 1979. Charan Singh opposed both the Zamindars and also, in effect, the marginal peasants for being 'less efficient'. The success of his middle peasant parties contributed to the decline of the old socialist parties (in their many shifting guises), especially between 1971 and 1974. Nearly half the district committee chairmen of the Lok Dal were Yadavs in 1984. Lok Dal championing of the middle or backward Hindu castes has sometimes deterred Muslim voters (who tend to oppose Congress-I in eastern UP). However, the appeal of the Lok Dal was probably more to social and political grievances (reservations etcetera) of the middle and backward castes against both lower and upper castes than to class grievances of the middle peasants. The class strategy of the Bharatiya Kranti Dal ignored marginal farmers and agricultural labourers, pitching its appeal to owners of 2.5 to 27.5 acres, ie. all owners from small to very large, but excluding ex-Zamindar owners of 'estates' and marginal mini-farmers.

Kohli (1987) argues that Janata's victory in 1977 depended heavily on the support of the medium and rich landowning peasants and thus precluded any continuation of Congress (I)'s minuscule and already faltering programme of land redistribution.

Since the late 1980s the Bharatiya Janata Party (the old Jan Sangh) has risen to become the main opposition party, both nationally and in UP. It even enjoyed a brief period of power in UP during 1991-2. The BJP has certainly exploited communalism and Hindu frustrations (notably of the backward castes) but it has also taken advantage of Congress(I) weaknesses and its (albeit sometimes shaky) secularism and championing of many (but not all) Muslim causes. The dangerous, mortal farce being played out at Ayodhya (Ram's alleged birthplace and the site of the now destroyed Babri Mosjid) has vastly increased tension between Hindus and Muslims and led to the BJP government being replaced by Presidential Rule in December 1992 (Cf. 1968 and 1980). The main rural classes who support the BJP include some big landlords, probably backed by many rural police.

The rise of the BJP and associated decline of other non-communal populist parties (such as Lok Dal/Janata) probably represents increasing urban influence, especially of the commercial and petty bourgeoisie.

The rise of the rural middle ranks has both helped the success of new opposition parties and also served to increase the pluralism, competitiveness and indeed, arguably, the ruthlessness of UP politics. This has coincided with the partial criminalisation of politics and the politicisation of many criminals. The ruling party now has to try to please the middle and/or backward castes as well as the scheduled and Muslims (traditionally the pawns of Congress-I?), as well as reserving some surplus spoils for the upper caste/upper class. In 1982 thoughtful people were worried that UP might 'go the Bihar way' and become as seriously problematic and 'ungovernable' as Kohli (1991) has subsequently described Bihar to now be. The criminalisation of politics (and other institutions) is an insidious process. Politicians may begin by hiring or using criminals either to protect them or to intimidate the opposition and/or the electorate. Criminals then have increased expectations of reciprocity such as politicians representing their interests and protecting them against the police and due process of law. The next stage is for legitimate politicians to become involved, voluntarily or involuntarily, directly or indirectly, in the criminal process itself. Finally, the professional criminal decides to short circuit the representation by using his powers of intimidation and harassment to seek election to office himself. In this way the criminalisation of politics, particularly at state level, is now well under way and even non-criminal MLAs may find it difficult either to keep free of criminal elements or, in extremis, to stay alive.

A Brief Political History of Uttar Pradesh

In 47 years there has been a total of 27 administrations, including three periods of Presidential rule (such as between December 1992 and November 1993). Fourteen of the 24 Chief Ministers (16 individuals, because some have served two or three times) have been either Brahmin (10) or Thakur (4) whilst a Bania ruled three times and a Kayastha twice. Whilst there have been 19 Chief Ministers from the upper castes, there have been only five from the middle castes (a Jat twice, one Yadav twice and another once). No Chief Minister from the lower castes nor from the Muslims has emerged to date and even those from the middle castes date from 1967 onwards.

Pant (1947-54), with Charan Singh, abolished Zamindari ('feudal' landlordism) in 1951. He also began mild agrarian (mainly tenurial) reform and promoted the interests of the middle peasantry as the dynamic force for rural growth. The 1951 Act did not impose any ceiling on landownership. Sampurnand (1954-60) favoured the élite castes and industrialists at the expense of the rural sector and especially its lower classes. Gupta (1960-3) promoted urban interests, notably industrial and commercial business, and increased rural taxation through higher land revenue charges. He also imposed the first (but rather pointless) ceiling on landownership: 40 acres per person or 64 acres per family. Mrs Kripalani (1963-7) was the wife of a Gandhian socialist but her unhappy ministry coincided with poor harvests, food shortages and widespread discontent among many classes, not least the urban middle class, stricken by inflation. Gupta (1967) formed a brief government, mainly of Brahmins and his fellow Banias. Charan Singh (1967-8), a Jat, became the first Chief Minister from a backward caste. He cobbled together a very wide non-Congress SVD coalition of left and right, which failed to abolish either grain procurement or land revenue.

The period from 1967 to 1969 marks a watershed in UP politics, ending automatic Congress dominance and beginning the rise of Charan Singh and his successive, populist, middle peasant, backward caste and non-socialist parties (epitomised by the Lok Dal). There was President's Rule (1968-9) after the collapse of the uneasy coalition of the SVD. Gupta (1969-70) returned for Congress and Singh's Bharatiya Kranti Dal, now the largest opposition party with 21 percent of the vote, forced the government to give more attention to the middle peasantry. Charan Singh (1970) allied his BKD briefly with Congress (I) to produce a new coalition government which reduced land ceilings from 40 to 30 acres. However, very little of the surplus was redistributed to the landless and Singh dealt firmly with 'land grabs' sponsored by both the CPI and the Samyukta

Socialist Party.

The year 1970 marks another watershed, as Mrs Gandhi began to intervene quite blatantly in the government and politics of UP. Charan Singh, reluctantly and under the influence of the Congress partners in his coalition, abolished land revenue for smaller peasants (5 bighas, equalling 3.1 acres, or less). His ostensible defence of princely rights prompted Mrs Gandhi to undermine him. T.N. Singh (1970-1) organised a new BKD-led coalition and extended the exemption from payment of land revenue to a much wider category, all those owning 6.25 acres and less. This exempted not only all small peasants but also some lower middle peasants as well.

There then followed three successive Congress (I) governments from 1971 to 1977. Between April 1967 and April 1971 there had been only 12 months of Congress rule, under Gupta. The new gharibi-hataoing Congress (I) sought to outbid the Bharatiya Kranti Dal in its appeal to the poorer peasants and landless. In 1972 land ceilings were reduced (in law, if not in practice) from 30 to 18 irrigated acres and from a range between 42 and 148 acres to a maximum of 48 non-irrigated acres. More vigour was displayed in confiscating illegal surplus lands (some of 500 or more acres) on the estates and 'educational trusts' of ex-Zamindars and ex-Talukdars, especially after the Emergency was declared in the June heat of 1975. Under the 20-point programme, aid to the small farmer, the landless and the rural poor was provided in the form of the Integrated Rural Development Programme, a plethora of other special programmes, public works, allotment of surplus land, including house sites, and of drinking wells.

This autocratic brand of populism and developmentalism was not sufficient to save Mrs Gandhi and Congress (I) from the mighty electoral backlash against the Emergency in 1977. R.N. Yadav (1977-9) became the second Chief Minister from the backward castes. He led a Janata coalition which consisted of the populist, pro-rural Bharatiya Lok Dal and the rightist, communal Jan Sangh. This was perhaps the first government of UP which had been unambiguously voted into power by the 'rising' (and now possibly even dominant?) rich and middle peasants and/or backward castes. Kohli (1987) characterises Yadav as a relatively unsophisticated politician who was happy so long as resources were allocated to the rural sector, perhaps irrespective of which classes in the countryside benefited. In practice, public investment was used to 'buttress the profitability of commercial farmers, especially those in the western half of the state' (1987:202). In February 1979 Yadav simplified land tenure to two basic categories, bhumidhars (permanent owners) and asamis (occupancy tenants). Debt relief was expanded and even partly extended to include some richer peasants. (The Debt Relief Act of 1977 had liquidated the debts of landless agricultural labourers, marginal farmers, rural artisans and other poor households with an annual income of less than Rs 2,400.) The effects of debt cancellation proved somewhat perverse and the benefits were much less than anticipated.

Yadav eventually fell out with his Jan Sangh partners and he was replaced by Das (1979-80), who led another Janata coalition, this time consisting of the BLD and Congress for Democracy. Das mainly represented continuity in policy but he was able to make some gestures which pleased the richer farmers. In particular, he raised the price for sugarcane, a crop important for cash (especially in the west) but virtually useless for nutrition. The procurement price for wheat was also raised and this too benefited western farmers more than eastern. The tractor trolley tax was abolished and proposals for land reform were dumped. Das was also on the point of ending job reservations for the scheduled when Presidential Rule was imposed in UP and eight other states, pending elections.

Congress (I) won the election in June 1980 and returned to power, with V.P. Singh (1980-2) as its new Chief Minister. He was only the second Thakur to govern UP and this marked the beginning of a nine-year period of alternating rule between Thakur and Brahmin Chief Ministers. 'Raja Sahib' comes from an ex-Zamindar family in Nehru territory (Allahabad district). He cultivated a new and rather conspicuous display of integrity, culminating in an 'honourable resignation' after the apparent 'failure' of his policy on law and order (which mainly consisted of killing or capturing 'dacoits'). His resignation was generally greeted as a refreshing gesture of honour in an age when ministers clung to their posts, whatever the infamy, but the self-sacrifice was soon rewarded by a post in the central cabinet. His successor in Lucknow was R.P. Misra (1982-4), the ex-speaker and appointee of Mrs Gandhi. Weak and unpopular, he was hastily replaced by Tiwari before the 1984 general election. Tiwari (1984-5) embarked on a pre-election spending spree. He paid large and long overdue arrears to sugarcane farmers, again mainly benefiting the richer west. He began nearly 1,000 new rural link roads and facilitated rural bank loans of Rs 6,000 to Rs 100,000 to poor borrowers at 4 percent interest. He increased the electricity supply to villages, repaired state tubewells and set up a corporation to finance industrial enterprises for minorities (mostly Muslims). He also doubled the foodgrain payments to 700,000 rural workers. In short, this was a classic (and ultimately highly successful) electoral strategy to sprinkle a little to many different classes and categories, especially in the richer (and more opposition-prone?) west. This produced more votes than large amounts to fewer, more selective, more finely targeted and more needy persons from the lower classes and castes. Despite this multi-class wizardry, Congress (I) dropped 11 percent of its vote between the general and the state election. Much of this went to a new party, the Dalit Mazdoor Krishak (Oppressed Labourer and Peasant) Party, which fared well in eastern UP as the Congress (I) vote slumped. Once Tiwari had got these two elections in the bag, he lost little time in resigning and was replaced by B.B. Singh (1985-8), a rather less emollient operator. Singh was a supporter (and nominee?) of Arun Nehru (Brahmin cousin of Rajiv Gandhi). As a rather rustic politician from the crime-infested district of Gorakhpur (in the east), Singh was considered tough enough to deal with the increasingly rough and criminalised politics of UP but the smoother Tiwari (1988-9) was again brought back to handle the 1989 election. Once this was won, he was again quickly succeeded by M.S. Yadav (1989-91). He is best remembered for aggressive, if not always sensitive, championing of secular values and Muslim interests (especially with the now national focus of communal conflict at Ayodhya, in eastern UP) against the communal politicking, posturing, pilgrimageing and bricklaying of the Bharatiya Janata Party and its associated Hindu organisations.

In June 1991 the Bharatiya Janata Party increased its seats from 57 to 211 and Congress (I) was forced into third place, after the Janata Dal. Kalyan Singh (1991-2) concentrated on law and order, especially campaigns against 'mafia dons' in the west, and there was little interest in development. In December 1992, despite a formal assurance to the Supreme Court, the BJP government failed to protect the Babri mosque at Ayodhya from being destroyed by Hindu militants and the Congress (I) central government dismissed the BJP government the same day. For the third time in its history UP settled down again to Presidential Rule via its governor and this remained the situation until a Socialist - BSP alliance won the election in November 1993. The current concentration on Hindu-Muslim conflict serves to distract (or serve as displacement?) from underlying class divisions, except insofar as many Hindus and Muslims also confront each other across class as well as religious and communal barriers. In addition, the whipping up of Hindu militancy can perhaps help to paper over the cracks between backward and upper caste Hindus. Positions on the Mandal and other reports advocating affirmative policies and reservations are complex but perhaps the gut reaction of both high caste and more communally minded Hindus is opposition, because reservation (especially for the backward castes) is deeply divisive for Hindus and also because affirmative policies in general could be used to help Muslims at the expense of equally disadvantaged Hindus.

The potted history outlined above may help to explain why redistribution of wealth and income and associated improvements in the nutrition and health of the rural poor have not been higher on the agenda in UP. With 27 administrations in 47 years, each government has lasted an average of only 21 months (17 months since 1967), compared with 55 months at the centre. Some Chief Ministers have been reluctant recruits, others have stayed just long enough to 'fix' elections and others have hardly had time to elect their ministers (or have them selected for them?). The worst have simply been the cronies or 'chamchas' (spoons) of the Prime Minister and of the High Command of Congress (I). Even if they had the will for reform, few survive long enough these days to learn the complexity of successful governance in such a large, populous, densely populated, heterogeneous and problematic state. Delhi is only one hour away by air and no more than 10 hours away by train from Lucknow. Increasing intervention from the centre complicates UP government and politics and adds another dimension of power which can in theory be manipulated to some extent by all the competing forces in UP but in practice it is the upper castes and classes which ultimately seem to benefit most from a form of interference which might at first sight appear to promise some help to the lower ranks.

Agrarian Reform in Uttar Pradesh

One of the masterminds of Zamindari Abolition was Charan Singh. He wished to get rid of large landlords and 'non-viable', marginal farmers, leaving agriculture to a sturdy, progressive and highly productive (implicitly capitalist) class of small, middle and fairly rich peasants (owning 2.5 to 27.5 or 30 acres). These farmers would supply raw materials to new rural industries which could provide employment to marginal farmers who needed to be displaced because of their alleged low productivity.

By 1971 over 41 types of land tenure had been reduced to two: bhumidhars, with permanent, heritable and transferable rights; and asamis, occupancy tenants with rights which are heritable but neither permanent nor transferable. Asamis could still lose their land if it remained unused for two consecutive years. Those sirdars who had not purchased bhumidhari rights became bhumidhars automatically in 1977, without payment. (Earlier, sirdars had constituted the majority of owners, with permanent, heritable but non-transferable, including non-saleable, rights.) Adhivasis, tenants of sirdars, had already been made sirdars in 1954.

In 1951 Zamindars lost their right to collect and keep a large share of land revenue. Some of the biggest and most absentee Zamindars also lost some land but the rest hung onto over 8 million excess acres (about 16% of total taxable land) by pretending that they had been previously cultivating it, as khudkasht. The long delay between establishing the committee in 1946 and implementing the legislation from 1952 gave most Zamindars ample time to plan for contingencies and to take evasive action. Compensation was generous and not progressively scaled. Many other provisions were biased in favour of the rich. Brass agrees with Neale (1965) and Reeves that abolition 'changed very little either in the agrarian structure or the pattern of political domination in UP' (1965:12). The tenants now paid their land revenue to the State, instead of mainly to the Zamindar, but most had acquired higher rights of ownership, especially by 1977. On the other hand, the number of marginal holdings, the target of Charan Singh's social engineering, had actually increased between 1953 and 1971. Overall, the State is the 'new Zamindar' and State power (and its richer peasant allies and dependents) has increased at the expense of the private, 'feudal' ex-Zamindars.

The imposition of ceilings on landownership, first in 1960 and subsequently in 1972, yielded 1.4 million and 0.12 million acres respectively of surplus land. The total area redistributed was probably as low as 0.15 million acres or only 0.3 percent of taxable land. Kohli (1987) doubts whether more than 0.7 percent of total land was actually redistributed during the peak of such activity, between 1972 and 1977. With the failure to redistribute land early on, the incidence of renting land, especially through sharecropping, actually increased between 1953-4 and 1970-1, even though it was technically illegal. Consolidation may have benefited richer peasants who can sometimes seize the opportunity to select the best land. A huge and quite disproportionate amount of legislative time has been wasted on arguing about whether to abolish or grant exemptions from land revenue, which in any case yields fairly modest income to the state and represents a derisory and non-progressive element of taxation for some of the peasantry, especially its richer members. Holdings of one acre and less were exempted from a 25 percent increase of land revenue in 1962. Later, in 1967, owners of

6.25 acres or less had their revenue dues halved and in 1970 land revenue was abolished on holdings of 3.1 acres or less (raised to 6.25 acres or less in 1971 and later reduced again to 3.1 acres or less). Land revenue rates in 1970-1 were still highly regressive and so Congress tried to introduce a progressive acreage-based scale of levies in the 1970s. Some irrigation charges have also been regressive.

The effects of other policies have been mixed. Crop procurement prices and practices have rarely been popular among the 9 million or so farmers of UP but prices have sometimes favoured the larger producers of sugarcane and wheat, who are mainly in the west. Real wages of agricultural labourers stagnated or fell at least up to the 1970s and minimum wage legislation has been neither implemented, inspected or sanctioned. Similarly, the central government legislated against bonded labour in 1976 but this was still a problem in 1982.

Income Distribution and Health in Uttar Pradesh

Inequality of consumption and poverty intensity decreased between 1957-8 and 1973-4. By 1977-8 the rural incidence of poverty (below Rs 656) and extreme poverty (below Rs 360) was 49 percent and 6 percent respectively. At least one million out of over 17 million households in UP were extremely poor. Kohli (1987) estimates that in 1979-80 there were 40 million (about 38%) below the poverty line in UP as a whole, including 20 million marginal farmers and sharecroppers (commoner in the east) and another 20 million landless labourers (more frequent in the west).

Life expectancy was still as low as 46 in 1986. This is the lowest life expectancy for any administrative unit in the world with such a large population (nearly 147 million in 1994). Only Nigeria, with 115 million, and Bangladesh, with 107 million, are remotely comparable and they had LEs of 52 and 51 respectively in 1991. The crude death rate in UP was still 15.8 in 1985 and infant mortality was 142 (166 in rural areas). As recently as the 1960s the female rural IMR was as high as 259. However, previously low expenditure on health rose faster in UP than in most states between 1976 and 1987. Jain (1988) reports a major increase in immunisation against tetanus after 1977 and a dramatic fall in IMR by 14 points in 1985.

The rural-urban gradient for the crude death rate in 1973 was 154 percent, slightly lower than the all-India gradient of 163 percent in 1978. The gender gradients for heights and weights of 18 to 40 year olds in 1980 were 107 percent and 113 percent respectively.

POLITICS, INCOME DISTRIBUTION AND HEALTH IN A VILLAGE IN CENTRAL UP

From 1981 to 1983, during the Congress (I) governments of V.P. Singh and then of R.P. Misra, a study was made of the politics, economy and health of a medium-sized village in Barabanki district, which forms part of the central plain of Uttar Pradesh. The village selected was Basauli, which is located in Suratganj block, in the east central part of Fatehpur tahsil. The Pradhan or chairman of the gram panchayat of Basauli gaon sabha was Thakur Sahib, an ex-Zamindar who belonged to the Bais subcaste of Thakur.

In 1901 the main castes in Barabanki district were Kurmi (about 14%), Ahir (12%), Pasi and Pathan (each 11%), Chamar (8%), Brahmin (7%), Thakur (3.5%), Lodh, Sheikh and Julaha (each 3%), Kahar (2%) and Bania (1%). Muslims comprised nearly 17 percent of the population. There were 43 Thakur 'tribes' and by far the most numerous subcaste was Bais (1%). Raikwar was the fifth largest. In 1981 the district was predominantly Congress (I), with at least one Congress (I) MP and four MLAs, plus two MLAs from the Lok Dal (a Yadav and a scheduled). However, Congress (I) lost three of its MLAs in 1985, probably to the Lok Dal, which in 1981 was the main opposition party in the district. Congress (I) in the district was said to be dominated alternately by Brahmins and Thakurs. In 1981 Thakurs seemed to have the upper hand, possibly reflecting the situation at state level. At that time the MLA for the constituency which contained Ramnagar block in the south and Suratganj block to the north was Gajendra Singh, a Thakur landlord with a very large estate of at least 50 acres. The previous MLA had been a Kurmi and now Gajendra Singh was being challenged by a Brahmin of Awasthi subcaste who had migrated from a poor 'interior' village in the locality to the city of Lucknow, where he had made some money.

The landlord class in both Suratganj and Ramnagar blocks was mainly Thakur and Brahmin. In Suratganj block the most populous subcaste of Thakur was Raikwar. Other smaller Zamindars in Suratganj block included Kurmis and Banias, the latter having acquired Zamindari through purchase of mortgaged land which the mortgageors could not afford to redeem. The two most powerful ex-Zamindars affecting Basauli were the Raja of Ramnagar, a Thakur of the Raikwar subcaste, and, to a much less extent, the Raja of Mahmoodabad, a Shia Muslim. The third most important landowning caste was Kurmi and, as Kurmis had risen in wealth and power, they were able to join Thakurs and Brahmins in three-cornered political fights. In 1982 Ramnagar block was still dominated by Thakurs whereas Suratganj block had been dominated by Kurmis for some time but they were now being challenged, particularly by Thakurs. The Pramukh of the block development committee in Suratganj was still a Kurmi but in the election of May 1983 he was defeated by Thakur Sahib, the Pradhan of Basauli gaon sabha.

A Village in Central UP

Basauli gaon sabha consists of two revenue villages, Basauli itself and the smaller village of Imlipur. Together, in 1981 these had a total area of 1,015 acres, a resident population of 1,425 and therefore an average of 0.71 acres per person. Basauli is a roadside 'village' about four kilometres from the block headquarters in Suratganj and 11 kilometres from the tahsil headquarters at Fatehpur. The tahsil forms the northeastern and perhaps most isolated quadrant of Barabanki district, which adjoins Lucknow district to the west. The district used to be part of the central heartland of the old Shia kingdom of Avadh ('Oudh') and it still retains some of the social and political features of that 'feudal', princely Shia state. Economically, in 1976-7 Barabanki district ranked twenty-second out of 56 districts in terms of per capita income. This high ranking was mainly due to a high level of irrigation (59%) and Barabanki district had very little urbanisation, electrification or industry. In 1981 population density was high (457 persons per km^2) and small farmers, with less than 5 acres, cultivated 59 percent of the total area. Fatehpur was probably the least developed of the four tahsils but a tarmac road built in 1959 had begun to open up Suratganj block to more commercial activity.

The 263 households of Basauli were divided among 26 caste groups, including two 'tribal' groups. In terms of caste strata, 23 percent of the population belonged to high castes, 56% percent to middle castes (including 15.5% Muslim) and over 20 percent to scheduled castes and tribes. The most numerous castes were Lodh (14%), Brahmin and Chamar (each 9%), Kurmi (8%), Mahabrahmin (8%), (Muslim) Pathan (7%), Thakur (nearly 6%) and (scheduled) Pasi (5%). This does not include temporary residents such as the 'Reza Adivasis', tribals from Bihar, and others working as labourers at a brickworks just beyond the village. Traditionally, and indeed still part of the time in 1981, the Mahabrahmins were employed to perform rituals related to cremation and as such were looked down on, particularly by other high castes. Mahabramins are also employed in farming and other occupations and one Mahabrahmin family, with a large joint household of 26 members, has become quite rich, through farming, milling and commerce. The family landholding status had changed from medium peasant (8 acres) to large peasant (25 acres, including 12.5 acres irrigable). This family forms the core of the opposition to the Thakur Pradhan. Arguably, the Pathans are the Muslim equivalent of Thakurs, whom they usually supported.

The largest Zamindar family in Basauli had been Thakur which had dominated the locality since at least 1880. In 1950 the father of Thakur Sahib collected malguzari (land revenue) worth about Rs 10,000 (at least Rs 30,000 at 1982 prices) from about 1,000 acres in 16 villages. He lost all this in 1952 but received some compensation, possibly in cash, over a 5-year period. The Zamindar's spacious house is located in the western mohalla (ward) and is partially surrounded by the densely packed housing of Pathans, Ahirs and some of the Lodhs.

Thakurs were not the only caste which suffered because of Abolition of Zamindari. The Zamindars had employed quite a large retinue of functionaries, such as guards, priests, managers, clerks and feudal retainers, some of them hereditary. Thakur Sahib's family had employed 16 such persons, mainly as guards, and three or four other Thakur families employed up to four guards. Most were Brahmins and so they lost an important source of employment after Abolition.

Kurmis in particular and also Lodhs were said to have benefited most from

Zamindari Abolition. As asamis or occupancy tenants they became full owners and they also had their malguzari reduced to 25 percent of earlier payments, which had included a 75 percent share to the Zamindar as tax collector.

At that time the scheduled castes were mainly labourers and were thus unable to benefit. In the 1970s the gram samaj distributed about 40 acres (4.4% of cultivable area) from gaon sabha land after Consolidation in 1968 and the main beneficiaries were Chamars, Pasis and (Muslim) Dhobes.

The average areas of total and irrigable land were 0.46 and 0.28 acres per person, respectively. Indices of total area per person were 156 percent of the average for high castes, 87 percent for middle castes and 61 percent for the scheduled. Inequalities were even greater for irrigable land per person: high caste 171 percent, middle caste 86 percent and scheduled 43 percent. Thus the high caste-scheduled gradients for total and irrigable land per person were 256 percent and 398 percent respectively. Comparing individual castes, a Punjabi Sikh immigrant family had the most irrigable land per person (949% of the average), followed by the biggest landowning caste, the Thakurs (370%), Kurmis (310%) and Mahabramins (122%). Major castes with less irrigable land included the Lodhs (91% of the average), Pasis (52%), Pathans (47%), Brahmins (42%) and Chamars (35%). Ahirs actually owned no irrigable land at all but had more than average of other land.

Twenty farmers owned a total of 21 pumpsets, including 5 Kurmis, 5 Lodhs, 4 Thakurs, 2 Mahabrahmins (including the opposition leader, with two) and one each among Pathans, Dhobes, Chamars and Pasis. Fourteen of the pumpsets had been purchased between 1978 and 1981. Some farmers had drilled 'borings' and hired engines to irrigate. These included four Thakurs, one Brahmin and four others.

Bais Thakurs owned four times the average amount of irrigated land and were also much better educated than other major groups. Some Bais had thus been able to secure jobs in government or other service, mostly locally. Raikwar Thakurs enjoyed almost similar advantages.

Thakurs were divided politically and not necessarily on the basis of subcaste. In 1982 Thakur Sahib, a Bais, was supported by about 30% of the Raikwars. In 1956 a Raikwar from the opposition faction had been elected Pradhan but TS claimed that the Raikwar had been unable to dominate in the way that TS was subsequently able to do.

The Pradhan was solidly and sometimes aggressively supported by the Pathans, whose illiterate head ('Khalipha') was also leader of the mosque. Thakur Sahib resonated sensitively both to Muslim religious interests and also to the concerns of the Pathans who were mostly fairly poor. The main opposition in 1982 included a large core of Brahmins and Mahabrahmins who would have found it difficult to reach out to Muslims. However, in 1975 the Pathans had switched their support temporarily to the Thakur-led opposition. (They were to desert Thakur Sahib's side again in the 1983 election, soon after Thakur Sahib had replaced the illiterate 'Khalipha' as a candidate for member by his more educated son.)

Until 1982 the Deputy Pradhan was the priest of the temple built by Thakur Sahib's ancestor. The priest was a Dube Brahmin.

Thakur Sahib was also supported by the richest Lodh farmer but only about 41% of this numerous, and politically rather crucial, caste group supported TS in the 1982 election. These probably included some of the 20 percent and 42 percent who lived in western Basauli and in Imlipur respectively. Later, when TS reversed an earlier judgment in a house land dispute between Lodhs and Ahirs, Lodh support for TS sank to 20 percent. The Pathans, Lodhs and other middle castes (such as Dhobes and Gadarias), plus lower castes (such as Pasis, Patharkots and Radhikas) usually acted as a 'militia' to defend the Pradhan against attack. Since Pathan and Ahir neighbours were usually in conflict and since Lodhs and Ahirs (again including neighbours) were mostly in even more deadly enmity (especially over housing land in the relatively overcrowded western mohalla), it was unusual for TS to be able to attract any Ahirs to his side. The above suggests that it was more complicated than a Thakur-Yadav conflict, though hostilities between Thakurs and Yadavs were common in UP, both locally and at state level.

The political role of the Kurmis seemed rather muted. They appeared to be more interested in agriculture and household matters, including the building of pacca housing. Only about a quarter of the Kurmis supported TS in 1982. The Sikhs, recent immigrants and arguably vulnerable, were extremely careful to stick to economic activities and, in their desire to avoid politics, they had not even registered as voters.

The main opposition to the Pradhan included the Mahabrahmins, some Shukla Brahmins, many other (but not all) Brahmins of other subcastes, a majority of the Raikwar Thakurs, and the Ahirs/Yadavs (as enemies of the Pathans). (No Ahirs supported TS in the election of April 1982 but by August they had shifted to his side after TS had quarrelled with the Lodhs of the western mohalla.) Two-thirds of the Chamars also supported the opposition.

Perhaps the most powerful opponent of Thakur Sahib was the large household of S. Mahabrahmin, which had risen from being poor dependents (possibly even servants?) of the main Zamindar family to become prosperous cultivators and businessmen. The family's business interests included two tubewells, tobacco cultivation, a grain mill, a pumpset agency in Fatehpur and commodity trade (which was alleged to have included some smuggling). Their house, which was the only one which had electricity in 1982, was located in the eastern mohalla, where most of the Brahmins, Mahabrahmins and Chamars lived.

The political conflict at village level encompassed divisions between two strong personalities, two rich families, the two richest upper castes (with contrasting cultures) and it was also between two elements of the upper class, a declining 'post-feudal', ex-Zamindar family and a rising, capitalist farmer and businessman. Whilst the Thakur ex-Zamindar was Chairman of the block committee of the Congress (I), the nephew of the Mahabrahmin businessman was secretary of the tahsil branch of the CPI(M), an opposition party with very little influence in the locality. The conflict on occasions had become violent, particularly between the younger generations. A country 'bomb' had been thrown at the youngest son of Thakur Sahib but he had escaped injury. Since then an uneasy peace and mutual avoidance by leading persons had prevailed. During the gram panchayat election of April 1982 there was a moderately serious encounter, involving use of firearms and 'fireworks', which had led to government intervention in the form of the joint appearance of the District Superintendent of Police and the District Commissioner, who were touring the booths to ensure calm.

Thakur Sahib expressed concern that Charan Singh and the Lok Dal, by championing the backward castes, had aroused 'casteism' (jatiwadi). He feared that the main conflict within Basauli was changing from factionalism within a single caste (the dominant Thakurs) to a more pervasive and damageing intercaste struggle between the three main upper castes, particularly Thakurs versus Brahmins and Mahabrahmins. This widened the core arena of conflict from 13 to 57 households (22% of the total). TS was particularly anxious to avoid Thakur-Brahmin conflict, for a variety of reasons. Insofar as the opposition continued to include a large number of Thakur dissidents, it almost seemed as if this were a political price worth paying, simply to avoid the more dangerous polarisation within upper caste ranks. To a large extent the main conflict continued to be between the Thakur ex-Zamindar who had also been the elected leader (Pradhan) continuously for the past 21 years, plus his supporters (especially the Pathans, and other Muslims, middle and lower castes in the western mohalla and the Pasis of Purwa hamlet) and any rich and powerful upper caste villager who was bold enough to oppose the hegemony of the ex-Zamindar.

Thakur power in Basauli had declined between 1950 and 1982, for several reasons. Firstly, the heirs to the largest Zamindari were uterine descendants, who had in-migrated quite a long distance, in fact from another district. Secondly, the Thakurs were segmented between a small minority subcaste group of Bais (who were mostly immigrants from different places and not interrelated) and the local Raikwar majority, who were themselves often split by kinship, faction and other divisions. Thirdly, Zamindari Abolition led to loss of income from land tax and also to costly litigation between pattidars. A few educated Thakurs had found salaried employment in government service (including Thakur Sahib himself, for a brief period in the 1950s). Few had been as dynamic or successful in commercial farming as at least five farmers of middle caste. Fourthly, Thakurs had sold about 30 percent of their land, mainly to Lodhs, Punjabis and various other castes. Fifthly, greater interests in proficiency at, and profits from, agriculture increased the relative wealth, income and power of certain middle castes, some of whom opposed the Pradhan. Despite decline, the Pradhan had retained the position for 21 years. However, there had only been one election since 1971 and in his third election, in 1982, Thakur Sahib only won by a very narrow majority.

Some Thakurs put their faith in technology and hoped that investment in a tractor would enable them to recapture the economic initiative and reverse the relatively greater progress of farmers from Lodh, Kurmi and other middle and lower castes. By 1985 Thakur Sahib had purchased a tractor and several other

Thakurs were considering it.

Thakur Sahib

Thakur Sahib was born in 1928, the son of a Talukdar of Bais Thakur caste in Rae Bareli district, who was also a Gandhian social worker and homeopathic practitioner. During the 1930s TS received a fair education as far as tenth class at a good English-medium school in Lucknow. His father's father owned over 120 acres in Rae Bareli. In 1944 his father inherited 70 acres in Basauli from his mother's mother (nanni), probably a Raikwar. Thakur Sahib and his father were obliged to leave the 'better social atmosphere' of Rae Bareli district, with its larger and more educated Talukdars and by 1952 they had settled permanently in Basauli, possibly to avoid being absentee landlords, which were proscribed by the new legislation. After Zamindari Abolition TS worked seasonally as a supervisor of sugarcane purchase for a sugar mill in Gonda (his first wife's district) and also, briefly, as a Naib Tahsildar in Gonda district. By 1982 TS claimed to own at least 28 acres (including 14.5 acres of irrigable land) or roughly 40 percent of his original inheritance. The land was valued at about Rs 200,000 in 1982 prices and the total net income of his household was said to be about Rs 16,000 per year.

In 1982 Thakur Sahib's family was at a stage in the development cycle when only one out of four adult sons was working and it was proving quite difficult to find a suitable groom for his younger daughter. Three of his sons were still studying at college and the expense of this, plus the need to find at least Rs 10,000 for his younger daughter's dowry, was imposing a strain on his finances. By 1983 the two middle sons had both completed postgraduate training and the eldest son, after a brief and abortive spell as a trainee revenue accountant, was intending to start as a building contractor. The two youngest sons hoped to find clerical employment, with the help of sofarish from MLA contacts of their father. The elder daughter had been married for some time to a bank official and the younger daughter eventually married someone with a diploma in electrical engineering. By 1985 the second son had a legal practice in Fatehpur and was intending to move to Barabanki. The third son had passed his MA in Sociology and was working 'as a research scholar'. The youngest had passed his BA and was working on the farm, with a tractor. The eldest son was also 'busy in agricultural work'. Many of TS's relatives were employed in the urban service sector, particularly in banking and in construction. (Thakur Sahib had himself undertaken one or two works of construction, including the building of the village school.)

Thakur Sahib was only 21 when he won his first election to become Pradhan (Chairman) of the gram panchayat (village committee) of Basauli goan sabha. In those days elections were conducted by a show of hands and TS won against a Kurmi. In 1956 TS was unable to be a candidate because of service and so he proposed J.S. Raikwar, who was elected unopposed. The latter proved autocratic and unpopular, surrounded by other Thakurs whom people found rough and oppressive. TS claims that in 1961 he was urged to stand for election by Thakurs, Brahmins and others. TS won and JS left the village to become a sadhu. In 1971 TS again won, by 320 votes to 207, a handsome margin of 113. Again there was a very long interval between elections and in fact by 1982 at least two of the 12 members had died. In the ten years TS had (perhaps inevitably) made a number of enemies and in 1982 he won by the narrow majority of only 34, against BBS, a Raikwar Thakur. Thakur Sahib had dropped the Dube Brahmin priest as candidate for Deputy Pradhan and DNS Raikwar crossed over from the opposition to become Deputy. TS was supported by Bais Thakurs; Pathans, Dhobes and Kabarias (nearly all Muslim); Gadarias (of middle caste status); Pasis (scheduled caste); and Patharkots and Radhikas (both scheduled 'tribes'). TS was opposed by most of the Raikwar Thakurs, Mahabrahmins, Brahmins and all the Ahirs (who were in litigation with the Pathans), Barhais and Telis. The members of the new panchayat were much younger, more educated and now included more opposition members (4 out of 12). The number of scheduled members also increased marginally from two to three, at the expense of the higher castes.

In May 1983 TS won the election for block Pramukh and a new election was held for Pradhan. TS supported DNS Raikwar, his Thakur Deputy, but he was defeated by RP Misra, the nephew of the richest Mahabrahmin. The margin was extremely close (only 6 votes) and the Thakur lost mainly because of a crucial defection by 70 percent of the Muslims and all the Lodhs of the western mohalla. This defection was possibly connected with TS having dropped CK Pathan from his list of candidates and also possibly by the switch in TS's support from Lodh to Ahir in a legal dispute.

Thakur Sahib had long been the Chairman of the block committee of Congress (I). As a village Pradhan he had also been a member of the development committee in Suratganj block for 21 years. In 1982 he decided to stand as a candidate for Pramukh (Chairman) of the block development committee. The electorate consisted of the Pradhans of the 125 gaon sabhas in the block, plus about 16 nominated members. In 1982 there were 142 members of the committee, including up to 40 Brahmins, 32 Kurmis, 30 Thakurs, 13 Muslims, 20 from the backward castes (including 8 Yadavs) and 9 scheduled (including 2 Pasis). The elections were originally timetabled for February 1982 but the government postponed them to May 1983, ostensibly to allow elections for a new generation of Pradhans to take place in April 1982. There were six candidates for Pramukh, including three Thakurs, two Brahmin lawyers and one Kurmi businessman (the previous Pramukh, from Dafarpur village). The two lawyers were not local politicians and it transpired that their main interest in the post of Pramukh was as a means to gain membership of the District Development Committee. Despite the proliferation of Thakur candidates and, with the help of energetic but gentle canvassing, by cycling round 'the interior', Thakur Sahib won by a margin of 13 votes and he claims that, but for a mistake by 14 voters over the preference system, the majority would have been 27. He had hoped to be supported by most of the Thakur, Muslim, Pasi and backward caste Pradhans, as well as a majority of the Brahmins, half the Yadavs and perhaps a third of the Kurmis. TS hoped to have another try at getting a state tubewell for the poorer villagers in the southeastern section of Basauli, as well as various benefits for the poorer, isolated and northwest 'interior' of the block.

Overall, it has to be said that Thakur Sahib represented a more educated, more liberal and also, incidentally, much less commercial and non-mercenary example of a Thakur ex-Zamindar, an ex-feudal whose participation and local leadership within the major 'democratic' political party had helped him to adapt moderately well to gradual social change in rural north India.

Thakur Sahib and his family had suffered several premature deaths. The first wife of TS died of septicemia when she was only about 20, during the birth of her second child. This child itself died two months later. His second wife produced four sons and a daughter. The wife of the eldest son died of a gastric upset, possibly severe food poisoning, in 1981 at the age of about 25. The wife of the second son gave birth to a stillborn daughter in 1982. TS, like his father, practised some homeopathy but he seemed to receive very few patients, perhaps mainly because of prolonged absence from the village and his intense involvement in politics. It seemed quite common for politicians to have some interest in health care, particularly in traditional or 'alternative' systems. From at least 1982 TS was himself suffering from low blood pressure.

The Economy of the Village

In 1981 the high castes owned an average of 3.6 bighas per person, middle castes 2.0, lower castes 1.4 and the overall average was 2.3. Thakurs owned 6.5 bighas per person and paid 25 percent of total land revenue. The Muslims owned an average of only 0.99 bighas per person, including 0.44 irrigated bighas (Cf. the average of 1.37). Assuming that the poverty line were Rs 810, then 51 percent of the sample and 56 percent of all households were below the poverty line. The highest household per capita income was more than five times that of the lowest. The sample average per capita income was Rs 913, which was 59 percent of the average for India, 71 percent of the average for UP in 1980-1 and probably 106 percent of the average for Barabanki district. Poverty incidence in the higher, middle and lower castes was 33 percent, 46 percent and 82 percent respectively. When per capita income was weighted for adult consumption units, these ratios fell to 21 percent, 29 percent and 55 percent respectively. The sample of 102 households was probably about 12 percent richer than the overall population.

Household heads were asked whether their standard of living had improved between 1971 and 1981. Altogether, 30 percent claimed that it had, including 33 percent of high castes, 36 percent of middle castes and only 14 percent of the scheduled. Among individual castes, the highest rates of improvement were affirmed by Thakurs (75%), Lodhs (67%), Dhobes (60%) and Gadarias (40%) whilst Kurmis (11%) probably under-reported their progress by as much as 30 percent. Mahabrahmins (29%) and Brahmins (23%) were also not very upbeat about improvement.

Six percent claimed a big improvement and 24 percent some improvement in standard of living. A plurality (36%) reported no change and 26 percent and 7 percent reported decline and serious decline respectively. Improvement seemed to correlate with purchase of land, development of the existing holding and with education beyond fifth class. Small grants of mostly poor quality land had not improved the standard of living of many households. Out of over Rs 157,000 in grants and loans to villagers since 1975, nearly 23 percent went to Chamars, 18 percent to Mahabrahmins, 16 percent each to Lodhs and Thakurs and 15 percent to Pasis.

The average area cropped was 3.4 acres. About 39 percent of household heads were exclusively farmers who did no labouring. A further 20 percent combined farming, mostly small-scale, with labouring. Seven percent worked in service, either in white collar jobs or as shopkeepers. The proportions of the sample in the high, medium and low classes were 22 percent, 24 percent and 54 percent respectively. In the total population most labourers, other than two annual and 11 biannual labourers, worked on a daily or short-term basis. They received from two to five rupees, usually with some food, but no one normally received the legal minimum daily wage (Rs 7), except at harvest and other peak times. Labourers were not organised into a trade union or other association. A major dispute between Kurmi farmers and Chamar labourers in a neighbouring village was mediated by the Pradhan of Basauli. He, as a fairly large scale employer of labour himself, engineered a compromise which was more favourable to the Kurmi employers. Biannual labourers were paid from Rs 30 to 70, per month, usually with food. At least 25 men from Basauli worked for about eight months of the year at the local brickworks. They were paid Rs 6 to 12 per day for carrying bricks and an average of Rs 10 per day for moulding the clay. Other villagers worked for the Public Works Department or for local building contractors. Many of these were paid Rs 5 or so rather than the statutory minimum of Rs 7 per day, on various pretexts.

HEALTH OF VILLAGERS IN A CENTRAL UP VILLAGE

A survey was made of the 582 members of the 102 households, which formed a 39 percent sample of all households in the gaon sabha. The introduction of potatoes and other changes in the 1970s had probably improved the general diet and nutrition, though the position on milk, pulses and fats seemed to have worsened. The heights and weights of 483 villagers were measured in August 1982 (a month of low income and worse health for many). Average heights for men and women aged 21 and over were 164.7 and 150.8 centimetres respectively. These were 101 percent of a male and 99 percent of a female sample of 18 to 40 year olds taken in UP as a whole in 1980 (see Bardhan 1984:88). Floud (1988:237) shows that the average height of Basauli men compared well with Italians in 1875 (162 cm), and most Africans and also Jamaicans (163 to 169 cm) but less favourably with the British in about 1983 (172 to 175 cm), American soldiers (177 cm) and new recruits to the Netherlands Army (181 cm). The average height of women in Britain ranged regionally from 159 to 162 centimetres. Basauli men and women were thus about 95 percent and 94 percent respectively of the average height of British counterparts.

Average weights for men and women aged 21 and over were 46.8 and 39.3 kilograms respectively. These were 94 percent of the male and 90 percent of the female sample in UP (with its younger age range). Twelve-year olds in Basauli were about 37 percent lighter than their British counterparts. The average weight for height of men and women was .284 and .261 respectively.

The crude death rate in 1982 was estimated to be at least 14, compared with 17 in rural UP and nearly 14 in rural India during 1979. Only 6.2 percent of the sample were aged over 60. Mothers aged 45 to 49 had had an average of 7.6 births (Cf. 5.1 in all India) and an average of 3.7 had died in stillbirth, childhood or adulthood. This represents 48 percent of ever born. This percentage is considerably inflated, mostly for females, because of a silly mistake in the survey. The majority of children who had survived to marry or leave the household for some other reason were not recorded. Consequently, only 195 female births were recorded, as against 293 male. This has increased the mortality rate, particularly of females and more especially of those born before about 1965 (insofar as they were more likely to have flown the nest). Despite this rather basic error, the infant and under five mortality rates for Basauli are not so different from those for rural UP as a whole but the under five mortality rate was 43 percent higher than in the western villages of Jhakri and Dharmnagri (JD), studied by Jeffery (1989). However, excess mortality in Basauli over JD was actually lower for those born before 1966 (27% higher) than for those born subsequently (53% higher). The methodological flaw, though serious, need not necessarily affect comparison of health inequalities (other than gender), insofar as the omission is likely to affect all categories more or less equally. Nevertheless these data weaknesses may have other unforeseen effects and need to be constantly borne in mind.

The stillbirth rate was 62, more than double the rate for JD and about ten times that of the UK. The average infant mortality rate between about 1941 and 1981 was 206, almost double the IMR in JD (108). The neonatal rates were similar in the two areas and the higher IMR in Basauli was due to its postneonatal rate (136) being three times that of JD (45). In general, a high ratio of postneonatal deaths is characteristic of less developed areas. The postneonatal rate for males in Basauli fell from 200 in the 1940s to 100 in 1970-4.

Up to 1965 male, female and total IMRs were 220, 504 (obviously inflated) and 278 respectively. Even with this inflation, the overall rate was not much in excess of the rate for rural UP (over 250), though it was much higher than in JD (147). From 1966 the male, female and total rates in Basauli fell to 180, 224 and 200 respectively. The rate was then still well over 160 in rural UP but down to only 86 in JD. As IMRs have fallen in both areas, the excess IMR in Basauli over JD has actually increased from 89 percent earlier to 133 percent later. Male rates in Basauli were more reliable, especially latterly, and had only fallen from 220 earlier to 180 later (though they were down to 133 by 1975-9). The female rate declined from 504 to 224 and was still 258 in 1975-9.

The under five mortality rate between about 1941 and 1982 was 371 per 1000 live births, compared with 259 for the period between about 1941 and 1985 in JD, ie. an excess in Basauli of 43 percent. Altogether, only 62 percent of babies in Basauli had survived to reach the age of five (Cf. 74% in JD). This is inflated by the under-recording of female births. If this is adjusted, assuming an equal number of male and female births, the under five rate would still remain high (about 312 or 371 x 515 ÷ 613).

The progeny of household heads also die after the age of five, including in adulthood, and, out of 501 ever born, 260 (52%) had survived and 48 percent had died by 1982.

Illness was recorded for a period of up to 420 days between January 1981 and the time of the interviews in January and February 1982. Altogether, 338 persons (58% of the sample 582) had experienced 382 bouts of illness, 0.65 episodes per person and 1.1 episodes per sick person. Each bout lasted an average of about 60 days but poor definition of what constituted a 'day of illness' probably means that morbidity has been overstated. All household members averaged 39 days of illness and sick members averaged 68 days. In a 12 month period, male adults experienced 52 days illness, and poorer household heads were ill for 83 days. In England and Wales during 1971 the comparable rates for working males and unskilled manual workers were 9 and 18 days respectively. Even if men in Basauli worked on half their days of illness, their morbidity rates would still be at least double those of England and Wales.

The most common illnesses were fevers and infections, which accounted for 32 percent of total episodes. The incidence of other aggregated categories were 27 percent of episodes for colds, coughs and pulmonary problems; 17 percent for gastro-intestinal problems; 10 percent for 'other illness'; 10 percent for skin problems; and 4 percent for aches, pains and fractures. As for serious illnesses before 1981, 39 percent of those mentioned were fevers and infections, followed by gastro-intestinal problems (20%).

In terms of days of sickness, gastro-intestinal problems were responsible for by far the largest share (27% of total days of illness). Skin problems accounted for nearly 16 percent of total days and the remaining four categories each comprised about 14 percent of days of illness. In disaggregated terms, 43 percent of days of illness were due to four types of problem: stomach complaints (18%), fevers (11%), colds, coughs and sore throat (9%) and diarrhea, dysentery and 'cholera' (5%).

Persons over 60 suffered most illness (average 85 days), followed by males and females aged 16 to 60 (57 and 46 days respectively), then girls (21 days) and boys (15 days). Overall <u>reported</u> female morbidity was only 83 percent of that of males. However, it is possible that both overall and male morbidity have been overstated but female morbidity somewhat underreported. About half the sample had experienced a serious illness before 1981. The lack of definition of 'days of illness' is an obvious weakness (Cf. Blaxter 1989).

Illness varied seasonally, with peak visits to the Primary Health Centre from its catchment area in August (66 per day) and the minimum in January and February (33 per day). Given seasonal variations in employment, income and health, there is a need for future studies to examine seasonal fluctuations in various gradients of health inequality.

HEALTH INEQUALITIES IN RURAL UP

Health inequalities between caste strata (especially between Muslims and high caste Hindus), individual castes, income categories, landowning classes and genders in Basauli were analysed. Gradients of inequality were calculated by expressing the health performance of the lower category as a percentage of that of the higher category.

Caste Stratum Gradients of Health

Caste stratum refers to combinations of individual castes: high, middle and low caste Hindus, plus Muslim castes. If key indicators are combined to produce an aggregate health index, then high castes emerge as the healthiest and Muslim castes as the least healthy in the sample. Surprisingly, the low or scheduled castes come second and the middle castes follow close behind. The relatively good performance of the scheduled, with the lowest under five mortality, may reflect the benefits of affirmative policies or could be explained by underreporting of health problems, due to higher thresholds of tolerance, illiteracy or other causes. High castes had the heaviest weight for height and the greatest expenditure on health care, relative to morbidity. Middle castes reported the lowest morbidity and the highest health expenditure, both per household and per person. Muslims scored worst on literally every major health indicator and were well below average on five key indicators. Under five mortality is the only indicator which provides evidence of change over time and this suggests that the relative excess mortality of Muslim children actually increased from 1966 onwards, as mortality of children in general fell.

Muslim-Hindu Gradients of Health

There were 17 Muslim households in the sample: 6 Pathans, 5 Dhobes, 3 Kabarias, 2 Telis and 1 Bhurji. The proportion of Muslim persons in the total population was 15.5 percent and this was 16 percent of households in the total population and 17 percent in the sample. In the total population there were 17 Pathan households, 7 Dhobes (ie. over-represented in the sample), 8 Kabarias, 5 Nais, 3 Telis and probably 2 of the 4 Bhurjis were Muslim (total 42 households and 220 persons, ie. 5.2 per household). Nine out of the 17 Muslim households (53%) in the sample were below the poverty line.

The Muslim and Hindu indices of under five mortality were 130 and 95 respectively. Thus the Muslim-Hindu gradient of under five mortality was 137 percent. This child mortality rate can be compared for live births in the earlier period up to 1965 and in the later period from 1966 to 1977. As the mortality rate fell by 39 percent in the second period, the Muslim index increased from 115 to 156, mainly due to the very high index (259) for females in richer households. The Muslim-Hindu gradient increased from an earlier 118 percent to 172 percent later, ie. as Hindu mortality improved, the relative mortality of Muslims worsened.

Comparison with JD (where, remember, the under five mortality rate was 30% lower) reveals more or less the same Muslim indices both for the whole period (130), for the earlier period (115) and for the later period (155), when the mortality rate fell by 49 percent, ie. even more than in Basauli. The Muslim-Hindu gradients in JD were 155 percent for the whole period, 124 percent earlier and 251 percent later, ie. the inequality between Muslims and Hindus was greater in western UP and most of this higher inequality occurred in the later, post-1965 period of reduced mortality. It might seem tempting to launch into general comparisons of central and western UP, in search of an explanation (especially economic) of the greater post-1965 inequality in the west. At this stage it must suffice to observe, firstly, that the Muslim population of JD included an above average majority (63%) of rich and middle peasants and even their share of landless persons (28%) was only slightly above average. Secondly, Muslims accounted for 35 percent of households in JD, compared with only 16 percent of households in the total population of Basauli. In the later period the Muslim-caste Hindu gradient in JD doubled from the earlier 137 percent to 287 percent and even the Muslim-scheduled gradient also more or less doubled from 104 percent to 204 percent.

Whereas the index of Muslim under five mortality in Basauli was 130, the index of Muslim morbidity was 142, with correspondingly higher gradients. The Muslim-high caste gradients for days illness of household heads, their wives and all household members were 161 percent, 232 percent and 156 percent respectively.

Whilst the Muslim-high caste gradient of morbidity of household heads was high (161%), the inequality of their health expenditure was far greater (444%). As a consequence, the gradient of expenditure on health care relative to morbidity or need was 728 percent. The scheduled-high caste gradient for this was almost as high (674%) but the middle caste-high caste gradient was only 124 percent.

Overall, for nearly every indicator of health, Muslims in Basauli performed below average and the high castes were above average. The Muslim-high caste gradient for the aggregate health index was 137 percent.

For some indicators, notably deaths of progeny at any age and also for morbidity of the household head's wife, it is noticeable that richer Muslims had worse health than poorer Muslims in Basauli.

Lower Caste-High Caste Gradients of Health

Lower caste here refers to middle caste Hindus, the scheduled and also Muslims. The lower caste-high caste gradient for the aggregate health index was 114 percent and all the individual gradients were positive. The highest gradients were for days illness of wives (187%), days illness of household head (118%) and deficiency in female weight for height (110%, a high gradient for this indicator, where the range of performance is narrower).

Income Gradients of Nutrition

Income here refers to household income per capita weighted in relation to the number of adult male equivalent consumption units in the household. The poorer-richer income gradients for weight and height of males aged 18 and over were 106 percent and 102 percent respectively. The gradient of male weight for height was 104 percent. In the case of females, poorer women were slightly heavier, as tall as, and had slightly greater weight for height than richer women. The gradients were 98 percent for weight, 100 percent for height and 98 percent with weight for height. The income gradient of weight for height of those measured, of all ages who belonged to sample households, was 106 percent.

Income Gradients of Child Mortality

Poorer refers to those with a weighted per capita income of Rs 950 and below and richer relates to those with Rs 951 and above (given an estimated poverty line of Rs 810). Against expectation, the income inequalities of child mortality were mostly small. In the case of stillbirth, the income gradient was actually negative (61%), ie. richer households had a much higher rate. The indices for under five mortality of poorer and richer households were 104 and 96. The income gradient for child mortality was thus 108 percent for the period from about 1941 to 1982. However, it is interesting and, indeed, it may even be highly significant that the gradient has been reversed from quite strongly positive (139%) in the earlier period to quite strongly negative (70%) in the later period, referring to live births between 1966 and 1977. This could be taken as evidence of major improvement in the relative mortality of the poorer households between the two periods. It should also be noted that this reversal, and thus improvement, was almost exclusive to, and particularly marked among, the middle Hindu castes whose income gradient changed drastically from 201 percent to 65 percent. The pattern for Muslims was somewhat different but also showed a sharp reversal, in this case from a negligible income gradient (106%) earlier to a steep negative one later (39%). The implication is that, as the rate for child mortality fell from (an inflated) 460 earlier to 281 later, the reported rates have fallen more rapidly among poorer households (especially in middle Hindu castes). This was so even though poorer households did not report that they had experienced a particularly high rate of improvement in standard of living during the 1970s.

When deaths of progeny at later ages are also included, the poorer-richer gradient actually falls to 96 percent.

It is possible to compare the income gradient in Basauli with the class gradient of under 5 mortality in JD:

REDUCTION IN INCOME OR CLASS GRADIENT OF CHILD MORTALITY

	BIRTHS TO 1965	BIRTHS 1966-77 OR 1966-80	TOTAL BIRTHS
UNDER 5 MORTALITY RATE			
Basauli	460	281	371
Jhakri-DharmnagrI	361	184	259
INCOME/CLASS GRADIENT			
Basauli	139	70	108
Jhakri-Dharmnagri	142	101	133

Class in JD is based on landownership per able-bodied adult man, the level of technology used and whether the household deployed only adult family labour, hired in labourers or had to seek employment themselves (Jeffery 1989:17). The indices for under five mortality of poorer and richer were 87 and 116 respectively, producing a gradient of 133 percent, ie. considerably steeper than in Basauli. However, the indices were amazingly similar for the period up to 1965 and the earlier gradient for JD (142%) was almost identical with that of Basauli (139%). The difference in the gradients of JD and Basauli derive from the sharply contrasting trend in child deaths among those born after 1965. Whereas the mortality index for 1966-77 in Basauli was higher for the richer households, giving a negative gradient of 70 percent, mortality indices for richer and poorer peasants in JD more or less equalised, giving a virtual non-gradient of 101 percent. Whilst noting the difference between these later gradients of 70 percent and 101 percent, the most important point is that the trend in both areas has been towards an improvement in the relative mortality of the poorer households. One puzzling difference between the two areas in UP is that for the whole period the income gradients were low, both for males and for females, except in the case of males in JD (153%). Closer examination shows that the highest income/class gradient was for males in JD during the earlier period (187%, and actually 305% among caste Hindu males but equal for all males in the later period).

Taking income/class gradients of mortality of male and female children respectively in the later period, there is only a small difference between those for males and females in Basauli and none at all in JD. The pattern is less consistent in the earlier period (when data for both areas may be less reliable and are known to be inflated for Basauli, especially for females). In fact the most aberrant index is for earlier females in Basauli (148) and, unlike in JD, the gradient for females (153%) exceeds that for males (129%) in Basauli.

Another very interesting difference between Basauli and JD is in the indices and income/class gradients of Muslims in the later period. Whilst the indices of Muslims were identical for the two areas in both periods, in the later period the Basauli income gradient is strongly negative (39%) and the JD class gradient strongly positive (155%). Insofar as the numbers involved are larger in JD (375 live births, compared with only 64 in Basauli) and the class gradient in JD more in conformity with expectations, perhaps the Basauli data need examination.

Thus, as child mortality rates fell between the two periods, the income gradient of under five mortality reversed from a positive 139 percent to a negative 70 percent in Basauli and from a positive 142 percent to 101 percent in JD. This trend towards equality in JD and towards relatively lower mortality among the poorer in Basauli seems in very distinct contrast to what appears to have been happening in the past 60 years in Britain, where many, if not most, class gradients of both mortality and morbidity have remained positive and in fact increased, in many cases. There are a number of possible explanations for the apparent trends in Basauli and JD. Firstly, the income distribution in Basauli and the land distribution in JD might reasonably be regarded as only reflecting the times when they were observed (in 1982 and 1985 respectively). Though there is evidence of some land redistribution and perhaps more changes in land distribution via market and other private forces, as well as changes in the standard of living of 30 percent of households, in Basauli, it cannot be claimed that the overall structure of ownership had changed sufficiently to explain such a major reversal of the gradient. The changes of land and income distribution in JD also need to be investigated. Given that the gradients for the earlier period are positive in both areas (and, being positive, ostensibly and arguably need less explanation than the later, negative gradients), it could perhaps be assumed that the general patterns of distribution have been fairly stable. Individual households have been rising and falling, but the general structural inequality has remained, albeit probably reduced. Insofar as there has been redistribution and change, it may be that, despite what was reported by sample households in Basauli, households that were poorer in 1982 were even poorer in previous times. This is, of course, pure speculation but not totally unreasonable.

A second possible explanation for this trend might be that richer household heads have better education, greater health consciousness or superior reporting capacity and so give a fuller account of child mortality. However, this would not explain why richer heads reported selectively in a more full way for the later period than they did for the earlier period. This explanation is therefore rejected, though the general suspicion remains that better educated informants with lower pain thresholds may have reported all health problems more exhaustively. A third possibility is that some households recorded as 'richer' in 1982 had actually been poorer before 1966 but their improvement in income had not produced a commensurate advancement in health, because of sociocultural or even medical 'lags'. Or, more speculatively, the effort in improving on the economic front had increased various pressures, risks and costs on the medical front. Related to this is the possibility that the health problems for richer households (analogous to 'diseases of affluence') had increased for various reasons in the later period. The question arises whether health problems increased more for those who were continuously richer in both periods or for those who were upward mobile. Another possibility is that categories do not conform completely to reality. The definition and treatment of the household unit is more rigorous in the Jefferys' study of JD. For example, a clear distinction is made between households (chulhas) and farms or other production units. Chulhas were allocated to the same class as the farm or other production unit of which they formed a part. In this way, it is possible that a poorer brother (say, in a stage of the development cycle when he has more dependents and fewer workers than an older brother) may still be categorised in the same class as a richer brother, with whom he was farming jointly. A further explanation could be that the data, especially on land, income and mortality, are wrong. Data and other imperfections are freely acknowledged for Basauli but it is still interesting that two very different studies in widely separated (and, arguably, contrasting) areas of UP do produce some ostensibly similar indices and trends, despite large differences in actual mortality rates. Finally, the relationship between income or landownership class and mortality could be purely random. The steepness of the slope of the gradients suggests that this is not the case.

Income Gradients of Morbidity

The poorer-richer gradient of days illness of household heads in Basauli was 155 percent, ie. much more positive than the mere 108 percent for under five mortality. The poorest-richest gradient of days illness of heads was actually 247 percent and it should perhaps be mentioned that, even for under five mortality, the gradient was 151 percent. On the other hand, the poorer-richer gradient of morbidity of wives of household heads was strongly negative (51%) and, for all household members, it was slightly negative (89%). When the relative morbidity of wives of richer heads from the middle Hindu castes is assessed, the index goes to 180. The poorer-richer gradient for morbidity of middle caste wives was as low as 11 percent. This fits in with the various suggestions in Jeffery (1989) that women on middle caste, medium to large area farms suffered greater workloads, stress and ill-health. These richer women were expected to do more work in the less protected and more stressful environment beyond their courtyards. Apart from being less private and less leisurely work, it often involved looking after more animals (which some poorer households lacked altogether), making cowdung cakes and being exposed to more diseases (such as tetanus) which are transmitted by or through animals.

It should be noted that, though the poorest-richest gradient for all household members was negligible (103%), the gradient for household heads was 247 percent. (The morbidity indices for the richest 16 and the poorest 8 household heads were 70 and 173 respectively.) The gradient of 247 percent may be compared with 181 percent in the rural communes of Finland and only 141 percent for those aged 31-50 in the rural areas of Zala county in Hungary, where the poor were compared to middle income villagers (Blaxter 1989:222). The only gradients comparable to 247 percent are not rural. It should also be noted that the poor rural-rich urban gradient of being 'unhealthy' in Zala county was 254 percent, among those aged 31 to 50.

POPULATION	GRADIENT: POOREST AS % OF RICHEST
Britain, c 1984: Males with high rates of symptoms aged 40-59	269%
Finland, urban communes c 1972: Persons with chronic illness	233%
France, c 1968: Persons with chronic illness	188%
Hungary, urban areas of Zala county c 1977: Persons 'unhealthy' aged 31-50	177%
Britain, c 1984: Females with high rates of symptoms aged 40-59	166%
Norway, c 1978: Persons with chronic illness	133%

Source: adapted from Blaxter 1989:222

Income Gradients of Health Expenditure

Whilst the poorer-richer gradient of days illness of household heads was 155 percent, the gradient for expenditure on their health was 424 percent (and even 800% for poorest-richest). When this expenditure is related to the number of days that they were ill, the gradient increases still further to 677 percent (and the really enormous, international-type gradient of 1,977 percent for poorest-richest). The poorer-richer gradient of total household expenditure on health care was 370 percent but slightly less (303%) in per capita terms.

Class Gradients of Health

Households in Basauli were divided into three classes. The high class included households containing salaried workers and/or owning and cropping at least four acres. The medium class owned and cropped two to four acres and the low class less than two acres, with or without heavy dependence on income from hiring out their manual labour. The low class-high class gradient of weight for height of some sample members was 108 percent, ie. very similar to the income gradient of 106 percent. The low-high class gradient for mortality of progeny at any age was 117 percent (Cf. 94% for poorer-richer). Comparable gradients for morbidity of household heads and their wives were 130 percent and 49 percent respectively. The gradient for all household members was only 108 percent. However, the low-high class gradient for health expenditure of household heads was 692 percent and, for expenditure related to days of illness, the inequality rose to 903 percent. Overall, the morbidity of the medium class tended to be closer to that of the high class but medium class expenditure on health was nearer to the low class level.

The health of tribal women, their children and other poor migrant workers, who seemed badly exploited and were housed in very poor conditions at the local brickworks, was not studied. This was an opportunity which was, most regrettably, missed, mainly because they were not actually residents of Basauli.

Gender Gradients of Health

The gender gradient is expressed here by the female index as a percentage of the male index. For those aged 18 and over, males weighed 17 percent more than females and were 10 percent taller (Cf. about 8% taller in Britain). The gender gradient of weight for height was thus 108 percent. This relative smallness of females was itself, of course, in comparison with Basauli males, who were both short and lightweight by international standards.

The gender gradient for stillbirths was 66 percent, which probably conforms with the normal pattern elsewhere. However, the gender gradient for under five mortality was 124 percent for the whole period. The situation for female children improved between the two periods, with the gradient falling from an earlier 141 percent (similar to the income gradient up to 1965) to a later 117 percent. Some of the female excess mortality among live births from about 1941 to 1965 ought to be attributable to under-recording of female births and survivors who had left the household. Without wishing to de-emphasise the effect of this bias, it is nevertheless remarkable that in JD the indices for the whole period were virtually identical, those for the earlier period were similar and it was, oddly, the indices for the *later* period which differed more (though only slightly) from that of Basauli. The gender gradient for under five mortality in JD was identical (124%) and the gradient fell from an earlier 135 percent to a later 105 percent, ie. rather more sharply from an expected lower original base. Given the under-recording of female births in Basauli, one would have expected the earlier Basauli gradient (142%) to have been inflated way above the earlier JD gradient (135%), especially given a mortality rate in the earlier period which was 27 percent higher than that of JD.

Comparison of rural areas and historical periods should not be allowed to obscure the two main points, namely, that females had about 12 percent excess mortality, above the average, for the whole period and that this had fallen from 20 percent earlier to about 6 percent later. The female-male gender gradient among Muslims was particularly high (about 130% in both areas) and this inequality actually increased from 116 percent earlier to 151 percent later in Basauli. In both areas the gender gradient for child mortality improved the most among the scheduled and in Basauli the fall was dramatic, from 255 percent to 63 percent. As with other bases of inequality, sometimes a low or seemingly reduced gender gradient is more indicative of bad or worsened health of males as of female improvement.

The gender gradient of morbidity of household members was 85 percent but this female superiority may reflect underreporting by household heads who were nearly all male. Gender gradients of morbidity varied with age and kinship status and were worst for household heads (165%) but only seven were female, all widows. Expenditure on treatment of wives of household heads was only 60 percent of that for their husbands. Given an even lower gradient for morbidity (50%), this meant that the wives did relatively better on expenditure related to morbidity (gradient 120%).

COMPARISON OF HEALTH INEQUALITIES

The final question concerns which type of social inequality is associated with the highest gradients of ill-health.

Under five mortality is arguably the most serious indicator of ill health for which data was collected. The highest gradient of inequality was between caste strata, more specifically between Muslim and Hindu castes (144%). The next largest gradient between caste strata was between medium and high castes but this was only 112 percent. In comparison with Muslim-Hindu inequality, the gender gradient was considerably smaller (124%) and the income gradient, surprisingly, was almost negligible. However, the Muslim plus scheduled-caste Hindu gradient was even less (98%). Interestingly, the Muslim-high caste gradient increased by 71 percentage points after 1965 whilst the income gradient fell 69 percentage points to a negative gradient of 70 percent. The gender gradient improved, from 141 percent to 117 percent, but much less than in the case of income.

Once again comparison with child mortality in the western villages of JD reveals a remarkably similar pattern. The Muslim-high caste gradient (171%) and the landowning class gradient (133%) were both greater than their nearest equivalents in Basauli. The gender gradient was identical with that of Basauli. The Muslim-Hindu gradient has more than doubled to 287 percent while the class gradient has fallen by 42 percentage points to 100 percent, ie. equality. The gender gradient has fallen to 105 percent, approaching equality. Ostensibly, it seems that Muslims were the most disadvantaged low status category in both Basauli and JD and that their relative mortality has worsened more in the western, probably more commercialised, village with its higher population of Muslims. The poorer households appear to have improved their relative child mortality considerably more, and females slightly less, in Basauli than in JD.

The gender gradient of weight for height (108%) was the largest and those for income (104%) and Muslim-high caste inequality (103%) were smaller. The same was true of weight and height respectively. In addition, the gradients of weight were larger than those of height, whether for gender, income or caste strata. The gender gradient for weight was 117 percent.

In the case of morbidity, the Muslim-high caste gradient of days illness of all household members was by far the highest (156%) and the only other positive gradient was for class (108%). The gradients for income (89%) and for gender (85%) were both negative. However, data on illness of household heads were probably more reliable than for other household members. Gender, Muslim-high caste and income gradients of morbidity of household heads were all high (165%, 161% and 154% respectively) and the class gradient was not far behind. For morbidity of wives, the Muslim-high caste inequality was extremely high (232%) but the income and class gradients were negative (51% and 49% respectively).

Perhaps predictably, income gradients for both total and per capita household expenditure on health were higher (370% and 303% respectively) than the Muslim-high caste gradients (227% and 217%). There was not much difference between the income and caste gradients for either expenditure on household heads (417% and 454%) or expenditure relative to days illness of household heads (625% and 714%). The class gradient for the latter was the highest of all (909%). The gender gradient for health expenditure on household heads was much lower (167%) than for caste or income and the gender gradient for this expenditure relative to days illness was actually negative (83%). (NB. These gradients of expenditure have been reversed, so as to demonstrate the degree of disadvantage, in a way consistent with the other indicators.)

Overall, the evidence suggests that inequalities between Muslims and high caste Hindus were the most serious, averaging 160 percent for a selection of indicators. The next largest gradient was for gender (average 121%). The average gradients for income (103%) and class (95%) were small and quite close to equality. It should be noted that comparison of Muslim and high castes involves a more extreme comparison of smaller and narrower categories than simply comparing broader bands of poorer and richer (roughly halves) or even low and high class (roughly thirds of the sample).

CONCLUSION

Briefly, the findings have various implications which require consideration of possible recommendations:

In reducing the incidence of major causes of death, the social distribution of these is an important consideration, though not necessarily always the most important consideration.

In 1990 ten categories of disease or injury accounted for almost 82 percent of the nearly 50 million global deaths. Cardiovascular disease (28.7% of deaths) and cancers (12.3%) caused 41 percent of total deaths. Of these, ischaemic heart disease or 'heart attacks' were responsible for 10.3 percent, and cerebrovascular problems (such as 'strokes') for 9.3 percent. Cancer deaths included those of trachea, bronchus and lung (1.9%), stomach (1.5%), colon and rectum (1.0%) and liver (0.9%). Respiratory infections accounted for 8.6 percent of deaths (including TB 4.0%), diarrheal diseases (5.7%) and non-infectious respiratory diseases a further 5.7 percent. Unintentional injuries or accidents led to 5.6 percent of deaths (including 1.7 percent in motor vehicle accidents, 0.8 percent through drowning and 0.5 percent from falls). Perinatal problems still produced 5.0 percent of deaths and five childhood diseases 3.7 percent (including measles 2.0%, tetanus 1.0%, pertussis or whooping cough 0.6%, and polio and diphtheria 0.1%). Digestive diseases accounted for 3.7 percent of the total and intentional injuries 2.9 percent (including self-inflicted injuries 1.6 percent, war 0.6 percent and homicide and violence 0.6 percent). Apart from these top ten causes of mortality, malaria (1.8%), cirrhosis (1.4%), diabetes mellitus (1.3%), and HIV (0.6%) were other major killers (World Bank 1993). Certain diseases, such as tuberculosis, are more related to poverty and harsh living and working conditions (see Packard 1989). Others may be more neutral in their social distribution. With changes in the relative weighting of the major diseases and injuries which cause death, there will be associated changes in the international social distribution of ill-health. Policy makers need to consider the implications of increase (and decrease) in the incidence of particular diseases for health inequalities. For example, the World Bank (1993) estimates that annual mortality from tobacco-related heart disease and cancer may double to 2 million deaths by 2010 and possibly to 12 million by 2025. Malaria mortality could also almost double to nearly 2 million and AIDS mortality could increase by a factor of six to 1.8 million by the year 2000. (AIDS morbidity could reach 30 or even 40 million.) Clearly, such potential trends for these and for other diseases will affect the future distribution of ill health, both social and spatial.

Reduce the largest and most serious health inequalities first and these are mostly international, not intra-national.

This implies targeting both the most unhealthy countries, LDCs (mainly in Africa) with life expectancies below 50, and also major killer diseases which affect mainly the poor. It also implies increase in both wealth and income in these countries, international redistribution of wealth and income and also more direct assistance in health. A corollary of targeting countries with low LE is less emphasis on prolonging longevity in countries with high LE, except insofar as this is mainly targeted on categories within MDCs which have below average LE. Unless Alzheimer's disease, other senile dementias and comparable problems can be prevented, some of the investment in prolongation of life in MDCs seems low priority, if not possibly misguided. Alongside this ideal (or idealist?) approach, the many and complex implications of the DNA revolution and of genetic engineering or gene therapy need to be anticipated, thought through and 'dealt with' by health planners, sociologists and political economists (see Jones 1993).

Though donors of international health aid do need to tackle international inequality as a priority, they also need to reduce health inequalities within their own boundaries.

Reduction of health inequalities within Britain and other donor countries is important for three reasons. Firstly, it is all too easy for aid to become a transfer of resources from poor people in rich countries to rich people in poor countries. Secondly, donor countries need to experiment with domestic policies to equalise health, since the process is not fully understood nor so easy to implement. Thirdly, research on the process is relatively new, gaining momentum in the late 1970s, and it needs more work, both in MDCs and LDCs.

A main criterion for targeting international aid should be health.

Since health is an irreducible and indispensable component of welfare, it should take precedence over geopolitical, military, political, economic, social (but perhaps not environmental?) criteria for selection of partners in aid, trade, investment and other development. This again implies giving priority to countries with very low or low life expectancy, most of which are in Africa.

Another criterion should be the total burden of disease and, on this criterion, India deserves highest priority.

Key components in international aid should be health, nutrition and population.

However, health aid is probably most effective when it is not exclusively to the health and related sectors and possibly the best assistance to health in the least healthy countries is not through aid at all (health or non-health) but through non-aid, especially trade, investment and economic growth. In fact the health share in total development aid declined slightly from 7 to 6 percent in the 1980s and total disbursements of international health aid amounted to only $4.8 billion in 1990. International aid contributed only 2.5 percent of total LDC direct expenditure on health (World Bank 1993).

The unhealthiest nations can learn from lower income countries with disproportionately high life expectancy.

Poor countries with high life expectancy include China, Sri Lanka and the Dominican Republic, with low average 'cost' per year of life expectancy. Among lower medium income countries, Cuba, Costa Rica, Dominica and Jamaica have particularly high life expectancy.

The governments of India and of the Indian states should be able to learn from the example of Kerala, the healthiest state in the union.

Kerala now has a life expectancy of about 70, compared with 60 in India as a whole and under 50 in the unhealthiest states, including Uttar Pradesh. Kerala has improved the conditions of women and of the poor through agrarian reforms, increased wages, education and family planning.

Impressive as Kerala's health record undoubtedly is, there is some danger of treating Kerala as some kind of utopian enclave within an otherwise quite hopeless subcontinent. In fact Kerala has many problems, such as relatively high poverty, below average PCI, poor nutrition, a very high proportion of labourers, high unemployment, high morbidity, suicide, mental illness, some signs of incipient deterioration in health, and other problems which seem to be associated with relatively rapid social change (see Chatterjee 1988; Sibbons 1992). Recently, new problems have arisen, such as tentative communalism and effects of the Gulf crisis, including migrants returning from Kuwait and Saudi recruiting of Keralan health workers to replace 'pro-Iraqui' Yemenis. Conversely, the rest of India can report some modest successes, including nutrition programmes in Tamil Nadu. This final note of caution partly arises because any discussion of differing political economies in the kind of federal state that India is must be sensitive to the limitations that this kind of federalism and the (perhaps associated?) increasing pressure towards centralisation imposes on individual states. For example, West Bengal complains of being starved of all-Indian and international investment and also of inordinate delay in the Presidential assent to further legislation on land reform.

In spite of all this, significant differences in both the general political economy and also the political economy of health obviously do exist at the extremes, between Kerala and UP. Kerala has a much larger labouring class and an educated, relatively heterogeneous and fairly cosmopolitan population. It has long and strong tradition of Communist party organisation and a relatively weak Congress tradition. Even so, communist influence in Kerala has been tempered by its intermittent control of state government, its need to share power in Left Front coalitions and by the balancing power and often active interference from the centre. Even without these restraints, the CPI in Kerala has sometimes combined pragmatism (and conservatism) with its more usual radicalism.

India needs to increase the income of the poor, especially the rural poor and particularly the poorest 20%.

This requires lowering of the landownership ceiling to 7.5 irrigated or 15 nonirrigated acres per household; and increase in the minimum wage for agricultural workers. Even if there were any uncertainty about the effect of such measures on health, they have their own intrinsic value. However, the political obstacles to a serious programme of land reform should not be underestimated. The political ground needs to be prepared: a civil war between landlords and poor peasants has not improved health (nor sometimes land distribution) in certain parts of the world. The issue of minimum wages is also obviously a complicated one, especially for economists. The fact remains that certain levels of wage payment are so low as to be incompatible with minimal health of labourers, however adept they may be at resource allocation. It implies the need for organisation or strengthening of trade unions and associations for poorer peasants and the landless. Resources need to be diverted from the urban to the rural sector but this needs to be a discriminating redistribution to the poorest and least healthy categories of the rural population. Overall, endowments (genetic, land, water, animals, labour power or human capital) and entitlements need to be equalised and strengthened for the weakest. As with entitlements to food, health can be acquired by entitlements through production, exchange of commodities (trade), labour and hire of labour power, transfer payments and other transactions with the State (and with other public agencies), inheritance and other private transfers, plus through non-entitlements such as theft. Drèze and Sen (1989) provide an analytical and policy framework for tackling hunger which can probably be adapted to wider health problems (see also Sen 1981 on famine).

India needs to give priority to health improvement in the most unhealthy states, which are mainly in north India.

Among the most unhealthy states, Uttar Pradesh represents the largest concentration of population on this earth with such a low average life expectancy. For this reason it represents the priority target number one, both internationally and also nationally within India, for health aid.

Priority needs to be given to female health, not least among Muslims.

The education, employment, income, property and other legal rights, health care, contraceptive and child care services for women need to be improved.

The health problems of Muslims need to be addressed but this has to be done without antagonising Hindus and exacerbating the already serious (and worsening?) communal conflict.

Insofar as the inferior health of Muslims is due to economic causes, then they can be helped through programmes which are not labelled as being for one community or another. Insofar as they are related to sociocultural factors such as education, especially of women, or to Muslim fertility (assuming they are), then a more difficult and more sensitive policy will be needed.

Finally, the whole question of changes in health inequalities, as average health by and large improves, needs to be researched further.

The comparison of local trends in a few villages in Uttar Pradesh with national trends in Britain or India is obviously most unsatisfactory, particularly given the methodological and other flaws in the Basauli study. Even the British studies are highly problematic in terms of method, interpretation and conclusions. Blaxter (1989) goes so far as to suggest that definitions and concepts of health and ill health vary so much between nations that international comparison may be impossible. In a world where average income and health standards continue somehow to improve (against all and perhaps increasingly heavy odds?), the problem of increasing unequalisation (albeit partial and certainly not on all fronts) and of huge pockets of income and health deprivation pose not only a moral, medical and economic problem but, more seriously, (for a mainly complacent western dominant affluent class) a political problem. Academically, the interesting question is what happens to health distribution and inequalities as economic growth and ostensible socio-economic development proceed (Cf. the comparable, rather more developed research on the effect of economic growth and development on social and regional inequalities of wealth and income.) Practically, the key issue is how to improve average health whilst at the same time reducing health inequality, on various social axes and in its various manifestations.

ACKNOWLEDGEMENTS

Grateful thanks to Professor D.P. Singh, his charming family and very helpful colleagues (especially Dr M.S. Verma) at the Institute of Public Administration, University of Lucknow, for extremely generous hospitality, warm friendship and academic support; Rudra Narain Singh ('Thakur Sahib') and the people of Basauli for hospitality, camaraderie and humour, as well as information; Thakur Sahib's wife and other family members for excellent food; his four sons, Satish Pratap ('Lal'), Manojpal ('Munnu'), Somesh Pratap and Anang Pal ('Annu') for much practical help, patience and good humour; Rajendra Pratap Singh for research assistance, interpreting, advice and also invaluable information in the early writing; Mrs I.B. (Padma) Sinha for raksha bandhan and Hindi tuition; Praveen Sinha for help with interviewing; Ram Advani for friendship, books and hospitality; Paul Brass for much stimulation and also a privileged insight into his fieldwork; Dr K.S. Vigh for help at Suratganj PHC and hospitality in Lucknow; Naresh Dayal, DC Barabanki district, for assistance in selecting the village; Manohar and other staff at the IPA hostel for innumerable services and favours; the nafasat and nazakat of the friendly people in the beautiful city of Lucknow; Glenys Bridges, Mary Owens, Denise Johns, Karen Davies and especially Gwyneth Goodhead for word processing and endless patience; John Verge for help with maps; Junior McDougall for revising the index; the British Council for travel and other invaluable support; colleagues in the Centre for Development Studies, Swansea for friendship, much tolerance and support; and, above all, to Billie and Polly.

The map of India is from J.M. Brown, 1985, Modern India: The Origins of an Asian Democracy, Oxford UP, page xviii and is reproduced by permission of Oxford University Press.

The map of Uttar Pradesh is adapted from Z. Hasan, 1989, Power and Mobilisation: Patterns of Resilience and Change in Uttar Pradesh Politics, in F. Frankel and M.S.A. Rao (eds) Dominance and State Power in Modern India: Decline of a Social Order, Vol. 1, Oxford UP, Delhi, page 136. The inset, showing regions of UP, is extracted from a larger map in B.D. Graham, 1990, Hindu Nationalism and Indian Politics: The Origins and Development of the Bharatiya Jana Sangh, Cambridge UP, page 221.

The map of Barabanki district is from Director of Census Operations, 1972, District Census Handbook, Barabanki, Series 21, Uttar Pradesh, Part 10A, Town and Village Directory, Lucknow, facing the title page.

Bibliography

ADLAKHA, A. and D. KIRK 1974 Vital Rates in India 1961-71. POPULATION STUDIES, 28:381-400.

AGARWAL, S.K. 1966 Consolidation of Holdings: A Case Study of Lucknow District. AICC ECONOMIC REVIEW, 28, 10.

AGARWAL, B. 1989 Rural Women, Poverty and Natural Resources. ECONOMIC AND POLITICAL WEEKLY, 24,43:WS46-66 (28 Oct).

AHLUWALIA, M.S. 1978 Rural Poverty in India: 1956-57 to 1973-74. In M.S. Ahluwalia (ed) India: Occasional Papers. Staff Working Paper 279. Washington DC: World Bank.

AHLUWALIA, M. 1978a Rural Poverty and Agricultural Performance in India. J. OF DEVELOPMENT STUDIES, 14, 3:298-323.

AHMED, I. and N.C. SAXENA 1985 Caste, Land and Political Power in Rural Uttar Pradesh. Paper to Conference on Class, Caste and Dominance at the U. of Pennsylvania (May).

AKHTAR, R. and A.T.A. LEARMONTH (eds) 1985 Geographical Aspects of Health and Disease in India. N. Delhi: Concept.

ALAVI, H. 1975 India and the Colonial Mode of Production. ECONOMIC AND POLITICAL WEEKLY, 10, 33-5:1235-62 (also in R. Miliband, ed, Socialist Register 1975:160-97).

ALAVI, H. 1983 Class and State. In H. Gardezi and J. Rashid (eds) Pakistan. The Roots of Dictatorship. The Political Economy of a Praetorian State. London: Zed Press, pp.40-93.

ALAVI, H. and J. HARRISS (eds) 1989 South Asia. Basingstoke: Macmillan.

ALI, S.M. 1993 The Fearful State. Power, People and Internal War in South Asia. London: Zed.

ALI, T. 1985 The Nehrus and the Gandhis. An Indian Dynasty. London: Picador.

AMBANNAVAR, J.P. 1975 Population. Second India Series. N. Delhi: Macmillan.

ANTONOVSKY, A. and J. BERNSTEIN 1977 Social Class and Infant Mortality. SOCIAL SCIENCE AND MEDICINE, 11:453-70.

ANTONOVSKY, A. 1989 Social Inequalities in Health: A Complementary Perspective. In J.Fox (ed) Health Inequalities in European Countries. Aldershot: Gower, pp 386-97.

APPADORAI, A. 1981 Gastropolitics in Hindu South Asia. AMERICAN ETHNOLOGIST, 8:494-511.

ARBER, S. 1989 Gender and Class Inequalities in Health: Understanding the Differentials. In J.Fox (ed) Health Inequalities in European Countries. Aldershot: Gower, pp 250-79.

BAILEY, F.G. 1988 Humbuggery and Manipulation. Ithaca, N. York: Cornell.

BAIROGI, R. and others 1982 Age Misstatement for Young Children in Rural Bangladesh. DEMOGRAPHY, 19, 4:447-58 (Nov).

BALASUBRAMANYAM, V.N. 1984 The Economy of India. London: Weidenfeld.

BANDYOPADHYAY, D. 1986 Land Reforms in India: An Analysis. ECONOMIC AND POLITICAL WEEKLY, 21, 25-26:A50-56.

BANERJI, D. 1982 Poverty, Class and Health Culture in India. Vol. 1. N. Delhi: Prachi Prakashan.

BARDHAN, P. 1982 Little Girls and Death in India. ECONOMIC AND POLITICAL WEEKLY, 17, 36:1448-50 (4 Sept).

BARDHAN, P. 1982a Agrarian Class Formation in India. J. OF PEASANT STUDIES, 10, 1:73-94.

BARDHAN, P. 1984 The Political Economy of Development in India. Oxford: Blackwell.

BARDHAN, P. 1988 Dominant Proprietary Classes and India's Democracy. In A. Kohli (ed) India's Democracy: An Analysis of Changing State-Society Relations. Princeton UP.

BARDHAN, P. (ed) Forthcoming. Measurement Problems of Socio-economic Change. Papers to Workshop on Measuring Economic Change in S. Asia: Differences in Approach between Large-Scale Surveys and Intensive Micro-Studies, Bangalore, August 1985.

BASCH, P.F. 1990 Textbook of International Health. Oxford UP. 2nd Edn.

BAXI, U. 1982 The Crisis of the Indian Legal System. N. Delhi: Vikas.

BEHRMAN, J. 1987 Nutrition, Health, Birth Order and Seasonality: Intrahousehold Allocation among Children in Rural India. J. DEVELOPMENT ECONOMICS, 28, 1:43-62.

BEHRMAN, J.R. and B.L. WOLFE 1984 More Evidence on Nutrition Demand: Income Seems Overrated and Women's Schooling Underemphasised. J. DEVELOPMENT ECONOMICS, 14, 1-2:105-28.

BEHRMAN, J.R. and A.B. DEOLALIKAR 1987 Will Developing Country

Nutrition Improve with Incomes? A Case Study for Rural South India. J. OF POLITICAL ECONOMY, 95, 3:492-507.

BELL, C. and R. RICH 1990 Rural Poverty and Agricultural Performance in India between 1956-57 and 1983-84. Background Paper to 1990 World Development Report. Washington DC: World Bank.

BETEILLE, A. 1992 The Backward Classes in Contemporary India. Oxford UP.

BHAT, L.S. and others 1982 Regional Inequalities in India: An Inter-State and Intra-State Analysis. N. Delhi: Society for the Study of Regional Disparities.

BHATIA, J.C. 1978 Ideal Number and Sex Preference of Children in India. J. OF FAMILY WELFARE, 24:3-16.

BHATIA, S. 1983 Traditional Practices Affecting Female Health and Survival: Evidence from Countries of South Asia. In A.D. Lopez and L.T. Ruzicka (eds) Sex Differentials in Mortality: Trends, Determinants and Consequences. Canberra: Australian National UP.

BLACKFORD, F.R. Jr. 1979 Belief and Psychotherapy in Banaras. PhD, U. of Pennsylvania.

BLANE, D. 1985 An Assessment of the Black Report's 'Explanation of Health Inequalities'. SOCIOLOGY OF HEALTH AND ILLNESS, 7, 3:423-5.

BLANE, D. 1986 Inequality and Social Class. In D.L. Patrick and G. Scambler (eds) Sociology as Applied to Medicine. London: Baillière Tindall, pp. 113-23.

BLAXTER, M. 1976 Social Class and Health Inequalities. In C. Carter and J. Peel (eds) Equalities and Inequalities in Health. London: Academic Press.

BLAXTER, M. 1987 Fifty Years On - Inequalities in Health. In J. Hobcraft and M. Murphy (eds) Proceedings of the British Society for Population Studies. Oxford UP.

BLAXTER, M. 1989 A Comparison of Measures of Inequality in Morbidity. In J. Fox (ed) Health Inequalities in European Countries. Aldershot: Gower, pp. 199-230.

BLISS, C.J. and N.H. STERN 1982 Palanpur: the Economy of an Indian Village. Delhi: Oxford UP (Moradabad district).

BONGAARTS, J. 1987 Does Family Planning Reduce Infant Mortality Rates? POPULATION AND DEVELOPMENT REVIEW, 13, 2:323-34.

BONNER, J.P. 1987 Land Consolidation and Economic Development in India. A Study of Two Haryana Villages. N. Delhi: Allied Publishers.

BOSE, A. and others (eds) 1977 Population Statistics in India. N. Delhi: Vikas.

BOUTON, M.M. 1985 Agrarian Radicalism in South Asia. Princeton UP.

BRASS, P.R. 1965 Factional Politics in an Indian State: The Congress Party in Uttar Pradesh. Berkeley: University of California Press.

BRASS, P.R. 1968 Uttar Pradesh. In M. Weiner (ed) State Politics in India. Princeton UP.

BRASS, P.R. 1972 The Politics of Ayurvedic Education: A Case Study of Revivalism and Modernization in India. In S.H. and L.I. Rudolph (eds) Education and Politics in India. Cambridge, Maryland: MIT Press.

BRASS, P.R. 1976 Leadership Conflict and the Disintegration of the Indian Socialist Movement: Personal Ambition, Power and Policy. J. COMMONWEALTH AND COMPARATIVE POLITICS, 14, 1:19-41.

BRASS, P.R. 1978 Indian Election Studies. SOUTH ASIA (New Series), 1, 2.

BRASS, P.R. 1980 The Politicization of the Peasantry in a North Indian State, Parts I and II. JOURNAL OF PEASANT STUDIES, 7, 4:395-426 (July) and 8, 1:3-36 (September) also in Brass 1984.

BRASS, P.R. 1981 Congress, the Lok Dal and Middle Peasant Castes: An Analysis of the 1977 and 1980 Parliamentary Elections in Uttar Pradesh. PACIFIC AFFAIRS, 54, 1:5-41.

BRASS, P.R. 1981a Class, Ethnic Group and Party in Indian Politics. WORLD POLITICS, 33, 3 (April).

BRASS, P. 1982 Pluralism, Regionalism and Decentralising Tendencies in Contemporary Indian Politics. In J. Wilson and D. Dalton (eds) The States of South Asia. London: Hurst.

BRASS, P.R. 1984 Caste, Faction and Party in Indian Politics. Vol. 1: Faction and Party. Delhi: Chanakya Publications.

BRASS, P.R. 1984a Division in the Congress and the Rise of Agrarian Interests and Issues in Uttar Pradesh Politics, 1952 to 1977. In J.R. Wood (ed) State Politics in Contemporary India: Crisis or Continuity. Boulder: Westview Press (also in Brass 1984:300-34).

BRASS, P.R. 1985 Caste, Faction and Party. Vol. 2. Election Studies. Delhi: Chanakya Publications.

BRASS, P.R. 1986 The 1984 Parliamentary Elections in Uttar Pradesh. ASIAN SURVEY, 26, 6.

BRASS, P.R. 1990 The Politics of India since Independence. Vol. IV.I of The New Cambridge History of India. Cambridge UP.

BRASS, P.R. and M.F. FRANDA (eds) 1973 Radical Politics in South Asia. Cambridge, Maryland: MIT Press.

BRASS, P.R. and F. ROBINSON (eds) 1987 The Indian National Congress and Indian Society: Ideology, Social Structure and Political Dominance. Delhi: Chanakya.

BRENNER, M.H. 1973 Fetal, Infant and Maternal Mortality during Periods of Economic Instability. INTL. J. OF HEALTH SERVICES, 3, 2.

BRENNER, M.H. 1976 Reply to Mr. Eyer. INTERNATIONAL JOURNAL OF HEALTH SERVICES, 6, 1:149-55.

BRENNER, M.H. 1977 Health Costs and Benefits of Economic Policy. INTERNATIONAL JOURNAL OF HEALTH SERVICES, 7, 4:581-623.

BRENNER, M.H. 1979 Mortality and the National Economy: A Review and the Experience of England and Wales 1936-1976. LANCET, pp. 568-73.

BRENNER, M.H. 1983 Mortality and Economic Instability: Detailed Analysis for Britain and Comparative Analysis for Selected Industrial Countries. INTERNATIONAL JOURNAL OF HEALTH SERVICES, 13, 4:563-619.

BROWN, J.M. 1985 Modern India. The Origins of an Asian Democracy. Oxford UP.

BURGER, A.S. 1969 Opposition in a Dominant Party System: A Study of the Jan Sangh, the Praja Socialist Party and the Socialist Party in Uttar Pradesh, India. Berkeley: University of California Press.

BUTLER, D., A. LAHIRI and P. ROY 1992 (and earlier) India Decides.

BYRES, T.J. 1981 The New Technology, Class Formation and Class Action in the Indian Countryside. JOURNAL OF PEASANT STUDIES, 8, 4:405-54.

BYRES, T.J. 1982 The Political Economy of Technological Innovation in Indian Agriculture. In R.S. Anderson and others (eds) Science, Politics and the Agricultural Revolution in Asia. Boulder, Colorado: Westview.

BYRES, T.J. 1982a The Dialectic of India's Green Revolution. SOUTH ASIAN REVIEW, 5, 2:99-116 (Jan).

BYRES, T.J. 1988 Charan Singh 1902-87: An Assessment. JOURNAL OF PEASANT STUDIES, 15, 2:139-89 (Jan).

BYRES, T.J. (ed) 1994 The State and Development Planning in India. N. Delhi: Oxford UP.

BYRES, T.J. and B. CROW 1985 The Green Revolution in India. Milton Keynes: Open University Press.

CALDWELL, J.C. 1986 Routes to Low Mortality in Poor Countries. POPULATION AND DEVELOPMENT REVIEW, 12, 2:171-220 (June).

CALDWELL, J.C., P.H. READY and P. CALDWELL 1982 The Causes of Demographic Change in South India. POPULATION AND DEVELOPMENT REVIEW, 8:689-727.

CALDWELL, J.C. and others 1983 The Social Component of Mortality Decline: An Investigation in South India, Employing Alternative Methodologies. POPULATION STUDIES, 37, 2:185-205 (July).

CASH, R. and others (eds) 1987 Child Health and Survival: the UNICEF GOBI-FFF Program. London: Croom Helm.

CASSEN, R. 1978 India: Population, Economy and Society. London: Macmillan.

CENTRE FOR MONITORING THE INDIAN ECONOMY (CMIE) 1985 Profiles of Districts: Part 1, A-K. Bombay: CMIE.

CENTRE FOR SCIENCE AND THE ENVIRONMENT 1982 and later The State of India's Environment: A Citizen's Report. N. Delhi (N. York: Council on International and Public Affairs); 1994 Floods, Flood Plains and Environmental Myths. Third Report. N. Delhi: The Centre for Science and Environment.

CHAMBERS, R. 1982 Health, Agriculture and Rural Poverty: Why Seasons Matter. JOURNAL OF DEVELOPMENT STUDIES, 18, 2.

CHAMBERS, R. 1988 Poverty in India: Concepts, Research and Reality. Discussion Paper 241. Brighton: Institute of Development Studies at the University of Sussex.

CHAMBERS, R. and others (eds) 1981 Seasonal Dimensions to Rural Poverty. London: Frances Pinter.

CHAND, Prem 1936, 1975 Godan (Gift of a Cow). Allahabad; 2nd Edn. 1979 Jaico (Novel).

CHARANJI, K. 1994 The Cancer Stick Invasion. DOWN TO EARTH, 3, 6:31-6 (15 Aug) N. Delhi.

CHATTERJEE, M. 1988 Implementing Health Policy. N. Delhi: Manohar.

CHAUHAN, S.K. 1984 Suicide in India. SOCIAL CHANGE, 14,3:17-29 (Sept).

CHEN JUNSHI and others 1990 Diet, Life-style and Mortality in China. A Study of the Characteristics of 65 Chinese Counties. Oxford UP.

CHEN, L.C. and others 1981 Sex Bias in the Family Allocation of Food and Health Care in Rural Bangladesh. POPULATION AND DEVELOPMENT REVIEW, 7, 1:55-70.

CHENERY, H. and others 1975 Redistribution with Growth. Oxford UP.

CORNIA, G.A., R. JOLLY and F. STEWART (eds) 1987 Adjustment with a Human Face. 2 Vols. Oxford: Clarendon.

CRAWLEY, W.F. 1971 Kisan Sabhas and Agrarian Revolt in the United Provinces. MODERN ASIAN STUDIES, 5, 2 (April).

CUTLER, P. 1984 The Measurement of Poverty: A Review of Attempts to Quantify the Poor, with Special Reference to India. WORLD DEVELOPMENT, 12, 11-12:1119-30.

DANDEKAR, V.M. and N. RATH 1971 Poverty in India: Dimensions and Trends. ECONOMIC AND POLITICAL WEEKLY, 6, 1:25-48 (2 January) and 6, 2:106-46 (9 January).

DAS GUPTA, M. 1987 Selective Discrimination against Female Children in Rural Punjab, India. POPULATION AND DEVELOPMENT REVIEW, 13:77-100.

DAVEY-SMITH, G., M. BARTLEY and D. BLANE 1990 The Black Report on Socio-economic Inequalities in Health: Ten Years On. BRITISH MEDICAL JOURNAL, 301.

DAVIS, K. 1951 The Population of India and Pakistan. Princeton UP.

DAWOOD, R. 1992 Travellers' Health. How to Stay Healthy Abroad. OUP.

DERR, B.W. 1979 The Growing Abundance of Food and Poverty in a North Indian Village: Karimpur 1925-1975. PhD, Syracuse U.

DESAI, A.R. (ed) 1979 Peasant Struggles in India. Delhi: Oxford UP.

DJURFELDT, G. and S. LINDBERG 1975 Pills against Poverty. A Study of the Introduction of Western Medicine in a Tamil Village. London: Curzon.

DONOSO, G. 1979 Weanling Diarrhoea: Overview of its Nutrition and Public Health Significance. INDIAN J. OF NUTRITION AND DIETETICS, 16, 4:103-13.

DORSCHNER, J.P. 1981 Alcohol Consumption in a Village in North India. PhD, U. of Arizona (on Rajputs in Rajasthan).

DREZE, J. and A. SEN 1989 Hunger and Public Action. Oxford: Clarendon.

DREZE, J., P. LANJOUW and N. STERN c1986 Identifying and Reaching the Poor: Principles and Some Examples from a N. Indian Village. Mimeo, London School of Economics (Moradabad district).

DUA, B.D. 1985 Federalism or Patrimonialism: The Making and Unmaking of Chief Ministers in India. ASIAN SURVEY, 25, 8 (Aug).

DUNCAN, R.I. 1987 Party Politics and the North Indian Peasantry: The Rise of the Bharatiya Kranti Dal in Uttar Pradesh. Mimeo, School of African and Asian Studies. Brighton: U. of Sussex.

DUNCAN, R.I. 1979 Levels, the Communication of Programmes and the Sectional Strategies in Indian Politics. BKD and the Republican Party of India in UP and Aligarh district. PhD, University of Sussex.

DYSON, T. 1975. India's Population: an Analysis of its Size, Age-structure, Fertility and Mortality. IDS Discussion Paper 72. Brighton: Institute of Development Studies, U. of Sussex.

DYSON, T. and M. MOORE 1983 On Kinship Structure, Female Autonomy and Demographic Behaviour in India. POPULATION AND DEVELOPMENT REVIEW, 9, 1:35-60.

DYSON, T. 1984 Excess Male Mortality in India. ECONOMIC AND POLITICAL WEEKLY, 9, 10:422-26 (10 March).

DYSON, T. Forthcoming. Excess Female Mortality in India: Uncertain Evidence on a Narrowing Differential. In K. Srinavan and S. Mukerji (eds) Dynamics of Population and Family Welfare. Bombay: Himalaya.

DYSON, T. and N. CROOK (eds) 1984 India's Demography. Essays on the Contemporary Population. N. Delhi: South Asian Publishers.

ECONOMIC AND POLITICAL WEEKLY (EPW, Bombay). No index but indexed either in The Social Sciences Citation Index or now on computer via the Bath Information and Data Services (BIDS) programme in any British university library. Articles on UP include 1992:27, 1-2; 25-7; 27, 18:933-4; 27, 40:2158-9; 27, 41:2208; and 1993:28, 6:207-8; 28, 12-13:502-3; 28, 24:1215-16; 28, 27-28:1421-2.

ECONOMIC AND SOCIAL COMMISSION FOR ASIA AND THE PACIFIC 1985.

ECONOMIST INTELLIGENCE UNIT 1989 India, Nepal. Country Profile 1989-90. London: EIU (Annual Survey, now Quarterly).

ELDER, J.W. 1962 Land Consolidation in an Indian Village: A Case Study of the Consolidation of Holdings Act in Uttar Pradesh. ECONOMIC DEVELOPMENT AND CULTURAL CHANGE, 11, 1.

EUROPA PUBLICATIONS 1990 The Europa World Year Book 1990. London: Europa Publications (Annual).

EYER, J. 1975 Hypertension as a Disease of Modern Society. INTERNATIONAL JOURNAL OF HEALTH SERVICES, 5, 4.

EYER, J. 1976 Rejoinder to Dr Brenner. INTERNATIONAL JOURNAL OF HEALTH SERVICES, 6, 1:157-68.

EYER, J. 1977 Prosperity as a Cause of Death. INTERNATIONAL JOURNAL OF HEALTH SERVICES, 7, 1.

EYER, J. 1977a Does Employment Cause the Death Rate Peak in Each Business Cycle? INTL. J. OF HEALTH SERVICES, 7, 4.

EYER, J. 1984 Capitalism, Health and Illness. In J.B. McKinlay (ed) Issues in the Political Economy of Health Care. N. York: Tavistock.

EYER, J. and P. STERLING 1977 Stress-related Mortality and Social Organisation. REVIEW OF RADICAL POLITICAL ECONOMICS, 9,

1:1-44.

FARMER, B.H. 1986 Perspectives on the 'Green Revolution' in South Asia. MODERN ASIAN STUDIES, 20, 1:175-99 (February).

FLOUD, R. 1989 Measuring European Inequality: the Use of Height Data. In J. Fox (ed) Health Inequalities in European Countries. Aldershot: Gower, pp. 231-49.

FOX, J. (ed) 1989 Health Inequalities in European Countries. Aldershot: Gower.

FRANKEL, F.R. 1977 Problems of Correlating Electoral and Economic Variables: An Analysis of Voting Behaviour and Agrarian Modernization in Uttar Pradesh. In M. Weiner and J.O. Field (eds) Electoral Politics in the Indian States. Vol. 3: The Impact of Modernization. Delhi: Manohar.

FRANKEL, F.R. 1978 India's Political Economy 1947-1977. The Gradual Revolution. Princeton UP.

FRANKEL, F.R. and M.S.A. RAO (eds) 1989 and 1990 Dominance and State Power in Modern India: Decline of a Social Order. 2 Vols. Delhi: Oxford UP.

FREED, R.S. and S.A. 1979 Shanti Nagar: the Effects of Urbanization in a Village in N. India. 3. Sickness and Health. N. York: Anthropological Papers of the American Museum of Natural History.

GALANTER, M. 1984 Competing Equalities. Law and the Backward Classes in India. Berkeley: University of California Press; Delhi: Oxford UP.

GHATE, P. 1984 Direct Attack on Rural Poverty: Policy, Programmes and Implementation. N. Delhi: Concept Publishing.

GHOSH, S. and others 1977 Bio-Social Determinants of Birth Weight. INDIAN PEDIATRICS, 14, 2:107-14 (Feb).

GILLESPIE, S.R. 1988 Social and Economic Aspects of Malnutrition and Health among South Indian Tribal Groups. PhD, London School of Hygiene and Tropical Medicine, U. of London.

GOPAL, S. (ed) 1992 Anatomy of a Confrontation. Ayodhya and the Rise of Communal Politics in India. London: Zed.

GOPALAN, C. 1983 Promoting Child Health and Nutrition in India. FOOD POLICY, 8, 1:23-30.

GOPALAN, C. 1984 Nutrition and Health Care: Problems and Policies. N. Delhi: Nutrition Foundation of India.

GOPALAN, C. 1985 The Mother and Child in India. ECONOMIC AND POLITICAL WEEKLY, 20, 4:159-166.

GOPALAN, C. 1992 Undernutrition: Concepts, Measurement and Implications. In S.R. Osmani (ed) Nutrition and Poverty. Oxford: Clarendon.

GOPALAN, C. and M. CHATTERJEE 1985 Use of Growth Charts for Promoting Child Nutrition. N. Delhi: Nutrition Foundation of India.

GORTMAKER, D.L. 1979 Poverty and Infant Mortality in the US. AMERICAN SOCIOLOGICAL REVIEW, 44:280-97.

GOUGH, K. 1974 Indian Peasant Uprisings. ECONOMIC AND POLITICAL WEEKLY:1391-1412 (Aug). Also in BULLETIN OF CONCERNED

ASIAN SCHOLARS, July 1976, 8, 3.

GRANT, J.P. 1978 Disparity Reduction Rates in Social Indicators. Washington DC: Overseas Development Council.

GOVERNMENT OF GUJARAT 1976 Report of the Socially and Educationally Backward Classes Commission. 2 Vols. Ahmedabad: The Commission (The Bakshi Report, after its chairman, A.R. Bakshi).

GOVERNMENT OF INDIA (GOI)

Backward Classes Commission 1981 Report 7 Vols. in 2. N. Delhi: Controller of Publications (The Mandal Report, after its chairman, B.P. Mandal).

Census 1972 District Census Handbook, Census 1971. Series 21, Uttar Pradesh. Director of Census Operations. Allahabad: Bansal Press.

Census 1981 Series 22, Uttar Pradesh Papers of 1981. Supplement, Provisional Population Totals.

Central Bureau of Health Intelligence 1980 Pocket Book of Health Statistics in India. N. Delhi: Director General of Health Services.

Central Bureau of Health Intelligence 1986 Health Statistics of India 1985. N. Delhi: Director General of Health Services, Ministry of Health and Family Welfare.

Ministry of Health and Family Welfare 1988 Family Welfare Programme in India Yearbook 1986-87. N. Delhi: Dept. of Family Welfare.

Ministry of Information and Broadcasting 1988 India 1987. A Reference Annual. N. Delhi: Publications Division.

Ministry of Welfare 1986 Handbook on Social Welfare Statistics. N. Delhi.

Office of the Registrar General 1980 Sample Registration Scheme 1979-80. N. Delhi.

Office of the Registrar General 1981 Survey on Infant and Child Mortality 1979. N. Delhi: Ministry of Home Affairs.

Office of the Registrar General 1983 Survey of Causes of Death (Rural) 1980. A Report. N. Delhi: Vital Statistics Division, Ministry of Home Affairs.

Planning Commission 1964 Report of Joint Study Team, Uttar Pradesh (Eastern Districts): Ghazipur, Azamgarh, Deoria, Jaunpur. Delhi: Govt. of India Press.

Planning Commission 1980 Sixth Five-Year Plan. 1980-85.

Planning Commission 1988

GOVERNMENT OF UTTAR PRADESH (GOUP)

Board of Revenue 1973 Agricultural Census in Uttar Pradesh 1970-71. Lucknow.

Board of Revenue 1980 Agricultural Census in Uttar Pradesh 1976-77. Lucknow.

Government Press 1903, 1921 Bara Banki. A Gazetteer. Vol. 48 of the District Gazetteers of the United Provinces of Agra and Oudh. Compiled and

edited by H.R. Nevill. Allahabad.
Planning Dept. 1980 Sixth Five-Year Plan, 1980-85. Lucknow: State Planning Institute.
Planning Dept. 1982 Annual Plan, 1983-84. Lucknow: State Planning Institute.
Planning Dept. 1983 Draft Seventh Five-Year Plan, 1985-90. Lucknow: State Planning Institute.
State Planning Institute 1979 Basic Statistics Relating to the Uttar Pradesh Economy 1950-51 to 1977-78. Lucknow.

GRAHAM, B.D. 1990 Hindu Nationalism and Indian Politics. The Origins and Development of the Bharatiya Jana Sangh. Cambridge UP.
GRAY, A.M. 1982 Inequalities in Health. The Black Report: A Summary and Comment. INTERNATIONAL JOURNAL OF HEALTH SERVICES, 12, 3:349-79.
GROSSE, N. 1980 Interrelation Between Health and Population: Observations Derived from Field Experiences. SOCIAL SCIENCE AND MEDICINE, 14C, 2 (Kanpur district).
GROSSE, R.N. and B.H. PERRY 1983 Correlates of Life Expectancy in LDCs. In I. Sirageldin and others (eds) Human Capital and Development Vol. 3. Health and Development. N. York: JAI Press.
GUHAN, S., B. HARRISS and R. CASSEN (eds) Forthcoming. Poverty in India. Delhi: Oxford UP.
GUPTA, D. 1988 Country-Town Nexus and Agrarian Mobilization: Bhartiya Kisan Union. ECONOMIC AND POLITICAL WEEKLY, 2'3.
GUPTA, G.R. (ed) 1981 The Social and Cultural Context of Medicine in India. N. Delhi: Vikas.
GUPTA, R. 1982 Census of India 1981, Series 2. Uttar Pradesh, Paper 1 of 1982: Final Population Totals. Lucknow: Director of Census Operations.
HAINES, A. 1990 The Implications for Health. In J. Leggett (ed) Global Warming. The Greenpeace Report. Oxford UP, pp. 149-62.
HARDIMAN, D. 1982 The Indian Faction. A Political Theory Examined. In R. Guha (ed) Subaltern Studies. Vol. 1. Delhi: Oxford UP.
HARRISS, B. 1986 The Intra-Family Distribution of Hunger in S. Asia. In A. Sen and J. Drèze (eds) Proceedings of the Conference on Food Strategies of the Project: Food and Hunger - the Poorest Billion. Helsinki: WIDER.
HARRISS, B. 1987 Poverty in India: Micro Level Evidence. Paper for Workshop on Poverty in India at Queen Elizabeth House, Oxford, October.
HARRISS, B. 1990 Child Nutrition and Poverty in South India. N. Delhi: Concept.
HARRISS, B. 1990a Poverty and Malnutrition at Extremes of South Asian Food Systems. ECONOMIC AND POLITICAL WEEKLY, 25, 51:2783-99.
HARRISS, B. Forthcoming. Differential Female Mortality and Health Care in South Asia. J. OF SOCIAL STUDIES.
HART, H. (ed) 1980 Indira Gandhi's India. Boulder, Colorado: Westview.
HART, N. 1990 Health and Inequality. London: Macmillan.

HASAN, K.A. 1967, 1979 The Cultural Frontier of Health in Village India. Bombay: Manek Talas (1979 title: The Medical Sociology of Rural India. Ajmer: Sachin Publications) Lucknow district.

HASAN, Z. 1989 Power and Mobilisation: Patterns of Resilience and Change in Uttar Pradesh Politics. In F.R. Frankel and M.S.A. Rao (eds) Dominance and State Power in Modern India: Decline of a Social Order. Vol. 1. Delhi: Oxford UP, pp 133-203.

HASAN, Z. 1989a Class and Caste: The Dynamics of Political Change in Uttar Pradesh. In Z. Hasan and R. Khan (eds) The State, Political Processes and Identity. Reflections on Modern India. N. Delhi: Sage, pp. 256-69.

HASAN, Z. 1989b Dominance and Mobilisation: Rural Politics in Western Uttar Pradesh 1930-80. N. York: Sage.

HASAN, Z. 1990 Self-Serving Guardians: Formation and Strategy of the Bhartiya Kisan Union. ECONOMIC AND POLITICAL WEEKLY, 24, 48:2663-70 (2 Dec).

HELMAN, C.G. 1984, 1990 Culture, Health and Illness. An Introduction for Health Professionals. London: Wright. 2nd Edn.

HERRING, R.J. 1983 Land to the Tiller. The Political Economy of Agrarian Reform in South Asia. Oxford UP.

HITCHCOCK, J.T. and L. MINTURN 1966 The Rajputs of Khalapur. N. York: Wiley.

HJORTSHOJ, K.G. 1977 Kerbala in Context: A Study of Mohurram in Lucknow, India. PhD, Cornell U.

HOBCRAFT, J.N. and others 1985 Demographic Determinants of Infant and Early Child Mortality: A Comparative Analysis. POPULATION STUDIES, 39, 3:363-85.

HOBSBAWM, E.J. 1954 Primitive Rebels. Manchester UP.

HOPPER, W.D. 1957 The Economic Organisation of a Village in North Central India. PhD, Cornell University (Senapur, Jaunpur district).

HUSSAIN, A. 1979 Sunlight on a Broken Column. Delhi: Arnold Heinemann.

HUSSAIN, F. (ed) 1984 Muslim Women. London: Croom Helm.

ILLSLEY, R. 1986 Occupational Class, Selection and the Production of Inequalities in Health. QUARTERLY JOURNAL OF SOCIAL AFFAIRS, 2, 2:151-65.

ILLSLEY, R. 1987 Occupational Class, Selection and Inequalities in Health - Rejoinder to Richard Wilkinson's Reply. QUARTERLY JOURNAL OF SOCIAL AFFAIRS, 3, 3:213-23.

ILLSLEY, R. and J. LE GRAND 1987 The Measurement of Inequality in Health. In A. Williams (ed) Economics and Health. London: Macmillan.

INDIAN COUNCIL OF SOCIAL SCIENCE RESEARCH and INDIAN COUNCIL OF MEDICAL RESEARCH 1981 Health for All. An Alternative Strategy. Pune: Indian Institute of Education.

INDIAN EXPRESS National Daily Newspaper (Delhi).

INDIA TODAY (IT) Fortnightly, Delhi, 1975 onwards: various issues (esp. 31 Jan 1982; 15 April 1984).

INDRIS, M.Z. and others 1981 Feeding Practices and Diarrhoeal Episodes Among Rural and Urban Infants of Lucknow. INDIAN PEDIATRICS, 18, 5:311-16 (May).

ISELEY, B.J. 1981 Social Correlates of Sex Differences in Mortality in a Small Area of South India. PhD, U. of Oregon.

JAIN, A.K. and P. VISARIA (eds) 1988 Infant Mortality: Differentials and Determinants. N. Delhi: Sage.

JALOTA, R. 1992 Medical Choice in an Urban Village: A Study of Zamrudpur, Delhi. M. Litt thesis, Cambridge U.

JEFFERY, P. 1979 Frogs in a Well: Indian Women in Purdah. London: Zed.

JEFFERY, P. and R., and A. LYON 1989 Labour Pains and Labour Power: Women and Childbearing in India. London: Zed Books.

JEFFERY, R. 1985 Health and the State in India. 2 Vols. PhD, U. of Edinburgh.

JEFFERY, R. 1986 Health Planning in India 1951-84: the Role of the Planning Commission. HEALTH POLICY AND PLANNING, 1:127-37.

JEFFERY, R. 1988 The Politics of Health in India. Berkeley: California UP.

JEFFERY, R. and P.M. 1984 Female Infanticide and Amniocentesis: a Research Note. SOCIAL SCIENCE AND MEDICINE, 19, 11:1207-12.

JEFFERY, R. and P.M., and A. LYON 1984 Only Cord-Cutters? Midwifery and Childbirth in Rural North India. SOCIAL ACTION, 27:1-37.

JEFFERY, R. and P.M., and A. LYON 1988 Traditional Birth Attendants in Rural North India. Paper to Wenner-Gren Conference on Analysis in Medical Anthropology, Portugal.

JESUDASON, V. and M. CHATTERJEE (eds) 1979 Health Status and Behaviour of Two Rural Communities. N. Delhi: Council for Social Development.

JHA, P.S. 1980 India: A Political Economy of Stagnation. Bombay: OUP.

JOHNSON, M. 1975 The Relation between Land Settlement and Party Politics in UP, India 1950-69. PhD, University of Sussex.

JOLLY, H. 1981, 1985 Book of Child Care: Complete Guide for Today's Parents. London: Allen and Unwin.

JONES, S. 1993 Language of the Genes. London: Harper-Collins.

JUSTICE, J. 1986 Policies, Plans and People: Culture and Health Development in Nepal. Berkeley: California UP.

KAKAR, D.N. 1980 Dais: The Traditional Birth Attendant in Village India. Delhi: New Age.

KAKWANI, N. and K. SUBBARAO 1990 Rural Poverty and its Alleviation in India. ECONOMIC AND POLITICAL WEEKLY, 25, 13:A2-16.

KAMATH, K.R. and others 1979 Infection and Disease in a Group of South Indian Families. II. General Morbidity Patterns of Families and Family Members. AMERICAN JOURNAL OF EPIDEMIOLOGY, 80:375-83.

KARKAL, M. 1985 Maternal and Infant Mortality. ECONOMIC AND POLITICAL WEEKLY, 20:1835-37.

KEESING'S RECORD OF WORLD EVENTS (Monthly) Harlow: Longman

(previously Keesing's Contemporary Archive).
KENT, G. 1991 The Politics of Child Survival. N. York: Praeger.
KIELMANN, A.A. and others 1983 Child and Maternal Health Services in Rural India: The Narangwal Experiment. Vol. 1. Baltimore: Johns Hopkins UP.
KLEIN, I. 1973 Death in India 1871-1921. J. ASIAN STUDIES, 32.
KNIGHT, I. 1984 The Height and Weight of Adults in Great Britain. Office of Population Censuses and Surveys. London: Her Majesty's Stationery Office.
KOHLI, A. 1987 The State and Poverty in India. The Politics of Reform. Cambridge UP.
KOHLI, A. (ed) 1988 India's Democracy: An Analysis of Changing State-Society Relations. Princeton UP.
KOHLI, A. 1991 Democracy and Discontent. India's Growing Crisis of Governability. Cambridge UP.
KOHLI, K.L. 1977 Mortality in India. A Statewise Study. N. Delhi: Sterling.
KRISHNA, R. 1983 Growth, Investment and Poverty in Mid-term Appraisal of Sixth Plan. ECONOMIC AND POLITICAL WEEKLY, 18, 47:1972-77.
KRISHNAJI, N. 1984 Family Size, Levels of Living and Differential Mortality in Rural India. ECONOMIC AND POLITICAL WEEKLY, 19:248-58.
KUMAR, A. and others 1982 Report of Evaluation of Traditional Birth Attendants (Dais) in the State of Uttar Pradesh. Lucknow: Population Centre, Dept of Economics, University of Lucknow.
KUZNETS, S. 1983 Economic Change: Selected Essays in Business Cycles, National Income and Economic Growth. London: Greenwood Press.
LECLERC, A. 1989 Differential Mortality by Cause of Death: Comparison between Selected European Countries. In J. Fox (ed) Health Inequalities in European Countries. Aldershot: Gower, pp 92-108.
LE GRAND, J. 1987 An International Comparison of Inequalities of Health. No. 16 in the Welfare State Programme of STICERD. London School of Economics.
LE GRAND, J. 1989 An International Comparison of Distributions of Ages-at-Death. In J. Fox (ed) Health Inequalities in European Countries. Aldershot: Gower, pp. 75-91.
LE GRAND, J. and M. RABIN 1986 Trends in British Health Inequality 1931-1983. In A.J. Culyer and B. Jönsson (eds) Public and Private Health Services. Oxford: Blackwell.
LERNER, M. 1969 Social Differences in Physical Health. In J. Kosa and others (eds) Poverty and Health: A Sociological Analysis. Cambridge: Harvard UP, pp. 69-112.
LIPTON, M. 1977 Why Poor People Stay Poor: A Study of Urban Bias in World Development. London: Temple Smith.
LIPTON, M. 1983 Demography and Poverty. Staff Working Paper 623. Washington DC: World Bank.
LIPTON, M., with R. LONGHURST 1989 New Seeds and Poor People.

London: Unwin Hyman.
LUSCHINSKY, M.S. 1962 The Life of Women in a Village of North India: A Study of Role and Status. PhD, Cornell U.
LYON, A. 1989 One or Two Sons: Class, Gender and Fertility in North India. PhD, Edinburgh U. (Bijnor district).
MACDORNAN, M. 1986 Contemporary Marriage Practices in North India: Evidence from Three Uttar Pradesh Villages. PhD, Australian National U.
MACKAY, J. 1993 The State of Health Atlas. N. York: Simon and Schuster.
MADDISON, A. 1971 Class Structure and Economic Growth. India and Pakistan since the Moghuls. London: Allen & Unwin.
MAHADEVAN, K. (ed) 1986 Fertility and Mortality: Theory, Methodology and Empirical Issues. N. Delhi: Sage.
MARI BHAT, P.N. and others 1984 Vital Rates in India 1961-1981. Washington, DC: National Academy Press for the Panel on India, Committee on Population and Demography.
MARSHALL, J.F. 1972 Culture and Contraception: Response Determinants to a Family Planning Programme in a North Indian Village. PhD, U. of Hawaii.
MATHEWS, C.M.E. 1979 Health and Culture in South Indian Villages. New Delhi: Sterling.
MATHEWS, C.M.E. and V. BENJAMIN 1981 Changing Health Beliefs and Practices in Rural Tamil Nadu. N. Delhi: Sterling.
MATHUR, A. 1983 Regional Development and Income Disparities in India: A Sectoral Analysis. ECONOMIC DEVELOPMENT AND CULTURAL CHANGE, 31, 3:475-505.
MATHUR, M.B. 1981 Uttar Pradesh. N. Delhi: National Book Trust.
McKINLAY, J.B. (ed) 1984 Issues in the Political Economy of Health Care. N. York: Tavistock.
MENCHER, J. 1974 Problems of Analysing Rural Class Structure. ECONOMIC AND POLITICAL WEEKLY (31 Aug).
METCALF, T.R. 1971 Landlords without Land: The UP Zamindars Today. PACIFIC AFFAIRS, 40 (Spring).
METCALF, T.R. 1979 Land, Landlords and the British Raj: Northern India in the Nineteenth Century. Berkeley: University of California Press.
MEYER, R.C. 1969 Political Elite in an Underdeveloped Society: The Case of Uttar Pradesh. PhD, U. of Pennsylvania.
MILLER, B. 1980 Female Neglect and the Costs of Marriage in Rural India. CONTRIBUTIONS TO INDIAN SOCIOLOGY, 14:95-129.
MILLER, B. 1981 The Endangered Sex: Neglect of Female Children in Rural North India. Ithaca, N. York: Cornell UP.
MINHAS, B.S. and others 1987 On the Choice of Appropriate Consumer Price Indices and Data Sets for Estimating the Incidence of Poverty in India. INDIAN ECONOMIC REVIEW, 12:19-49.
MISRA, 1982 The Indian Administrative Service. PhD, Lucknow University.
MITRA, A. (Economist) 1977 Terms of Trade and Class Relations. London:

Cass.
MITRA, A. (Demographer) 1978 India's Population: Aspects of Quality and Control. 2 Vols. N. Delhi: Abhinav Publications.
MITRA, S.K. 1990 Postcolonial State of India: Dialectics of Politics and Government. Brighton: Harvester Wheatsheaf.
MOHAMMAD, A. 1977 Food and Nutrition in India. N. Delhi: KB Publications (3 districts, including Barabanki).
MOHIUDDIN, I. 1968 Land Use and Nutrition in Lucknow District. M Phil thesis, U. of Lucknow.
MONTGOMERY, R.H. 1992 From Cattle to Cane: the Economic and Social Transformation of a Tarai Village, North India. PhD, Cambridge U. (Lakhimpur-Kheri district).
MOORE, F.J. and C.A. FREYDIG 1955 Land Tenure Legislation in Uttar Pradesh. Berkeley: University of California Press.
MUKERJEE, S.B. 1976 The Age Distribution of the Indian Population. Honolulu: East-West Centre.
MUNDLE, S. 1984 Recent Trends in the Condition of Children in India: A Statistical Profile. In R. Jolly and G.A. Cornia (eds) The Impact of World Recession on Children. Oxford: Pergamon, pp. 127-38 (also in WORLD DEVELOPMENT 1984, 12, 3:297-307).
MURTHY, N. 1982 Reluctant Patients: The Women of India. WORLD HEALTH FORUM, 3:315-16.
MUSGROVE, P. 1986 Measurement of Equity in Health. WORLD HEALTH STATISTICS QUARTERLY, 39:325-35.
NAG, M. 1985 The Impact of Social and Economic Development on Mortality: A Comparative Study of Kerala and West Bengal. In S.B. Halstead and others (eds) Good Health at Low Cost. N. York: Rockefeller Foundation (also in ECONOMIC AND POLITICAL WEEKLY, May 1983:877-900).
NARAIN, I. (ed) 1976 State Politics in India. Meerut: Meenakshi Prakashan.
NARAYANA, G. and J. ACHARYA 1981 Problems of Field Workers: Study of Eight Primary Health Centres in Four States. Hyderabad: Administrative Staff College of India.
NATH, U.R. 1985 Smoking. Third World Alert. Oxford UP.
NATIONAL NUTRITION MONITORING BUREAU (NNMB) 1980 Report for 1979. Hyderabad: NNMB, NIN and the Indian Council for Medical Research.
NAYYAR, R. 1977 Wages, Employment and Standard of Living of Agricultural Labourers in Uttar Pradesh. In ILO (ed) Poverty and Landlessness in Rural Asia. Geneva: International Labour Office, pp. 61-74 (see EPW 6 Nov, 1976).
NEALE, W.C. 1962 Economic Change in Rural India: Land Tenure and Reform in Uttar Pradesh 1800-1955. New Haven: Yale UP.
NEVILL, H.R. 1903, 1921 Bara Banki: A Gazetter. Vol. 48 of the District Gazetteers of the United Provinces of Agra and Oudh. Allahabad: Govt. Press.

NEWELL, C. 1988 Methods and Models in Demography. London: Belhaven.
NEWELL, R.S. 1966 Congress Agrarian Reform Policy. A Case Study of Land Redistribution in Northern India. PhD, U. of Pennsylvania.
NICHTER, M.A. 1977 Health Ideologies and Medical Cultures in the South Kanara Areca-Nut Belt. PhD, U. of Edinburgh.
NORTHERN INDIA PATRIKA (NIP) Daily Newspaper, Lucknow.
NOSSITER, T.J. 1985 Communism in Rajiv Gandhi's India. THIRD WORLD QUARTERLY, 7, 4:924-41 (Oct).
NOSSITER, T.J. 1986 Marxist State Governments in India. London: Pinter.
OFFICE OF POPULATION CENSUSES AND SURVEYS (OPCS) 1978 Occupational Mortality. Decennial Supplement, 1970-72, England and Wales. London: Her Majesty's Stationery Office.
OFFICE OF POPULATION CENSUSES AND SURVEYS 1986 Registrar General's Decennial Supplement on Occupational Mortality 1979-83. London: Her Majesty's Stationery Office (Pt 1 Commentary; and Pt 2 Tables on microfiche).
OSMANI, S.R. (ed) 1992 Nutrition and Poverty. Oxford: Clarendon.
OTTEN, M.W. and others 1990 The Effect of Known Risk Factors on the Excess Mortality of Black Adults in the US. JOURNAL OF THE AMERICAN MEDICAL ASSOCIATION, 263, 6:845-50.
PACKARD, R.M. 1989 White Plague, Black Labour. Tuberculosis and the Political Economy of Health and Disease in South Africa. Berkeley: University of California Press.
PAMUK, E.R. 1985 Social Class Inequality in Mortality from 1921-1972 in England and Wales. POPULATION STUDIES, 39:17-31.
PANDEY, G. 1978 The Ascendancy of the Congress in Uttar Pradesh 1926-1934. A Study in Imperfect Mobilisation. Oxford UP.
PANIKAR, P.G.K. and S.R. SOMAN 1984 Health Status of Kerala. The Paradox of Economic Backwardness and Health Development. Trivandrum: Centre for Development Studies.
PAPOLA, T.S. 1980 Informal Sector: Concept and Policy. ECONOMIC AND POLITICAL WEEKLY (3 May).
PAPOLA, T.S. and FAHIMUDDIN 1985 Industrial Spurt in Uttar Pradesh. ECONOMIC AND POLITICAL WEEKLY, 20, 7:269-73 (16 Feb).
PAPOLA, T.S. and others (eds) 1979 Studies in the Development of Uttar Pradesh. Lucknow: Giri Institute of Development Studies.
PATNAIK, U. 1972 The Organisational Basis of Indian Agriculture with Special Reference to the Development of Capitalist Farming. PhD, Oxford.
PATNAIK, U. 1976 Class Differentiation within the Peasantry. ECONOMIC AND POLITICAL WEEKLY, 2, 39.
PATNAIK, U. 1978 In A. Rudra (ed) Studies in the Development of Capitalism in India. Lahore: Vanguard.
PATNAIK, U. 1986 Reflections on the Agrarian Question and the Development of Capitalism in India. First Daniel Thorner Memorial Lecture. Delhi.
PATNAIK, U. 1987 Peasant Class Differentiation: a Study in Method, with

Reference to Haryana. Oxford UP.

PAUL, S. 1984 Mid-Term Appraisal of the Sixth Plan: Why Poverty Alleviation Lags Behind. ECONOMIC AND POLITICAL WEEKLY, 19, 18:760-66 (5 May).

PETTIGREW, J. 1989 Problems of Medical Prevention in a Punjab Village. ECONOMIC AND POLITICAL WEEKLY, 24, 50:2784-89 (16 Dec).

PIONEER Daily Newspaper, Lucknow.

POFFENBERGER, T. 1981 Child Rearing and Social Structure in Rural India: Toward a Cross-Cultural Definition of Child Abuse and Neglect. In J.E. Korbin (ed) Child Abuse and Neglect: Cross-cultural Perspectives. Berkeley: University of California Press.

PRADHAN, M.C. 1986 The Political System of the Jats of Northern India. Bombay: Oxford UP.

PRAHLADACHAR, M. 1983 Income Distribution Effects of the Green Revolution in India: A Review of Empirical Evidence. WORLD DEVELOPMENT, 11, 11:927-44.

PRASAD, B.G. and others 1969 A Study on Beliefs and Customs in a Lucknow Village in Relation to Certain Diseases, Menstruation, Child Birth and Family Planning. INDIAN JOURNAL OF SOCIAL WORK, 30:45-54.

PRASAD, P.H. 1989 Lopsided Growth. Political Economy of Indian Development. Delhi: Oxford UP.

PRESTON, S.H. 1980 Causes and Consequences of Mortality Declines in LDCs during the Twentieth Century. In R.A. Easterlin (ed) Population and Economic Change in Developing Countries. Chicago UP.

PRESTON, S.H. 1985 Mortality in Childhood: Lessons from the World Fertility Survey. In J.C. Cleland and J.W. Hobcraft (eds) Reproductive Change in Developing Societies. London: Oxford UP, pp. 253-72.

PRESTON, S. and others 1981 Effects of Industrialisation on Mortality in Developed Countries. In International Union of Scientific Study of Population. Solicited Papers. Vol 2. 19th International Population Conference, Manila. Part 2. Liège: Imprimerie Derouaux, pp. 233-54.

PRESTON, S. and P.N. MARI BHAT 1984 New Evidence on Fertility and Mortality Trends in India. POPULATION AND DEVELOPMENT REVIEW, 10, 3:481-503.

RAJALAKSHMI, R., R.P. DEVADAS and R. KAVERI 1981 Influence of Family Income and Parents' Education on the Nutritional Status of Preschool Children. INDIAN J. OF NUTRITIONAL DEFICIENCY, 17, 7:237-44.

RAMASUBBAN, R. 1984 The Development of Health Policy in India. in T. Dyson and N. Crook (eds) India's Demography. N. Delhi: South Asian Publishers, pp. 97-116.

RAO, C.H.H. and P. RANGASWAMY 1988 Efficiency of Investments in IRDP: A Study of Uttar Pradesh. ECONOMIC AND POLITICAL WEEKLY, 23, 26:A69 (25 June).

RAO, K.G. and S. KUMAR No date. Impact of Health Services on Health

Status of Women in Post-Independence India. N. Delhi: National Institute of Health and Family Welfare.

RATCLIFFE, J. 1983 Social Justice and the Demographic Transition: Lessons from India's Kerala State. In D. Morley (ed) Practising Health for All. Oxford UP.

REEVES, P. 1985 The Congress and the Abolition of Zamindari in Uttar Pradesh. SOUTH ASIA (New Series), 13, 1 and 2.

REEVES, P.D. 1991 Landlords and Governments in Uttar Pradesh. A Study of their Relations until Zamindari Abolition. Oxford UP.

RODGERS, G.B. 1979 Income and Inequality as Determinants of Mortality: An International Cross-section Analysis. POPULATION STUDIES, 33, 2:343-51.

ROHDE, J. 1982 Why the Other Half Dies: The Science and Politics of Child Mortality in the Third World. Lecture at University of Birmingham. Paris: UNESCO.

ROSENZWEIG, M.R. and T.P. SCHULTZ 1982 Market Opportunities, Genetic Endowments and the Intra-Family Distribution of Resources. AMERICAN ECONOMIC REVIEW (Sept).

ROWE, W.L. 1960 Social and Economic Mobility in a Low Caste North Indian Community. PhD, Cornell University (Senapur, Jaunpur district).

RUDOLPH, L.I. and S.H. 1987 In Pursuit of Lakshmi: The Political Economy of the Indian State. University of Chicago Press; Bombay: Orient Longman.

RUTSTEIN, S.O. 1984 Infant and Child Mortality: Levels, Trends and Demographic Differentials. WORLD FERTILITY SURVEY, COMPARATIVE STUDIES, No. 43. Voorburg, Netherlands: International Statistical Institute.

RUZICKA, L.T. 1984 Mortality in India: Past Trends and Future Prospects. In T. Dyson (ed) India's Demography. N. Delhi: South Asian Publishers.

SAGAN, L.A. 1987 The Health of Nations: True Causes of Sickness and Wellbeing. N. York: Basic Books.

SAHA, S.K. and K. SRIVASTA 1983 Federalism and Inter-regional Resource Allocation Policy in India. THIRD WORLD PLANNING REVIEW, 5,1:37-56.

SAHOTA, G.S. and C.K. 1975 Green Revolution and Population Dynamics in India. Research Report to the Smithsonian Institution, Washington DC. Nashville, Tennessee: Vanderbilt University.

SARKAR, S. 1983 Modern India: 1885-1947. Madras: Macmillan.

SARVEKSHANA 1983 (Journal for the National Sample Survey).

SAXENA, N.C. 1985 Caste and Zamindari Abolition in UP. MAINSTREAM, 15 June:15-19.

SCRIMSHAW, S.C.M. 1978 Infant Mortality and Fertility Behaviour in the Regulation of Family Size. POPULATION AND DEVELOPMENT REVIEW, 4, 3:383-403.

SEN, A.K. 1973 Poverty, Inequality, Unemployment: Some Conceptual Issues in Measurement. ECONOMIC AND POLITICAL WEEKLY, 8, Special Number (August)

SEN, A. 1981 Poverty and Famines. Oxford UP.

SEN, A.and S. SENGUPTA 1983 Malnutrition of Rural Children and the Sex Bias. ECONOMIC AND POLITICAL WEEKLY, 18:855-62.

SEN, A.K. 1993 The Economics of Life and Death. SCIENTIFIC AMERICAN (May):18-25.

SHANKAR, K. 1991 Politics of Land Distribution in Uttar Pradesh. ECONOMIC AND POLITICAL WEEKLY, 26, 17:1086-87.

SHARMA, M. 1978 The Politics of Inequality: Competition and Control in an Indian Village. Honolulu: University Press of Hawaii; and Delhi: Hindustan Publishing Corporation (a Thakur village near Varanasi).

SHARMA, M. 1985 Caste, Class and Gender: Production and Reproduction in North India. JOURNAL OF PEASANT STUDIES, 12:57-88.

SHARMA, S. 1993 Landlords and Governments in UP. A Study of their Relations until Zamindari Abolition. INDIAN ECONOMIC AND SOCIAL HISTORY REVIEW, 30, 1:124-26.

SHARMA, U. 1980 Women, Work and Property in North-West India. London: Tavistock.

SHEPPERDSON, M. 1988 The Political Economy of Health in India. In Shepperdson, M. and C. Simmons (eds) The Indian National Congress and the Political Economy of India 1885-1985. Aldershot: Avebury, pp. 304-71.

SHIVA, V. 1991 The Violence of the Green Revolution: Third World Agriculture, Ecology and Politics. London: Zed.

SHRIMALI, P.D. 1981 Agrarian Change, Agrarian Tensions, Peasant Movements and Organisations in Uttar Pradesh. Mimeo. Dept. of Economics, U. of Lucknow.

SIBBONS, M. 1992 Health for All by the Year 2000: The Good Example of Kerala? Centre for Development Studies, University College of Swansea.

SIMMONS, G.B. and S. BERNSTEIN 1982 The Educational Status of Parents and Infant Mortality in Rural North India. HEALTH POLICY, 2, 3-4:349-67.

SIMMONS, G.B., C. SMUCKER, B.D. MISRA and P. MAJUMDAR 1978 Patterns and Causes of Infant Mortality in Rural Uttar Pradesh. JOURNAL OF TROPICAL PEDIATRICS, 24, 5:207-16.

SIMMONS, G.B., C. SMUCKER and B.D. MISRA 1979 Some Aspects of Infant and Child Mortality in Rural North India. SOCIAL ACTION, 29, 3.

SIMMONS, G.B. and others 1982 Post-neonatal Mortality in Rural India: Implications of an Economic Model. DEMOGRAPHY, 19, 3:371-89.

SIMON, S.R. 1966 Changes in Income, Consumption and Investment in an Eastern Uttar Pradesh Village, 1954 to 1964-65. PhD, Cornell University (Senapur, Jaunpur district).

SINGH, A.K. 1987 Agricultural Development and Rural Poverty. N. Delhi:

Ashish Publishing House.
SINGH, B. and S. MISRA 1964 A Study of Land Reforms in Uttar Pradesh. Honolulu: East-West Centre Press.
SINGH, Charan 1964 India's Poverty and its Solution. Bombay: Asia PH.
SINGH, Charan 1970 The Story of New Congress - BKD Relations. How New Congress Broke the UP Coalition. Lucknow: Bharatiya Kranti Dal.
SINGH, Charan 1981 Economic Nightmare of India: Its Cause and Cure. N. Delhi: National.
SINGH, Charan 1981a Land Reform in UP and the Kulaks. Delhi: Vikas PH.
SINGH, J. 1988 Changing Agrarian Relations and Politics in Western Uttar Pradesh: A Study of Meerut District 1952-85. PhD, Jawaharlal Nehru University.
SINGH, K. and others 1993 Analysis of Birth Intervals in India. UP and Kerala States. JOURNAL OF BIOSOCIAL SCIENCE, 25, 2:143-53 (see also SOCIAL BIOLOGY 1993, 39, 3-4:292-8).
SINGH, R. 1980-1 Caste, Land and Power in UP 1775-1970. TEACHING POLITICS.
SINGH, V.B. and S. BOSE 1988 State Elections in India. Data Handbooks on Vidhan Sabha Elections 1952-85. Vol. 4: The North (Part 2). N. York and N. Delhi: Sage.
SINHA, U.P. and S. LAHIRI 1976 Life Tables for the States of India 1951-1961. Deonar-Bombay: International Institute for Population Studies.
SMART, N. and S. THAKUR (eds) 1993 Ethical and Political Dilemmas of Modern India. N. York: St. Martin's Press.
SMUCKER, C.M., G.B. SIMMONS, S. BERNSTEIN and B.D. MISRA 1980 Neo-natal Mortality in South Asia: the Special Role of Tetanus. POPULATION STUDIES, 34, 2:321-35.
SRIVASTAVA, S. 1976 Uttar Pradesh: Politics of Neglected Development. In I. Narain (ed) State Politics in India. Meerut: Meenakshi Prakashan.
STOECKEL, J. and A.K.M. ALAUDDIN CHOWDHURY 1972 Neo-natal and Post-neonatal Mortality in a Rural Area of Bangladesh. POPULATION STUDIES, 26 (March).
STOKES, E. 1975 The Structure of Land Holding in UP 1860-1948. INDIAN ECONOMIC AND SOCIAL HISTORY REVIEW (Delhi) 12, 2 (April-June).
SUBBARAO, K. 1985 Regional Variation in Impact of Anti-Poverty Programmes: a Review of Evidence. ECONOMIC AND POLITICAL WEEKLY, 20, 43:1829-34 (26 Oct).
SUKHATME, P.V. 1977 Malnutrition and Poverty. N. Delhi: Indian Council of Agricultural Research.
SUKHATME, P.V. 1978 Assessment of Adequacy of Diets at Different Income Levels. ECONOMIC AND POLITICAL WEEKLY, 12, 31-33:1373-84.
SUNDRUM, R.M. 1987 Growth and Income Distribution in India. Policy and Performance Since Independence. N. Delhi: Sage.
THAKUR, D.S. 1985 A Survey of Literature on Rural Poverty in India.

MARGIN:32-49 (April).
THOMAS, V.K. 1982 New Indicators of Development: Analysis of India's PQLI. PRODUCTIVITY, 22, 4:97-104 (compares UP and Kerala).
TODARO, M.P. 1979 Economic Development in the Third World. London: Longman.
TOWNSEND, P. 1990a Widening Inequalities of Health in Britain: A Rejoinder to Rudolf Klein. INTERNATIONAL J. OF HEALTH SERVICES, 20, 3:363-72.
TOWNSEND, P. 1990 Individual or Social Responsibility for Premature Death? Current Controversies in the British Debate about Health. INTERNATIONAL JOURNAL OF HEALTH SERVICES, 20, 3:373-92.
TOWNSEND, P., N. DAVIDSON and M. WHITEHEAD 1988 Inequalities in Health. Including P. Townsend and N. Davidson (eds), The Black Report; and M. Whitehead, The Health Divide. Penguin.
TOYE, J.F.J. 1981 Public Expenditure and Indian Development Policy 1960-1970. Cambridge UP.
TOYE, J. 1988. Political Economy and the Analysis of Indian Development. MODERN ASIAN STUDIES, 22, 1:97-122.
TRUSSELL, J. 1988 Does Family Planning Reduce Infant Mortality? An Exchange. POPN. AND DEVELOPMENT REVIEW, 14, 1:171-78.
TUCKER, P.R. 1979 Maa-Baap in Contemporary Uttar Pradesh. Bureaucracy and Democracy in an Indian State. PhD, University of Missouri.
TULLY, M. 1992 No Full Stops in India. Penguin.
TURSHEN, M. 1989 The Politics of Public Health. London: Zed.
UNDP 1990 Human Development Report 1990 Washington DC: United Nations Development Programme (and annually since 1990).
UNICEF 1981 The State of the World's Children 1980. Oxford UP.
UNICEF 1984 Analysis of the Situation of Children in India. Washington DC.
UNICEF 1990 State of the World's Children. London: Oxford UP for United Nations Children's Fund (and annually).
UNITED NATIONS 1974 and 1980 Demographic Year Book. N. York: UN.
VAIDYANATHAN, A. 1986 On the Validity of NSS Consumption Data. ECONOMIC AND POLITICAL WEEKLY, 21, 3:129-37 (18 Jan).
VAIDYANATHAN, A. 1987 Poverty and Economy: the Regional Dimension. Paper to Workshop on Poverty in India, Queen Elizabeth House, Oxford.
VANAIK, A. 1990 Painful Transition: Bourgeois Democracy in India. London: Verso.
VERMA, H.S. 1980 Post-Independence Change in Rural India: a Pilot Study of an Uttar Pradesh Village. Delhi: Inter-India Publications.
VISARIA, L. 1972 Religious and Regional Differences in Mortality and Fertility in the Indian Subcontinent. PhD, Princeton University.
VISARIA, L. 1985 Infant Mortality in India: Levels, Trends and Determinants. ECON. AND POLITICAL WEEKLY, 20:1352-59, 1399-1405, 1447-50.
VISARIA, L. and P. 1983 Population (1757-1947). In D. Kumar (ed) Cambridge Economic History of India. Vol. 2. c1757-1970. Cambridge UP.

VISARIA, P. 1969 Mortality and Fertility in India 1951-1961. MILBANK MEMORIAL FUND QUARTERLY, 47:91-116.

VISARIA, P. 1971 The Sex Ratio of the Population of India. Monograph 10. N. Delhi: Office of the Registrar-General.

VISARIA, P. 1981 Poverty and Unemployment in India: An Analysis of Recent Evidence. WORLD DEVELOPMENT, 9, 3:277-300.

VISARIA, P. and L. 1981 Indian Population Scene after the 1981 Census. ECONOMIC AND POLITICAL WEEKLY, 16,44-6:1727-80.

WADLEY, S.S. and B. DERR 1986 Child Survival and Economic Status in a North Indian Village. European Modern S. Asia Studies Conference, Heidelberg.

WALT, G. 1994 Health Policy. An Introduction to Process and Power. London:Zed.

WEINER, M. 1986 The Political Economy of Industrial Growth in India. WORLD POLITICS, 38, 4:596-610 (July).

WILKINSON, R.G. 1986 Occupational Class Selection and Inequalities in Health: A Reply to Raymond Illsley. QUARTERLY JOURNAL OF SOCIAL AFFAIRS, 3, 3:225-28.

WILKINSON, R. G. (ed) 1986a Class and Health: Research and Longitudinal Data. London: Tavistock.

WILKINSON, R.G. 1992 Income Distribution and Life Expectancy. BRITISH MEDICAL JOURNAL, 304:165-68 (Jan).

WINGATE, P. 1988 The Penguin Medical Encyclopaedia. Penguin. 3rd Edition.

WISER, W.H. and C.V. 1971 Behind Mud Walls 1930-1960, with a Sequel: the Village in 1970. Berkeley: University of California Press.

WOLFE, B.L. and J.R. BEHRMAN 1983 Is Income Overrated in Determining Adequate Nutrition? ECONOMIC DEVELOPMENT AND CULTURAL CHANGE, 31, 3:525-49.

WOOD, J.R. (ed) 1984 State Politics in Contemporary India. Boulder, Colorado: Westview Press.

WORLD BANK 1981 Economic Situation and Prospects of India. Report 3401-IN, S. Asia Region. Washington DC.

WORLD BANK 1984 Situation and Prospects of the Indian Economy. A Medium Term Perspective. 3 Volumes. Washington DC.

WORLD BANK 1993 World Development Report: Investing in Health. Washington, DC: Oxford UP (and earlier annual issues).

WORLD HEALTH ORGANISATION 1982

WORLD HEALTH ORGANISATION 1989 World Health Statistics Annual. Geneva: WHO (and other years).

WORLDWATCH INSTITUTE 1993 Vital Signs. Washington DC.

ZACHARIA, K.C. and S. PATEL 1983 Trends and Determinants of Infant and Child Mortality in Kerala. JANASAMKHYA, 1, 2:125-41 (Dec).

ZAIDI, S.A. 1988 Poverty and Disease: Need for Structural Change. SOCIAL SCIENCE AND MEDICINE, 27, 2:119-27.

INDEX OF AUTHORS

f indicates following page(s)
t includes a reference in a table

INDEX OF POLITICIANS

INDEX OF SUBJECTS

including glossary and acronyms